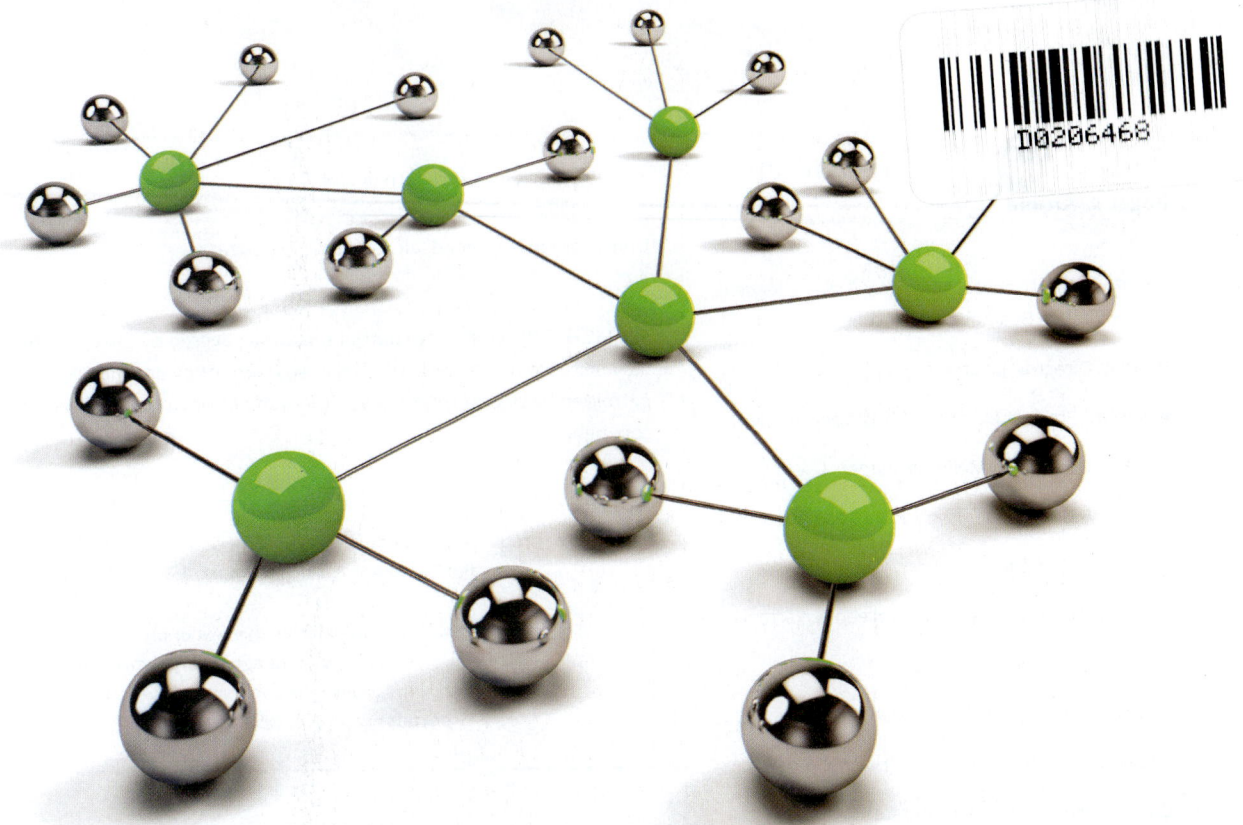

MICROECONOMICS

Thirteenth Edition

Roger A. Arnold

California State University
San Marcos

 CENGAGE

Australia • Brazil • Mexico • Singapore • United Kingdom • United States

Microeconomics, **Thirteenth Edition**
Roger A. Arnold

Vice President, General Manager, Social Science & Qualitative Business: Erin Joyner

Product Director: Jason Fremder

Associate Product Manager: Christopher Rader

Content Developer: Molly Umbarger

Product Assistant: Denisse Zavala-Rosales

Executive Marketing Manager: John Carey

Sr. Content Project Manager: Colleen A. Farmer

Production Service: SPi Global

Sr. Art Director: Michelle Kunkler

Cover and Internal Designer: Tippy McIntosh

Cover Image: Sashkin/Shutterstock.com

Internal design images: Igor Shikov/Shutterstock.com (Office Hours feature); Nobelus/Shutterstock.com (Does it Matter feature); PictureStudio/Shutterstock.com (Hear What and How feature); Sashkin/Shutterstock.com

Intellectual Property

   Analyst: Jennifer Bowes

   Project Manager: Carly B. Belcher

For product information and technology assistance, contact us at
Cengage Customer & Sales Support, 1-800-354-9706

For permission to use material from this text or product, submit all requests online at **www.cengage.com/permissions**
Further permissions questions can be emailed to
permissionrequest@cengage.com

Library of Congress Control Number: 2017952171

ISBN: 978-1-337-61740-6

Cengage
20 Channel Center Street
Boston, MA 02210
USA

Cengage is a leading provider of customized learning solutions with employees residing in nearly 40 different countries and sales in more than 125 countries around the world. Find your local representative at **www.cengage.com**

Cengage products are represented in Canada by Nelson Education, Ltd.

To learn more about Cengage platforms and services, visit **www.cengage.com**

To register or access your online learning solution or purchase materials for your course, visit **www.cengagebrain.com**

Printed in the United States of America
Print Number: 01   Print Year: 2017

To Sheila, Daniel, and David

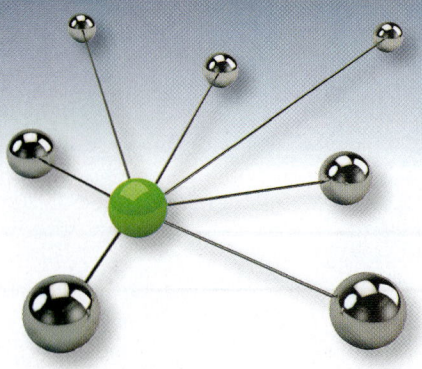

BRIEF CONTENTS

CONTENTS

AN INTRODUCTION TO ECONOMICS

Part 1   Economics: The Science of Scarcity

ECONOMICS 24/7

OFFICE HOURS

OFFICE HOURS

MICROECONOMICS

Part 2   Microeconomic Fundamentals

ECONOMICS 24/7

OFFICE HOURS

ECONOMICS 24/7

OFFICE HOURS

Part 3   Product Markets and Policies

ECONOMICS 24/7

The Digital Revolution, Price, and Marginal Cost 246

How Is High-Quality Land Like a Genius Software Engineer? 257

OFFICE HOURS

"Do You Have to Know the *MR* = *MC* Condition in Order to Be Successful in Business?" 259

ECONOMICS 24/7

Monopoly and the Boston Tea Party 266

Religion and Monopoly 277

One for $40 or Two for $70 279

Do Colleges and Universities Price Discriminate? 281

Buying a Computer and Getting a Printer for $100 Less Than the Retail Price 283

OFFICE HOURS

"Does the Single-Price Monopolist Lower Price Only on the Additional Unit?" 284

ECONOMICS 24/7

The People Wear Prada 291

How Is a New Year's Resolution Like a Cartel Agreement? 296

OFFICE HOURS

"Are Firms (as Sellers) Price Takers or Price Searchers?" 306

ECONOMICS 24/7

Thomas Edison and Hollywood 311

Why It May Be Hard to Dislodge People from Facebook 316

High-Priced Ink Cartridges and Expensive Minibars 317

OFFICE HOURS

"What Is the Advantage of the Herfindahl Index?" 325

Part 4   Factor Markets and Related Issues

ECONOMICS 24/7

OFFICE HOURS

"Why Do Economists Think in Twos?" 351

ECONOMICS 24/7

Technology, the Price of Competing Factors, and Displaced Workers 360

Are You Ready for Some Football? 366

OFFICE HOURS

"Don't Higher Wages Reduce Profits?" 368

ECONOMICS 24/7

Statistics Can Mislead If You Don't Know How They Are Made 375

OFFICE HOURS

"Are the Number of Persons in Each Fifth the Same?" 385

OFFICE HOURS

"How Is Present Value Used in the Courtroom?" 405

Part 5 Market Failure, Public Choice, and Special-Interest Group Politics

An Unintended Effect of Social Media 412

Tribes, Transaction Costs, and Social Media 418

"They Paved Paradise and Put Up a Parking Lot" 426

Arriving Late to Class, Grading on a Curve, and Studying Together for the Midterm 431

OFFICE HOURS

"Doesn't It Seem Wrong to Let Some Business Firms Pay to Pollute?" 432

Part 6   Economic Theory-Building and Everyday Life

THE GLOBAL ECONOMY

Part 7 International Economics and Globalization

ECONOMICS 24/7

Dividing the Work 489

Offshore Outsourcing, or Offshoring 497

OFFICE HOURS

"Should We Impose Tariffs if They Impose Tariffs?" 499

ECONOMICS 24/7

The U.S. Dollar as the Primary Reserve Currency 509

Chinese Imports and the U.S. Economy 512

WEB CHAPTERS

OFFICE HOURS

"I Have Three Questions."
557

Roger Arnold's **MICROECONOMICS** opens up the world of economic analysis. Substantive content, detailed diagrams, popular economic features, and innovative pedagogy are just the beginning. **MICROECONOMICS** continues to blaze the trail for constantly updated content and applications balanced with unequaled media and study assets, including the new Adaptive Test Prep app.

Only available in MindTap®, the new Adaptive Test Prep helps students prepare for test success by allowing them to generate multiple practice tests across chapters. Once a practice test is complete, the student is presented with a personalized Study Plan featuring a series of highly targeted remediation resources, including "Teachable Moment" videos created by author, Roger Arnold.

Adaptive Test Prep helps students more effectively gauge their understanding before taking an exam.

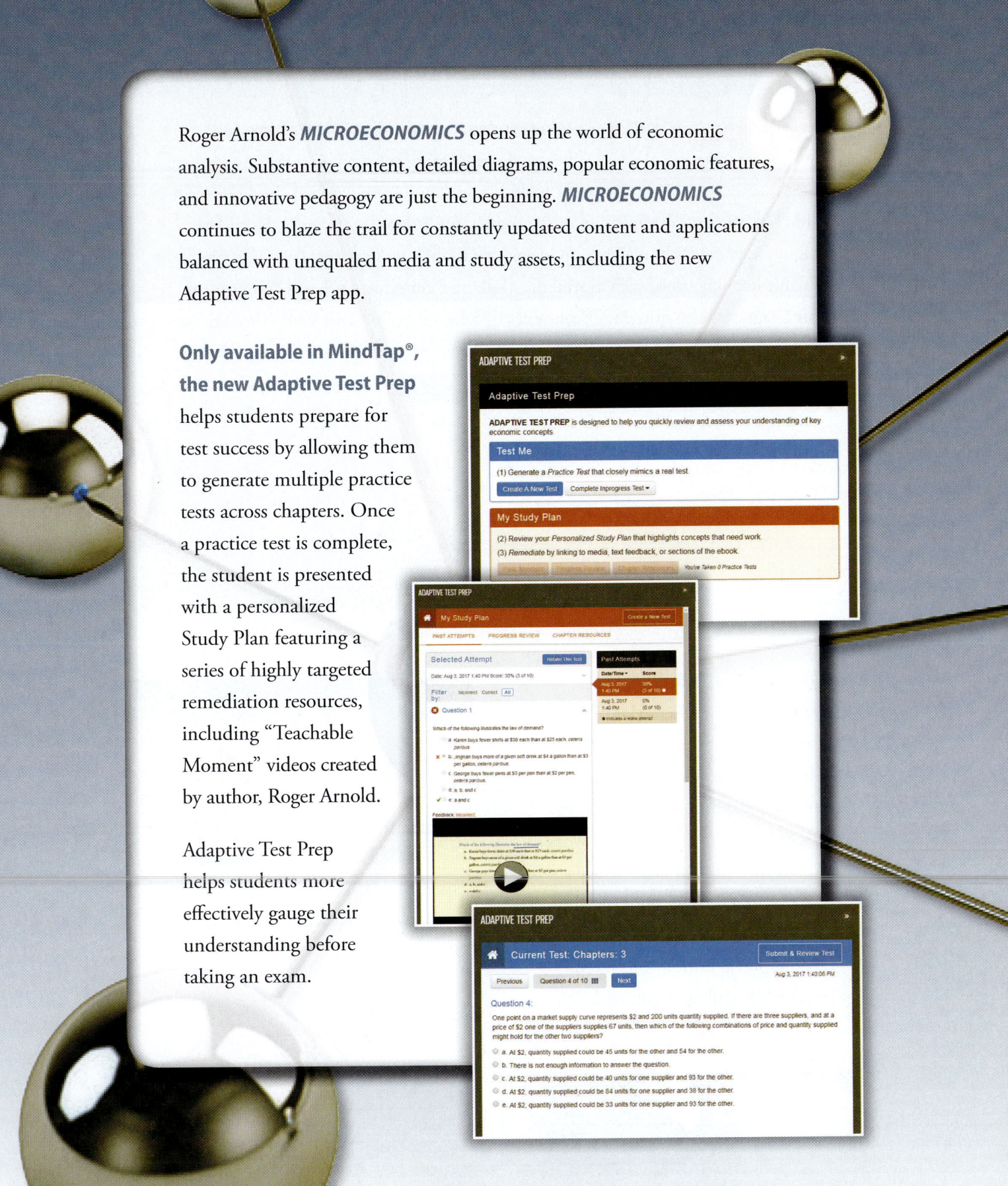

MINDTAP
From Cengage

MindTap Microeconomics 13th Edition is a personalized learning solution empowering students to analyze, apply, and improve their thinking. With MindTap, students can measure their progress and improve outcomes. Using the unique Learning Path in MindTap, students can follow prescribed steps that highlight valuable learning tools, such as readings, Talking Economics, What is Wrong With This Diagram video quizzing, Economics in 5 minutes, Problem Walk-Through videos, End-of-Chapter practice problems, the new Adaptive Test Prep App, new Graph Builders in the eReader, ConceptClip videos, Aplia, and much more.

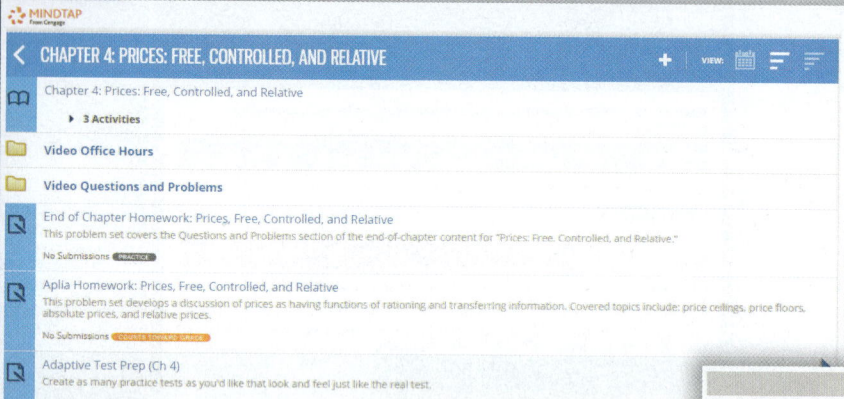

NEW! Graph Builder

Available in MindTap. Many economic graphs have been digitally enhanced in Arnold's eReader using our new Graph Builder technology. This feature allows students to work at their own pace in order to see a complex graph being built step-by-step. Progression Graphs decompose each graphical exhibit into several layers while still maintaining a rich, economic pedagogy.

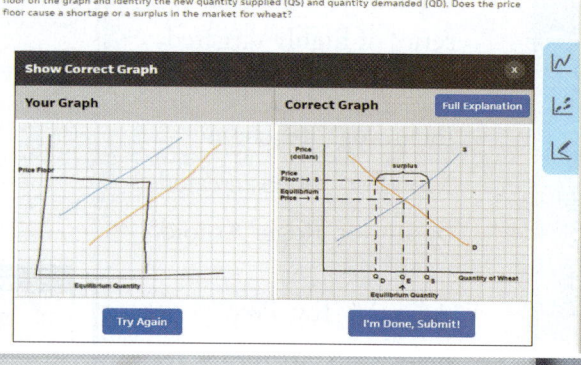

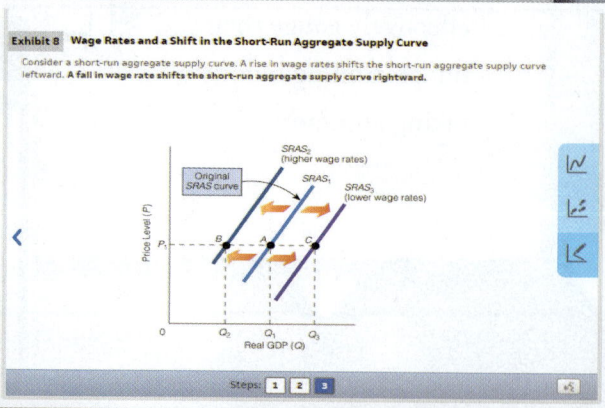

Aplia is the most successful and widely used homework solution in the Economics market, with over 1 billion answers entered. Online interactive problem sets, analyses, tutorials, experiments, and critical-thinking exercises give students hands-on application without adding to instructors' workload. Based on discovery learning, Aplia requires students to take an active role in the learning process—helping them improve their economic understanding and ability to relate to the economic concepts presented. Instructors can assign homework that is automatically graded and recorded.

Embedded in the Aplia product for Arnold's 13th Edition is the fully interactive, media rich eReader. Combining the functionality you and your students are coming to expect from a modern eReader (text search, highlighting, note-taking) with our exclusive embedded media—Video Questions and Problems, and ConceptClips—this robust reading experience is just a click away as students work through their Aplia problem sets.

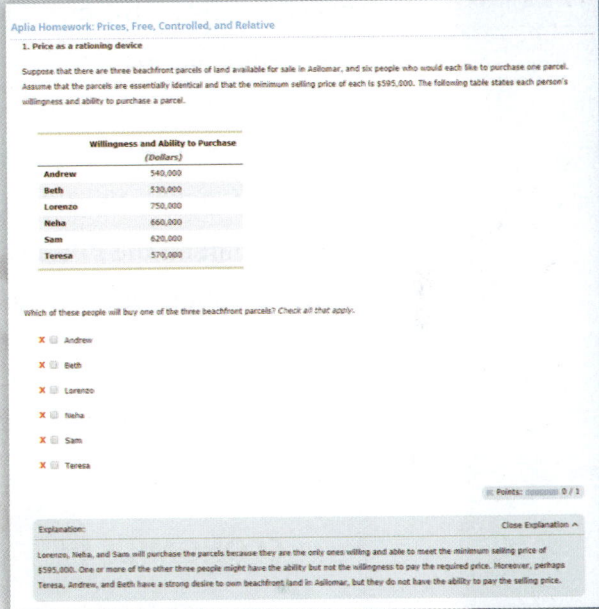

"What's Wrong With This Diagram?" assignable video quizzing walks students through the creation of a diagram, then stops the video and provides assessment that is focused on what is wrong with the newly created diagram. Once answered, the video continues to play and provides remediation and explanation. These activities are available in MindTap.

Because cultivating an economic way of thinking requires building on a foundation of theory and its application to real-world examples, *MICROECONOMICS, 13e* continues to set the standard for thoroughly updated content. In this edition, "Here What and How the Economist Thinks" and "Does It Matter to You If . . .?" are two new features included in every chapter. The first feature gives insight into just how economists go about thinking about various topics. The second feature ties what students read in an economics principles book—on such subjects as market structures, interest rates, regulation and antitrust—directly to how each affects them. Does It Matter To You If You are Efficient or Not? or If the Economy is at One Point on the PPF Instead of Another? or If Something You Buy Is Taxed or Subsidized? It certainly does.

ECONOMICS 24/7

Obesity and a Soda Tax

The percentage of the U.S. population that is deemed obese today is higher than it was 20 years ago. Obesity is a health problem, so we often hear proposals directed at trying to reduce the obesity rate in the country. One proposal is to place a tax on high-fat, high-calorie so-called junk food. A similar proposal is to place a tax on soda.

We now know that a tax placed on one good (but not on another) will change the relative prices of the two goods. Placing a tax on good X, but not on good Y, will make good X relatively more expensive and Y relatively cheaper, prompting consumers to purchase relatively less X and relatively more Y.

Consider a tax placed on soda. We would expect the absolute (money) price of soda to rise. And if the tax is placed only on soda, its relative price will rise too. As soda becomes relatively more expensive, we would expect fewer sodas to be consumed and obesity to decline. Right? Well, fewer sodas might be purchased and consumed, but whether obesity will decline is not so clear. Consider soda and sugared iced tea. Both soda and sugared iced tea are sweet drinks. They might even be substitutes. With this idea in mind, suppose the absolute price of a soda is $1 and the absolute price of an iced tea (with sugar) is 50¢. It follows that the relative prices are

$$1 \text{ soda} = 2 \text{ sugared iced teas}$$
$$1 \text{ sugared iced tea} = \tfrac{1}{2} \text{ soda}$$

Now let's place a tax on soda that drives its price up to $2. The new relative prices for soda and iced tea are

$$1 \text{ soda} = 4 \text{ sugared iced teas}$$
$$1 \text{ sugared iced tea} = \tfrac{1}{4} \text{ soda}$$

As a result of the tax on soda, its relative price has risen, but the relative price of sugared iced tea has fallen. We would thus expect people to consume relatively less soda and relatively more sugared iced tea.

Obesity is lessened by ingesting fewer calories, not the same number or more calories. Simply put, the soda tax might reduce the consumption of sodas, but it doesn't necessarily reduce obesity. Although the soda tax makes soda relatively more expensive, it makes soda substitutes (such as sugared iced tea) relatively less expensive and thus makes a rise in the consumption of sugared iced tea more likely.

Patti McConville / Alamy Stock Photo

IN APPRECIATION

Many colleagues have contributed to the success of this text over the last twelve editions. Their feedback continues to influence and enhance the text and ancillary package and I'm grateful for their efforts. Now into our 13th edition, space dictates that we can no longer list the names of all reviewers for each past edition; we are including here instructors who contributed to the development of the 13th edition, but continue to be grateful for the improvements suggested by all of the reviewers and contributors to this product over the years.

Randy Barcus
Embry Riddle Aeronautical University - Daytona Beach Daytona Beach, FL

Yosef Bonaparte
University of British Columbia Kelowna, BC

Anthony Chan
Santa Monica College Los Angeles, CA

Amy Chataginer
Mississippi Gulf Coast Community College Biloxi, MS

Megan Cummins
Mt. San Jacinto College Long Beach, CA

Ribhi Daoud
Sinclair Community College Dayton, OH

Carol Decker
Tennessee Wesleyan College Niota, TN

Brittany Dobill
John A Logan College Carterville, IL

Tila Dorina
Embry Riddle Aeronautical University - Daytona Beach, FL

Matthew Dudman
California State University - Maritime Vallejo, CA

Harry Ellis
University of North Texas Denton, TX

Susan Emens
Kent State University - Trumbull Warren, OH

Fidel Ezeala-Harrison
Jackson State University Jackson, MS

John Finley
Columbus State University Columbus, GA

Lea Frances
Germanna Community College Orange, VA

John Gaughan
Penn State University Lehigh Valley Center Valley, PA

Sherry Grosso
University of South Carolina Sumter, SC

Travis Hayes
Dalton State College Dalton, GA

Aubrey Haynes
Southwest Texas Jr College Uvalde, TX

Dewey Heinsma
Mt. San Jacinto College Yucaipa, CA

Tony Hunnicutt
College of the Ouachitas Malvern, AR

Joe Hutlak
Union County College Cranford, NJ

Andres Jauregui
Columbus State University Columbus, GA

Deb Jones
Iowa Lakes Community College Emmetsburg, IA

Barry Kotlove
Edmonds Community College Lynnwood, WA

Katie Lotz
Lake Land College Mattoon, IL

Brian Lynch
Lake Land College Mattoon, IL

Michael Machiorlatti
Oklahoma City Community College Oklahoma City, OK

Mehrdad Madresehee
Lycoming College Williamsport, PA

Mike McGay
Wilmington University Newark, DE

Shah Mehrabi
Montgomery College Arlington, VA

José Mendez
John A Logan College Carterville, IL

Elizabeth Moorhouse
Lycoming College Williamsport, PA

Edward Murphy
Embry Riddle Aeronautical University - Daytona Beach Daytona Beach, FL

Charles Myrick
Oklahoma City Community College Warr Acres, OK

Charles Newton
Houston Community College Stafford, TX

Ogbonnaya Nwoha
Grambling State University Ruston, LA

Charles Parker
Wayne State College Wayne, NE

Van Pham
Salem State University Salem, MA

John Pharr
Brookhaven College Garland, TX

Germain Pichop
Oklahoma City Community College
Oklahoma City, OK

Craig Richardson
Winston-Salem State University
Winston-Salem, NC

April Ruhmann
Southwest Texas Jr College Uvalde, TX

Sara Saderion
Houston Community College
Houston, TX

Richard Sarkisian
Camden County College Blackwood, NJ

Daniel Saros
Valparaiso University Valparaiso, IN

Anthony Sawyer
Paris Junior College Paris, TX

Bill Schweizer
University of Mount Union
Alliance, OH

Matt Shekels
North Arkansas College Harrison, AR

Kent Sickmeyer
Kaskaskia College Centralia, IL

Donald Sparks
The Citadel Charleston, SC

Boo Su
College of the Canyons Santa
Clarita, CA

Omari Swinton
Howard University Upper Marlboro, MD

Krystal Thrailkill
Rich Mountain Community College
Mena, AR

Kelly Whealan-George
Embry-Riddle Aeronautical University
South Riding, VA

Beth Wilson
Humboldt State University Arcata, CA

Davin Winger
Oklahoma Panhandle State University
Goodwell, OK

Peter Wui
University of Arkansas Pine Bluff
Little Rock, AR

Mustafa Younis
Jackson State University Jackson, MS

Evaristo Zapata
Southwest Texas Jr College Eagle Pass, TX

I would like to thank Peggy Crane of Southwestern College, who revised the Test Bank and wrote the questions for the Adaptive Test Prep. I owe a debt of gratitude to all the fine and creative people I worked with at Cengage Learning. These persons include Erin Joyner, Vice President and General Manager (Social Science and Qualitative Business); Jason Fremder, Product Director; Chris Rader, Associate Product Manager; John Carey, Executive Marketing Manager; Molly Umbarger, Content Developer; Colleen Farmer, Senior Content Project Manager; and Michelle Kunkler, Senior Art Director.

My deepest debt of gratitude goes to my wife, Sheila, and to my two sons, David and Daniel. They continue to make all my days happy ones.

Roger A. Arnold

WHAT ECONOMICS IS ABOUT

Denise Lett/Shutterstock.com

INTRODUCTION

You are about to begin your study of economics. Before discussing particular topics in economics, we think it best to give you an overview of what economics is and of some of the key concepts. The key concepts can be compared to musical notes: Just as musical notes are repeated in any song (you hear the musical note G over and over again), so are the key concepts in economics repeated. Some of these concepts are scarcity, opportunity cost, efficiency, marginal decision making, incentives, and exchange.

1-1 YOUR LIFE, 2019–2029

What will your life be like during the years 2019–2029? What kind of work will you do after college? How much will you earn in that first job after college? Where will you be living and who will your friends be? How many friends will you have? Will you buy a house in the next few years? If so, how much will you pay for the house? And, perhaps most importantly, will you be happy?

The specific answers to these questions and many more have to do with economics. For example, the salary you will earn has to do with the economic concept of *opportunity cost*. What you will do in your first job after college has to do with the *state of the economy* when you graduate. The price you pay for a house has to do with the state of the *housing market*. How many friends you have has to do with the economic concept of *scarcity*. Whether you are happy will depend on such things as the *net benefits* you receive in various activities, the *utility* you gain by doing certain things, and more.

In this chapter, we begin our study of economics. As you read the chapter (and those which follow), ask yourself how much of what you are reading is relevant to your life today and tomorrow. Ask: What does what I am reading have to do with *my* life? Our guess is that after answering this question a few dozen times, you will be convinced that economics explains much about your present and future.

1-2 A DEFINITION OF ECONOMICS

In this section, we discuss a few key economic concepts; then we incorporate knowledge of these concepts into a definition of economics.

1-2a Goods and Bads

Economists talk about *goods* and *bads*. A **good** is anything that gives a person **utility**, or satisfaction. Here is a partial list of some goods: a computer, a car, a watch, a television set, friendship, and love. You will notice from our list that a good can be either tangible or intangible. A computer is a tangible good; friendship is an intangible good. Simply put, for something to be a good (whether tangible or intangible), it only has to give someone utility or satisfaction.

A **bad** is something that gives a person **disutility** or dissatisfaction. If the flu gives you disutility or dissatisfaction, then it is a bad. If the constant nagging of an acquaintance is something that gives you disutility or dissatisfaction, then it is a bad.

People want goods, and they do not want bads. In fact, they will pay to get goods ("Here is $1,000 for the computer"), and they will pay to get rid of bads ("I'd be willing to pay you, doctor, if you can prescribe something that will shorten the time I have the flu").

Can something be a *good* for one person and a *bad* for another person? Smoking cigarettes gives some people utility; it gives others disutility. We conclude that smoking cigarettes can be a *good* for some people and a *bad* for others. This must be why the wife tells her husband, "If you want to smoke, you should do it outside." In other words, "Get those *bads* away from me."

1-2b Resources

Goods do not just appear before us when we snap our fingers. It takes resources to produce goods. (Sometimes *resources* are referred to as *inputs* or *factors of production.*)

Generally, economists divide resources into four broad categories: *land, labor, capital,* and *entrepreneurship.*

- **Land** includes natural resources, such as minerals, forests, water, and unimproved land. For example, oil, wood, and animals fall into this category. (Sometimes economists refer to the category simply as *natural resources.*)

- **Labor** consists of the physical and mental talents that people contribute to the production process. For example, a person building a house is using his or her own labor.

- **Capital** consists of produced goods that can be used as inputs for further production. Factories, machinery, tools, computers, and buildings are examples of capital. One country might have more capital than another; that is, it has more factories, machinery, tools, and the like.

- **Entrepreneurship** refers to the talent that some people have for organizing the resources of land, labor, and capital to produce goods, seek new business opportunities, and develop new ways of doing things.

1-2c Scarcity and a Definition of Economics

We are now ready to define a key concept in economics: *scarcity.* **Scarcity** is the condition in which our wants (for goods) are greater than the limited resources (land, labor, capital, and entrepreneurship) available to satisfy those wants. In other words, we want goods, but not enough resources are available to provide us with all the goods we want.

Look at it this way: Our wants (for goods) are infinite, but our resources (which we need to produce the goods) are finite. Scarcity is the result of our infinite wants hitting up against finite resources.

Good
Anything from which individuals receive utility or satisfaction.

Utility
The satisfaction one receives from a good.

Bad
Anything from which individuals receive disutility or dissatisfaction.

Disutility
The dissatisfaction one receives from a bad.

Land
All natural resources, such as minerals, forests, water, and unimproved land.

Labor
The work brought about by the physical and mental talents that people contribute to the production process.

Capital
Produced goods, such as factories, machinery, tools, computers, and buildings that can be used as inputs for further production.

Entrepreneurship
The talent that some people have for organizing the resources of land, labor, and capital to produce goods, seek new business opportunities, and develop new ways of doing things.

Scarcity
The condition in which our wants are greater than the limited resources available to satisfy those wants.

Many economists say that if scarcity didn't exist, neither would economics. In other words, if our wants weren't greater than the limited resources available to satisfy them, there would be no field of study called economics. This is similar to saying that if matter and motion didn't exist, neither would physics or that if living things didn't exist, neither would biology. For this reason, we define **economics** in this text as the science of scarcity. More completely, *economics is the science of how individuals and societies deal with the fact that wants are greater than the limited resources available to satisfy those wants.*

Economics
The science of scarcity; the science of how individuals and societies deal with the fact that wants are greater than the limited resources available to satisfy those wants.

THINKING LIKE AN ECONOMIST

Scarcity Affects Everyone Everyone in the world—even a billionaire—has to face scarcity. Billionaires may be able to satisfy more of their wants for tangible goods (houses, cars) than most people, but they still may not have the resources to satisfy all their wants. Their wants might include more time with their children, more friendship, no disease in the world, peace, and a hundred other things that they don't have the resources to "produce."

Thinking in Terms of Scarcity's Effects Scarcity has effects. Here are three: (1) the need to make choices, (2) the need for a rationing device, and (3) competition.

Choices People have to make choices because of scarcity. Because our unlimited wants are greater than our limited resources, some wants must go unsatisfied. We must choose which wants we will satisfy and which we will not. Jeremy asks, "Do I go to Hawaii or do I pay off my car loan earlier?" Ellen asks, "Do I buy the new sweater or two new shirts?"

Need for a Rationing Device A **rationing device** is a means of deciding who gets what of available resources and goods. Scarcity implies the need for a rationing device. If people have infinite wants for goods and if only limited resources are available to produce the goods, then a rationing device is needed to decide who gets the available quantity of goods. Dollar price is a rationing device. For instance, 100 cars are on the lot, and everyone wants a new car. How do we decide who gets what quantity of the new cars? The answer is to use the rationing device called *dollar price*. The people who pay the dollar price for a new car end up with one.

Rationing Device
A means for deciding who gets what of available resources and goods.

Scarcity and Competition Do you see competition in the world? Are people competing for jobs? Are states and cities competing for businesses? Are students competing for grades? The answer to all these questions is yes. The economist wants to know why this competition exists and what form it takes. First, the economist concludes, competition exists because of scarcity. If there were enough resources to satisfy all our seemingly unlimited wants, people would not have to compete for the available, but limited, resources.

Second, the economist sees that competition takes the form of people trying to get more of the rationing device. If dollar price is the rationing device, people compete to earn dollars. Look at your own case. You are a college student working for a degree. One reason (but perhaps not the only reason) you are attending college is to earn a higher income after graduation. But why do you want a higher income? You want it because it will allow you to satisfy more of your wants.

Suppose muscular strength (measured by lifting weights), instead of dollar price, were the rationing device. Then people with more muscular strength would receive more resources and goods than people with less muscular strength. In that case, people would compete for muscular strength. (Would they spend more time at the gym lifting weights?) The lesson is simple: *Whatever the rationing device is, people will compete for it.*

FINDING ECONOMICS

At the campus bookstore   To learn economics well, you must practice what you learn. One of the ways to practice economics is to find it in everyday life. Consider the following scene: You are in the campus bookstore buying a book for your computer science course, and you are handing over $85 to the cashier. Can you find the economics in this simple scene? Before you read on, think about it for a minute.

Let's work backward to find the economics. You are currently handing the cashier $85. We know that dollar price is a rationing device. But let's now ask ourselves why we would need a rationing device to get the book. The answer is scarcity. In other words, scarcity is casting its long shadow there in the bookstore as you buy a book. We have found one of the key economic concepts—scarcity—in the campus bookstore. (If you also said that a book is a good, then you have found even more economics in the bookstore. Can you find more than scarcity and a good?)

SELF-TEST

(Answers to Self-Test questions are in Answers to Self-Test Questions at the back of the book.)

1. True or false? Scarcity is the condition of finite resources. Explain your answer.

2. How does competition arise out of scarcity?

3. How does choice arise out of scarcity?

1-3   KEY CONCEPTS IN ECONOMICS

A number of key concepts in economics define the field. We discuss a few of these concepts next.

1-3a Opportunity Cost

So far, we have established that people must make choices because scarcity exists. In other words, because our seemingly unlimited wants push up against limited resources, some wants must go unsatisfied. We must therefore *choose* which wants we will satisfy and which we will not. The most highly valued opportunity or alternative forfeited when we make a choice is known as **opportunity cost**. Every time you make a choice, you incur an opportunity cost. For example, you have chosen to read this chapter. In making this choice, you denied yourself the benefits of doing something else. You could have watched television, written text messages to a friend, taken a nap, eaten a few slices of pizza, read a novel, shopped for a new computer, and so on. Whatever you *would have chosen* to do is the opportunity cost of your reading this chapter. For instance, if you would have watched television instead of reading this chapter—if that was your next best alternative—then the opportunity cost of reading the chapter is watching television.

Opportunity Cost
The most highly valued opportunity or alternative forfeited when a choice is made.

There Is No Such Thing as a Free Lunch   Economists are fond of saying that "there is no such thing as a free lunch." This catchy phrase expresses the idea that opportunity costs are incurred whenever choices are made. Perhaps this is an obvious point, but consider how often people mistakenly assume that there *is* a free lunch. For example, some parents think that education is free, because they do not pay tuition for their children to attend public elementary school. That's a misconception. "Free" implies no sacrifice and no opportunities forfeited, but an elementary school education requires resources that could be used for other things.

Consider the people who speak about free medical care, free housing, free bridges ("there's no charge to cross it"), and free parks. Again, free medical care, free housing, free bridges, and free parks are misconceptions. The resources that provide medical care, housing, bridges, and parks could have been used in other ways.

ECONOMICS 24/7

Rationing Spots at Yale

Each year, Yale University receives more applications for admission to the freshmen class than spots are available. In most years, for every 100 applications for admission that Yale receives, it can accept only seven applicants for admission. What Yale has to do, then, is ration its available admission spots.

How does it ration its available spots? One way is simply to use money as a rationing device. In other words, raise the dollar amount of attending Yale to a high enough level so that the number of spots equals the number of students willing and available to pay for admission. To illustrate, think of Yale as auctioning off spots in its freshman class. It calls out a price of $50,000 a year, and at this price more people wish to be admitted to Yale than there are spots available. Yale keeps on raising the price until the number of students who are willing and able to pay the tuition is equal to the number of available spots. Maybe this price is, say, $200,000.

As we know, Yale does not ration its available spots this way. In fact, it uses numerous rationing devices in an attempt to whittle down the number of applicants to the number of available spots. For example, it might use the rationing device of high school grades. Anyone with a GPA in high school of less than, say, 3.50 is not going to be admitted. If, after doing this, Yale still has too many applicants, it might then make use of the rationing device of standardized test scores. Anyone with an SAT score of under, say, 2100 is eliminated from the pool of applicants. If there are still too many applicants, then perhaps other rationing devices will be used, such as academic achievements, community service, degree of interest in attending Yale, and so on.

iStock.com/peterspiro

Yale might also decide that it wants to admit certain students over others, even if the two categories of students have the same academic credentials. For example, suppose Yale wants at least one student from each state in the country, and only 10 students from Wyoming have applied to go to Yale whereas 500 students from California have applied. Then Yale could very well use the rationing device of state diversity to decide in favor of the student from Wyoming instead of the applicant from California.

In the first week of April each year, Yale sends out many more rejection letters than acceptance letters. No doubt, some students who are rejected by Yale feel that some of the students who were accepted might not be as academically strong as they are. No doubt, the student with a 4.00 GPA and a perfect SAT score of 2400 feels that he might have been slighted by Yale when he learns that a student in his high school with a 3.86 GPA and SAT score of 2180 was chosen over him. What did the 3.86–2180 student have that he didn't have? What rationing device benchmark did the rejected student score lower on?

In life, you will often hear people arguing over what the rationing device for certain things should be. Should high school grades and standardized test scores be the only two rationing devices for college admission? What role should money play as a rationing device when a high school graduate applies to college? What role should ethnic or racial diversity, or state diversity, or income diversity play in the application process? Our point is a simple one: With scarcity comes the need for a rationing device. More people want a spot at Yale than there are spots available. Yale has to use one or more rationing devices to decide who will be accepted and who will be rejected.

THINKING LIKE AN ECONOMIST

Zero Price Doesn't Mean Zero Cost   A friend gives you a ticket to an upcoming concert for zero price (i.e., you pay nothing). Does it follow that zero price means zero cost? No. There is still an opportunity cost of attending the concert. Whatever you would be doing if you don't go to the concert is the opportunity cost of attending. To illustrate, if you don't attend the concert, you would hang out with friends. The value you place on hanging out with friends is the opportunity cost of your attending the concert.

1-3b Opportunity Cost and Behavior

Economists believe that a change in opportunity cost can change a person's behavior. For example, Ryan, who is a sophomore at college, attends classes Monday through Thursday of every week. Every time he chooses to go to class, he gives up the opportunity to do something else, such as earn $15 an hour working at a job. The opportunity cost of Ryan's spending an hour in class is $15.

Now let's raise the opportunity cost of attending class. On Tuesday, we offer Ryan $70 to skip his economics class. He knows that if he attends his economics class, he will forfeit $70. What will Ryan do? An economist would predict that as the opportunity cost of attending class increases relative to the benefits of attending, Ryan is less likely to go to class.

This is how economists think about behavior: *The higher the opportunity cost of doing something, the less likely it is that it will be done.* This is part of the economic way of thinking.

Look at Exhibit 1, which summarizes some of the things about scarcity, choice, and opportunity cost up to this point.

EXHIBIT 1

Scarcity and Related Concepts

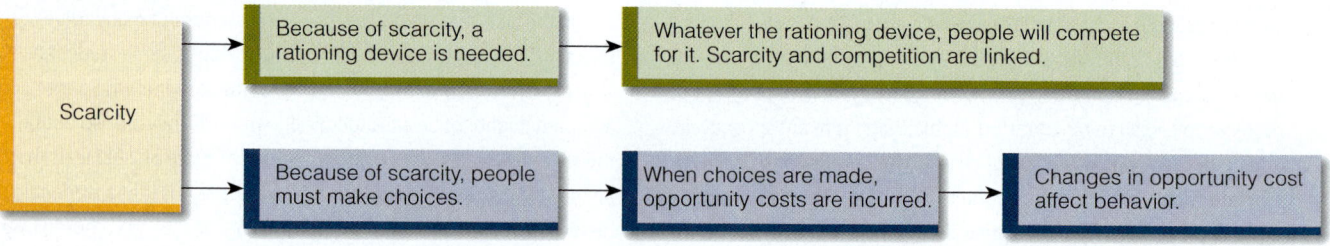

FINDING ECONOMICS

In Being Late to Class   John is often a few minutes late to his biology class. The class starts at 10 a.m., but John usually walks into the class at 10:03 a.m. The instructor has asked John to be on time, but John usually excuses his behavior by saying that the traffic getting to college was bad or that his alarm didn't go off at the right time or that something else happened to delay him. One thing the instructor observes, though, is that John is never late when it comes to test day. He is usually in class a few minutes before the test begins. Where is the economics?

We would expect behavior to change as opportunity cost changes. When a test is being given in class, the opportunity cost of being late to class is higher than when a test is not being given and the instructor is simply lecturing. If John is late to class on test day, he then has fewer minutes to complete the test, and having less time can adversely affect his grade. In short, the higher the opportunity cost of being late to class, the less likely it is that John will be late.

1-3c Benefits and Costs

If we could eliminate air pollution completely, should we do it? If your answer is yes, then you are probably focusing on the *benefits* of eliminating air pollution. For example, one benefit might be healthier individuals. Certainly, individuals who do not breathe polluted air have fewer lung disorders than people who do breathe polluted air.

But benefits rarely come without costs. The economist reminds us that, although eliminating pollution has its benefits, it has costs too. To illustrate, one way to eliminate all car pollution tomorrow is to pass a law stating that anyone caught driving a car will go to prison for 40 years. With such a draconian law in place and enforced, very few people would drive cars and all car pollution would be a thing of the past. Presto! Cleaner air! However, many people would think that the cost of obtaining that cleaner air is too high. Someone might say, "I want cleaner air, but not if I have to completely give up driving my car. How will I get to work?"

What distinguishes the economist from the noneconomist is that the economist thinks in terms of *both* costs *and* benefits. Often, the noneconomist thinks in terms of one or the other. Studying has its benefits, but it has costs too. Coming to class has benefits, but it has costs too. Getting up early each morning and exercising has its costs, but let's not forget that there are benefits too.

1-3d Decisions Made at the Margin

It is late at night, and you have already studied three hours for your biology test tomorrow. You look at the clock and wonder if you should study another hour. How would you summarize your thinking process? What question or questions do you ask yourself to decide whether to study another hour?

Perhaps without knowing it, you think in terms of the costs and benefits of further study. You probably realize that studying an additional hour has certain benefits (you may be able to raise your grade a few points), but it has costs too (you will get less sleep or have less time to watch television or talk on the phone with a friend). *That* you think in terms of costs and benefits, however, doesn't tell us *how* you think in terms of costs and benefits. For example, when deciding what to do, do you look at the *total costs* and *total benefits* of the proposed action, or do you look at something less than the total costs and benefits? According to economists, for most decisions, you think in terms of *additional*, or *marginal*, costs and benefits, not *total* costs and benefits. That's because most decisions deal with making a small, or additional, change.

To illustrate, suppose you just finished eating a hamburger and drinking a soda for lunch. You are still a little hungry and are considering whether to order another hamburger. An economist would say that, in deciding whether to order another hamburger, you compare the additional benefits of the second hamburger with its additional costs. In economics, the word *marginal* is a synonym for *additional*. So, we say that you compare the **marginal benefits (MB)** of the (next) hamburger to its **marginal costs (MC)**. If the marginal benefits are greater than the marginal costs, you obviously expect a net benefit to ordering the next hamburger, and therefore you order another. If, however, the marginal benefits are less than the marginal costs, you obviously expect a net cost to ordering the next hamburger, and therefore you do not order another. Logically, the situation is as follows:

Marginal Benefits (MB)
Additional benefits; the benefits connected with consuming an additional unit of a good or undertaking one more unit of an activity.

Marginal Costs (MC)
Additional costs; the costs connected with consuming an additional unit of a good or undertaking one more unit of an activity.

Condition	Action
MB of next hamburger > MC of next hamburger	Buy next hamburger
MB of next hamburger < MC of next hamburger	Do not buy next hamburger

What you don't consider when making this decision are the *total* benefits and *total* costs of hamburgers. That's because the benefits and costs connected with the first hamburger (the one you have already eaten) are no longer relevant to the current decision. You are not deciding between eating two hamburgers or eating no hamburgers; your decision is whether to eat a second hamburger after you have already eaten one.

According to economists, when individuals make decisions by comparing marginal benefits with marginal costs, they are making **decisions at the margin**. The employee makes a decision at the margin in deciding whether to work two hours overtime; the economics professor makes a decision at the margin in deciding whether to put an additional question on the final exam.

Decisions at the Margin
Decision making characterized by weighing the additional (marginal) benefits of a change against the additional (marginal) costs of a change with respect to current conditions.

ECONOMICS 24/7

When Is It Too Costly to Attend College?

Look around your class. Are there any big-name actors, sports stars, or comedians between the ages of 18 and 25 in your class? Probably not. The reason is that, for these people, the opportunity cost of attending college is much higher than it is for most 18-to-25-year-olds. Think of LeBron James, a basketball star, Chris Rock, a comedian, Johnny Depp, an actor, Will Smith, also an actor—these people and many more like them chose not to go to college. Why didn't they go to college? The fact is that they didn't go to college because it was too expensive for them to go to college. Not "too expensive" in the sense that the "tuition was too high," but expensive in terms of what they would have had to give up if they attended college—expensive in opportunity cost terms.

To understand this idea, think of what it's costing you to attend college. If you pay $3,000 tuition a semester for eight semesters, the full tuition amounts to $24,000. However, $24,000 is not the full cost of attending college, because if you were not a student, you could be earning income working at a job. For example, you could be working at a full-time job earning $32,000 annually. Certainly, this $32,000, or at least part of it if you are currently working part time, is forfeited because you are attending college. It is part of the total cost of your attending college.

The *tuition cost* may be the same for everyone who attends your college, but the *opportunity cost* is not. Some people have higher opportunity costs of attending college than others. It just so happens that Johnny Depp, LeBron James, Will Smith, and Chris Rock had extremely high opportunity costs of attending college. Each would have to give up hundreds of thousands of dollars if he were to attend college on a full-time basis.

Simply put, our story illustrates two related points we have made in this chapter. First, earlier we said that *the higher the opportunity cost of doing something, the less likely it will be done*. The opportunity cost of attending college is higher for some people than others, and that is why not everyone who can pay for college chooses to attend college.

Kent Smith/NBAE/Getty Images

Second, we said that economists believe that *individuals think and act in terms of costs and benefits and that they undertake actions only if they expect the benefits to outweigh the costs*. Thus, Johnny Depp, LeBron James, Will Smith, and Chris Rock saw certain benefits to attending college—just as you see certain benefits to attending college. But those benefits—although they may be the same for you and everyone else—are not enough to get everyone to attend college. That's because the benefits are not all that matters. The costs matter, too. In the case of Johnny Depp, LeBron James, Will Smith, and Chris Rock, the costs of attending college were much higher than the benefits, so they chose not to attend college. In your case, the benefits are higher than the costs, so you have decided to attend college.

1-3e **Efficiency**

What is the right amount of time to study for a test? In economics, the *right amount* of anything is the *optimal* or *efficient* amount—the amount for which the marginal benefits equal the marginal costs. Stated differently, you have achieved **efficiency** when the marginal benefits equal the marginal costs.

Suppose you are studying for an economics test, and for the first hour of studying, the marginal benefits (*MB*) are greater than the marginal costs (*MC*):

> MB studying first hour > MC studying first hour

Given this condition, you will certainly study for the first hour, because it is worth it: The additional benefits are greater than the additional costs, so there is a net benefit to studying.

Suppose, for the second hour of studying, the marginal benefits are still greater than the marginal costs:

> MB studying second hour > MC studying second hour

Then you will study for the second hour, because the additional benefits are still greater than the additional costs. In other words, studying the second hour is worthwhile. In fact, you will continue to study as long as the marginal benefits are greater than the marginal costs. Exhibit 2 illustrates this discussion graphically.

Efficiency
Exists when marginal benefits equal marginal costs.

EXHIBIT 2

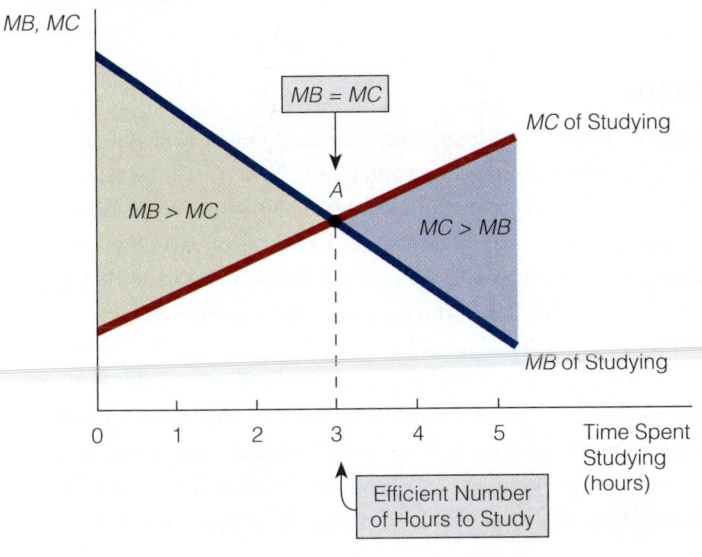

Efficiency

MB = marginal benefits and *MC* = marginal costs. In the exhibit, the *MB* curve of studying is downward sloping and the *MC* curve of studying is upward sloping. As long as *MB* > *MC*, the person will study. The person stops studying when *MB* = *MC*. This point is where efficiency is achieved.

The *MB* curve of studying is downward sloping because we have assumed that the benefits of studying for the first hour are greater than the benefits of studying for the second hour and so on. The *MC* curve of studying is upward sloping because we have assumed that studying the second hour costs a person more (in terms of goods forfeited) than studying the first hour, studying the third hour costs more than studying the second, and so on. (If we assume that the additional costs of studying are constant over time, the *MC* curve is horizontal.)

In the exhibit, the marginal benefits of studying equal the marginal costs of studying at three hours. So, three hours is the *efficient* length of time to study in this situation. At less than three hours, the marginal benefits of studying are greater than the marginal costs; thus, at all these hours, studying has net benefits. At more than three hours, the marginal costs of studying are greater than the marginal benefits, so studying beyond three hours is not worthwhile.

Maximizing Net Benefits   Take another look at Exhibit 2. Suppose you had stopped studying after the first hour (or, equivalently, after the 60th minute). Would you have given up anything? Yes, you would have given up the *net benefits* of studying longer. To illustrate, notice that between the first and the second hour, the *MB* curve lies above the *MC* curve. This means that studying the second hour has net benefits. But if you hadn't studied that second hour—if you had stopped after the first hour—then you would have given up the opportunity to collect those net benefits. The same analysis holds for the third hour. We conclude that, by studying three hours (but not one minute longer), you have maximized net benefits. In short, efficiency, which is consistent with $MB = MC$, is also consistent with maximizing net benefits.

THINKING LIKE AN ECONOMIST

No $10 Bills on the Sidewalk   An economist says that people try to maximize their net benefits. You ask for proof. The economist says, "You don't find any $10 bills on the sidewalk." What is the economist getting at by making this statement? Keep in mind that you don't find any $10 bills on the sidewalk because, if there were a $10 bill on the sidewalk, the first person to see it would pick it up; when you came along, it wouldn't be there. But why would the first person to find the $10 bill pick it up? The reason is that people don't pass by net benefits, and picking up the $10 bill comes with net benefits. The *benefits* of having an additional $10 are obvious; the *costs* of obtaining the additional $10 bill are simply what you give up during the time you are stooping down to pick it up. In short, the marginal benefits are likely to be greater than the marginal costs (giving us net benefits), and that is why the $10 bill is picked up. Saying that there are no $10 bills on the sidewalk is the same as saying that no one leaves net benefits on the sidewalk. In other words, people try to maximize net benefits.

Does It Matter to You . . .
If You Are Efficient or Not?

The efficient amount of an activity is the amount at which the marginal benefits (*MB*) of the activity equal the marginal costs (*MC*). With this in mind, look at Exhibit 3. The activity of bowling is on the horizontal axis, measured in minutes. The marginal benefits and costs of bowling are on the vertical axis. The efficient amount of time spent bowling—the time at which the marginal benefits of bowling are equal to the marginal costs of bowling—is 60 minutes.

Now let's ask what is so special about the efficient amount of bowling? Why, in our example, is 60 minutes of bowling preferred to, say, 30 minutes of bowling? To answer the question, consider what the net benefits of bowling are at 30 minutes and at 60 minutes.

The net benefits of bowling 30 minutes are shown in the diagram as the shaded red area. To understand why this area represents the net benefits of bowling for 30 minutes, consider that from 0 minutes through 30 minutes, the *MB* curve lies above the *MC* curve. In other words, from 0 minutes through 30 minutes the marginal benefits of bowling are greater than the marginal costs, leaving us with net benefits. We have assigned a dollar figure of $8 to these net benefits.

Now if a person stopped bowling after 30 minutes, he or she would have received $8 worth of net benefits. That is not bad, but things

Action Plus Sports Images/Alamy Stock Photo

could be better. Notice that there are net benefits gained by bowling additional minutes. In fact, there are net benefits gained by bowling 30 additional minutes (from the 31st through the 60th minute). The area of net benefits is shown in the diagram as the shaded blue area. We have assigned a dollar figure of $6 to these net benefits.

Is it better to bowl 30 minutes or 60 minutes? The answer is 60 minutes, because having bowled 60 minutes a person receives overall net benefits of $8 plus $6 or $14. But bowling only 30 minutes leaves a person having gained only $8 worth of net benefits. In other words, by not bowling after the 30th minute, it is as if a person is leaving $6 (worth of net benefits) on the table. That's sort of like leaving $6 on the street instead of picking it up.

We started with a question: Does it matter if you are efficient or not? The answer is that it does matter. If you are efficient, you have done as well as can be done; you have maximized net benefits.

Now, if 60 minutes of bowling is better than 30 minutes, then why isn't 75 minutes of bowling better than 60 minutes? If you look at the diagram, the answer is obvious. Because bowling for more than 60 minutes comes with marginal benefits less than marginal costs. The shaded green area in the exhibit represents the net costs of bowling from the 60th minute to the 75th minute. We have assigned a dollar value of $4 to this net cost. What then would your overall net benefits be if you bowled 75 minutes instead of 60 minutes? They would be equal to $8 + $6 − $4 or $10. And that, we notice, is a lower overall net benefit than one receives by bowling just 60 minutes.

EXHIBIT 3

The Efficient Amount of Time to Bowl

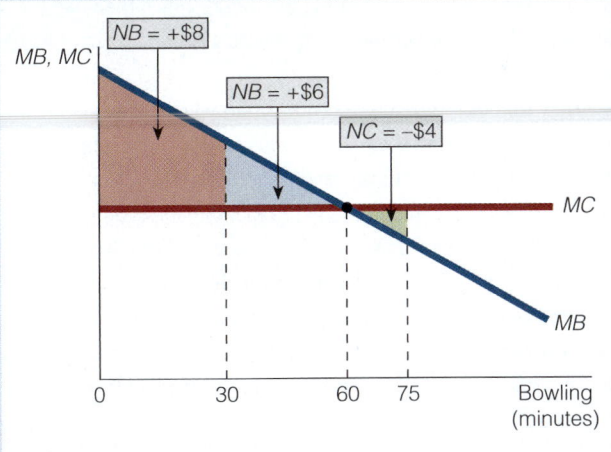

1-3f   Economics Is About Incentives

Incentive
Something that encourages or motivates a person to undertake an action.

An **incentive** is something that encourages or motivates a person to undertake an action.

Often, what motivates a person to undertake an action is the belief that, by taking that action, she can make herself better off. For example, if we say that Dawn has an incentive to study for the upcoming exam, we imply that, by studying, Dawn can make herself better off, probably in terms of receiving a higher grade on the exam than if she didn't study.

Incentives are closely related to benefits and costs. Individuals have an incentive to undertake actions for which the benefits are greater than the costs or, stated differently, for which they expect to receive net benefits (benefits greater than costs).

ECONOMICS 24/7

Can Incentives Make You Smarter?

Most people seem to think themselves smarter when it comes to some things than other things. For example, a person may say that she is fairly smart when it comes to learning biology, but not so smart when it comes to learning mathematics. Another person might say that he is smart when it comes to fixing cars, but not so smart when it comes to learning foreign languages.

Now ask yourself if incentives can affect how smart you are when it comes to any given subject: economics, mathematics, biology, history, and so on. Consider the experiment described next, and consider what you think the results of the experiment are likely to be.

An economics instructor teaches two classes of economics, A and B. In each class there are 45 students, and in each class the instructor gives the same eight quizzes. In class A, the instructor tells each student that, for every quiz on which the student receives a grade of 90 or higher, he or she will receive $100. In class B, the instructor offers no such incentive.

Now predict whether grades in the two classes will be the same or different? If different, in which class, A or B, are students likely to earn higher grades? Finally, ask yourself if you would study harder for a quiz given in class A or class B? If your answer to the last question is class A (in which there is a chance of earning $800 over eight quizzes), then it is very likely that your grades will be higher in class A than in class B. In fact, by studying harder and earning higher grades, you might even end up concluding that you are smarter when it comes to economics than you thought you were. It's very likely that the incentive encouraged

wavebreakmedia/Shutterstock.com

or motivated you to study harder (and more), which then had the unintended effect of getting you to realize you were smarter than you initially thought.

Now suppose someone asks how smart you are when it comes to physics or mathematics. If you feel that these subjects are beyond you somehow, you might say, "I don't think I'm that smart when it comes to physics or mathematics. I don't really understand a lot that is taught in those subjects." But perhaps the correct answer is, "I'm not sure how smart or not I am when it comes to physics or mathematics. A lot depends on the incentives that exist to learn physics and mathematics. Under certain incentives, I seem to be smarter than under other incentives."

Economists are interested in what motivates behavior. Why does the person buy more of good *X* when its price falls? Why might a person work longer hours when income tax rates decline? Why might a person buy more of a particular good today if he expects the price of that good to go up next week? The general answer to many of these questions is that people do what they have an incentive to do. Economists then hunt for what the incentive is. For example, if a person buys more of good *X* when its price goes down, what specifically is the incentive? How, specifically, does the person make himself better off by buying a good when its price declines. Does he get more utility or satisfaction? Or how does a person make herself better off if she buys a good today that she expects will go up in price next week?

1-3g Unintended Effects

Economists think in terms of unintended effects. For instance, Andrés, 16 years old, currently works after school at a grocery store. He earns $9.50 an hour.

Suppose the state legislature passes a law specifying that the minimum dollar wage a person can be paid to do a job is $15 an hour. The legislators' intention in passing the law is to help people like Andrés earn more income.

Will the $15-an-hour legislation have the intended effect? Perhaps not. The manager of the grocery store may not find it worthwhile to continue employing Andrés if she has to pay him $15 an hour. In other words, Andrés may have a job at $9.50 an hour but not at $15 an hour. If the law specifies that no one may earn less than $15 an hour and the manager of the grocery store decides to fire Andrés rather than pay that amount, then an unintended effect of the legislation is Andrés losing his job.

As another example, let's analyze mandatory seat-belt laws to see whether they have any unintended effects. States have laws that require drivers to wear seat belts. The intended effect is to reduce the number of car-related fatalities by making it more likely that drivers will survive accidents.

Could these laws have an unintended effect? Some economists think so. They look at accident fatalities in terms of this equation:

$$\text{Total number of fatalities} = \text{Number of accidents} \times \text{Fatalities per accident}$$

For example, if there are 200,000 accidents and 0.10 fatality per accident, the total number of fatalities is 20,000.

The objective of a mandatory seat-belt program is to reduce the total number of fatalities by reducing the number of fatalities per accident (the fatality rate). Many studies have found that wearing seat belts does just that. If you are in an accident, you have a better chance of not being killed if you are wearing a seat belt.

Let's assume that, with seat belts, there is 0.08, instead of 0.10, fatality per accident. If there are still 200,000 accidents, then the total number of fatalities falls from 20,000 to 16,000. Thus, as the following table shows, the total number of fatalities drops if the number of fatalities per accident is reduced and the number of accidents is constant:

Number of Accidents	Fatalities per Accident	Total Number of Fatalities
200,000	0.10	20,000
200,000	0.08	16,000

However, some economists wonder whether the number of accidents stays constant. Specifically, they suggest that seat belts may have an unintended effect: *The number of accidents may increase* because wearing seat belts may make drivers feel safer. Feeling safer may cause them to take chances that they wouldn't ordinarily take, such as driving faster or more aggressively, or concentrating less on their driving and more on the music on the radio. For example, if the number of accidents rises to 250,000, then the total number of fatalities is again 20,000:

Number of Accidents	Fatalities per Accident	Total Number of Fatalities
200,000	0.10	20,000
250,000	0.08	20,000

We conclude the following: If a mandatory seat-belt law reduces the number of fatalities per accident (the intended effect) but increases the number of accidents (an unintended effect), then the law may not, contrary to popular belief, reduce the total number of fatalities. In fact, some economics studies show just that.

What does all this mean for you? You may be safer if you know that this unintended effect exists and you adjust accordingly. To be specific, when you wear your seat belt, your chances of getting hurt in a car accident are less than if you don't wear your seat belt. But if this added sense of protection causes you to drive less carefully than you would otherwise, then you could unintentionally offset the measure of protection your seat belt provides. To reduce the probability of hurting yourself and others in a car accident, *the best policy is to wear a seat belt and to drive as carefully as you would if you weren't wearing a seat belt.* Knowing about the unintended effect of wearing your seat belt could save your life.

1-3h Exchange

Exchange, or **trade**, is the giving up of one thing for something else. Economics is sometimes called the *science of exchange* because so much that is discussed in economics has to do with exchange.

We start with a basic question: Why do people enter into exchanges? The answer is that they do so to make themselves better off. When a person voluntarily trades $100 for a jacket, she is saying, "I prefer to have the jacket instead of the $100." And, of course, when the seller of the jacket voluntarily sells the jacket for $100, he is saying, "I prefer to have the $100 instead of the jacket." In short, through trade or exchange, each person gives up something he values less for something he values more.

You can think of trade in terms of utility or satisfaction. Imagine a utility scale that goes from 1 to 10, with 10 being the highest utility you can achieve. Now, suppose you currently have $40 in your wallet and you are at 7 on the utility scale. A few minutes later, you are in a store looking at some new shirts. The price of each is $20, and you end up buying two shirts for $40.

After you traded your $40 for the shirts, are you still at 7 on the utility scale? The likely answer is no. If you expected to have the same utility after the trade as you did before, you probably would not have traded your $40 for the shirts. The only reason you entered into the trade is that you *expected* to be better off after the trade than you were before it. In other words, you thought that trading your $40 for the shirts would move you up the utility scale from 7 to, say, 8.

ECONOMICS 24/7

Why Didn't I Think of That? The Case of Uber and Airbnb

Consider two companies, both headquartered in San Francisco. The first is Uber and the second is Airbnb. Uber is a company that operates a mobile-app-based transportation network. Here are how things work. One person needs transportation from his home to the airport. Another person, with a car, who is in the vicinity of this first person, is willing and able to drive the person to the airport for a fee. Uber takes a percentage of the dollar transaction between driver and rider. In a way, you could say that Uber is a taxi company, but owns no taxis.

svetikd/E+/Getty Images

Now consider Airbnb, which is essentially a website. Here are how things work at the website. One person wants to rent a room in a house, or an entire house, or say a couch in the living room of someone's house for a night, a week, or more. Another person, with a room or a house or a couch in the living room, is willing to accommodate this person. What Airbnb essentially does is put these two people in contact with each other and Airbnb charges a fee. In a way, you could say that Airbnb is a hotel, but owns no rooms.

Now what many people think when first learning about Uber and Airbnb is to ask themselves: Why didn't I think of that? How ingenious to start your own taxi business but not own any taxis, or to start your own hotel businesses but not own any rooms.

Now what must the founders of Uber and Airbnb have been thinking that others didn't? Whether they knew it or not, what they were thinking about was exchange or trade. As we stated earlier, exchange or trade is giving up one thing for something else. In the case of Uber, one person is giving up money for a ride to the airport. The other person is giving up his time and his car to drive the first person to the airport for money. In the case of Airbnb, one person is giving up money for a week's stay in a house. The other person is giving up his occupancy of his house for money.

Now what Uber and Airbnb essentially do is bring people together who want to trade with each other. Uber knows that there are people who want to be transported from one location to another and other people who want to do the transporting. Uber brings these two sets of people together. Airbnb knows that there are people who want to rent a room or a house in, say, Miami Beach for a day or a week and other people who want to rent out their room or a house in Miami for a day or a week. Airbnb brings these two sets of people together.

So, how does one come up with the Uber or Airbnb ideas? Basically, both ideas have to do with trying to answer this question: *How do I bring together people who want to trade with each other, but who are not currently trading with each other?* That is the question the founders of both Uber and Airbnb asked and answered, albeit the first with respect to transportation and the second with respect to lodging. Are there other instances where people who want to trade with each are just waiting to be brought together?

SELF-TEST

1. Give an example to illustrate how a change in opportunity cost can affect behavior.

2. Studying has both costs and benefits. If you continue to study (e.g., for a test) for as long as the marginal benefits of studying are greater than the marginal costs, and you stop studying when the two are equal, will your action be consistent with having maximized the net benefits of studying? Explain your answer.

3. You stay up an additional hour to study for a test. The intended effect is to raise your test grade. What might be an unintended effect of staying up another hour to study?

1-4 *CETERIS PARIBUS* AND THEORY

We cover two important topics in this section: (1) *ceteris paribus* and (2) theory.

1-4a *Ceteris Paribus* Thinking

Wilson has eaten regular ice cream for years, and for years his weight has been 190 pounds. One day, Wilson decides he wants to lose weight. With this objective in mind, he buys a new fat-free ice cream at the grocery store. The fat-free ice cream has half the calories of regular ice cream.

Wilson eats the fat-free ice cream for the next few months. He then weighs himself and finds that he has gained two pounds. Does this mean that fat-free ice cream causes people to gain weight and regular ice cream does not? The answer is no. Why did Wilson gain weight when he substituted fat-free ice cream for regular ice cream? Perhaps Wilson ate three times as much fat-free ice cream as regular ice cream. Or perhaps during the time he was eating fat-free ice cream, he wasn't exercising, and during the time he was eating regular ice cream, he was exercising. In other words, a number of factors—such as eating more ice cream or exercising less—may have offset the weight loss that Wilson would have experienced had these other factors not changed.

Now, suppose you want to make the point that Wilson would have lost weight by substituting fat-free ice cream for regular ice cream had these other factors not changed. What would you say? A scientist would say, "If Wilson has been eating regular ice cream and his weight has stabilized at 190 pounds, then substituting fat-free ice cream for regular ice cream will lead to a decline in weight, *ceteris paribus.*"

Ceteris Paribus
A Latin term meaning *all other things constant* or *nothing else changes.*

The term **ceteris paribus** means *all other things constant* or *nothing else changes.* In our ice cream example, if nothing else changes—such as how much ice cream Wilson eats, how much exercise he gets, and so on—then switching to fat-free ice cream will result in weight loss. This expectation is based on the theory that a reduction in calorie consumption will result in weight loss and an increase in calorie consumption will result in weight gain.

Using the *ceteris paribus* assumption is important because, with it, we can clearly designate what we believe is the correct relationship between two variables. In the ice cream example, we can designate the correct relationship between calorie intake and weight gain.

Economists don't often talk about ice cream, but they will often make use of the *ceteris paribus* assumption. An economist might say, "If the price of a good decreases, the quantity of it consumed increases, *ceteris paribus.*" For example, if the price of Pepsi-Cola decreases, people will buy more of it, assuming that nothing else changes.

But some people ask, "Why would economists want to assume that when the price of Pepsi-Cola falls, nothing else changes? Don't other things change in the real world? Why make assumptions that we know are not true?"

Of course, economists do not specify *ceteris paribus* because they want to say something false about the world. They specify it because they want to clearly define what they believe to be the real-world relationship between two variables. Look at it this way: If you drop a ball off the roof of a house, it will fall to the ground, unless someone catches it. This statement is true, and probably everyone would willingly accept it as true. But here is another true statement: If you drop a ball off the roof of a house, it will fall to the ground, *ceteris paribus.* In fact, the two statements are identical in meaning. This is because adding the phrase "unless someone catches it" in the first sentence is the same as saying "*ceteris paribus*" in the second sentence. If one statement is acceptable to us, the other should be too.

1-4b What Is a Theory?

Almost everyone, including you, builds and tests theories or models on a regular basis. (In this text, the words *theory* and *model* are used interchangeably.) Perhaps you thought that only scientists and others with high-level mathematics at their fingertips built and tested theories. However, theory building and testing is not the domain of only the highly educated and mathematically proficient. Almost everyone builds and test theories.

People build theories any time they do not know the answer to a question. Someone asks, "Why is the crime rate higher in the United States than in Belgium?" Or, "Why did Aaron's girlfriend break up with him?" Or, "Why does Professor Avalos give easier final exams than Professor Shaw, even though they teach the same subject?" If you don't know the answer to a question, you are likely to build a theory so that you can provide an answer.

What exactly is a theory? To an economist, a **theory** is an abstract representation of the world. In this context, **abstract** means that you omit certain variables or factors when you try to explain or understand something. For example, suppose you were to draw a map for a friend, showing him how to get from his house to yours. Would you draw a map that showed every single thing your friend would see on the trip, or would you simply draw the main roads and one or two landmarks? If you'd do the latter, you would be abstracting from reality; you would be omitting certain things.

You would abstract for two reasons. First, to get your friend from his house to yours, you don't need to include everything on your map. Simply noting main roads may be enough. Second, if you did note everything on your map, your friend might get confused. Giving too much detail could be as bad as giving too little.

When economists build a theory or model, they do the same thing you do in drawing a map. They abstract from reality; they leave out certain things. They focus on the major factors or variables that they believe will explain the phenomenon they are trying to understand.

Suppose a criminologist's objective is to explain why some people turn to crime. Before actually building the theory, he considers a number of variables that may explain why some people become criminals: (1) the ease of getting a gun, (2) child-rearing practices, (3) the neighborhood a person grew up in, (4) whether a person was abused as a child, (5) family education, (6) the type of friends a person has, (7) a person's IQ, (8) climate, and (9) a person's diet.

The criminologist may think that some of these variables greatly affect the chance that a person will become a criminal, some affect it only slightly, and others do not affect it at all. For example, a person's diet may have only a 0.0001 percent effect on the person becoming a criminal, whereas whether a person was abused as a child may have a 30 percent effect.

A theory emphasizes only the variables that the theorist believes are the main or critical ones that explain an activity or event. Thus, if the criminologist in our example thinks that parental child-rearing practices and family education are likely to explain much more about criminal behavior than the other variables are, then his (abstract) theory will focus on these two variables and ignore the others.

All theories are abstractions from reality. But it doesn't follow that (abstract) theories cannot explain reality. The objective in theory building is to ignore the variables that are essentially irrelevant to the case at hand, making it easier to isolate the important variables that the untrained observer would probably miss.

In the course of reading this text, you will come across numerous theories. Some of these theories are explained in words, and others are represented graphically. For example, Chapter 3 presents the theory of supply and demand. First, the parts of the theory are explained. Then the theory is represented graphically in terms of a supply curve and a demand curve.

Theory
An abstract representation of the real world designed with the intent to better understand it.

Abstract
The process (used in building a theory) of focusing on a limited number of variables to explain or predict an event.

What to Ask a Theorist Physicists, chemists, and economists aren't the only persons who build and test theories. Historians, sociologists, anthropologists, and many others build and test theories. In fact, as suggested earlier in this section, almost everyone builds theories (although not everyone tests theories).

Anytime you listen to someone expound on a theory, you should always ask a key question: "If your theory is correct, what do you predict we will see in the world?" To illustrate, let's consider a very simple example. Suppose your history professor comes to class each day clean shaven and dressed in slacks, shirt, and sports jacket. One day he comes to class unshaven and dressed in jeans and a somewhat wrinkled T-shirt. The difference in appearance is obvious. You turn to your friend who sits next to you in class and ask, "What do you think explains the difference in his appearance and dress?"

Notice that you have asked a question that does not have an obvious answer. Such questions are ripe for theory building. Your friend proposes an explanation. She says, "I think the professor forgot to set his alarm clock last night. He got up late this morning and didn't have time to shave or to dress the way he usually does. He just threw on the first clothes he found and rushed to class."

Your friend has advanced a theory of sorts. She has implicitly assumed that the professor wants to shave and dress in slacks, shirt, and sports jacket but that some unusual event prevented him from doing so today.

Somehow, you don't think your friend's theory is correct. Instead, you think your history professor has decided to make a life change of some sort. He has decided to look more casual, to take life a little easier, to be less formal. You tell your friend what you think explains your professor's new behavior.

You, like your friend, have advanced a theory of sorts. Whose theory, if either, is correct? Now is the time for you to ask your friend, and your friend to ask you, "If your theory is correct, what do you predict we will see in the world?"

Your friend's answer should be, "If *my* theory is correct, then the next time the professor comes to class, he will be clean shaven and dressed in his old way—slacks, shirt, and sports jacket." Your answer should be, "If *my* theory is correct, then the next time the professor comes to class, he will be unshaven and dressed as he is today—in jeans, T-shirt, and the like."

The question—If your theory is correct, what do you predict we will see in the world?—gives us a way to figure out who might be closer to the truth when people disagree. It minimizes talk and maximizes the chances of establishing who is correct and who is incorrect.

Hear What and How the Economist Thinks . . .
About Theories

The economist hears two people talking:

First person says: "People are always advancing theories to explain this or that. They advance theories to explain things like the climate, crime, rising unemployment, poverty, and so much more. I only accept those theories that sound reasonable or right to me. "

Second person says: "I agree. You have to use your common sense when deciding who has the right theory. For example, if someone comes up with a theory that says that 'little aliens in a faraway galaxy are controlling our every move,' that sounds just ridiculous. No need to accept that theory."

Hear what and how the economist thinks:

Using the criterion of accepting a theory only if it "sounds reasonable" doesn't always guarantee that we will get things correct. To illustrate, suppose you lived 500 years ago and someone proposed the flat Earth theory. That theory essentially says that the earth is flat. Probably everyone 500 years ago would accept that theory because it "sounded reasonable." Fact is, though, the flat Earth theory is wrong: the Earth is not flat.

Now consider a theory which, upon first hearing it, might sound unreasonable. Albert Einstein proposed the theory of general relativity in a paper published in 1916. The theory stated that Sun's gravity would bend light. For many people, that might "sound unreasonable," thus, they conclude, it is wrong. But how a theory "sounds to us" is not the right criterion by which to evaluate a theory. For Einstein, as for many scientists, it is how well the theory predicts that matters. As a test of his theory, he predicted that a photo taken during a solar eclipse would show that the Sun's gravity would bend light. Specifically, starlight passing near the Sun would bend, and the stars would show up in just slightly the wrong place. Pictures of

Marcel Clemens/Shutterstock.com

the 1919 eclipse show the exact amount of bending that Einstein predicted.

There are plenty of examples of theories that "sound reasonable" that turn out to be wrong and theories that "sound unreasonable" that turn out to be right. Because of this, we need something better than "how a theory sounds to me" as a criterion by which to evaluate theories. Generally, economists use the criterion of how well a theory predicts when evaluating theories.

Questions to Think About:

1. Can you think of a theory that "sounded reasonable" to you that turned out to be wrong? Can you think of a theory that "sounded unreasonable" to you that turned out to be right?

2. Two people consider the validity of theory A. If both people use the "sounds reasonable" criterion by which to evaluate the theory, will both people necessarily agree as to whether the theory is correct or not? Explain your answer.

SELF-TEST

1. What is the purpose of building a theory?
2. How might a theory of the economy differ from a description of it?
3. Why is it important to test a theory? Why not simply accept a theory if it sounds right?
4. Your economics instructor says, "If the price of going to the movies goes down, people will go to the movies more often." A student in class says, "Not if the quality of the movies goes down." Who is right, the economics instructor or the student?

1-5 ECONOMIC CATEGORIES

Economics is sometimes broken down into different categories according to the type of questions asked. Four common economic categories are positive economics, normative economics, microeconomics, and macroeconomics.

1-5a Positive Economics and Normative Economics

Positive Economics
The study of *what is* in economics.

Normative Economics
The study of *what should be* in economics.

Positive economics attempts to determine *what is*. **Normative economics** addresses *what should be*. Essentially, positive economics deals with cause-effect relationships that can be tested. Normative economics deals with value judgments and opinions that cannot be tested.

Many topics in economics can be discussed in both a positive and a normative framework. Consider a proposed cut in federal income taxes. An economist practicing positive economics would want to know the *effect* of a cut in income taxes. For example, she may want to know how a tax cut will affect the unemployment rate, economic growth, inflation, and so on. An economist practicing normative economics would address issues that directly or indirectly relate to whether the federal income tax *should* be cut. For example, he may say that federal income taxes should be cut because the income tax burden on many taxpayers is currently high.

This book deals mainly with positive economics. For the most part, we discuss the economic world as it is, not the way someone might think it should be. Keep in mind, too, that no matter what your normative objectives are, positive economics can shed some light on how they might be accomplished. For example, suppose you believe that absolute poverty should be eliminated and that the unemployment rate should be lowered. No doubt you have ideas as to how these goals can be accomplished. But will your ideas work? For example, will a greater redistribution of income eliminate absolute poverty? Will lowering taxes lower the unemployment rate? There is no guarantee that the means you think will bring about certain ends will do so. This is where sound positive economics can help us see what is. As someone once said, "It is not enough to want to do good; it is important also to know how to do good."

1-5b Microeconomics and Macroeconomics

Microeconomics
The branch of economics that deals with human behavior and choices as they relate to relatively small units: an individual, a firm, an industry, a single market.

Macroeconomics
The branch of economics that deals with human behavior and choices as they relate to highly aggregate markets (e.g., the market for goods and services) or the entire economy.

It has been said that the tools of microeconomics are microscopes and the tools of macroeconomics are telescopes. Macroeconomics stands back from the trees to see the forest. Microeconomics gets up close and examines the tree itself—its bark, its limbs, and its roots. **Microeconomics** is the branch of economics that deals with human behavior and choices as they relate to relatively small units: an individual, a firm, an industry, a single market. **Macroeconomics** is the branch of economics that deals with human behavior and choices as they relate to an entire economy. In microeconomics, economists discuss a single price; in macroeconomics, they discuss the price level. Microeconomics deals with the demand for a particular good or service; macroeconomics deals with aggregate, or total, demand for goods and services. Microeconomics examines how a tax change affects a single firm's output; macroeconomics looks at how a tax change affects an entire economy's output.

Microeconomists and macroeconomists ask different types of questions. A microeconomist might be interested in answering such questions as the following:

- How does a market work?
- What level of output does a firm produce?
- What price does a firm charge for the good it produces?
- How does a consumer determine how much of a good to buy?
- Can government policy affect business behavior?
- Can government policy affect consumer behavior?

A macroeconomist, by contrast, might be interested in answering such questions as these:

- How does the economy work?
- Why is the unemployment rate sometimes high and sometimes low?

- What causes inflation?
- Why do some national economies grow faster than others?
- What might cause interest rates to be low one year and high the next?
- How do changes in the money supply affect the economy?
- How do changes in government spending and taxes affect the economy?

OFFICE HOURS

"I Don't Believe That Every Time a Person Does Something, He Compares the Marginal Benefits and Costs"

STUDENT: In class yesterday, you said that individuals compare the marginal benefits (*MB*) of doing something (say, exercising) with the marginal costs (*MC*). If the marginal benefits are greater than the marginal costs, they exercise; if the marginal costs are greater than the marginal benefits, they don't. Here is what I am having a problem with: I don't believe that every time people do something, they compare the marginal benefits and costs. I think people do some things without thinking of benefits and costs; they do some things instinctively or because they have always done them.

INSTRUCTOR: Can you give an example?

STUDENT: I don't think of the benefits and costs of eating breakfast in the morning; I just eat breakfast. I don't think of the benefits and costs of doing my homework; I just do the homework before it is due. For me, many activities are automatic; I do them without thinking.

INSTRUCTOR: It doesn't necessarily follow that you are not considering benefits and costs when you do something automatically. All you have to do is sense whether doing something comes with net benefits (benefits greater than costs) or net costs (costs greater than benefits). All you have to do is sense whether something is likely to make you better off or worse off. You eat breakfast in the morning because you have decided that it makes you better off. But making you better off is no different from saying that you receive net benefits from eating breakfast, which is no different from saying that the benefits of eating breakfast are greater than the costs. In other words, *better off* equals *net benefits* equals *benefits greater than costs*.

STUDENT: I see what you're saying. But then how would you explain the fact that Smith smokes cigarettes and Jones does not. If both Smith and Jones consider the benefits and costs of smoking cigarettes, then it seems that either both would have to smoke or both would have to not smoke.

The fact that different people do different things tells me that not everyone is considering the costs and benefits of their actions. If everyone did, they would all do the same thing.

INSTRUCTOR: I disagree. Not everyone sees the costs and benefits of the same thing the same way. Smith and Jones may not see the benefits or costs of smoking the same way. For Smith, the benefits of smoking may be high, but for Jones they may be low. It is no different from saying different people estimate the benefits of playing chess or eating a doughnut or riding a bicycle differently. The same holds for costs. Not everyone will estimate the costs of playing chess or eating a doughnut or riding a bicycle the same way. The costs of a person with diabetes eating a doughnut are much higher than the costs of a person without diabetes eating a doughnut.

STUDENT: Let me see if I have this right. You are making two points. First, not everyone has the same benefits and costs of, say, running a mile. Second, everyone who does run a mile believes that the benefits are greater than the costs, and everyone who does not run a mile believes that the costs are greater than the benefits.

INSTRUCTOR: Yes, that's it. Everybody is trying to make himself better off (reap net benefits), but not everybody will do *X* because not everybody will be made better off by doing *X*.

Points to Remember

1. If you undertake those actions for which you expect to receive net benefits, then you are "thinking" in terms of costs and benefits. Specifically, you expect the marginal benefits to be greater than the marginal costs.
2. The costs and benefits of doing any activity are not necessarily the same for everybody. Smith may expect higher benefits than Jones when it comes to doing *X*; Jones may expect higher costs than Smith when it comes to doing *X*.

CHAPTER SUMMARY

GOODS, BADS, AND RESOURCES

- A good is anything that gives a person utility or satisfaction.
- A bad is anything that gives a person disutility or dissatisfaction.
- Economists divide resources into four categories: land, labor, capital, and entrepreneurship.
- Land includes natural resources, such as minerals, forests, water, and unimproved land.
- Labor is brought about by the physical and mental talents that people contribute to the production process.
- Capital consists of produced goods, such as machinery, tools, computers, trucks, buildings, and factories, that can be used as inputs for further production.
- Entrepreneurship is the talent that some people have for organizing the resources of land, labor, and capital to produce goods, seek new business opportunities, and develop new ways of doing things.

SCARCITY

- Scarcity is the condition in which our wants are greater than the limited resources available to satisfy them.
- Scarcity implies choice. In a world of limited resources, we must choose which wants will be satisfied and which will go unsatisfied.
- Because of scarcity, there is a need for a rationing device. A rationing device is a means of deciding who gets what quantities of the available resources and goods.
- Scarcity implies competition. If resources were ample to satisfy all our seemingly unlimited wants, people would not have to compete for the available, but limited, resources.

OPPORTUNITY COST

- Every time a person makes a choice, he or she incurs an opportunity cost. Opportunity cost is the most highly valued opportunity or alternative forfeited when a choice is made. The higher the opportunity cost of doing something, the less likely it is that it will be done.

COSTS AND BENEFITS

- What distinguishes the economist from the noneconomist is that the economist thinks in terms of *both* costs and benefits. Asked what the benefits of taking a walk may be, an economist will also mention the related costs. Asked what the costs of studying are, an economist will also point out its benefits.

DECISIONS MADE AT THE MARGIN

- Marginal benefits and costs are not the same as total benefits and costs. When deciding whether to talk on the phone one more minute, an individual would not consider the total benefits and total costs of speaking on the phone. Instead, the person would compare only the marginal benefits (additional benefits) of talking on the phone one more minute with the marginal costs (additional costs) of talking on the phone one more minute.

INCENTIVES

- An incentive is something that encourages or motivates a person to undertake an action. Incentives are closely related to benefits and costs. Individuals have an incentive to undertake actions for which the benefits are greater than the costs or, stated differently, for which they expect to receive some net benefits (benefits greater than costs).

EFFICIENCY

- As long as the marginal benefits of an activity are greater than its marginal costs, a person gains by continuing to do the activity—whether the activity is studying, running, eating, or watching television. The net benefits of an activity are maximized when the marginal benefits of the activity equal its marginal costs. Efficiency exists at this point.

UNINTENDED EFFECTS

- Economists often think in terms of causes and effects. Effects may be either intended or unintended. Economists want to denote both types of effects when speaking of effects in general.

EXCHANGE

- Exchange, or trade, is the process of giving up one thing for something else. People enter into exchanges to make themselves better off.

CETERIS PARIBUS

- *Ceteris paribus* is a Latin term that means "all other things constant" or "nothing else changes." *Ceteris paribus* is used to designate what we believe is the correct relationship between two variables.

THEORY

- Economists build theories to explain and predict real-world events. Theories are necessarily abstractions from, as opposed to descriptions of, the real world.

- All theories abstract from reality; they focus on the critical variables that the theorist believes explain and predict the phenomenon in question.

ECONOMIC CATEGORIES

- Positive economics attempts to determine what is; normative economics addresses what should be.

- Microeconomics deals with human behavior and choices as they relate to relatively small units: an individual, a firm, an industry, a single market. Macroeconomics deals with human behavior and choices as they relate to an entire economy.

KEY TERMS AND CONCEPTS

Good	Entrepreneurship	Decisions at the Margin	Positive Economics
Utility	Scarcity	Efficiency	Normative Economics
Bad	Economics	Incentive	Microeconomics
Disutility	Rationing Device	Exchange (Trade)	Macroeconomics
Land	Opportunity Cost	*Ceteris Paribus*	
Labor	Marginal Benefits	Theory	
Capital	Marginal Costs	Abstract	

QUESTIONS AND PROBLEMS

1. The United States is considered a rich country because Americans can choose from an abundance of goods and services. How can there be scarcity in a land of abundance?

2. Give two examples for each of the following: (a) an intangible good, (b) a tangible good, (c) a bad.

3. Give an example of something that is a good for one person and a bad for someone else.

4. What is the difference between labor as a resource and entrepreneurship as a resource?

5. Can either scarcity or one of the effects of scarcity be found in a car dealership? Explain your answer.

6. Explain the link between scarcity and each of the following: (a) choice, (b) opportunity cost, (c) the need for a rationing device, and (d) competition.

7. Is it possible for a person to incur an opportunity cost without spending any money? Explain.

8. Discuss the opportunity costs of attending college for four years. Is college more or less costly than you thought it was? Explain.

9. Explain the relationship between changes in opportunity cost and changes in behavior.

10. Smith says that we should eliminate all pollution in the world. Jones disagrees. Who is more likely to be an economist, Smith or Jones? Explain your answer.

11. A friend pays for your lunch. Is this an example of a free lunch? Why or why not?

12. A layperson says that a proposed government project simply costs too much and therefore shouldn't be undertaken. How might an economist's evaluation be different?

13. Economists say that individuals make decisions at the margin. What does this mean?

14. How would an economist define the efficient amount of time spent playing tennis?

15. Ivan stops studying before the point at which his marginal benefits of studying equals his marginal costs. Is Ivan forfeiting any net benefits? Explain your answer.

16. What does an economist mean if she says that there are no $10 bills on the sidewalk?

17. A change in X will lead to a change in Y. The predicted change is desirable, so we should change X. Do you agree or disagree? Explain.

18. Why do people enter into exchanges?

19. When two individuals enter into an exchange, you can be sure that one person benefits and the other person loses. Do you agree or disagree with this statement? Explain your answer.

20. What is the difference between positive economics and normative economics? Between microeconomics and macroeconomics?

21. Would there be a need for a rationing device if scarcity did not exist? Explain your answer.

22. Jackie's alarm clock buzzes. She reaches over to the small table next to her bed and turns it off. As she pulls the covers back up, Jackie thinks about her 8:30 American history class. Should she go to the class today or sleep a little longer? She worked late last night and really hasn't had enough sleep. Besides, she's fairly sure her professor will be discussing a subject she already knows well. Maybe it would be okay to miss class today. Is Jackie more likely to miss some classes than she is to miss other classes? What determines which classes Jackie will attend and which classes she won't?

23. If you found $10 bills on the sidewalk regularly, we might conclude that individuals don't try to maximize net benefits. Do you agree or disagree with this statement. Explain your answer.

24. The person who smokes cigarettes cannot possibly be thinking in terms of costs and benefits because it has been proven that cigarette smoking increases one's chances of getting lung cancer. Do you agree or disagree with the part of the statement that reads "the person who smokes cigarettes cannot possibly be thinking in terms of costs and benefits"? Explain your answer.

25. Janice decides to go out on a date with Kyle instead of Robert. Do you think Janice is using some kind of rationing device to decide whom she dates? If so, what might that rationing device be?

26. A theory is an abstraction from reality. What does this statement mean?

WORKING WITH NUMBERS AND GRAPHS

1. Suppose the marginal costs of reading are constant and the marginal benefits of reading decline (over time). Initially, the marginal benefits of reading are greater than the marginal costs. Draw the *marginal-benefit (MB)* curve and *marginal-cost (MC)* curve of reading, and identify the efficient amount of reading. Next, explain why the efficient point is the point at which the net benefits of reading are maximized.

2. Using the diagram you drew in question 1, lower the marginal costs of reading and identify the new efficient amount of reading. Also, identify the additional net benefits derived as a result of the lower marginal cost of reading.

3. Jim could undertake activity X, but chooses not to. Draw how the *marginal-benefit (MB)* and *marginal-cost (MC)* curves look for activity X from Jim's perspective.

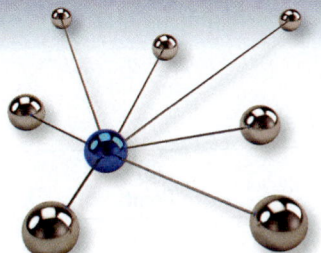

WORKING WITH DIAGRAMS

Most of the diagrams in this book represent the relationship between two variables. Economists compare two variables to see how a change in one variable affects the other.

Suppose our two variables of interest are *consumption* and *income*. We want to show how consumption changes as income changes. We collect the data in Table 1. Simply by looking at the data in the first two columns, we can see that as income rises (column 1), consumption rises (column 2). If we wanted to show the relationship between income and consumption on a graph, we could place *income* on the horizontal axis, as in Exhibit 1, and *consumption* on the vertical axis. Point A represents income of $0 and consumption of $60, point B represents income of $100 and consumption of $120, and so on. If we draw a straight line through the points we have plotted, we have a picture of the relationship between income and consumption, based on the data we collected.

Notice that the line in Exhibit 1 slopes upward from left to right. As income rises, so does consumption. For example, as you move from point A to point B, income rises from $0 to $100 and consumption rises from $60 to $120. The line in Exhibit 1 also shows that as income falls, so does consumption. For example, as you move from point C to point B, income falls from $200 to $100 and consumption falls from $180 to $120. When two variables—such as consumption and income—change in the same way, they are said to be **directly related**.

Now let's take a look at the data in Table 2. Our two variables are the *price of compact discs (CDs)* and the quantity demanded of CDs. Just by looking at the data in the first two columns, we see that as price falls (column 1), quantity demanded rises (column 2). Suppose we want to plot these data. We could place *price of CDs* on the vertical axis, as in Exhibit 2, and *quantity demanded of CDs* on the horizontal axis. Point A represents a price of $20 and a quantity demanded

EXHIBIT 1

A Two-Variable Diagram Representing a Direct Relationship

The data in Table 1, plotted. Then points are connected with a straight line. The data represent a direct relationship: As one variable (say, income) rises, the other variable (consumption) rises too.

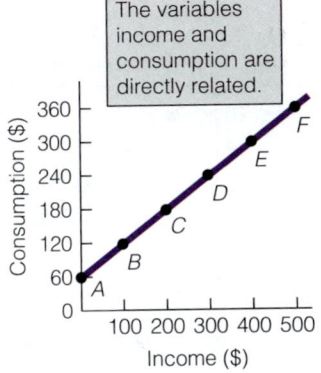

The variables income and consumption are directly related.

Directly Related

Two variables are directly related if they change in the same way.

Table 1

(1) When Income Is ($)	(2) Consumption Is ($)	(3) Point
0	60	A
100	120	B
200	180	C
300	240	D
400	300	E
500	360	F

Table 2

(1) When Price of CDs Is ($)	(2) Quantity Demanded of CDs Is	(3) Point
20	100	A
18	120	B
16	140	C
14	160	D
12	180	E

EXHIBIT 2

A Two-Variable Diagram Representing an Inverse Relationship

The data in Table 2, plotted. The points are connected with a straight line. The data represent an inverse relationship: As one variable (price) falls, the other variable (quantity demanded) rises.

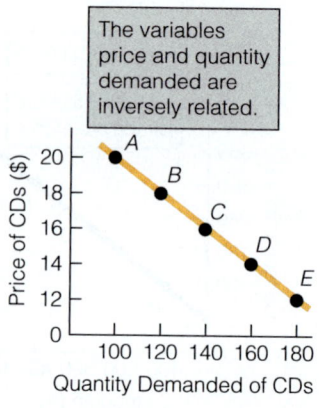

The variables price and quantity demanded are inversely related.

Inversely Related
Two variables are inversely related if they change in opposite ways.

Independent
Two variables are independent if, as one changes, the other does not.

Slope
The ratio of the change in the variable on the vertical axis to the change in the variable on the horizontal axis.

of 100, point *B* represents a price of $18 and a quantity demanded of 120, and so on. If we draw a straight line through the plotted points, we have a picture of the relationship between price and quantity demanded, based on the data in Table 2.

Notice:

- As price falls, the quantity demanded rises. For example, as price falls from $20 to $18, the quantity demanded rises from 100 to 120.

- As price rises, the quantity demanded falls. For example, when price rises from $12 to $14, quantity demanded falls from 180 to 160.

When two variables—such as price and quantity demanded—change in opposite ways, they are said to be **inversely related**.

As you have seen so far, variables may be directly related (when one increases, the other also increases) or inversely related (when one increases, the other decreases). Variables can also be **independent** of each other if, as one variable changes, the other does not.

In Exhibit 3(a), as the *X* variable rises, the *Y* variable remains the same (at 20). Obviously, the *X* and *Y* variables are independent of each other: As one changes, the other does not.

In Exhibit 3(b), as the *Y* variable rises, the *X* variable remains the same (at 30). Again, we conclude that the *X* and *Y* variables are independent of each other: As one changes, the other does not.

A-1 SLOPE OF A LINE

In addition to knowing *how* two variables are related, we also often need to know *how much* one variable changes as the other changes. To find out, we need to only calculate the slope of the line. The **slope** is the ratio of the change in the variable on the vertical axis to the change in the variable on the horizontal axis. For example, if *Y* is on the vertical axis and *X* is on the horizontal axis, the slope is equal to $\Delta Y / \Delta X$. (The symbol "Δ" means "change in.")

$$\text{slope} = \frac{\Delta Y}{\Delta X}$$

EXHIBIT 3

Two Diagrams Representing Independence Between Two Variables

In parts (a) and (b), the variables X and Y are independent: As one changes, the other does not.

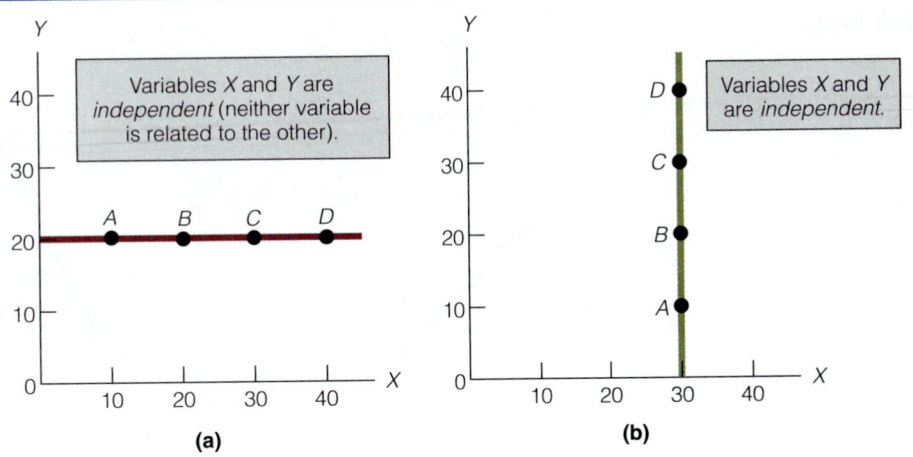

(a)

(b)

Exhibit 4 shows four lines. In each case, the slope is calculated. After studying parts (a)–(d), see if you understand why the slopes are negative, positive, zero, and infinite.

A-2 SLOPE OF A LINE IS CONSTANT

Look again at the line in Exhibit 4(a). The slope between points A and B is computed to be -1. If we had computed the slope between points B and C or between points C and D, would it still be -1? Let's compute the slope between points B and C. Moving from point B to point C, the change in Y is -10 and the change in X is $+10$. So, the slope is -1, as it was between points A and B. Now let's compute the slope between points A and D. Moving from point A to point D, the change in Y is -30 and the change in X is $+30$. Again, the slope is -1. Our conclusion is that the slope between any two points on a straight line is always the same as the slope between any other two points. To see this for yourself, compute the slope between points A and B and between points A and C using the line in Exhibit 4(b).

A-3 SLOPE OF A CURVE

In addition to straight lines, economics graphs use curves. The slope of a curve is not constant throughout, as it is for a straight line. The slope of a curve varies from one point to another. Calculating the slope of a curve at a given point requires two steps, as illustrated for point A in Exhibit 5. First, draw a line tangent to the curve at the point (a tangent line is one that just touches the curve but does not cross it). Second, pick any two points on the tangent line and determine the slope. In Exhibit 5, the slope of the line between points B and C is 0.67. The slope of the curve at point A (and only at point A) is therefore 0.67.

A-4 THE 45-DEGREE LINE

Economists sometimes use a *45-degree line* to represent data. This is a straight line that bisects the right angle formed by the intersection of the vertical and horizontal axes (see Exhibit 6). As a result, the 45-degree line divides the space enclosed by the two axes into *two equal parts*, as shown

EXHIBIT 4

Calculating Slopes

The slope of a line is the ratio of the change in the variable on the vertical axis to the change in the variable on the horizontal axis. In (a)–(d), we have calculated the slope.

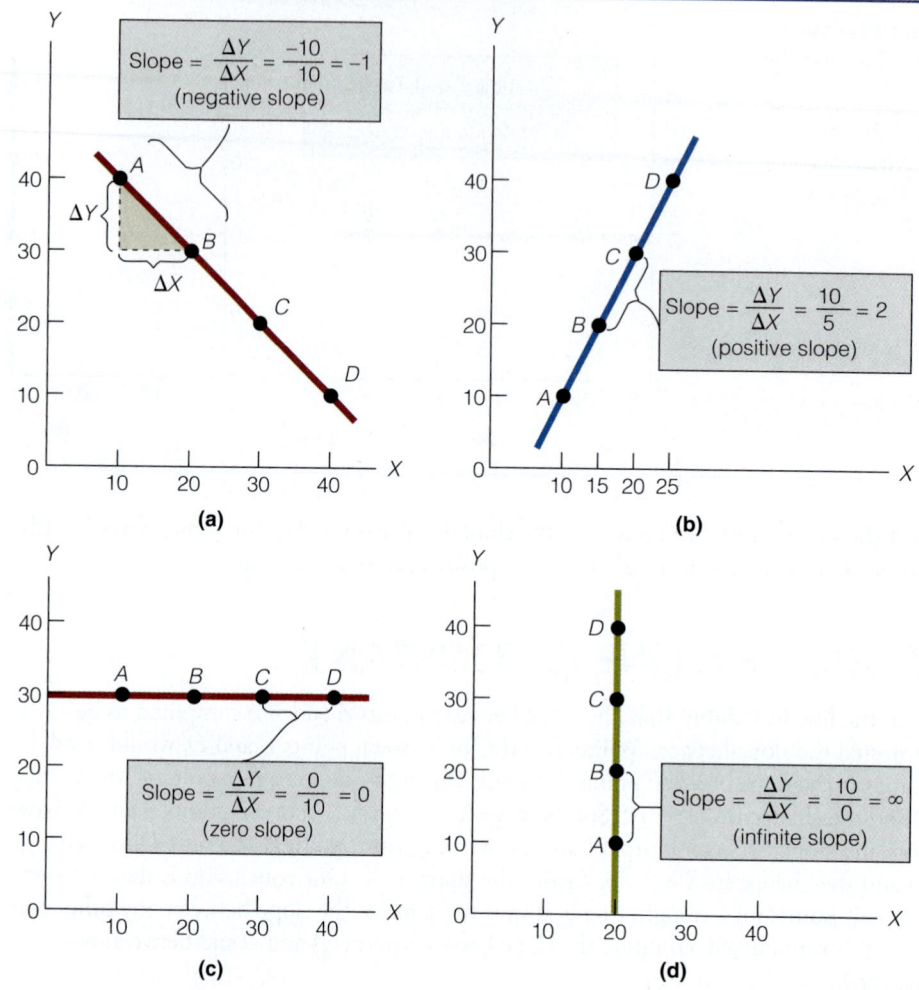

EXHIBIT 5

Calculating the Slope of a Curve at a Particular Point

The slope of the curve at point A is 0.67. This is calculated by drawing a line tangent to the curve at point A and then determining the slope of the line.

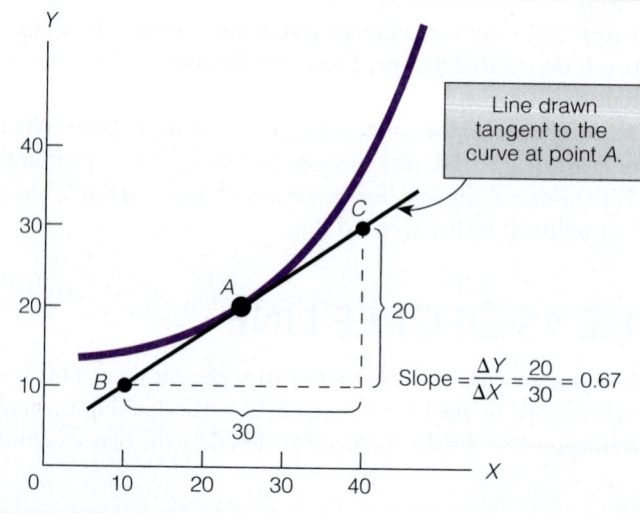

in the exhibit by the shading in different colors. The major characteristic of the 45-degree line is that any point on it is equidistant from both the horizontal and vertical axes. For example, point A is exactly as far from the horizontal axis as it is from the vertical axis. Thus, point A represents as much X as it does Y. Specifically, in the exhibit, point A represents 20 units of X and 20 units of Y.

A-5 PIE CHARTS

Pie charts appear in numerous places throughout this text. A pie chart is a convenient way to represent the different parts of something that when added together equal the whole. Let's consider a typical 24-hour weekday for Charles Myers. On a typical weekday, Charles spends 8 hours sleeping, 4 hours taking classes at the university, 4 hours working at his part-time job, 2 hours doing homework, 1 hour eating, 2 hours watching television, and 3 hours doing nothing in particular ("hanging around"). Exhibit 7 shows the breakdown of a typical weekday for Charles in pie chart form.

Pie charts send a quick visual message about rough percentage breakdowns and relative relationships. For example, Exhibit 7 clearly shows that Charles spends twice as much time working as doing homework.

A-6 BAR GRAPHS

The *bar graph* is another visual aid that economists use to convey relative relationships. Suppose we want to represent the gross domestic product for the United States in different years. The **gross domestic product (GDP)** is the value of the entire output produced annually within a country's borders. The bar graph in Exhibit 8 is a quick picture not only of the actual GDP for each year but also of the relative relationships between the GDP numbers for different years. For example, the graph makes it easy to see that the GDP in 2015 was more than double what it was in 1995.

Gross Domestic Product (GDP)
The value of the entire output produced annually within a country's borders.

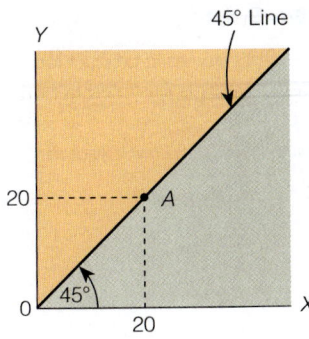

EXHIBIT 6

The 45-Degree Line

Any point on the 45-degree line is equidistant from each axis. For example, point A is the same distance from the vertical axis as it is from the horizontal axis.

EXHIBIT 7

A Pie Chart

The breakdown of activities for Charles Myers during a typical 24-hour weekday is represented in pie chart form.

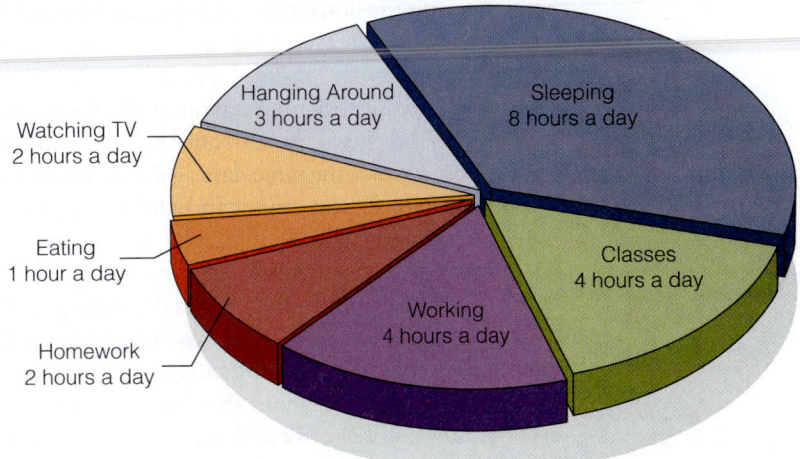

EXHIBIT 8

A Bar Graph

U.S. gross domestic product for different years is illustrated in bar graph form.

Source: Bureau of Economic Analysis.

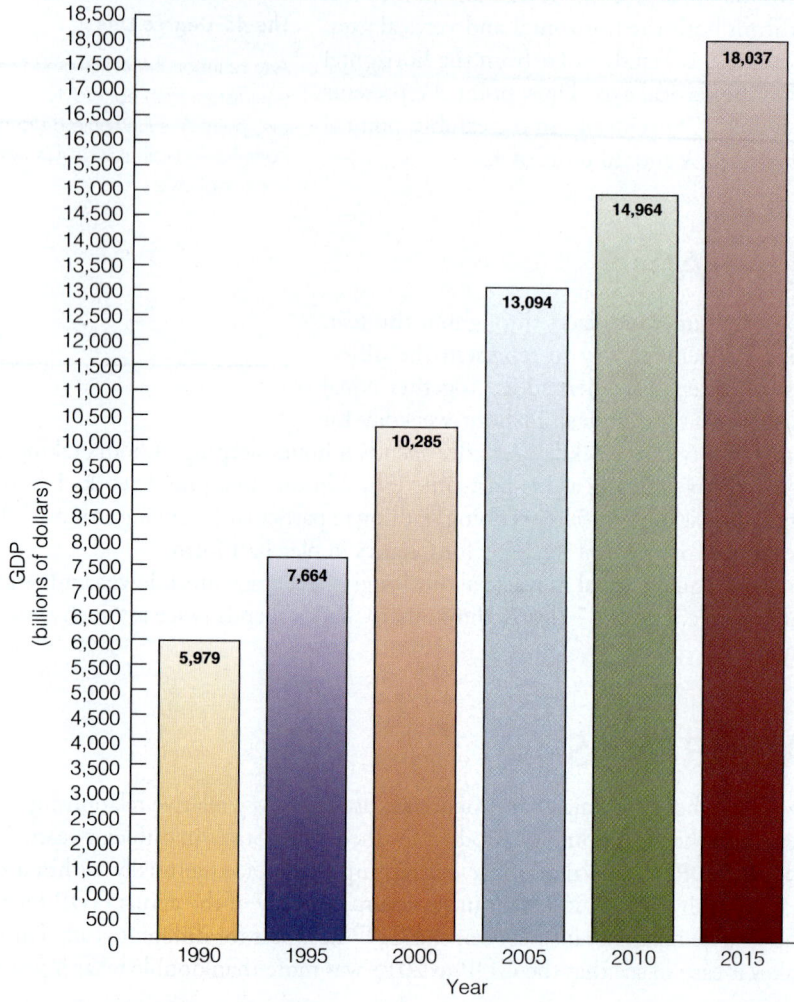

A-7 LINE GRAPHS

Sometimes information is best and most easily displayed in a *line graph*, which is particularly useful for illustrating changes in a variable over a time period. Suppose we want to illustrate the variations in average points per game for a college basketball team over a number of years. The line graph in Exhibit 9(a) shows that the basketball team was on a roller coaster during the years 2004–2017. Perhaps the visual message is that the team's performance has not been consistent from one year to the next.

Suppose we plot the same data again, except this time using a different measurement scale on the vertical axis. As you can see in Exhibit 9(b), the variation in the team's performance appears much less pronounced than in part (a). In fact, we could choose a scale that, if we were to plot the data, would give us something close to a straight line. The point is simple: Data plotted in a line graph may convey different messages depending on the measurement scale used.

Sometimes economists show two line graphs on the same axes. Usually, the purpose is to draw attention to either (1) the *relationship* between two variables or (2) the *difference* between them. In Exhibit 10, the line graphs show the variation and trend in (1) projected federal government expenditures and (2) projected tax receipts for the years 2013–2017, drawing attention to the "gap" between the two over the years.

EXHIBIT 9

The Two Line Graphs Plot the Same Data

(a) The average numbers of points per game for a college basketball team in different years are plotted. The variation between the years is pronounced. (b) The same data as in (a), but the variation in the performance of the team appears much less pronounced than in part (a).

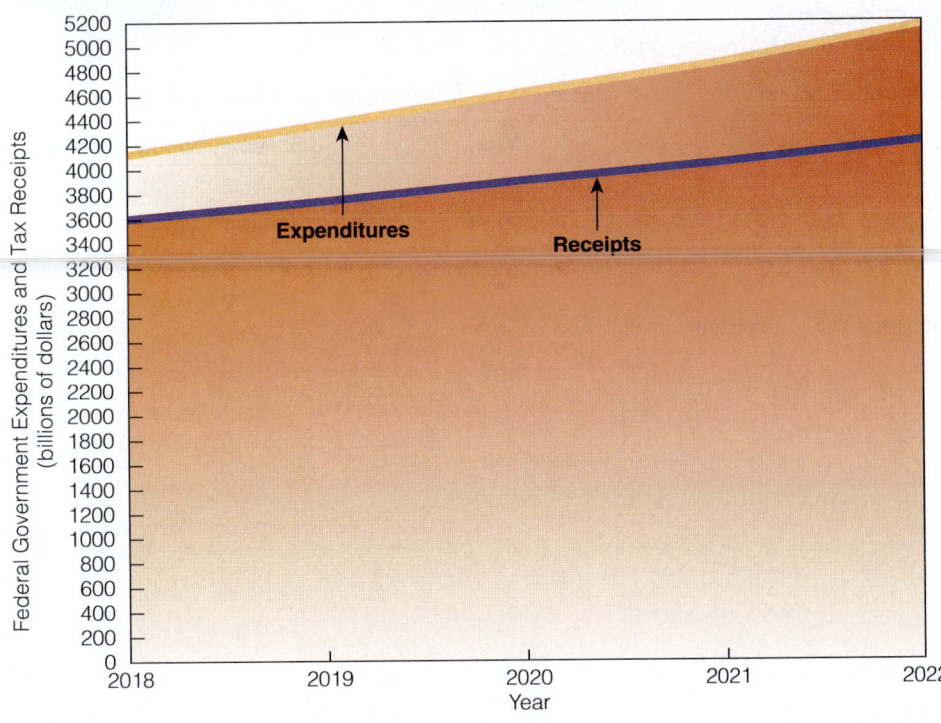

Year	Average Number of Points per Game
2004	50
2005	40
2006	59
2007	51
2008	60
2009	50
2010	75
2011	63
2012	60
2013	71
2014	61
2015	55
2016	70
2017	64

EXHIBIT 10

Projected Federal Government Expenditures and Tax Receipts, 2018–2022

Projected federal government expenditures and tax receipts are shown in line graph form for the period 2018–2022. Numbers are in billions of dollars.

Year	Expenditures	Receipts
2018	4,120	3,600
2019	4,370	3,745
2020	4,614	3,900
2021	4,853	4,048
2022	5,166	4,212

Source: Congressional Budget Office.

APPENDIX SUMMARY

- Two variables are directly related if one variable rises as the other rises.
- An upward-sloping line (left to right) represents two variables that are directly related.
- Two variables are inversely related if one variable rises as the other falls.
- A downward-sloping line (left to right) represents two variables that are inversely related.
- Two variables are independent if one variable rises as the other remains constant.
- The slope of a line is the ratio of the change in the variable on the vertical axis to the change in the variable on the horizontal axis. The slope of a straight line is the same between any two points on the line.

- To determine the slope of a curve at a point, draw a line tangent to the curve at the point and then determine the slope of the tangent line.
- Any point on a 45-degree line is equidistant from the two axes.
- A pie chart is a convenient way to represent the different parts of something that when added together equal the whole. A pie chart visually shows rough percentage breakdowns and relative relationships.
- A bar graph is a convenient way to represent relative relationships.
- Line graphs are particularly useful for illustrating changes in one or more variables over time.

KEY TERMS AND CONCEPTS

Directly Related

Inversely Related

Independent

Slope

Gross Domestic Product (GDP)

QUESTIONS AND PROBLEMS

1. What type of relationship would you expect between the following?
   a. Sales of hot dogs and sales of hot dog buns
   b. The price of winter coats and sales of winter coats
   c. The price of personal computers and the production of personal computers
   d. Sales of toothbrushes and sales of cat food
   e. The number of children in a family and the number of toys in a family

2. Represent the following data in bar graph form.

Year	U.S. Money Supply ($ billions)
2012	2,458
2013	2,641
2014	2,924
2015	3,079
2016	3,278

3. Plot the following data, and specify the type of relationship between the two variables. (Place "Price" on the vertical axis and "Quantity Demanded" on the horizontal axis.)

Price of Apples ($)	Quantity Demanded of Apples
0.25	1,000
0.50	800
0.70	700
0.95	500
1.00	400
1.10	350

4. In Exhibit 4(a), determine the slope between points C and D.

5. In Exhibit 4(b), determine the slope between points A and D.

6. What is the special characteristic of a 45-degree line?

7. What is the slope of a 45-degree line?

8. When is a pie chart better than a bar graph for illustrating data?

9. Plot the following data, and specify the type of relationship between the two variables. (Place "Price" on the vertical axis and "Quantity Supplied" on the horizontal axis.)

Price of Apples ($)	Quantity Supplied of Apples
0.25	350
0.50	400
0.70	500
0.95	700
1.00	800
1.10	1,000

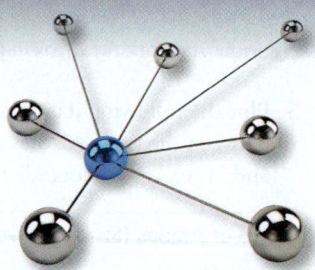

SHOULD YOU MAJOR IN ECONOMICS?

You are probably reading this textbook as part of your first college course in economics. You may be taking the course to satisfy a requirement in your major. Economics courses are sometimes required for students who plan to major in business, history, liberal studies, social science, or computer science.

Or you may be planning to major in economics. If you are like many college students, you may complain that not enough information is available about the various majors at your college or university. For example, students who major in business sometimes say that they are not quite certain what a business major is all about, but then they add that majoring in business is a safe bet. "After all," they assert, "you're pretty sure of getting a job if you have a business degree. That's not always the case with other degrees."

Many college students choose their majors on the basis of their high school courses. History majors, for example, might say that they decided to major in history because they "liked history in high school." Similarly, chemistry, biology, and math students say they chose their majors on the basis of their experiences in high school. If a student found both math and economics easy and interesting in high school, then she is likely to major in math or economics. Conversely, if a student had a hard time with chemistry in high school and found it boring, then he doesn't usually want to major in chemistry in college.

Students also often look to the dollars at the end of the college degree. A student may enjoy history and want to learn more of it in college, but she may tell herself that she will earn a higher starting salary after graduation if she majors in computer science or engineering. Thus, when choosing a major, students often consider (1) how much they enjoy studying a particular subject, (2) what they would like to see themselves doing in the future, and (3) what their income prospects are.

People may weight these three factors differently, but, regardless of the weighting, having more information is better than not having it, *ceteris paribus*. (We note "*ceteris paribus*" because having more information is not better if you have to pay more for it than it is worth. Who wants to pay $10 for information that provides only $1 in benefits? This appendix is therefore a low-cost way of providing you with more information about an economics major.)

We start by dispelling some of the misinformation about an economics major. Stated bluntly, some perceptions about an economics major and about a career in economics are just not true. For example, some people think that economics majors almost never study social relationships, but rather only such things as inflation, interest rates, and unemployment. Not true. Economics majors study some of the same things that sociologists, historians, psychologists, and political scientists study.

In addition to busting myths, the appendix also provides you with information about economics as a major: what courses you study, how many courses you are likely to have to take, and more.

Finally, we tell you something about a career in economics. If you have opted to become an economics major, the day will come when you have your degree in hand. What's next? What is your starting salary likely to be? What will you be doing? Are you going to be happy doing what economists do? (If you never thought economics was about happiness, you already have some misinformation about the field. Contrary to what most laypeople think, economics is not just about money. It is about happiness too.)

B-1 FIVE MYTHS ABOUT ECONOMICS AND BEING AN ECONOMICS MAJOR

Myth 1: Economics Is All Mathematics and Statistics. Some students choose not to major in economics because they think that economics is all mathematics and statistics. Math and statistics *are* used in economics, but certainly not overwhelmingly at the undergraduate degree level. Economics majors are usually required to take one statistics course and one math course (usually an introductory calculus course). Even students who say, "Math isn't my subject," are sometimes happy with the amount of math they need in economics. The fact is that, at the undergraduate level at many colleges and universities, economics is not a very math-intensive course of study. Economics uses many diagrams, but not a large amount of math.

A proviso: The amount of math in the economics curriculum varies across colleges and universities. Some economics departments do not require their students to learn much math or statistics; others do. The majority of economics departments do not require much math or statistics at the undergraduate level. The graduate level is a different story.

If you are thinking of pursuing economics at the graduate level, you should enroll in numerous mathematics and statistics courses as an undergraduate.

Myth 2: Economics Is Only About Inflation, Interest Rates, Unemployment, and Other Such Things. If you study economics at college and then go on to become a practicing economist, no doubt people will ask you certain questions when they learn your chosen profession. Here are some:

- Do you think the economy is going to pick up?

- Do you think the economy is going to slow down?

- What stocks would you recommend?

- Do you think interest rates are going to fall?

- Do you think interest rates are going to rise?

- What do you think about buying bonds right now? Is it a good idea?

People ask these kinds of questions because most believe that economists study only stocks, bonds, interest rates, inflation, unemployment, and so on. Although economists do study these topics, they are only a tiny part of what economists study. It is not hard to find many economists today, both inside and outside academia, who spend most of their time studying anything but inflation, unemployment, stocks, bonds, and the like.

In fact, much of what economists study may surprise you. Some economists use their economic tools and methods to study crime, marriage, divorce, sex, obesity, addiction, sports, voting behavior, bureaucracies, presidential elections, and much more. In short, today's economics is not your grandfather's economics. Many more topics are studied today in economics than were studied in years past.

Myth 3: People Become Economists Only If They Want to "Make Money." A while back we asked a few well-respected and well-known economists what got them interested in economics. Here is what some of them had to say:[1]

---

[1] See various interviews in Roger A. Arnold, *Economics*, 2nd ed. (St. Paul, MN: West Publishing Company, 1992).

Gary Becker, the 1992 winner of the Nobel Prize in Economics, said,

> *I got interested in economics when I was an undergraduate in college. I came into college with a strong interest in mathematics and at the same time with a strong commitment to do something to help society. I learned in the first economics course I took that economics could deal rigorously, à la mathematics, with social problems. That stimulated me because, in economics, I saw that I could combine both the mathematics and my desire to do something to help society.*

Vernon Smith, the 2002 winner of the Nobel Prize in Economics, said,

> *My father's influence started me in science and engineering at Cal Tech, but my mother, who was active in socialist politics, probably accounts for the great interest I found in economics when I took my first introductory course.*

Alice Rivlin, an economist and former member of the Federal Reserve Board, said,

> *My interest in economics grew out of concern for improving public policy, both domestic and international. I was a teenager in the tremendously idealistic period after World War II when it seemed terribly important to get nations working together to solve the world's problems peacefully.*

Allan Meltzer, economist, said,

> *Economics is a social science. At its best it is concerned with ways (1) to improve well-being by allowing individuals the freedom to achieve their personal aims or goals and (2) to harmonize their individual interests. I find working on such issues challenging, and progress is personally rewarding.*

Robert Solow, the 1987 winner of the Nobel Prize in Economics, said,

> *I grew up in the 1930s, and it was very hard not to be interested in economics. If you were a high school student in the 1930s, you were conscious of the fact that our economy was in deep trouble and no one knew what to do about it.*

Charles Plosser, former president of the Federal Reserve Bank of Philadelphia and co-coiner of the term "real business cycle," said,

> *I was an engineer as an undergraduate with little knowledge of economics. I went to the University of Chicago Graduate School of Business to get an MBA and there became fascinated with economics. I was impressed with the seriousness with which economics was viewed as a way of organizing one's thoughts about the world to address interesting questions and problems.*

Walter Williams, professor of economics at George Mason University and winner of numerous fellowships and awards, said,

> *I was a major in sociology in 1963 and I concluded that it was not very rigorous. Over the summer I was reading a book by W. E. B. DuBois, Black Reconstruction, and somewhere in the book it said something along the lines that blacks could not melt into the mainstream of American society until they understood economics, and that was something that got me interested in economics.*

Murray Weidenbaum, former professor of economics at Washington University of St. Louis and former chairman of the Council of Economic Advisors, said,

> *A specific professor got me interested in economics. He was very prescient: He correctly noted that while lawyers dominated the policy-making process up until the 1940s, in the future economics would be an important tool for developing public policy. And he was right.*

Irma Adelman, former professor of agricultural and resource economics at the University of California at Berkeley, said,

> I hesitate to say because it sounds arrogant. My reason [for getting into economics] was that I wanted to benefit humanity. And my perception at the time was that economic problems were the most important problems that humanity has to face. That is what got me into economics and into economic development.

Lester Thurow, economist and former dean of the MIT Sloan School of Management, said,

> [I got interested in economics because of] the belief—some would see it as naïve belief—that economics was a profession where it would be possible to help make the world better.

Myth 4: Economics Wasn't Very Interesting in High School, So It's Not Going to Be Very Interesting in College. A typical high school economics course emphasizes, and spends much time discussing, consumer economics. Students learn about credit cards, mortgage loans, budgets, buying insurance, renting an apartment, and other such things. These are important topics because not knowing their ins and outs can make your life much harder. Still, many students come away from high school thinking that economics is always and everywhere about consumer topics.

However, a high school economics course and a college economics course are usually as different as day and night. Simply leaf through this book and look at the variety of topics covered, compared with those you might have covered in high school economics. Go on to look at texts used in other economics courses—ranging from law and economics, to the history of economic thought, to international economics, to sports economics—and you will see what we mean.

B-2 WHAT AWAITS YOU AS AN ECONOMICS MAJOR?

If you become an economics major, what courses will you take? What are you going to study?

At the lower division level, economics majors must take courses in the principles of macroeconomics and the principles of microeconomics. They usually also take a statistics course and a math course (usually calculus).

At the upper division level, they must take intermediate microeconomics and intermediate macroeconomics, along with a certain number of electives. Some of the elective courses, among many others, are as follows:

- Money and banking
- Law and economics
- History of economic thought
- Behavioral economics
- Public finance
- Labor economics
- International economics
- Antitrust and regulation
- Health economics
- Economics of development

- Urban and regional economics
- Econometrics
- Mathematical economics
- Environmental economics
- Public choice
- Global managerial economics
- Economic approach to politics and sociology
- Sports economics

Most economics majors take between 12 and 15 economics courses.

One of the attractive things about studying economics is that you will acquire many of the skills employers value highly. First, you will have the quantitative skills that are important in many business and government positions. Second, you will acquire the writing skills necessary in almost all lines of work. Third, and perhaps most importantly, you will develop the thinking skills that almost all employers agree are critical to success.

A study published in the 1998 edition of the *Journal of Economic Education* ranked economics majors as having the highest average scores on the Law School Admission Test (LSAT). Also, consider the words of the Royal Economic Society:

> One of the things that makes economics graduates so employable is that the subject teaches you to think in a careful and precise way. The fundamental economic issue is how society decides to allocate its resources: how the costs and benefits of a course of action can be evaluated and compared, and how appropriate choices can be made. A degree in economics gives a training in decision making principles, providing a skill applicable in a very wide range of careers.

Keep in mind, too, that economics is one of the most popular majors at some of the most respected universities in the country. As of this writing, economics is the top major at Harvard, Princeton, Columbia, Stanford, the University of Pennsylvania, and the University of Chicago. It is the second most popular major at Brown, Yale, and the University of California at Berkeley. It is the third most popular major at Cornell and Dartmouth.

B-3 WHAT DO ECONOMISTS DO?

Today, economists work in many and varied fields. Here are some of the fields and some of the positions that economists hold in those fields:

Education

College professor

Researcher

High school teacher

Journalism

Researcher

Industry analyst

Economic analyst

Accounting

- Analyst
- Auditor
- Researcher
- Consultant

General Business

- Chief executive officer
- Business analyst
- Marketing analyst
- Business forecaster
- Competitive analyst

Government

- Researcher
- Analyst
- Speechwriter
- Forecaster

Financial Services

- Business journalist
- International analyst
- Newsletter editor
- Broker
- Investment banker

Banking

- Credit analyst
- Loan officer
- Investment analyst
- Financial manager

Other

- Business consultant
- Independent forecaster
- Freelance analyst
- Think tank analyst
- Entrepreneur

Economists do a myriad of things, including the following:

- In business, economists often analyze economic conditions, make forecasts, offer strategic-planning initiatives, collect and analyze data, predict exchange rate movements, and review regulatory policies, among other things.

- In government, economists collect and analyze data, analyze international economic situations, research monetary conditions, advise on policy, and do much more.

- As private consultants, economists work with accountants, business executives, government officials, educators, financial firms, labor unions, state and local governments, and others.

In May 2015, the median annual wage and salary earnings of economists were $99,180. The lowest 10 percent earned less than $52,540, and the top 10 percent earned more than $176,960. In May 2015, the average annual salary for economists employed by the federal government was $110,570.

B-4 PLACES TO FIND MORE INFORMATION

If you are interested in a major and perhaps a career in economics, here are some places you can go to and people you can speak with to acquire more information:

- To learn about the economics curriculum, speak with the economics professors at your college or university. Ask them what courses you would have to take as an economics major and what elective courses are available. In addition, ask them why they chose to study economics: What is it about economics that interested them?

- For more information about salaries and what economists do, you may want to visit the *Occupational Outlook Handbook* website (http://www.bls.gov/ooh/).

B-5 CONCLUDING REMARKS

Choosing a major is a big decision and therefore should not be made quickly and without much thought. This short appendix has provided you with some information about an economics major and a career in economics. Economics is not for everyone, but it may be right for you. A major in economics trains you in today's most marketable skills: good writing, quantitative analysis, and rigorous thinking. It is a major in which professors and students daily ask and answer some very interesting and relevant questions. It is a major that is highly regarded by employers. It may just be the right major for you. Give it some thought.

PRODUCTION POSSIBILITIES FRONTIER FRAMEWORK

INTRODUCTION

In the last chapter, you learned about various economic concepts, such as scarcity, choice, and opportunity cost. In this chapter, we develop a graphical framework of analysis for understanding these concepts and others. Specifically, we develop the production possibilities frontier.

2-1 THE PRODUCTION POSSIBILITIES FRONTIER

Think of yourself as being alone on an island. You can produce two goods and only two goods: coconuts and pineapples. Because your resources are limited, producing more of one good means producing less of the other. That type of thinking is the intuition behind the *production possibilities frontier*. Now keep that intuition in mind as we proceed.

2-1a The Straight-Line PPF: Constant Opportunity Costs

In Exhibit 1(a), we have identified five combinations of books and shirts that can be produced in an economy. For example, combination *A* is 4 books and 0 shirts, combination *B* is 3 books and 1 shirt, and so on. Next, we plotted these five combinations of books and shirts in Exhibit 1(b), with each combination representing a different point. For example, the combination of 4 books and 0 shirts is represented by point *A*. The line that connects points *A–E* is the production possibilities frontier. A **production possibilities frontier (PPF)** is the combination of two goods that can be produced in a certain span of time under the conditions of a given state of technology and fully employed resources.

Production Possibilities Frontier (PPF)
The possible combinations of two goods that can be produced during a certain span of time under the conditions of a given state of technology and fully employed resources.

Notice that the PPF is a straight line. This is because the opportunity cost of books and shirts (in our example) is constant:

$$\text{Straight-line PPF} = \text{Constant opportunity costs}$$

To illustrate what *constant opportunity costs* means, suppose the economy were to move from point A to point B. At point A, 4 books and 0 shirts are produced; at point B, 3 books and 1 shirt are produced:

- Point A: 4 books and 0 shirts
- Point B: 3 books and 1 shirt

What does the economy have to forfeit (in terms of books) to get 1 shirt? The answer is 1 book. We conclude that, in moving from point A to point B, the opportunity cost of 1 shirt is 1 book.

Now let's move from point B to point C. At point B, 3 books and 1 shirt are produced; at point C, 2 books and 2 shirts are produced:

- Point B: 3 books and 1 shirt
- Point C: 2 books and 2 shirts

So, how many books does the economy have to forfeit to get another shirt? The answer is 1 book. We conclude that, in moving from point B to C, the opportunity cost of 1 shirt is 1 book.

In fact, when we move from C to D or from D to E, we also notice that the opportunity cost of 1 shirt is 1 book. This is what we mean when we speak of constant opportunity costs: The opportunity cost of 1 shirt is *always* 1 book. And because opportunity costs are constant, the PPF in Exhibit 1(b) is a straight line. When opportunity costs are not constant, the PPF will not be a straight line, as you will see next.

2-1b The Bowed-Outward (Concave-Downward) PPF: Increasing Opportunity Costs

In Exhibit 2(a), we have identified five combinations of cell phones and coffee makers that can be produced in an economy. For example, combination A is 10 cell phones and 0 coffee makers, combination B is 9 cell phones and 1 coffee maker, and so on. We plotted these five combinations of cell phones and coffee makers in Exhibit 2(b), again with each combination representing a different point. The curved line that connects points A–E is

---

EXHIBIT 1

Production Possibilities Frontier (Constant Opportunity Costs)

The economy can produce any of the five combinations of books and shirts in part (a). We have plotted these combinations in part (b). The PPF in part (b) is a straight line because the opportunity cost of producing either good is constant.

Combination	Books	Shirts	Point in Part (b)
A	4	0	A
B	3	1	B
C	2	2	C
D	1	3	D
E	0	4	E

(a)

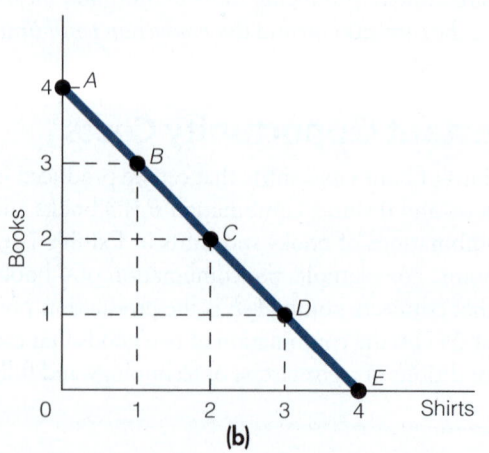

(b)

EXHIBIT 2

Production Possibilities Frontier (Increasing Opportunity Costs)

The economy can produce any of the five combinations of cell phones and coffee makers in part (a). We have plotted these combinations in part (b). The PPF in part (b) is bowed outward because the opportunity cost of producing coffee makers increases as more coffee makers are produced.

Combination	Cell Phones	Coffee Makers	Point in Part (b)
A	10	0	A
B	9	1	B
C	7	2	C
D	4	3	D
E	0	4	E

(a)

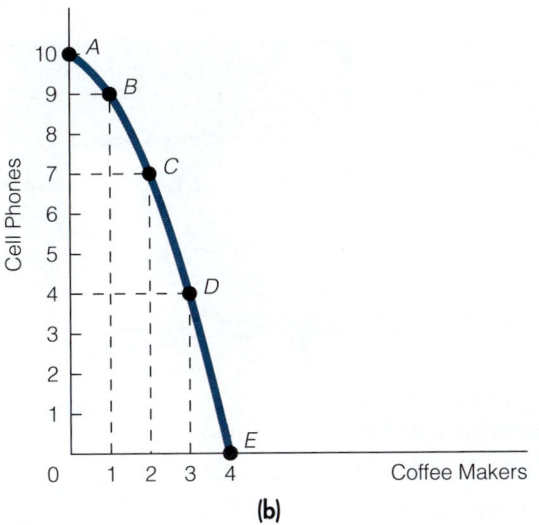

(b)

the PPF. In this case, the production possibilities frontier is bowed outward (concave downward) because the opportunity cost of coffee makers increases as more coffee makers are produced:

$$\text{Bowed-outward PPF} = \text{Increasing opportunity costs}$$

To illustrate, let's start at point *A*, where the economy is producing 10 cell phones and 0 coffee makers, and move to point *B*, where the economy is producing 9 cell phones and 1 coffee makers:

- Point *A*: 10 cell phones and 0 coffee makers
- Point *B*: 9 cell phones and 1 coffee makers

What is the opportunity cost of a coffee maker in moving from point *A* to point *B*? Stated differently, what does the economy have to forfeit (in terms of cell phones) to get 1 coffee maker? The answer is 1 cell phone.

Now let's move from point *B* to point *C*. At point *B*, the economy is producing 9 cell phones and 1 coffee maker; at point *C*, the economy is producing 7 cell phones and 2 coffee makers:

- Point *B*: 9 cell phones and 1 coffee makers
- Point *C*: 7 cell phones and 2 coffee makers

Now how many cell phones does the economy have to forfeit to get 1 additional coffee maker? The answer this time is 2 cell phones. We conclude that, in moving from point *A* to point *B*, the opportunity cost of 1 coffee maker was 1 cell phone, but that, in moving from point *B* to point *C*, the opportunity cost of 1 (additional) coffee makers is 2 cell phones. If we were to continue

Does It Matter to You . . .
If the Economy Is at One Point on the PPF Instead of Another?

In Exhibit 3 we have shown a production possibilities frontier (PPF). On the horizontal axis we have placed good *X*; on the vertical axis, good *Y*. On the PPF itself, we have identified three points, labeled points 1, 2, and 3. Does it matter to you if the economy is at one point instead of another? For example, does it matter to you if the economy is located at point 1 instead of point 3? To help us get at the answer, consider that at point 1 the economy is producing more of good *Y* and less of good *X* than at point 3. At point 3, the economy is producing more of good *X* and less of good *Y* that a point 1.

Consider the case in which there is no international trade. In this case, the point at which the economy is located on the PPF has a lot to say as to what people in the economy end up consuming. Specifically, an economy in which a lot of Y but very little X is produced is an economy in which people will most likely end up consuming much more Y than X.

In fact, it is more likely to be the case that because people want to consume more Y than X that firms end up producing more Y than X.

Monkey Business Images/Shutterstock.com

Consumption, to a large extent, directs production. If people want to consume numerous iPads and smartphones and very few V-neck sweaters, then it is likely that producers will end up producing what they think will sell. In this case, iPads and smartphones, and not so many V-neck sweaters.

We return to our original question: Does it matter to you if the economy is at one point of the PPF instead of another? To a large degree, it matters as to what you consume.

It also is likely to matter to your employment. You are more likely to end up working in an industry in which a lot of a particular good is produced than in an industry in which very little of some good is produced. In terms of our PPF diagram, if the economy is located at point 1 instead of point 3, you are more likely to work—as an accountant, attorney, factory worker, janitor, clerical worker, and so on—in the industry that produces good *Y* than in the industry that produces good *X*.

Now think about the following. Suppose that government decides that it wants to put more resources into a particular area, such as health care. Might this end up moving the economy from one point to another on the PPF, thus affecting your consumption and your employment? In other words, government raises taxes, then takes the increased tax revenue and directs them into health care. As a result, more health care is produced in the economy as it moves from one point to another point on the PPF—from a point that represents less health care to one that represents more health care. Could this affect you? It certainly could, after all if more health care is produced, you now have a greater probability of working—once again, as an accountant, attorney, clerical worker, and so on—in the health care industry than had the government not directed more resources into health care. In fact, directing more resources into the health care industry—thus moving the economy from one point to another on the PPF—can influence what work for which you train. For example, if the health care industry is expanding, you might end up training to be a nurse instead of an accountant, a lab technician, or radiologist instead of a teacher.

EXHIBIT 3

A PPF and 3 points

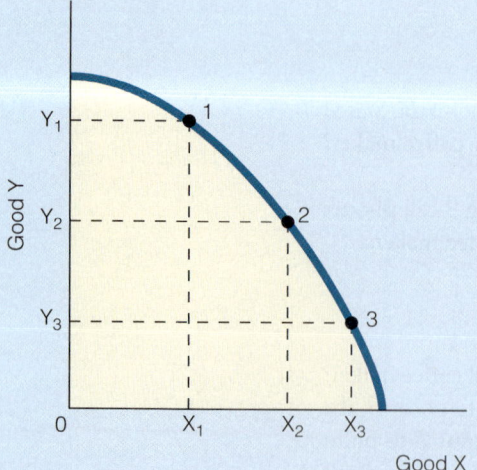

producing additional coffee makers, we would see that we would have to give up increasingly more cell phones. You can see this easily if you consider the economy moving from point C to point D (where the opportunity cost of producing an additional coffee makers is 3 cell phones) or moving from point to D to point E (where the opportunity cost of producing an additional coffee makers is 4 cell phones). We end with a question: Why is the PPF in Exhibit 2(b) bowed outward? The reason is the increasing opportunity costs of producing coffee makers.

2-1c Law of Increasing Opportunity Costs

We know that the shape of the PPF depends on whether opportunity costs (1) are constant or (2) increase as more of a good is produced. In Exhibit 1(b), the PPF is a straight line; in Exhibit 2(b), it is bowed outward (curved). In the real world, most PPFs are bowed outward. In other words, for most goods, the opportunity costs *increase* as more of the good is produced. This relationship is referred to as the **law of increasing opportunity costs.**

The law of increasing opportunity costs holds for most goods because people have varying abilities. For example, some individuals are better suited to building houses than others are. When a construction company first starts building houses, it employs the people most skilled at doing so. The most skilled persons can build houses at lower opportunity costs than others can. But as the construction company builds more houses, it finds that it has already employed the most skilled builders; so, it must employ those who are less skilled at building houses. The less skilled people build houses at higher opportunity costs: Whereas three skilled house builders could build a house in a month, as many as seven unskilled builders may be required to build one as fast. Exhibit 4 summarizes the points in this section.

Law of Increasing Opportunity Costs
As more of a good is produced, the opportunity costs of producing that good increase.

EXHIBIT 4

A Summary Statement About Increasing Opportunity Costs and a Production Possibilities Frontier That Is Bowed Outward (Concave Downward)

Many of the points about increasing opportunity costs and a PPF that is bowed outward are summarized here.

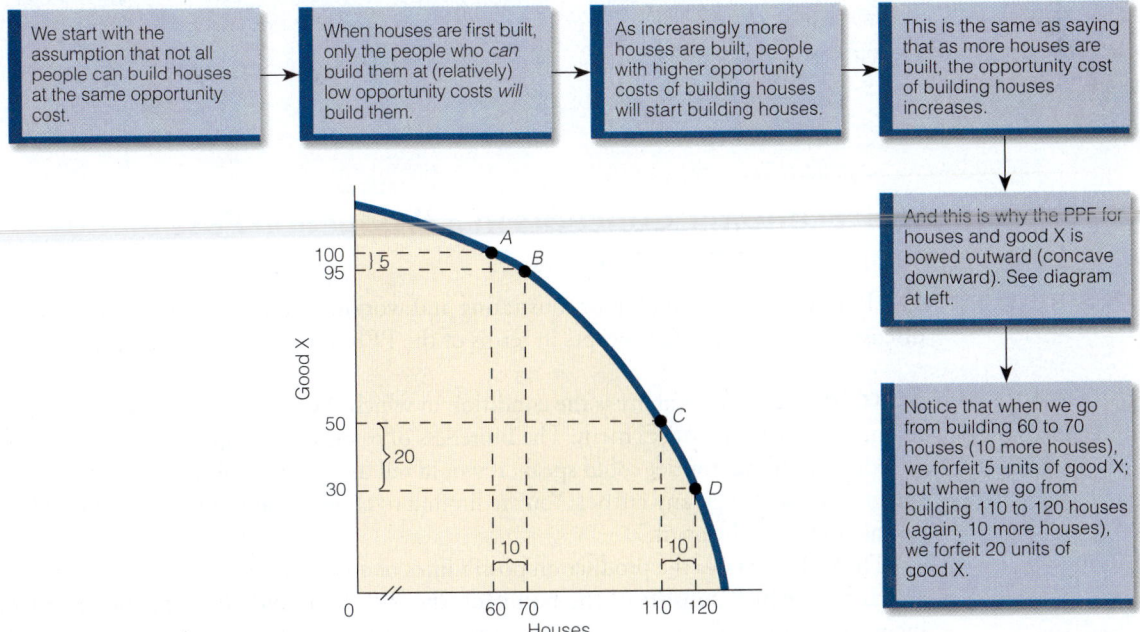

We start with the assumption that not all people can build houses at the same opportunity cost.

When houses are first built, only the people who *can* build them at (relatively) low opportunity costs *will* build them.

As increasingly more houses are built, people with higher opportunity costs of building houses will start building houses.

This is the same as saying that as more houses are built, the opportunity cost of building houses increases.

And this is why the PPF for houses and good X is bowed outward (concave downward). See diagram at left.

Notice that when we go from building 60 to 70 houses (10 more houses), we forfeit 5 units of good X; but when we go from building 110 to 120 houses (again, 10 more houses), we forfeit 20 units of good X.

ECONOMICS 24/7

Deducing Where Sherlock Holmes Was on His Production Possibilities Frontier?

Of Sherlock Holmes, it has been said that "his ignorance was as remarkable as his knowledge."[1] In fact, his companion, Dr. Watson, said, "Of contemporary literature, philosophy and politics he appeared to know next to nothing…. My surprise reached a climax, however, when I found incidentally that he was ignorant of the Copernican Theory and of the composition of the Solar System. That any civilized being in this nineteenth century should not be aware that the earth travelled round the sun appeared to be to me such an extraordinary fact that I could hardly realize it."[2]

When Dr. Watson expressed his surprise to Sherlock Holmes, Holmes told Watson that now that Watson had told him that the earth revolves around the sun, he would try his best to forget it. Holmes said, "You see, I consider that a man's brain originally is like a little empty attic, and you have to stock it with such furniture as you choose. A fool takes in all the lumber of every sort that he comes across, so that the knowledge which might be useful to him gets crowded out…. He will have nothing but the tools which may help him in doing his work…. Depend upon it there comes a time when for every addition of knowledge you forget something that you knew before."[3]

Time Life Pictures/Getty Images

Holmes was interested in solving crimes, and he wanted his brain filled with only the things that would help him achieve his sole purpose. If he learned something that was irrelevant to this task, then something that was relevant to the purpose at hand would be discarded. In other words, he was on his PPF and more of one thing necessarily meant less of something else.

Not only that, but Holmes wanted to stay at a particular point on his PPF. But which point? Well, let's deduce the answer together. Suppose that on the vertical axis there is "knowing more about things about the world, none of which is helpful in solving crime" and on the horizontal axis is "number of crimes solved." Now, if Holmes wants to solve as many crimes as possible, obviously he wants to be on his PPF at the point where it touches the horizontal axis. He wants to solve as many crimes as possible, given his resources (physical and mental). In other words, he wants to use all of his resources to do one thing and one thing only: solve crimes.

1. Sir Arthur Conan Doyle, "A Study in Scarlet," *The Adventures of Sherlock Holmes*, Modern Library paperback edition (New York: Random House, 2003), chapter 2.
2. Ibid.
3. Ibid.

2-1d Economic Concepts in a *Production Possibilities Frontier* Framework

The PPF framework is useful for illustrating and working with economic concepts. This section discusses seven economic concepts in terms of the PPF framework. (See Exhibit 5.)

Scarcity Recall that scarcity is the condition in which the wants (for goods) are greater than the resources available to satisfy them. The finiteness of resources is graphically portrayed by the PPF in Exhibit 6. If the frontier could speak, it would tell us, "At this point in time, that's as far as you can go. You cannot go any farther. You are limited to choosing any combination of the two goods on the frontier or below it."

The PPF separates the production possibilities of an economy into two regions: (1) an attainable region, which consists of the points on the PPF itself and all points below it (this region includes points *A–F*), and (2) an unattainable region, which consists of the points above and

EXHIBIT 5

The PPF Economic Framework

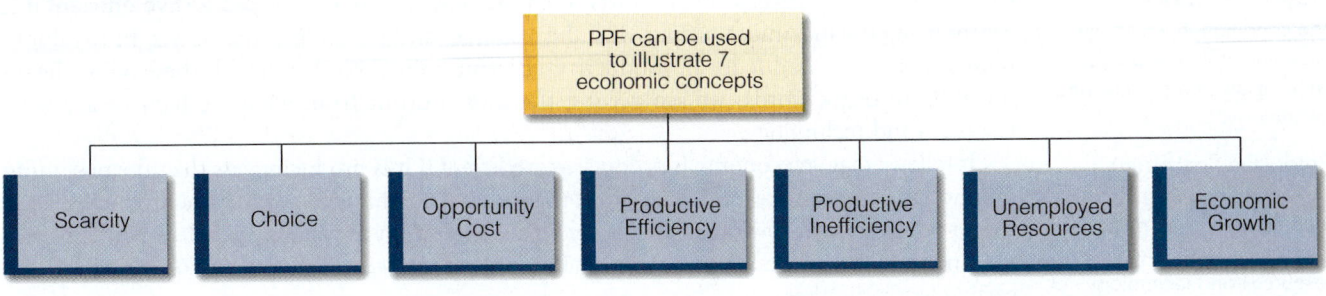

beyond the PPF (such as point *G*). Recall that scarcity implies that some things are attainable and others are unattainable. Point *A* on the PPF is attainable, as is point *F*; point *G* is not.

Choice and opportunity cost are also shown in Exhibit 6. Note that, within the attainable region, individuals must choose the combination of the two goods they want to produce. Obviously, hundreds of combinations exist, but let's consider only two, represented by points *A* and *B*, respectively. Which of the two will individuals choose? They can't be at both points; they must make a choice.

Opportunity cost is illustrated as we move from one point to another on the PPF in Exhibit 6. Suppose we are at point *A* and choose to move to point *B*. At point *A*, we have 55,000 television sets and 5,000 cars; at point *B*, we have 50,000 television sets and 15,000 cars. What is the

EXHIBIT 6

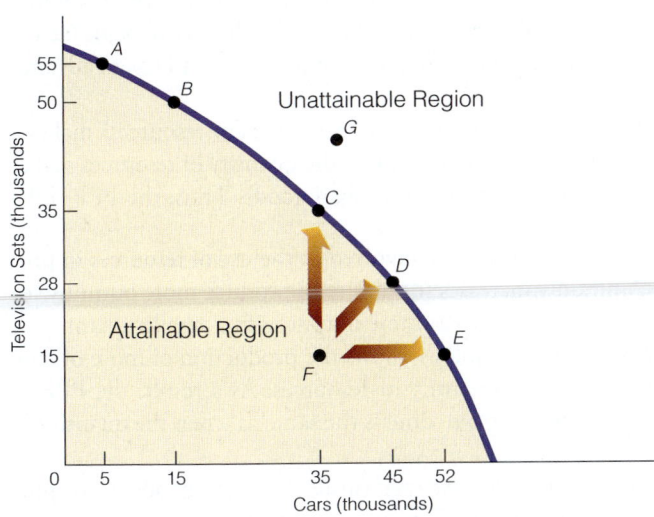

The PPF and Various Economic Concepts

The PPF can illustrate various economic concepts:

(1) Scarcity is illustrated by the frontier itself. Implicit in the concept of scarcity is the idea that we can have some things but not all things. The PPF separates an attainable region from an unattainable region.

(2) Choice is represented by our having to decide among the many attainable combinations of the two goods. For example, will we choose the combination of goods represented by point *A* or by point *B*?

(3) Opportunity cost is most easily seen as movement from one point to another, such as movement from point *A* to point *B*. More cars are available at point *B* than at point *A*, but fewer television sets are available. In short, the opportunity cost of more cars is fewer television sets.

(4) Productive efficiency is represented by the points *on* the PPF (such as *A–E*), while productive inefficiency is represented by any point *below* the PPF (such as *F*).

(5) Unemployment (in terms of resources being unemployed) exists at any productive-inefficient point (such as *F*), whereas resources are fully employed at any productive-efficient point (such as any point in the range *A–E*).

opportunity cost of a car? Because 10,000 *more* cars come at a cost of 5,000 *fewer* television sets, the opportunity cost of 1 car is ½ television set.

Productive Efficiency   Economists often say that an economy is **productive efficient** if it is producing the maximum output with the resources and technology that it has. In Exhibit 6, points *A*, *B*, *C*, *D*, and *E* are all productive-efficient points. Notice that all these points lie on the PPF. In other words, we are getting the most output from what we have of available resources and technology.

It follows that an economy is **productive inefficient** if it is producing less than the maximum output with the resources and technology that it has. In Exhibit 6, point *F* is a productive-inefficient point. It lies below the PPF; it is below the outer limit of what is possible. In other words, we can produce more goods with the available resources, or we can get more of one good without getting less of another.

To illustrate, suppose we move from inefficient point *F* to efficient point *C*. We produce more television sets and no fewer cars. What if we move from *F* to *D*? We produce more television sets and more cars. Finally, if we move from *F* to *E*, we produce more cars and no fewer television sets. Thus, moving from *F* can give us more of at least one good and no less of another good. In short, productive inefficiency implies that gains are possible in one area without losses in another.

Unemployed Resources   When the economy exhibits productive inefficiency, it is not producing the maximum output with the available resources and technology. One reason may be that the economy is not using all of its resources; that is, some of its resources are unemployed, as at point *F* in Exhibit 6.

When the economy exhibits productive efficiency, it is producing the maximum output with the available resources and technology. In other words, it is using all its resources to produce goods; its resources are fully employed, and none are unemployed. At the productive-efficient points *A–E* in Exhibit 6, no resources are unemployed.

Economic Growth   The term *economic growth* refers to the increased productive capabilities of an economy. Economic growth is illustrated by an outward shift in the PPF. Two major factors that produce economic growth are (1) an increase in the quantity of resources and (2) an advance in technology.

An increase in the quantity of resources (e.g., through a discovery of new resources) makes a greater quantity of output possible. In Exhibit 7(a), an increase in the quantity of resources makes it possible to produce both more military goods and more civilian goods. Thus, the PPF shifts outward from PPF_1 to PPF_2.

Technology refers to the body of skills and knowledge involved in the use of resources in production. An advance in technology commonly increases the ability to produce more output with a fixed quantity of resources or the ability to produce the same output with a smaller quantity of resources. For example, suppose an advance in technology allows the production of more of *both* military goods and civilian goods with the same quantity of resources. As a result, the PPF in Exhibit 7(a) shifts outward from PPF_1 to PPF_2. The outcome is the same as when the quantity of resources is increased.

If the advance in technology allows only more of *one good* (instead of both goods) to be produced with the same quantity of resources, then the PPF shifts outward, but not in the same way as shown in Exhibit 7(a). To illustrate, suppose an advance in technology allows only more civilian goods to be produced but not more military goods. Therefore, the maximum amount of military goods that can be produced does not change, but the maximum amount of civilian goods rises. This situation gives us the shift from PPF_1 to PPF_2 shown in Exhibit 7(b).

Productive Efficient
The condition in which the maximum output is produced with the given resources and technology.

Productive Inefficient
The condition in which less than the maximum output is produced with the given resources and technology. Productive inefficiency implies that more of one good can be produced without any less of another being produced.

Technology The body of skills and knowledge involved in the use of resources in production. An advance in technology commonly increases the ability to produce more output with a fixed amount of resources or the ability to produce the same output with fewer resources.

EXHIBIT 7

Economic Growth Within a PPF Framework

An increase in resources or an advance in technology (that can lead to more of both goods being produced) can increase the production capabilities of an economy, leading to economic growth and a shift outward in the PPF, as shown in part (a). If the advance in technology leads to the greater production of only one good (such as civilian goods in this exhibit), then the PPF shifts outward, as shown in (b).

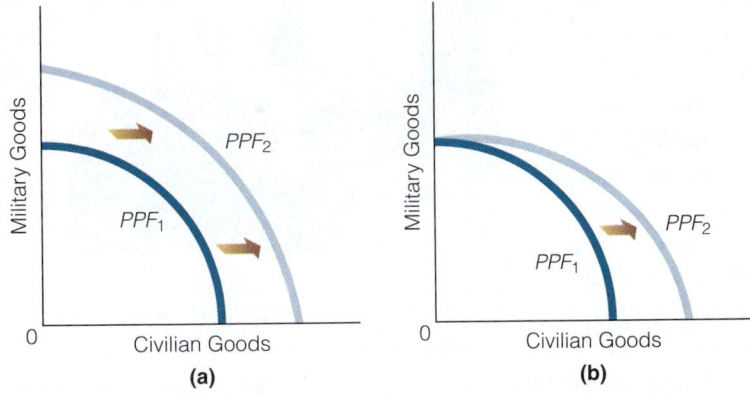

(a)

(b)

FINDING ECONOMICS

In an Online Travel Agency   You are online at Travelocity.com, the online travel agency, booking a flight to New York City. Where is the economics?

Let's first talk about brick-and-mortar travel agencies. Before the Internet, it was common for people to book airline flights, vacations, and cruises through a brick-and-mortar travel agency. A person might get into his car, drive to the travel agency, walk into the agency, talk to an agent about where he or she wanted to go and wanted to see, and the agent then would book the flights, hotels, rental cars, and more. The Internet has largely changed that. Today, there are appreciably fewer brick-and-mortar travel agencies. Most people book their travel arrangements online. Because of the technological advancement, witnessed in the Internet, many people who were once travel agents, or who would have become travel agents, had to find other things to do. Where did all the travel agents go? They went into other occupations. No doubt some decided to become teachers, factory workers, computer technicians, police officers.

What we learn from this is that a technological advancement in one sector of the economy can have ripple effects throughout the economy. We also learn that a technological advancement can affect the composition of employment.

SELF-TEST

(Answers to Self-Test questions are in Answers to Self-Test Questions at the back of the book.)

1. What does a straight-line PPF represent? What does a bowed-outward PPF represent?

2. What does the law of increasing costs have to do with a bowed-outward PPF?

3. A politician says, "If you elect me, we can get more of everything we want." Under what condition is the politician telling the truth?

4. In an economy, only one combination of goods is productive efficient. True or false? Explain your answer.

ECONOMICS 24/7

Studying and Your PPF

You have your own PPF; you just may not know it. Suppose you are studying for two upcoming exams. You have only a total of six hours before you have to take the first exam, after which you will immediately proceed to take the second exam. Thus, time spent studying for the first exam (in economics) takes away from time that could be spent studying for the second exam (in math), and vice versa. Also, *time spent studying* is a resource in the production of a good grade: Less time spent studying for the economics exam and more time spent studying for the math exam means a higher grade in math and a lower grade in economics. For you, the situation may look as it does in Exhibit 8(a). We have identified four points (1–4) in the exhibit that correspond to the four combinations of two grades (one grade in economics and one grade in math).

Notice that each grade comes with a certain amount of time spent studying. This time is specified under the grade.

Monkey Business Images/Shutterstock.com

Given the resources you currently have (your labor and time), you can achieve any of the four combinations. For example, you can spend six hours studying for economics and get a *B* (point 1), but then you study math for zero hours and get an F in that course. Or you can spend four hours studying for economics and get a *C* (point 2), leaving you two hours to study for math, in which you get a *D*.

What do you need to get a higher grade in one course without getting a lower grade in the other course? You need more resources, which in this case is more time. If you have eight hours to study, your PPF shifts rightward, as in Exhibit 8(b). Now point 5 is possible (whereas it was not possible before you got more time). At point 5, you can get a C in economics and in math, an impossible combination of grades when you had less time (a PPF closer to the origin).

EXHIBIT 8

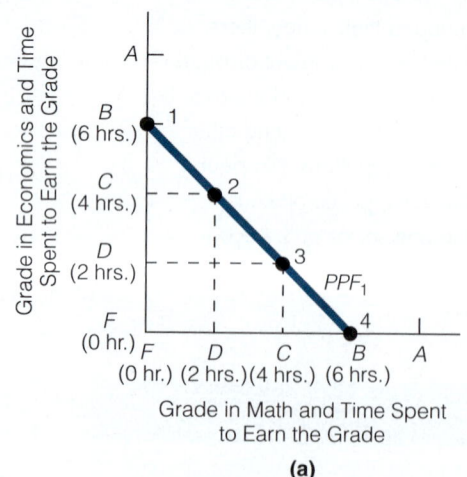

(a)

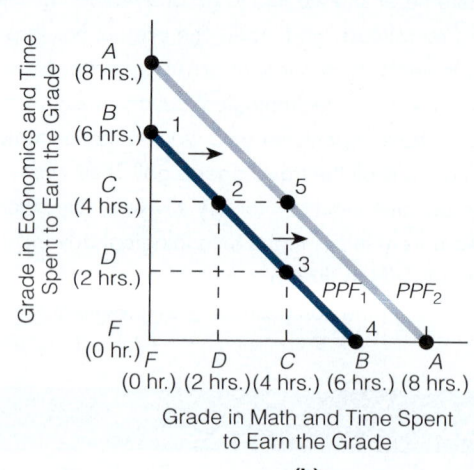

(b)

2-2 SPECIALIZATION AND TRADE CAN MOVE US BEYOND OUR PPF

In this section, we explain how a country that specializes in the production of certain goods and then trades those goods to countries for other goods can make itself better off. In terms of its PPF, it can consume at a level *beyond* its PPF.

2-2a A Simple Two-Person PPF Model

Two individuals, Elizabeth and Brian, live near each other, and each engages in two activities: baking bread and growing apples. Let's suppose that, within a certain period, Elizabeth can produce 20 loaves of bread and no apples, or 10 loaves of bread and 10 apples, or no bread and 20 apples. (See Exhibit 9.) In other words, three points on Elizabeth's PPF correspond, respectively, to 20 loaves of bread and no apples, 10 loaves of bread and 10 apples, and no bread and 20 apples. As a consumer, Elizabeth likes to eat both bread and apples; so she decides to produce (and consume) 10 loaves of bread and 10 apples. This combination is represented by point *B* in Exhibit 9(a).

During the same period, Brian can produce 10 loaves of bread and no apples, or 5 loaves of bread and 15 apples, or no bread and 30 apples. In other words, these three combinations correspond, respectively, to three points on Brian's PPF. Brian, like Elizabeth, likes to eat both bread and apples; so he decides to produce and consume 5 loaves of bread and 15 apples. This combination is represented by point *F* in Exhibit 9(b).

Elizabeth thinks that both she and Brian may be better off if each specializes in producing only one of the two goods and trading it for the other. In other words, Elizabeth should produce either bread or apples but not both. Brian thinks that this may be a good idea but is not sure which good each person should specialize in producing.

An economist would advise each to produce the good that he or she can produce at a lower cost. In economics, a person who can produce a good at a lower cost than another person is said to have a **comparative advantage** in the production of the good.

Comparative Advantage
The situation in which someone can produce a good at lower opportunity cost than someone else can.

Exhibit 9 shows that, for every 10 units of bread Elizabeth does not produce, she can produce 10 apples. In other words, the opportunity cost of producing 1 loaf of bread *(B)* is 1 apple *(A)*:

$$\text{Opportunity costs for Elizabeth}: \quad 1B = 1A$$
$$1A = 1B$$

For every 5 loaves of bread that Brian does not produce, he can produce 15 apples. So, for every 1 loaf of bread he does not produce, he can produce 3 apples. Therefore, for every 1 apple he chooses to produce, he forfeits 1/3 loaf of bread:

$$\text{Opportunity costs for Brian}: \quad 1B = 3A$$
$$1A = 1/3B$$

Comparing opportunity costs, we see that Elizabeth can produce bread at a lower opportunity cost than Brian can. (Elizabeth forfeits 1 apple when she produces 1 loaf of bread, whereas Brian forfeits 3 apples for 1 loaf of bread.) By contrast, Brian can produce apples at a lower opportunity cost than Elizabeth can. We conclude that Elizabeth has a comparative advantage in the production of bread and Brian has a comparative advantage in the production of apples.

Suppose both individuals specialize in the production of the good in which they have a comparative advantage. Then Elizabeth produces only bread and makes 20 loaves. Brian produces only apples and grows 30 of them.

Now suppose that Elizabeth and Brian decide to trade 8 loaves of bread for 12 apples. In other words, Elizabeth produces 20 loaves of bread and then trades 8 of them for 12 apples. After

EXHIBIT 9

Elizabeth's PPF, Brian's PPF

In (a) we show the combination of the two goods that Elizabeth can produce, first in terms of a table and then in terms of a PPF. Because Elizabeth wants to consume some of both goods, she chooses to produce the combination of the two goods represented by point B.

In (b) we show the combination of the two goods that Brian can produce, first in terms of a table and then in terms of a PPF. Because Brian wants to consume some of both goods, he chooses to produce the combination of the two goods represented by point F.

Elizabeth	
Bread	**Apples**
20	0
10	10
0	20

Brian	
Bread	**Apples**
10	0
5	15
0	30

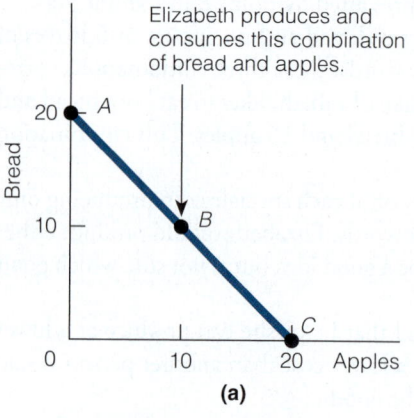

Elizabeth produces and consumes this combination of bread and apples.

(a)

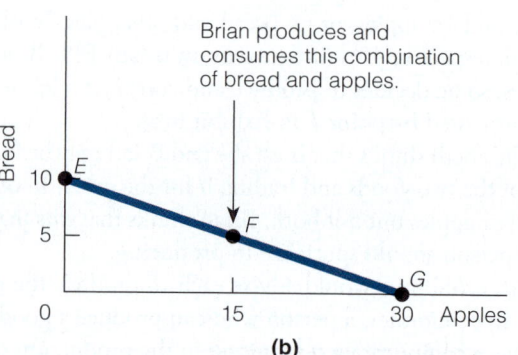

Brian produces and consumes this combination of bread and apples.

(b)

the trade, Elizabeth consumes 12 loaves of bread and 12 apples. Compare this situation with what she consumed when she didn't specialize and didn't trade. In that situation, she consumed 10 loaves of bread and 10 apples. Clearly, Elizabeth is better off when she specializes and trades than when she does not.

But what about Brian? He produces 30 apples and trades 12 of them to Elizabeth for 8 loaves of bread. In other words, he consumes 8 loaves of bread and 18 apples. Compare this situation with what he consumed when he didn't specialize and didn't trade. In that situation, he consumed 5 loaves of bread and 15 apples. Thus, Brian is also better off when he specializes and trades than when he does not.

2-2b On or Beyond the PPF?

In Exhibit 10(a), we show the PPF for Elizabeth. When she was not specializing and not trading, she consumed the combination of bread and apples represented by point B (10 loaves of bread and 10 apples). When she did specialize and trade, her consumption of both goods increased, moving her to point D (12 loaves of bread and 12 apples). Here is the lesson learned: Through specialization and trade, Elizabeth's consumption moved beyond her PPF. It is easy to see the benefits of specialization and trade.

In Exhibit 10(b), we show the PPF for Brian. When he was not specializing and not trading, he consumed the combination of bread and apples represented by point F (5 loaves of bread and

Hear What and How the Economist Thinks . . .
About Manufacturing Jobs

The economist is reading an opinion piece in a news magazine. Part of the article reads:

The United States is losing jobs manufacturing jobs to other countries. The number of manufacturing jobs has fallen in the United States in recent years. If the current trend in manufacturing jobs continues, the day will soon come in the United States when Americans produce no manufactured goods. Something has to be done to reverse this trend, and the sooner the better.

Yuangeng Zhang/Shutterstock.com

Hear what and how the economist thinks:

The person who wrote this opinion piece seems to think that as the number of jobs in the manufacturing sector declines, so falls the number of manufactured goods produced in the United States. In other words, more jobs means more output and fewer jobs means less output.

First, let's think of an example that counteracts this relationship. There used to be time in the United States when a fairly high percentage of the labor force was in agriculture. But today only a small percentage (1.5 percent) of the labor force is in agriculture. In other words, the country has lost agriculture jobs; it has lost many of its farmers. But does it follow that because there are a small percentage of workers in agriculture today—as well as a smaller absolute number of farmers—that there is less food produced in the United States today than in the past. The answer is no. In fact, more food is produced in the country today with fewer farmers than was the case in the past with more farmers.

Think in terms of a production possibilities frontier (PPF). Suppose manufactured goods are on the vertical axis and services are on the horizontal axis. What can shift the PPF rightward such that it intersects both the vertical and horizontal axes further away from the origin? Well, an increase in resources will do it, but also an advancement in technology. As economists know, an advance in technology commonly increases the

ability to produce more output with a fixed quantity of resources. Now, if an advance in technology increases the ability to produce more output with a fixed quantity of resources (e.g., it allows 100 people to produce 1,000 units of a good instead of 700 units), it then follows that an advance in technology also makes it possible to produce the same amount of a good with fewer resources (e.g., it allows 80 instead of 100 people to produce 1,000 units of a good.)

Could that be the case in manufacturing? Could it be that there have been technological developments in manufacturing in the United States, such that fewer workers in manufacturing can produce the same number of manufacturing goods as it took more workers to produce in the past? It certainly could be. Case in point: While manufacturing employment in the United States was lower in 2016 than in 2001, manufacturing output was higher in 2016 than 2001.

The person who wrote the opinion piece linking a decline in the number of jobs in manufacturing with less manufacturing output missed an important point: It is possible, with developments in technology in manufacturing, to produce the same amount of manufacturing output with fewer manufacturing workers or even more manufacturing output with fewer workers.

Questions to Think About:

1. Think of the total output produced in an economy in a year. Say the dollar amount of this output, adjusted for price changes, is $500 billion in year 1. In year 2, it falls to $490 billion. Also in year 2 it happens that the number of jobs in one particular industry declined from 1,000 to 900. Does it follow that the number of jobs declining in one particular industry was the cause of the decline in total output produced?

2. Suppose higher-level educational output is measured by how many college students graduate with an undergraduate degree in a year. Also, suppose that the number of instructors in colleges declines. Does it follow that higher-level educational output will decline too? Why or why not?

15 apples). When he did specialize and trade, his consumption of both goods increased, moving him to point *H* (8 loaves of bread and 18 apples). Here is *this* lesson learned: Through specialization and trade, Brian's consumption moved beyond his PPF.

EXHIBIT 10

Consumption for Elizabeth and Brian With and Without Specialization and Trade

A comparison of the consumption of bread and apples before and after specialization and trade shows that both Elizabeth and

Brian benefit from producing the good in which each has a comparative advantage and trading for the other good.

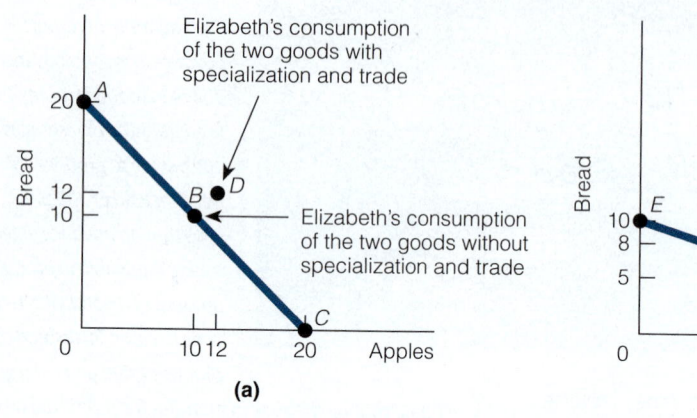

(a)

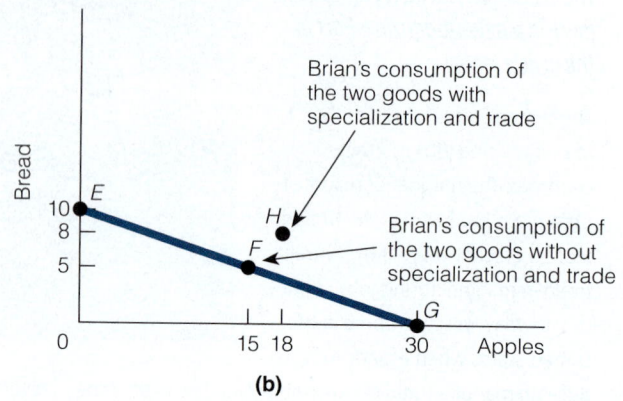

(b)

What holds for Elizabeth and Brian through specialization and trade holds for countries too. For example, if both Americans and Brazilians specialize in producing those goods for which they have a comparative advantage and then trade some of those goods for the other's goods, both Americans and Brazilians can consume more of both goods than if they don't specialize and don't trade.

A Benevolent and All-Knowing Dictator Versus the Invisible Hand Suppose a benevolent dictator governs the country where Brian and Elizabeth live. We assume that this benevolent dictator knows everything about almost every economic activity in his country. In other words, he knows Elizabeth's and Brian's opportunity costs of producing bread and apples.

Because the dictator is benevolent and because he wants the best for the people who live in his country, he orders Elizabeth to produce only loaves of bread and Brian to produce only apples. Next, he tells Elizabeth and Brian to trade 8 loaves of bread for 12 apples.

Afterward, he shows Exhibit 10 to Elizabeth and Brian. They are both surprised that they are better off having done what the benevolent dictator told them to do.

Now in the original story of Elizabeth and Brian, there was no benevolent, all-knowing dictator. There were only two people who were guided by their self-interest to specialize and trade. In other words, self-interest did for Elizabeth and Brian what the benevolent dictator did for them.

Adam Smith, the eighteenth-century Scottish economist and founder of modern economics, spoke about the *invisible hand* that "guided" individuals' actions toward a positive outcome that they did not intend. That is what happened in the original story about Elizabeth and Brian. Neither intended to increase the overall output of society; each intended only to make himself or herself better off.

FINDING ECONOMICS

At the Airport   Suppose you wake up in the morning and drive to the airport. You have your bags checked curbside at the airport. You tip the person who checks your luggage. You then line up to go through security. Once on the plane, you hear the pilot telling you the flying time for today's flight. Later in the flight, the flight attendant brings you a soft drink and a snack. What you see at the airport and on board the plane is different people performing different tasks. The pilot is flying the plane, the customer service person at the check-in counter is receiving your luggage, and so on. Can you find the economics in this situation? Think about it for a minute before you read on.

What you see at the airport and on board the plane is specialization. The pilot isn't flying the plane and checking your luggage too. He is only flying the plane. The flight attendant isn't serving you food and checking you through security too. He is only serving you food. Why do people specialize? Largely, it's because individuals have found that they are better off specializing than not specializing. And usually what people specialize in is that activity in which they have a comparative advantage.

OFFICE HOURS

"What Purpose Does the PPF Serve?"

STUDENT: Economists seem to have many uses for the PPF. For example, they can talk about scarcity, choice, opportunity costs, and many other topics in terms of the PPF. Beyond this capability, however, what purpose does the PPF serve?

INSTRUCTOR: One purpose is to ground us in reality. For example, the frontier (or boundary) of the PPF represents scarcity, which is a fact of life. In other words, the frontier of the PPF is essentially saying, "Here is scarcity. Work with it." One of the important effects of acknowledging this fact is that we come to understand what *is* and what *is not* possible. For example, if the economy is currently on the frontier of its PPF, producing 100 units of X and 200 units of Y, then getting more of X is possible, but not without getting less of Y. In other words, the frontier of the PPF grounds us in reality: More of one thing means less of something else.

STUDENT: But isn't this something we already knew?

INSTRUCTOR: We understand that more of X means less of Y once someone makes this point, but think of how often we might act as if we didn't know it. John thinks he can work more hours at his job and get a good grade on his upcoming chemistry test. Well, he might be able to get a good grade

(say, a 90), but this possibility ignores how much higher the grade could have been (say, five points higher) if he hadn't worked more hours at his job. The frontier of the PPF reminds us that there are trade-offs in life. That is an important reality to be aware of. We ignore it at our own peril.

STUDENT: I've also heard that the PPF can show us what is necessary before the so-called average person in a country can become richer? Is this true? And how much richer do we mean here?

INSTRUCTOR: We are talking about becoming richer in terms of having more goods and services. It's possible for the average person to become richer through economic growth. In other words, the average person in society becomes richer if the PPF shifts rightward by more than the population grows. To illustrate, suppose that a 100-person economy is currently producing 100 units of X and 200 units of Y. The average person can then have 1 unit of X and 2 units of Y. Now suppose there is economic growth (shifting the PPF to the right) and the economy can produce more of both goods, X and Y. It produces 200 units of X and 400 units of Y. If the population has not changed (if it is still 100 people), then the average person can now have 2 units of X and 4 units of Y.

The average person is richer in terms of both goods. If we change things and let the population grow from 100 persons to, say, 125 persons, it is still possible for the average person to have more through economic growth. With a population of 125 people, the average person now has 1.6 units of *X* and 3.2 units of good *Y*. In other words, as long as the productive capability of the economy grows by a greater percentage than the population, the average person can become richer (in terms of goods and services).

STUDENT: Even if the economy is producing more of both goods (*X* and *Y*), the average person isn't necessarily better off in terms of goods and services, right? Can't all the extra output end up in the hands of only a few people instead of being evenly distributed across the entire population.

INSTRUCTOR: That's correct. What we are assuming when we say that the average person can be better off is that, if we took the extra output and divided it evenly across the population, then the average person would be better off in terms of having more goods and services. By the way, this idea is exactly what economists mean when they say that the output (goods and services) per capita in a population has risen.

Points to Remember

1. The PPF grounds us in reality. It tells us what is and what is not possible in terms of producing various combinations of goods and services.

2. The PPF tells us that when we have efficiency (i.e., when we are at a point on the frontier itself), more of one thing means less of something else. In other words, the PPF tells us life has its trade-offs.

3. If the PPF shifts rightward and the population does not change, then output per capita rises.

CHAPTER SUMMARY

AN ECONOMY'S PRODUCTION POSSIBILITIES FRONTIER

- An economy's PPF represents the possible combinations of two goods that the economy can produce in a certain span of time under the conditions of a given state of technology and fully employed resources.

INCREASING AND CONSTANT OPPORTUNITY COSTS

- A straight-line PPF represents constant opportunity costs: Increased production of a good comes at a constant opportunity cost.

- A bowed-outward (concave-downward) PPF represents the law of increasing opportunity costs: Increased production of a good comes at an increasing opportunity cost.

THE PRODUCTION POSSIBILITIES FRONTIER AND VARIOUS ECONOMIC CONCEPTS

- The PPF can be used to illustrate various economic concepts. Scarcity is illustrated by the frontier itself. Choice is illustrated by the fact that we have to find a point either on or below the frontier. In short, of the many attainable positions, one must be chosen. Opportunity cost is illustrated by a movement from one point to another on the PPF. Unemployed resources and productive inefficiency are illustrated by a point below the PPF. Productive efficiency and fully employed resources are illustrated by a point on the PPF. Economic growth is illustrated by a shift outward in the PPF.

SPECIALIZATION, TRADE, AND THE PPF

- Individuals can make themselves better off by specializing in the production of the good in which they have a comparative advantage and then trading some of that good for other goods. Someone who can produce the good at a lower opportunity cost than another person can has a comparative advantage in the production of the good.

- By specializing in the production of the good for which they have a comparative advantage and then trading it for other goods, people can move beyond their PPF.

KEY TERMS AND CONCEPTS

Production Possibilities
  Frontier (PPF)

Law of Increasing
  Opportunity Costs

Productive Efficient
Productive Inefficient

Technology
Comparative Advantage

QUESTIONS AND PROBLEMS

1. Describe how each of the following would affect the U.S. PPF: (a) a war that takes place on U.S. soil, (b) the discovery of a new oil field, (c) a decrease in the unemployment rate, and (d) a law that requires individuals to enter lines of work for which they are not suited.

2. Explain how the following can be represented in a PPF framework: (a) the finiteness of resources implicit in the scarcity condition, (b) choice, (c) opportunity cost, (d) productive efficiency, and (e) unemployed resources.

3. What condition must hold for the PPF to be bowed outward (concave downward)? To be a straight line?

4. Look back at Exhibit 4 and notice that the slope between points A and B is relatively flatter than it is between points C and D. What does the slope of a curve between two points have to do with the opportunity cost of producing additional units of a good?

5. Give an example to illustrate each of the following: (a) constant opportunity costs and (b) increasing opportunity costs.

6. Why are most PPFs for goods bowed outward (concave downward)?

7. Within a PPF framework, explain each of the following: (a) a disagreement between a person who favors more domestic welfare spending and one who favors more national defense spending, (b) an increase in the population, and (c) a technological change that makes resources less specialized.

8. Explain how to derive a PPF. For instance, how is the extreme point on the vertical axis identified? How is the extreme point on the horizontal axis identified?

9. If the slope of the PPF is the same between any two points, what does this relationship imply about costs? Explain your answer.

10. Suppose a nation's PPF shifts inward as its population grows. What happens, on average, to the material standard of living of the people? Explain your answer.

11. Can a technological advancement in sector X of the economy affect the number of people who work in sector Y of the economy? Explain your answer.

12. Use the PPF framework to explain something in your everyday life that was not mentioned in the chapter.

13. What exactly allows individuals to consume more if they specialize and trade than if they don't?

WORKING WITH NUMBERS AND GRAPHS

1. Illustrate constant opportunity costs in a table similar to the one in Exhibit 1(a). Next, draw a PPF that is based on the data in the table.

2. Illustrate increasing opportunity costs (for one good) in a table similar to the one in Exhibit 2(a). Next, draw a PPF based on the data in the table.

3. Draw a PPF that represents the production possibilities for goods X and Y if there are constant opportunity costs. Next, represent an advance in technology that makes it possible to produce more of X but not more of Y. Finally, represent an advance in technology that makes it possible to produce more of Y but not more of X.

4. In the following figure, which graph depicts a technological breakthrough in the production of good X only?

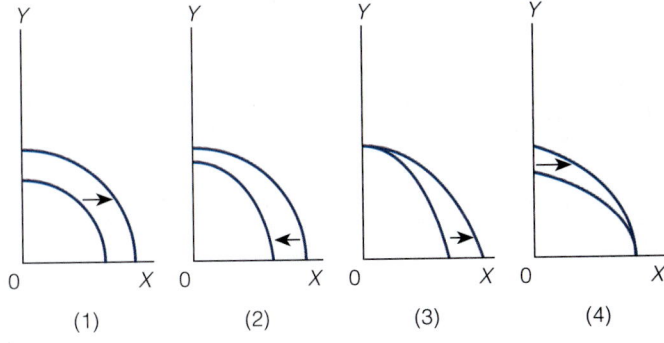

5. In the preceding figure, which graph depicts a change in the PPF that is a likely consequence of war?

6. If PPF_2 in the graph that follows is the relevant PPF, then which points are unattainable? Explain your answer.

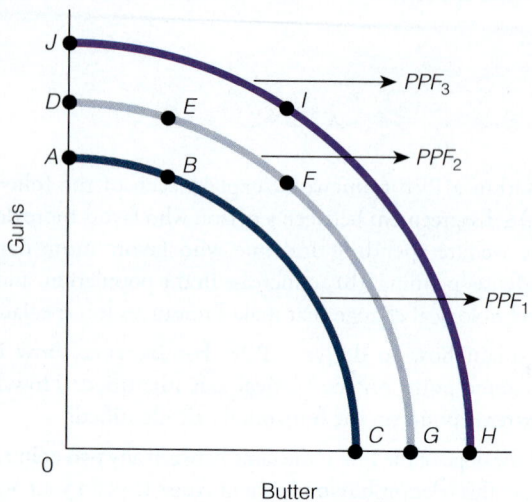

7. If PPF_1 in the preceding figure is the relevant PPF, then which point(s) represent productive efficiency? Explain your answer.

8. Tina can produce any of the following combinations of goods X and Y: (a) 100 X and 0 Y, (b) 50 X and 25 Y, and (c) 0 X and 50 Y. David can produce any of the following combinations of X and Y: (a) 50 X and 0 Y, (b) 25 X and 40 Y, and (c) 0 X and 80 Y. Who has the comparative advantage in the production of good X? Of good Y? Explain your answer.

9. Using the data in problem 8, prove that both Tina and David can be made better off through specialization and trade.

10. Suppose there is a PPF with two goods, X and Y. Suppose the economy is located at a point on the PPF. Does this point represent some of both goods or only one good and not the other?

11. The economy is producing 100X and 200Y, but it could produce 200X and 300Y with the given resources and technology. Does it follow that when the economy is producing 100X and 200Y that it is productive inefficient and that when it is producing 200X and 300Y it is productive efficient? Explain your answer.

12. A person can produce the following combinations of goods A and B: 20A and 0B, 15A and 5B, 10A and 10B, 5A and 15B, and 0A and 20B. What is the opportunity cost of producing 1B? 1A?

SUPPLY AND DEMAND: THEORY

Semmick Photo/Shutterstock.com

Semmick Photo/Shutterstock.com

INTRODUCTION

Supply and demand have been called the "bread and butter" of economics. In this chapter, we discuss them, first separately and then together.

A **market** is any place people come together to trade. Economists often say that every market has *two* sides: a buying side and a selling side. The buying side of the market is usually referred to as the *demand* side; the selling side is usually referred to as the *supply* side. Let's begin with a discussion of *demand*.

3-1 WHAT IS DEMAND?

The word **demand** has a precise meaning in economics. It refers to:

1. the willingness and ability of buyers to purchase different quantities of a good,[1]

2. at different prices

3. during a specific period (per day, week, etc.).

For example, we can express part of John's demand for magazines by saying that he is willing and able to buy 10 magazines a month at $4 per magazine and that he is willing and able to buy 15 magazines a month at $3 per magazine.

Remember this important point about demand: Unless both willingness and ability to buy are present, there is neither demand nor a buyer. For example, Josie may be willing to buy a computer

Market
Any place people come together to trade.

Demand
The willingness and ability of buyers to purchase different quantities of a good at different prices during a specific period.

---

[1] Demand takes into account services as well as goods. A few examples of goods are shirts, books, and TV sets. A few examples of services are dental care, medical care, and an economics lecture. To simplify the discussion, we refer only to goods.

but be unable to pay the price; Tanya may be able to buy a computer but be unwilling to do so. Neither Josie nor Tanya demands a computer, and neither is a buyer of a computer.

3-1a   The Law of Demand

Law of Demand

As the price of a good rises, the quantity demanded of the good falls, and as the price of a good falls, the quantity demanded of the good rises, *ceteris paribus*.

Will people buy more units of a good at lower prices than at higher prices? For example, will people buy more shirts at $10 apiece than at $70 apiece? If your answer is yes, you instinctively understand the law of demand. The **law of demand** states that as the price of a good rises, the quantity demanded of the good falls, and that as the price of a good falls, the quantity demanded of the good rises, *ceteris paribus*. Simply put, the law of demand states that the price of a good and the quantity demanded of it are inversely related, *ceteris paribus*. That is,

$$P\uparrow Q_d\downarrow$$
$$P\downarrow Q_d\uparrow, ceteris\ paribus$$

where P = price and Q_d = quantity demanded.

Quantity demanded is the number of units of a good that individuals are willing and able to buy at a particular price during a particular period. For example, suppose individuals are willing and able to buy 100 TV dinners per week at a price of $4 per dinner. Therefore, 100 units is the quantity demanded of TV dinners at $4 per dinner.

A warning: We know that the words "demand" and "quantity demanded" sound alike, but be aware that they do not describe the same thing. Demand is different from quantity demanded. Keep that in mind as you continue to read this chapter. For now, remind yourself that demand speaks to the willingness and ability of buyers to buy different quantities of a good at different prices. Quantity demanded speaks to the willingness and ability of buyers to buy a specific quantity (say, 100 units of a good) at a specific price (say, $10 per unit).

3-1b   Four Ways to Represent the Law of Demand

Here are four ways to represent the law of demand:

- *In Words.* We can represent the law of demand in words; we have done so already. Earlier we said that as the price of a good rises, quantity demanded falls, and as price falls, quantity demanded rises, *ceteris paribus*. That was the statement (in words) of the law of demand.

- *In Symbols.* We can also represent the law of demand in symbols, as we have also already done. In symbols, the law of demand is

$$P\uparrow Q_d\downarrow$$
$$P\downarrow Q_d\uparrow, ceteris\ paribus$$

Demand Schedule

The numerical tabulation of the quantity demanded of a good at different prices. A demand schedule is the numerical representation of the law of demand.

- *In a Demand Schedule.* A **demand schedule** is the numerical representation of the law of demand. A demand schedule for good X is illustrated in Exhibit 1(a).

- *As a Demand Curve.* In Exhibit 1(b), the four price–quantity combinations in part (a) are plotted and the points connected, giving us a (downward-sloping) demand curve. A (downward-sloping) **demand curve** is the graphical representation of the inverse relationship between price and quantity demanded specified by the law of demand. In short, a demand curve is a picture of the law of demand.

Demand Curve

The graphical representation of the law of demand.

EXHIBIT 1

Demand Schedule and Demand Curve

Part (a) shows a demand schedule for good X. Part (b) shows a demand curve, obtained by plotting the different price–quantity combinations in part (a) and connecting the points. On a demand curve, the price (in dollars) represents price per unit of the good. The quantity demanded, on the horizontal axis, is always relevant for a specific period (a week, a month, etc.).

Demand Schedule for Good X

Price (dollars)	Quantity Demanded	Point in Part (b)
4	10	A
3	20	B
2	30	C
1	40	D

(a)

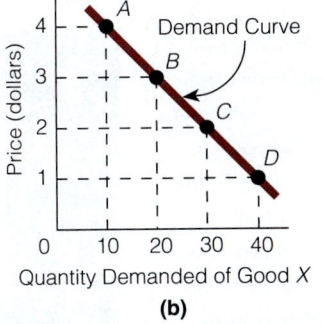

(b)

FINDING ECONOMICS

In a Visit Home to See Mom A friend tells you that she flies home to see her mother only once a year. You ask why. She says, "Because the price of the ticket to fly home is $1,100." She then adds, "If the price were, say, $600 instead of $1,100, I'd fly home twice a year instead of once." Can you find any economics in what she is telling you? If you listen closely to what she says, she has identified two points on her demand curve for air travel home: One point corresponds to $1,100 and buying one ticket home, and the other point corresponds to $600 and buying two tickets home.

3-1c Why Does Quantity Demanded Go Down as Price Goes Up?

The law of demand states that price and quantity demanded are inversely related. This much you know. But do you know *why* quantity demanded moves in the direction opposite that of price? We identify two reasons.

The first reason is that *people substitute lower priced goods for higher priced goods*. Often, many goods serve the same purpose. Many different goods will satisfy hunger, and many different drinks will satisfy thirst. For example, both orange juice and grapefruit juice will satisfy thirst. On Monday, the price of orange juice equals the price of grapefruit juice, but on Tuesday the price of orange juice rises. As a result, people will choose to buy less of the relatively higher priced orange juice and more of the relatively lower priced grapefruit juice. In other words, a rise in the price of orange juice will lead to a decrease in the quantity demanded of it.

The second reason for the inverse relationship between price and quantity demanded has to do with the **law of diminishing marginal utility**, which states that, over a given period, the marginal (or additional) utility or satisfaction gained by consuming equal successive units of a good will decline as the amount of the good consumed increases. For example, you may receive more utility,

Law of Diminishing Marginal Utility
Over a given period, the marginal (or additional) utility or satisfaction gained by consuming equal successive units of a good will decline as the amount consumed increases.

ECONOMICS 24/7

What Do the Following Have in Common? Losing One's Temper, Arriving to Class Late, and Buying the Textbook for a Class

The answer is that they all abide by the law of demand.

The law of demand states that the price of a good and the quantity demanded of that good are inversely related, *ceteris paribus*. Applied to losing one's temper, this law means that a person is more likely to lose his or her temper with someone who charges a low price than a high price.

Doug Jones/Portland Press Herald/Getty Images

The price of something is what you have to give up to get it. Usually, we speak about price in monetary terms. But there are also nonmonetary prices. Consider a person's boss and the person's girlfriend. If a person loses his temper in front of his boss, he might end up "paying a high price" for that. In fact, he could lose his job or end up not getting that promotion. But if he loses his temper in front of his girlfriend, he isn't likely to pay as high a price. On the basis of the law of demand, then, we predict that people will lose their temper more often when the price of losing one's temper is low rather than high.

The same goes for arriving late to class. Very rarely are students late to class when they have to take an exam. That's because, if they are late on exam dates, they will end up with less time to complete the exam, and that can adversely affect their grade. In other words, the price of arriving late to class on exam day is fairly high compared with arriving late to class on a non-exam day.

Lastly, will everyone buy the textbook for a given course? What we observe is that, the higher the price of a text is, the fewer the number of students who will buy the text and the greater the number of students who will try to find a substitute for the assigned text—such as an older edition of it.

or satisfaction, from eating your first hamburger at lunch than from eating your second and, if you continue, more utility from your second hamburger than from your third.

What does marginal utility have to do with the law of demand? Economists state that, the more utility you receive from a unit of a good, the higher the price you are willing to pay for it, and the less utility you receive from a unit of a good, the lower the price you are willing to pay for it. According to the law of diminishing marginal utility, individuals obtain less utility from additional units of a good. Therefore, they will buy larger quantities of a good only at lower prices, and their behavior reflects the law of demand.

3-1d Individual Demand Curve and Market Demand Curve

There is a difference between an individual demand curve and a market demand curve.

An individual demand curve represents the price–quantity combinations of a particular good for a *single buyer*. For example, an individual demand curve could show Jones's demand for CDs. By contrast, a market demand curve represents the price–quantity combinations of a good for *all buyers*. In this case, the demand curve would show all buyers' demand for CDs.

A market demand curve is derived by adding up individual demand curves, as shown in Exhibit 2. The demand schedules for Jones, Smith, and other buyers are shown in part (a). The market demand schedule is obtained by adding the quantities demanded at each price. For example, at

EXHIBIT 2

Deriving a Market Demand Schedule and a Market Demand Curve

Part (a) shows four demand schedules combined into one table. The market demand schedule is derived by adding the quantities demanded at each price. In (b), the data points from the demand schedule are plotted to show how a market demand curve is derived. Only two points on the market demand curve are noted.

		Quantity Demanded		
Price	Jones	Smith	Other Buyers	All Buyers
$15	1	2	20	23
14	2	3	45	50
13	3	4	70	77
12	4 +	5 +	100 =	109
11	5 +	6 +	130 =	141
10	6	7	160	173

(a)

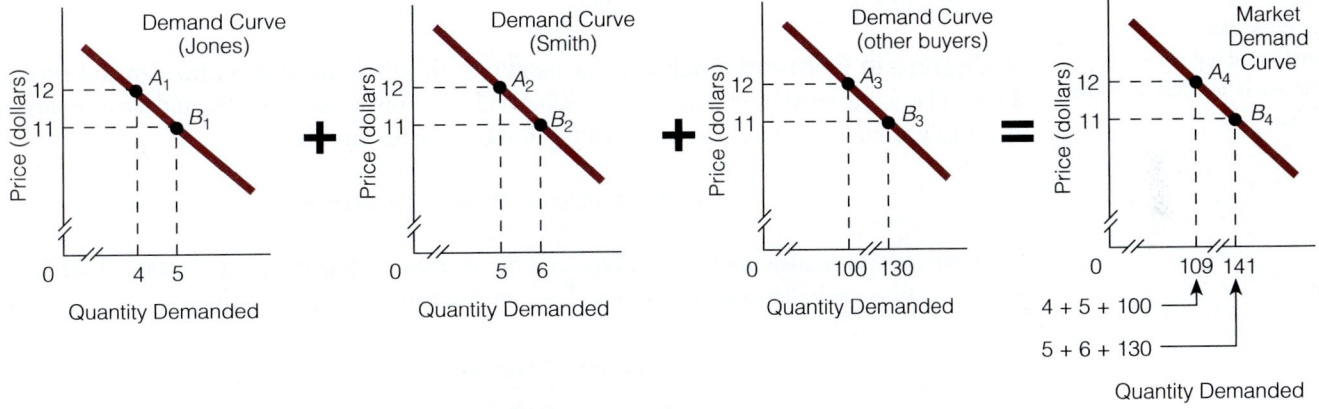

(b)

$12, the quantities demanded are 4 units for Jones, 5 units for Smith, and 100 units for other buyers. Thus, a total of 109 units are demanded at $12. In part (b), the data points for the demand schedules are plotted and added to produce a market demand curve. The market demand curve could also be drawn directly from the market demand schedule.

3-1e A Change in Quantity Demanded Versus a Change in Demand

Economists often talk about (1) a change in quantity demanded and (2) a change in demand. As stated earlier, although the phrase "quantity demanded" may sound like "demand," the two are not the same. In short, a change in quantity demanded *is not* the same as a change in demand. (Read the last sentence at least two more times.) We use Exhibit 1 to illustrate the difference between a change in quantity demanded and a change in demand.

A Change in Quantity Demanded Look at Exhibit 1. The horizontal axis is labeled "Quantity Demanded of Good *X*." Notice that quantity demanded is a *number*—such as 10, 20, 30, 40, and so on. More specifically, it is the number of units of a good that individuals are willing and able to buy at a particular price during some period. In Exhibit 1, if the price is $4, then the quantity demanded is 10 units of good *X*; if the price is $3, then the quantity demanded is 20 units of good *X*. In general,

Quantity demanded = The *number* of units of a good that individuals are willing and able
to buy at a particular price

Now, again looking at Exhibit 1, see if you can figure out what can change quantity demanded from 10 (which it is at point *A*) to 20 (which it is at point *B*). Or what has to change before quantity demanded will change. The answer is on the vertical axis of Exhibit 1. The only thing that can change the quantity demanded of a good is its price:

Change in quantity demanded = A movement from one point to another point on the same demand
curve that is caused by a change in the price of the good

Own Price
The price of a good. For example, if the price of oranges is $1, this is its own price.

The price of a good is also called **own price**.

A Change in Demand Look again at Exhibit 1, this time focusing on the demand curve. Demand is represented by the *entire* curve. When talking about a change in demand, an economist is actually talking about a change—or shift—in the entire demand curve:

Change in demand = Shift in demand curve

Demand can change in two ways: Demand can increase and demand can decrease. Let's look first at an *increase* in demand. Suppose we have the following demand schedule:

Demand Schedule A

Price	Quantity Demanded
$20	500
$15	600
$10	700
$5	800

The demand curve for this demand schedule will look like the demand curve labeled D_A in Exhibit 3(a).

What does an increase in demand mean? It means that individuals are willing and able to buy more units of the good at each and every price. In other words, demand schedule *A* will change as follows:

Demand Schedule B (increase in demand)

Price	Quantity Demanded	
$20	~~500~~	600
$15	~~600~~	700
$10	~~700~~	800
$5	~~800~~	900

EXHIBIT 3

Shifts in the Demand Curve

In part (a), the demand curve shifts rightward from D_A to D_B. This shift represents an increase in demand. At each price, the quantity demanded is greater than it was before.

For example, the quantity demanded at $20 increases from 500 units to 600 units. In part (b), the demand curve shifts leftward from D_A to D_c. This shift represents a decrease in demand. At each price, the quantity demanded is less. For example, the quantity demanded at $20 decreases from 500 units to 400 units.

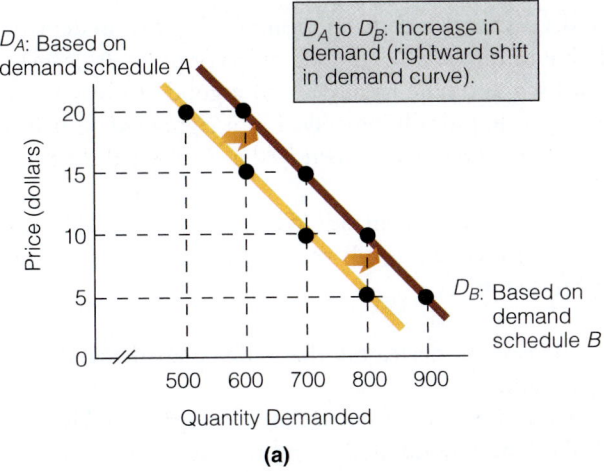

D_A: Based on demand schedule A

D_A to D_B: Increase in demand (rightward shift in demand curve).

D_B: Based on demand schedule B

(a)

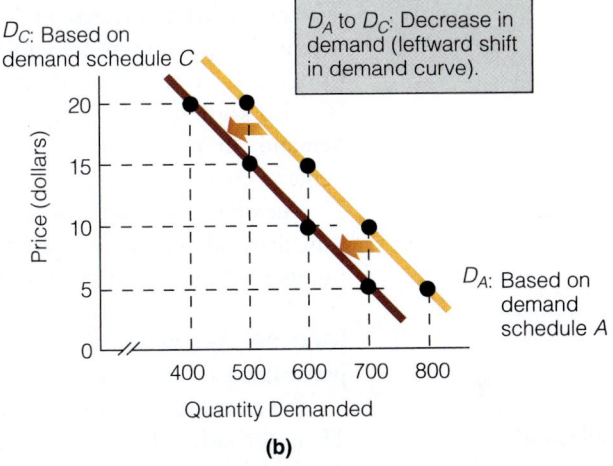

D_C: Based on demand schedule C

D_A to D_C: Decrease in demand (leftward shift in demand curve).

D_A: Based on demand schedule A

(b)

Whereas individuals were willing and able to buy 500 units of the good at $20, now they are willing and able to buy 600 units of the good at $20; whereas individuals were willing and able to buy 600 units of the good at $15, now they are willing and able to buy 700 units of the good at $15, and so on.

As shown in Exhibit 3(a), the demand curve that represents demand schedule B (D_B) lies to the right of the demand curve that represents demand schedule A (D_A). We conclude that *an increase in demand is represented by a rightward shift in the demand curve and means that individuals are willing and able to buy more of a good at each and every price:*

Increase in demand = Rightward shift in the demand curve

Now let's look at a decrease in demand. A decrease in demand means that individuals are willing and able to buy less of a good at each and every price. In this case, demand schedule A will change as follows:

Demand Schedule C (decrease in demand)

Price	Quantity Demanded
$20	~~500~~ 400
$15	~~600~~ 500
$10	~~700~~ 600
$5	~~800~~ 700

As shown in Exhibit 3(b), the demand curve that represents demand schedule $C(D_C)$ obviously lies to the left of the demand curve that represents demand schedule $A(D_A)$. We conclude that a *decrease in demand is represented by a leftward shift in the demand curve and means that individuals are willing and able to buy less of a good at each and every price:*

Decrease in demand = Leftward shift in the demand curve

3-1f What Factors Cause the Demand Curve to Shift?

We know what an increase in demand and a decrease in demand mean: An increase in demand means that consumers are willing and able to buy *more* of a good at every price. A decrease in demand means that consumers are willing and able to buy *less* of a good at every price. We also know that an increase in demand is graphically portrayed as a rightward shift in a demand curve and that a decrease in demand is graphically portrayed as a leftward shift in a demand curve.

But what factors or variables can increase or decrease demand? What factors or variables can shift demand curves? They are (1) income, (2) preferences, (3) prices of related goods, (4) the number of buyers, and (5) expectations of future prices.

Income As a person's income changes (increases or decreases), that individual's demand for a particular good may rise, fall, or remain constant.

For example, suppose Jack's income rises and, as a consequence, his demand for CDs rises. Then, for Jack, CDs are a normal good. For a **normal good**, demand rises as income rises and demand falls as income falls:

Normal Good
A good for which demand rises (falls) as income rises (falls).

X is a normal good: If income↑, then D_X↑ If income↓, then D_X↓

Now suppose Marie's income rises and, as a consequence, her demand for canned baked beans falls. Then, for Marie, canned baked beans are an inferior good. For an **inferior good**, demand falls as income rises and demand rises as income falls:

Inferior Good
A good for which demand falls (rises) as income rises (falls).

Y is an inferior good: If income↑, then D_Y↓ If income↓, then D_Y↑

Finally, suppose that, when George's income rises, his demand for toothpaste neither rises nor falls. Then, for George, toothpaste is neither a normal good nor an inferior good. Instead, it is a **neutral good**. For a neutral good, demand does not change as income rises or falls.

Neutral Good
A good for which demand does not change as income rises or falls.

Preferences People's preferences affect the amount of a good they are willing to buy at a particular price. A change in preferences in favor of a good shifts the demand curve rightward. A change in preferences away from the good shifts the demand curve leftward. For example, if people begin to favor Elmore Leonard novels to a greater degree than previously, the demand for his novels increases and the demand curve shifts rightward.

Prices of Related Goods There are two types of related goods: substitutes and complements. Two goods are substitutes if they satisfy similar needs or desires. For many people, Coca-Cola and Pepsi-Cola are substitutes. If two goods are **substitutes**, then, as the price of one rises (falls), the demand for the other rises (falls). For instance, higher Coca-Cola prices will increase the demand for Pepsi-Cola as people substitute Pepsi for the higher priced Coke. [See Exhibit 4(a).]

Substitutes
Two goods that satisfy similar needs or desires.

Other examples of substitutes are coffee and tea, corn chips and potato chips, different brands of margarine, and foreign and domestic cars. Generalizing, we obtain

$$X \text{ and } Y \text{ are substitutes: If } P_X\uparrow, \text{ then } D_Y\uparrow \text{ If } P_X\downarrow, \text{ then } D_Y\downarrow[2]$$

Two goods are **complements** if they are consumed jointly. For example, tennis rackets and tennis balls are used together to play tennis. If two goods are complements, then, as the price of one rises (falls), the demand for the other falls (rises). For example, higher tennis racket prices will decrease the demand for tennis balls, as Exhibit 4(b) shows. Other examples of complements are cars and tires, lightbulbs and lamps, and golf clubs and golf balls. Generalizing yields the following relationship:

Complements
Two goods that are used jointly in consumption.

$$X \text{ and } Y \text{ are complements: If } P_X\uparrow, \text{ then } D_Y\downarrow \text{ If } P_X\downarrow, \text{ then } D_Y\uparrow[3]$$

EXHIBIT 4

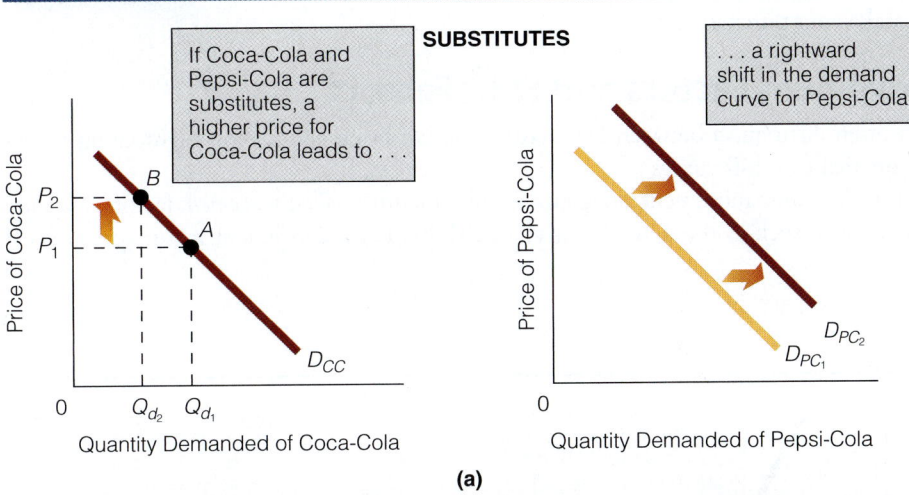

(a)

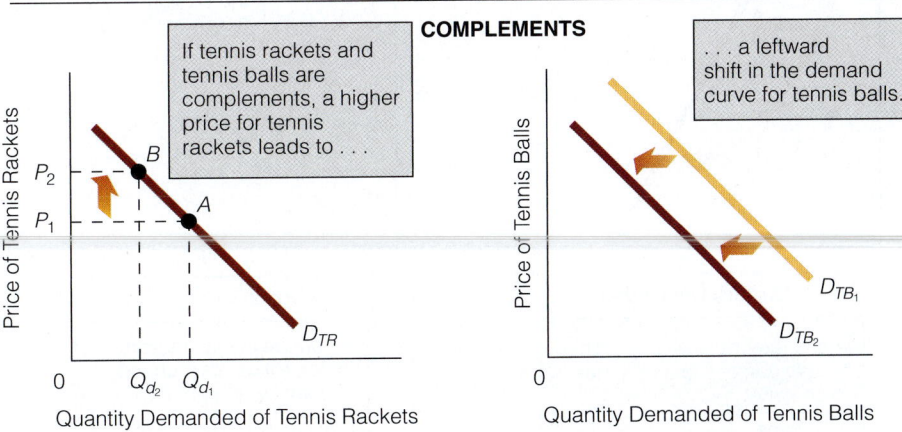

(b)

Substitutes and Complements

(a) Coca-Cola and Pepsi-Cola are substitutes: The price of one and the demand for the other are directly related. As the price of Coca-Cola rises, the demand for Pepsi-Cola increases. (b) Tennis rackets and tennis balls are complements: The price of one and the demand for the other are inversely related. As the price of tennis rackets rises, the demand for tennis balls decreases.

[2] The relationship specified here holds if the initial price change (in X) is the result of a change in supply and not demand. You can read more about this at the end of the chapter in the section titled: *It Is Important to Know Why the Price Changed.*

[3] This relationship holds if the initial price change (in X) is due to a change in supply and not demand. You can read more about this at the end of the chapter in the section titled: *It Is Important to Know Why the Price Changed.*

Number of Buyers The demand for a good in a particular market area is related to the number of buyers in the area: more buyers means higher demand; fewer buyers means lower demand. The number of buyers may increase owing to a heightened birthrate, rising immigration, the migration of people from one region of the country to another, and so on. The number of buyers may decrease owing to an increased death rate, war, the migration of people from one region of the country to another, and so on.

Expectations of Future Price Buyers who expect the price of a good to be higher next month may buy it now, thus increasing the current (or present) demand for the good. Buyers who expect the price of a good to be lower next month may wait until next month to buy it, thus decreasing the current (or present) demand for the good.

For example, suppose you are planning to buy a house. One day, you hear that house prices are expected to go down in a few months. Consequently, you decide to delay your purchase for a while. Alternatively, if you hear that prices are expected to rise in a few months, you might go ahead and make your purchase now.

3-1g Movement Factors and Shift Factors

Economists often distinguish between (1) factors that can bring about movement along curves and (2) factors that can shift curves.

The factors that cause movement along curves are sometimes called *movement* factors. In many economic diagrams, such as the demand curve in Exhibit 1, the movement factor (price) is on the vertical axis.

EXHIBIT 5

A Change in Demand Versus a Change in Quantity Demanded

(a) A change in demand refers to a shift in the demand curve. A change in demand can be brought about by a number of factors. (see the exhibit and the text.)

(b) A change in quantity demanded refers to a movement along a given demand curve. A change in quantity demanded is brought about only by a change in (a good's) own price.

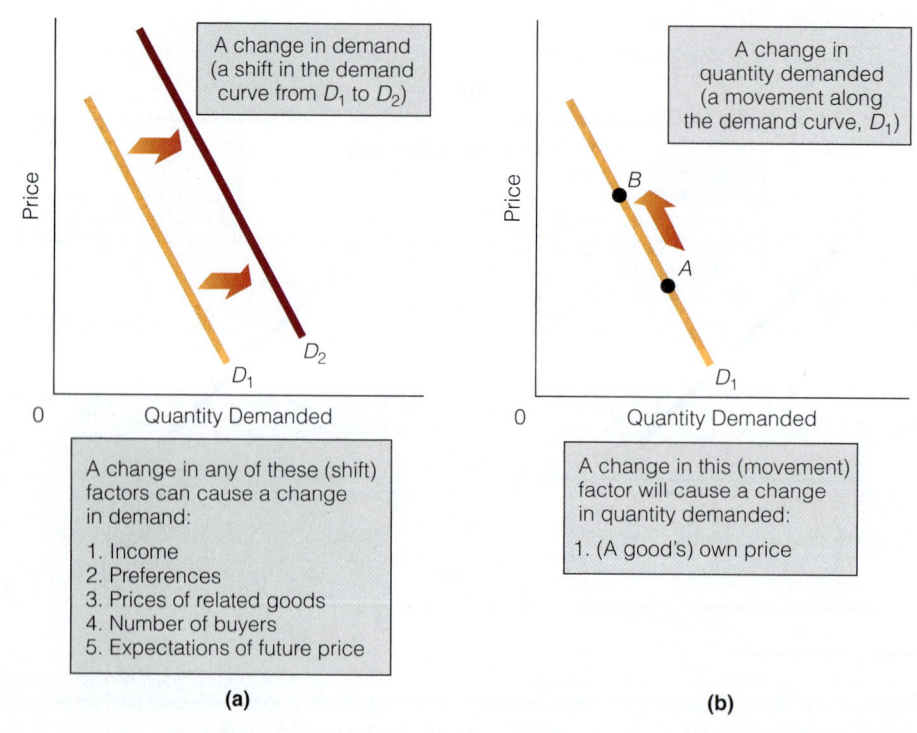

A change in demand (a shift in the demand curve from D_1 to D_2)

A change in quantity demanded (a movement along the demand curve, D_1)

A change in any of these (shift) factors can cause a change in demand:

1. Income
2. Preferences
3. Prices of related goods
4. Number of buyers
5. Expectations of future price

A change in this (movement) factor will cause a change in quantity demanded:

1. (A good's) own price

(a)

(b)

The factors that actually shift the curves are sometimes called *shift* factors. The shift factors for the demand curve are income, preferences, the price of related goods, and so on. Often, shift factors do not appear in the economic diagrams. For example, although in Exhibit 1 the movement factor—price—is on the vertical axis, the shift factors do not appear anywhere in the diagram. We just know what they are and that they can shift the demand curve.

When you see a curve in this book, first ask which factor will move us along the curve. In other words, what is the movement factor? Second, ask which factors will shift the curve. In other words, what are the shift factors? Exhibit 5 summarizes the shift factors that can change demand and the movement factors that can change quantity demanded.

SELF-TEST

(Answers to Self-Test questions are in Answers to Self-Test Questions at the back of the book.)

1. As Sandi's income rises, her demand for popcorn rises. As Mark's income falls, his demand for prepaid telephone cards rises. What kinds of goods are popcorn for Sandi and telephone cards for Mark?

2. Why are demand curves downward sloping?

3. Give an example that illustrates how to derive a market demand curve.

4. What factors can change demand? What factors can change quantity demanded?

3-2 SUPPLY

Just as the word "demand" has a specific meaning in economics, so does the word "supply." **Supply** refers to:

1. the willingness and ability of sellers to produce and offer to sell different quantities of a good,

2. at different prices

3. during a specific period (per day, week, etc.).

Supply
The willingness and ability of sellers to produce and offer to sell different quantities of a good at different prices during a specific period.

3-2a The Law of Supply

The **law of supply** states that as the price of a good rises, the quantity supplied of the good rises, and as the price of a good falls, the quantity supplied of the good falls, *ceteris paribus*. Simply put, the price of a good and the quantity supplied of the good are directly related, *ceteris paribus*. (The quantity supplied is the number of units that sellers are willing and able to produce and offer to sell at a particular price.) The **(upward-sloping) supply curve** is the graphical representation of the law of supply. (see Exhibit 6.) The law of supply can be summarized as

$$P\uparrow Q_s\uparrow$$
$$P\downarrow Q_s\downarrow, ceteris\ paribus$$

where P = price and Q_s = quantity supplied.

Law of Supply
As the price of a good rises, the quantity supplied of the good rises, and as the price of a good falls, the quantity supplied of the good falls, *ceteris paribus*.

(Upward-Sloping) Supply Curve
The graphical representation of the law of supply.

The law of supply holds for the production of most goods. It does not hold when there is no time to produce more units of a good. For example, suppose a theater in Atlanta is sold out for tonight's play. Then, even if ticket prices increased from $30 to $40, the theater would have no additional seats and no time to produce more. The supply curve for theater seats is illustrated in Exhibit 7(a). It is fixed at the number of seats in the theater, 500.[4]

EXHIBIT 6

A Supply Curve

The upward-sloping supply curve is the graphical representation of the law of supply, which states that price and quantity supplied are directly related, *ceteris paribus*. On a supply curve, the price (in dollars) represents the price per unit of the good. The quantity supplied, on the horizontal axis, is always relevant for a specific period (a week, a month, etc.).

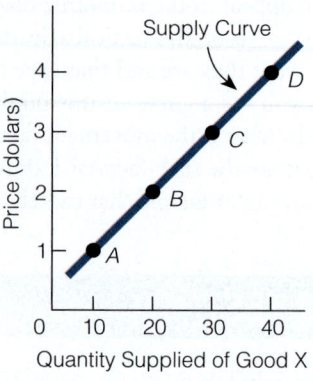

EXHIBIT 7

Supply Curves When There Is No Time to Produce More or When No More Can Be Produced

The supply curve is not upward sloping when there is no time to produce additional units or when additional units cannot be produced. In those cases, the supply curve is vertical.

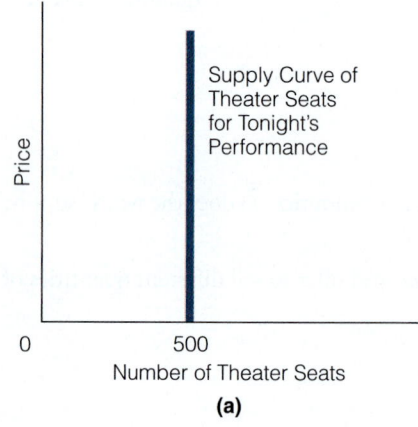

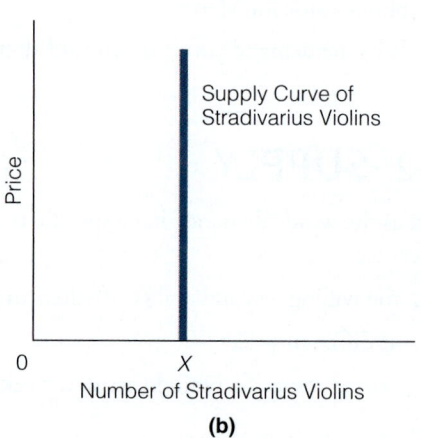

The law of supply also does not hold for goods that cannot be produced over any period. For example, the violin maker Antonio Stradivari died in 1737, so, because he cannot produce any violins anymore, a rise in the price of Stradivarius violins does not affect the number of Stradivarius violins supplied, as Exhibit 7(b) illustrates.

3-2b Why Most Supply Curves Are Upward Sloping

Most supply curves are upward sloping. The fundamental reason for this behavior involves the *law of diminishing marginal returns*, discussed in a later chapter. Here, suffice it to say that an upward-sloping supply curve reflects the fact that, under certain conditions, a higher price is an incentive to producers to produce more of the good. The incentive comes in the form of higher profits. For example, suppose the price of good X rises, and nothing else (such as the per-unit costs

---

4. The vertical supply curve is said to be *perfectly inelastic*.

of producing good X) changes. In that case, the producers of good X will earn higher profits per unit and are thus encouraged to increase the quantity of good X that they supply to the market.

Generally, though, producing more of a good does not come with constant per-unit costs. As we learned in Chapter 2, the law of increasing opportunity costs is usually at work. In other words, the increased production of a good comes at increased opportunity costs. An upward-sloping supply curve simply reflects the fact that costs rise when more units of a good are produced.

The Market Supply Curve An individual supply curve represents the price–quantity combinations for a single seller. The market supply curve represents the price–quantity combinations for all sellers of a particular good. Exhibit 8 shows how a market supply curve can be derived by adding individual supply curves. In part (a), a **supply schedule**, the numerical tabulation of the quantity supplied of a good at different prices is given for Brown, Alberts, and other suppliers. The market supply schedule is obtained by adding the quantities supplied at each price, *ceteris paribus*. For example, at $11, the quantities supplied are 2 units for Brown, 3 units for Alberts, and 98 units for the other suppliers. Thus, 103 units are supplied at $11. In part (b), the data points for the supply schedules are plotted and added to produce a market supply curve (which could also be drawn directly from the market supply schedule).

Supply Schedule
The numerical tabulation of the quantity supplied of a good at different prices. A supply schedule is the numerical representation of the law of supply.

EXHIBIT 8

Price	Brown		Alberts		Other Suppliers		All Suppliers
				Quantity Supplied			
$10	1		2		96		99
11	2	+	3	+	98	=	103
12	3	+	4	+	102	=	109
13	4		5		106		115
14	5		6		108		119
15	6		7		110		123

(a)

Deriving a Market Supply Schedule and a Market Supply Curve

Part (a) shows four supply schedules combined into one table. The market supply schedule is derived by adding the quantities supplied at each price. In (b), the data points from the supply schedules are plotted to show how a market supply curve is derived. Only two points on the market supply curve are noted.

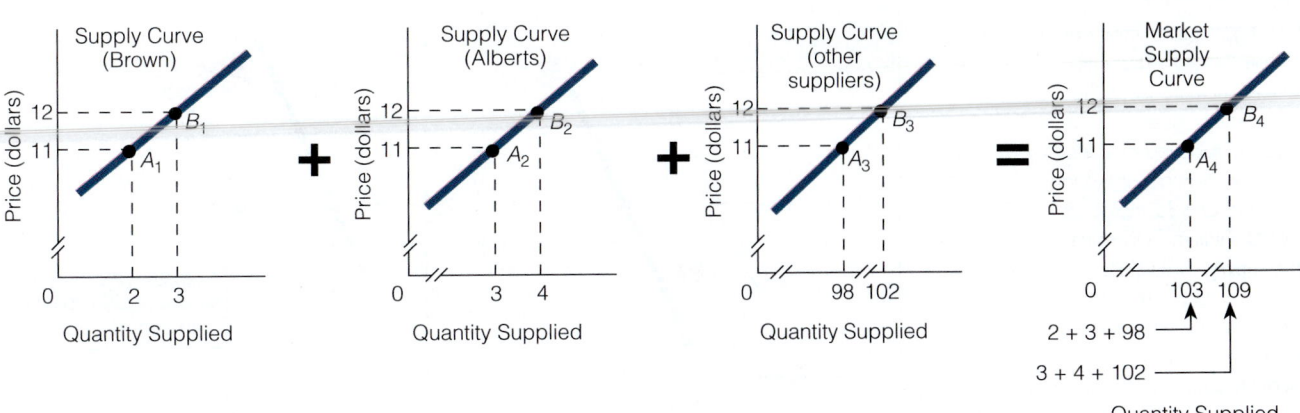

(b)

3-2c Changes in Supply Mean Shifts in Supply Curves

Just as demand can change, so can supply. The supply of a good can rise or fall. An increase in the supply of a good means that suppliers are willing and able to produce, and offer to sell more of, the good at all prices. For example, suppose that in January sellers are willing and able to produce and offer for sale 600 shirts at $25 each and that in February they are willing and able to produce and sell 900 shirts at $25 each. Then an increase in supply shifts the entire supply curve to the right, as shown in Exhibit 9(a).

The supply of a good decreases if sellers are willing and able to produce and offer to sell less of the good at all prices. For example, suppose that in January sellers are willing and able to produce and offer for sale 600 shirts at $25 each and that in February they are willing and able to produce and sell only 300 shirts at $25 each. Then a decrease in supply shifts the entire supply curve to the left, as shown in Exhibit 9(b).

3-2d What Factors Cause the Supply Curve to Shift?

We know that the supply of any good can change, but what causes supply to change? What causes supply curves to shift? The factors that can change supply include (1) the prices of relevant resources, (2) technology, (3) the prices of related goods, (4) the number of sellers, (5) expectations of future price, (6) taxes and subsidies, and (7) government restrictions.

Prices of Relevant Resources　Resources are needed to produce goods. For example, wood is needed to produce doors. If the price of wood falls, producing doors becomes less costly. How will door producers respond? Will they produce more doors, the same number, or fewer? With lower costs and prices unchanged, the profit from producing and selling doors has increased; as a result, the (monetary) incentive to produce doors is increased. So, door producers will produce and offer to sell more doors at each and every price. Thus, the supply of doors will increase, and the supply curve of doors will shift rightward. If the price of wood rises, producing doors becomes more costly. Consequently, the supply of doors will decrease, and the supply curve of doors will shift leftward.

Technology　In Chapter 2, technology was defined as the body of skills and knowledge involved in the use of resources in production. Also, an advance in technology was said to refer to the ability

---

EXHIBIT 9

Shifts in the Supply Curve

(a) The supply curve shifts rightward from S_1 to S_2. This shift represents an increase in the supply of shirts: At each price, the quantity supplied of shirts is greater. For example, the quantity supplied at $25 increases from 600 shirts to 900 shirts. (b) The supply curve shifts leftward from S_1 to S_2. This shift represents a decrease in the supply of shirts: At each price, the quantity supplied of shirts is less. For example, the quantity supplied at $25 decreases from 600 shirts to 300 shirts.

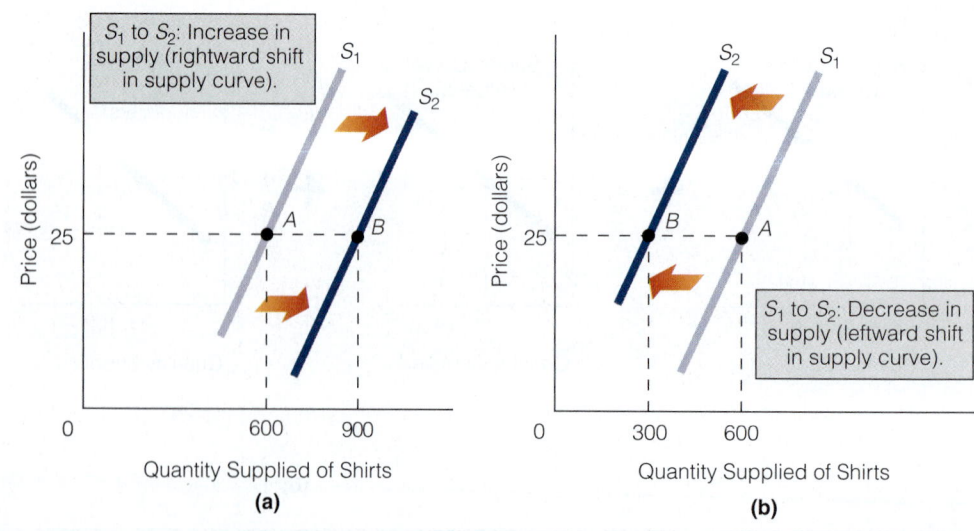

to produce more output with a fixed amount of resources, reducing per-unit production costs. To illustrate, suppose it takes $100 to produce 40 units of a good. Then the per-unit cost is $2.50. If an advance in technology makes it possible to produce 50 units at a cost of $100, then the per-unit cost falls to $2.00.

We expect that if the per-unit production costs of a good decline, then the quantity supplied of the good at each price will increase. Why? Lower per-unit costs increase profitability and therefore provide producers with an incentive to produce more. For example, if corn growers develop a way to grow more corn by using the same amount of water and other resources, then per-unit production costs will fall, profitability will increase, and growers will want to grow and sell more corn at each price. The supply curve of corn will shift rightward.

Prices of Other Goods Think of a farmer who is producing wheat. Suddenly, the price of something he is not producing (say, corn) rises relative to the price of wheat. The farmer might then shift his farming away from wheat to corn. In other words, as the price of corn rises relative to wheat, the farmer switches from wheat production to corn production. We conclude that a change in the price of one good can lead to a change in the supply of another good.

Number of Sellers If more sellers begin producing a good, perhaps because of high profits, the supply curve will shift rightward. If some sellers stop producing a good, perhaps because of losses, the supply curve will shift leftward.

Expectations of Future Price If the price of a good is expected to be higher in the future, producers may hold back some of the product today (if possible—perishables cannot be held back). Then they will have more to sell at the higher future price. Therefore, the *current* supply curve will shift leftward. For example, if oil producers expect the price of oil to be higher next year, some may hold oil off the market this year to be able to sell it next year. Similarly, if they expect the price of oil to be lower next year, they might pump more oil this year than previously planned.

Taxes and Subsidies Some taxes increase per-unit costs. Suppose a shoe manufacturer must pay a $2 tax per pair of shoes produced. This tax leads to a leftward shift in the supply curve, indicating that the manufacturer wants to produce and offer to sell fewer pairs of shoes at each price. If the tax is eliminated, the supply curve shifts rightward.

Subsidies have the opposite effect. Suppose the government subsidizes the production of corn by paying corn farmers $2 for every bushel of corn they produce. Then, because of the subsidy, the quantity supplied of corn is greater at each price and the supply curve of corn shifts rightward. The removal of the subsidy shifts the supply curve of corn leftward. A rough rule of thumb is that we get more of what we subsidize and less of what we tax.

Subsidy
A monetary payment by government to a producer of a good or service.

Government Restrictions Sometimes government acts to reduce supply. Consider a U.S. import quota—a quantitative restriction on foreign goods—on Japanese television sets. The quota reduces the supply of Japanese television sets in the United States. It thus shifts the supply curve leftward. The elimination of the import quota allows the supply of Japanese television sets in the United States to shift rightward.

Licensure has a similar effect. With licensure, individuals must meet certain requirements before they can legally carry out a task. For example, owner–operators of day-care centers must meet certain requirements before they are allowed to sell their services. No doubt this requirement reduces the number of day-care centers and shifts the supply curve of day-care centers leftward.

3-2e A Change in Supply Versus a Change in Quantity Supplied

A change in *supply* is not the same as a change in *quantity supplied*. A change in supply is a shift in the supply curve, as illustrated in Exhibit 10(a). For example, saying that the supply of oranges has increased is the same as saying that the supply curve for oranges has shifted rightward. The factors that can change supply (i.e., shift the supply curve) are prices of relevant resources, technology, prices of other goods, the number of sellers, expectations of future prices, taxes and subsidies, and government restrictions.

A change in quantity supplied refers to a movement along a supply curve, as in Exhibit 10(b). The only factor that can directly cause a change in the quantity supplied of a good is a change in the price of the good.

EXHIBIT 10

A Change in Supply Versus a Change in Quantity Supplied

(a) A change in supply refers to a shift in the supply curve. A change in supply can be brought about by several factors. (See the exhibit and the text.)

(b) A change in quantity supplied refers to a movement along a given supply curve. A change in quantity supplied is brought about only by a change in (a good's) own price.

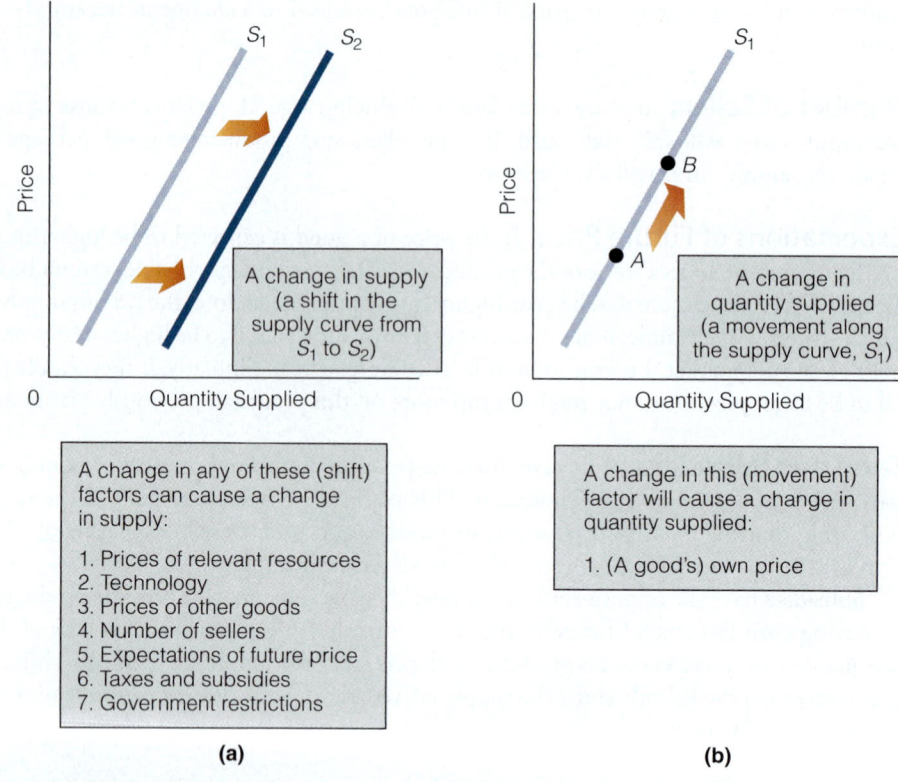

A change in supply (a shift in the supply curve from S_1 to S_2)

A change in quantity supplied (a movement along the supply curve, S_1)

A change in any of these (shift) factors can cause a change in supply:

1. Prices of relevant resources
2. Technology
3. Prices of other goods
4. Number of sellers
5. Expectations of future price
6. Taxes and subsidies
7. Government restrictions

A change in this (movement) factor will cause a change in quantity supplied:

1. (A good's) own price

(a)   (b)

SELF-TEST

1. What would the supply curve for houses (in a given city) look like for a period of (a) the next 10 hours and (b) the next three months?

2. What happens to the supply curve if each of the following occurs?

   a. The number of sellers decreases.

   b. A per-unit tax is placed on the production of a good.

   c. The price of a relevant resource falls.

3. "If the price of apples rises, the supply of apples will rise." True or false? Explain your answer.

3-3 THE MARKET: PUTTING SUPPLY AND DEMAND TOGETHER

In this section, we put supply and demand together and discuss the market. The purpose of the discussion is to gain some understanding about how prices are determined.

3-3a Supply and Demand at Work at an Auction

In Exhibit 11, the supply curve of corn is vertical. It intersects the horizontal axis at 40,000 bushels; that is, the quantity supplied is 40,000 bushels. The demand curve for corn is downward sloping.

Now, suppose you are at a computerized auction where bushels of corn are bought and sold. At this auction, the auctioneer will adjust the corn price to sell all the corn offered for sale. Each potential buyer of corn is sitting in front of a computer and can immediately input the number of bushels he or she wants to buy. For example, if Nancy wants to buy 5,000 bushels of corn, she simply keys "5,000" into her computer. The total number of bushels that all potential buyers are willing and able to buy appears on the auctioneer's computer screen.

The auction begins. Follow along in Exhibit 11 as it develops. The auctioneer announces the price on the computer screens:

- *$9.00!* The potential buyers think for a second and then register the numbers of bushels they are willing and able to buy at that price. On the auctioneer's screen, the total is 10,000 bushels, which is the quantity demanded of corn at $9.00. The auctioneer, realizing that 30,000 bushels of corn ($40,000 - 10,000 = 30,000$) will go unsold at this price, decides to lower the price per bushel.

- *$8.00!* The quantity demanded increases to 20,000 bushels, but still the quantity supplied of corn at this price is greater than the quantity demanded. The auctioneer tries again.

- *$7.00!* The quantity demanded increases to 30,000 bushels, but the quantity supplied at $7.00 is still greater than the quantity demanded. The auctioneer drops the price further.

- *$4.25!* At this price, the quantity demanded jumps to 60,000 bushels, but that is 20,000 bushels more than the quantity supplied. The auctioneer calls out a higher price.

- *$5.25!* The quantity demanded drops to 50,000 bushels, but buyers still want to buy more corn at this price than there is corn to be sold. The auctioneer calls out one more time.

- *$6.10!* At this price, the quantity demanded of corn is 40,000 bushels and the quantity supplied of corn is 40,000 bushels. The auction stops. Sold! The 40,000 bushels of corn are bought and sold at $6.10 per bushel.

EXHIBIT 11

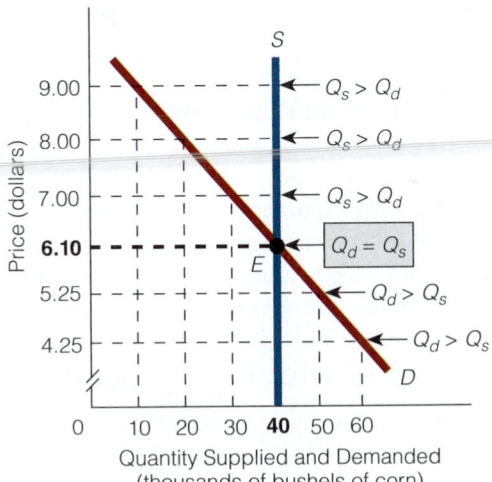

Supply and Demand at Work at an Auction

Let Q_d = quantity demanded and Q_s = quantity supplied. The auctioneer calls out different prices, and buyers record how much they are willing and able to buy. At prices of $9.00, $8.00, and $7.00, $Q_s > Q_d$. At prices of $4.25 and $5.25, $Q_d > Q_s$. At a price of $6.10, $Q_d = Q_s$.

Surplus (Excess Supply)
A condition in which the quantity supplied is greater than the quantity demanded. Surpluses occur only at prices above the equilibrium price.

Shortage (Excess Demand)
A condition in which the quantity demanded is greater than the quantity supplied. Shortages occur only at prices below the equilibrium price.

Equilibrium Price (Market-Clearing Price)
The price at which the quantity demanded of a good equals the quantity supplied.

Equilibrium Quantity
The quantity that corresponds to the equilibrium price. The quantity at which the amount of the good that buyers are willing and able to buy equals the amount that sellers are willing and able to sell, and both equal the amount actually bought and sold.

Disequilibrium Price
A price other than the equilibrium price. A price at which the quantity demanded does not equal the quantity supplied.

Disequilibrium
A state of either surplus or shortage in a market.

Equilibrium
Equilibrium means "at rest." Equilibrium in a market is the price–quantity combination from which buyers or sellers do not tend to move away. Graphically, equilibrium is the intersection point of the supply and demand curves.

3-3b   The Language of Supply and Demand: A Few Important Terms

If the quantity supplied is greater than the quantity demanded, a **surplus**, or **excess supply**, exists. If the quantity demanded is greater than the quantity supplied, a **shortage**, or **excess demand**, exists. In Exhibit 11, a surplus exists at $9.00, $8.00, and $7.00. A shortage exists at $4.25 and $5.25. The price at which the quantity demanded equals the quantity supplied is the **equilibrium price**, or **market-clearing price**. In our example, $6.10 is the equilibrium price. The quantity that corresponds to the equilibrium price is the **equilibrium quantity**. In our example, it is 40,000 bushels of corn. Any price at which quantity demanded is not equal to quantity supplied is a **disequilibrium price**.

A market that exhibits either a surplus ($Q_s > Q_d$) or a shortage ($Q_d > Q_s$) is said to be in **disequilibrium**. A market in which the quantity demanded equals the quantity supplied ($Q_d = Q_s$) is said to be in **equilibrium** (point E in Exhibit 11).

3-3c   Moving to Equilibrium: What Happens to Price When There Is a Surplus or a Shortage?

What did the auctioneer do when the price was $9.00 and there was a surplus of corn? He lowered the price. What did the auctioneer do when the price was $5.25 and there was a shortage of corn? He raised the price. The behavior of the auctioneer can be summarized in this way: If a surplus exists, lower the price; if a shortage exists, raise the price. That is how the auctioneer moved the corn market into equilibrium.

Not all markets have auctioneers. (When was the last time you saw an auctioneer in the grocery store?) But many markets act *as if* an auctioneer were calling out higher and lower prices until the equilibrium price is reached. In many real-world, auctioneerless markets, prices fall when there is a surplus and rise when there is a shortage. Why?

Why Does Price Fall When There Is a Surplus? In Exhibit 12, there is a surplus at a price of $15: The quantity supplied (150 units) is greater than the quantity demanded (50 units). At $15, suppliers will not be able to sell all they had hoped to sell. As a result, their inventories will grow beyond the level they hold in preparation for changes in demand. Sellers will then want to reduce their inventories. Some will lower prices to do so, some will cut back on production, and others will do a little of both. As shown in the exhibit, price and output tend to fall until equilibrium is achieved.

Why Does Price Rise When There Is a Shortage In Exhibit 12, there is a shortage at a price of $5: The quantity demanded (150 units) is greater than the quantity supplied (50 units). At $5, buyers will not be able to buy all they had hoped to buy. Some buyers will then bid up the price to get sellers to sell to them instead of to other buyers. Some sellers, seeing buyers clamor for the goods, will realize that they can raise the price of the goods they have for sale. Higher prices will also call forth added output. Thus, price and output tend to rise until equilibrium is achieved.

Exhibit 13 brings together much of what we have discussed about supply and demand.

3-3d   Speed of Moving to Equilibrium

On March 15, 2017, at 9:05 a.m. (Eastern time), the price of a share of IBM stock was $174.75. A few minutes later, the price had risen to $175.20. Obviously, the stock market equilibrates quickly. If demand rises, then initially there is a shortage of the stock at the current equilibrium price. The price is then bid up, and there is no longer a shortage. All this happens in seconds.

EXHIBIT 12

Moving to Equilibrium

If there is a surplus, sellers' inventories rise above the level the sellers hold in preparation for changes in demand. Sellers will want to reduce their inventories. As a result, price and output fall until equilibrium is achieved. If there is a shortage, some buyers will bid up the price of a good to get sellers to sell to them instead of to other buyers. Some sellers will realize that they can raise the price of the goods they have for sale. Higher prices will call forth added output. Price and output rise until equilibrium is achieved. (*Note:* Recall that price, on the vertical axis, is price per unit of the good, and quantity, on the horizontal axis, is for a specific period. In this text, we do not specify those qualifications on the axes themselves, but consider them to be understood.)

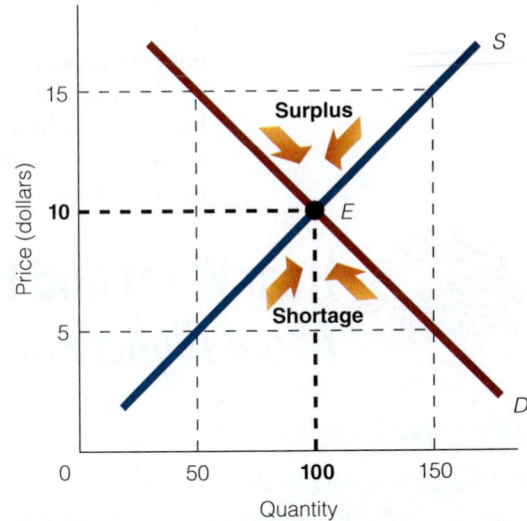

Price	Q_s	Q_d	Condition
$15	150	50	Surplus
10	100	100	Equilibrium
5	50	150	Shortage

EXHIBIT 13

A Summary Exhibit of a Market (Supply and Demand)

This exhibit ties together the topics discussed so far in the chapter. A market is composed of both supply and demand. Also shown are the factors that affect supply and demand and therefore indirectly affect the equilibrium price and quantity of a good.

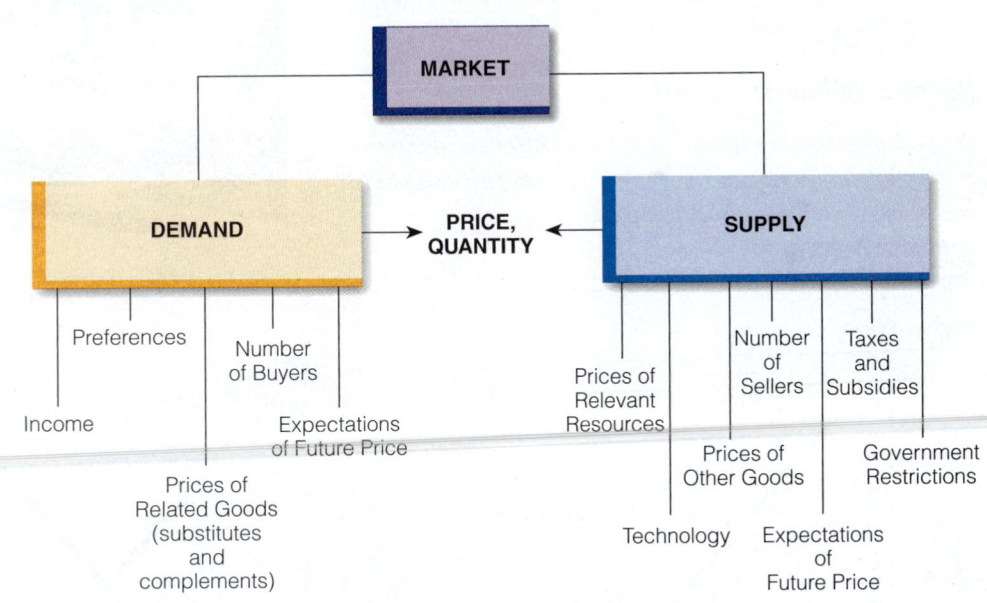

Now consider a house offered for sale in any city in the United States. The sale price of a house may remain the same even though the house does not sell for months. For example, a person offers to sell her house for $400,000. One month passes, no sale; two months pass, no sale; three months pass, no sale; and so on. Ten months later, the house is still not sold and the price is still $400,000.

Is $400,000 the equilibrium price of the house? Obviously not. At the equilibrium price, there would be a buyer for the house and a seller of the house: The quantity demanded would equal the quantity supplied. At a price of $400,000, there is a seller but no buyer. The $400,000 price is above the equilibrium price. At $400,000, the housing market has a surplus; equilibrium has not been achieved.

Some people may be tempted to argue that supply and demand are at work in the stock market but not in the housing market. A better explanation, though, is that *not all markets equilibrate at the same speed.* Although the stock market may take only seconds to go from surplus or shortage to equilibrium, the housing market may take months to do so.

Hear What and How the Economist Thinks . . .
About Higher Prices and Buying More

The economist hears someone say:

It seems to me that the law of demand has to be wrong in some cases. There are plenty of examples of the price of a good rising and people buying more of the good. For example, during the period 2000–2006, house prices were rising (sometimes quite rapidly) in the United States and all you heard about back then was how house sales were up. In other words, prices were up and house sales were up. That seems to me to contradict the law of demand, which states that if prices rise, sales will go down.

Here what and how the economist thinks:

This person is making a very fundamental mistake. He thinks that the higher price is what causes people to buy more, when it is people who want to buy more that causes the higher price.

Think of a downward sloping demand curve, like the one shown in Exhibit 14(a). At a price of $10, the quantity demanded is 100; and at the higher price of $12, the quantity demanded is 80. This

Carolyn Franks/Shutterstock.com

EXHIBIT 14

Higher Prices

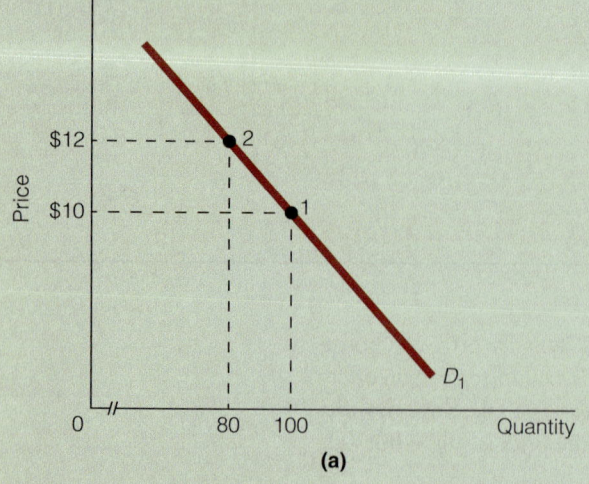

(a)

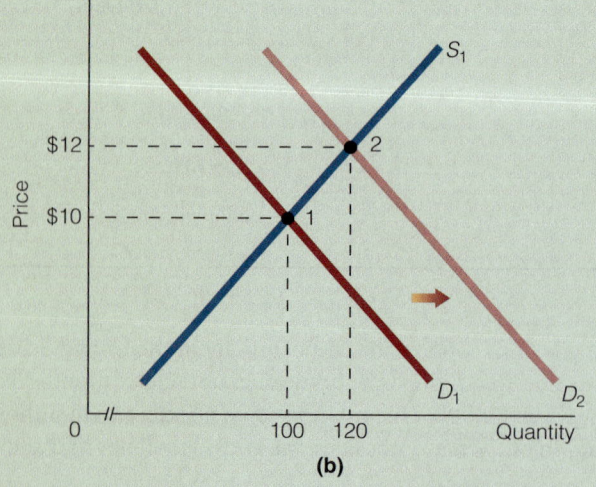

(b)

illustrates the law of demand: a higher price brings about a lower quantity demanded.

Now look at panel (b) in Exhibit 14(b). When the demand curve is D_1, and the equilibrium price is $10, the quantity demanded is 100. Now suppose demand rises, and the demand curve shifts rightward from D_1 to D_2. First, what happens to the equilibrium price of the good? It rises from $10 to $12. Now ask yourself what the quantity demanded is at $12, given that the demand curve has shifted rightward? The answer is that it is 120. In other words, we see that the quantity demanded is higher at $12 than it was at $10—but this is because the demand curve shifted rightward, it is not because of the higher price alone.

Let's now think about what was happening in the period 2000–2006 when house prices were rising and house sales were rising too.

Was it the higher house prices that caused the greater house sales? No. Instead, it was the increased demand for houses that caused both the higher house prices and the higher house sales.

Questions to Think About:

1. Suppose the equilibrium price of a good is currently $4. Then something happens to cause it to rise to $6. Under what condition will quantity demanded be higher at $6 than at $4? Under what condition will quantity demanded be lower at $6 than at $4?

2. The law of demand states that as the price of a good rises, quantity demanded falls; and as the price of a good falls, quantity demanded rises. Is it important to add that the law of demand holds when all other things are held constant or nothing else changes? Explain your answer in terms of the person who argued that house prices increased and house sales increased too.

3-3e Moving to Equilibrium: Maximum and Minimum Prices

There is another way to demonstrate how a market moves to equilibrium. Exhibit 15 shows the market for good X. Look at the first unit of good X. What is the *maximum price buyers are willing to pay* for it? The answer is $70. Just follow the dotted line up from the first unit of the good to the demand curve. What is the *minimum price sellers need to receive before they are willing to sell* this unit of good X? It is $10. Follow the dotted line up from the first unit to the supply curve. Because the maximum buying price is greater than the minimum selling price, the first unit of good X will be exchanged.

EXHIBIT 15

Moving to Equilibrium in Terms of Maximum and Minimum Prices

As long as the maximum buying price of a good is greater than the minimum selling price, an exchange will occur. This condition is met for units 1–4. The market converges on equilibrium through a process of mutually beneficial exchanges.

Units of Good X	Maximum Buying Price	Minimum Selling Price	Result
1st	$70	$10	Exchange
2nd	60	20	Exchange
3rd	50	30	Exchange
4th	40	40	Exchange
5th	30	50	No exchange

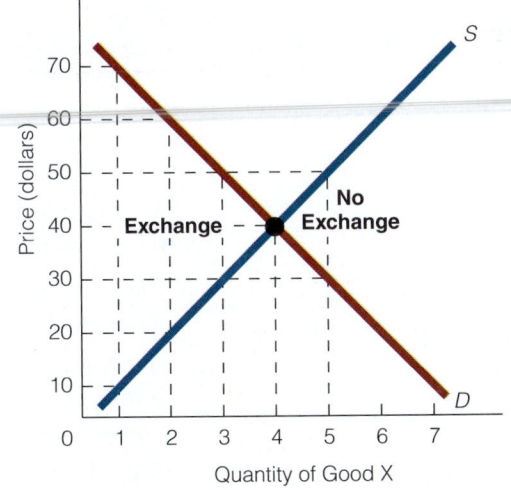

What about the second unit? For the second unit, buyers are willing to pay a maximum price of $60 and sellers need to receive a minimum price of $20. Thus, the second unit of good X will be exchanged. In fact, exchange will occur as long as the maximum buying price is greater than the minimum selling price. The exhibit shows that a total of four units of good X will be exchanged. The fifth unit will not be exchanged, because the maximum buying price ($30) is less than the minimum selling price ($50).

In this process, buyers and sellers trade money for goods as long as both benefit from the trade. The market converges on a quantity of 4 units of good X and a price of $40 per unit. This point is the equilibrium point. In other words, mutually beneficial trade drives the market to equilibrium.

3-3f The Connection Between Equilibrium and Predictions

In a market setting, both equilibrium and disequilibrium are real-world states. A market is in disequilibrium if there is either a shortage or a surplus in the market. In other words, if quantity demanded is not equal to quantity supplied, the market is in disequilibrium. In contrast, if quantity demanded equals quantity supplied, the market is in equilibrium.

Besides being real-world states, equilibrium and disequilibrium are mental constructs that economists use to think about things. As a mental construct, equilibrium represents a balance of forces from which there is no tendency to move. Disequilibrium represents an imbalance, from which there is a tendency to move. To illustrate, when a market is in disequilibrium, such as when quantity demanded is greater than quantity supplied, price will *move up*. When quantity supplied is greater than quantity demanded, price will *move down*. In other words, disequilibrium, as a mental construct, means that something is going to happen. What exists now won't continue to exist for long. The last page of the book has yet to be read.

Seen in this light, the concepts of equilibrium and disequilibrium are used by economists to "foreshadow" what is about to happen. Hence, both concepts are related to the predictions that economists make.

To see this relationship explicitly, consider again a market in disequilibrium: The quantity demanded of a good is greater than the quantity supplied. For the economist, this state of affairs is temporary. The market, currently in disequilibrium, will soon edge its way over to equilibrium. The economist, then, knows where the market is headed. Knowing where it is headed—to equilibrium—he then makes a prediction that might sound something like this:

The market is currently in disequilibrium, with quantity demanded being greater than quantity supplied. A state of equilibrium exists when quantity demanded equals quantity supplied. So, disequilibrium will soon turn into equilibrium. (Notice here that the economist is making a prediction: Disequilibrium will turn into equilibrium.) It follows that things will soon change. How will they change, you ask? Well, quantity demanded will need to go down, and quantity supplied will need to rise, so that they equal each other. (Again, the economist is making a prediction of what is to come.) And how will this state of affairs come about? By price rising (again, another prediction).

We conclude that the economist's concept of equilibrium is related to the economist's predictions. It is a two-step process:

1. *The economist compares "what is" with what exists in equilibrium. For example, the market shortage is compared with market equilibrium.*

2. *If "what is" is not what exists in equilibrium, then the economist predicts the path the market will take to get from "what is" to equilibrium. For example, price will rise until quantity demanded and quantity supplied are equal.*

In short, the economist uses the concepts of disequilibrium and equilibrium in much the same way that a person uses a map. We are at point X and we want to go to point Y. The shortest route is this way. The economist says, the market is in disequilibrium and soon it will be in equilibrium. Here is the "path" (I predict) that the market will follow to get from disequilibrium to equilibrium.

3-3g Equilibrium in Terms of Consumers' and Producers' Surplus

Equilibrium can be viewed in terms of two important economic concepts: consumers' surplus and producers' (or sellers') surplus. **Consumers' surplus (CS)** is the difference between the maximum buying price and the price paid by the buyer:

$$\text{Consumers' surplus} = \text{Maximum buying price} - \text{Price paid}$$

For example, if the highest price you would pay to see a movie is $10 and you pay $7 to see it, then you have received a $3 consumers' surplus. Obviously, the more consumers' surplus that consumers receive, the better off they are. Wouldn't you have preferred to pay, say, $4 to see the movie instead of $7? If you had paid only $4, your consumers' surplus would have been $6 instead of $3.

Producers' (or sellers') surplus (PS) is the difference between the price received by the producer or seller and the minimum selling price:

$$\text{Producers' (sellers') surplus} = \text{Price received} - \text{Minimum selling price}$$

Suppose the minimum price the owner of the movie theater would have accepted for admission is $5. But she sells admission for $7, not $5. Her producers' or sellers' surplus is therefore $2. A seller prefers a large producers' surplus to a small one. The theater owner would have preferred to sell admission to the movie for $8 instead of $7 because then she would have received a $3 producers' surplus.

Total surplus (TS) is the sum of consumers' surplus and producers' surplus:

$$\text{Total surplus} = \text{Consumers' surplus} + \text{Producers' surplus}$$

In Exhibit 16(a), consumers' surplus is represented by the shaded triangle. This triangle includes the area under the demand curve and above the equilibrium price. According to the definition, consumers' surplus is the highest price that buyers are willing to pay (the maximum buying price) minus the price they pay. For example, the window in part (a) shows that buyers are willing to pay as high as $7 for the 50th unit but they pay only $5. Thus, the consumers' surplus on the 50th unit of the good is $2. If we add the consumers' surplus on each unit of the good between the first and the 100th unit, inclusive (the equilibrium quantity), we obtain the shaded consumers' surplus triangle.

In Exhibit 16(b), producers' surplus is also represented by a shaded triangle. This triangle includes the area above the supply curve and under the equilibrium price. Keep in mind the definition of producers' surplus: the price received by the seller minus the lowest price the seller would accept for the good. The window in part (b) shows that sellers would have sold the 50th unit for as low as $3 but actually sold it for $5. Thus, the producers' surplus on the 50th unit of the good is $2. If we add the producers' surplus on each unit of the good between the first and the 100th unit, inclusive, we obtain the shaded producers' surplus triangle.

Now consider consumers' surplus and producers' surplus at the equilibrium quantity. Exhibit 17 shows that the consumers' surplus at equilibrium is equal to areas $A + B + C + D$ and the producers' surplus at equilibrium is equal to areas $E + F + G + H$. At any other exchangeable quantity, such as 25, 50, or 75 units, both consumers' surplus and producers' surplus are less. For

Consumers' Surplus (CS)
The difference between the maximum price a buyer is willing and able to pay for a good or service and the price actually paid. (CS = Maximum buying price − Price paid)

Producers' (Sellers') Surplus (PS)
The difference between the price sellers receive for a good and the minimum or lowest price for which they would have sold the good. (PS = Price received − Minimum selling price.)

Total Surplus (TS)
The sum of consumers' surplus and producers' surplus. ($TS = CS + PS$.)

EXHIBIT 16

Consumers' and Producers' Surplus

(a) *Consumers' surplus.* As the shaded area indicates, the difference between the maximum, or highest, amount that buyers would be willing to pay for a good and the price that they actually pay is consumers' surplus. (b) *Producers' surplus.* As the shaded area indicates, the difference between the price that sellers receive for a good and the minimum or lowest price they would be willing to sell the good for is producers' surplus.

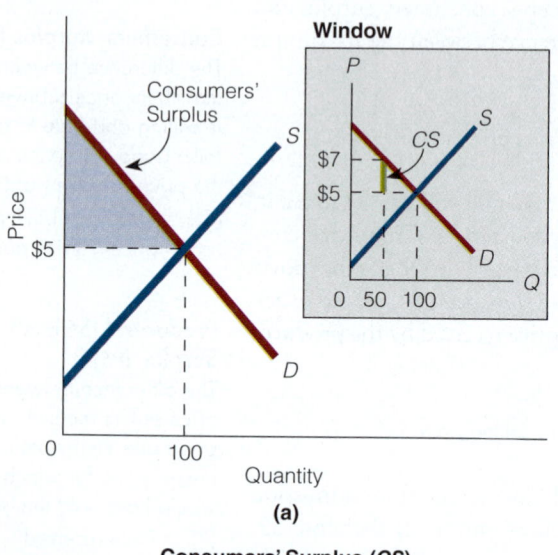

(a)

Consumers' Surplus (CS)

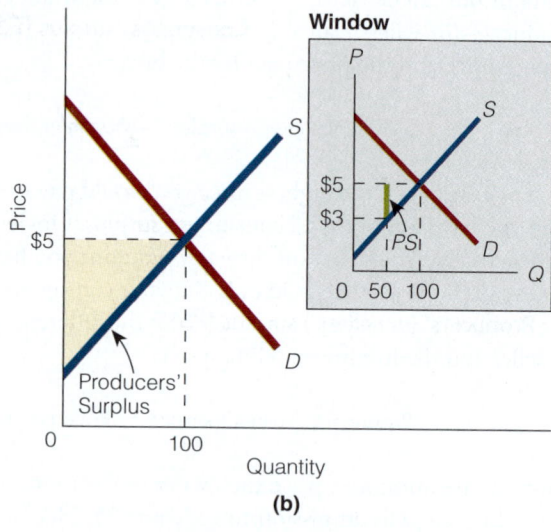

(b)

Producers' Surplus (PS)

example, at 25 units, consumers' surplus is equal to area *A* and producers' surplus is equal to area *E.* At 50 units, consumers' surplus is equal to areas *A* + *B* and producers' surplus is equal to areas *E* + *F.*

Equilibrium has a special property: At equilibrium, both consumers' surplus and producers' surplus are maximized. In short, total surplus is maximized.

EXHIBIT 17

Equilibrium, Consumers' Surplus, and Producers' Surplus

Consumers' surplus is greater at the equilibrium quantity (100 units) than at any other exchangeable quantity. Producers' surplus is greater at the equilibrium quantity than at any other exchangeable quantity. For example, consumers' surplus is areas *A* + *B* + *C* at 75 units, but areas *A* + *B* + *C* + *D* at 100 units. Producers' surplus is areas *E* + *F* + *G* at 75 units, but areas *E* + *F* + *G* + *H* at 100 units.

Quantity (units)	Consumers' Surplus	Producers' Surplus
25	*A*	*E*
50	*A* + *B*	*E* + *F*
75	*A* + *B* + *C*	*E* + *F* + *G*
100 (equilibrium)	*A* + *B* + *C* + *D*	*E* + *F* + *G* + *H*

(a)

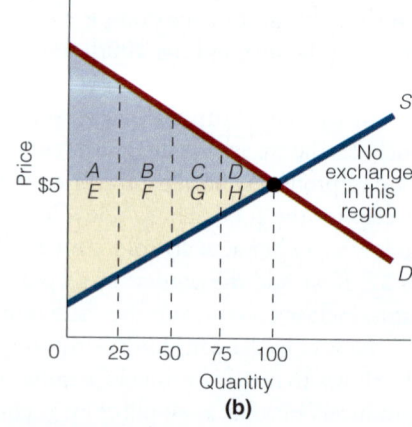

(b)

Does It Matter to You . . .
If You Pay Equilibrium Prices or Not?

There are two sides to a market—a buying or demand side and a selling or supply side. Since most of us buy many more goods and services than we sell, let's consider the price a buyer pays for a good or service.

There are two kinds of prices—equilibrium prices and disequilibrium prices. If equilibrium price exists in a market for a good, then the quantity of the good that buyers want to buy is equal to the quantity of the good that sellers want to sell. If a disequilibrium price exists, then either the quantity of the good that buyers want to buy is greater than or less than the quantity that sellers want to sell. In other words, either a shortage or surplus of the good exists in the market.

If the disequilibrium price is *below* the equilibrium price (e.g., the equilibrium price is $10 and the disequilibrium price is $7), then a shortage of the good exists. If the disequilibrium price is *above* the equilibrium price (e.g., the equilibrium price is $10 and the disequilibrium price is $14), then a surplus of the good exists.

So, let's take our original question—Does it matter to you if you pay equilibrium prices or not?—and ask instead, Does it matter to you if either shortages or surpluses in the market matter to you as a buyer?

If a shortage exists, this means that you, as a buyer, may be willing to buy the good, but be unable to buy it. After all, when there is a shortage of a good, it holds that some buyers are going to be unable to buy the good. You may want to buy the bread, but you can't; you may want to buy the medicine, but you can't; you may want to buy the car, but you can't.

Now if a surplus exists, this means that you, as a buyer, will pay more for the good you are buying than you would have paid at equilibrium. What this translates into is less consumers' surplus for you. Remember, consumers' surplus is the difference between the maximum price you are willing to pay for a good and the price you pay. When equilibrium price is, say, $10, and the maximum price you are willing to pay is $15, you receive $5 worth of consumers' surplus. But when the price you pay is above equilibrium, say, $12, and the maximum price you are willing to pay is $15, then you receive $3 worth of consumers' surplus.

Once again, does it matter to you if you pay equilibrium price or not? It matters quite a lot because if you don't pay equilibrium price you may not be able to buy the good you want to buy (the case when a shortage exists) or you end up with less consumers' surplus (the case when a surplus exists).

RanaPhotos/Alamy Stock Photo

3-3h What Can Change Equilibrium Price and Quantity?

Equilibrium price and quantity are determined by supply and demand. Whenever demand changes, or supply changes, or both change, equilibrium price and quantity change. Exhibit 18 illustrates eight different cases where this scenario occurs. Cases (a)–(d) illustrate the four basic changes in supply and demand: either supply changes or demand changes. Cases (e)–(h) illustrate changes in both supply and demand.

- *Case (a):* Demand rises (the demand curve shifts rightward from D_1 to D_2), and supply is constant (the supply curve does not move). As a result of demand rising and supply remaining constant, the equilibrium price rises from P_1 to P_2 and the equilibrium quantity

EXHIBIT 18

Equilibrium Price and Quantity Effects of Supply Curve Shifts and Demand Curve Shifts

The exhibit illustrates the effects on equilibrium price and quantity of a change in demand, a change in supply, and a change in both. Below each diagram, the condition leading to the effects is noted, using the following symbols: (1) a bar over a letter means *constant* (thus, $\bar{S}$ means that supply is constant); (2) a downward-pointing arrow ($\downarrow$) indicates a fall; and (3) an upward-pointing arrow ($\uparrow$) indicates a rise. A rise (fall) in demand is the same as a rightward (leftward) shift in the demand curve. A rise (fall) in supply is the same as a rightward (leftward) shift in the supply curve.

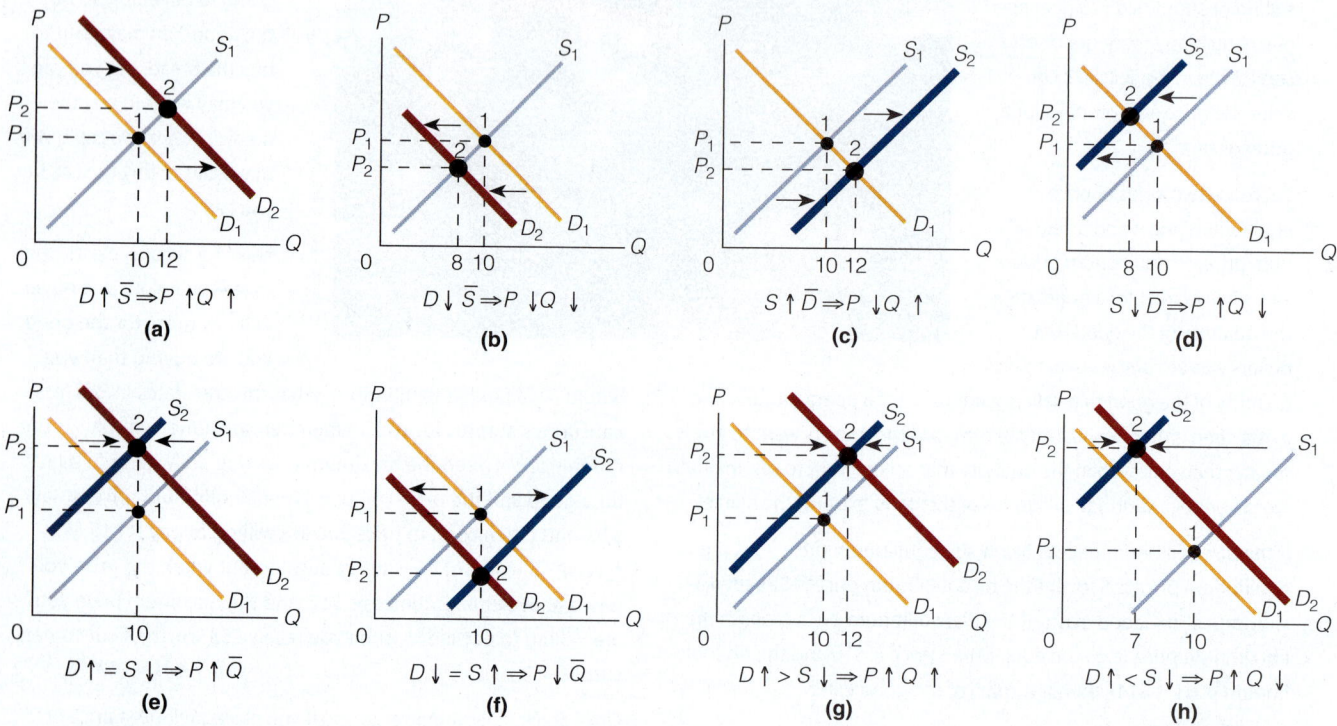

rises from 10 units to 12 units. Now, let's see if you can identify what has happened to quantity supplied (not supply) as price has risen from P_1 to P_2. (Remember, quantity supplied changes if *price* changes.) As price rises from P_1 to P_2, quantity supplied rises from 10 units to 12 units. We see this situation as a movement up the supply curve from point 1 to point 2, corresponding (on the horizontal axis) to a change from 10 units to 12 units.

- *Case (b):* Demand falls (the demand curve shifts leftward from D_1 to D_2), and supply is constant. As a result, the equilibrium price falls from P_1 to P_2 and the equilibrium quantity falls from 10 to 8 units. Now ask, has the quantity supplied (not supply) changed? Yes, it has. As a result of price falling from P_1 to P_2, we move down the supply curve from point 1 to point 2 and the quantity supplied falls from 10 units to 8 units.

- *Case (c):* Supply rises (the supply curve shifts rightward from S_1 to S_2), and demand is constant. As a result, the equilibrium price falls from P_1 to P_2 and the equilibrium quantity rises from 10 units to 12 units. Now ask, has the quantity demanded (not demand) changed? Yes, it has. As a result of price falling from P_1 to P_2, we move down the demand curve from point 1 to point 2 and the quantity demanded rises from 10 units to 12 units.

- *Case (d):* Supply falls (the supply curve shifts leftward from S_1 to S_2), and demand is constant. As a result, the equilibrium price rises from P_1 to P_2 and the equilibrium quantity falls from 10 to 8 units. One last time: Has quantity demanded (not demand) changed? Yes, it has. As a result of price rising from P_1 to P_2, we move up the demand curve from point 1 to point 2, and quantity demanded falls from 10 units to 8 units.

- *Case (e):* Demand rises (the demand curve shifts from D_1 to D_2), and supply falls (the supply curve shifts leftward from S_1 to S_2) by an equal amount. As a result, the equilibrium price rises from P_1 to P_2 and the equilibrium quantity remains constant at 10 units.

- *Case (f):* Demand falls (the demand curve shifts leftward from D_1 to D_2), and supply rises (the supply curve shifts rightward from S_1 to S_2) by an equal amount. As a result, the equilibrium price falls from P_1 to P_2 and the equilibrium quantity is constant at 10 units.

- *Case (g):* Demand rises (the demand curve shifts rightward from D_1 to D_2) by a greater amount than supply falls (the supply curve shifts leftward from S_1 to S_2). As a result, the equilibrium price rises from P_1 to P_2 and the equilibrium quantity rises from 10 units to 12 units.

- *Case (h):* Demand rises (the demand curve shifts rightward from D_1 to D_2) by a smaller amount than supply falls (the supply curve shifts leftward from S_1 to S_2). As a result, the equilibrium price rises from P_1 to P_2 and the equilibrium quantity falls from 10 units to 7 units.

ECONOMICS 24/7

Are You Buying More Than You Want to Buy?

Consumers' surplus is the difference between the maximum buying price and the price paid. If you'd be willing to pay a maximum of $10 for good *X*, but you pay only $4 for the good, then your consumers' surplus is $6.

Now, suppose you receive $10 consumers surplus on the first unit of good *X* that you buy, $9 on the second unit of good *X*, $8 on the third unit, and so on. How many units of the good will you buy? The answer is that you will continue to buy additional units of the good as long as you receive positive consumers' surplus. You will receive positive consumers' surplus on items 1 through 10. You will not receive any consumers' surplus on the 11th unit, so you will stop buying at the 10th unit.

goodluz/Shutterstock.com

Now suppose that the seller of good *X* comes to you and says this: No longer will I allow you to buy individual units of good *X*. From now on, you must buy either 11 units or nothing at all. In other words, the seller of good *X* presents you with an "all-or-nothing" deal: Either buy all that he says you will buy (11), or buy nothing.

What would you do?

The answer is, it depends on the negative consumers' surplus you would receive on the 11th unit? If things follow the path we have outlined—according to which, for each additional unit of the good you buy, you receive $1 less in consumers' surplus than you received for the previous unit purchased—then you will receive $1 in negative consumers' surplus on the 11th unit. So, will you buy the 11 units or zero units?

Think things through in this way: If you buy 11 units, you will receive positive consumers' surplus on units 1–10 and negative consumers' surplus on the 11th unit. Thus, on units 1–10, you will receive a total positive consumers' surplus of $55 ($10 on the first unit + $9 on the second unit + $8 on the third unit and so on) and you will receive a negative $1 in consumers' surplus on the 11th unit. Fifty-five dollars minus $1 leaves you with $54 in consumers' surplus if you buy all 11 units. Of course, if you don't buy all 11 units, but instead choose to buy zero units, you will receive zero dollars in consumers' surplus. So, the choice is between buying 11 units and receiving $54 in consumers' surplus or buying zero units and receiving $0 in consumer's surplus. Better the $54 in consumers' surplus than the zero dollars.

Better to accept the "all" than the "nothing." Of course, it is still better to buy only 10 units of good X than 11 units, but 10 units was no longer a choice. It was 11 or nothing. The all-or-nothing deal ended up reducing your consumers' surplus (from $55 to $54).

Now think of two institutions that sometimes offer, or threaten to offer, all-or-nothing deals. One is private firms. A cable company could offer you 100 channels to choose from for, say, $2 a channel a month. If you want to purchase 10 channels, then purchase 10 channels; if you want to purchase 14 channels, then purchase 14 channels. But cable companies do not usually sell channels this way. Instead, they offer a number of all-or-nothing packages. Buy these 10 channels or buy nothing; buy these 50 channels or buy nothing. It could very well be that some of the channels a consumer buys offer either no or negative consumers' surplus, but still the overall package comes with positive consumers' surplus, albeit not quite as much as would be the case if channels were selected one by one.

Or consider the purchase of a cell phone or cell phone plan. Often, you choose a particular plan or a particular phone with a host of features. Your phone and plan may come with more features than you would buy if you purchased each feature separately. Still, both the plan and the phone may be worth it to you because, overall, you receive positive consumers' surplus, albeit once again not as much as you might have received had you been able to decide on each feature separately.

Now move from private firms to government. There may be some things you receive from government—roads, schools, national defense, and so on—for which you receive positive consumers' surplus. In other words, what you would have been willing to pay for each of these goods or services that you consume is more than what you pay in taxes. But then there might be some things you receive from government for which you receive negative consumers' surplus.

While government doesn't have to be an all-or-nothing deal—it is possible to cut some things out of government and keep other things—often elected government officials threaten to cut some of the things for which people receive a positive consumers' surplus if they aren't willing to pay (through taxes) for some of the things for which they might receive negative consumers' surplus. Here is a fictional, yet representative, scenario of how things might proceed at a local government public meeting:

Taxpayers:	We don't want to pay higher taxes.
City Council:	Then we will have to cut services.
Taxpayers:	Maybe that is the right thing to do, given these tight budgetary times.
City Council:	Well, then, we might have to cut police and fire protection.
Taxpayers:	But what about cutting all the waste in government? Why not start there? Or what about cutting your salaries or putting off some of your proposed projects?
City Council:	That might be very hard to do. We might need to start with police and fire protection.
Taxpayers:	Give us a few minutes to think.
City Council:	Take your time.

3-3i It Is Important to Know Why the Price Changed: Back to Substitutes and Complements

According to our discussion of substitutes (on pages 66–67), two goods are substitutes if, as the price of one rises (falls), the demand for the other rises (falls). For example, consider the substitutes coffee and tea: As the price of coffee rises, it makes sense to think that people will cut back on buying as much coffee (the quantity demanded of coffee declines) and increase their demand for tea.

But will a higher price of coffee always cause this set of events? The answer depends on *why* the price of coffee increases? Is it because the supply of coffee decreases or because the demand for coffee increases?

If the supply of coffee decreases, the price of coffee will rise. This will cause people to cut back on buying coffee (the quantity demanded of coffee declines) and increase their demand for tea.

Now suppose the demand for coffee rises—say, because peoples' preference for coffee becomes stronger. The price of coffee will rise. This time, however, the higher price of coffee *will not* cause people to increase their demand for tea. If coffee becomes more expensive because the demand for coffee increases, it seems peculiar to think that the demand for tea also increases. (If pears become more expensive because the demand for pears increases, does the demand for apples have to increase too? No. If pens become more expensive because the demand for pens increases, does the demand for pencils have to increase too? No.)

So, when it's said that "two goods are substitutes if as the price of one rises (falls), the demand for the other rises (falls)," is this correct? It is, as long as the initial price rise or fall is due to a change in supply and not a change in demand.

Now let's turn to complements. According to our discussion of complements (on page 67), two goods are complements if, as the price of one rises (falls), the demand for the other falls (rises). For example, consider the complements, pasta and pasta sauce: As the price of pasta rises, it makes sense to think that people will cut back on buying as much pasta (the quantity demanded of pasta declines) and therefore decrease their demand for pasta sauce.

But will a higher price of pasta always cause this set of events? The answer depends on *why* the price of pasta increases? Is it because the supply of pasta decreases or because the demand for pasta increases?

If the supply of pasta decreases, the price of pasta will rise. This will cause people to cut back on buying as much pasta (quantity demanded of pasta falls) and decrease their demand for pasta sauce.

Now suppose the demand for pasta rises—say, because peoples' preferences for pasta becomes stronger. The price of pasta will rise. This time, though, the higher price of pasta will not cause people to decrease their demand for pasta sauce. If anything, they will want to buy more pasta sauce to go with the increased pasta they have purchased.

So, when it's said that "two goods are complements if as the price of one rises (falls), the demand for the other falls (rises)," is this correct? It is, as long as the initial price rise or fall is due to a change in supply and not a change in demand.

There is an important lesson to be learned from our discussion of price, substitutes, and complements. It is that we should never "reason from" or "start an economic explanation with" a price change. ("Price changed and then the following happened . . . "). Instead, we should start an economic explanation one step before the price changed. We should start it with *why* the price changed. (Demand increased and then price increased or supply decreased and then price increased). That's because, as we have seen here, *why* price changes matters.

3-3j Epilogue: Who Feeds Cleveland?

Here is a question to think about: Who feeds Cleveland? If you have a hard time answering the question, or even making sense of the question, then that is probably for one of two reasons. First, asking "who" feeds Cleveland is an odd question. No one person feeds Cleveland. We can't point to the president of the United States, or to the CEO of a large company, or to a specific farmer, and say, "He feeds Cleveland." That's why the "who feeds" question may initially draw a blank stare.

But more importantly, the question is hard to answer because we have been born into a world where food always has existed for people in Cleveland. We never hear of any stories of mass starvation in Cleveland. We never hear that the people in Cleveland are hungry. We have just taken it for granted—and never really given it much thought—that people in Cleveland eat, just as people in New York, Los Angeles, or Topeka, Kansas, eat.

But still, the question nags at us. Obviously, there must be some reason that the people in Cleveland always seem to have food to eat. Who or what is it that makes this possible? Is there a government agency called the Department of Food located in Washington, D.C., that gives orders to people to send food to Cleveland? We know there isn't. Well, then, how does Cleveland get all the food that it consumes? Who or what does feed Cleveland?

The answer is "the market." The market feeds Cleveland. It also feeds every other city in the country. Here is how the market works: The people in Cleveland want to eat. They want to eat all kinds of things: steaks, potato chips, chicken, tomatoes, carrots, bananas, and bread. There are other people who produce these items. They produce these items for one single reason: because they want to sell them for money, which they can then use to buy themselves things they want.

The producers and sellers of these food items send these items to Cleveland. Some of these people even build stores and restaurants in Cleveland where this food can be purchased or eaten. The people who build these stores and restaurants in Cleveland do what they do for the same reason that the producers of the food items did what they did because they want to sell what they have to sell for money, which they can then use to buy themselves things they want.

Now let's enter a grocery store in Cleveland. The manager of the store is walking down the snacks aisle when she notices that Oreo cookies are leaving the shelves more quickly than before. She thinks to herself that people must really want to buy Oreo cookies. So, she places an order for Oreo cookies that is larger than the order she placed last week. If the same thing is happening in other grocery stores—if Oreo cookies are flying off the shelves—then other managers are doing the same thing too: placing larger orders for Oreo cookies. The manufacturers of Oreo cookies end up producing more Oreo cookies and sending them out to grocery stores to be sold. If Oreo cookies have been flying off the shelves faster than ever because the demand for Oreo cookies has increased, Oreo cookies might go up in price.

The higher price of Oreo cookies might then prompt other cookie manufacturers to come out with a cookie that is similar to an Oreo cookie. After all, almost nothing is copied as often as success.

Now leave the grocery store and go to a restaurant. On the menu at the restaurant are numerous items. Some of those items sell better than other items. If an item sells well, the restaurant keeps the item on the menu. If an item sells poorly, it removes the item from the menu. For example, if, for some reason, peoples' preferences for food changes from Mexican cuisine to Italian cuisine, then the Mexican restaurants either convert to Italian restaurants or go out of business.

So, we now know that "the market" feeds Cleveland, and we have some idea of exactly how it feeds Cleveland, namely, sellers of food get together with buyers of food and then trade their food for money. Also, as the demand for a food item changes, the producers or sellers of food respond in a way that the buyers of food want them to respond. When the buyers want more cookies, the suppliers of cookies give them more cookies; when the buyers want more Italian food and less Mexican food, the restaurateurs deliver.

Now, if "the market" were an invention, much the way a car or TV or personal computer were invented, we'd have to say that it is quite some invention. It would be a more significant invention than almost anything you can think of because "the market" does something as important as feed Cleveland. It is also "the thing" within which other inventions appear. If there were no market, would there be any reason to invent cars, computers, cell telephones, and so on?

So, if "the market" were an invention, it would be a most important invention, if not the most important invention of all time. But, alas, no one invented the market. The market is simply the very quiet and invisible manifestation of the actions of millions of people simply trying to make themselves better off.

The market—that "thing" that ends up feeding Cleveland, making more Oreo cookies, changing the menu when restaurant goers want a change in the menu, and so on—is a **spontaneous order**. It is something that emerged as an unintended effect of peoples' actions directed at trying to make themselves better off.

Spontaneous Order
The spontaneous and unintended emergence of order out of the self-interested actions of individuals; an unintended consequence of human action, with emphasis placed on the word "unintended."

ECONOMICS 24/7

"Sorry, But This Flight Has Been Overbooked"

Airlines often overbook flights; that is, they accept more reservations than they have seats available on a flight. Airlines know that a certain (usually small) percentage of individuals with reservations will not show up. An empty seat means that the airline's cost per actual passenger on board is higher than it would be if the seat were occupied by a paying passenger. So, airlines try to make sure to have few empty seats. One way to reduce the number of empty seats is to overbook.

Filipe Frazao/Shutterstock.com

In the past, when more people with reservations showed up for a flight than there were seats available, the airline simply "bumped" passengers. In other words, the airline would tell some passengers that they could not fly on that flight. Understandably, the bumped passengers were disappointed and angry.

One day while shaving, economist Julian Simon (1932–1998) came up with a better way to deal with overbooking. He argued that the airline should enter into a market transaction with the ticket holders who had reserved seats for an overbooked flight. Instead of bumping people randomly, an airline should ask passengers to sell their seats back to the airline. Passengers who absolutely had to get from one city to another would not sell their seats, but passengers who did not have to fly right away might be willing to sell their tickets for, say, first class on a later flight or some other compensation.

Simon wrote the executives of various airlines and outlined the details of his plan. He even told them that the first airline

which enacted the plan would likely reap larger sales. The airline could, after all, guarantee its passengers that they would not get bumped. Most airline executives wrote back and told him that his idea was a reasonably good one but was unworkable.

Simon then contacted various economists and asked them to support his idea publicly. Some did; some didn't. For years, Simon pushed his idea with airline executives and government officials.

Then Alfred Kahn, an economist, was appointed chairman of the Civil Aeronautics Board. Simon contacted Kahn with his plan, and Kahn liked it. According to Simon, "Kahn announced something like the scheme in his first press conference. He also had the great persuasive skill to repackage it as a 'voluntary' bumping plan, and at the same time to increase the penalties that airlines must pay to involuntary bumpees, a nice carrot-and-stick combination."

The rest, as people say, is history. Simon's plan has been in operation since 1978. Simon wrote, "The volunteer system for handling airline oversales exemplifies how markets can improve life for all concerned parties. In case of an oversale, the airline agent proceeds from lowest bidder upwards until the required number of bumpees is achieved. Low bidders take the next flight, happy about it. All other passengers fly as scheduled, also happy. The airlines can overbook more, making them happy too."

SELF-TEST

1. When a persowm goes to the grocery store to buy food, there is no auctioneer calling out prices for bread, milk, and other items. Therefore, supply and demand cannot be operative. Do you agree or disagree? Explain your answer.

2. The price of a personal computer of a given quality is lower today than it was five years ago. Is this necessarily the result of a lower demand for computers? Explain your answer.

3. What is the effect on equilibrium price and quantity of the following?

   a. A decrease in demand that is greater than the increase in supply

   b. An increase in supply

   c. A decrease in supply that is greater than the increase in demand

   d. A decrease in demand

4. At equilibrium quantity, what is the relationship between the maximum buying price and the minimum selling price?

5. If the price paid for a certain item is $40 and the consumers' surplus is $4, then what is the maximum buying price for that item? If the minimum selling price is $30 and the producers' surplus is $4, then what is the price received by the seller?

OFFICE HOURS

"I Thought Prices Equaled Costs Plus 10 Percent"

STUDENT: My uncle produces and sells lamps. I asked him once how he determines the price he sells his lamps for. He said he takes his costs and adds 10 percent. In other words, if it cost him $200 to make a lamp, he sells it for a price of $220. If all sellers do the same thing, then prices aren't being determined by supply and demand, are they?

INSTRUCTOR: Supply and demand could still be at work, even given what your uncle said. For example, the $220 could be the equilibrium price (determined by supply and demand) for the type of lamps your uncle is producing and selling. Look at it this way: If your uncle could sell the lamps for, say, $250 each, then he would have told you that he takes his cost (of $200) and adds on 25 percent ($50) to get "his price" of $250.

STUDENT: Is the point that what looks like *cost plus 10 percent* to me could really be supply and demand?

INSTRUCTOR: Yes, that's the point. But we can add something else to make the point stronger. Think of the housing market for a minute. Are the prices of houses determined by *cost plus 10 percent* or by supply and demand? Let's see if we can think through an example together. Suppose you buy a house for $400,000 in one year and then decide to sell it 10 years later. What price do you charge for the house? Do you charge the (market) equilibrium price for that house, or do you charge what you paid for the house ($400,000) plus 10 percent ($40,000), for a total of $440,000?

STUDENT: Oh, I think I see what you mean. You mean that if the equilibrium price for the house happened to be $650,000, I wouldn't charge only $440,000.

INSTRUCTOR: Exactly. In other words, the price determined by supply and demand would take precedence over the cost-plus-10-percent price. Now, going back to your uncle, we see that he might have just thought that he was charging a price of cost plus 10 percent because the equilibrium price for the good he produced and sold happened to be 10 percent higher than his cost. But, as stated before, if that equilibrium price had been 25 percent higher, your uncle would have told you that his price was determined by his taking his costs and adding 25 percent. The equilibrium price was determining the percentage that your uncle said he added to costs; he didn't just pick a percentage out of thin air.

Points to Remember

1. What looks like cost plus 10 percent (cost plus some markup) could instead be supply and demand at work.

2. Supply and demand are obviously determining prices at, say, an auction. A single good (say, a painting) is for sale, and numerous buyers bid on it. The bidding stops when only one buyer is left. At the price the last bidder bid, the quantity demanded (of the painting) equals the quantity supplied, and both equal 1. Even if you do not see supply and demand at work in nonauction settings, supply and demand are still at work determining prices.

CHAPTER SUMMARY

DEMAND

- The law of demand states that as the price of a good rises, the quantity demanded of it falls, and that as the price of a good falls, the quantity demanded of it rises, *ceteris paribus*. The law of demand holds that price and quantity demanded are inversely related.

- Quantity demanded is the total number of units of a good that buyers are willing and able to buy at a particular price.

- A (downward-sloping) demand curve is the graphical representation of the law of demand.

- Factors that can change demand and cause the demand curve to shift are income, preferences, the prices of related goods (substitutes and complements), the number of buyers, and expectations of future price.

- The only factor that can directly cause a change in the quantity demanded of a good is a change in the good's own price.

SUPPLY

- The law of supply states that as the price of a good rises, the quantity supplied of the good rises, and that as the price of a good falls, the quantity supplied of the good falls, *ceteris paribus*. The law of supply asserts that price and quantity supplied are directly related.

- The law of supply does not hold when there is no time to produce more units of a good during a given period or when goods cannot be produced at all over that period.

- An upward-sloping supply curve is the graphical representation of the law of supply. More generally, a supply curve (no matter how it slopes) represents the relationship between the price and quantity supplied.

- Factors that can change supply and cause the supply curve to shift are the prices of relevant resources, technology, the prices of other goods, expectations of future price, taxes and subsidies, and government restrictions.

- The only factor that can directly cause a change in the quantity supplied of a good is a change in the good's own price.

THE MARKET

- Demand and supply together establish the equilibrium price and equilibrium quantity.

- A surplus exists in a market if, at some price, the quantity supplied is greater than the quantity demanded. A shortage exists if, at some price, the quantity demanded is greater than the quantity supplied.

- Mutually beneficial trade between buyers and sellers drives the market to equilibrium.

CONSUMERS' SURPLUS, PRODUCERS' SURPLUS, AND TOTAL SURPLUS

- Consumers' surplus is the difference between the maximum buying price and the price paid by the buyer:

  Consumers' surplus = Maximum buying price − Price paid

- Producers' (or sellers') surplus is the difference between the price the seller receives and the minimum selling price:

  Producers' surplus = Price received − Minimum selling price

- The more consumers' surplus that buyers receive, the better off they are. The more producers' surplus that sellers receive, the better off they are. Total surplus is the sum of consumers' surplus and producers' surplus.

- Total surplus (the sum of consumers' surplus and producers' surplus) is maximized at equilibrium.

KEY TERMS AND CONCEPTS

Market	Normal Good	Supply Schedule	Disequilibrium
Demand	Inferior Good	Subsidy	Equilibrium
Law of Demand	Neutral Good	Surplus (Excess Supply)	Consumers' Surplus (*CS*)
Demand Schedule	Substitutes	Shortage (Excess Demand)	Producers' (Sellers') Surplus
Demand Curve	Complements	Equilibrium Price (Market-	(*PS*)
Law of Diminishing	Supply	Clearing Price)	Total Surplus (*TS*)
Marginal Utility	Law of Supply	Equilibrium Quantity	Spontaneous Order
Own Price	Upward-Sloping Supply Curve	Disequilibrium Price	

QUESTIONS AND PROBLEMS

1. What is wrong with the following statement? Demand refers to the willingness of buyers to purchase different quantities of a good at different prices during a specific period.

2. What is the difference between *demand* and *quantity demanded*?

3. True or false? As the price of oranges rises, the demand for oranges falls, *ceteris paribus*. Explain your answer.

4. "The price of a bushel of wheat, which was $3.00 last month, is $3.70 today. The demand curve for wheat must have shifted rightward between last month and today." Discuss.

5. Some goods are bought largely because they have "snob appeal." For example, the residents of Beverly Hills gain prestige by buying expensive items. In fact, they won't buy some items unless they are expensive. The law of demand, which holds that people buy more at lower prices than higher prices, obviously doesn't hold for the residents of Beverly Hills. The following rules apply in Beverly Hills: high prices, buy; low prices, don't buy. Discuss.

6. "The price of T-shirts keeps rising and rising, and people keep buying more and more. T-shirts must have an upward-sloping demand curve." Identify the error.

7. With respect to each of the following changes, identify whether the demand curve will shift rightward or leftward:

   a. An increase in income (the good under consideration is a normal good)
   b. A rise in the price of a substitute good (caused by a decline in supply)
   c. A rise in expected future price
   d. A fall in the number of buyers

8. What does a sale on shirts have to do with the law of demand (as applied to shirts)?

9. What is wrong with this statement: As the price of a good falls, the supply of that good falls, *ceteris paribus*.

10. In the previous chapter, you learned about the law of increasing opportunity costs. What does this law have to do with an upward-sloping supply curve?

11. How might the price of corn affect the supply of wheat?

12. What is the difference between supply and quantity supplied?

13. What is the difference between a movement factor and a shift factor?

14. Compare the ratings for television shows with prices for goods. How are ratings like prices? How are ratings different from prices? (*Hint:* How does rising demand for a particular television show manifest itself?)

15. At equilibrium in a market, the maximum price that buyers would be willing to pay for the good is equal to the minimum price that sellers need to receive before they are willing to sell the good. Do you agree or disagree with this statement? Explain your answer.

16. Must consumers' surplus equal producers' surplus at the equilibrium price? Explain your answer.

17. Many movie theaters charge a lower admission price for the first show on weekday afternoons than they do for a weeknight or weekend show. Explain why.

18. A Dell computer is a substitute for an HP® computer. What happens to the demand for HP computers and the quantity demanded of Dell computers as the price of a Dell falls (as a result of a change in supply)?

19. Describe how each of the following will affect the demand for personal computers:

   a. A rise in income (assuming that computers are a normal good)
   b. A lower expected price for computers
   c. Cheaper software
   d. Computers that are simpler to operate

20. Describe how each of the following will affect the supply of personal computers:

   a. A rise in wage rates
   b. An increase in the number of sellers of computers
   c. A tax placed on the production of computers
   d. A subsidy for the production of computers

21. The price of good X is higher in year 2 than in year 1 and people are buying more of good X in year 2 than year 1. Obviously, the law of demand does not hold. Do you agree or disagree? Explain your answer.

22. Use the law of diminishing marginal utility to explain why demand curves slope downward.

23. Explain how the market moves to equilibrium in terms of shortages and surpluses and in terms of maximum buying prices and minimum selling prices.

24. Identify what happens to equilibrium price and quantity in each of the following cases:

   a. Demand rises and supply is constant.
   b. Demand falls and supply is constant.
   c. Supply rises and demand is constant.
   d. Supply falls and demand is constant.
   e. Demand rises by the same amount that supply falls.
   f. Demand falls by the same amount that supply rises.

g. Demand falls less than supply rises.
h. Demand rises more than supply rises.
i. Demand rises less than supply rises.
j. Demand falls more than supply falls.
k. Demand falls less than supply falls.

25. Suppose the demand curve for a good is downward sloping and the supply curve is upward sloping. Now suppose demand rises. Will producers' surplus rise or fall? Explain your answers.

26. When speeding tickets were $100, usually 500 speeders were on the roads each month in a given city; when ticket prices were raised to $250, usually 215 speeders were on the roads in the city each month. Can you find any economics in this observation?

27. On most days, more people want to see the taping of *The Tonight Show Starring Jimmy Fallon* (in New York City) than there are seats in the taping studio. What might explain this shortage?

28. What does it mean to say that "the market" feeds Cleveland, Austin, Atlanta, or Indianapolis?

WORKING WITH NUMBERS AND GRAPHS

1. Suppose the price is $10, the quantity supplied is 50 units, and the quantity demanded is 100 units. For every $1 rise in price, the quantity supplied rises by 5 units and the quantity demanded falls by 5 units. What is the equilibrium price and quantity?

2. Using numbers, explain how a market demand curve is derived from two individual demand curves.

3. Draw a diagram that shows a larger increase in demand than the decrease in supply.

4. Draw a diagram that shows a smaller increase in supply than the increase in demand.

5. At equilibrium in the following figure, what area(s) represent consumers' surplus? producers' surplus?

6. At what quantity in the preceding figure is the maximum buying price equal to the minimum selling price?

7. In the figure that follows, can the movement from point 1 to point 2 be explained by a combination of an increase in the price of a substitute and a decrease in the price of nonlabor resources? Explain your answer.

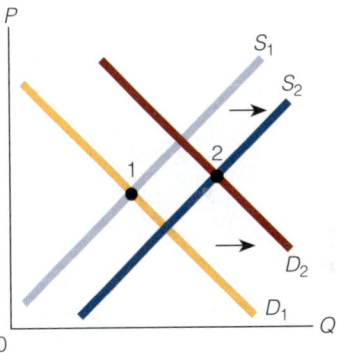

8. Suppose the demand curve is downward sloping, the supply curve is upward sloping, and the equilibrium quantity is 50 units. Show on a graph that the difference between the maximum buying price and minimum selling price is greater at 25 units than at 33 units.

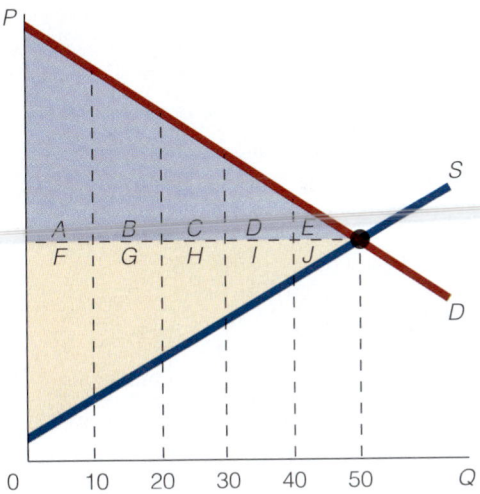

9. Fill in the blanks in the following table.

This Happens ...	Does equilibrium price rise, fall, or remain unchanged?	Does equilibrium quantity rise, fall, or remain unchanged?
Demand rises and supply remains constant	A	B
Supply declines more than demand rises	C	D
Demand rises more than supply rises	E	F
Demand rises by the same amount as supply rises	G	H
Supply falls and demand remains constant	I	J
Demand falls more than supply falls	K	L

PRICES: FREE, CONTROLLED, AND RELATIVE

INTRODUCTION

In the last chapter, we discussed supply and demand. Mainly, we saw how supply and demand work together to determine prices. In this chapter, we discuss prices at greater length. First, we discuss two of the key "jobs" that price performs: (1) rationing resources and goods and (2) transmitting information. Second, we discuss government controls that can be imposed on prices. Specifically, we discuss both price ceilings and price floors. Third, we discuss two types of price: absolute (or money) price and relative price.

4-1 PRICE

To most people, price is a number with a dollar sign in front of it, such as $10. But price is much more. Price performs two major jobs: It acts (1) as a rationing device and (2) as a transmitter of information.

4-1a Price as a Rationing Device

In Chapter 1, we said that wants (for goods) are unlimited and resources are limited, so scarcity exists. As a result of scarcity, a rationing device is needed to determine who gets what of the available limited resources and goods. (Because resources are limited, goods are also, given that the production of goods requires resources.) Price serves as that rationing device. It rations resources to the producers who pay the price for the resources. It rations goods to those buyers who pay the price for the goods. The process is as simple as this: Pay the price, and the resources or goods are yours. Don't pay the price, and they aren't.

Is dollar price a fair rationing device? Doesn't it discriminate against the poor? After all, the poor have fewer dollars than the rich, so the rich can get more of what they want than can the poor. True, dollar price does discriminate against the poor. But then, as economists know, every rationing device discriminates against someone. To illustrate, suppose for some reason that tomorrow dollar price could not be used as a rationing device. Some rationing device would still be necessary, because scarcity would still exist. How would we ration gas at the gasoline station, food in the grocery store, or tickets for the Super Bowl? Let's consider some alternatives to dollar price as a rationing device.

Suppose *first come, first served* is the rationing device. For example, suppose only 40,000 Super Bowl tickets are available. If you are one of the first 40,000 in line for a Super Bowl ticket, you get a ticket. If you are person number 40,001 in line, you don't. Such a method discriminates against those who can't get in line quickly enough. What about slow walkers or people with disabilities? What about people without cars who can't drive to where the tickets are distributed?

Or suppose *brute force* is the rationing device. For example, of the 40,000 Super Bowl tickets, you get one as long as you can take it away from someone else. Against whom does this rationing method discriminate? Obviously, it discriminates against the weak and nonaggressive.

Or suppose *beauty* is the rationing device. The more beautiful you are, the better your chances are of getting a Super Bowl ticket. Again, the rationing device discriminates against someone.

These and many other alternatives to dollar price could be used as rationing devices. However, each discriminates against someone, and none is clearly superior to dollar price.

In addition, if first come, first served, brute force, beauty, or another alternative to dollar price is the rationing device, what incentive would the producer of a good have to produce the good? With dollar price as a rationing device, a person produces computers and sells them for money. He then takes the money and buys what he wants. But if the rationing device were, say, brute force, he would not have an incentive to produce. Why produce anything when someone will end up taking it away from you? In short, in a world where dollar price isn't the rationing device, people are likely to produce much less than in a world where dollar price is the rationing device.

4-1b Price as a Transmitter of Information

Rationing isn't the only job that price performs. Price also *transmits information*. That may sound odd. Consider the following story: On Saturday, Noelle walks into a local grocery store and purchases a half gallon of orange juice for $2.50. On Sunday, unknown to her, a cold spell hits Florida and wipes out half the orange crop. The cold spell ends up shifting the supply curve of oranges leftward, which drives up the price of oranges. Because oranges are a resource in the production of orange juice, the supply curve of orange juice shifts leftward and the price of orange juice rises.

Noelle returns to the grocery store in a week. She notices that the half gallon of orange juice she bought last week for $2.50 has now risen to $3.50. Because Noelle has a downward-sloping demand curve for orange juice, she ends up buying less orange juice. She buys only a quart of orange juice instead of a half gallon.

What role did price play in Noelle's decision to cut back on the consumption of orange juice? It played a major role. If the price hadn't risen, Noelle probably wouldn't have reduced her purchases and consumption of orange juice. Noelle reacted to the price rise, but what the price rise was "saying"—if we had ears to hear it—is this: "The relative scarcity of a good has risen because of a cold spell in Florida. In other words, the gap between people's wants for orange juice and the amount of orange juice available to satisfy those wants has widened."

Now, we know that Noelle might not have "heard" price saying this. But if you understand economics, that is just what price *is* saying. In other words, price is a transmitter of information that often relates to the relative scarcity of a good. A market system, oddly enough, is powerful enough to have people respond in appropriate ways to the information that price is transmitting, even if the people do not fully hear or understand that information. In the case of Noelle, her cutting back on the consumption of orange juice conserves orange juice in the face of an act of nature that ended up making orange juice relatively scarcer.

Think of how this reaction is similar to what people who tell you to conserve water want. For example, in California in the summer of 2015, public messages on television asked people to cut back on their consumption of water because water in the state was in short supply. The appropriate behavior to take was to cut back on the consumption of water, because it had become relatively scarcer. You were being civic minded if you did so. Well, movements in price can get you to be civic minded too. When the price of orange juice rises because of a cold spell in Florida, you might automatically cut back on your consumption, thus conserving on the consumption of a good that has become relatively scarcer.

SELF-TEST

(Answers to Self-Test questions are in Answers to Self-Test Questions at the back of the book.)

1. Why is there a need for a rationing device, whether it is price or something else?

2. If price is not the rationing device used, then individuals won't have as sharp an incentive to produce. Explain.

3. What kind of information does price often transmit?

4-2 PRICE CONTROLS

A rationing device—such as dollar price—is needed because scarcity exists. But price is not always allowed to be a rationing device. Sometimes price is controlled. There are two types of price controls: price ceilings and price floors. In the discussion of price controls, the word "price" is used in the generic sense. It refers to the price of an apple, for example, the price of labor (a wage), the price of credit (the interest rate), and so on.

4-2a Price Ceiling

Definition and Effects A **price ceiling** is a government-mandated maximum price above which legal trades cannot be made. For example, suppose the government mandates that the maximum price at which good X can be bought and sold is $8. Therefore, $8 is a price ceiling. If $8 is below the equilibrium price of good X, as in Exhibit 1, any or all of the following effects may arise:[1] shortages, fewer exchanges, nonprice-rationing devices, buying and selling at prohibited prices, and tie-in sales.

Price Ceiling
A government-mandated maximum price above which legal trades cannot be made.

---

[1]. If the price ceiling is above the equilibrium price (e.g., $8 is the price ceiling and $4 is the equilibrium price), the ceiling has no effect. Usually, however, a price ceiling is below the equilibrium price.

EXHIBIT 1

A Price Ceiling

The price ceiling is $8 and the equilibrium price is $12. At $12, quantity demanded = quantity supplied. At $8, quantity demanded > quantity supplied. (Recall that price, on the vertical axis, always represents price per unit. Quantity, on the horizontal axis, always holds for a specific period.)

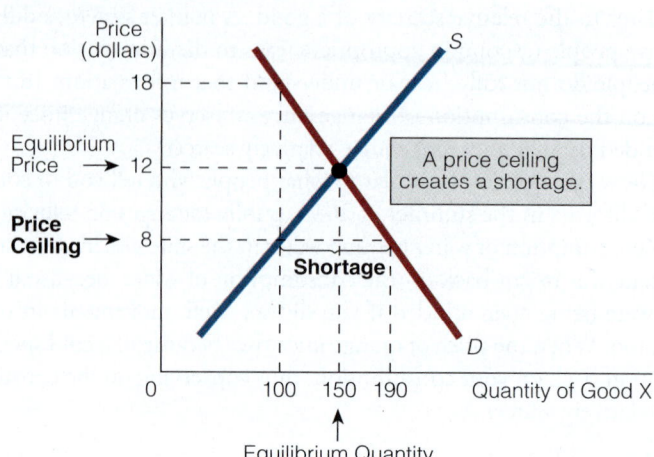

Shortages At the $12 equilibrium price in Exhibit 1, the quantity demanded of good X (150) is equal to the quantity supplied (150). At the $8 price ceiling, a shortage exists: The quantity demanded (190) is greater than the quantity supplied (100). When a shortage exists, price and output tend to rise to equilibrium. But when a price ceiling exists, they cannot rise to equilibrium because it is unlawful to trade at the equilibrium price.

Fewer Exchanges At the equilibrium price of $12 in Exhibit 1, 150 units of good X are bought and sold. At the price ceiling of $8, 100 units of good X are bought and sold. (Buyers would prefer to buy 190 units, but only 100 are supplied.) We conclude that price ceilings cause fewer exchanges to be made.

Notice in Exhibit 1 that the demand curve is above the supply curve for all quantities less than 150 units. (At 150 units, the demand curve and the supply curve intersect and thus share the same point in the two-dimensional space.) Thus, the maximum buying price is greater than the minimum selling price for all units less than 150. In particular, the maximum buying price is greater than the minimum selling price for units 101–149. For example, buyers might be willing to pay $17 for the 110th unit, and sellers might be willing to sell the 110th unit for $10. But no unit after the 100th unit (not the 110th unit, not the 114th unit, not the 130th unit) will be produced and sold because of the price ceiling. In short, the price ceiling prevents mutually advantageous trades from being realized.

Nonprice-Rationing Devices If the equilibrium price of $12 fully rations good X before the price ceiling is imposed, then a lower price of $8 only partly rations this good. In short, price ceilings prevent price from rising to the level sufficient to ration goods fully. But if price is responsible for only part of the rationing, what accounts for the rest?

The answer is that some other (nonprice) rationing device, such as first come, first served. In Exhibit 1, 100 units of good X will be sold at $8, although buyers are willing to buy 190 units at this price. What happens? Possibly, good X will be sold on a first-come, first-served basis for $8 per unit. In other words, to buy good X, a person must not only pay $8 per unit but also be one of the first people in line.

Buying and Selling at a Prohibited Price Buyers and sellers may regularly circumvent a price ceiling by making their exchanges under the table. For example, some buyers may offer some sellers more than $8 per unit for good *X*. No doubt, some sellers will accept the offers. But why would some buyers offer more than $8 per unit when they can buy good *X* for $8? Because not all buyers can buy the amount of good *X* they want at $8. As Exhibit 1 shows, there is a shortage. Buyers are willing to buy 190 units at $8, but sellers are willing to sell only 100 units. In short, 90 fewer units will be sold than buyers would like to buy. Some buyers will go unsatisfied. How, then, does any one buyer make it more likely that sellers will sell to him or her instead of to someone else? The answer is by offering to pay a higher price. However, because it is illegal to pay a higher price, the transaction must be made under the table.

Tie-In Sales In Exhibit 1, the maximum price buyers would be willing and able to pay per unit for 100 units of good *X* is $18. (This is the price on the demand curve at a quantity of 100 units.) The maximum legal price, however, is $8. The difference between the two prices often prompts a **tie-in sale**, a sale whereby one good can be purchased only if another good is also purchased. For example, if Ralph's Gas Station sells gasoline to customers only if they buy a car wash, the two goods are linked in a tie-in sale.

> **Tie-in Sale**
> A sale whereby one good can be purchased only if another good is also purchased.

Suppose that the sellers of good *X* in Exhibit 1 also sell good *Y*. Then they might offer to sell buyers good *X* at $8 only if the buyers agree to buy good *Y* at, say, $10. We choose $10 as the price for good Y because $10 is the difference between the maximum per-unit price buyers are willing and able to pay for 100 units of good *X* ($18) and the maximum legal price ($8).

In New York City and other communities with rent-control laws, tie-in sales sometimes result from rent ceilings on apartments. Occasionally, to rent an apartment, an individual must agree to buy the furniture in the apartment.

Buyers and Higher and Lower Prices Do buyers prefer lower to higher prices? "Of course," you might say, "buyers prefer lower prices to higher prices. What buyer would want to pay a higher price for anything?" And yet, even though price ceilings are often lower than equilibrium prices, does it follow that buyers prefer price ceilings to equilibrium prices? Not necessarily. Price ceilings have effects that equilibrium prices do not: shortages, the use of first come, first served as a rationing device, tie-in sales, and so on. A buyer could prefer to pay a higher price (an equilibrium price) than pay a lower price and have to deal with the effects of a price ceiling. All we can say for certain is that buyers prefer lower prices to higher prices, *ceteris paribus*. As in many cases, the *ceteris paribus* condition makes all the difference.

Price Ceilings and False Information Let's go back to the orange juice example in the first section of this chapter. In that example, a cold spell destroys part of the orange crop, leading to a higher price for oranges and orange juice. The market price of orange juice then rises from $2.50 to $3.50 a half gallon.

Now let's change things. Suppose that, instead of letting the new, lower supply of orange juice and demand for orange juice determine the market price of orange juice at $3.50 a half gallon, government imposes a price ceiling on orange juice at $2.50 a half gallon. Think about what the price ceiling does to prevent price from transmitting information. Specifically, the price ceiling prevents the correct information about the increased relative scarcity of orange juice (due to the cold spell) from getting through to consumers. It's as if price is a radio signal and the price ceiling jams the signal. Because of the jammed price signal, consumers mistakenly believe that nothing has changed. As far as they are concerned, they can continue buying orange juice at the same rate of consumption they did earlier. But, of course, they can't: There are fewer oranges and less orange juice in the world. One way or another, some people are going to have to curtail their consumption of orange juice.

The lesson is simple: Price ceilings (that are below the equilibrium price) distort the flow of accurate information to buyers. Buyers get a false view of reality; they then base their buying behavior on incorrect information. Problems follow, and the unintended, unexpected, and undesirable effects of price ceilings soon occur.

THINKING LIKE AN ECONOMIST

Look for the Unintended Effects Economists think in terms of unintended effects. For example, a price ceiling policy intended to lower prices for the poor may cause shortages, the use of nonprice rationing devices, illegal market transactions, and tie-in sales. When we consider both the price ceiling and its effects, whether the poor have been helped is not so clear. The economist knows that wanting to do good (for others) is not sufficient: Knowing how to do good is important too.

ECONOMICS 24/7

A Price Ceiling in the Kidney Market

Just as some people want to buy houses, computers, and books, others want to buy kidneys. These people have kidney failure, and they will either die without a new kidney or have to endure years of costly and painful dialysis. This demand for kidneys is shown as D_K in Exhibit 2, and the supply of kidneys is shown as S_K.

Notice that, at a $0 price, the quantity supplied of kidneys is 350. These kidneys are from people who donate their kidneys to others, asking nothing in return. They may donate upon their death,

or they may donate one of their two kidneys while living. We have drawn the supply curve as upward sloping because we assume that some people who today are unwilling to donate a kidney for $0 might be willing to do so for some positive dollar amount. Specifically, we assume that, as the price of a kidney rises, the quantity supplied of kidneys also will rise.

If there were a free market in kidneys, the price of a kidney would be P_1 in Exhibit 2. At this price, 1,000 kidneys would be purchased and sold; that is, 1,000 kidney transplants would occur.

EXHIBIT 2

The Market for Kidneys

We have identified the demand for kidneys as D_K and the supply of kidneys as S_K. Given the demand for and supply of kidneys, the equilibrium price of a kidney is P_1. It does not follow, though, that simply because there is an equilibrium price, people will be allowed to trade at that price. Today, it is unlawful to buy and sell kidneys at *any* positive price. In short, there is a price ceiling in the kidney market, and the ceiling is $0. At the price ceiling, there are at least four effects: a shortage of kidneys, a nonprice-rationing device for kidneys (first come, first served), fewer kidney transplants (than there would be at P_1), and illegal purchases and sales of kidneys.

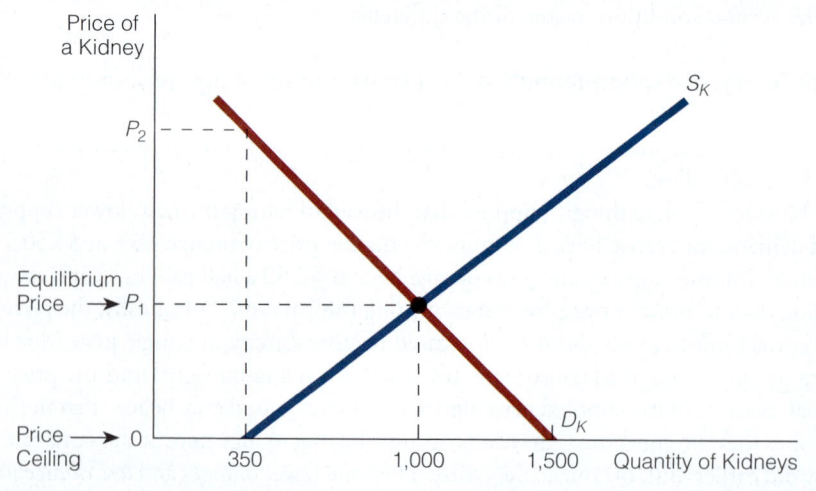

Today, there is no free market in kidneys. Buying or selling kidneys is illegal at any dollar amount. In essence, then, there is a price ceiling in the kidney market, and the ceiling is set at $0. What is the effect of the ceiling?

If the demand curve for kidneys and the supply curve of kidneys intersected at $0, there would be neither a surplus nor a shortage of kidneys. But there is evidence that the demand and supply curves do not intersect at $0; they look more like the curves shown in Exhibit 2. In other words, there is a shortage of kidneys at $0: The quantity supplied of kidneys is 350, and the quantity demanded is 1,500.

(Although these are not the actual numbers of kidneys demanded and supplied at $0, they are representative of the current situation in the kidney market.)

This chapter has described the possible effects of a price ceiling set below the equilibrium price: shortages, nonprice-rationing devices, fewer exchanges, tie-in sales, and buying and selling at prohibited prices (in other words, illegal trades). Are any of these effects actually occurring in the kidney market?

First, there is evidence of a shortage. In almost every country in the world, more people on national lists want a kidney than there are kidneys available. Some of these people die waiting for a transplant.

Second, as just intimated, the nonprice-rationing device used in the kidney market is (largely) first come, first served. A person who wants a kidney registers on a national waiting list. How long people wait is a function of how far down the list their names appear.

Third, there are fewer exchanges, so not everyone who needs a kidney gets one. With a price ceiling of $0, only 350 kidneys are supplied. All these kidneys are from people who freely donate their kidneys. If P_1 were permitted, some people who are unwilling to supply a kidney (at $0) would be willing to do so. In short, monetary payment would provide the incentive for some people to supply a kidney. At P_1, 1,000 kidneys are demanded and supplied, so more people would get kidney transplants when the price of a kidney is P_1 (1,000 people in all) than when the price of a kidney is $0 (350 people). More transplants, of course, means that fewer people die waiting for a kidney.

Fourth, kidneys are bought and sold at prohibited prices. People buy and sell kidneys today; they just do so illegally. People are reported to have paid between $25,000 and $200,000 for a kidney.

Some argue that a free market in kidneys would be wrong. Such a system would place the poor at a disadvantage. Think of it: A rich person who needed a kidney could buy one, but a poor person could not. The rich person would get a second chance at life, whereas the poor person would not. No one enjoys contemplating this stark reality.

But consider another stark reality. If it is unlawful to pay someone for a kidney, fewer kidneys will be forthcoming. In other words, the quantity supplied of kidneys is less at $0 than at, say, $20,000. Fewer kidneys supplied means fewer kidney transplants. And fewer kidney transplants means that more people will die from kidney failure.

ECONOMICS 24/7

1973 and 1979

In 1973, there were gas lines in the United States. Drivers in their cars waited in long lines to buy gas. Sometimes they waited a couple of hours or more. In some states, a person couldn't buy gas on just any day of the week. Those who had a license plate number that ended with an odd number (such as TBN-347) could buy gas on odd-numbered days of the month, while those who had a license plate number that ended with an even number (such as BNR-874) could buy gas on even-numbered days of the month. In 1979, it was much the same: long lines of drivers waiting to buy gas.

In 1965, there were no long lines of drivers waiting to buy gas, nor was this the case in, say, 1987, 1995, or 2016. What was so different about 1973 and 1979? In those two years, the federal government imposed price ceilings on gasoline. The price ceilings made all the difference, because, as we have pointed out in this chapter, price ceilings lead to shortages and shortages lead to rationing devices other than only money price being used to ration goods. One common nonprice-rationing device is first come, first served, which leads to long lines.

As you might expect, sometimes those long lines produced certain problems, as when someone tried to cut in front of drivers waiting in line. In one case, an attendant at the gas station tried to prevent someone from cutting into line and was almost run over by the driver of the car. In many cases, fights broke out among drivers waiting in line.

McDonald's ran a television ad in 1979 based on gas lines. In fact, the ad was titled "Gas Line." The scene is a gas station with a long line of drivers in cars waiting to buy gas. One man says to another right behind him in line, "Excuse me, would you watch my place in line, I'm just going to run over to McDonald's." The second man responds, "Yeah," and then asks the first man if he could bring him back a Big Mac. On his way to McDonald's, other drivers in cars ask for a variety of McDonald's products: fries, a Coke, a strawberry shake, and so on. The last scene shows everyone eating their McDonald's products and having a good time but still waiting in the gas line. If you would like to see the actual ad, it can be found on YouTube at http://www.youtube.com/watch?v=tjXhwevOVAE.

AP Images

Hear What and How the Economist Thinks . . .
About Price Ceilings and the Value of Money

The economist hears on a radio news show:

The government has today imposed a price ceiling on gasoline purchased at the pump. As one member of Congress said, "It was done to keep gasoline prices within the reach of the poor and the middle-class. It was also done to make our money more valuable." When asked how a price ceiling made "our money more valuable" the Congressman said, "At $4 a gallon of gas, $1 buys 1/4 gallon of gas, but at a price ceiling of $3 a gallon of gas, $1 buys 1/3 gallon of gas. In other words, with a $3 price ceiling, a dollar buys more gas than it did at $4 a gallon."

Hear what and how the economist thinks:

There is no doubt that if the price of gas is $4 a gallon, $1 buys 1/4 gallon of gas and at $3 a gallon, $1 buys 1/3 gallon of gas. That much the Congressman has correct. But what the Congressman doesn't understand is that there is a difference between the situation in which $3 is the equilibrium price of gas and when it is a price ceiling (below equilibrium price) and the equilibrium price of gas is $4.

When $3 is the equilibrium price, money fully rations gasoline. There are no other rationing devices involved—such as first-come, first-served, and so on. But when the equilibrium price is $4 and $3 is a price ceiling (that is, when it is a legislated below-equilibrium price), money does not fully ration gasoline. At the $3 price ceiling, there is now going to be a shortage of gasoline in the gasoline market, and some rationing device along with money is going to emerge to ration gasoline. Usually, it is first-come, first-served. So, people are going to have to line up in gas lines to buy gas when the price ceiling is operational. Because of the shortage, some people who want to buy gas will be unable to buy gas.

The Congressman said that the price ceiling made money more valuable, but really how valuable is money if it doesn't get you what you want to buy? How valuable is money to the person at the end of the gas line who is willing to pay $3 for the gallon of gas, but can't use his money to buy the gasoline because with the shortage of gas caused by the price ceiling, some people are going to have to do without gas.

What the Congressman, and so many others often forget, is that it matters how the $3 price of gasoline comes to exist. If it is the result of market forces, if it is the result of supply and demand equilibrating

4-2b Price Floor: Definition and Effects

A **price floor** is a government-mandated minimum price below which legal trades cannot be made. For example, suppose the government mandates that the minimum price at which good X can be sold is $20. Then the $20 minimum is a price floor. (See Exhibit 3.)

Effects of a Price Floor If the price floor is above the equilibrium price, the following two effects arise:[2] surpluses and fewer exchanges.

Surpluses At the $15 equilibrium price in Exhibit 3, the quantity demanded of good X (130) is equal to the quantity supplied (130). At the $20 price floor, a surplus exists.

The quantity supplied (180) is greater than the quantity demanded (90). Usually, a surplus is temporary. When a surplus exists, price and output tend to fall to equilibrium. But when a price floor exists, they cannot fall to equilibrium because it is unlawful to trade at the equilibrium price.

Fewer Exchanges At the equilibrium price in Exhibit 3, 130 units of good X are bought and sold. At the price floor, 90 units are bought and sold. (Sellers want to sell 180 units, but buyers buy only 90.) Thus, price floors cause fewer exchanges to be made.

Price Floor
A government-mandated minimum price below which legal trades cannot be made.

EXHIBIT 3

A Price Floor

The price floor is $20 and the equilibrium price is $15. At $15, quantity demanded = quantity supplied. At $20, quantity supplied > quantity demanded.

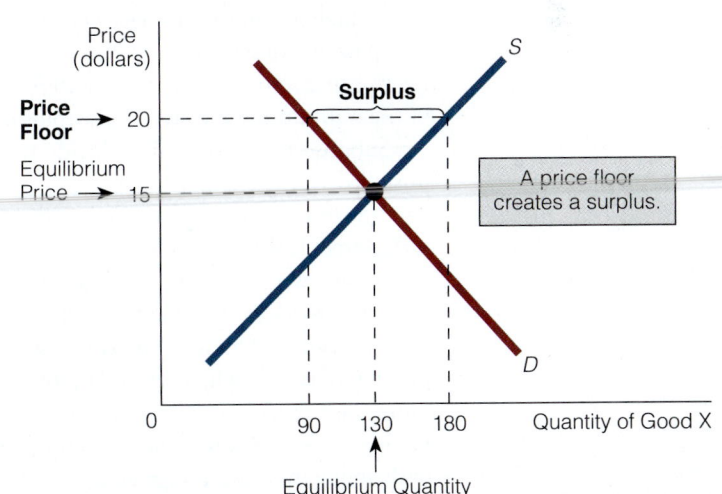

A price floor creates a surplus.

---

[2] If the price floor is below the equilibrium price (e.g., $20 is the price floor and $25 is the equilibrium price), then the price floor has no effects. Usually, however, a price floor is above the equilibrium price.

EXHIBIT 4

Effects of the Minimum Wage

At a minimum wage of W_M an hour, there is a surplus of workers and fewer workers are employed than would be employed at the equilibrium wage W_E.

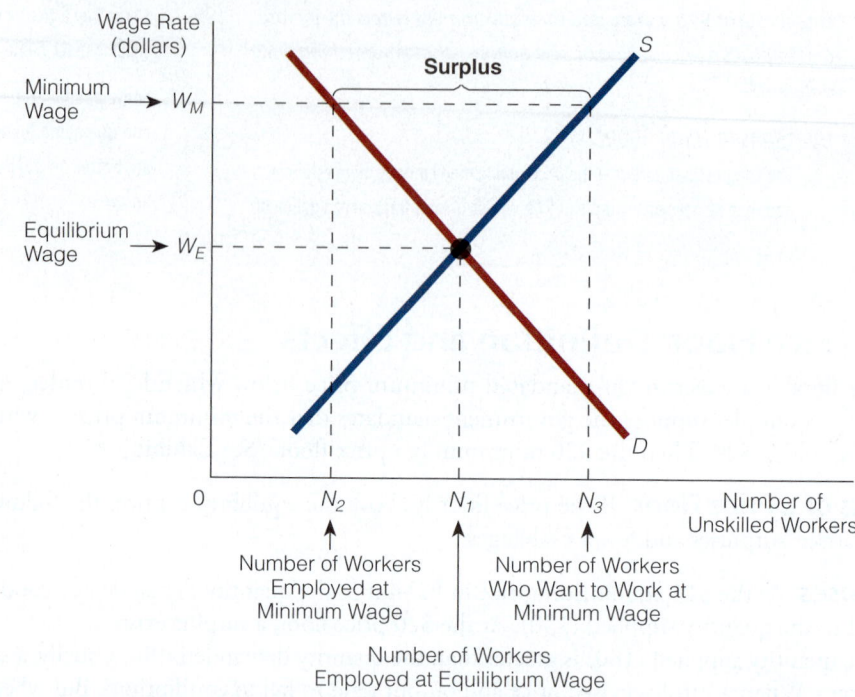

The Minimum Wage If a price floor is a legislated minimum price below which trades cannot legally be made, then the *minimum wage* is a price floor—a government-mandated minimum price for labor. It affects the market for unskilled labor. In Exhibit 4, we assume that the minimum wage is W_M and the equilibrium wage is W_E. At the equilibrium wage, N_1 workers are employed. At the higher minimum wage, N_3 workers want to work but only N_2 actually do work. There is a surplus of workers equal to $N_3 - N_2$ in this unskilled labor market. In addition, fewer workers are working at the minimum wage (N_2) than at the equilibrium wage (N_1). Overall, the effects of the minimum wage are (1) a surplus of unskilled workers and (2) fewer workers employed.

Suppose two economists decide to test the theory that as the minimum wage rises some unskilled workers will lose their jobs. They look at the number of unskilled workers before and after the minimum wage is raised, and surprisingly they find that the number of unskilled workers is the same. Is this sufficient evidence to conclude that an increase in the minimum wage does not cause some workers to lose their jobs?

The answer to that question depends on whether the economists have adequately tested their theory. Instead of focusing on the number of people who lose their jobs, suppose they look at the number of people who keep their jobs but have their hours reduced as a result of the higher minimum wage. Let's look at an example. Suppose a local hardware store currently employs David and Francesca to work after school cleaning up and stocking shelves. The owner of the store pays each of them the minimum wage of, say, $7.25 an hour. Then the minimum wage is raised to $10.75 an hour. Will either David or Francesca lose their jobs as a result? Not necessarily. Instead, the owner of the store could reduce the number of hours he employs the two workers. For example, instead of having each of them work 20 hours a week, he might ask each to work only 14 hours a week.

Now let's consider our original question again: Has the higher minimum wage eliminated jobs? In a way, no. It has, however, reduced the number of hours a person works in a job. (Of course, if we define a job as including both a particular task and a certain number of hours taken to complete that task, then the minimum wage increase has eliminated "part" of the job.) This discussion argues for changing the label on the horizontal axis in Exhibit 4 from "Number of Unskilled Workers" to "Number of Unskilled Labor Hours."

THINKING LIKE AN ECONOMIST

Direction Versus Magnitude In economics, some questions relate to direction and some to magnitude. For example, suppose someone asks, "If the demand for labor is downward sloping and the labor market is competitive, how will a minimum wage that is above the equilibrium wage affect employment?" This person is asking a question that relates to the direction of the change in employment. Usually, these types of questions can be answered by applying a theory. Applying the theory of demand, an economist might say, "At higher wages, the quantity demanded of labor, or the employment level, will be lower than at lower wages." The word "lower" speaks to the *directional change* in employment.

Now suppose someone asks, "How much will employment decline?" This question relates to *magnitude*. Usually, questions that deal with magnitude can be answered only through some kind of empirical (data collection and analysis) work. In other words, we would have to collect employment figures at the equilibrium wage and at the minimum wage and then find the difference.

 **Does it Matter to You . . .**
If the Demand Curve for Unskilled Labor Is Steep or Not?

Suppose the U.S. Congress is considering raising the federal minimum wage by $5. Some people say that the $5 higher minimum wage will lead to a higher unemployment rate among unskilled laborers in the country. Others argue that there will be almost no increase in the unemployment rate among the unskilled. You are not quite sure what to think. Whether a $5 raise in the federal minimum wage will lead to a higher unemployment or not depends upon how steep the demand curve for unskilled labor is.

Take a look at the two demand curves for unskilled labor in Exhibit 5. Demand curve D_1 is steeper than demand curve D_2. Now suppose the supply of unskilled labor intersects both demand curves at point 1 and the equilibrium wage rate—no matter which demand curve represents the buying side of the labor market—is $10. At this wage rate,

Jacob Lund/Shutterstock.com

we see that the number of people who will have jobs in this market is N_1. Let's also assume that $10 is the current minimum wage.

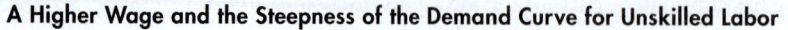

A Higher Wage and the Steepness of the Demand Curve for Unskilled Labor

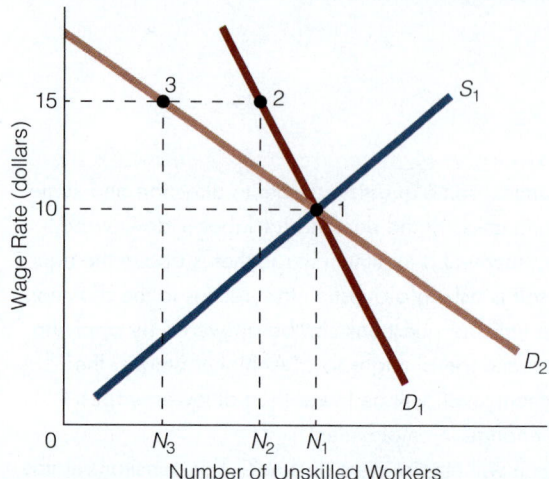

If the U.S. Congress raises the minimum wage by $5, the new minimum wage becomes $15. With either D_1 or D_2, there is going to be a cutback in the number of people with jobs, but with D_1 the cutback is smaller (N_1 to N_2) than with D_2 (N_1 to N_3). In other words, the steeper the demand curve for unskilled labor, the smaller the cutback in the number of people with jobs.

Put yourself in the position of an unskilled worker. Would the higher minimum wage matter to you? If you keep your job at the higher minimum wage, you are now earning $5 more an hour than you did before. But you may not keep your job at the higher minimum wage. After all, some people are not going to have the job at $15 an hour that they had at $10 an hour. Obviously, if you are one of these people, the minimum wage has hurt you by pricing you out of the unskilled labor market.

But let's not leave it there. Let's think of how the higher minimum wage, and the degree of steepness of the demand curve for unskilled labor, can affect what you see in a restaurant you regularly attend. Perhaps you have noticed that in some restaurants today there are tablets at restaurant tables that one can use to order food. That is, instead of having a server come

to a table and take your order, it is now possible in some food establishments to sit down at a table and place your order via a tablet. Just tap on the items you want to purchase—a hamburger with lettuce, tomato, and mayonnaise, with a small order of fries, and a large soft drink. Once your order is submitted, it takes just a short while before someone delivers your order to your table.

With tablets for ordering, the restaurant does not need to hire as many servers. With tablets, possibly three servers can now do what it took six servers to do previously. What does this have to do with the minimum wage and the degree of steepness of the demand curve for unskilled labor? Quite a bit. The higher the minimum wage above the equilibrium wage, and the less steep the demand curve for labor, the greater the cutback in the number of servers (who are often paid the minimum wage) a restaurant is likely to hire, or keep employed, and the greater the likelihood the restaurant will "employ" tablets to replace the servers. In the end, an uptick in the minimum wage, the steepness of the demand curve for unskilled labor, and tablets at your restaurant table are linked.

Price Floors, Changes in Consumers' and Producers' Surplus, and Deadweight Losses

We now turn to a discussion of consumers' surplus, producers' surplus, and price floors in terms of a specific example: a price floor on an agricultural foodstuff.

Exhibit 6 shows the demand for and supply of an agricultural foodstuff (corn, wheat, soybeans, etc.). If the market is allowed to move to equilibrium, the equilibrium price will be P_1 and the equilibrium quantity will be Q_1. Consumers' surplus will equal the area under the demand curve and above the equilibrium price: areas $1 + 2 + 3$. Producers' surplus will equal the area under the equilibrium price and above the supply curve: areas $4 + 5$. Total surplus, of course, is the sum of consumers' surplus and producers' surplus: areas $1 + 2 + 3 + 4 + 5$.

EXHIBIT 6

Agricultural Price Floors

The demand for and supply of an agricultural foodstuff are shown in this exhibit. The equilibrium price is P_1; consumers' surplus (CS) is areas $1 + 2 + 3$; producers' surplus is areas $4 + 5$. A price floor of P_F effectively transfers some of the consumers' surplus to producers in the form of a gain in producers' surplus. Specifically, at P_F, consumers' surplus is area 1 and producers' surplus is areas $2 + 4$. Consumers are net losers because consumers' surplus has decreased by areas $2 + 3$. Producers are net gainers because producers' surplus has increased from areas $4 + 5$ to areas $2 + 4$ and area 2 is larger than area 5. Overall, the economic pie of $CS + PS$ has decreased from areas $1 + 2 + 3 + 4 + 5$ to areas $1 + 2 + 4$.

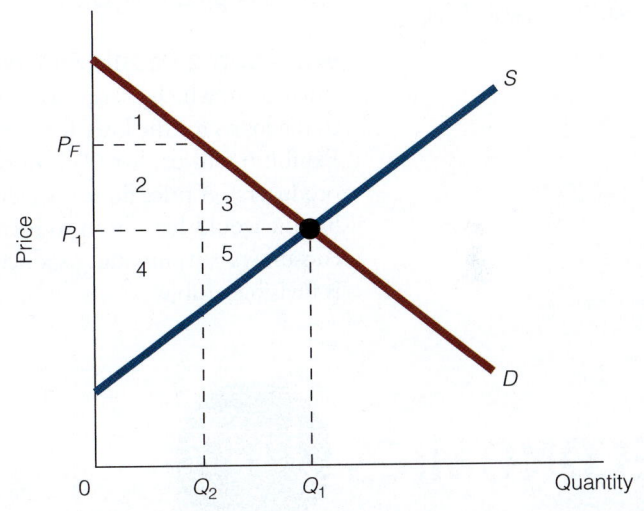

Now, suppose that the suppliers of the foodstuff argue for (and receive) a price floor P_F. At this higher price, consumers do not buy as much as they once did. They now buy Q_2, whereas they used to buy Q_1. In addition, consumers' surplus is now only area 1, and producers' surplus is areas $2 + 4$.

Obviously, consumers have been hurt by the increased (government-mandated) price P_F; specifically, they have lost consumers' surplus equal to areas $2 + 3$.

How have suppliers fared? Whereas their producers' surplus was equal to areas $4 + 5$ at P_1, it is now equal to areas $2 + 4$. (Area 2, which used to be part of consumers' surplus, has been transferred to producers and is now part of producers' surplus.) Whether producers are better off depends on whether area 2 (what they gain from P_F) is larger than area 5 (what they lose from P_F). Visually, we can tell that area 2 is larger than area 5, so producers are better off.

What is the overall effect of the price floor? Have producers gained more than consumers have lost, or have consumers lost more than producers have gained? To answer this question, we note that consumers lose areas 2 and 3 in consumers' surplus and producers gain area 2 in producers' surplus and lose area 5 in producers' surplus. So, the gains and losses are as follows:

Losses to consumers:	areas $2 + 3$
Gains to producers:	area 2
Losses to producers:	area 5

Part of the loss to consumers is offset by the gain to producers (area 2), so net losses amount to areas 3 + 5. In other words, the total surplus—the sum of consumers' surplus and producers' surplus—is lower than it was. Whereas it used to be areas 1 + 2 + 3 + 4 + 5, it now is areas 1 + 2 + 4. The total surplus lost is in areas 3 + 5. In short, (1) consumers lose, (2) producers gain, and (3) society (which is the sum of consumers and producers) loses.

You can think of this example in terms of a pie. Initially, the pie was made up of areas 1 + 2 + 3 + 4 + 5. This rather large pie registered all the gains of consumers and producers. After the price floor P_F was imposed, the pie shrank to areas 1 + 2 + 4; in other words, the pie was smaller by areas 3 + 5.

A loss in total surplus—in our example, areas 3 + 5—is sometimes called a **deadweight loss**. This is the loss to society of not producing the competitive, or supply-and-demand-determined, level of output. In terms of Exhibit 6, it is the loss to society of producing Q_2 instead of producing Q_1.

Deadweight Loss
The loss to society of not producing the competitive, or supply-and-demand-determined, level of output.

What Some People Get Wrong   In sum, some persons argue that a price floor creates a situation in which (1) someone wins and someone loses and (2) the gains for the winner are equal to the losses for the loser (e.g., one person loses $5 and another person wins $5). A quick look at Exhibit 6 tells us that (2) is not true. The losses (for consumers) are not offset by the gains (for producers). A price floor ends with a *net loss*, or *deadweight loss*, of areas 3 + 5. Now think of how hard it would have been to identify this deadweight loss without the tools of supply, demand, consumers' surplus, and producers' surplus. Economic tools often have the ability to make what is invisible visible.

ECONOMICS 24/7

What Does Price Have to Do with Being Late to Class?

Class starts at 10 o'clock in the morning. At 10:09, Pam Ferrario walks in late. She apologizes to the instructor, saying, "I've been on campus 20 minutes, but I couldn't find a parking spot." Her classmates nod, knowing full well what she is talking about. Here at the university, especially between the hours of 9 a.m. and 2 p.m., parking spots are hard to come by.

This scene is replayed every day at many universities and colleges across the country. Students are late for class because on many days there isn't a parking space to be found.

iStock.com/Kerstin Waurick

Think of the ways in which parking spaces can be rationed at a college campus. One way is on a first-come, first-served basis. In other words, students are not charged a fee to park; they just park where spaces are available. At zero price for parking, the quantity demanded of spaces is likely to be greater than the quantity supplied and a shortage of parking spaces will result at certain times of the day. To deal with this shortage, students will likely try to be "first in line" for a parking spot, causing them to leave for the campus earlier than they would otherwise. Instead of leaving home at 9:40 a.m. for a 10 o'clock class, one leaves at 9:30 a.m. Now, who pays for the first-come, first-served parking scheme? Of course, the students do, not in money, but in time.

Naturally, if the student doesn't leave home early enough to get a parking spot, then perhaps he or she will end up going up and down the parking aisles looking for an open spot. This way, the student ends up paying for a parking spot by being late to class.

So, if parking spaces are allocated on a first-come, first-served basis, it is likely that the student will end up paying in terms of time or in terms of being late to class.

The alternative is to pay in terms of money price. The university could, say, install parking meters and adjust the parking fee in such a way as to have the quantity demanded of parking spaces equal the quantity supplied of parking spaces at various times of the day.

Of course, if, by chance, the university sets the parking fee at a level below the equilibrium price, then the student will end up paying for the parking scheme in terms of both money price and first come, first served, because a parking fee below equilibrium will generate a shortage of parking spaces, and thus spaces will be rationed on a first-come, first-served basis.

You may often hear people say that price is a bad way to ration parking spaces at a college campus. But, then, what is the alternative? If price does not ration parking spots, something else will. In short, students who want to park on campus are going to have to pay for parking; it is just a question of *how* they pay. Do they pay in terms of their time, in being late to class, or in money price?

SELF-TEST

1. Do buyers prefer lower prices to higher prices?
2. "When there are long-lasting shortages, there are long lines of people waiting to buy goods. It follows that the shortages cause the long lines." Do you agree or disagree? Explain your answer.
3. Who might argue for a price ceiling? A price floor?

4-3 TWO PRICES: ABSOLUTE AND RELATIVE

In everyday language, we often use the word "price" without specifying the kind of price. Economists often distinguish the *absolute*, or *money*, *price* of a good from the *relative price* of a good.

4-3a Absolute (Money) Price and Relative Price

The **absolute (money) price** is the price of the good in money terms. For example, the absolute price of a car might be $30,000. The **relative price** is the price of the good *in terms of another good*. To illustrate, suppose the absolute price of a car is $30,000 and the absolute price of a computer is $2,000. Then the relative price of the car—that is, the price of the car *in terms of computers*—is 15 computers. A person gives up the opportunity to buy 15 computers when buying a car:

Absolute (money) Price
The price of a good in money terms.

Relative Price
The price of a good in terms of another good.

$$\text{Relative price of a car (in terms of computer)} = \frac{\text{Absolute price of a car}}{\text{Absolute price of a computer}}$$
$$= \frac{\$30,000}{\$2,000}$$
$$= 15$$

Now let's compute the relative price of a computer—that is, the price of a computer in terms of a car:

$$\text{Relative price of a computer (in terms of car)} = \frac{\text{Absolute price of a computer}}{\text{Absolute price of a car}}$$

$$= \frac{\$2,000}{\$30,000}$$

$$= \frac{1}{15}$$

Thus, the relative price of a computer in this example is 1/15 of a car. A person gives up the opportunity to buy 1/15 of a car when buying a computer.

Now consider this question: What happens to the relative price of a good if its absolute price rises and nothing else changes? For example, if the absolute price of a car rises from \$30,000 to \$40,000, what happens to its relative price? Obviously, the relative price rises from 15 computers to 20 computers. In short, if the absolute price of a good rises and nothing else changes, then its relative price rises too.

THINKING LIKE AN ECONOMIST

Higher Absolute Price Can Sometimes Mean Lower Relative Price   Economists know that a good can go up in price at the same time that it becomes relatively cheaper. How can this happen? Suppose the absolute price of a pen is \$1 and the absolute price of a pencil is 10¢. The relative price of 1 pen, then, is 10 pencils.

Now let the absolute price of a pen rise to \$1.20 at the same time that the absolute price of a pencil rises to 20¢. As a result, the relative price of 1 pen falls to 6 pencils. In other words, the absolute price of pens rises (from \$1 to \$1.20) at the same time that pens become relatively cheaper (in terms of how many pencils you have to give up to buy a pen).

How does this phenomenon happen? Well, the absolute price of a pen went up by 20 percent (from \$1 to \$1.20) at the same time that the absolute price of a pencil doubled (from 10¢ to 20¢). Because the absolute price of a pen went up by *less than* the absolute price of a pencil increased, the relative price of a pen fell.

4-3b Taxes on Specific Goods and Relative Price Changes

Suppose that the equilibrium price of good X is \$10 and that the equilibrium price of good Y is \$20. The relative price of good X is therefore ½ unit of good Y, and the relative price of good Y is 2 units of good X:

$$1X = \tfrac{1}{2}Y$$

$$1Y = 2X$$

Given these relative prices of X and Y, consumers will buy some combination of the two goods. For example, a given consumer might end up buying 10 units of X each week and 12 units of Y.

Now suppose that the government imposes a tax only on the purchase of good X. Then the tax effectively raises the price the consumer pays for the good from \$10 to \$15. Because no tax is placed on good Y, its price remains at \$20.

The tax thus changes the relative prices of the two goods. The after-tax relative prices are

$$1X = \tfrac{3}{4}Y$$
$$1Y = 1.33X$$

Comparing the new relative prices with the old relative prices, we recognize that the tax makes X relatively more expensive (going from ½ Y to ¾ Y) and makes Y relatively cheaper (going from $2X$ to $1.33X$). In other words, a tax placed only on X ends up making X relatively more expensive and Y relatively cheaper. As a result, we would expect consumers to buy relatively less X and relatively more Y. Think in terms of two familiar goods: Coke and Pepsi. A tax placed on Coke, but not on Pepsi, will induce consumers to buy relatively less Coke and relatively more Pepsi.

ECONOMICS 24/7

Obesity and a Soda Tax

The percentage of the U.S. population that is deemed obese today is higher than it was 20 years ago. Obesity is a health problem, so we often hear proposals directed at trying to reduce the obesity rate in the country. One proposal is to place a tax on high-fat, high-calorie so-called junk food. A similar proposal is to place a tax on soda.

We now know that a tax placed on one good (but not on another) will change the relative prices of the two goods. Placing a tax on good X, but not on good Y, will make good X relatively more expensive and Y relatively cheaper, prompting consumers to purchase relatively less X and relatively more Y.

Consider a tax placed on soda. We would expect the absolute (money) price of soda to rise. And if the tax is placed only on soda, its relative price will rise too. As soda becomes relatively more expensive, we would expect fewer sodas to be consumed and obesity to decline. Right? Well, fewer sodas might be purchased and consumed, but whether obesity will decline is not so clear. Consider soda and sugared iced tea. Both soda and sugared iced tea are sweet drinks. They might even be substitutes. With this idea in mind, suppose the absolute price of a soda is $1 and the absolute price of an iced tea (with sugar) is 50¢. It follows that the relative prices are

$$1\text{ soda} = 2\text{ sugared iced teas}$$
$$1\text{ sugared iced tea} = \tfrac{1}{2}\text{ soda}$$

Now let's place a tax on soda that drives its price up to $2. The new relative prices for soda and iced tea are

$$1\text{ soda} = 4\text{ sugared iced teas}$$
$$1\text{ sugared iced tea} = \tfrac{1}{4}\text{ soda}$$

As a result of the tax on soda, its relative price has risen, but the relative price of sugared iced tea has fallen. We would thus expect people to consume relatively less soda and relatively more sugared iced tea.

Obesity is lessened by ingesting fewer calories, not the same number or more calories. Simply put, the soda tax might reduce the consumption of sodas, but it doesn't necessarily reduce obesity. Although the soda tax makes soda relatively more expensive, it makes soda substitutes (such as sugared iced tea) relatively less expensive and thus makes a rise in the consumption of sugared iced tea more likely.

Patti McConville/Alamy Stock Photo

Does It Matter to You . . .
If Something You Buy Is Taxed or Subsidized?

Monkey Business Images/Shutterstock.com

We learned earlier that if one good is taxed, and another is not, that the good that is taxed becomes relatively more expensive and the good that is not taxed becomes relatively cheaper. In other words, if soda is taxed, and fruit is not, then soda becomes relatively more expensive and fruit becomes relatively cheaper. In turn, a change in relative prices leads to a change in how much of each good is purchased and consumed.

Now consider a subsidy, which can be viewed as a negative tax. While a tax makes a good relatively more expensive, a subsidy makes a good relatively cheaper. To illustrate, suppose the price of one unit of good X is $10 and the price of one unit of good Y is $20.

$$1X = \$10$$
$$1Y = \$20$$

It follows that the relative price of each good is:

$$1X = \tfrac{1}{2}Y$$
$$1Y = 2X$$

Now suppose the purchase of good X is subsidized, but the purchase of good Y is not. If you buy good X (for $10), you will get $2

back, which makes the price you end up paying for good X $8. Here, then, are the new prices for goods X and Y:

$$1X = \$8$$
$$1Y = \$20$$

Now the relative price of each good is:

$$1X = \tfrac{2}{5}Y$$
$$1Y = 2.5X$$

The subsidy has made good X relatively cheaper (2/5Y instead of 1/2Y) and it has made good Y relatively more expensive (2.5X instead of 2X). These changes in relative prices are likely to change consumption patterns—buyers are likely to buy relatively more X and relatively less Y.

Now consider that there are two goods, higher education and "all other goods" lumped together and called good AOG. The nonsubsidized price of each good is:

$$\text{Higher education} = \$40,000$$
$$\text{AOG} = \$20,000$$

The relative price of each good is:

$$\text{Higher education} = 2 \text{ AOG}$$
$$\text{AOG} = \tfrac{1}{2} \text{ higher education}$$

If we subsidize higher education so that the price people pay for it is $10,000, it follows that the relative price of each good becomes:

$$\text{Higher education} = \tfrac{1}{2} \text{ AOG}$$
$$\text{AOG} = 2 \text{ higher educations}$$

Subsidizing higher education has made it relatively cheaper while making all other goods (AOG) relatively more expensive. This change in relative prices will lead to a change in the consumption of each of the goods. Relatively more higher education will be purchased and relatively less of all other goods will be purchased.

SELF-TEST

1. If the absolute (or money) price of good *A* is $40 and the absolute price of good *B* is $60, what is the relative price of each good?

2. Someone says, "The price of good *X* has risen, so good *X* is more expensive than it used to be." In what sense is this statement correct? In what sense is this statement either incorrect or misleading?

OFFICE HOURS | "I Thought Price Ceilings Were Good for Consumers"

STUDENT: I still don't quite understand how a price ceiling can hurt consumers. After all, a price ceiling is usually set below the equilibrium price of a good, and everyone knows that consumers prefer lower prices to higher prices.

INSTRUCTOR: The problem is that when a price ceiling is imposed on a good, certain things happen that don't benefit consumers. Look at it this way: Consumers like the lower price that goes along with the price ceiling, but what they don't like are some of the effects of the price ceiling.

STUDENT: But it seems to me that if you picked 100 consumers at random and asked them whether they preferred the price of bread to be $1 a loaf as opposed to $2, all 100 consumers would say they prefer the lower price. Because a price ceiling is usually lower than the equilibrium price, doesn't this example prove that consumers benefit from price ceilings? After all, why would they say they prefer paying $1 than $2 for a loaf of bread if they didn't see it benefiting them?

INSTRUCTOR: A couple of things could be going on here. First, consumers might intuitively take the question to mean, do they prefer the *$1 price determined by supply and demand* to the *$2 price determined by supply and demand*? If this is how they understand the question, then it certainly seems reasonable for them to say they prefer the lower price to the higher price. You might not get the same response from consumers, though, if you asked them this question:

Which of the following two options do you prefer?

Option A:
　$2 (equilibrium) price of bread

Option B:
　$1 (price ceiling) price of bread + shortages of bread + lines of people waiting to buy bread, and so on.

STUDENT: In other words, your point is that consumers prefer lower to higher prices, assuming that nothing else changes but the price of the good. But if lower prices, as the result of price ceilings, come with shortages and long lines of people waiting to buy bread, then they may not prefer lower to higher prices.

INSTRUCTOR: Yes, that is the point.

STUDENT: A slightly different question: Do you think that all consumers know the adverse effects of price ceilings?

INSTRUCTOR: Probably not. In fact, even after government imposes a price ceiling and certain adverse effects (shortages, long lines, etc.) set in, consumers may fail to relate the cause to the effects of the price ceiling. In other words, *X* causes *Y*, but individuals either don't understand how (so they don't connect the two), or they believe that something else—*Z*—causes *Y*.

Points to Remember

1. Consumers may prefer a lower to higher price, *ceteris paribus*, but not necessarily a lower price with shortages to a higher price without shortages.

2. *X* may cause *Y*, but it doesn't necessarily follow that everyone will understand that *X* causes *Y*.

CHAPTER SUMMARY

PRICE

- As a result of scarcity, a rationing device is needed to determine who gets what of the available limited resources and goods. Price serves as a rationing device.
- Price acts as a transmitter of information relating to the change in the relative scarcity of a good.

PRICE CEILINGS

- A price ceiling is a government-mandated maximum price. If a price ceiling is below the equilibrium price, some or all of the following effects arise: shortages, fewer exchanges, nonprice-rationing devices, buying and selling at prohibited prices, and tie-in sales.
- Consumers do not necessarily prefer (lower) price ceilings to (higher) equilibrium prices. They may prefer higher prices

and none of the effects of price ceilings to lower prices and some of the effects of price ceilings. All we can say for sure is that consumers prefer lower prices to higher prices, *ceteris paribus*.

PRICE FLOORS

- A price floor is a government-mandated minimum price. If a price floor is above the equilibrium price, the following effects arise: surpluses and fewer exchanges.

ABSOLUTE PRICE AND RELATIVE PRICE

- The absolute price of a good is the price of the good in terms of money.
- The relative price of a good is the price of the good in terms of another good.

KEY TERMS AND CONCEPTS

Tie-in Sale
Price Ceiling

Price Floor
Deadweight Loss

Absolute (Money) Price
Relative Price

QUESTIONS AND PROBLEMS

1. "If price were outlawed as the rationing device used in markets, there would be no need for another rationing device to take its place. We would have reached utopia." Discuss.
2. What kind of information does price transmit?
3. Should grades in an economics class be "rationed" according to dollar price instead of how well a student does on exams? If they were and prospective employers learned of it, what effect might this have on the value of your college degree?
4. Think of ticket scalpers at a rock concert, a baseball game, or an opera. Might they exist because the tickets to these events were originally sold for less than the equilibrium price? Why or why not? In what way is a ticket scalper like and unlike your retail grocer, who buys food from a wholesaler and then sells it to you?
5. Many of the proponents of price ceilings argue that government-mandated maximum prices simply reduce producers' profits and do not affect the quantity supplied of a good on the market. What must the supply curve look like if the price ceiling does not affect the quantity supplied?

6. James lives in a rent-controlled apartment and has for the past few weeks been trying to get the supervisor to fix his shower. What does waiting to get one's shower fixed have to do with a rent-controlled apartment?
7. Explain why fewer exchanges are made when a disequilibrium price (below the equilibrium price) exists than when the equilibrium price exists.
8. Buyers always prefer lower prices to higher prices. Do you agree or disagree with this statement? Explain your answer.
9. What is the difference between a price ceiling and a price floor? What effect is the same for both a price ceiling and a price floor?
10. If the absolute price of good X is \$10 and the absolute price of good Y is \$14, then what is (a) the relative price of good X in terms of good Y and (b) the relative price of good Y in terms of good X?
11. Give a numerical example that illustrates how a tax placed on the purchase of good X can change the relative price of good X in terms of good Y.

WORKING WITH NUMBERS AND GRAPHS

1. In the diagram, what areas represent the deadweight loss due to the price ceiling (P_C)?

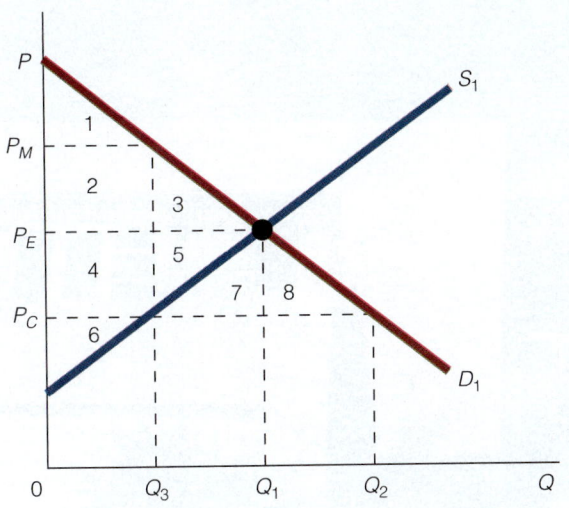

2. In the preceding diagram, what areas represent consumers' surplus at the equilibrium price of P_E? At P_C? (Keep in mind that, at P_C, the equilibrium quantity is neither produced nor sold.)

3. Using Exhibit 1 in the chapter, suppose the price ceiling is $13 instead of $8. Would the consequences of the price ceiling we identified in the text (such as a shortage, fewer exchanges, etc.) arise? Why or why not?

4. Draw a market that is in equilibrium, and identify the area of consumers' surplus and producers' surplus. Now place a price ceiling in the market, and identify the rise and fall in consumers' surplus. Finally, identify the decline in producers' surplus.

5. The absolute prices of goods X, Y, and Z are $23, $42, and $56, respectively. What is the relative price of X in terms of Y? What is the relative price of Y in terms of Z? What is the relative price of Z in terms of X?

6. There are two goods: X and Y. The absolute price of X rises and the absolute price of Y does not change. Prove that the relative price of X rises in terms of Y.

CHAPTER

5

SUPPLY, DEMAND, AND PRICE: APPLICATIONS

INTRODUCTION

In the previous two chapters, we discussed supply, demand, and price. In this chapter, we *work with* supply, demand, and price. The theory of supply and demand is not very useful to you unless you can use it to explain some of the things you see around you in everyday life. In this chapter, we discuss medical care, changing house prices, college classes at 10 a.m., driving on a freeway, standardized tests (such as the SAT), college athletes, and more—all in the general framework of supply and demand.

5-1 APPLICATION 1: U-HAUL RATES AND DEMAND[1]

Suppose you want to rent a 10-ft U-Haul truck to move from Columbus, Ohio to Austin, Texas. Will that truck cost you the same dollar amount as it would if you want to move from Austin to Columbus? The answer is no. Here are the rates:

> Columbus Ohio to Austin, Texas : $1,071
>
> Austin, Texas to Columbus, Ohio : $630

Why is it more expensive to rent a U-Haul truck going from Columbus to Austin than from Austin to Columbus?

[1] The idea for this feature came from Mark Perry's discussion of U-Haul rates at his blog, AEI/ Carpe Diem at http://www.aei.org/publication/blog/carpe-diem/.

Before we answer that question, consider the U-Haul rates for the following combinations of cities:[2]

Las Vegas, Nevada to Roanoke, Virginia : $925

Roanoke, Virginia to Las Vegas, Nevada : $1,573

Tampa, Florida to Oklahoma City, Oklahoma : $853

Oklahoma City, Oklahoma to Tampa, Florida : $1,228

Nashville, Tennessee to Detroit, Michigan : $357

Detroit, Michigan to Nashville, Tennessee : $552

Now what you will notice in the four combinations of cities that we have cited is that it is more expensive to rent a truck that goes in one direction than it is to rent a truck that goes in the reverse direction. It is more expensive to go from Detroit to Nashville than from Nashville to Detroit; it is more expensive to go from Oklahoma City to Tampa than from Tampa to Oklahoma.

Why is this? The answer has to do with the demand of going from point 1 to 2 relative to the demand of going from point 2 to 1. In 2016, some of the cities that people were moving to in large numbers were Austin, Las Vegas, Tampa, and Nashville. We can say that the "demand" to move to these cities was much higher than it was for many other cities. Given the higher demand to move to the cities, the demand for U-Haul trucks to move to these cities was higher than the demand for U-Haul trucks to move to many other cities (e.g., Columbus, Oklahoma City, etc.). Higher demand translated into higher U-Haul rental rates.

SELF-TEST

(Answers to Self-Test questions are in Answers to Self-Test Questions at the back of the book.)

1. If more people want to move from California to Texas than want to move from Texas to California, might U-Haul rates reflect this difference? Explain your answer.

2. Why might median house prices be higher in one city than in another?

5-2 APPLICATION 2: SUBSIDIZING THE CONSUMPTION OF ANYTHING CAN RAISE ITS PRICE

Any point on a demand curve represents the highest price (maximum buying price) buyers will pay per unit for a specific quantity of a good. With this in mind, look at Exhibit 1(a). Focus first on the demand curve, D_1. The highest price that buyers will pay for the first unit of the good here is $10.

---

[2] All U-Haul rates in this feature are based on the one-way rental of a 10-ft truck on November 17, 2016.

EXHIBIT 1

Subsidies and Demand

In (a) we show that the highest price buyers will pay for the first unit of the good is $10 if D_1 holds. If government offers a $1 subsidy for each unit of the good the buyer purchases, then the highest price buyers will pay for the first unit of the good is $11. D_2 is the demand curve with the subsidy of $1. In (b) we show the demand for the good with and without the subsidy. Notice that price ends up higher ($5.50) when a subsidy (for the purchase of the good) exists than when it does not exist ($5.00).

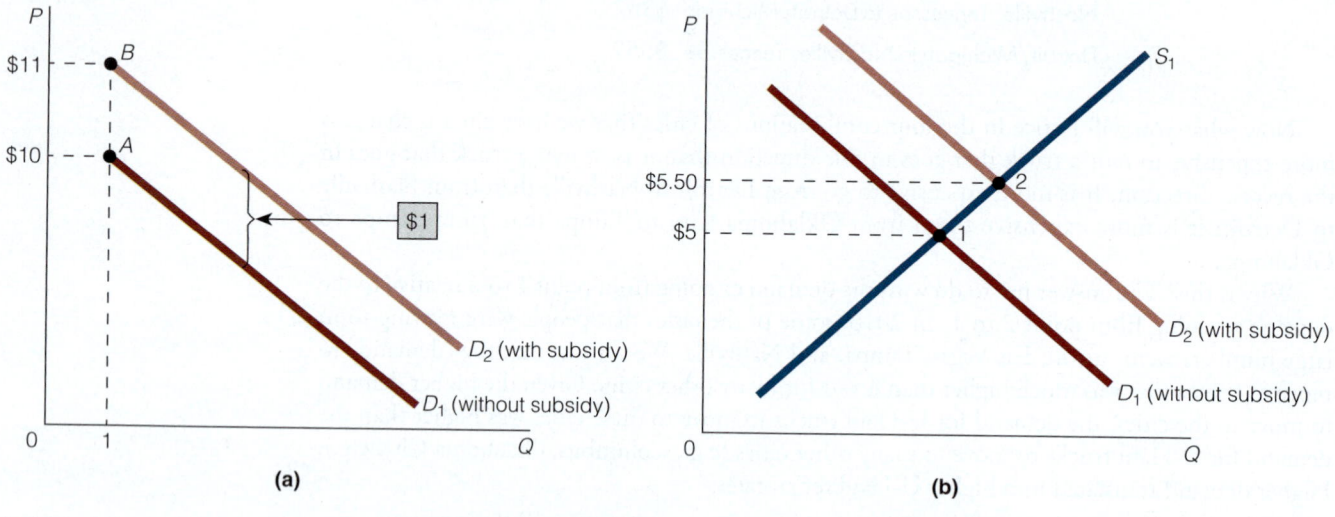

(a)   (b)

Now ask yourself what will happen to the demand curve D_1 if government were to subsidize the purchases of the good. Suppose government were to give $1 to each person who purchased a unit of the good. Now the highest price that buyers would be willing to pay for the first unit of the good would be $11 instead of $10. That's because paying $11 and getting $1 from the government is the same as paying $10 and not getting anything from the government.

As a result of the subsidy, (for purchasing the good), the demand curve for the good now moves upward from D_1 to D_2. At each quantity (on the horizontal axis), the new demand curve, D_2 (which is the demand curve with the subsidy) lies $1 higher than the old demand curve, D_1 (which is the demand curve without the subsidy).

Now in Exhibit 1(b), we put both D_1 and D_2 together with the supply curve for the good. Notice that when the purchases of the good are not subsidized—when D_1 holds—the equilibrium price for the good is lower ($5) than when the purchases of the good are subsidized ($5.50)—that is, when D_2 holds. We conclude that a government subsidy that is applied to the purchases (and consumption) of a good ends up raising the price of the good.

Now consider the following. Someone argues that both health care and higher education are expensive for many people. He argues that the government should subsidize buyers of both health care and higher education. For example, tell a college student that for every $100 she pays for college, the government will give her $40. Or tell a person that is buying health care that for every $100 he pays for health care, the government will give him $30. What is likely to happen as a consequence? Both the demand for health care and for education will rise and, along with higher demand, will come higher prices for both health care and higher education.

SELF-TEST

1. If a subsidy is provided for the consumption of good X, and the subsidy is different for different units of good X (e.g., $40 subsidy on the first unit of good X and $32 on the second unit of good X, etc.), would the demand curve without a subsidy be parallel to the demand curve with a subsidy, as is the case in Exhibit 1? Explain your answer.

2. Suppose a subsidy is provided to the buyers of solar panels. What is likely to happen to the price of solar panels? Explain your answer.

Tomasz Bidermann/Shutterstock.com

5-3 APPLICATION 3: 10 A.M. CLASSES IN COLLEGE

Suppose an economics class is offered in the same classroom twice in a day: at 10 a.m. in the morning and at 8 p.m. at night. Most students would prefer the 10 a.m. class to the 8 p.m. class. So, in Exhibit 2, the supply of seats in the class is the same at each time but the demand to occupy those seats is not. Because the demand is greater for the 10 a.m. class than for the 8 p.m. class, the equilibrium price for the morning class is higher than the equilibrium price for the evening class.

But the university or college charges the same tuition no matter what time students choose to take the class. The university doesn't charge students a higher tuition if they enroll in 10 a.m. classes than if they enroll in 8 p.m. classes.

Suppose that tuition T_1 is charged for all classes and that T_1 is the equilibrium tuition for 8 p.m. classes. (See Exhibit 2.) T_1 is therefore below the equilibrium tuition for 10 a.m. classes: At T_1, the quantity demanded of seats for the morning classes will be greater than the quantity supplied; more students will want the earlier class than there is space available.

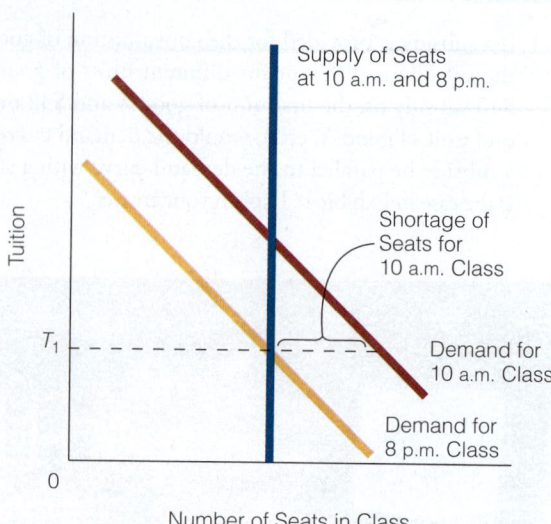

EXHIBIT 2

The Supply of and Demand for College Classes at Different Times

A given class is offered at two times, 10 a.m. and 8 p.m. The supply of seats in the classroom is the same at both times; however, student demand for the 10 a.m. class is higher than that for the 8 p.m. class. The university charges the same tuition, T_1, regardless of which class a student takes. At this tuition level, there is a shortage of seats for the 10 a.m. class. Seats are likely to be rationed on a first-come, first-served (first to register) basis or on seniority (seniors take precedence over juniors, juniors over sophomores, etc.).

How will the university allocate the available seats? It may do so on a first-come, first-served basis. Students who are first to register get the 10 a.m. class; the latecomers have to take the 8 p.m. class. Or the university could ration the high-demand classes by giving their upper-class students (seniors) first priority.

THINKING LIKE AN ECONOMIST

Remembering Price Upon seeing students clamoring to get 10 a.m. classes, lay-people conclude that the demand is high for mid-morning classes. They then wonder why the university doesn't schedule more 10 a.m. classes. The economist knows that what laypeople see is as much an effect of price as of demand. The demand for 10 a.m. classes may be high, but the quantity demanded may not be if the price is high enough. In fact, even though the demand for classes at certain times may vary, some set of prices will make the quantity demanded of each class the same.

SELF-TEST

1. Suppose college students are given two options. With option *A*, the price a student pays for a class is always the equilibrium price. For example, if the equilibrium price to take Economics 101 is $600 at 10 a.m. and $400 at 4 p.m., then students pay more for the early class than they do for the later class. With option *B*, the price a student pays for a class is the same regardless of the time the class is taken. Given the choice between options *A* and *B*, many students would say that they prefer option *B* to option *A*. Is this the case for you? If so, why would that be your choice?

2. How is the analysis of the 10 a.m. class similar to the analysis of a price ceiling in a market?

5-4 APPLICATION 4: WHY DO COLLEGES USE GPAs, ACTs, AND SATs FOR PURPOSES OF ADMISSION?

At many colleges and universities, students pay part of the price of their education (in the form of tuition payments) and taxpayers and private donors pay part (by way of tax payments and charitable donations, respectively). Thus, the tuition that students pay to attend colleges and universities is usually less than the equilibrium tuition. To illustrate, suppose a student pays tuition T_1 at a given college or university. As shown in Exhibit 3, T_1 is below the equilibrium tuition T_E. At T_1, the number of students who want to attend the university (N_1) is greater than the number of openings at the university (N_2); that is, quantity demanded is greater than quantity supplied. The university receives more applications for admission than there are places available. Something has to be done. But what?

EXHIBIT 3

College and University Admissions

If the college or university charges tuition T_1, then if T_E is the equilibrium tuition, a shortage will be generated. The college or university will then use some nonprice-rationing device, such as GPAs, ACTs, and SATs, as an admission criterion.

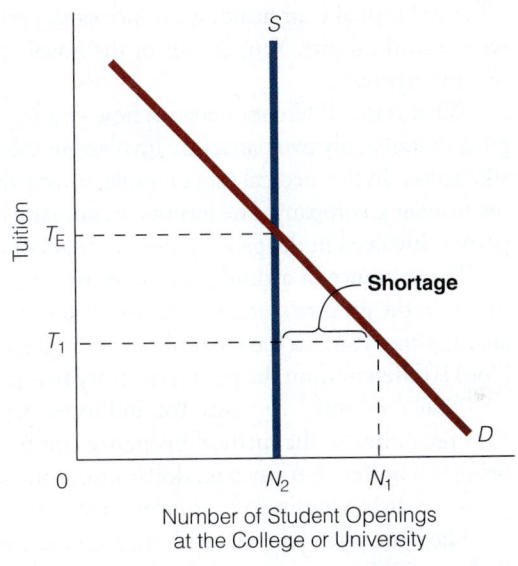

The college or university is likely to ration its available space by a combination of money price and some nonprice-rationing devices. The student must then pay the tuition T_1 *and* meet the standards of the nonprice-rationing devices. Colleges and universities typically use such things as GPAs (grade point averages), ACT scores, and SAT scores as rationing devices.

THINKING LIKE AN ECONOMIST

Identifying Rationing Devices The layperson sees a GPA of 3.8 and an SAT score of 1300 or better as requirements for admission. Economists see them as a rationing device. Economists then go on to ask why this particular nonprice-rationing device is used. They reason that a nonprice-rationing device *would not* be needed if the (dollar) price were fully rationing the good or service.

1. The demand rises for admission to a university, but both the tuition and the number of openings in the entering class remain the same. Will this change affect the admission standards of the university? Explain your answer.

2. Administrators and faculty at state colleges and universities often say that their standards of admission are independent of whether there is a shortage or surplus of openings at the university. Do you think that this statement is true? Do you think that faculty and administrators ignore surpluses and shortages of openings when setting admission standards? Explain your answer.

5-5 APPLICATION 5: WHY IS MEDICAL CARE SO EXPENSIVE?

Think of how you buy groceries. You go to the store, place certain products in your basket, and then pay for them at the cash register.

Now think of how you buy medical care. You go to the doctor or hospital, give the doctor's office or hospital your health insurance card, perhaps make a co-payment of $10 or $20, and then receive medical care. Your doctor or the hospital then bills your insurance company for the bulk of your expenses.

What is the difference between how you buy groceries and how you buy medical care? In the grocery store, only two parties are involved in the transaction: you (the buyer) and the grocery store (the seller). In the medical care example, three parties are involved: you, the doctor or hospital, and the insurance company. The insurance company is often referred to as the "third party." So no third party is involved in the grocery store transaction, but one is involved in purchasing medical care.

The existence of a third party separates the buying of something from the paying for something. In the grocery store, the person who buys the groceries and the person who pays for them are the same (you). In the medical care example, the person who buys and receives the medical care (you) is different from the person or entity that pays for the medical care (the insurance company).

"Wait a minute," you say. "You indirectly pay for your medical care by paying monthly insurance premiums to the medical insurance company." That is partly true, but what happens is like being at a buffet. You pay a set dollar price for the buffet, and then you can eat all you want. Our guess is that at a buffet you eat more than you would if you had to pay for each plateful.

The same often happens with medical care. You pay a set premium to the insurance company (let's say, $250 a month), and then you enter the health care buffet line. Might you end up buying more health care than you would if each doctor visit and lab test at the health care buffet were priced separately?

Before we continue, let's consider two objections to this analogy.

First, you might say, "But I don't buy medical care as I buy food in the food buffet line. I like shrimp, steak, salads, and desserts, but who likes being X-rayed, being prodded and poked by doctors, and taking medicine? No one buys MRIs as if they were shrimp cocktails."

That objection is true, of course, but it begs the point: Once you get sick and go to the doctor or hospital, the existence of a third party (who pays for your medical care) makes it easier for your doctor or the hospital to opt for more medical examinations or procedures and care than you need. For example, a conversation in your doctor's office may go like this:

Doctor: I think you have condition X, but just to be sure, let's order some blood tests and get an MRI too.

You: Whatever you think is best.

Now ask yourself how you might respond if you had to pay—out of pocket—for the blood test and MRI. The dialogue might change:

Doctor: I think you have condition X, but just to be sure, let's order some blood tests and get an MRI too.

You: How much is this going to cost me, doctor? And is all this really necessary?

The point is simple: Once you have paid your insurance premium, the price you pay for medical care amounts only to your co-payment (which is usually minimal). For all practical purposes, the dollar amount you pay for medical care, out of pocket, is close to zero—a fairly low price for health care. We can expect that the quantity demanded of medical care would be greater at zero than at some positive dollar amount.

Second, let's link the *quantity demanded* for medical care in general (which is high if the price of medical care is zero) with the *demand for specific items* that make up medical care. (In our food buffet example, we would link the *quantity demanded* of food with the *demand* for specific food items—shrimp, chocolate ice cream, a Caesar salad, and the like.)

If the quantity demanded of medical care is higher at a zero price than at some positive price, then we would expect the demand for the *specific items* that make up medical care to be higher than it would be if the quantity demanded of medical care were lower. This situation is shown diagrammatically in Exhibit 4. In Exhibit 4(a), the demand for medical care is downward sloping. If the price is zero for health care, then the quantity demanded of medical care is 100 units. But if the price is some positive dollar amount (such as P_1), then the quantity demanded of medical care is 50 units.

Exhibit 4(b) does not show the demand for medical care in general, just the demand for a specific item of medical care: X-rays. Of the two demand curves in panel (b), the first (D_1) is the

EXHIBIT 4

The Price of Medical Care and the Demand for X-rays

(a) If the price of medical care is low (e.g., zero), the quantity demanded of medical care is 100 units. If the price of medical care for you is P_1, the quantity demanded of medical care for you is 50 units. (b) The lower the price of medical care and the higher the quantity demanded of medical care in panel (a), the higher is the demand curve for X-rays in (b). (c) The higher the demand for X-rays, the higher the price of X-rays is.

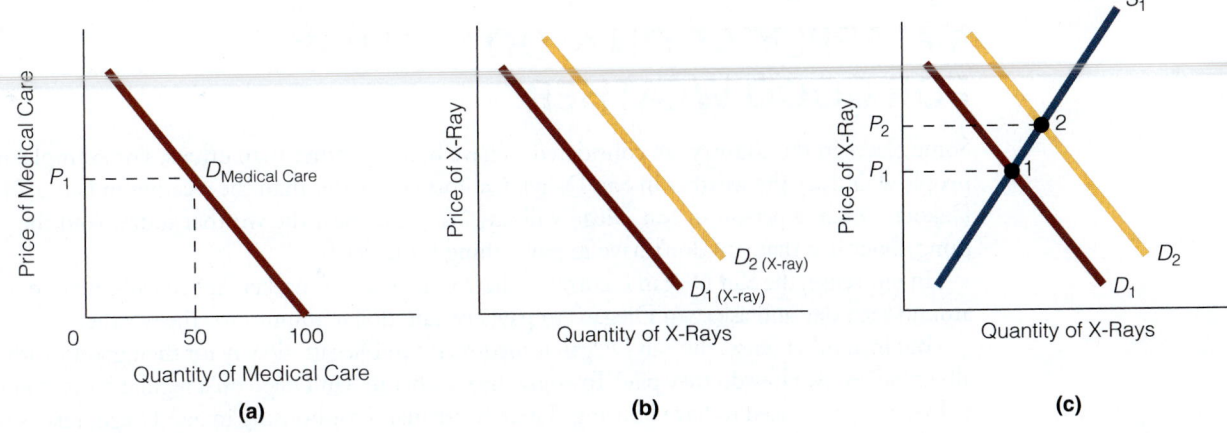

demand that exists for X-rays if the *quantity demanded of medical care* is 50 units in panel (a); it is the demand for X-rays if the price for medical care (shown in panel a) is P_1. The second demand curve (D_2) is the demand curve for X-rays if the *quantity demanded of medical care* is 100 units in panel (a); it is the demand for X-rays if the price for medical care (shown in panel a) is zero.

Here is the point in a nutshell:

1. The *lower* the price of medical care, the higher the quantity demanded of medical care and the demand for X-rays will be. That is,

    Price of medical care is low → Quantity demanded of medical care is high →

    Demand for X-rays is high

2. The *higher* the price of medical care, the lower the quantity demanded of medical care and the demand for X-rays will be. That is,

    Price of medical care is high → Quantity demanded of medical care is low →

    Demand for X-rays is low

Now, the question is, what does a high demand for X-rays do to the price of an X-ray? Obviously, it pushes the price upward. [See Exhibit 4(c).]

As a result, the health insurance company finds itself paying more for the X-rays you receive. Can you see what will happen next? The health insurance company makes the argument that, with rising medical costs, the premiums for your coverage need to rise too.

Why is health insurance as expensive as it is? You now have a large part of the answer. Think buffet.

SELF-TEST

1. Suppose food insurance exists. You pay the food insurance company a certain dollar amount each month, and then you purchase all the food you want from your local grocery store. The grocery store sends the bill to your food insurance company. What will happen to the price of food and to the premium you pay for food insurance?

2. In Exhibit 4(a), suppose that the price a person has to pay for medical care is between P_1 and zero. Where would the demand for X-rays in panel (b) be in relationship to D_1 and D_2?

5-6 APPLICATION 6: DO YOU PAY FOR GOOD WEATHER?

Some places in the country are considered to have better weather than others. For example, most people would say the weather in San Diego, California is better than the weather in Fargo, North Dakota. Often, a person in San Diego will say, "You can't beat the weather today. And the good thing about it is that you don't have to pay a thing for it. It's free."

In one sense, the San Diegan is correct: There is no weather market. Specifically, no one comes around each day and asks San Diegans to pay a certain dollar amount for the weather.

But in another sense, the San Diegan is incorrect: San Diegans do pay for their good weather—albeit indirectly. How do they pay? To enjoy the weather in San Diego on a regular basis, you have to live there; you need to have housing. There is a demand for housing in San Diego, just as there is a demand for housing in other places. Is the demand for housing in San Diego higher than it would be if the weather were not so good? Without the good weather, living in San Diego would not be as pleasurable, and therefore the demand to live there would be lower. (See Exhibit 5.)

In short, the demand for housing in San Diego is higher because the city enjoys good weather. It follows that the price of housing is higher too (P_2, as opposed to P_1, in Exhibit 5). Thus, San Diegans indirectly pay for their good weather because they pay higher housing prices than they would if the area had bad weather.

Was our representative San Diegan right when he said that the good weather was free?

EXHIBIT 5

The Price of Weather and the Price of Housing

We show two demand curves, D_1 and D_2. D_1 represents the demand for housing in San Diego if the weather were not so good. The higher demand curve D_2 shows the demand for housing in San Diego given that the weather is good. Notice that the price of housing in San Diego is higher because the weather there is good. Lesson learned: You pay for good weather (in San Diego) in terms of higher house prices.

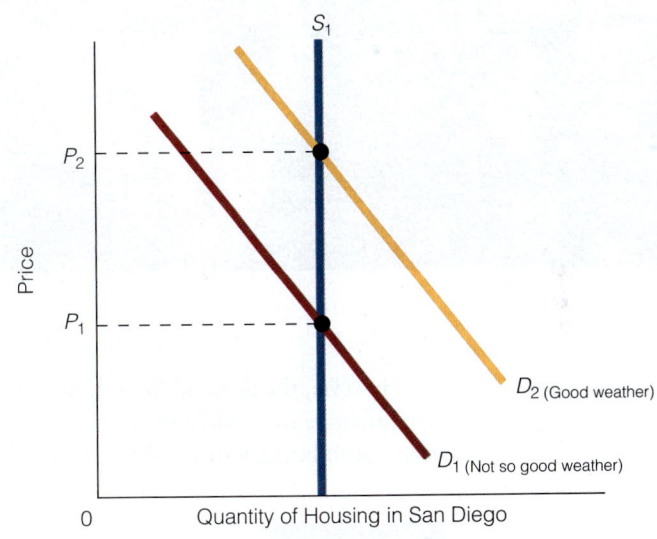

FINDING ECONOMICS

Good Schools and House Prices Suppose there are two neighborhoods, A and B. The kids who live in neighborhood A go to school A, and the kids who live in neighborhood B go to school B. Currently, school A has a much better academic reputation than school B. Can you find the economics?

This case is really no more than a disguised version of our good-weather example. If school A is better than school B, then the equilibrium price of houses in neighborhood A is likely to be higher than the equilibrium price of similar houses in neighborhood B. Just as we pay for good weather in terms of house prices, we pay for good schools in terms of house prices too.

SELF-TEST

1. Give an example to illustrate that someone may "pay" for clean air in much the same way that she "pays" for good weather.

2. If people pay for good weather, who ultimately receives the "good-weather payment"?

5-7 APPLICATION 7: THE PRICE OF AN AISLE SEAT

Most airlines will reserve an assigned seat for you when you buy a ticket. For example, if you want to buy an airline ticket from American Airlines, you can go online, purchase the ticket, and then look at a graphic that shows unreserved seats. If seat 13A is the one you want and no one has chosen it, then it is yours if you click it in the graphic.

Southwest Airlines does things differently. You do not reserve a seat when you book a flight. You choose a seat when you board the plane. If you are one of the first to board, you have your pick of many seats; if you are one of the last, you have your pick of very few seats.

Keep in mind that aisle seats are more popular than middle seats. Usually, for every aisle seat, there is a middle seat (assuming that the row of seats on each side of the plane consists of 3 seats: window, middle, and aisle). So, if the plane has 50 aisle seats, it also has 50 middle seats. In other words, the supply of middle seats equals the supply of aisle seats.

However, the demand for aisle seats is higher than the demand for middle seats. If price were to equilibrate the middle seats market and the aisle seats market, we would expect the price of an aisle seat to be higher than that of a middle seat. (See Exhibit 6.)

EXHIBIT 6

The Market for Middle and Aisle Seats on Airline Flights

We have assumed that the supply of aisle seats is equal to the supply of middle seats. Because the demand for aisle seats is higher than the demand for middle seats, we conclude that the equilibrium price for an aisle seat is higher than the equilibrium price for a middle seat. In the diagram, P_2 is the equilibrium price for an aisle seat, and P_1 is the equilibrium price for a middle seat.

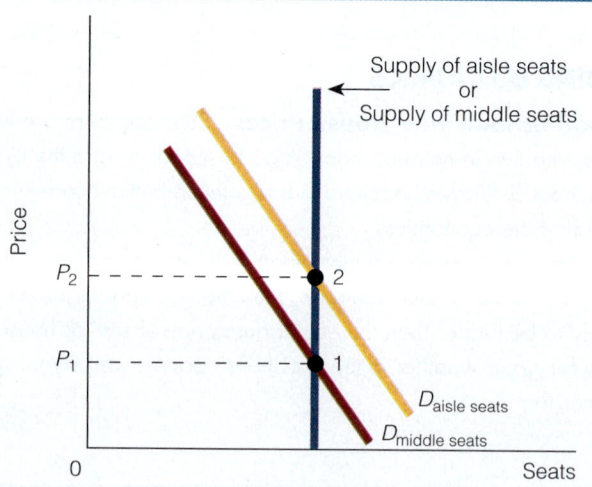

Does Southwest charge more for an aisle seat than a middle seat? Perhaps if you asked the airline this question, its answer would be no. But Southwest does charge more for priority boarding. If you want to board before others, you must choose the Business Select option when purchasing a ticket. If you board before others, you obviously have a larger selection of seats to choose from than later boarders do. Because most people prefer aisle to middle seats, those who board the plane first will probably choose the aisle seats.

So, does Business Select come with an additional charge? Yes. On the day we checked, the added charge was $20. In effect, Southwest was charging $20 more for an aisle seat than a middle seat, as we would expect, because the demand for aisle seats is higher than the demand for middle seats whereas the supply of each is the same.

SELF-TEST

1. If the equilibrium price is $400 for an aisle seat and $350 for a middle seat but an airlines company charges $350 for each seat, we would expect a shortage to appear in the aisle seat market. (More people will want aisle seats than there are aisle seats available.) How will the airlines decide who gets an aisle seat?

2. Suppose the supply of aisle, middle, and window seats is each 100 seats but the demand for aisle seats is greater than the demand for window seats, which, in turn, is greater than the demand for middle seats. If the equilibrium price of an aisle seat is $300, where do the equilibrium prices of middle and window seats stand in relation to this price?

5-8 APPLICATION 8: COLLEGE SUPERATHLETES

Suppose a young man, 17 years old, is one of the best high school football players in the country. As a superathlete, the young man will be recruited by football coaches at many colleges and universities. Every one of those schools will likely want its coach to be successful at signing up the young athlete; after all, at many universities, athletics is a moneymaker.

Suppose our superathlete decides to attend college A, where he receives a "full ride"—a full scholarship. How should this full scholarship be viewed? One way is to say that the superathlete is charged zero tuition to attend the college. (In other words, whereas some students pay a price of $30,000 a year to attend, the superathlete pays nothing.)

Another way to view the full scholarship is as a two-step process. First, the college pays the superathlete a dollar amount equal to the full tuition. Second, it charges the superathlete the full tuition. (In other words, the college gives the athlete $30,000 with one hand and then collects it with the other.)

Either way we view the scholarship, the effect is the same for the athlete. For purposes of our analysis, let's view it the second way: as a payment to the athlete, combined with full price being charged. This view leads to two important questions:

1. Can the college pay the athlete more than the full tuition? In other words, if the full tuition is $30,000 a year, can the college pay the athlete, say, $35,000 a year?

2. Is the superathlete being paid what he is worth?

Because of National Collegiate Athletic Association (NCAA) rules, the answer to the first question is essentially no. The NCAA states that a college or university cannot pay a student to attend, and for all practical purposes, the NCAA views payment as anything more than a full scholarship. The NCAA position is that college athletes are amateurs and amateurs cannot be paid to play their sport.

How does the NCAA rule affect the second question? What if the athlete's worth to the college or university is greater than the dollar amount of the full tuition? For example, suppose the athlete will increase the revenues of the college by $100,000 a year and the full tuition is $30,000 a year. In this case, the NCAA rule is actually a price ceiling (a below-equilibrium imposed price) on what the college may pay an athlete.

What is the effect of this price ceiling? Let's consider the demand (on the part of various colleges) for a single superathlete and the supply of this single superathlete. (See Exhibit 7.) We assume that the supply curve for athletic services is vertical at 1. Then, if the representative college charges $30,000 in tuition because of the NCAA rule, that dollar amount is the effective price ceiling (or wage ceiling). If the single athlete's market equilibrium wage is $35,000 and the NCAA rule did not exist, the athlete's wage would rise to $35,000. This dollar amount is equal to areas $B + C$ in Exhibit 7. The consumers' surplus for the college that buys the athlete's services for $35,000 is obviously equal to area A.

However, the NCAA rule stipulates that the college cannot pay the athlete more than $30,000 (full tuition). So the athlete's payment falls from $35,000 to $30,000, or from areas $B + C$ to simply area C. The college's consumers' surplus then increases to areas $A + B$. Essentially, the NCAA rule transfers part of the athlete's income—area B—to the college in the form of greater consumers' surplus.

EXHIBIT 7

The College Athlete

The exhibit shows the demand for and supply of a college athlete. If the market wage for the college athlete is $35,000, then the buyer of the athlete—in this case, the college—receives consumers' surplus equal to area A. If the wage can be held down to the tuition cost of attending the college—$30,000 in this example—then the college receives consumers' surplus of areas A + B.

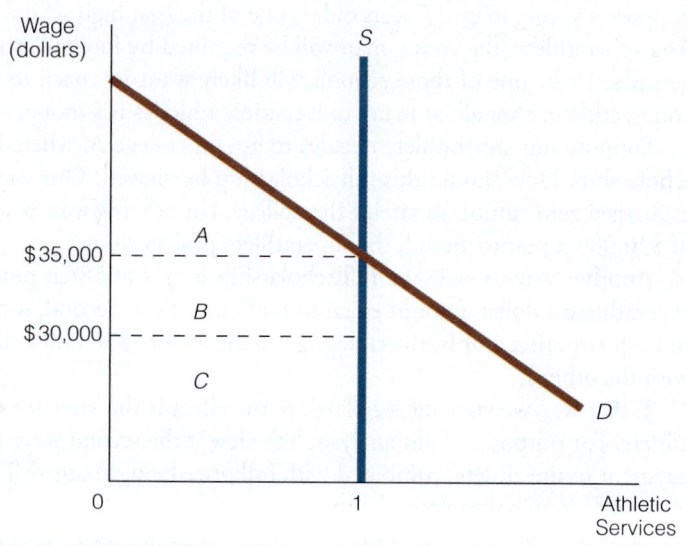

SELF-TEST

1. University X is a large school with a major football team. A new field house and track were just added to the campus. How is this addition related to the discussion in this application?

2. Sometimes it is argued that, if colleges paid student athletes, the demand for college sports would decline. In other words, the demand for college sports is as high as it is because student athletes are not paid (in the same way that professional athletes are paid). How would the analysis in this application change if we assume the preceding argument to be true?

5-9 APPLICATION 9: EASIER-TO-OBTAIN LOANS AND HIGHER HOUSING PRICES

If the federal government wants to make it easier for people to buy houses, one thing it can do is push for lowered lending standards. For example, suppose that lenders require individuals who want a mortgage loan to buy a house to make a down payment of 20 percent of the sale price. Now suppose that the government passes a law stating that no lender can require more than a 5 percent down payment before granting a loan. Will this law make it easier for individuals to buy homes? Not necessarily. The interest rate on a mortgage loan that requires only a 5 percent down payment might be higher than the rate on one that requires a 20 percent down payment.

Can government do *anything* now? Well, it could undertake specific monetary actions that have the effect of lowering interest rates. (We will discuss these actions in detail in a later chapter.)

Then what happens? The government seems to have met its objective of making it easier for individuals to buy houses. After all, prospective buyers now have to come up with only a 5 percent down payment (instead of 20 percent), and they end up paying lower interest rates for the loans they receive. So, are home buyers necessarily better off with this kind of government assistance? Not exactly.

By making mortgage loans easier to get, the government has indirectly increased the demand for houses. As the demand for houses rises, so do house prices. In short, making it easier to get home mortgage loans (as described) results in rising home prices, which make buying a house all the harder:

Lower down payments + Lower interest rates → Easier-to-obtain loans →

Higher demand for houses → Higher house prices

The main point is simply this: Government set out to make buying a home easier for more people by passing laws that forced lenders to accept lower down payments and by undertaking actions to put downward pressure on interest rates. But making it easier for individuals to get loans had the effect of raising the demand for, and the prices of, houses. Higher house prices made it harder for people to buy homes.

Continuing on with the story, suppose government now states that individuals need even more help to get a home because housing prices have risen. So, in its attempt to help people buy a house, government pushes for even lower lending standards (maybe requiring only a 1 percent down payment) and lower interest rates. Will that do the trick? Not likely: The lower lending standards and interest rates will probably stimulate greater demand for housing, leading to even higher housing prices.

SELF-TEST

1. If lowering lending standards can indirectly raise housing prices, can increasing lending standards lower housing prices? Explain.

2. Suppose anyone who buys a house in a certain year gets to pay $1,000 less in income taxes (assuming that the tax owed is greater than $1,000). Would the tax credit affect house prices? Explain your answer.

5-10 APPLICATION 10: SPECULATORS, PRICE VARIABILITY, AND PATTERNS

Think of an abstract good, say, *X*. Let's suppose that the price of good *X* initially varies over a month. Sometimes it is $10, other times it is $13, and at other times it is $12. Usually, when prices fluctuate, speculators will enter the market. That's because, when prices fluctuate, there is profit to be earned by buying low and selling high. In terms of our example so far, there is profit to be earned by buying at $10 and selling at $13.

The common view of speculators is that they somehow hurt others by trying to make themselves better off. Well, they certainly might be trying to make themselves better off, but it doesn't necessarily follow that, because they are doing what is in their best interest, others will be made worse off.

To understand why, suppose that on Monday through Wednesday of every week the price of good *X* is $10 and that on Thursday of every week the price of good *X* rises to $14. Clearly, then, there is price variability over part of the week. How will speculators respond to this variability? Obviously, they will buy good *X* on Monday through Wednesday and sell it on Thursday.

But their buying good *X* on Monday through Wednesday will drive up the price of good *X* on those days, and their selling good *X* on Thursday will drive down the price. In other words, speculators will end up changing the Monday-through-Thursday pattern of the price of good *X*. No longer will the pattern be $10 on Monday through Wednesday and $14 on Thursday. The price will be higher than $10 on Monday through Wednesday and lower than $14 on Thursday. In fact, speculators will continue to buy and sell good *X* until the price of good *X* is the same on every day. For example, the price of good *X* may end up being $11 every day of the week.

Essentially, the speculators have done three things: (1) bought low and sold high; (2) changed the pattern of price from $10 on three days and $14 on one day to $11 for each of four days; and (3) moved some of the supply of good X from certain days to other days.

Now, with this example in mind, let's think of a possible real-world scenario. Suppose that unusually bad weather for growing crops threatens the Midwest of the United States. High prices for food are expected as a result. Are speculators likely to respond to the news of impending bad weather? Most likely, they will translate bad weather into higher food prices. Given their objective to buy low and sell high, they will likely buy certain (food) crops today (before the bad weather hits) and sell those crops later (after the bad weather has hit). Speculators' actions will end up making food a little more expensive today and a little less expensive later. In other words, instead of a loaf of bread being $2 today and $5 later, a loaf of bread may end up being $3.50 both today and later.

What speculators essentially do, then, as a byproduct of buying low and selling high, is "spread out" the pain of bad weather (on food prices) over a longer time. Instead of taking all the "hurt" of high prices after the bad weather has hit, speculators move some of the "hurt" to before the bad weather hits. As a result, there will be less "hurt" after the bad weather hits.

Now, to see even more dramatically what happens as a result of speculators "buying low and selling high," suppose we change our example and have the bad weather result in no crops and thus no food. Under these dire circumstances, wouldn't the activities of the speculators—reallocating the current supply of food away from today to later and thereby changing the pattern of prices—be truly lifesaving?

SELF-TEST

1. Speculators can benefit themselves and others at the same time. Do you agree or disagree with this statement? Explain your answer with an example.

2. The price of a given good is likely to be less variable with than without speculators. Explain.

5-11 APPLICATION 11: SUPPLY AND DEMAND ON A FREEWAY

What does a traffic jam on a busy freeway in any large city have to do with supply and demand? Actually, it has quite a bit to do with supply and demand. Look at the question this way: There is a demand for driving on the freeway and a supply of freeway space. The supply of freeway space is fixed. (Roadways do not expand and contract over a day, week, or month.) The demand, however, fluctuates: It is higher at some times than at others. For example, we would expect the demand for driving on the freeway to be higher at 8 a.m. (the rush hour) than at 11 p.m. But even though the demand may vary, the money price for driving on the freeway is always the same: zero. A zero money price means that motorists do not pay tolls to drive on the freeway.

Exhibit 8 shows two demand curves for driving on the freeway: $D_{8a.m.}$ and $D_{11p.m.}$. We have assumed the demand at 8 a.m. to be greater than at 11 p.m. We have also assumed that, at $D_{11p.m.}$ and zero money price, the freeway market clears: The quantity demanded of freeway space equals the quantity supplied. At the higher demand, $D_{8a.m.}$, this is not the case. At zero money price, a shortage of freeway space exists: The quantity demanded of freeway space is greater than the quantity supplied. The shortage appears as freeway congestion and bumper-to-bumper traffic. One way to eliminate the shortage is through an increase in the money price of driving on the freeway at 8 a.m. For example, as Exhibit 8 shows, a toll of 70¢ would clear the freeway market at 8 a.m.

EXHIBIT 8

Freeway Congestion, and Supply and Demand

The demand for driving on the freeway is higher at 8 a.m. than at 11 p.m. At zero money price and D_{11} p.m., the freeway market clears. At zero money price and D_8 a.m., there is a shortage of freeway space, which shows up as freeway congestion. At a price (toll) of 70 cents, the shortage is eliminated and freeway congestion disappears.

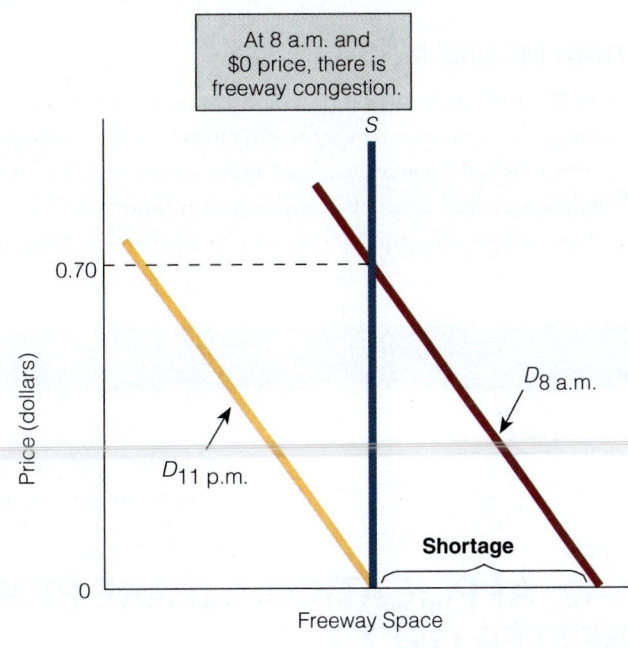

If charging different prices (tolls) on freeways, depending on the time of day, sounds like an unusual idea, consider how Miami Beach hotels price their rooms. They charge different prices for their rooms, depending on the time of year. During the winter months, when the demand for vacationing in Miami Beach is high, the hotels charge higher prices than when the demand is (relatively) low. If different prices were charged for freeway space, depending on the time of day, freeway space would be rationed the same way Miami Beach hotel rooms are rationed.

Finally, consider three alternatives usually proposed to counter freeway congestion:

- *Tolls:* Tolls deal with the congestion problem by adjusting price to its equilibrium level, as shown in Exhibit 8.

- *Building more freeways:* Building more freeways deals with the problem by increasing supply. In Exhibit 8, the supply curve of freeway space would have to be shifted to the right so that there is no longer any shortage of space at 8 a.m.

- *Encouraging carpooling:* More carpooling deals with the problem by decreasing demand. Two people in one car take up less space on a freeway than two people in two cars. In Exhibit 8, if, through carpooling, the demand at 8 a.m. begins to look like the demand at 11 p.m., then there is no longer a shortage of freeway space at 8 a.m.

A final note: A fee to drive in the Central London area was introduced in 2003. Anyone going into or out of the Central London area between 7:00 a.m. and 6:30 p.m., Monday through Friday, must pay a fee of approximately $15. (Not everyone has to pay the fee. For example, taxi drivers, ambulance drivers, drivers of police vehicles, motorcycle drivers, and bicyclists are exempt. The residents who live in the area receive a 90 percent discount.) Many people have claimed the fee a success because it has cut down on traffic and travel times and reduced pollution in the area.

Some people have urged New York City to institute a fee program to drive on certain streets in the city. On any given day in New York City, approximately 800,000 cars are on the streets south of 60th Street in Manhattan. According to many, the city is "choking in traffic." We will have to wait to see whether New York City goes the way of London.

THINKING LIKE AN ECONOMIST

It's One of Three   The economist knows that when there are buyers and sellers of anything (bread, cars, or freeway space), only three conditions are possible: equilibrium, shortage, or surplus. When the economist sees traffic congestion, the first thing that comes to mind is the shortage of road space. But why is there a shortage? The economist knows that shortages occur at prices below the equilibrium price. In other words, the price of driving on the road is too low.

SELF-TEST

1. In Exhibit 8, at what price is there a surplus of freeway space at 8 a.m.?

2. If the driving population increases in an area and the supply of freeway space remains constant, what will happen to freeway congestion? Explain your answer.

5-12 APPLICATION 12: ARE RENTERS BETTER OFF?

We begin with an analysis of two laws related to the eviction of a renter:

- Under law 1, a renter has 30 days to vacate an apartment after being served with an eviction notice.

- Under law 2, the renter has 90 days to vacate.

Landlords will find it less expensive to rent apartments under law 1 than under law 2. Under law 1, the most money a landlord can lose after serving an eviction notice is 30 days' rent. Under law 2, a landlord can lose up to 90 days' rent. Obviously, losing 90 days' rent is more costly than losing 30 days' rent.

A different supply curve of apartments exists under each law. The supply curve under law 1 (S_1 in Exhibit 9) lies to the right of the supply curve under law 2 (S_2). It is less expensive to supply apartments under law 1 than under law 2.

If the supply curve is different under the two laws, the equilibrium rent will be different too. As shown in Exhibit 9, the equilibrium rent will be lower under law 1 (R_1) than under law 2 (R_2). So,

- Under law 1, a renter pays lower rent (good) and has fewer days to vacate the apartment (bad).

- Under law 2, a renter pays a higher rent (bad) and has more days to vacate the apartment (good).

Who pays for the additional days to vacate the apartment under law 2? The renter pays for them by paying a higher rent.

EXHIBIT 9

Apartment Rent and the Law

Under law 1, a renter has 30 days to leave an apartment after receiving an eviction notice from his or her landlord. Under law 2, a renter has 90 days to leave an apartment after receiving an eviction notice. The cost to the landlord of renting an apartment is higher under law 2 than law 1, so the supply curve of apartments under law 1 lies to the right of the supply curve of apartments under law 2. Different supply curves mean different rents. Apartment rent is higher under law 2 (R_2) than under law 1 (R_1).

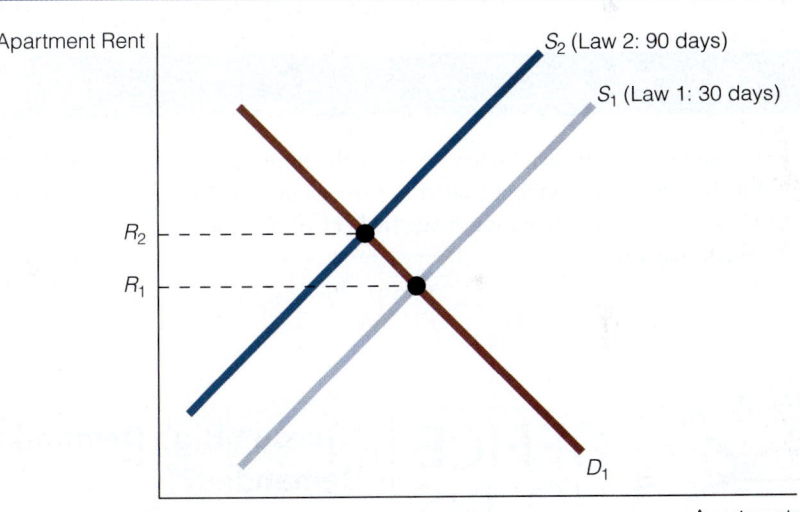

FINDING ECONOMICS

In an HMO You may frequently hear people complain about their health maintenance organizations (HMOs). Of the diverse and wide-ranging complaints, a common one is that patients usually cannot sue their HMOs in state courts for denial of benefits and poor-quality care. Some people argue that patients should have the right to sue their HMOs.

Let's consider two settings: one in which patients cannot sue their HMOs and one in which they can. If patients cannot sue, an HMO's liability cost is lower than if patients can sue. A difference in liability costs is then reflected in different supply curves.

To illustrate, recall that any single point on a supply curve is the minimum price sellers need to receive for them to be willing and able to sell that unit of a good. Suppose that, when patients cannot sue, an HMO is willing and able to provide health care to John for $300 a month. If patients can sue, is the HMO still willing and able to provide the service for $300 a month? Not likely. Because of the higher liability cost due to patients' ability to sue, the HMO is still willing and able to provide health care to John, but for, say, $350 month, not $300.

Saying that a seller's minimum price for providing a good or service rises is the same as saying that the seller's supply curve has shifted upward and to the left. In other words, the supply curve of HMO-provided health care will shift upward and to the left if patients have the right to sue. This is how the supply curve of apartments moved in Exhibit 8. So, will a difference in supply curves affect the price patients pay for their HMO-provided health care coverage? Yes. One effect of moving from a setting in which patients do not have the right to sue to one in which they do is that patients will have to pay more for their HMO-provided health care coverage.

Economists don't determine whether a patient having the right to sue is good or bad or right or wrong. Economists use their tools (in this instance, supply and demand) to point out that the things people want, such as the right to sue their HMOs, often come with price tags. Individuals must decide whether the price they pay is worth what they receive in return.

SELF-TEST

1. Economists often say, "There is no such thing as a free lunch." How is this saying related to patients moving from a system in which they cannot sue their HMOs to one in which they can?

2. A professor tells her students that they can have an extra week to complete their research papers. Under what condition are the students better off with the extra week? Can you think of a case where the students would actually be worse off with the extra week?

OFFICE HOURS | "Doesn't High Demand Mean High Quantity Demanded?"

STUDENT: The other day in class, you said, "The demand for 10 a.m. classes may be high, but the quantity demanded may not be if the price is high enough." In other words, you were saying that high demand doesn't necessarily mean high quantity demanded. But I thought it did. Could you explain?

INSTRUCTOR: Let me explain what's going on by first showing you the demand schedule for two goods, A and B:

Good A Demand Schedule		Good B Demand Schedule	
Price	Quantity Demanded	Price	Quantity Demanded
$6	100	$6	200
7	80	7	150
8	60	8	125
9	40	9	90

As you can see from the two schedules, the demand for good *B* is greater than the demand for good *A*. In other words, if we were to derive a demand curve for each good (based on its demand schedule), the demand curve for good *B* would lie farther to the right than the demand curve for good *A*.

Now, suppose we look at quantity demanded for each good at the price of $6. The quantity demanded of good *A* (the low-demand good) is 100 units, and the quantity demanded of good *B* (the high-demand good) is 200 units. What can we conclude? At the same price for each good ($6), the quantity demanded is higher when demand is higher.

But now let's consider quantity demanded for each good when the price of good *A* is $6 and the price of good *B* is $9. The quantity demanded of good *A* (the low-demand good) is 100 units, and the quantity demanded of good *B* (the high-demand good) is 90 units. In other words, if the price is high enough for good *B* (the high-demand good), then the quantity demanded of good *B* may be lower than the quantity demanded of good *A* (the low-demand good).

Now let's go back and repeat the statement I made in class: "The demand for 10 a.m. classes may be high, but the quantity demanded may not be if the price is high enough." Now do you understand what I was saying?

STUDENT: Yes, I think I do. You were saying that high demand doesn't necessarily mean high quantity demanded if we are dealing with different prices.

INSTRUCTOR: Yes, that's it.

Points to Remember

1. High demand means high quantity demanded, but only if the prices for the high-demand good and the low-demand good are the same. From our example, at a price of $6, the quantity demanded for the high-demand good *B* is greater than quantity demanded for the low-demand good *A*.

2. The quantity demanded for the low-demand good can be higher than the quantity demanded for the high-demand good if the prices for the two goods are not the same and the price for the high-demand good is high enough. From our example, at a price of $9 for good *B* (the high-demand good), the quantity demanded is lower than the quantity demanded for good *A* (the low-demand good) at a price of $6.

CHAPTER SUMMARY

U-HAUL RATES AND DEMAND

- We might think that the U-Haul rate to go from location X to location Y would be the same as to go from Y to X, but this isn't always so. If the demand to go from X to Y is greater than the demand to go from Y to X, then the U-Haul rate is likely to be higher going from X to Y than from Y to X.

SUBSIDIZING THE CONSUMPTION OF ANYTHING CAN RAISE ITS PRICE

- A subsidy placed on the purchase of a good will raise the demand curve for that good by the amount of the subsidy.
- Subsidizing the consumption of a good will often lead to a higher equilibrium price for the good.

10 A.M. CLASSES IN COLLEGE

- Colleges usually charge the same tuition for a class no matter when it is taken. The supply of seats in the class may be the same for each time slot, but the demand for the class may be different. At least for some classes, the quantity demanded of seats will be greater than the quantity supplied. Thus, some nonprice-rationing device will have to be used to achieve equilibrium.

WHY DO COLLEGES USE GPAs, ACTs, AND SATs FOR PURPOSES OF ADMISSION?

- Colleges and universities charging students less than the equilibrium tuition for admission create a shortage of spaces at their schools. Consequently, colleges and universities have to impose some nonprice-rationing device, such as GPAs or ACT or SAT scores.

WHY IS MEDICAL CARE SO EXPENSIVE?

• When it comes to medical care, often three parties are involved: the person who sells medical care, the person who buys medical care, and the person who (directly) pays for the medical care (the third party).

• Once a person has paid her medical insurance premium, the price paid thereafter for medical care may amount to no more than a copayment (usually minimal). For all practical purposes, then, the dollar amount she has to pay out of pocket to get medical care is zero. We thus expect the quantity demanded of medical care to be greater than it would be at some positive dollar amount.

DO YOU PAY FOR GOOD WEATHER?

• If good weather gives people utility, then the demand for and the price of housing will be higher in a city with good weather than in a city with bad weather *ceteris paribus*. Thus, people who buy houses in good-weather locations indirectly pay for the good weather.

THE PRICE OF AN AISLE SEAT

• If the supply of aisle and middle seats is the same, but the demand for aisle seats is greater, then the equilibrium price for aisle seats will be greater than the equilibrium price of middle seats.

COLLEGE SUPERATHLETES

• A college superathlete may receive a full scholarship to play a sport at a university, but the full scholarship may be less than the equilibrium wage for the superathlete (because of a mandate that the athlete cannot be paid the difference between his higher equilibrium wage and the dollar amount of his full scholarship). In such a case, the university gains at the expense of the athlete.

GOVERNMENT, LOANS, AND HOUSING PRICES

• Lower lending standards and lower interest rates make it easier to get a mortgage loan. But as getting a mortgage loan becomes easier, the demand for housing rises. As the demand for housing rises, house prices rise.

SPECULATORS, PRICE VARIABILITY, AND PATTERNS

• Speculators try to make themselves better off by buying a product at a low price and then selling it (later) at a high price. In pursuit of profit, they often reallocate a good from a period where it is greater in supply to a period where it is lesser in supply. As a result of reallocating supply, price patterns are changed too. As an example, suppose unusually bad weather for growing crops threatens the Midwest of the United States. High prices for food are expected as a result. Given their objective to buy low and sell high, speculators will likely buy certain (food) crops today (before the bad weather hits) and sell those crops later (after the bad weather has hit). Speculators' actions will end up making food a little more expensive today and a little less expensive later. Instead of taking all the "hurt" of high prices after the bad weather has hit, speculators move some of the "hurt" to before the bad weather hits. As a result, there will be less "hurt" after the bad weather hits.

SUPPLY AND DEMAND ON A FREEWAY

• The effect of a disequilibrium price (below the equilibrium price) for driving on a freeway is a traffic jam. If the price to drive on a freeway is $0 and, at this price, the quantity demanded of freeway space is greater than the quantity supplied, then a shortage of freeway space will result, in the form of freeway congestion.

ARE WE REALLY MAKING RENTERS BETTER OFF?

• If renters have 90 days instead of 30 days to vacate an apartment, the supply curve of apartments will shift upward and to the left. As a result, renters will pay higher rents when they have 90 days to vacate an apartment.

QUESTIONS AND PROBLEMS

1. Explain how lower lending standards and lower interest rates can lead to higher house prices.

2. If there were no third parties in medical care, medical care prices would be lower. Do you agree or disagree? Explain your answer.

3. Harvard, Yale, and Princeton all charge relatively high tuition. Still, each uses ACT and SAT scores as admission criteria. Are charging a relatively high tuition and using standardized test scores as admission criteria inconsistent? Explain your answer.

4. What do the applications about freeway congestion and 10 a.m. classes have in common?

5. Economics has been called the "dismal science" because it sometimes "tells us" that things are true when we would prefer them to be false. For example, although there are no free lunches, might we prefer that there were? Was there anything in this chapter that you learned was true that you would have preferred to be false? If so, identify it. Then explain why you would have preferred it to be false.

6. In the discussion of health care and the right to sue your HMO, we state, "Saying that a seller's minimum price for providing a good or service rises is the same as saying that the seller's supply curve has shifted upward and to the left." Does it follow that, if a seller's minimum price falls, the supply curve shifts downward and to the right? Explain your answer.

7. Application 6 explains that even though no one directly and explicitly pays for good weather ("Here is $100 for the good weather"), you may pay for good weather indirectly, such as through housing prices. Identify three other things (besides good weather) that you believe people pay for indirectly.

8. Suppose there exists a costless way to charge drivers on the freeway. Under this costless system, tolls on the freeway would be adjusted according to traffic conditions. For example, when traffic is usually heavy, as it is from 6:30 a.m. to 9:00 a.m. on a weekday, the toll to drive on the freeway would be higher than when traffic is light. In other words, freeway tolls would be used to equate the demand for freeway space with its supply. Would you be in favor of such a system to replace our current (largely zero price) system? Explain your answer.

9. Wilson walks into his economics class 10 minutes late because he couldn't find a place to park. Because of his tardiness, he doesn't hear the professor tell the class that there will be a quiz at the next session. Consequently, Wilson is unprepared for the quiz and ends up failing it. Might Wilson's failing the quiz have anything to do with the price of parking?

10. University A charges more for a class for which there is high demand than for a class for which there is low demand. University B charges the same for all classes. All other things being equal between the two universities, which university would you prefer to attend? Explain your answer.

11. Suppose the equilibrium wage for a college athlete is $40,000, but, because of NCAA rules, the university can offer him only $22,000 (full tuition). How might the university administrators, coaches, or university alumni lure the college athlete to choose their school over others?

12. Consider the theater in which a Broadway play is performed. If tickets for all seats are the same price (say, $70), what economic effect might arise?

13. What is the relationship between the probability of a person being admitted to the college of his choice and the tuition the college charges?

14. Samantha is flying from San Diego, California to Arlington, Texas, on a commercial airliner. She asks for an aisle seat, but only middle seats are left. Why aren't any aisle seats left? (*Hint:* The airline charges the same price for an aisle seat as a middle seat.)

15. Speculation (on prices) leads to gains for the speculator and losses for others. Do you agree or disagree? Explain your answer.

16. Explain why subsidizing the purchase of good X could end up raising the price of good X.

WORKING WITH NUMBERS AND GRAPHS

1. Diagrammatically show and explain why there is a shortage of classroom space for some college classes and a surplus for others.

2. Smith has been trying to sell his house for six months, but so far he has had no buyers. Draw the market for Smith's house.

3. Think of two types of books, A and B. Book A can be purchased new by someone and resold as a used book. Book B can only be purchased new by someone. (It cannot be resold as a used book.) All other things being equal between the two books, draw the demand curve for each book.

4. As price declines, quantity demanded rises but quantity supplied does not change. Draw the supply and demand curves that represent this state of affairs.

5. As price declines, quantity demanded rises and quantity supplied falls. Draw the supply and demand curves that represent this state of affairs.

6. Explain diagrammatically why a good whose consumption is subsidized is likely to sell for a higher price than a good whose consumption is not subsidized.

6   ELASTICITY

INTRODUCTION

Suppose that, in New York City, a Broadway play is performed in a theater with 1,500 seats. Will the play take in more revenue if the average ticket price for a performance is $100 or if it is $200? If you said $200, consider some other questions: Will the play take in more revenue if the average price is $200 or $280? Will it take in more revenue if the average price is $280 or $320? Are you beginning to get suspicious? Perhaps the highest ticket price won't generate the greatest amount of revenue, but which ticket price will? The answer may surprise you.

Allen.G/Shutterstock.com

6-1 ELASTICITY: PART 1

The law of demand states that price and quantity demanded are inversely related, *ceteris paribus*. But it doesn't tell us by what percentage the quantity demanded changes as price changes. Suppose price rises by 10 percent. As a result, quantity demanded falls, but by what percentage does it fall? The notion of price elasticity of demand can help answer this question. The general concept of elasticity provides a technique for estimating the response of one variable to changes in another. It has numerous applications in economics.

6-1a Price Elasticity of Demand

The law of demand states that there is a *directional relationship* between price and quantity demanded: price and quantity demanded are inversely related. But the law of demand does *not* tell us *how much* quantity demanded declines as price rises. The *magnitudinal relationship* between price and quantity demanded brings us to a discussion of **price elasticity of demand**, which is a measure of the responsiveness of quantity demanded to changes in price. More specifically, it addresses the percentage change in quantity demanded for a given percentage change in price. (Keep in mind "percentage change," not just "change.")

Price Elasticity of Demand
A measure of the responsiveness of quantity demanded to changes in price.

Let's say that a seller of a good—a computer—raises the price by 10 percent and, as a result, the quantity demanded for the computer falls by 20 percent. The percentage change in quantity demanded (Q_d)—20 percent—divided by the percentage change in price (P)—10 percent—is called the *coefficient of price elasticity of demand* (E_d):

$$E_d = \frac{\text{Percentage change in quantity demand}}{\text{Percentage change in price}} = \frac{\%\Delta Q_d}{\%\Delta P}$$

In the formula, E_d = coefficient of price elasticity of demand, or simply elasticity coefficient; % = percentage; and Δ stands for "change in."

If we apply the calculation to our simple example—in which quantity demanded changes by 20 percent and price changes by 10 percent—we get 2. An economist would say either "The coefficient of price elasticity of demand is 2" or, more simply, "Price elasticity of demand is 2." Either expression means that the percentage change in quantity demanded will be two times any percentage change in price.[1] If price changes by 5 percent, the quantity demanded will change by 10 percent; if price changes by 10 percent, the quantity demanded will change by 20 percent.

Where Is the Missing Minus Sign? Price and quantity demanded move in opposite directions: When price rises, quantity demanded falls; when price falls, quantity demanded rises. In our example, when price rises by 10 percent, quantity demanded falls by 20 percent. When you divide a *negative 20 percent* by a *positive 10 percent*, you don't get 2; you get -2. Instead of saying that the price elasticity of demand is 2, you might think that price elasticity of demand is -2. However, by convention, economists usually simplify things by using the absolute value of the price elasticity of demand; thus, they drop the minus sign.

Formula for Calculating Price Elasticity of Demand Using percentage changes to calculate price elasticity of demand can lead to conflicting results, depending on whether price rises or falls. Therefore, economists use the following formula to calculate price elasticity of demand:[2]

$$E_d = \frac{\dfrac{\Delta Q_d}{Q_{d\ average}}}{\dfrac{\Delta P}{P_{average}}}$$

In the formula, ΔQ_d stands for the absolute change in Q_d. For example, if Q_d changes from 50 units to 100 units, then ΔQ_d is 50 units. ΔP stands for the absolute change in price. For example, if price changes from $12 to $10, then ΔP is $2. $Q_{d\ average}$ stands for the average of the two quantities demanded, and $P_{average}$ stands for the average of the two prices.

For the data on price and quantity demanded in Exhibit 1, the calculation is

$$E_d = \frac{\dfrac{50}{75}}{\dfrac{2}{11}} = 3.67$$

Because we use the average price and average quantity demanded in the equation for price elasticity of demand, 3.67 may be considered the price elasticity of demand at a point *midway between the*

---

[1] This statement assumes that we are changing price from its current level.

[2] This formula is sometimes called the *midpoint formula for calculating price elasticity of demand.*

EXHIBIT 1

Calculating Price Elasticity of Demand

We identify two points on a demand curve. At point A, price is $12 and quantity demanded is 50 units. At point B, price is $10 and quantity demanded is 100 units. When calculating price elasticity of demand, we use the *average* of the two prices and the *average* of the two quantities demanded. The formula for price elasticity of demand is

$$E_d = \frac{\dfrac{\Delta Q_d}{Q_{d\ average}}}{\dfrac{\Delta P}{P_{average}}}$$

For example, the calculation is:

$$E_d = \frac{\dfrac{50}{75}}{\dfrac{2}{11}} = 3.67$$

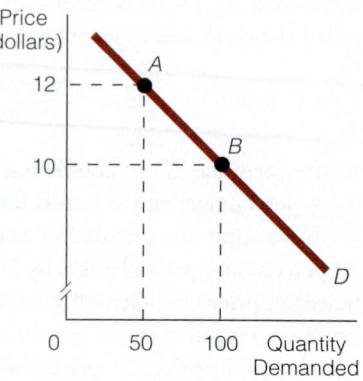

two points identified on the demand curve. For example, in Exhibit 1, 3.67 is the price elasticity of demand between points *A* and *B* on the demand curve.

6-1b Elasticity Is Not Slope

Some people think that slope and price elasticity of demand are the same, but they are not. Suppose we identify a third point on the demand curve in Exhibit 1. The following table shows the price and quantity demanded for our three points.

Point	Price	Quantity Demanded
A	$12	50
B	10	100
C	8	150

To calculate the *price elasticity of demand* between points *A* and *B*, we divide the percentage change in quantity demanded (between the two points) by the percentage change in price (between the two points). Using the formula for price elasticity of demand, we get 3.67.

The *slope of the demand curve* between points *A* and *B* is the ratio of the change in the variable on the vertical axis to the change in the variable on the horizontal axis. Thus, the slope of the demand curve reflects the *level* of change, not the *percentage* change:

$$\text{Slope} = \frac{\Delta \text{Variable on vertical axis}}{\Delta \text{Variable on horizontal axis}} = \frac{-2}{50} = -0.04$$

Now, let's calculate the price elasticity of demand and the slope between points *B* and *C*. The price elasticity of demand is 1.80; the slope is still −0.04.

6-1c From Perfectly Elastic to Perfectly Inelastic Demand

Look back at the equation for the elasticity coefficient and think of it as

$$E_d = \frac{\text{Percentage change in quantity demanded}}{\text{Percentage change in price}} = \frac{\text{Numerator}}{\text{Denominator}}$$

EXHIBIT 2

EXHIBIT 2

Price Elasticity of Demand	Demand may be elastic, inelastic, unit elastic, perfectly elastic, or perfectly inelastic.	

Elasticity Coefficient	Responsiveness of Quantity Demanded to a Change in Price	Terminology
$E_d > 1$	Quantity demanded changes proportionately more than price changes: $\%\Delta Q_d > \%\Delta P$.	Elastic
$E_d < 1$	Quantity demanded changes proportionately less than price changes: $\%\Delta Q_d < \%\Delta P$.	Inelastic
$E_d = 1$	Quantity demanded changes proportionately to price change: $\%\Delta Q_d = \%\Delta P$.	Unit elastic
$E_d = \infty$	Quantity demanded is extremely responsive to even very small changes in price.	Perfectly elastic
$E_d = 0$	Quantity demanded does not change as price changes.	Perfectly inelastic

Focusing on the numerator and denominator, we realize that the numerator can be (1) greater than, (2) less than, or (3) equal to the denominator. These three cases, along with two peripherally related cases, are discussed in the paragraphs that follow. Exhibits 2 and 3 provide summaries of the discussion.

Elastic Demand ($E_d > 1$) If the numerator (percentage change in quantity demanded) is greater than the denominator (percentage change in price), then the elasticity coefficient is greater than 1 and demand is elastic [see Exhibit 3(a)]:

$$\text{Percentage change in quantity demanded} > \text{Percentage change in price} \rightarrow$$
$$E_d > 1 \rightarrow \text{Demand is elastic}$$

Thus, $E_d > 1$ represents **elastic demand**; that is, the quantity demanded changes proportionately more than price changes. A 10 percent increase in price causes, say, a 20 percent reduction in quantity demanded ($E_d = 2$).

Inelastic Demand ($E_d < 1$) If the numerator (percentage change in quantity demanded) is less than the denominator (percentage change in price), then the elasticity coefficient is less than 1 and demand is inelastic [see Exhibit 3(b)]:

$$\text{Percentage change in quantity demanded} < \text{Percentage change in price} \rightarrow$$
$$E_d < 1 \rightarrow \text{Demand is inelastic}$$

Thus, $E_d < 1$ represents **inelastic demand**; that is, the quantity demanded changes proportionately less than price changes. A 10 percent increase in price causes, say, a 4 percent reduction in the quantity demanded ($E_d = 0.4$).

Unit Elastic Demand ($E_d = 1$) If the numerator (percentage change in quantity demanded) equals the denominator (percentage change in price), then the elasticity coefficient is 1 and we have unit elasticity of demand [see Exhibit 3(c)]:

$$\text{Percentage change in quantity demanded} = \text{Percentage change in price} \rightarrow$$
$$E_d = 1 \rightarrow \text{Demand is unit elastic}$$

Thus, $E_d = 1$ represents **unit elastic demand**; that is, the quantity demanded changes proportionately with price changes. For example, a 10 percent increase in price causes a 10 percent decrease in quantity demanded ($E_d = 1$).

Elastic Demand
The demand that occurs when the percentage change in quantity demanded is greater than the percentage change in price. Quantity demanded changes proportionately more than price changes.

Inelastic Demand
The demand that occurs when the percentage change in quantity demanded is less than the percentage change in price. Quantity demanded changes proportionately less than price changes.

Unit Elastic Demand
The demand that occurs when the percentage change in quantity demanded is equal to the percentage change in price. Quantity demanded changes proportionately to price changes.

EXHIBIT 3

Graphical Representation of Price Elasticity of Demand

(a) The percentage change in quantity demanded is greater than the percentage change in price: $E_d > 1$ and demand is elastic. (b) The percentage change in quantity demanded is less than the percentage change in price: $E_d < 1$ and demand is inelastic. (c) The percentage change in quantity demanded is equal to percentage change in price: $E_d = 1$ and demand is unit elastic. (d) A small change in price reduces quantity demanded to zero: $E_d = \infty$ and demand is perfectly elastic. (e) A change in price does not change quantity demanded: $E_d = 0$ and demand is perfectly inelastic.

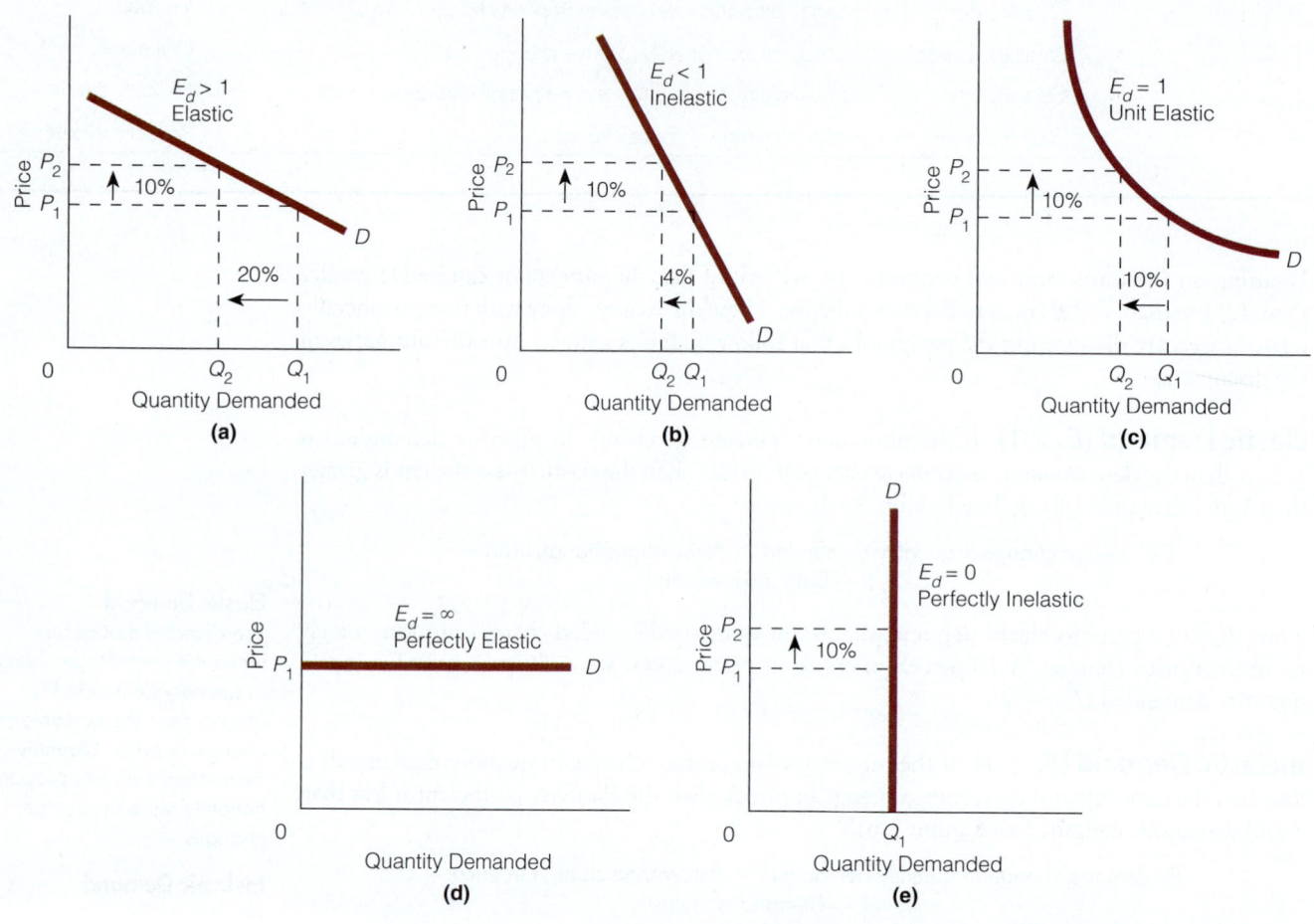

Perfectly Elastic Demand
The demand that occurs when a small percentage change in price causes an extremely large percentage change in quantity demanded (from buying all to buying nothing).

Perfectly Inelastic Demand
The demand that occurs when quantity demanded does not change as price changes.

Perfectly Elastic Demand ($E_d = \infty$) If quantity demanded is extremely responsive to changes in price, the result is **perfectly elastic demand** [see Exhibit 3(d)]. For example, suppose buyers are willing to buy all units of a seller's good at $5 per unit but nothing at $5.10. In other words, a small percentage change in price causes an extremely large percentage change in quantity demanded (from buying all to buying nothing). The percentage is so large, in fact, that economists say it is infinitely large.

Perfectly Inelastic Demand ($E_d = 0$) If quantity demanded is completely unresponsive to changes in price, the result is **perfectly inelastic demand** [see Exhibit 3(e)]. For example, suppose the price of Dogs Love It dog food rises 10 percent (from $2 to $2.20) and Jeremy doesn't buy any less of it per week for his dog. Then, a change in price causes no change in quantity demanded, and Jeremy's demand for *Dogs Love It* dog food is perfectly inelastic between a price of $2 and a price of $2.20.

Perfectly Elastic and Perfectly Inelastic Demand Curves Even though you are used to seeing a downward-sloping demand curve, Exhibit 3 shows two demand curves that are not downward sloping. But aren't *all* demand curves supposed to be downward sloping because, according to the law of demand, an inverse relationship exists between price and quantity demanded? In the real world, no demand curves are perfectly elastic (horizontal) or perfectly inelastic (vertical) at all prices. Thus, the perfectly elastic and perfectly inelastic demand curves in Exhibit 3 should be viewed as representations of the extreme limits between which all real-world demand curves fall.

However, a few real-world demand curves do *approximate* the perfectly elastic and inelastic demand curves in Exhibits 3(d) and (e); that is, they come very close. For example, the demand for a particular farmer's wheat approximates the perfectly elastic demand curve in Exhibit 3(d). A later chapter discusses the perfectly elastic demand curve for firms in perfectly competitive markets.

FINDING ECONOMICS

At the Local Coffee Bar Suppose you buy 7 coffees at the local coffee bar each week when the price of a cup of coffee is $2 and you buy 5 coffees a week when the price is $2.50. Where is the economics?

Actually, economics appears in two places. First, the law of demand is visible because you buy *fewer* cups of coffee at the higher price. Second, calculating your price elasticity of coffee between the lower and higher prices is easy. It is 1.5, which means that your demand for coffee is *elastic*.

6-1d Price Elasticity of Demand and Total Revenue (Total Expenditure)

The **total revenue (TR)** of a seller equals the price of a good times the quantity of the good sold.[3] For example, if the hamburger stand down the street sells 100 hamburgers today at $1.50 each, its total revenue is $150.

Suppose the hamburger vendor raises the price of a hamburger to $2. What do you predict will happen to total revenue? Most people, in the widespread belief that higher prices bring higher total revenue, say that total revenue will increase. However, total revenue may increase, decrease, or remain constant. To see how, suppose price rises to $2 but, because of the higher price, the quantity of hamburgers sold falls to 50. Then total revenue is now $100 (whereas it was $150). Whether total revenue rises, falls, or remains constant after a price change depends on whether the percentage change in the quantity demanded is, respectively, less than, greater than, or equal to the percentage change in price. Thus, price elasticity of demand influences total revenue.

Total Revenue (TR)
Price times quantity sold.

---

[3] In this discussion, "total revenue" and "total expenditure" are equivalent terms. *Total revenue* equals price times quantity sold. *Total expenditure* equals price times quantity purchased. If something is sold, it must be purchased, making total revenue equal to total expenditure. The term "total revenue" is used when one is looking at things from the point of view of the sellers in a market. The term "total expenditure" is used when one is looking at things from the point of view of the buyers in a market. Buyers make expenditures; sellers receive revenues.

6-1e Elastic Demand and Total Revenue

If demand is elastic, the percentage change in quantity demanded is greater than the percentage change in price. Given a price rise of, say, 5 percent, the quantity demanded falls by more than 5 percent—say, 8 percent—having an effect on total revenue. Because quantity demanded falls, or sales fall off, by a greater percentage than the percentage rise in price, total revenue decreases. In short, if demand is elastic, a price rise decreases total revenue:

$$\text{Demand is elastic: } P \uparrow \rightarrow TR \downarrow$$

If demand is elastic and price falls, the quantity demanded rises (price and quantity demanded are inversely related) by a greater percentage than the percentage drop in price, causing total revenue to increase. In short, if demand is elastic, a price decline increases total revenue:

$$\text{Demand is elastic: } P \downarrow \rightarrow TR \uparrow$$

Exhibit 4(a) shows the relationship between a change in price and total revenue if demand is elastic. Between points A and B on the demand curve, demand is elastic. At point A, price is P_1 and quantity demanded is Q_1. Total revenue is equal to the rectangle $0P_1AQ_1$. Now, suppose we lower price to P_2. After the price decline, total revenue is now the rectangle $0P_2BQ_2$, which, as you can see, is larger than rectangle $0P_1AQ_1$. In other words, if demand is elastic and price declines, then total revenue will rise.

Of course, when price moves in the opposite direction, rising from P_2 to P_1, then the total-revenue rectangle becomes smaller. In other words, if demand is elastic and price rises, then total revenue will fall.

EXHIBIT 4

Price Elasticity of Demand and Total Revenue

In (a), demand is elastic between points A and B. Thus, a drop in price from P_1 to P_2 will increase the size of the total revenue rectangle from $0P_1AQ_1$ to $0P_2BQ_2$. A rise in price from P_2 to P_1 will decrease the size of the total revenue rectangle from $0P_2BQ_2$ to $0P_1AQ_1$. In other words, when demand is elastic, price and total revenue are inversely related. In (b), demand is inelastic between points A and B. Therefore, a drop in price from P_1 to P_2 will decrease the size of the total revenue rectangle from $0P_1AQ_1$ to $0P_2BQ_2$. A rise in price from P_2 to P_1 will increase the size of the total revenue rectangle from $0P_2BQ_2$ to $0P_1AQ_1$. In other words, when demand is inelastic, price and total revenue are directly related.

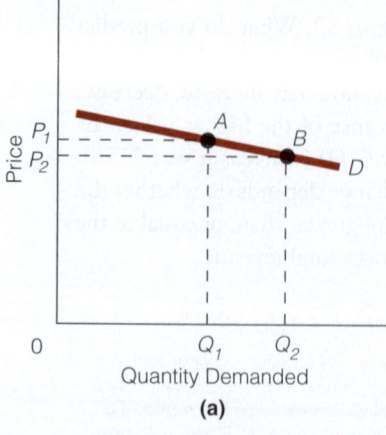

(a)

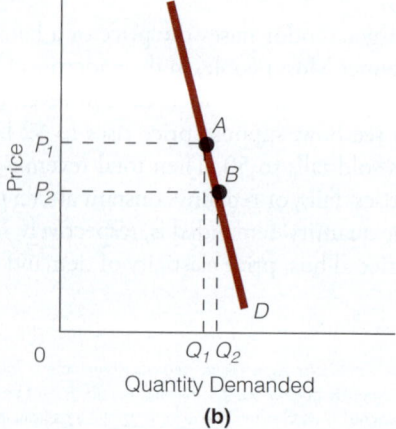

(b)

ECONOMICS 24/7

Drug Busts and Crime

Most people agree that the sale or possession of drugs such as cocaine and heroin should be illegal, but sometimes laws may have unintended effects. Do drug laws have unintended effects? Let's analyze the enforcement of drug laws in terms of supply, demand, and price elasticity of demand.

Suppose that, for every $100 of illegal drug sales, 60 percent of the $100 paid is obtained by illegal means. That is, buyers of $100 worth of illegal drugs obtain $60 of the purchase price from criminal activities such as burglaries, muggings, and similar illegal acts.

In Exhibit 5, the demand for and supply of cocaine in a particular city are represented by D_1 and S_1, respectively. The equilibrium price of $50 an ounce and the equilibrium quantity of 1,000 ounces give cocaine dealers a total revenue of $50,000. If 60 percent of this total revenue is obtained by the criminal activities of cocaine buyers, then $30,000 worth of crime has been committed to purchase the $50,000 worth of cocaine.

Now, suppose that a drug bust in the city reduces the supply of cocaine. Then, the supply curve shifts leftward from S_1 to S_2, the equilibrium price rises to $120 an ounce, and the equilibrium quantity falls to 600 ounces. The demand for cocaine is inelastic between the two prices, at 0.607. When demand is inelastic, an increase in price will raise total revenue, so the total revenue received by

cocaine dealers is now $72,000. If, again, we assume that 60 percent of the total revenue paid comes from criminal activity, then $43,200 worth of crime has been committed to purchase the $72,000 worth of cocaine.

Therefore, if the demand for cocaine is inelastic and people commit crimes to buy drugs, then a drug bust can actually increase the amount of drug-related crime. Obviously, this is an unintended effect of the enforcement of drug laws.

EXHIBIT 5

Drug Busts and Drug-Related Crime

In the exhibit, P = price of cocaine, Q = quantity of cocaine, and TR = total revenue from selling cocaine. At a price of $50 for an ounce of cocaine, the equilibrium quantity is 1,000 ounces and total revenue is $50,000. If $60 of every $100 cocaine purchase is obtained through crime, then $30,000 worth of crime

is committed to purchase $50,000 worth of cocaine. As a result of a drug bust, the supply of cocaine shifts leftward; the price rises and the quantity falls. Because we have assumed that the demand for cocaine is inelastic, total revenue rises to $72,000. As the accompanying table shows, 60 percent of this dollar amount, or $43,200, comes from criminal activities.

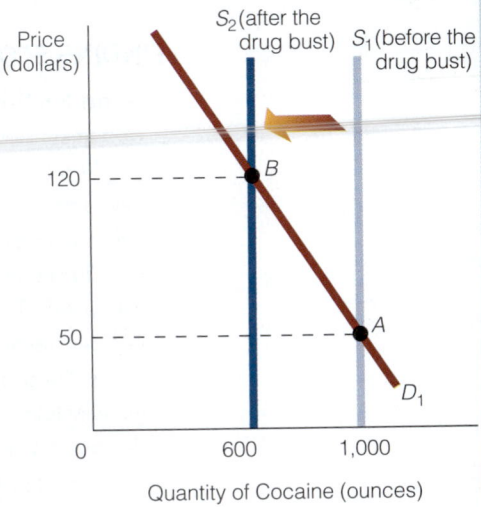

	P	Q	TR	Dollar Amount of *TR* Obtained Through Crime
Before Drug Bust	$50	1,000	$50,000	$30,000
After Drug Bust	120	600	72,000	43,200

Inelastic Demand and Total Revenue If demand is inelastic, the percentage change in quantity demanded is less than the percentage change in price. That is, if price rises, then quantity demanded falls, but by a smaller percentage than the percentage rise in price. As a result, total revenue increases. So, if demand is inelastic, a price rise increases total revenue. However, if price falls, then quantity demanded rises by a smaller percentage than the percentage fall in price and total revenue decreases. In other words, if demand is inelastic, then a price decline decreases total revenue. In sum, price and total revenue are directly related:

$$\text{Demand is inelastic} : P \uparrow \rightarrow TR \uparrow$$

$$\text{Demand is inelastic} : P \downarrow \rightarrow TR \downarrow$$

You can see the relationship between inelastic demand and total revenue in Exhibit 4(b), where demand is inelastic between points A and B on the demand curve. If we start at P_1 and lower price to P_2, then the total-revenue rectangle goes from $0P_1AQ_1$ to the smaller rectangle $0P_2BQ_2$. In other words, if demand is inelastic and price falls, then total revenue will fall.

Moving from the lower price, P_2, to the higher price, P_1, does just the opposite: If demand is inelastic and price rises, then the total revenue rectangle becomes larger; that is, total revenue rises.

Unit Elastic Demand and Total Revenue If demand is unit elastic, the percentage change in quantity demanded equals the percentage change in price. That is, if price rises, then quantity demanded falls by the same percentage as the percentage rise in price. Total revenue does not change. If price falls, then quantity demanded rises by the same percentage as the percentage drop in price. Again, total revenue does not change. If demand is unit elastic, a rise or fall in price leaves total revenue unchanged. (For a review of the relationship between price elasticity of demand and total revenue, see Exhibit 6.)

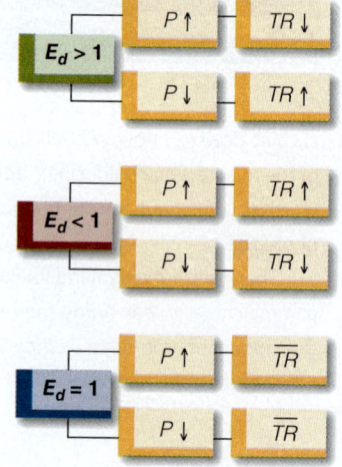

FINDING ECONOMICS

In an Earthquake Suppose an earthquake in Los Angeles destroys 10 percent of the apartment stock. Where is the economics?

As a result of the earthquake, we can expect the average rent for an apartment in the city to rise. Some people go further and argue that, because of the earthquake, landlords will take in more total revenue than they did before the earthquake, but that is not necessarily true. To see why, suppose the rent before the earthquake is $2,000 and 100,000 apartments are rented. Then the monthly total revenue is $200 million. Now, suppose the earthquake reduces the number of apartments to 90,000. Then, as a result of a lower supply of apartments, the average rent rises to, say, $2,100 a month. At this higher rent per month, the monthly total revenue from apartments is $189 million. Total revenue is lower because the demand for apartments between the lower rent and the higher rent is elastic. If demand is elastic and price rises, then total revenue falls.

ECONOMICS 24/7

Elasticity and the Issue of "How Much"

Elasticity is a measurement of how much one thing changes given how much something else changes. Price elasticity of demand is the percentage change in quantity demanded given some percentage change in price. Income elasticity of demand is the percentage change in the quantity demanded of a good given some percentage change in income. Price elasticity of supply is the percentage change in the quantity supplied of a good given some percentage change in price.

Elasticity—of demand, income, or supply, or even some other type of elasticity—is often the right concept to consider in discussing various topics. Let's illustrate. Suppose someone says, "If we raise income tax rates, people will work much less. After all, who will work as much when she has to pay 60 cents out of every dollar earned as when she has to pay 30 cents out of every dollar earned? Well, it could be true that higher income tax rates will dampen the incentive to earn income through work, but *how much* it dampens the incentive to work depends on an elasticity concept—specifically, how much work declines as taxes rise. For example, if tax rates rise by 10 percent, do people end up working 10 percent less, more than 10 percent less, or less than 10 percent less. And might the answer depend upon whether we're raising, say, the highest marginal tax rate from 30 percent to 33 percent or from 20 percent to 22 percent?

Or consider someone who argues that if the minimum wage rate is raised by, say, $2, then the number of people hired (at the new, higher) minimum wage will fall. If the demand for labor is downward sloping, then certainly, fewer people will be hired at a

iStock.com/damircudic

higher than a lower wage, but *what percentage fewer* will be hired depends upon an elasticity concept. In other words, as wage rate rises by, say, 5 percent, what is the percentage decline in the quantity demanded of labor—more than 5 percent, less than 5 percent, or exactly 5 percent?

Or, finally, suppose someone says that, if we tax cigarettes at a higher rate than we do now, teenagers are less likely to start smoking or to continue smoking and therefore the higher tax will end up saving a generation from starting and developing the habit of cigarette smoking. No doubt, a tax on cigarettes will make cigarettes more expensive to purchase, likely leading to a cutback in the purchases of cigarettes. But *how much* of a cutback will there be? Will there be a large cutback (because the demand for cigarettes is highly elastic), a small cutback (because the demand for cigarettes is highly inelastic), or no cutback at all (because the demand for cigarettes is perfectly inelastic).

As you can tell from our examples, the concept of elasticity is relevant to the question of how much or what percentage something will change as a result of something else changing. And sometimes, knowing the answer to that question is extremely important to the issue at hand. For example, if higher taxes on cigarettes really don't reduce cigarette consumption very much, then perhaps there is a better way than taxes to reduce the consumption of cigarettes among the young, should that be the objective.

ECONOMICS 24/7

When Is a Half-Packed Auditorium Better Than a Packed One?

Oliver Gutfleisch/imageBROKER/Alamy Stock Photo

Suppose you are the manager of a famous rock group that will soon go on a tour of 30 U.S. cities. In each of the 30 cities, the group will play in an auditorium. The auditorium in St. Louis, Missouri, seats, let's say, 20,000 people. Is it better to sell all 20,000 tickets for the rock group's performance or to sell less than 20,000 tickets—maybe 10,000 tickets?

Most people will say that it is better to sell 20,000 tickets than 10,000 tickets. But is it necessarily better? To sell 20,000 tickets, the price per ticket will have to be lower than the price per ticket to sell 10,000 tickets. For example, suppose that, to sell all 20,000 tickets, the ticket price must be $50. In that case, the total revenue will be $1 million. Suppose, however, that, at $120 per ticket, 10,000 tickets (and no more) can be sold. In that case, the total revenue will be $1.2 million. In other words, a $50 ticket price fills the auditorium to capacity and generates $1 million. A $120 ticket price fills only half the auditorium but generates $1.2 million.

Of course, our analysis here implicitly assumes that only one ticket price, either $50 or $120, can be charged. If more than one price can be charged, then the 10,000 good seats in the auditorium might be sold for $120 each and the remaining 10,000 not-so-good seats might be sold for $50 each. The total revenue would be $1.7 million. In short, if only one price can be charged, then a half-packed auditorium may, under certain conditions, generate more revenue than a packed auditorium. But if two prices can be charged, then a packed auditorium is preferable to a half-packed auditorium. In fact, charging a higher price for good seats and a lower price for not-so-good seats actually happens at rock concerts, plays, basketball games, and more. Now we know why.

SELF-TEST

(Answers to Self-Test questions are in Answers to Self-Test Questions at the back of the book.)

1. On Tuesday, the price and quantity demanded are $7 and 120 units, respectively. Ten days later, the price and quantity demanded are $6 and 150 units, respectively. What is the price elasticity of demand between the $7 and $6 prices?

2. What does a price elasticity of demand of 0.39 mean?

3. Identify what happens to total revenue as a result of each of the following:

   a. Price rises and demand is elastic.

   b. Price falls and demand is inelastic.

   c. Price rises and demand is unit elastic.

   d. Price rises and demand is inelastic.

   e. Price falls and demand is elastic.

4. Alexi says, "When a seller raises his price, his total revenue rises." What is Alexi implicitly assuming?

6-2 ELASTICITY: PART 2

EXHIBIT 7

This section discusses the elasticity ranges of a straight-line downward-sloping demand curve and the determinants of price elasticity of demand.

6-2a Price Elasticity of Demand Along a Straight-Line Demand Curve

The price elasticity of demand for a straight-line downward-sloping demand curve varies from highly elastic to highly inelastic. Consider the price elasticity of demand at the upper range of the demand curve in Exhibit 7(a). Whether the price falls from $9 to $8 or rises from $8 to $9, using the formula for price elasticity of demand, we calculate the price elasticity of demand as 5.66.[4]

Now, consider the price elasticity of demand at the lower range of the demand curve in Exhibit 7(a). Whether the price falls from $3 to $2 or rises from $2 to $3, we calculate the price elasticity of demand as 0.33.

In other words, along the range of the demand curve identified, price elasticity goes from being greater than 1 (5.66) to being less than 1 (0.33). Obviously, on its way from being greater than 1 to being less than 1, price elasticity of demand must be equal to 1 somewhere on the curve. In Exhibit 7(a), we have identified the price elasticity of demand as equal to 1 at the *midpoint* of the demand curve.[5]

The elastic and inelastic ranges along the straight-line downward-sloping demand curve can be related to a total revenue curve [see Exhibit 7(b)]. If we start in the elastic range of the demand curve in Exhibit 7(a) and lower price, then total revenue rises, as shown in Exhibit 7(b). That is, as price is coming down within the elastic range of the demand curve in part (a), total revenue is rising in part (b).

When price has fallen enough that we move into the inelastic range of the demand curve in part (a), further price declines simply lower total revenue, as shown in part (b). Therefore, total revenue is at its highest—its peak—when price elasticity of demand equals 1.

Price Elasticity of Demand Along a Straight-Line Demand Curve

In (a), the price elasticity of demand varies along the straight-line downward-sloping demand curve. The curve has an elastic range (where $E_d > 1$) and an inelastic range (where $E_d < 1$). At the midpoint of any straight-line downward-sloping demand curve, price elasticity of demand is equal to 1 ($E_d = 1$).

Part (b) shows that, in the elastic range of the demand curve, total revenue rises as price is lowered. In the inelastic range of the demand curve, further price declines result in declining total revenue. Total revenue reaches its peak when price elasticity of demand equals 1.

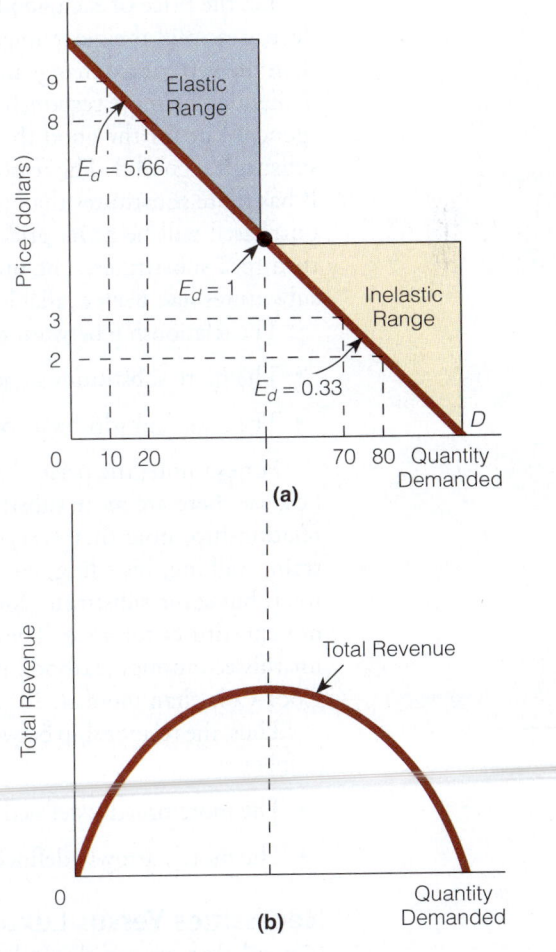

---

4. Keep in mind that our formula uses the average of the two prices and the average of the two quantities demanded. You may want to look back at the formula to refresh your memory.

5. For any straight-line downward-sloping demand curve, price elasticity of demand equals 1 at the midpoint of the curve.

6-2b Determinants of Price Elasticity of Demand

Four factors are relevant to the determination of price elasticity of demand:

1. Number of substitutes
2. Necessities versus luxuries
3. Percentage of one's budget spent on the good
4. Time

Because all four factors interact, we hold all other things constant as we discuss each factor.

Number of Substitutes Suppose good A has 2 substitutes and good B has 15 substitutes. Assume that each of the 2 substitutes for good A is as good a substitute (or a good enough substitute) for that good as each of the 15 substitutes is for good B.

Let the price of each good rise by 10 percent. Then, the quantity demanded of each good decreases. Will the percentage change in the quantity demanded of good A be greater or less than the percentage change in quantity demanded of good B? In other words, will the quantity demanded be more responsive to the 10 percent price rise for the good that has 2 substitutes (good A) or for the good that has 15 substitutes (good B)? The answer is the good with 15 substitutes, good B. The reason is that the greater the opportunities are for substitution (good B has more substitutes than good A has), the greater the cutback in the quantity of the good purchased will be as its price rises. When the price of good A rises 10 percent, people can turn to 2 substitutes. The quantity demanded of good A falls, but not by as much as if 15 substitutes had been available, as there are for good B.

The relationship between the availability of substitutes and price elasticity is clear:

- The more substitutes a good has, the higher the price elasticity of demand will be.
- The fewer substitutes a good has, the lower the price elasticity of demand will be.

For example, the price elasticity of demand for Chevrolets is higher than that for all cars because there are more substitutes for Chevrolets than there are for cars. To understand this relationship, note that everything that is a substitute for a car (taking a bus, getting on a train, walking, bicycling, etc.) is also a substitute for a specific type of car, such as a Chevrolet, but some substitutes for a Chevrolet (Ford, Toyota, Chrysler, Mercedes-Benz, etc.) are not substitutes for a car. They are simply types of cars. Similarly, there are more substitutes for this economics textbook than there are for textbooks, and there are more substitutes for Coca-Cola than there are for soft drinks.

Thus, the relationship between the availability of substitutes and price elasticity can be restated as follows:

- The more broadly defined the good, the fewer substitutes it will have.
- The more narrowly defined the good, the more substitutes it will have.

Necessities Versus Luxuries Generally, the more that a good is considered a luxury (a good that we can do without) rather than a necessity (a good that we cannot do without), the higher the price elasticity of demand will be. For example, consider two goods: jewelry and a medicine for controlling high blood pressure. If the price of jewelry rises, cutting back on purchases is easy: No one really needs jewelry to live. However, if the price of the medicine for controlling one's high blood pressure rises, cutting back is not so easy. We expect the price elasticity of demand for jewelry to be higher than that for high blood pressure medicine.

ECONOMICS 24/7

Price Elasticity of Demand and Health Care

Consider a health care system in which the customers have to pay some percentage of their health care bill and taxpayers pay the remainder. For example, if could be that, for every $100, the customer pays $30 and taxpayers pay $70. We'll call this system the 30-percent co-pay system (because the customer has a 30 percent co-payment).

Now, suppose someone argues that the 30 percent co-payment is too high; he supports bringing it down to 10 percent. So, for every $100, the customer pays $10 and the taxpayers pay $90. First question: Will the lower co-payment increase the quantity demanded of health care? It will, unless the demand for health care is perfectly inelastic. With a perfectly inelastic demand curve, the quantity demanded of health care is the same whether the customer pays $10 of each $100 or $100 of $100.

But now suppose the demand for health care is elastic. In this case, a lower price for health care (a lower co-payment) will lead to a percentage increase in the quantity demanded of health care that is greater than the percentage decrease in price. This will result in an increase in the total dollar amount spent on health care.

Now, some studies have shown that the demand for health care is fairly elastic . In other words, small declines in price (that customers pay) are going to increase the quantity demanded much more

Rob Hainer/Shutterstock.com

than proportionally. For example, if price elasticity of demand is, say, 2.22, then a 10 percent decline in price is going to increase quantity demanded of health care by 22.2 percent. Some economists have wondered whether the hospitals and doctors could deal with all the extra work. Would some kind of non-price rationing device have to be instituted?

In one study, it was noted that if customers paid much less than 30 percent of their own health care bills, the demand for health care was highly elastic. What would this observation mean for the taxpayers in our health care system? It would mean that they would end up paying much larger bills for health care because, if demand is highly elastic and price is lowered, then the total amount spent on health care is going to increase dramatically. (Think of this situation in terms of total revenue for a good: If demand is elastic and price declines, total revenue will rise. Similarly, if demand is elastic for health care at low prices, and the price the customer pays drops, then the total amount of spending on health care—much of which will have to be picked up by the taxpayer—will definitely increase.)

Percentage of One's Budget Spent on the Good Claire Rossi has a monthly budget of $3,000. Of this monthly budget, she spends $3 per month on pens and $400 per month on dinners at restaurants. In terms of percentages, she spends 0.1 percent of her monthly budget on pens and 13 percent of her monthly budget on dinners at restaurants. Suppose both the price of pens and the price of dinners at restaurants double. Claire is likely to be more responsive to the change in the price of restaurant dinners than to the change in the price of pens. She feels the pinch of a doubling in the price of a good on which she spends 0.1 percent of her budget a lot less than a doubling in price of a good on which she spends 13 percent. So, Claire is more likely to ignore the increased price of pens than she is to ignore the heightened price of restaurant dinners. Claire's behavior illustrates the idea that buyers are (and thus quantity demanded is) more responsive to price as the percentage of their budget that goes for the purchase of the good increases. In general,

- The greater the percentage of one's budget that goes to purchase a good, the higher the price elasticity of demand will be.

- The smaller the percentage of one's budget that goes to purchase a good, the lower the price elasticity of demand will be.

Time   As time passes, buyers have greater opportunities to be responsive to a price change. For example, if the price of electricity went up today and you knew about it, you probably would not change your consumption of electricity today as much as you would three months from today. As time passes, you have more chances to change your consumption by finding substitutes (natural gas), changing your lifestyle (buying more blankets and turning down the thermostat at night), and so on. Thus,

- The more time that passes (since the price change), the higher the price elasticity of demand for the good will be.

- The less time that passes, the lower the price elasticity of demand for the good will be.

In other words, the price elasticity of demand for a good is higher in the long run than in the short run.

ECONOMICS 24/7

Tuition Hikes at the College or University

Suppose you are the seller of some good. You have many customers who buy your good, and each customer has his or her own demand for your good. Let's suppose that some of your customers currently have elastic demand for your good, others inelastic demand, and still others unit elastic demand. What does this then mean for you? It means that if you raise the price of your good, everyone will cut back on buying your good, but some will cut back by a larger percentage than the percentage increase in price (these are the ones who have elastic demand), others will cut back by a smaller percentage than the percentage increase in price (there are the ones who have inelastic demand), and still others will cut back by the same percentage as the percentage increase

in price (these are the ones with unit elastic demand). In other words, your customers will all cut back on buying your good if you raise your price, but not everyone will cut back by the same magnitude.

Now is a price increase a good idea? Well, for those customers who have inelastic demand, a price increase will result in greater total revenue for you. For those customers who have elastic demand, a price increase will result in lower total revenue for you. And for those customers who have unit elastic demand, a price increase will result in the same revenue for you. In all, for two of the three groups (the inelastic and unit elastic demand groups), a price increase either helps you or leaves you the same. But for the one of the three groups, the elastic demand group, a price increase lowers your total revenue.

iStock.com/dszc

What to do? Ideally, what you might want to do is raise the price to the inelastic demand group (and possibly the unit elastic demand group too), but leave the price unchanged for the elastic demand group. In other words, charge two groups the higher price, but leave the price unchanged for the other group.

But often this is hard to do because you post a single price to everyone. Think of this in terms of a restaurant owner. On the menu, a shrimp dinner has one price, not one price for people with inelastic demand and another price for people with elastic demand.

Now, one way to get around being locked into one price is to post one, but not actually charge one price. In other words, tell everyone the price is being raised from, say, $15 to $20, but then give some people a discount on price depending on their elasticity of demand for the good.

One institution that often does this is the college or university. The college or university raises tuition, but then gives some students a "discount" in the form of more financial aid. (Both universities and the federal government can and do give financial aid. The university can then raise tuition for some and not for others by "increasing" the tuition for all, knowing full well that students receiving financial aid may have their financial aid package increased by the federal government.) The students it gives a discount to in the form of more financial aid tend to be students whose income (or parent's income) makes paying for education a larger percentage of their budget than others. Recall from our earlier discussion *that the larger the percentage of one's budget spent on a good, the higher the price elasticity of demand will be.* In other words, the college or university figures out a way to raise the tuition for those whose demand for the education being sold is likely to be inelastic and keep it the same (or nearly the same) for those whose demand for the education is likely to be elastic. Financial aid has a lot more to do with total revenue and price elasticity of demand than you may have originally thought.

Hear What and How the Economist Thinks . . .
About the Prevalence of Elasticity

The economist hears each of the following statements made by different people:

- Statement 1: Businesses always want to sell their products at higher prices, this way they take in greater revenue.
- Statement 2: If wages go up on average then the workers, the people who earn the wages, will, as a group, earn a greater income.

Hear what and how the economist thinks:

This is an elasticity issue again. Each of these statements could be true, but then again, each of the statements could be false. Let's consider statement 1 that businesses always want to sell their products at higher prices.

This is not always true. If it were true, then why wouldn't businesses continue to raise their prices? Why would a computer company sell its computers at $1,500 instead of $15,000? Why would a car company sell its cars for $30,000 instead of $300,000? Businesses face downward-sloping demand curves and, as prices rise, quantity demanded falls. What matters to total revenue are the percentage of price rises as compared to the percentage of quantity demanded that falls. As we know, if price elasticity of demand is greater than 1, then a rise in price will result in lower total revenue, not higher total revenue.

Now, consider statement 2 that holds if wages rise, wage-earners (as a group) will earn greater incomes. Consider the following: Suppose that the equilibrium wage is $20 an hour, and that 100 people are working at this wage. Their weekly total income as a group (if each person works 40 hours a week) is $80,000. Now suppose that, without any change in the supply of labor, the wage is raised to $22 an hour, which is $2 above the equilibrium wage. The demand curve for labor is downward-sloping, therefore, fewer people will be working at $22 an hour than at $20 an hour. Let's say that the quantity demanded of labor falls to 80 people. What is the weekly income of the wage-earners? Eighty individuals, each earning $22 an hour over 40 hours a week, turns out to be $70,400. In this case, the percentage rise in the wage was less than the percentage decline in the number of persons working, so that the total wage income fell. This is an elasticity concept—the elasticity of labor demand, which takes into account the percentage change in wages and the quantity demanded of labor.

SELF-TEST

1. If good X has 7 substitutes and demand is inelastic, then if there are 9 substitutes for good X, will demand be elastic? Explain your answer.

2. Price elasticity of demand is predicted to be higher for which good of the following combinations of goods?
   a. Dell computers or computers
   b. Heinz ketchup or ketchup
   c. Perrier water or water

   Explain your answers.

6-3 OTHER ELASTICITY CONCEPTS

This section looks at three other elasticities:

- Cross elasticity of demand
- Income elasticity of demand
- Price elasticity of supply

6-3a Cross Elasticity of Demand

Cross Elasticity of Demand
A measure of the responsiveness in quantity demanded of one good to changes in the price of another good.

Cross elasticity of demand measures the responsiveness in the quantity demanded of one good to changes in the price of another good. It is calculated by dividing the percentage change in the quantity demanded of one good by the percentage change in the price of another. That is,

$$E_c = \frac{\text{Percentage change in quantity demanded of one good}}{\text{Percentage change in price of another good}}$$

where E_c stands for the coefficient of cross elasticity of demand, or the elasticity coefficient.

This concept is often used to determine whether two goods are substitutes for or complements to each other and the degree to which one good is a substitute for or a complement to the other. Consider, for example, Skippy peanut butter and Jif peanut butter. Suppose that, when the price of Jif increases by 10 percent, the quantity demanded of Skippy increases by 45 percent. Then, the cross elasticity of demand for Skippy with respect to the price of Jif is

$$E_c = \frac{\text{Percentage change in quantity demanded of Skippy}}{\text{Percentage change in price of Jif}}$$

$$E_c = \frac{45}{10} = 4.5$$

In this case, the cross elasticity of demand is a positive 4.5. When the cross elasticity of demand is positive, the percentage change in the quantity demanded of one good (the good mentioned in the numerator) moves in the same direction as the percentage change in the price of the other good (the good mentioned in the denominator). A positive cross elasticity of demand is a characteristic of goods that are substitutes. As the price of Jif rises, the demand curve for Skippy shifts rightward, causing the quantity demanded of Skippy to increase at every price. So, if $E_c > 0$, the two goods are substitutes:

$$E_c > 0 \rightarrow \text{Goods are substitutes}$$

If the elasticity coefficient is negative ($E_c < 0$), then the two goods are complements:

$$E_c < 0 \rightarrow \text{Goods are complements}$$

A negative cross elasticity of demand occurs when the percentage change in the quantity demanded of one good (the good mentioned in the numerator) and the percentage change in the price of another good (the good mentioned in the denominator) move in opposite directions. For example, suppose the price of cars increases by 5 percent and the quantity demanded of car tires decreases by 10 percent. Calculating the cross elasticity of demand, we have -10 percent $\div$ 5 percent $= -2$. Thus, cars and car tires are complements.

The concept of cross elasticity of demand can be very useful. For instance, a company that sells cheese might ask what goods are substitutes for cheese. The answer would help the company identify its competitors. The company could identify substitutes for cheese by calculating the cross elasticity of demand between cheese and other goods. A positive cross elasticity of demand would indicate that the two goods were substitutes, and the higher the cross elasticity of demand is, the greater the degree of substitution will be.

6-3b Income Elasticity of Demand

Income elasticity of demand measures the responsiveness of quantity demanded to changes in income. It is calculated by dividing the percentage change in quantity demanded of a good by the percentage change in income. That is,

$$E_y = \frac{\text{Percentage change in quantity demanded}}{\text{Percentage change in income}}$$

where E_y denotes the coefficient of income elasticity of demand, or the elasticity coefficient.

Income elasticity of demand is positive ($E_y > 0$) for a *normal good*. Recall that a normal good is a good whose demand, and thus whose quantity demanded, increases, given an increase in income. Hence, for a normal good, the variables in the numerator and denominator in the formula for the income elasticity of demand move in the same direction:

$$E_y > 0 \rightarrow \text{Normal good}$$

In contrast to a normal good, the demand for an *inferior good* decreases as income increases. Income elasticity of demand for an inferior good is negative ($E_y < 0$):

$$E_y < 0 \rightarrow \text{Inferior good}$$

We calculate the income elasticity of demand for a good by using the same approach we used to calculate price elasticity of demand, namely,

$$E_y = \frac{\dfrac{\Delta Q_d}{Q_{d\ \text{average}}}}{\dfrac{\Delta Y}{Y_{\text{average}}}}$$

Income Elasticity of Demand
A measure of the responsiveness of quantity demanded to changes in income.

where $Q_{d\,average}$ is the average quantity demanded of the good and $Y_{average}$ is the purchaser's average income.

Now, suppose a person's income increases from \$500 to \$600 per month and, as a result, the quantity demanded of good X increases from 20 units to 30 units per month. Then we have income elasticity of 2.2, as shown here:

$$E_y = \frac{\dfrac{10}{25}}{\dfrac{100}{550}} = 2.2$$

Since E_y is a positive number, so good X is a normal good. Also,

- Because $E_y > 1$, demand for good X is said to be **income elastic**. In other words, the percentage change in quantity demanded of the good is greater than the percentage change in the purchaser's income.

- If $E_y < 1$, the demand for the good is said to be **income inelastic**.

- If $E_y = 1$, then the demand for the good is **income unit elastic**.

6-3c Price Elasticity of Supply

Price elasticity of supply measures the responsiveness of quantity supplied to changes in price. It is calculated by dividing the percentage change in the quantity supplied of a good by the percentage change in the price of the good. Mathematically,

$$E_s = \frac{\text{Percentage change in quantity supplied}}{\text{Percentage change in price}}$$

where E_s stands for the coefficient of price elasticity of supply, or the elasticity coefficient. We use the same approach to calculate the price elasticity of supply that we used to calculate the price elasticity of demand.

In addition, supply can be classified as elastic, inelastic, unit elastic, perfectly elastic, or perfectly inelastic:

- Elastic supply $(E_s > 1)$ refers to a percentage change in quantity supplied that is greater than the percentage change in price of the good [see Exhibit 8(a)]:

  Percentage change in quantity supplied > Percentage change in price →
  $E_s > 1 →$ Elastic supply

- Inelastic supply $(E_s < 1)$ refers to a percentage change in quantity supplied that is less than the percentage change in price of the good [see Exhibit 8(b)]:

  Percentage change in quantity supplied < Percentage change in price →
  $E_s < 1 →$ Inelastic supply

- Unit elastic supply $(E_s = 1)$ refers to a percentage change in quantity supplied that is equal to the percentage change in price of the good [see Exhibit 8(c)]:

  Percentage change in quantity supplied = Percentage change in price →
  $E_s = 1 →$ Unit elastic supply

- In the case of perfectly elastic supply $(E_s = \infty)$, a small change in price changes the quantity supplied by an infinitely large amount (and thus the supply curve, or a portion of the overall supply curve, is horizontal) [see Exhibit 8(d)].

Income Elastic
The condition that exists when the percentage change in quantity demanded of a good is greater than the percentage change in income.

Income Inelastic
The condition that exists when the percentage change in quantity demanded of a good is less than the percentage change in income.

Income Unit Elastic
The condition that exists when the percentage change in quantity demanded of a good is equal to the percentage change in income.

Price Elasticity of Supply
A measure of the responsiveness of quantity supplied to changes in price.

EXHIBIT 8

Price Elasticity of Supply

(a) The percentage change in quantity supplied is greater than the percentage change in price: $E_s > 1$ and supply is elastic. (b) The percentage change in quantity supplied is less than the percentage change in price: $E_s < 1$ and supply is inelastic. (c) The percentage change in quantity supplied is equal to the percentage change in price: $E_s = 1$ and supply is unit elastic. (d) A small change in price changes quantity supplied by an infinite amount: $E_s = \infty$ and supply is perfectly elastic. (e) A change in price does not change quantity supplied: $E_s = 0$ and supply is perfectly inelastic.

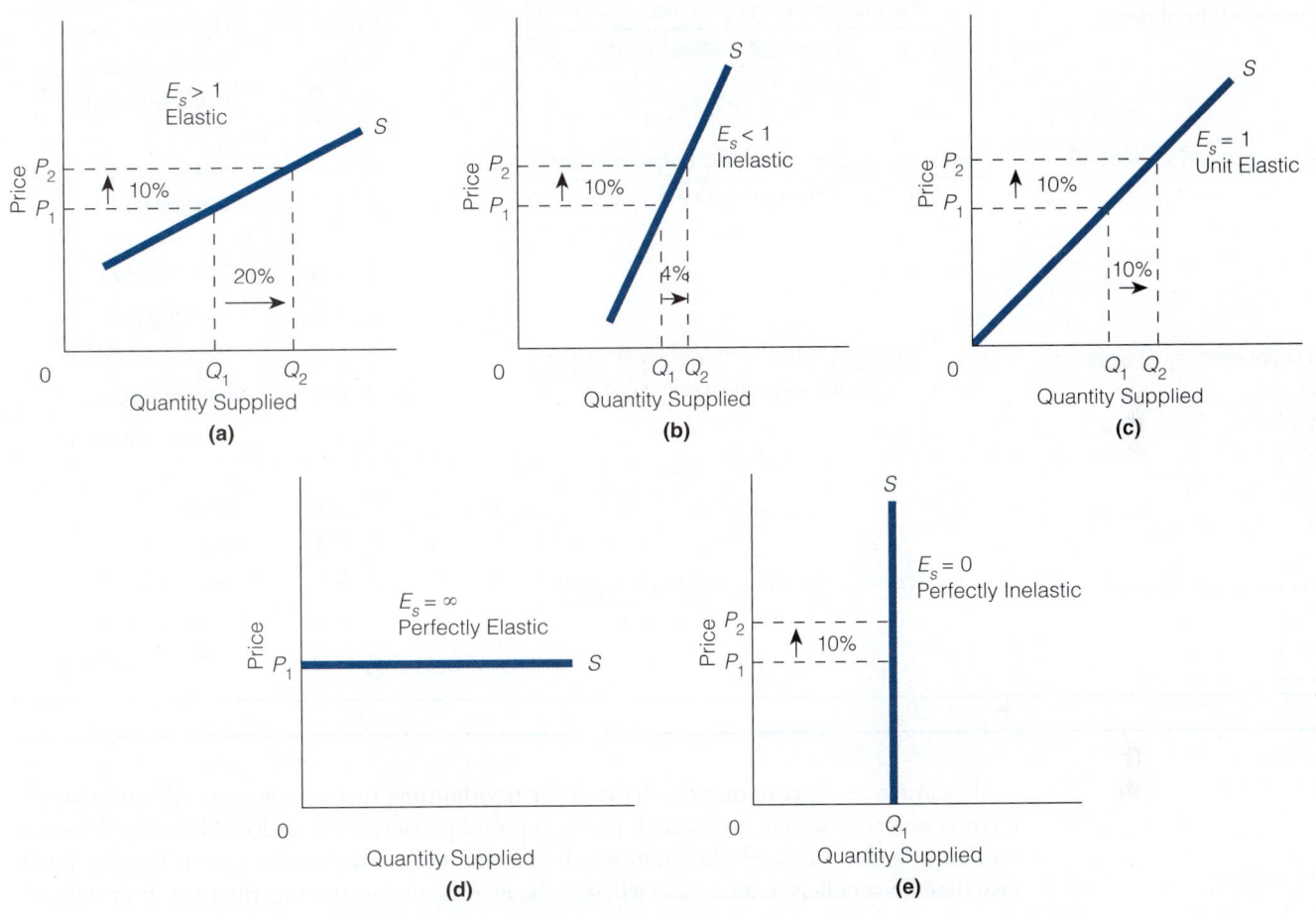

(a) (b) (c)

(d) (e)

- In the case of perfectly inelastic supply ($E_s = 0$), a change in price brings no change in quantity supplied (and thus the supply curve, or a portion of the overall supply curve, is vertical) [see Exhibit 8(e).]

(See Exhibit 9 for a summary of concepts related to elasticity.)

6-3d Price Elasticity of Supply and Time

For goods whose quantity supplied can increase with time—a characteristic of most goods (but not, e.g., original Picasso paintings)—the longer the period of adjustment is to a change in price, the higher the price elasticity of supply will be. The obvious reason is that additional production takes time or may be impossible.

EXHIBIT 9

Summary of the Four Elasticity Concepts

Type	Calculation	Possibilities	Terminology
Price elasticity of demand	$\dfrac{\text{Percentage change in quantity demanded}}{\text{Percentage change in price}}$	$E_d > 1$ $E_d < 1$ $E_d = 1$ $E_d = \infty$ $E_d = 0$	Elastic Inelastic Unit elastic Perfectly elastic Perfectly inelastic
Cross elasticity of demand	$\dfrac{\text{Percentage change in quantity demanded of one good}}{\text{Percentage change in price of another good}}$	$E_c < 0$ $E_c > 0$	Complements Substitutes
Income elasticity of demand	$\dfrac{\text{Percentage change in quantity demanded}}{\text{Percentage change in income}}$	$E_y > 0$ $E_y < 0$ $E_y > 1$ $E_y < 1$ $E_y = 1$	Normal good Inferior good Income elastic Income inelastic Income unit elastic
Price elasticity of supply	$\dfrac{\text{Percentage change in quantity supplied}}{\text{Percentage change in price}}$	$E_s > 1$ $E_s < 1$ $E_s = 1$ $E_s = \infty$ $E_s = 0$	Elastic Inelastic Unit elastic Perfectly elastic Perfectly inelastic

For instance, suppose that the demand for new housing increases in your city and that the increase occurs all at once on Tuesday, placing upward pressure on the price of housing. Then the number of houses supplied will not be much different on Saturday than it was on Tuesday. It will take time for suppliers to determine whether the increase in demand is permanent. If they decide that it is temporary, not much will change. If, however, they decide that the increase in demand is permanent, they need time to move resources from the production of other things into the production of new housing. Simply put, the change in quantity supplied of housing is likely to be different in the long run than in the short run, given a change in price. This effect translates into a higher price elasticity of supply in the long run than in the short run.

THINKING LIKE AN ECONOMIST

Think Ratios   In a way, this chapter is about ratios. A ratio describes how one thing changes (the numerator) relative to a change in something else (the denominator). For example, when we discuss price elasticity of demand, we investigate how quantity demanded changes as price changes; when we discuss income elasticity of demand, we explore how quantity demanded changes as income changes. Economists often think in terms of ratios because they frequently are comparing the change in one variable with the change in another.

ECONOMICS 24/7

House Prices and the Elasticity of Supply

House prices increased in the United States during the years 1998 through mid-2006. House prices did not rise by the same percentage in all cities and states, however. For example, house prices increased more in Los Angeles than in Houston. House prices increased more in Florida than in Idaho. Why didn't house prices rise by the same percentage in every location? Why did they rise more in some places than in others?

One reason could be that demand didn't increase by the same amount in all locations. The demand for houses in, say, San Francisco could have risen by more than the demand for houses in Topeka, Kansas. No doubt, this differential increase in demand is part of the explanation.

But another part of the explanation has to do with supply. As the price of a good rises, we expect the quantity supplied of the good to rise too. In other words, the supply curve of the good is upward sloping. But, although the supply curve of housing is upward sloping, not all supply curves have the same elasticity of supply.

For example, Exhibit 10 shows two supply curves, S_1 and S_2. S_1 has lower elasticity of supply than S_2. Now, suppose that S_1 represents the supply curve of housing in city 1 and that S_2 represents the supply curve of housing in city 2. Suppose also that the demand for housing in each city rises from D_1 to D_2, as in Exhibit 10. As a result, the price of houses rises in both cities, but it rises by more in city 1 than in city 2. In other words, the lower the elasticity of supply is, the greater the increase in price will be.

But why would the elasticity of supply be lower for housing in city 1 than in city 2? The answer could have to do with land use regulations. Suppose that each city has 1,000 vacant areas and that house developers are able to put houses up on only 10 percent of vacant land in city 1 but 70 percent of vacant land in city 2. Then, for a given rise in price, the developers in city 2 can put up more houses (of a given size of house and plot) than developers in city 1 can put up. As a result, if the demand for houses rises by the same amount in city 1 and city 2, more houses will be built in city 2 than in city 1, so the price of houses will rise by less in city 2 than in city 1.

EXHIBIT 10

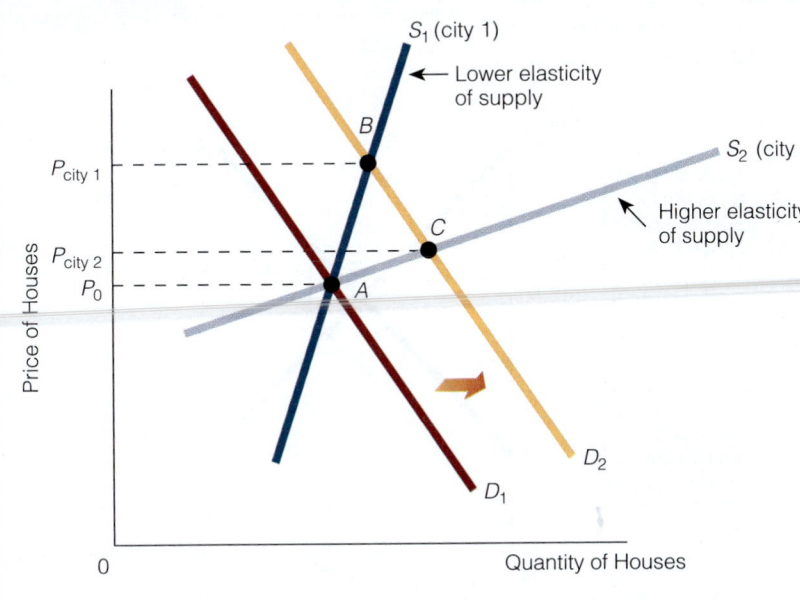

House Prices and Elasticity of Supply

S_1 represents the supply of housing in city 1, and S_2 represents the supply of housing in city 2. S_1 has lower elasticity of supply than S_2. Suppose the demand for housing in each city rises from D_1 to D_2. As a result, the price of houses rises in both cities but it rises by more in city 1 than city 2. In other words, the lower the elasticity of supply, the greater is the increase in price.

6-4 THE RELATIONSHIP BETWEEN TAXES AND ELASTICITY

Before explaining how elasticity affects taxes and tax revenues, we explore how supply and demand determine who pays a tax.

6-4a Who Pays the Tax?

Many people think that, if government places a tax on the seller of a good, the seller actually pays the tax. However, the *placement* of a tax is not the same as its *payment*, and placement does not guarantee payment. To see why, suppose the government imposes a tax on sellers of music digital video discs (DVDs). Then sellers are taxed $1 for every DVD they sell: sell a DVD, send $1 to the government. The government action changes the equilibrium in the DVD market. In Exhibit 11, before the tax is imposed, the equilibrium price and the quantity of tapes are $15 and Q_1, respectively. The tax per DVD shifts the supply curve leftward from S_1 to S_2. The vertical distance between the two supply curves represents the $1-per-DVD tax, because what matters to sellers is how much they keep for each DVD sold, not how much buyers pay. For example, if sellers are keeping $15 per DVD for Q_1 DVDs before the tax is imposed, then they will want to keep as much after the tax is imposed. But if the tax is $1, the only way they can keep $15 per DVD for Q_1 DVDs is to receive $16 per DVD. They receive $16 per DVD from buyers, turn over $1 to the government, and keep $15. In other words, each quantity on the new supply curve, S_2, corresponds to a $1 higher price than it did on the old supply curve, S_1.

EXHIBIT 11

Who Pays the Tax?

A tax placed on the sellers of DVDs shifts the supply curve from S_1 to S_2 and raises the equilibrium price from $15.00 to $15.50. Part of the tax is paid by buyers through a higher price paid ($15.50 instead of $15.00), and part of the tax is paid by sellers through a lower price kept ($14.50 instead of $15.00).

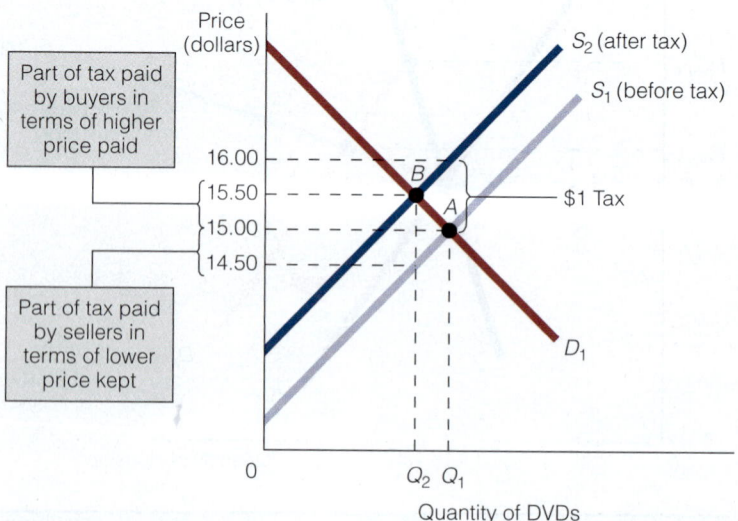

However, the new equilibrium price will not necessarily be $1 higher than the old equilibrium price. In this case, the new equilibrium happens to be at a price of $15.50 and a quantity Q_2. Buyers pay $15.50 per DVD after the tax is imposed, as opposed to $15.00 before the tax was imposed. The difference between the new and old prices is the amount of the $1.00 tax that buyers pay per DVD. In this example, buyers pay 50¢, or one-half of the $1.00 tax per DVD:

Before the tax, buyers pay $15.00.

After the tax, buyers pay $15.50.

The sellers receive $15.50 per DVD from buyers after the tax is imposed, as opposed to $15.00 per DVD before the tax was imposed, but they do not get to keep $15.50 per DVD. One dollar has to be turned over to the government, leaving the sellers with $14.50. Before the tax was imposed, however, sellers received and kept $15.00 per DVD. In this example, the difference between $15.00 and $14.50—50¢—is the amount of the tax per DVD that sellers pay:

Before the tax, sellers receive $15.00 and keep $15.00.

After the tax, sellers receive $15.50 and keep $14.50.

So, although the full tax was *placed* on the sellers, they *paid* only one-half of it; although none of the tax was placed on buyers, they paid one-half of it too. The lesson is that government can place a tax on whomever it wants, but the laws of supply and demand determine who actually ends up paying it.

THINKING LIKE AN ECONOMIST

Placement Can Be Different from Payment   According to a layperson, if the government places a tax on entity A, then entity A pays the tax. The economist knows that the placement and the payment of a tax are two different things. Government may determine the placement of a tax, but supply and demand determine who pays.

6-4b Elasticity and the Tax

In our tax example, buyers paid half of the $1 tax and sellers paid half, but that is not the outcome in every situation. In some situations, the buyer can pay more than half the tax. In fact, the buyer can pay the full tax if demand for the good is perfectly inelastic, as in Exhibit 12(a). Here, the tax shifts the supply curve from S_1 to S_2, and the equilibrium price rises from $15.00 to $16.00. In other words, if demand is perfectly inelastic and a tax is placed on the sellers of a good, buyers pay the full tax as part of a higher price.

Parts (b)–(d) of Exhibit 12 show other cases. In part (b), demand is perfectly elastic. The tax shifts the supply curve from S_1 to S_2, but the equilibrium price does not change. Sellers must therefore pay the full tax if demand is perfectly elastic. In part (c), supply is perfectly elastic, and buyers pay the full tax. In part (d), a change in price causes no change in quantity supplied. If sellers try to charge a higher price than $15 for their good (and thus try to get buyers to pay some of the tax), a surplus will result, driving the price back down to $15. In this case, sellers pay the full tax. Although the exhibit does not show it, sellers would receive $15, turn over $1 to the government, and keep $14 for each unit sold.

EXHIBIT 12

Different Elasticities and Who Pays the Tax

Four extreme cases are illustrated here. If demand is perfectly inelastic (a) or if supply is perfectly elastic (c), then buyers pay the full tax even though the tax may be placed entirely on sellers. If demand is perfectly elastic (b) or if supply is perfectly inelastic (d), then the full tax is paid by the sellers.

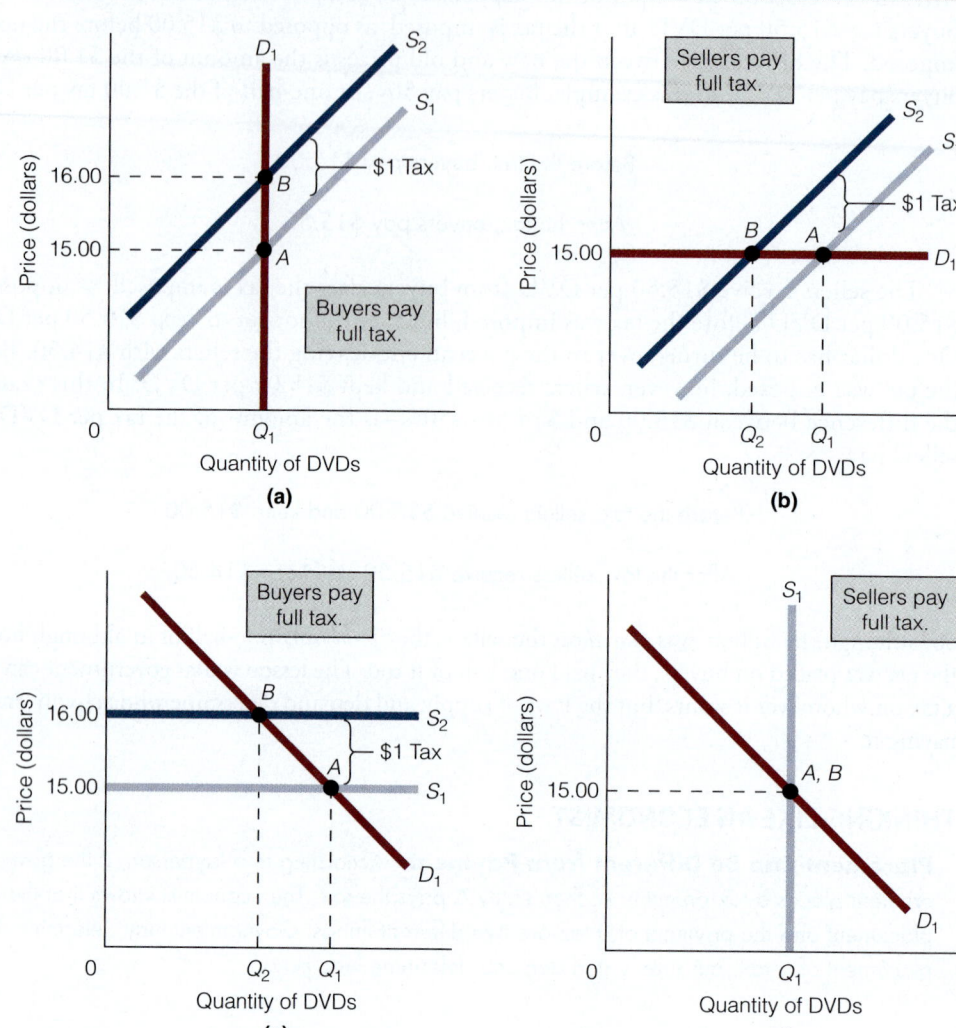

Does It Matter to You . . .
If There Are Few or Many Substitutes for the Goods You Buy?

Suppose you buy two goods, A and B, on a fairly regular basis. Good A has 10 substitutes for it and good B has 2 substitutes. Does one good having more substitutes than another good really make a difference? And, if it does, to what does it make a difference?

Consider that the more substitutes a good has, the greater is the price elasticity of demand for the good—holding all other things

constant. This means that the price elasticity of demand for good A (the good with 15 substitutes) will be higher than the price elasticity of demand for good B (the good with 2 substitutes).

But does it really matter if the price elasticity of demand for one good is higher than it is for another? It does once we consider how price elasticity of demand relates to the percentage of a tax that you, as a buyer, pay. We have learned that the lower the price elasticity of demand for a good is, the larger the percentage of the tax placed on the production of that good will be, which is paid by the buyer.

To illustrate, look again at Exhibit 12. In panel (a), the demand curve is perfectly inelastic, or price elasticity of demand is zero. Notice that, in this case, the tax of $1 is fully paid for by the buyers in terms of a higher price. But in panel (b), where the demand curve is perfectly elastic, the price elasticity of demand approaches infinity, it is the sellers who pay the full tax.

Does the number of substitutes a good has matter to you? It does if the percentage of a tax you pay matters.

6-4c Degree of Elasticity and Tax Revenue

Suppose that, of two sellers, seller A faces a perfectly inelastic demand for her product and is currently selling 10,000 units a month. Suppose also that seller B faces an elastic demand for his product and is currently selling 10,000 units a month. Government is thinking about placing a $1 tax per unit of product sold on one of the two sellers. If government's objective is to maximize tax revenues, it should tax seller A, because that seller is facing the inelastic demand curve.

In Exhibit 13, the demand curve facing seller A is D_1 and the demand curve facing seller B is D_2. S_1 represents the supply curve for both firms. Currently, both firms are at equilibrium at point A, selling 10,000 units. If government places a $1 tax per unit sold on seller A, then the supply curve shifts to S_2 and the equilibrium is now at point C. Because demand is perfectly inelastic, seller A still sells 10,000 units and the government's tax revenue from seller A equals the tax ($1) times 10,000 units, or $10,000. If government places the $1 tax per unit sold on seller B, then tax revenue will be only $8,000 Because, when the tax shifts the supply curve to S_2, the equilibrium moves to point B, at which only 8,000 units are sold.

EXHIBIT 13

Maximizing Tax Revenues

Two sellers, A and B, are each currently selling 10,000 units of their good. A faces the demand curve D_1 and B faces D_2. If the objective is to maximize tax revenues with a $1 tax per unit of product sold and if only one seller can be taxed, then taxing A will maximize tax revenues and taxing B will not. Note that, after the tax has been placed, the supply curve shifts from S_1 to S_2. Seller A is in equilibrium at point C, selling 10,000 units, and B is in equilibrium at point B, selling 8,000 units. Because tax revenues equal the tax per unit times the quantity of output sold, taxing A raises $10,000 in tax revenues whereas taxing B raises $8,000.

The lesson is that, given the $1 tax per unit sold, tax revenues are maximized by placing the tax on the seller who faces the more inelastic (less elastic) demand curve.

SELF-TEST

1. What does an income elasticity of demand of 1.33 mean?

2. What does perfectly inelastic supply signify?

3. Why will government raise more tax revenue if it applies a tax to a good with inelastic demand than if it applies the tax to a good with elastic demand?

4. Under what condition would a per-unit tax placed on the sellers of computers be fully paid by the buyers of computers?

OFFICE HOURS | "What Is the Relationship Between Different Price Elasticities of Demand and Total Revenue?"

STUDENT: I'm still not sure I understand the relationship between price elasticity of demand and total revenue.

INSTRUCTOR: Let's use some numbers to illustrate the relationship. Here we have identified two points on a demand curve:

Price	Quantity Demanded
$10	110
$12	100

The price elasticity of demand between these two points is 0.52, so demand is inelastic. Now let's find the total revenue at each price. If we assume that the economy is in equilibrium (at which quantity demanded is equal to quantity supplied), then total revenue at $10 is $1,100. (We get this amount by multiplying $10 by 110.) When price is $12, total revenue is $1,200. We conclude that if price elasticity of demand is less than 1 (demand is inelastic), then a price rise will raise total revenue. Therefore, if we lower the price (from $12 to $10), total revenue will decline.

Now let's change one of the numbers in the table—from 100 to 80. Then we have the following table:

Price	Quantity Demanded
$10	110
$12	80

If we compute the new price elasticity of demand, we get 1.73, meaning that demand is elastic. Now let's compute total revenue at each price. At $10, that's $1,100. At the higher price of $12, total revenue is $960. So, if price elasticity is greater than 1 (demand is elastic) and if price rises, total revenue falls. And, of course, if price falls (from $12 to $10), total revenue will rise.

STUDENT: So, in the first example, when demand was inelastic, we raised price and total revenue increased. But in the second example, when demand was elastic and we raised price, total revenue decreased.

INSTRUCTOR: Yes, that's correct. When demand is inelastic, the directional change in price brings about the same directional change in total revenue: When price rises, total revenue rises; when price falls, total revenue falls. But when demand is elastic, the directional change in price brings about an opposite directional change in total revenue: When price rises, total revenue falls; when price falls, total revenue rises.

Points to Remember

1. When demand is inelastic, price and total revenue move in the same direction.

2. When demand is elastic, price and total revenue move in opposite directions.

CHAPTER SUMMARY

PRICE ELASTICITY OF DEMAND

- Price elasticity of demand is a measure of the responsiveness of quantity demanded to changes in price.

- If the percentage change in quantity demanded is greater than the percentage change in price, demand is elastic.

- If the percentage change in quantity demanded is less than the percentage change in price, demand is inelastic.

- If the percentage change in quantity demanded is equal to the percentage change in price, demand is unit elastic.

- If a small change in price causes an infinitely large change in quantity demanded, demand is perfectly elastic.

- If a change in price causes no change in quantity demanded, demand is perfectly inelastic.

- The coefficient of price elasticity of demand (E_d) is negative, signifying the inverse relationship between price and quantity demanded. For convenience, however, the absolute value of the elasticity coefficient is used.

TOTAL REVENUE AND PRICE ELASTICITY OF DEMAND

- If demand is elastic, price and total revenue are inversely related: as price rises (falls), total revenue falls (rises).

- If demand is inelastic, price and total revenue are directly related: as price rises (falls), total revenue rises (falls).

- If demand is unit elastic, total revenue is independent of price: as price rises (falls), total revenue remains constant.

DETERMINANTS OF PRICE ELASTICITY OF DEMAND

- The more substitutes a good has, the higher is the price elasticity of demand for the good; the fewer substitutes a good has, the lower is the price elasticity of demand.

- The more that a good is considered a luxury instead of a necessity, the higher the price elasticity of demand will be.

- The greater the percentage of one's budget that goes to purchase a good, the higher the price elasticity of demand will be; the smaller the percentage of one's budget that goes to purchase a good, the lower the price elasticity of demand will be.

- The more time that passes (since a price change), the higher the price elasticity of demand will be; the less time that passes, the lower the price elasticity of demand.

CROSS ELASTICITY OF DEMAND

- Cross elasticity of demand measures the responsiveness in the quantity demanded of one good to changes in the price of another good.

- If $E_c > 0$, two goods are substitutes for each other. If $E_c < 0$ two goods are complements to each other.

INCOME ELASTICITY OF DEMAND

- Income elasticity of demand measures the responsiveness of quantity demanded to changes in income.

- If $E_y > 0$, the good is a normal good. If $E_y < 0$, the good is an inferior good.

- If $E_y > 1$, demand is income elastic. If $E_y < 1$, demand is income inelastic. If $E_y = 1$, demand is income unit elastic.

PRICE ELASTICITY OF SUPPLY

- Price elasticity of supply measures the responsiveness of quantity supplied to changes in price.

- If the percentage change in quantity supplied is greater than the percentage change in price, then supply is elastic.

- If the percentage change in quantity supplied is less than the percentage change in price, then supply is inelastic.

- If the percentage change in quantity supplied is equal to the percentage change in price, then supply is unit elastic.

- Price elasticity of supply is higher in the long run than in the short run.

TAXES AND ELASTICITY

- The placement of a tax is different from its payment. For example, a tax may be placed on the seller of a good, and both the seller and buyer end up paying the tax.

- In this chapter, we discuss a per-unit tax that was placed on the seller of a specific good (DVDs). This tax shifted the supply curve of DVDs leftward. The vertical distance between the old supply curve (before the tax) and the new supply curve (after the tax) was equal to the per-unit tax.

- If a per-unit tax is placed on the seller of a good, both the buyer and the seller will pay part of the tax if the demand curve is downward sloping and the supply curve is upward sloping.

- The more inelastic the demand, the larger the percentage of the tax that the buyer will pay.

- The more elastic the demand, the smaller the percentage of the tax that the buyer will pay.
- When demand is perfectly inelastic or supply is perfectly elastic, buyers pay the full tax.
- When demand is elastic or supply is perfectly inelastic, sellers pay the full tax.

KEY TERMS AND CONCEPTS

Price Elasticity of Demand
Elastic Demand
Inelastic Demand
Unit Elastic Demand

Perfectly Elastic Demand
Perfectly Inelastic Demand
Total Revenue (*TR*)
Cross Elasticity of Demand

Income Elasticity of
   Demand
Income Elastic
Income Inelastic

Income Unit Elastic
Price Elasticity of Supply

QUESTIONS AND PROBLEMS

1. Explain how a seller can determine whether the demand for his or her good is inelastic, elastic, or unit elastic between two prices.

2. For each of the following, identify where demand is elastic, inelastic, perfectly elastic, perfectly inelastic, or unit elastic:

   a. Price rises by 10 percent, and quantity demanded falls by 2 percent.

   b. Price falls by 5 percent, and quantity demanded rises by 4 percent.

   c. Price falls by 6 percent, and quantity demanded does not change.

   d. Price rises by 2 percent, and quantity demanded falls by 1 percent.

3. Prove that price elasticity of demand is not the same as the slope of a demand curve.

4. Suppose the current price of gasoline at the pump is $4 per gallon and that 1 million gallons are sold per day. A politician proposes to add a $1 tax to the price of a gallon of gasoline. She says that the tax will generate $1 million in tax revenues per day. What assumption is she making?

5. For each of the following, identify whether total revenue rises, falls, or remains constant:

   a. Demand is inelastic and price falls.

   b. Demand is elastic and price rises.

   c. Demand is unit elastic and price rises.

   d. Demand is inelastic and price rises.

   e. Demand is elastic and price falls.

6. Suppose a straight-line downward-sloping demand curve shifts rightward. Is the price elasticity of demand higher, lower, or the same between any two prices on the new (higher) demand curve than on the old (lower) demand curve?

7. Suppose a city is hit by a tornado that destroys 25 percent of the housing in the area. Would you expect the total expenditure on housing after the tornado to be greater than, less than, or equal to what it was before the tornado? Explain your answer.

8. For each of the following pairs of goods, which has the higher price elasticity of demand?

   a. Airline travel in the short run or airline travel in the long run

   b. Television sets or Sony television sets

   c. Cars or Fords

   d. Cell phones or Samsung cell phones

   e. Popcorn or Orville Redenbacher's popcorn

9. How might you determine whether toothpaste manufacturers and mouthwash manufacturers are competitors?

10. Suppose that the demand for product A is perfectly inelastic and that the buyers of A get the funds to pay for it by stealing.

    a. If the supply of A decreases, what happens to its price?

    b. What happens to the amount of crime committed by the buyers of A?

11. Suppose you learned that the price elasticity of demand for wheat is 0.7 between the current price for wheat and a price $2 higher per bushel. Do you think that farmers collectively would try to reduce the supply of wheat and drive the price up $2 higher per bushel? Explain your answer. Assuming

that they would try to reduce supply, what problems might they have in actually doing so?

12. In 1947, the U.S. Department of Justice brought a suit against the DuPont Company (which, at the time, sold 75 percent of all the cellophane in the United States) for monopolizing the production and sale of cellophane. In court, DuPont tried to show that cellophane was only one of several goods in the market in which it was sold. The company argued that its market was not the cellophane market but the flexible-packaging materials market, which included (besides cellophane) waxed paper, aluminum foil, and other such products. DuPont pointed out that it had only 20 percent of all sales in this more broadly defined market. Using this information, discuss how the concept of cross elasticity of demand would help establish whether DuPont should have been viewed as a firm in the cellophane market or as a firm in the flexible-packaging materials market.

13. "If government wishes to tax certain goods, it should tax goods that have inelastic rather than elastic demand." What is the rationale for this statement?

14. A tax is placed on the sellers of a good. What happens to the percentage of this tax that buyers pay as the price elasticity of demand for the good decreases? Explain your answer.

WORKING WITH NUMBERS AND GRAPHS

1. A college raises its annual tuition from $23,000 to $24,000, and its student enrollment falls from 4,877 to 4,705. Compute the price elasticity of demand. Is demand for the college elastic or inelastic?

2. As the price of good X rises from $10 to $12, the quantity demanded of good Y rises from 100 units to 114 units. Are X and Y substitutes or complements? What is the cross elasticity of demand?

3. The quantity demanded of good X rises from 130 to 145 units as income rises from $2,000 to $2,500 a month. What is the income elasticity of demand for good X?

4. The quantity supplied of a good rises from 120 to 140 as price rises from $4 to $5.50. What is the price elasticity of supply of the good?

5. In the accompanying figure, what is the price elasticity of demand between the two prices on D_1? On D_2?

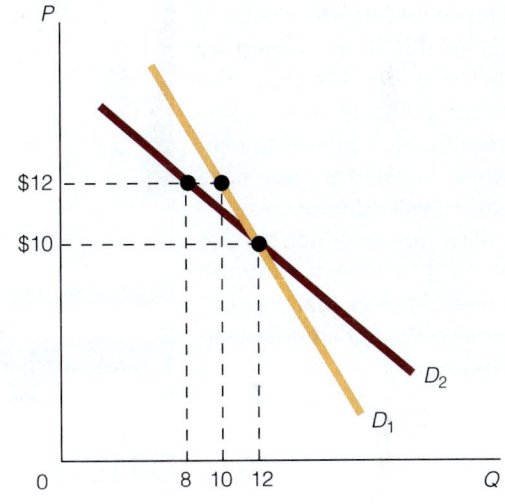

7 CONSUMER CHOICE: MAXIMIZING UTILITY AND BEHAVIORAL ECONOMICS

INTRODUCTION

Just before purchasing a computer, a book, or an iPad, what do you think about? Do you say, "Do I want this or not?" Many people would give this answer. Economists have put this response under the microscope and rephrased it: "The marginal utility of this item divided by its price is greater than the marginal utility of other items divided by their prices, so I am going to make this purchase because it will increase my overall utility." You may not believe now that you—or anyone else—would think that way, but you may believe it after reading this chapter.

7-1 UTILITY THEORY

Water is cheap, and diamonds are expensive. But water is necessary to life and diamonds are not. Isn't it odd—even paradoxical—that what is necessary to life is cheap and what is not necessary is expensive? Eighteenth-century economist Adam Smith wondered about this question. He observed that things with the greatest value in use (or that are the most useful) often have a relatively low price and things with little or no value in use have a high price. Smith's observation came to be known as the **diamond–water paradox**, or the paradox of value. The paradox challenged economists, and they sought a solution to it. This section begins to develop parts of the solution they found.

7-1a Utility: Total and Marginal

Saying that a good gives you **utility** is the same as saying that it has the power to satisfy your wants or that it gives you satisfaction. For example, suppose you buy your first unit of good X and you get a certain amount of utility, say, 10 **utils** from it. (Utils are an artificial construct used to measure utility; we realize that you have never seen a util—no one has.) You buy a second unit of good X, and, once again, you get a certain amount of utility from this second unit, say, 8 utils. You purchase

Diamond–Water Paradox
The observation that things with the greatest value in use sometimes have little value in exchange and things with little value in use sometimes have the greatest value in exchange.

Utility
A measure of the satisfaction, happiness, or benefit that results from the consumption of a good.

Util
An artificial construct used to measure utility.

a third unit and receive 7 utils. The sum of the number of utils (the amount of utility) you obtain from each of the 3 units is the total utility you receive from purchasing good X: 25 utils. Total utility is the total satisfaction one receives from consuming a particular quantity of a good (in this example, 3 units of good X).

Total utility is different from marginal utility. Marginal utility is the *additional* utility gained from consuming an additional unit of good X. **Marginal utility** (*MU*) is the change in total utility (Δ*TU*) divided by the change in the quantity (Δ*Q*) consumed of a good:

$$MU = \frac{\Delta TU}{\Delta Q}$$

The change in the quantity consumed of a good is usually stipulated to be equal to 1 unit.

To illustrate, suppose you receive 10 utils of total utility from consuming 1 apple and 19 utils of total utility from consuming 2 apples. Then the marginal utility of the second apple (the additional utility of consuming an additional apple) is 9 utils. As a person consumes more apples, total utility rises, but marginal utility (additional utility received from the additional apple) falls. In other words, total utility rises as marginal utility falls.

Total Utility
The total satisfaction a person receives from consuming a particular quantity of a good.

Marginal Utility
The additional utility a person receives from consuming an additional unit of a good.

THINKING LIKE AN ECONOMIST

Total Utility and Marginal Utility Can Move in Opposite Directions The economist knows that marginal utility and total utility can move in opposite directions. So, a rise in total utility doesn't mean that marginal utility is rising too. To illustrate, look at the following table:

(1) Number of Apples Consumed	(2) Total Utility (utils)	(3) Marginal Utility (utils)
1	10	10
2	19	9
3	27	8

Clearly, in moving from one, to two, to three apples, total utility rises but marginal utility falls.

7-1b Law of Diminishing Marginal Utility

Do you think that the marginal utility of the second unit is greater than, less than, or equal to the marginal utility of the first unit? To begin to answer this question, consider the difference in marginal utility between the third unit and the second unit and between the fifth unit and the fourth unit (had we extended the number of units consumed). In general, the question is whether the marginal utility of the unit that follows a given unit is greater than, less than, or equal to that of the unit that precedes the given unit.

Economists have generally answered "less than." The **law of diminishing marginal utility** states that, over a given period, the marginal utility gained by consuming equal successive units of a good declines as the amount consumed increases. In other words, the number of utils gained by consuming the first unit of a good is greater than the number of utils gained by consuming the second unit (which is greater than the number gained by the third, which is greater than the number gained by the fourth, and so on).

The law of diminishing marginal utility is illustrated in Exhibit 1. The table in part (a) shows both the total utility of consuming a certain number of units of a good and the marginal utility of consuming additional units. The graph in part (b) shows the total utility

Law of Diminishing Marginal Utility
The marginal utility gained by consuming equal successive units of a good will decline as the amount consumed increases.

EXHIBIT 1

(1) Units of Good X	(2) Total Utility (utils)	(3) Marginal Utility (utils)
0	0	–
1	10	10
2	19	9
3	27	8
4	34	7
5	40	6

(a)

Total Utility, Marginal Utility, and the Law of Diminishing Marginal Utility

TU = total utility and MU = marginal utility. (a) Both total utility and marginal utility are expressed in utils. Marginal utility is the change in total utility divided by the change in the quantity consumed of the good: $MU = \Delta TU / \Delta Q$. (b) Total utility curve. (c) Marginal utility curve. Together, (b) and (c) demonstrate that total utility can increase (b) as marginal utility decreases (c).

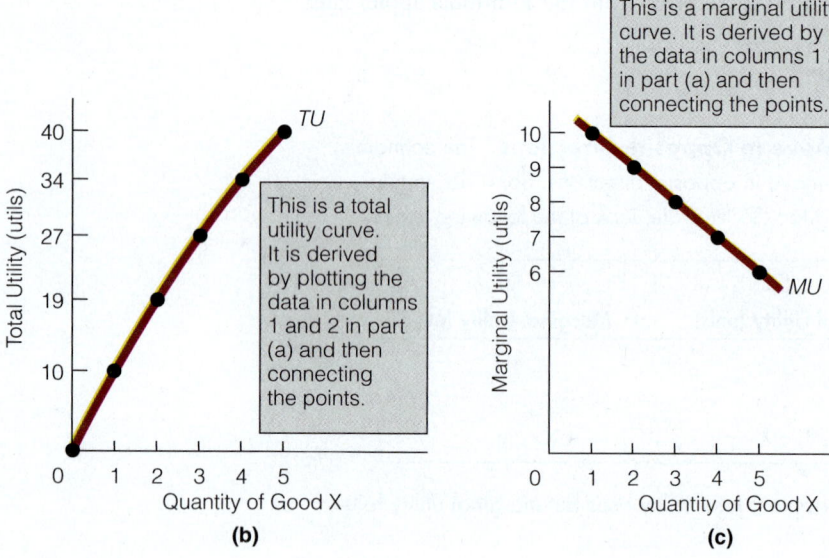

This is a marginal utility curve. It is derived by plotting the data in columns 1 and 3 in part (a) and then connecting the points.

This is a total utility curve. It is derived by plotting the data in columns 1 and 2 in part (a) and then connecting the points.

curve for the data in part (a), and the graph in part (c) shows the marginal utility curve for the data in part (a). The graphs in parts (b) and (c) show that total utility can increase as marginal utility decreases. This relationship between total utility and marginal utility is important in unraveling the diamond–water paradox.

The law of diminishing marginal utility is based on the idea that, if a good has a variety of uses but only 1 unit of the good is available, then the consumer will use the first unit to satisfy his or her most urgent want. If 2 units are available, the consumer will use the second unit to satisfy a less urgent want. Suppose that good X can be used to satisfy wants A through E, with A being the most urgent and E being the least. Also, B is more urgent than C, C is more urgent than D, and D is more urgent than E. We can chart the wants as follows:

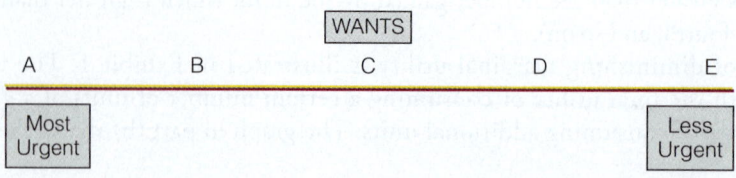

Suppose the first unit of good X can satisfy any one—but only one—of wants A through E. An individual will choose to satisfy the most urgent want, A, instead of B, C, D, or E, because people ordinarily satisfy their most urgent want before satisfying all others. If you were dying of thirst in a desert (having gone without water for, say, three days) and came across a quart of water, you would drink, not wash your hands; that is, you would satisfy your most urgent want first. Washing your hands in the water would give you less utility than drinking it.

The Millionaire and the Pauper: What the Law Says and Doesn't Say

Who gets more utility from one more dollar, a poor man or a millionaire? Most people would say that a poor man gets more utility from one more dollar because the poor man has far fewer dollars than the millionaire. To a millionaire, one more dollar is nothing. A millionaire has so many dollars, one more doesn't mean a thing.

Some people think that the law of diminishing marginal utility substantiates the claim that a millionaire gets less utility from one more dollar than a poor man does. Unfortunately, though, this interpretation is a misreading of the law. The law says that, for the millionaire or the poor man, an additional dollar is worth less than the dollar that preceded it. Let's say the millionaire has $2 million and the poor man has $1,000. We now give each of them one more dollar. The law of diminishing marginal utility says that (1) the additional dollar is worth less to the millionaire than her two-millionth dollar and (2) the additional dollar is worth less to the poor man than his one-thousandth dollar. That is all the law says. We do not, and cannot, know whether the additional dollar is worth more or less to the millionaire than it is to the poor man. In sum, the law says something about the millionaire and about the poor man (both persons value the last dollar less than the next-to-last dollar), but it does not say anything about the millionaire's utility compared to the poor man's utility.

To compare the utility the millionaire gets from the additional dollar with the utility the poor man gets from it is to fall into the trap of making an **interpersonal utility comparison**. The utility that one person gets cannot be scientifically or objectively compared with the utility that another person gets from the same thing because utility is subjective. Who knows for certain how much satisfaction (utility) the millionaire gets from the additional dollar, compared with that of the poor man? On the one hand, the poor man may care little for money; he may shun it, consider the love of it the root of all evil, and prefer to consume the things in life that do not require money. On the other hand, the millionaire may be interested only in amassing more money. We must not guess at the utility that someone obtains from consuming a certain item, compare it with our guess about the utility that another person obtains from consuming the same item, and then call our guesses scientific facts.

Interpersonal Utility Comparison
Comparing the utility one person receives from a good, service, or activity with the utility another person receives from the same good, service, or activity.

THINKING LIKE AN ECONOMIST

Seeming Reasonable Is Not Enough The economist knows that what looks true or seems true may not be true. Although assuming that the millionaire receives less utility from an additional dollar than a pauper may seem perfectly reasonable, the assumption does not make it so. At one time, believing that the world was flat seemed perfectly reasonable, but we know that the world is not flat.

7-1c The Solution to the Diamond–Water Paradox

Goods have both total utility and marginal utility. Water, for example, is extremely useful: we cannot live without it. Thus, we would expect its total utility (its total usefulness) to be high, but its marginal utility to be low because water is relatively plentiful. As the law of diminishing marginal utility states, the utility of successive units of a good diminishes as consumption of the good increases. In short, water is immensely useful, but there is so much of it that individuals place relatively little value on another unit of it.

In contrast, diamonds are not as useful as water. Hence, we would expect the total utility of diamonds to be lower than that of water, but their marginal utility to be high because there are relatively few diamonds in the world. In other words, the consumption of diamonds (in contrast to that of water) takes place at relatively high marginal utility. Diamonds, which are rare, are used only for their few valuable uses. Water, which is plentiful, gets used for its many valuable uses as well as for its not-so-valuable uses (e.g., spraying the car with the hose for 2 more minutes even though you are 99 percent sure that the soap is fully rinsed off).

So, the total utility of water is high because water is extremely useful. The total utility of diamonds is comparatively low because diamonds are not as useful as water. The marginal utility of water is low because water is so plentiful that people consume it at low marginal utility. The marginal utility of diamonds is high because diamonds are so scarce that people consume them at high marginal utility.

Prices therefore reflect marginal utility, not total utility.

SELF-TEST

(Answers to Self-Test questions are in Answers to Self-Test Questions at the back of the book.)

1. State and solve the diamond–water paradox.

2. What does falling total utility imply for marginal utility? Give an arithmetical example to illustrate your answer.

3. When would a good's total utility and marginal utility be the same?

ECONOMICS 24/7

The Gym and Diminishing Marginal Utility

Many people buy a gym membership but do not use it regularly. This is usually how things go: A person visits a gym. He sees people working out; he sees all the different exercise machines. A gym employee tells him that a membership is a great deal, only $1 a day. He signs up for a membership. He visits the gym every other day for the first week of his membership. Then weeks go by without his visiting. He begins to feel guilty about not using his membership, so he drags himself to the gym. A few more weeks pass, and then he drags himself to the gym one more time. Finally, three months pass without his going at all. One day he

wavebreakmedia/Shutterstock.com

gets on the phone and cancels his gym membership. He doesn't even want to add up how much he has spent for a gym membership he rarely used. He sits down, has a bowl of ice cream, and watches television.

What has happened is that our gym member has underestimated the law of diminishing marginal utility applied to exercising at a gym. When he first visits the gym and looks at all the people working out, he might feel that here is a place where utility can be gained. But that utility might simply be the utility he expects to receive on his *first visit* to the gym, times the number of visits he pays to the gym. In other words, he expects to receive, say, 100 utils on his first visit, and he plans to visit the gym 90 days a year. That is a total of 9,000 utils.

What our gym member overlooks is that the utility he receives on his second visit might be less than the utility he receives on his first visit. In other words, the law of diminishing marginal utility might apply to exercising at the gym. For all we know, there could be a dramatic drop-off in marginal utility with, say, the third or fourth visit. His marginal utility per visit might go something like this: first visit, 100 utils; second visit, 80 utils; third visit, 20 utils; fourth visit, 5 utils.

In short, our gym member's decision to join the gym might have been made on the basis of his thinking that he wouldn't experience diminishing marginal utility when, in fact, that is exactly what he does experience.

Now let's return to the gym employee who told our prospective gym member that the gym membership was a great deal: only $1 a day. That $1 a day might have been a great deal for the first day (the first visit to the gym), because our gym member received more than one dollar's worth of utility on the first visit. But then diminishing marginal utility kicked in, and by the time he got to the fifth visit, he no longer was receiving more than one dollar's worth of utility.

7-2 CONSUMER EQUILIBRIUM AND DEMAND

This section identifies the condition necessary for consumer equilibrium and then discusses the relationship between equilibrium and the law of demand. The analysis is based on the assumption that individuals seek to maximize utility.

7-2a Equating Marginal Utilities per Dollar

Suppose there are only two goods in the world: apples and oranges. At present, a consumer is spending his entire income consuming 10 apples and 10 oranges a week. For a particular week, the marginal utility (MU) and price (P) of each are as follows:[1]

$$MU_{oranges} = 30 \text{ utils}$$
$$MU_{apples} = 20 \text{ utils}$$
$$P_{oranges} = \$1$$
$$P_{apples} = \$1$$

So, the consumer's marginal (last) dollar spent on apples returns 20 utils per dollar, and his marginal (last) dollar spent on oranges returns 30 utils per dollar. The ratio MU_O/P_O (O = oranges) is greater than the ratio MU_A/P_A (A = apples):

$$\frac{MU_O}{P_O} > \frac{MU_A}{P_A}$$

---

[1] You may wonder where we get these marginal utility figures. They are points on hypothetical marginal utility curves, such as the one in Exhibit 1. What is important is that one number is greater than the other. We could easily have picked other numbers, such as 300 and 200.

If the consumer recognizes this fact one week, he might redirect his purchases of apples and oranges the next week: "If I buy an orange, I receive more utility [30 utils] than if I buy an apple [20 utils]. It's better to buy 1 more orange with $1 and 1 less apple. I gain 30 utils from buying the orange, which is 10 utils more than if I buy the apple."

As the consumer buys 1 more orange and 1 less apple, however, the marginal utility of oranges falls (recall what the law of diminishing marginal utility says about consuming additional units of a good), and the marginal utility of apples rises (the consumer is consuming fewer apples). Because the consumer has bought 1 more orange and 1 less apple, he now has 11 oranges and 9 apples. At this new combination of goods,

$$MU_O = 25 \text{ utils}$$
$$MU_A = 25 \text{ utils}$$
$$P_O = \$1$$
$$P_A = \$1$$

Now the ratio MU_O/P_O equals the ratio MU_A/P_A. The consumer is getting exactly the same amount of utility (25 utils) per dollar from each of the two goods. There is no way for the consumer to redirect his purchases (i.e., buy more of one good and less of another good) and have more utility. Thus, the consumer is in equilibrium; that is, he derives the same marginal utility per dollar for all goods. The condition for **consumer equilibrium** is

$$\frac{MU_A}{P_A} = \frac{MU_B}{P_B} = \frac{MU_c}{P_c} = \cdots = \frac{MU_Z}{P_Z}$$

where the letters A–Z represent all the goods a person buys.[2]

A person in consumer equilibrium has *maximized total utility*. By spending his or her dollars on goods that give the greatest marginal utility and, in the process, bringing about the consumer equilibrium condition, the consumer is adding as much to total utility as is possible.

Consumer Equilibrium
The equilibrium that occurs when the consumer has spent all of his or her income and the marginal utilities per dollar spent on each good purchased are equal: $MU_A/P_A = MU_B/P_B = \cdots = MU_Z/P_Z$, where the letters A–Z represent all the goods a person buys.

FINDING ECONOMICS

In Everyday Choices Suppose you are standing in a store trying to decide whether to buy another pair of shoes or one more sweater. What is the economics?

You might be seeking consumer equilibrium. Consumer equilibrium exists when the marginal utility–price (MU/P) ratios for all goods are the same—in this case, when the MU/P ratio for shoes is the same as the MU/P ratio for the sweater. As you are standing there trying to decide which to buy more of and which not to buy more of, you are deciding on how best you can spend that next dollar. If you feel that you will get more utility (or satisfaction) per dollar by buying one more pair of shoes instead of one more sweater, then you will buy another pair of shoes. If you feel that you will get more utility per dollar by buying one more sweater instead of one more pair of shoes, then you will buy another sweater. Maybe, as you read this material, you're thinking, "This is crazy. I know I never try to achieve consumer equilibrium. I don't even think about consumer equilibrium at all." But that is exactly what you do if you have purchased one more unit of one good instead of one more unit of another good because you thought it was "worth it."

[2] We are assuming that the consumer exhausts his or her income and that saving is treated as a good.

7-2b Maximizing Utility and the Law of Demand

Suppose a consumer of oranges and apples is currently in equilibrium; that is,

$$\frac{MU_O}{P_O} = \frac{MU_A}{P_A}$$

When in equilibrium, the consumer is maximizing utility. Now, suppose the price of oranges falls. Then the situation becomes

$$\frac{MU_O}{P_O} > \frac{MU_A}{P_A}$$

The consumer will attempt to restore equilibrium by buying more oranges. This behavior—buying more oranges when their price falls—is consistent with the law of demand.

Therefore, the consumer's attempt to reach equilibrium—which is another way of saying that the consumer is seeking to maximize utility—is consistent with the law of demand. In other words, maximization of utility is consistent with the law of demand. The next time someone says that she doesn't maximize utility, ask her if she buys more units of a good when the price is lowered, that is, whether her behavior is consistent with the law of demand. If she says yes, then you can be sure she maximizes utility, because maximization of utility is consistent with the law of demand.

7-2c Should the Government Provide the Necessities of Life for Free?

Some people argue that, because food and water are necessities of life and no one can live without them, charging for them is wrong. The government should provide them to everyone for free. Similarly, others argue that medical care is a necessity for those who are sick. Without proper care, sick people will either die or experience an extremely low quality of life. Making people pay for medical care is wrong: The government should provide it for free to those who need it. Each argument labels something as a necessity of life (food, water, medical care) and then makes the policy proposal that government should provide the necessity for free.

Suppose government did give food, water, and medical care to everyone for free—at zero price (although not at zero taxes). At zero price, people would want to consume these goods up to the point of zero marginal utility for each good. If the marginal utility of the good (expressed in dollars) is greater than its price, people can derive more utility from purchasing the good than they lose in parting with the dollar price of the good. For example, if the price of a good is $5, an individual will continue consuming the good as long as the marginal utility derived from it is greater than $5. If the price is $0, the person will continue to consume the good as long as the marginal utility derived from it is greater than $0.

Resources must be used to produce every unit of a good consumed. If the government uses scarce resources to provide goods with low marginal utility (which food, water, and medical care would have at zero price), then fewer resources are available to produce other goods. The resources could then be redirected to producing goods with a higher marginal utility, thereby raising total utility.

The people who argue that certain goods should be provided free implicitly assume that the not-so-valuable uses of food, water, and medical care are valuable enough to warrant a system of taxes to pay for the complete provision of them at zero price. It is questionable, however, whether the least valuable uses of food, water, and health care are worth the sacrifices of other goods that would necessarily be forfeited if more of these goods were produced.

Think about the question this way: Currently, water is relatively cheap, and people use it for its valuable purposes and its not-so-valuable purposes. But if water were cheaper than it is—if its price were zero—would it be used to satisfy its more valuable uses, its not-so-valuable uses, and its absolutely least valuable use? If food had a zero price, would it be used to satisfy its more valuable uses, its not-so-valuable uses, and its absolutely least valuable use (food fights perhaps)?

THINKING LIKE AN ECONOMIST

Yes, There Can Be Too Much of a Good Thing. As odd as it may sound to say so, there is such a thing as too much health care. The right amount of health care is the amount at which the marginal benefit or marginal utility (of an additional unit of health care) equals the marginal cost. Let's say that the marginal cost of health care is $40 but that, under a system of free health care for everyone, no one directly pays even one cent for personal health care. All health care bills are paid by the federal government with tax monies. In such a case, an individual is likely to continue consuming health care until his marginal utility equals zero. In other words, a person will consume, say, the one-hundredth unit of health care, even though the one-hundredth unit comes with only $0.0000001 worth of benefits to him and a cost of $40 to society at large. Economists say that, if individuals are getting not even a penny's worth of benefits from care that costs $40 to provide, then that is too much health care.

ECONOMICS 24/7

How You Pay for Good Weather

Suppose two cities are alike in every way except one: the weather. One city is called Good-Weather City (*GWC*) and the other Bad-Weather City (*BWC*). In *GWC*, temperatures are moderate all year (70 degrees) and the sky is always blue. In *BWC*, the winter brings snow and freezing rain and the summer brings high humidity and high temperatures. *BWC* has all the forms of weather that people dislike.

We assume that people get more utility from living in good weather than from living in bad weather and that the median price (*P*) of a home in the two cities is the same: $200,000. In terms of marginal utility and housing prices,

$$\frac{MU_{GMC}}{P_{H,GWC}} > \frac{MU_{BWC}}{P_{H,BWC}}$$

alexmisu/Shutterstock.com

That is, the marginal utility of living in *GWC* (*MU_{GWC}*), divided by the price of a house in *GWC* (*P_{H,GWC}*), is greater than the marginal utility of living in *BWC* (*MU_{BWC}*), divided by the price of a house in *BWC* (*P_{H,BWC}*). *GWC* offers greater utility per dollar than does *BWC*.

At least some people will move from *BWC* to *GWC*. The people in *BWC* who want to move will put their houses up for sale, increasing the supply of houses for sale and lowering the price. As these people

move to *GWC*, they increase the demand for houses there, and house prices in *GWC* begin to rise.

This process will continue until the price of a house in *GWC* has risen high enough, and the price of a house in *BWC* has fallen low enough, so that the *MU/P* ratios in the two cities are the same. In other words, the process continues until

$$\frac{MU_{GMC}}{P_{H,GWC}} = \frac{MU_{BWC}}{P_{H,BWC}}$$

At this point, a consumer receives the same utility per dollar in the two cities; the two cities are the same as regards the utility of a dollar.

Now, consider a young couple choosing which city to live in. The couple will not necessarily choose *GWC* because it has a better climate. *GWC* has a better climate than *BWC*, but *BWC* has lower housing prices. One partner says, "Let's live in *GWC*. Think of all that great weather we'll enjoy. We can go outside every day." The other partner says, "But if we live in *BWC*, we can have either a much bigger and better house for the money or more money to spend on things other than housing. Think of the better cars and clothes we'll be able to buy or the vacations we'll be able to take because we won't have to spend as much money to buy a house."

What has happened is that the initial greater satisfaction of living in *GWC* (the higher utility per dollar) has been eroded by people moving there, thereby raising housing prices. On the one hand, *GWC* doesn't look as good as it once did. On the other hand, *BWC* doesn't look as bad as it once did. It still doesn't have the good climate that *GWC* has, but it now has lower housing prices. The utility per dollar of living in *BWC* has risen as a consequence of lowered housing prices.

As long as one city is better (in some way) than another, people will move to it. In the process, they will change things just enough so that it is no longer relatively better. In the end, you have to pay for paradise.

Hear What and How the Economist Thinks . . .
About Towns, Pollution Standards, and Making the Invisible, Visible

The economist hears someone say the following:

The town adjacent to my own has just implemented tighter pollution standards. It turns out that, as a result, the air quality is better in that town than in the town I live in. I think that people moving into the area are going to prefer to live in the town with better air than in my town.

Hear what and how the economist thinks:

If everything between the two towns is the same except that one town has better air quality than the other, the person is right: people who move into the area will probably prefer to live in the town with better air. But this may not continue forever. Let's say that towns A and B are alike in all ways, except that town A has better air quality than town B. As a result, when deciding where to live, people moving into the area would probably see more benefits per $1 by moving into town A than B. But those who move into town A end up increasing the demand for housing in the area, and, eventually, house prices rise in town A relative to house prices in town B. Yes, there will be higher air quality in town A, but individuals will have to pay for it by paying higher prices on housing. (We discuss this phenomenon in our feature, "How You Pay for Good Weather.")

What people often do not see, because it is often difficult to see, is that even though people do not directly pay for something that they

want, that does not mean that they won't end up paying for it indirectly. In our example, no one comes around to the residents of town A and says that they each owe $100 a month for cleaner air. But that doesn't mean that people do not indirectly pay for the cleaner air. If, because of cleaner air, the demand for the houses in town A rise, the price of clean air will get incorporated into housing prices in town A.

It's been said that one of the jobs of the economist is to make what is invisible, visible. When the economist points out how we can end up paying for things that do not have a literal price tag attached to them, this is what he or she is doing.

For another example, let's think back to our discussion (in an earlier chapter) on price ceilings. Suppose the equilibrium price of a good is $4 per unit, and then the government imposes a price ceiling of $3 on the good. For many people, nothing will change other than they will end up paying less for the good instead of more—all benefits, no costs. However, the economist says that, because of the below-equilibrium price, both the quantity supplied and quantity demanded change. The quantity supplied falls (if the supply curve is upward-sloping) and the quantity demanded rises. Because of this, there is a shortage. And because of the shortage, there needs to be some rationing device other than price (since there is a ceiling on price) to deal with it. As a result, we get non-price rationing devices, such as first-come, first-served. Oftentimes, what happens *after the price ceiling has been imposed is invisible to many people. The economist's job is to make what comes after the price ceiling visible.*

Questions to Think About:

1. State governments will often rank the public schools in the state. Would you expect housing prices in neighborhoods where top-rated schools exist to be higher than in neighborhoods where low-rated schools exist? Explain your answer.

2. Real estate prices in New York City, especially Manhattan, are higher than real estate prices in Lake City, Florida (a city of about 12,000 people), although most people would likely consider the weather better in Lake City than in New York. Does this prove that people do not indirectly pay for good weather in housing prices? Explain your answer.

SELF-TEST

1. Alessandro purchases two goods, X and Y, and the utility gained for the last unit purchased of each is 16 utils and 23 utils, respectively. The prices of X and Y are $1 and $1.75, respectively. Is Alessandro in consumer equilibrium? Explain your answer.

2. In a two-good world (goods A and B), what does it mean to be in consumer disequilibrium?

7-3 BEHAVIORAL ECONOMICS

Economists are interested in how people behave with respect to marginal utility. Economic theory predicts that when the MU/P ratio for one good is greater than it is for another, individuals will buy more of the good with the higher MU/P ratio and less of the good with the lower MU/P ratio. Seeking to maximize their utility, individuals will buy more of one good and less of another until the MU/P ratios for all goods are the same.

In traditional economic theories and models, individuals are assumed to be rational, self-interested, and consistent. For about the last 30 years, however, behavioral economists have challenged the traditional economic models. Behavioral economists argue that some human behavior does not fit neatly—at a minimum, easily—into the traditional economic framework. In this section, we describe some of the findings of behavioral economists.

7-3a Are People Willing to Reduce Others' Incomes?

Two economists, Daniel Zizzo and Andrew Oswald, set up a series of experiments with four groups, each with four people. Each person was given the same amount of money and asked to gamble with it. At the end of each act of gambling, two of the four persons in each group had won some money and two had lost some. Then each of the four people in each group was given the opportunity to pay (or forfeit) some amount of money (to a bank) to reduce the take of the others in the group. To illustrate, in the group consisting of Smith, Matsui, Brown, and Rivera, Smith and Rivera had more money after gambling and Matsui and Brown had less. All four were given the opportunity to reduce the amount of money held by the others in the group. For example, Brown could pay to reduce Smith's money, Matsui could pay to reduce Rivera's, and so on.

A reasonable expectation is that no one will spend money to hurt someone else if doing so means leaving himself poorer. However, Zizzo and Oswald found that 62 percent of the participants did just that: They made themselves worse off to make someone else worse off.

Possibly, people behave this way because they are more concerned with relative rank and status than with absolute well-being. Thus, the poorer of the two individuals doesn't mind paying, say,

25¢ if he can reduce the richer person's take by, say, $1. After the poorer person pays 25¢, the gap between him and the richer person is smaller.

Some economists argue that such behavior is irrational and inconsistent with utility maximization. Other economists say it is no such thing. They argue that if people get utility from relative rank, then, in effect, they are buying a move up the relative rank ladder by reducing the size of the gap between themselves and others.

ECONOMICS 24/7

$800 for Sure or $1,000 with a Probability of 85 percent? An Experiment

Here is an experiment in which individuals are presented with two options:

Option A: Receive $800

Option B: Receive $1,000 with a probability of 85 percent and receive nothing with a probability of 15 percent.

In this experiment, there is a sure thing (option A) and an option that is a gamble (option B). The expected payoff for the two options is not the same. The expected payoff for option A is, of course, $800. In other words, a person is guaranteed (has a probability of 100 percent) of receiving $800. Under option B, one has an 85 percent chance of $1,000 and a 15 percent chance of receiving nothing. Here is the expected payoff:

$$0.85(\$1,000) + 0.15(\$0) = \$850$$

In conclusion, then, the expected payoff of option A is $800 and the expected payoff of option B is $850. Standard economics, built on men and women who seek to maximize their expected utility or net benefits, says that, given a choice between options A and B, individuals would choose option B over A. But is that what the

experiment found? Not at all: The overwhelming number of people chose option A, with the expected payoff of $800, instead of option B, with the expected payoff of $850. In other words, they opted for the sure thing instead of the gamble.

One criticism here is that the experiment itself has been called into question. To illustrate, in the experiment, individuals were offered the option of a sure thing with an expected payoff of $800 and the option of a gamble with an expected payoff of $850. Most people chose the sure thing, even though the expected payoff was $50 less than the expected payoff of the gamble. But would the experimental results be different if the expected payoff were larger than $50? Suppose the sure thing's expected payoff was $800 and the gamble's expected payoff was $1,000. Would people still go with the sure thing over the gamble if the gamble's expected payoff were $200 more, instead of $50 more, than the sure thing's payoff? Would people still go with the sure thing over the gamble if the gamble's expected payoff were $10,000 more, instead of $50 more, than the sure thing's payoff? In other words, the difference between the two expected payoffs (sure thing and gamble) may make all the difference as to how people decide.

7-3b Is One Dollar Always One Dollar?

Do people treat money differently depending on where it comes from? Traditional economics argues that they should not; after all, a dollar is a dollar is a dollar. Specifically, a dollar that someone gives you as a gift is no different from a dollar you earn or a dollar you find on the street. When people treat some dollars differently from other dollars, they are *compartmentalizing*: They are saying that dollars in some compartments (of their minds) are valued differently from dollars in other compartments.

Suppose you plan to see a Broadway play, the ticket for which costs $100. You buy the $100 ticket on Monday to see the play on Friday night. When Friday night arrives, you realize you have lost the ticket. Do you spend another $100 to buy another ticket (given that another ticket can be purchased)?[4]

Now let's change the circumstances slightly. Instead of buying the ticket on Monday, you plan to buy the ticket at the ticket window on Friday night. At the ticket window on Friday night, you realize you have lost $100 somewhere between home and the theater. Given that you still have enough money to buy a $100 ticket to the play, do you buy it?

Regardless of how you answer each question, some economists argue that your answers should be consistent. If you say no to the first question, you should say no to the second. If you say yes to the first, you should say yes to the second. The two questions, based on two slightly different settings, present you with essentially the same choice.

However, many people, when asked the two questions, say that they will not pay an additional $100 to buy a second ticket (having lost the first one) but will spend an additional $100 to buy a first ticket (having lost $100 in cash between home and the theater). Some people argue that spending an additional $100 on an additional ticket is the same as paying $200 to see the play—and that is just too much to pay. However, they don't see themselves as spending $200 to see the play when they lose $100 and pay $100 for a ticket. In either case, though, $200 is gone. Behavioral economists argue that people who answer the two questions differently (yes to one and no to the other) are compartmentalizing. They are treating two $100 amounts in two different ways, as if they come from two different compartments. For example, if a person will not buy a second $100 ticket (having lost the first $100 ticket) but will buy a first ticket (having lost $100 cash), her behavior is effectively indicating that $100 lost on a ticket is different from $100 lost in cash.

Consider another situation. Suppose you earn $1,000 by working hard at a job and also win $1,000 at the roulette table in Las Vegas. Would you feel freer to spend the $1,000 you won than to spend the $1,000 you earned? If the answer is yes, then you are treating money differently, depending on where it came from and on what you had to do to get it. Nothing is necessarily wrong or immoral about that, but it is interesting because $1,000 is $1,000 is $1,000—no matter where it came from and no matter what you had to do to get it.

Finally, consider an experiment conducted by two marketing professors. Drazen Prelec and Duncan Simester once organized a sealed-bid auction for tickets to a Boston Celtics basketball game. Half the participants in the auction were told that, if they had the winning bid, they had to pay in cash. The other half of the participants were told that, if they had the winning bid, they had to pay with a credit card.

Under the assumption that the two groups were divided randomly and that neither group showed a stronger or weaker preference for seeing the Celtics game, the average bid from the people who had to pay cash should have been the same as the average bid from the people who had to pay with a credit card. But that didn't happen; instead, the average bid of the people who had to pay with a credit card was higher than the average bid of the people who had to pay with cash. Using a credit card somehow caused people to bid higher dollar amounts than they would have bid if they had to pay cash. Money from the credit card compartment seemed to be more quickly or easily spent than money from the cash compartment.

7-3c Coffee Mugs and the Endowment Effect

In an economics experiment, coffee mugs were allocated randomly to half the people in a group. Each person with a mug was asked to state a price at which he would be willing to sell his mug. Each person without a mug was asked to state a price at which he would be willing to buy a mug.

---

4. This example comes from Gary Belsky and Thomas Gilovich, *Why Smart People Make Big Money Mistakes and How to Correct Them* (New York: Simon & Schuster, 1999).

Even though the mugs were allocated randomly (in other words, the people who received mugs did not necessarily value them more than those who did not receive them), the lowest price at which the owner would sell the mug was, on average, higher than the highest price at which a buyer would pay to buy a mug. For example, the sellers wouldn't sell the mugs for less than $15, and the buyers wouldn't pay more than $10.

This outcome—called the *endowment effect*—is odd. Even though we have no reason to believe that the people who received the mugs valued them more than the people who didn't receive them, people seem to place a high value on something (such as a mug) simply because they own it. In other words, they seem to show an inclination to hold on to what they have.

If this tendency applies to you, think of what it means. When you go into a store to buy a sweater, you might determine that a sweater is worth no more to you than, say, $40 and that you are not willing to pay more than $40 for it. But if someone gave you the sweater as a gift and you were asked to sell it, you wouldn't be willing to sell it for less than, say, $50. Owning the sweater makes it more valuable to you.

Economist David Friedman says that such behavior is not limited to humans.[5] He points out that some species of animals exhibit territorial behavior; that is, they are more likely to fight to keep what they have than to fight to get what they do not have. As Friedman notes, "It is a familiar observation that a dog will fight harder to keep his own bone than to take another dog's bone."

Friedman argues that this type of behavior in humans makes perfect sense in a hunter–gatherer society. Here is what Friedman has to say:

> Now consider the same logic [found in the fact that a dog will fight harder to keep the bone he has than to take a bone from another dog] in a hunter–gatherer society—in which there are no external institutions to enforce property rights. Imagine that each individual considers every object in sight, decides how much each is worth to him, and then tries to appropriate it, with the outcome of the resulting Hobbesian struggle determined by some combination of how much each wants things and how strong each individual is. It does not look like a formula for a successful society, even on the scale of a hunter–gatherer band.
>
> There is an alternative solution, assuming that humans are at least as smart as dogs, robins, and fish. Some method, possibly as simple as physical possession, is used to define what "belongs to" whom. Each individual then commits himself to fight very hard to protect his "property"—much harder than he would be willing to fight in order to appropriate a similar object from someone else's possession—with the commitment made via some psychological mechanism presumably hardwired into humans. The result is both a considerably lower level of (risky) violence and a considerably more prosperous society.
>
> The fact that the result is attractive does not, of course, guarantee that it will occur—evolution selects for the reproductive interest of the individual, not the group. But in this case they are the same. To see that, imagine a population in which some individuals have adopted the commitment strategy [outlined above—that is, fighting for what you physically possess], and some have adopted different commitment strategies—for example, a strategy of fighting to the death for whatever they see as valuable. It should be fairly easy to see that individuals in the first group will, on average, do better for themselves—hence have (among other things) greater reproductive success—than those in the second group.
>
> How do I commit myself to fight very hard for something? One obvious way is some psychological quirk that makes that something appear very valuable to me. Hence the same behavior

---

[5]. See his "Economics and Evolutionary Psychology" at his website, http://www.daviddfriedman.com/Academic/econ_and_evol_psych/economics_and_evol_psych.html.

pattern that shows up as territorial behavior in fish and ferocious defense of bones in dogs shows up in Cornell students [who were given the coffee mugs] as an endowment effect. Just as in the earlier cases, behavior that was functional in the environment in which we evolved continues to be observed, even in an environment in which its function has largely disappeared.[6]

7-3d Does the Endowment Effect Hold Only for New Traders?

The endowment effect has not gone untested. John List, an economist at the University of Chicago, wanted to know whether new traders were more likely than experienced traders to experience the endowment effect. He went to a sports card exchange where people trade regularly. In one experiment, he took aside a group of card fans and gave them such things as sports autographs and sports badges. He then gave them the opportunity to trade. He observed that the more experience traders had (at trading such items), the less prone they were to the endowment effect.

One criticism of this experiment was that new traders were less likely to trade than experienced traders because novices were not sure of the value of the sports autographs. To meet this criticism, List conducted another experiment with chocolate and coffee mugs, where he was sure everyone did know the values of the items. Once again, he observed some endowment effect, but it was not as evident as in the sports memorabilia case, and—more important—only newer traders demonstrated the effect. In other words, experience as a trader seems to make one less prone to the endowment effect.

We value X more highly if we have it than if we do not have it because such behavior at one point in our evolution made possible a system of property rights in a world where the alternative was the Hobbesian jungle.

Does It Matter to You . . .
If You Are Subject to the Endowment Effect?

Consider Isaac, who is currently getting ready to sell the house that he has owned and lived in for 20 years. He has decided that he will not sell his house for less than $600,000. His realtor tells him that comparable houses in the neighborhood are selling for $550,000 and that he has probably overpriced his house by $50,000. However, Isaac says that he believes his house is "worth" $600,000, and that he won't sell his house for any less. Isaac's realtor asks him how much he would be willing to pay for the house if he were buying it today. And he says that he would be willing to pay $550,000.

This is a case of the endowment effect: Isaac is placing a higher dollar value on the house he has owned for 20 years than he would place on the house if he didn't own it.

iStock.com/RichLegg

---

[6] Ibid., p. 10.

Does it matter if Isaac is subject to the endowment effect? It could very well matter. To illustrate just how, consider the following scenario. Isaac goes ahead and lists his house for $600,000. He has had people looking at his house, but so far, everyone who has looked at his house has offered $550,000 for it, which is the price he would likely offer if he were buying the house today. Isaac turns down every offer continuing to believe that his house is "worth" $600,000.

Over time Isaac begins to wonder if, perhaps, he should sell his house for $550,000. The reality of not receiving an offer of $600,000 for some time makes him believe that buyers may simply be unwilling to pay $600,000 for his house. Finally, he decides to lower the price of his house. But now, the market price of the house no longer appears to be $550,000. Demand for houses in his neighborhood has fallen recently, and now the market equilibrium price for his house appears to be $520,000. In the end, Isaac ends up selling his house for $520,000.

Does it matter to Isaac that he was subject to the endowment effect? It mattered $30,000, which is the difference between what he could have sold his house for when he first placed it on the market and what he ended up selling it for.

7-3e The Ultimatum Game—and Facebook, YouTube, and Wikipedia

Facebook, YouTube, and Wikipedia have provided people with online sites to visit. At those sites, people can do specific things. They can create a personal profile, post pictures, and share information (Facebook); upload audio and video files (YouTube); and create and edit encyclopedia articles (Wikipedia). Facebook, YouTube, and Wikipedia are among the top 10 most visited websites in the world.

Now, there is one important thing that these three websites have in common: The content on each is not produced by the owners of the sites or (in most cases) by the persons the owners of the sites employ. The vast majority of the content on each site comes from visitors to the site. If you have a Facebook profile, you produce some of the content that makes up Facebook; if you upload a video to YouTube, you produce some of the content that makes up YouTube; and if you have ever started or edited an article on Wikipedia, you have produced some of the content that makes up Wikipedia. In short, the actual "employees" who produce the content on each of the three websites are members of the general public who visit those sites. Members of the general public are, in a sense, the workers.

Now, what the owners of Facebook and YouTube do is sell that content and gain revenue in the process. That is, they charge advertisers to advertise on Facebook and YouTube. So, the whole process for Facebook and YouTube looks like this: (1) The owners of each site essentially tell members of the general public that there is now a place that they can come to produce content; (2) members of the general public go to the site and produce the content; and then (3) the owners of the site sell the content by charging fees to companies that want to advertise on the site.

In comparison to Facebook and YouTube, consider what Wikipedia does not do: sell content that members of the general public produce. There are no ads on Wikipedia. According to the Wikipedia Foundation:

> We never run ads on Wikipedia. Wikipedia is funded by more than a million donors, who give an average donation of less than 30 dollars. We run fundraising appeals, usually at the end of the year. If you're seeing advertisements for a for-profit industry … or anything but our fundraiser, then your web browser has likely been infected with malware.

So the question is why do Facebook and YouTube, but not Wikipedia, run ads? Some have argued that it's because, if they did, then the contributors to Wikipedia (i.e., the members of the general public who actually write and edit the Wikipedia articles) would leave the site. In fact, there is some evidence that many would.

In May 2001, the Spanish Wikipedia was launched. Not long after, there was talk that Wikipedia was thinking of selling advertising space. Many of the contributors to the Spanish Wikipedia were dismayed at hearing about the possibility of selling such space. That possibility was one of the main reasons most of the Spanish Wikipedia community took the content they had written to another server and set up their own encyclopedia, *Enciclopedia Libre Universal*. In response to this action, Larry Sanger, who cofounded Wikipedia with Jimmy Wales, had this to say (in Wikipedia):

> *I don't claim to understand fully why this effort has been undertaken. My vague understanding is that some people have objected to the fact that advertisements are planned. These people, however, seem not to have all the facts. Please, read the following—it's important. The mere fact that advertisements are presently being left open as an option should not be a reason for anyone to quit the project and start a competing one.*

There seems to be a difference between contributors to Facebook and YouTube and contributors to Wikipedia. Facebook and YouTube contributors are not against the owners of both sites earning revenue from their collective contributions, but Wikipedia contributors do seem to be against Wikipedia, the organization, earning revenue from their collective contributions.

With this information as background, consider the ultimatum game that is sometimes played in economic experiments (see the Economics 24/7 feature "$40 and Two People: The Ultimatum Game). In the game, two persons interact to divide a sum of money between them. One person chooses how to divide the money, and the other person decides to either accept or reject the particular division offered. If she accepts the offer, each person gets the amount the initial person divided up. If she rejects the offer, neither person gets any money. For example, let's say person A is chosen to divide up $10. She proposes $9.99 for herself and one cent for person B. Person B then has to either accept or reject the offer. If she accepts the offer, she gets one cent and A gets $9.99. If she rejects the offer, she gets nothing and A gets nothing.

Now, the thought is that the rational thing to do if you are person B is to accept the offer—even if it is only one cent. Why? Because it is better to have one cent than zero cents. But this is not usually what happens. Usually, person B is more likely to turn down any offer that doesn't provide her with at least 20 percent of the entire sum of money. In other words, what economic experiments of the ultimatum game show is that people are often willing to "make themselves worse off" in order to "make someone else worse off" if that someone else hasn't offered them what they consider to be a fair deal.

Now let's return to Facebook, YouTube, and Wikipedia. Obviously, Facebook and YouTube contributors are willing to accept the deal that Facebook and YouTube owners present to them, which is as follows: we will allow you to network with others, and upload audio and video files to share with others, if you let us sell advertising space and collect all the revenue. In other words, when it comes to dividing up the revenue, we take 100 percent of it and give you none of it. In terms of the ultimatum game, Facebook and YouTube contributors are closer to those persons who, in the game, willingly accept one cent of the $10 sum to be divided.

The Wikipedia contributors weren't willing to accept the same deal. They essentially said that if the Wikipedia organization takes 100 percent of the revenue it gets from ads, they will no longer contribute to Wikipedia. They are closer, in actions, to the persons in the ultimatum game who say, "Unless the way you divide up the money is closer to 60:40 or 50:50, we choose not to play—and while that might hurt us, it will certainly hurt you too."

Although the contributors to Wikipedia play the ultimatum game differently than the contributors to Facebook and YouTube do, this difference begs the question of *why* they play the game differently. One noticeable difference between Facebook and YouTube, on the one hand, and Wikipedia, on the other, is that contributors to Facebook and YouTube actually receive benefits from doing what they do on each platform. On Facebook, they get to network with their friends; Facebook is a way of keeping up with others, and there are some benefits derived from being able to do that. On YouTube, there is a benefit from posting a video that you can share with your friends or that may go viral. In other words, the contributors to both Facebook and YouTube are, in a way, already receiving some benefits and therefore don't feel as much need to also get part of the advertising revenues that both Facebook and YouTube receive.

But, of course, can't the same be said about those who contribute to Wikipedia? Don't they receive benefits from knowing that they are informing others on a particular topic or editing an article someone else has written? No doubt there are benefits from doing such things, but if the benefits of writing encyclopedia articles for free and then distributing them to others were high enough, people would have done that before Wikipedia—but they didn't. Pre-Facebook, people had always tried to network with friends; pre-YouTube, people had always shared their videos with friends. But pre-Wikipedia, no one seemed willing to write or edit encyclopedia articles and then pass them along to friends and acquaintances. What Facebook and YouTube allowed people to do is what they had always been doing (without pay), but just in an easier way and on a grander scale. Wikipedia, by contrast, allowed people to do something that they hadn't already been doing, but that some people did in the past only if they were paid. That is, before Wikipedia there were companies that published encyclopedias, but those companies paid employees to write the articles that made up the encyclopedia. When Wikipedia came along and did not offer to pay people to write and edit encyclopedia articles, Wikipedia contributors knew that they were not being paid for work which was paid for in the past, and they seemed all right with that as long as *no one* got paid for their encyclopedia contributions.

ECONOMICS 24/7

$40 and Two People: The Ultimatum Game[7]

The ultimatum game involves two people and one pot of money. One person divides the money between himself and the other person. The other person, who knows how much money has been allotted to him, can either accept his portion of the money or reject it. If he rejects it, then neither person gets any money. To illustrate, suppose Jack is going to divide $40 between himself and Bill. Jack gives himself $35, and he gives Bill $5. At this point, Bill can either accept or reject the $5 that Jack has apportioned to him. If he accepts it, then he gets the $5 and Jack gets the $35. But if he rejects it, neither he nor Jack gets any money.

In Bill's position, would you accept the $5 or reject it? Often, your strategy may depend on whether this is a one-time deal or there are other rounds of play. If there are other rounds of play, you might reject the initial offer of $5, so that you send a message to Jack: Either divide the money more nearly equal (closer to $20 each), or I will make sure you get nothing. Over several rounds of play, this strategy may give you the most money overall.

But if it is a one-round game, which is the way the ultimatum game is often played, does rejecting the deal make sense, no matter

how Jack divides the money? If Jack gives himself $35 and you $5 and if you reject the deal, you do not get the $5. If you accept the deal, you get at least the $5. When economists have experimented with the one-round ultimatum game, they find that many participants reject the money offer if it is not close to half the money. In other words, they are likely to reject an offer of $35–$5 (where they receive the $5) or an offer of $30–$10, whereas they are likely to accept an offer of $20–$20.

Some economists reason that this tendency to reject uneven splits of the money shows that people are more concerned with their relative income position than with their absolute income position. In other words, how much income one has does not seem to matter as much as how much income one has relative to others.

In one experiment, performed by economist Terence Burnham of Harvard University, the results showed that men with higher testosterone levels were more likely to reject unequal offers of money than those with lower testosterone levels. Five of 7 men with the highest testosterone levels in the group rejected an unequal offer, whereas only 1 of 19 men with lower testosterone levels rejected an unequal offer. Because high testosterone is highly correlated with social dominance (in many societies), one conclusion might be that the higher a man's testosterone level is, the more relative position (as opposed to absolute position) seems to matter.

Another way of looking at the results of the ultimatum game is to say that sometimes people are irrational. In other words, turning down, say, a $35–$5 offer is irrational because having $5 is better than not having $5. Of course, another perspective is that rejecting such an offer is not irrational at all for someone who is trying to maximize his or her relative position in society, not the number of dollars the person has. In such a case, rejecting offers that lower one's relative position *is* rational.

_____

7. This feature is based on "Money Isn't Everything" in *The Economist*, July 5, 2007.

7-3f Framing

In economics, the term *framing* refers to how a problem is presented. To illustrate, we draw on the work of Amos Tversky and Daniel Kahneman, who have shown that framing can influence the choices one makes. In fact, how a problem is framed can lead to a reversal of preferences.

Before getting to how problems are framed, consider the following two options, a sure thing and a gamble:

- *Sure Thing*. You are guaranteed a payment of $50.

- *Gamble*. A coin is tossed. If heads comes up, you win nothing; if tails comes up, you win $100.

The *expected payoff* of the sure thing is $50 ($50 × 100 percent = $50). The expected payoff of the gamble is $50 ($0 × ½ + $100 × ½ = $50). Notice that, in this example, the expected payoffs of the sure thing and the gamble are the same: $50. Three terms can be used to describe a person's attitude toward risk. Given a sure thing and a gamble that have the same expected payoff:

- A person who prefers the sure thing over the gamble is called *risk averse*.

- A person who prefers the gamble over the sure thing is *risk loving*.

- A person who is indifferent between the two options is *risk neutral*.

Tversky and Kahneman proposed an Asian disease problem: Suppose the United States is preparing for an outbreak of an unusual Asian disease, which could kill 600 people. A group of individuals is asked to choose between two options (programs) that have been proposed to combat the disease. The choice is framed as follows:

- *Option A (a sure thing)*. Two hundred people will be saved.

- *Option B (a gamble)*. There is a one-third probability that 600 people will be saved and a two-thirds probability that no one will be saved.

Notice that the expected payoff for each option is the same. In option A (the sure thing), 200 people will be saved and 400 people will die. In option B (the gamble), one-third of 600 people are expected to be saved, for an expected payoff of 200 lives saved and 400 lives lost. When Tversky and Kahneman surveyed people as to their preference between the two options, 72 percent of the people chose option A (the sure thing) and 28 percent chose option B (the gamble). Because options A and B have the same expected payoff and the majority of people chose the sure thing over the gamble, we conclude that people are generally risk averse.

In a second survey, a group of individuals was confronted with another two options, framed in the following way:

- *Option C (the sure thing)*. Four hundred people will die.
- *Option D (the gamble)*. There is a one-third probability that nobody will die and a two-thirds probability that 600 people will die.

The expected payoff in option C (the sure thing) is that 400 people will die and 200 people will be saved. The expected payoff in option D (the gamble) is that 400 people will die and 200 people will be saved ($600 \times 2/3 = 400$ die; $600 \times 1/3 = 200$ saved). Once again, the expected payoffs of the two options are the same. More importantly, the expected payoffs of options C and D are the same as the expected payoffs of options A and B from the previous survey. It is therefore reasonable to think that the results of the second survey would be similar to the results of the first survey.

As it turns out, the results were completely different: Only 22 percent of the persons surveyed chose the sure thing (as opposed to 72 percent in the first survey), and 78 percent chose the gamble (as opposed to 28 percent in the first survey). People were now overwhelmingly choosing the gamble over the sure thing. The conclusion from the second survey is that people are generally risk loving.

What made the difference in choosing between options A and B and between options C and D? The answer is that the options were framed differently. Options A and B were phrased in terms of *people saved*; options C and D were phrased in terms of *people dying*. When the options were phrased in terms of lives saved, the majority of people chose the sure thing and were risk averse. But when the options were phrased in terms of people dying, the majority of people chose the gamble and therefore were risk loving. Conclusion: *Even when the expected payoffs are the same, how the options are framed (people saved or people dying) can affect the choices people make*. In our example, framing caused risk-averse choosers to become risk-loving choosers.

7-3g Neuroeconomics

Neuroeconomics is a branch of behavioral economics. In neuroeconomics, the brain is studied with tools such as magnetic resonance imaging (MRI) to see what is happening when people make choices, have certain thoughts, try to solve certain problems, and so on. For a concrete example of an issue that might interest a neuroeconomist, consider choices that human beings make that involve two time references: the present and the future.

There are two key subsystems of the brain. One deals with how we feel emotionally, how we respond to people, and how we respond to what we consider fair and unfair. This is the limbic system. The other subsystem of the brain deals with calculating, conscious, future-oriented thinking. This is the analytic system.

Using magnetic resonance imaging, researchers find that both systems of the brain show activity when faced with some choices. For example, when individuals are asked to choose between receiving $20 now and receiving $23 in a month, both the limbic and analytic systems show activity. Notice that the choice here has to do with a present–future trade-off: Get something now, or get more of that something in the future.

When faced with present–future choices, the limbic system (which weights the present heavily) seems to win out over the analytic system: Individuals choose the present (receive $20 now) over the future (receive $23 in a month). Stated differently, temptation wins out over waiting. Brain researchers think that, when faced with a present–future trade-off, the brain might weight the present high and future low because responding quickly and definitively to present rewards might have come with an evolutionary advantage, since future rewards in an environment in which human evolution took place were so uncertain. Grab what you can now, for tomorrow may not come.

But what does the brain do when an individual is faced with *two future-oriented choices*, such as receiving $20 in two weeks (the future) or receiving $23 in a month (a slightly more distant future). In that case, researchers have found activity in the analytic system but not in the limbic system. It is as if the limbic system has dropped out of its tug-of-war with the analytic system. As a result, individuals often choose the later future-oriented choice: $23 in a month instead of $20 in two weeks.

SELF-TEST

1. Brandon's grandmother is very cautious about spending money. Yesterday, she gave Brandon a gift of $100 for his birthday. Brandon also received a gift of $100 from his father, who isn't nearly as cautious about spending money as Brandon's grandmother is. Brandon believes that buying frivolous things with his grandmother's gift would be wrong, but not with his father's gift. Is Brandon compartmentalizing? Explain your answer.

2. Summarize David Friedman's explanation of the endowment effect.

OFFICE HOURS | "Is There an Indirect Way of Proving the Law of Diminishing Marginal Utility?"

STUDENT: In class, you proved that the law of demand is consistent with utility maximization. This was an important proof for me because I had always accepted the law of demand as true, but I never really felt easy with the idea that individuals seek to maximize utility. Your proof that the law of demand is consistent with utility maximization helps put this earlier uneasiness of mine to rest.

Having said that, I want to know if there is any similar proof of the law of diminishing marginal utility? The law of diminishing marginal utility sounds true, but can it be proven so?

INSTRUCTOR: Yes, there is. To illustrate, let's start with something that we know is true because it is so obvious: People trade. Now, it's not likely that they would trade if the law of diminishing marginal utility did not hold.

STUDENT: In other words, you're saying that the law of diminishing marginal utility is consistent with the fact that people trade.

INSTRUCTOR: Yes. Consider two people, Smith and Jones. Smith has 100 apples and Jones has 100 oranges. As Smith consumes her apples, her marginal utility declines. Her tenth apple doesn't give her as much utility as her ninth, and so on. The same is true for Jones with respect to oranges. In other words, as Smith and Jones consume successive units of what they have, their respective marginal utilities fall.

At some point, Smith's marginal utility of consuming another apple is likely less than her marginal utility of consuming something different—such as an orange. And at some point, Jones's marginal utility of consuming another orange is likely less than his marginal utility of consuming something different—say, an apple. When this point comes, Smith and Jones will trade. For Smith, the marginal utility of consuming an apple will be less than the marginal utility of consuming an orange, and she will gladly trade an apple for an orange. For Jones, the marginal utility of consuming an orange will be less than the marginal utility of consuming an apple, and he will gladly trade an orange for an apple.

Now, suppose the law of diminishing marginal utility did not exist. Then Smith would have the same marginal utility when she consumed her first and her one-hundredth apple, and this marginal utility would always be greater than her marginal utility of consuming an orange. The situation would be reversed for Jones: He would have the same marginal utility when he consumed his first and his one-hundredth orange, and that marginal utility would always be greater than his marginal utility of consuming an apple. Thus, Smith and Jones would never trade with each other. The law of diminishing marginal utility, at work on both apples and oranges, eventually gets Smith and Jones to trade.

Points to Remember

1. The law of demand is consistent with utility maximization.
2. The law of diminishing marginal utility is consistent with the fact that individuals trade.

CHAPTER SUMMARY

THE LAW OF DIMINISHING MARGINAL UTILITY

- The law of diminishing marginal utility holds that, as the amount of a good consumed increases, the marginal utility of the good decreases.

- The law of diminishing marginal utility should not be used to make interpersonal utility comparisons. For example, the law does not say that a millionaire receives less (or more) utility from an additional dollar than a poor man does. All it says is that, for both the millionaire and the poor man, the last dollar has less value than the next-to-last dollar has.

THE DIAMOND–WATER PARADOX

- The diamond–water paradox states that what has great value in use sometimes has little value in exchange and that what has little value in use sometimes has great value in exchange. A knowledge of the difference between total utility and marginal utility is necessary to unravel the paradox.

- A good can have high total utility and low marginal utility. For example, water's total utility is high, but because water is so plentiful, its marginal utility is low. In short, water is immensely useful, but it is so plentiful that individuals place relatively low value on another unit of it. In contrast, diamonds are not as useful as water, but because there are few diamonds in the world, the marginal utility of diamonds is high. In sum, on the one hand, a good can be extremely useful and have a low price if the good is in plentiful supply (high value in use, low value in exchange); on the other hand, a good can be of little use and have a high price if the good is in short supply (low value in use, high value in exchange).

CONSUMER EQUILIBRIUM

- Individuals seek to equate marginal utilities per dollar. For example, if a person receives more utility per dollar spent on good A than on good B, she will reorder her purchases and buy more A and less B. The tendency is to move away from the condition $MU_A/P_A > MU_B/P_B$ and toward the condition $MU_A/P_A = MU_B/P_B$. The latter condition represents consumer equilibrium (in a two-good world).

MARGINAL UTILITY ANALYSIS AND THE LAW OF DEMAND

- Marginal utility analysis can be used to illustrate the law of demand, which states that price and quantity demanded are inversely related, *ceteris paribus*. Starting from consumer equilibrium in a world containing only two goods, A and B, a decline in the price of A will cause MU_A/P_A to be greater than MU_B/P_B. As a result, the consumer will purchase more of good A in order to restore herself to equilibrium.

BEHAVIORAL ECONOMICS

- Behavioral economists argue that some human behavior does not fit neatly—at a minimum, easily—into the traditional economic framework.

- Behavioral economists believe that they have identified human behaviors that are inconsistent with the model of men and women as rational, self-interested, and consistent: (1) Individuals are willing to spend some money to lower the incomes of others, even if doing so lowers their own incomes. (2) Individuals don't always treat one dollar as one dollar: some dollars seem to be treated differently than others. (3) Individuals sometimes value X more if it is theirs than if it isn't theirs and they are seeking to acquire it. (4) The way a set of options is framed (presented) can matter to the choices individuals make.

KEY TERMS AND CONCEPTS

Diamond–Water Paradox
Utility
Util

Total Utility
Marginal Utility
Law of Diminishing Marginal Utility

Interpersonal Utility Comparison
Consumer Equilibrium

QUESTIONS AND PROBLEMS

1. Give a numerical example that illustrates total utility rising as marginal utility declines.

2. The law of diminishing marginal utility is consistent with the fact that people trade. Do you agree or disagree? Explain your answer.

3. "If we take $1 away from a rich person and give it to a poor person, the rich person loses less utility than the poor person gains." Comment.

4. Is it possible to get so much of a good that it turns into a bad? If so, give an example.

5. If a person consumes fewer units of a good, will marginal utility of the good increase as total utility decreases? Why or why not?

6. The marginal utility of good A is 4 utils, and its price is $2. The marginal utility of good B is 6 utils, and its price is $1. Is the individual consumer maximizing (total) utility if she spends a total of $3 by buying one unit of each good? If not, how can more utility be obtained?

7. Individuals who buy second homes usually spend less for them than they do for their first homes. Why is this the case?

8. Describe five everyday examples of you or someone else making an interpersonal utility comparison.

9. Is there a logical link between the law of demand and the assumption that individuals seek to maximize utility? (*Hint:* Think of how the condition for consumer equilibrium can be used to express the inverse relationship between price and quantity demanded.)

10. List five sets of two goods each (i.e., each set is composed of two goods; for example, diamonds and water make up one set) such that the good with the greater value in use has a lower value in exchange than does the good with the lower value in use.

11. Do you think that people with high IQs are in consumer equilibrium (equating marginal utilities per dollar) more often than people with low IQs? Why or why not?

12. What is the endowment effect?

13. After each toss of a coin, one person has more money and one person has less. If the person with less money cares about relative rank and status, will he be willing to pay, say, $1 to reduce the other person's winnings by, say, 50¢? Will he be willing to pay 25¢ to reduce the other person's winnings by $1? Explain your answers.

14. How is buying a house in a good school district like sending children to a private school?

15. Of two similar houses on a street, one faces the ocean and the other does not. How might we determine the price of an ocean view? Explain your answer.

16. What is framing, and what effect can it have on the choices that individuals make?

WORKING WITH NUMBERS AND GRAPHS

1. The marginal utility for the third unit of X is 60 utils, and the marginal utility for the fourth unit of X is 45 utils. If the law of diminishing marginal utility holds, what is the minimum total utility of X?

2. Fill in blanks A–D in the following table.

Units of Good Consumed	Total Utility (utils)	Marginal Utility (utils)
1	10	10
2	19	A
3	B	8
4	33	C
5	35	D

3. The total utilities of the first 5 units of good X are 10, 19, 26, 33, and 40 utils, respectively. In other words, the total utility of 1 unit is 10 utils, the total utility of 2 units is 19 utils, and so on. What is the marginal utility of the third unit?

Use the following table to answer Questions 4 and 5:

Units of Good X	Total Utility of Good X (utils)	Units of Good Y	Total Utility of Good Y (utils)
1	20	1	19
2	35	2	32
3	48	3	40
4	58	4	45
5	66	5	49

4. If George spends $5 (total) a week on good X and good Y, and if the price of each good is $1 per unit, then how many units of each good does he purchase to maximize utility?

5. Given the number of units of each good that George purchases in Question 4, what is his total utility?

6. Draw the marginal utility curve for a good that has constant marginal utility.

7. The marginal utility curve for units 3–5 of good X is below the horizontal axis. Draw the corresponding part of the total utility curve for good X.

C

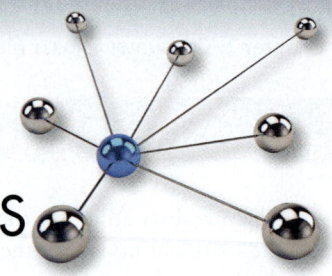

BUDGET CONSTRAINT AND INDIFFERENCE CURVE ANALYSIS

This chapter has used marginal utility theory to discuss consumer choice. Sometimes budget constraint and indifference curve analysis are used instead for the same purpose, especially in upper-division economics courses. We therefore examine this important topic here.

Budget Constraint

All the combinations, or bundles, of two goods a person can purchase, given a certain money income and prices for the two goods.

C-1 THE BUDGET CONSTRAINT

Societies have production possibilities frontiers, and individuals have **budget constraints**. A budget constraint is built on three components: two prices and the individual's income. To illustrate, suppose O'Brien has a monthly income of $1,200. Then, in a world of two goods, X and Y, O'Brien can spend his total income on X, he can spend his total income on Y, or he can spend part of his income on X and part on Y. Suppose the price of X is $100 and the price of Y is $80. Then, if O'Brien spends his total income on X, he can purchase a maximum of 12 units; if he spends his total income on Y, he can purchase a maximum of 15 units. Locating these two points on a two-dimensional diagram and then drawing a line between them, as shown in Exhibit 1, gives us O'Brien's budget constraint. Any point on the budget constraint, as well as any point in the triangular area between it and the origin, represents a possible combination (or bundle) of the two goods available to O'Brien.

The Budget Constraint

An individual's budget constraint gives us a picture of the different combinations (bundles) of two goods available to the individual. (We assume a two-good world; for a many-good world, we could put one good on one axis and all other goods on the other axis.) The budget constraint is derived by finding the two points representing the maximum amount of each good that an individual can consume (given his or her income and the prices of the two goods) and connecting those points.

$$\frac{\text{Income}}{\text{Price of good Y}} = \frac{\$1,200}{\$80} = 15$$

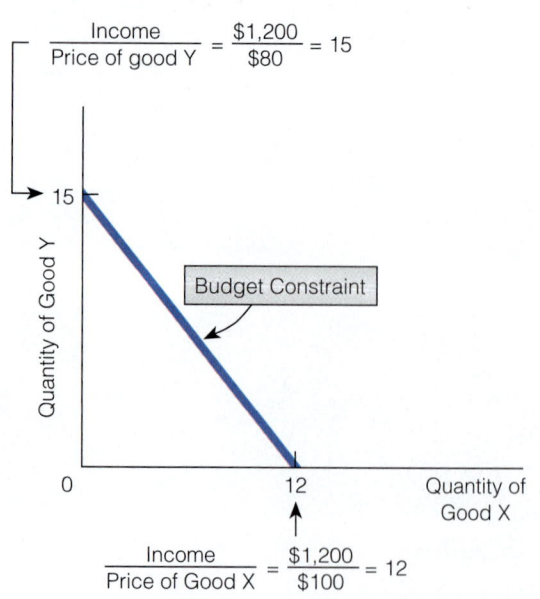

$$\frac{\text{Income}}{\text{Price of Good X}} = \frac{\$1,200}{\$100} = 12$$

C-1a Slope of the Budget Constraint

The slope of the budget constraint has special significance. The absolute value of the slope represents the relative prices of the two goods X and Y. In Exhibit 1, the slope, or P_X/P_Y, is equal to 1.25, indicating that the relative price of 1 unit of X is 1.25 units of Y.

C-1B WHAT WILL CHANGE THE BUDGET CONSTRAINT?

If any of the three variables—the two prices and the individual's income—changes, then the budget constraint changes. Not all changes are alike, however. Consider a fall in the price of good X from $100 to $60. With this change, the maximum number of units of good X purchasable with an income of $1,200 rises from 12 to 20. As a result, the budget constraint revolves away from the origin, as shown in Exhibit 2(a). The number of

EXHIBIT 2

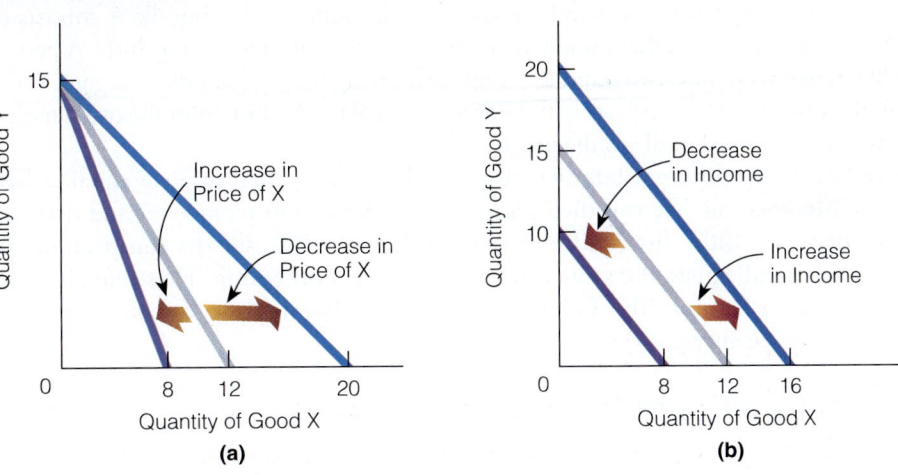

(a)

(b)

Changes in the Budget Constraint

(a) A change in the price of good X or good Y will change the slope of the budget constraint. (b) A change in income will change the position of the budget constraint while the slope remains constant. Whenever a budget constraint changes, the number of combinations (bundles) of the two goods available to the individual changes too.

O'Brien's possible combinations of the two goods increases: more bundles of the two goods are available after the price decrease than before.

Now consider what happens to the budget constraint if the price of good X rises. If it goes from $100 to, say, $150, then the maximum number of units of good X falls from 12 to 8. In this case, the budget constraint revolves *toward* the origin and the number of bundles available to O'Brien decreases. In sum, a change in the price of either good changes the slope of the budget constraint, with the result that relative prices and the number of bundles available to the individual also change.

We turn now to a change in income. If O'Brien's income rises to $1,600, the maximum number of purchasable units of X rises to 16 and the maximum number of purchasable units of Y rises to 20. The budget constraint then shifts rightward (away from the origin) and is parallel to the old budget constraint. As a consequence, the number of bundles available to O'Brien increases [Exhibit 2(b)]. If, by contrast, O'Brien's income falls from $1,200 to $800, the extreme endpoints on the budget constraint become X = 8 and Y = 10. Now the budget constraint shifts leftward (toward the origin) and is parallel to the old budget constraint. As a consequence, the number of bundles available to O'Brien falls.

C-2 INDIFFERENCE CURVES

An individual can, of course, choose any bundle of the two goods on the budget constraint or in the triangular area between it and the origin. If she spends her total income and therefore chooses a point on the budget constraint, this action raises two important questions: (1) Which bundle of the many bundles of the two goods does the individual choose? (2) How does the individual's chosen combination of goods change, given a change in prices or income? Both questions can be answered by combining the budget constraint with the graphical expression of the individual's preferences in an indifference curve.

C-3 CONSTRUCTING AN INDIFFERENCE CURVE

A person can be indifferent between two bundles of goods. Suppose that bundle A consists of 2 pairs of shoes and 6 shirts and that bundle B consists of 3 pairs of shoes and 4 shirts. A person who is indifferent between these two bundles is implicitly saying that one bundle is as good as the other. She is likely to say this, though, only if she receives equal total utility from the two bundles. If not, she would prefer one bundle to the other.

If we tabulate all the different bundles from which the individual receives equal utility, we have an **indifference set**. We can then plot the data in the indifference set and draw an **indifference curve**. Consider the indifference set in Exhibit 3(a). Of the four bundles of goods, A–D, each bundle gives the same total utility as every other one. These equal-utility bundles are plotted in Exhibit 3(b). Connecting these bundles in a two-dimensional space gives us an indifference curve.

Indifference Set

A group of bundles of two goods that give an individual equal total utility.

Indifference Curve

The curve that represents an indifference set and that shows all the bundles of two goods giving an individual equal total utility.

C-3a Characteristics of Indifference Curves

Indifference curves for goods have certain characteristics that are consistent with reasonable assumptions about consumer behavior:

1. *Indifference curves are downward sloping (from left to right).* The assumption that consumers always prefer more of a good to less requires that indifference curves slope downward from left to right. Consider the alternatives to downward sloping: vertical, horizontal, and upward sloping (from left to right). A horizontal or vertical curve would combine bundles of goods, some of which had more of one good and no less of another good than other bundles had [Exhibit 4(a–b)]. (If bundle B contains more of one good and no less of another good than bundle A does, an individual would not be indifferent between them. Remember, individuals prefer more to less.) An upward-sloping curve would combine bundles of goods, some of which had more of both goods than other bundles had [Exhibit 4(c)]. More simply, indifference curves are downward sloping because a person has to get more of one good in order to maintain the same level of satisfaction (utility) when giving up some of another good.

EXHIBIT 3

An Indifference Set and an Indifference Curve

An indifference set is a number of bundles of two goods such that each bundle yields the same total utility. An indifference curve represents an indifference set. In this exhibit, data from the indifference set (a) are used to derive an indifference curve (b).

	An Indifference Set	
	Milk	**Orange Juice**
Bundle	**(units)**	**(units)**
A	8	3
B	5	4
C	3	5
D	2	6

(a)

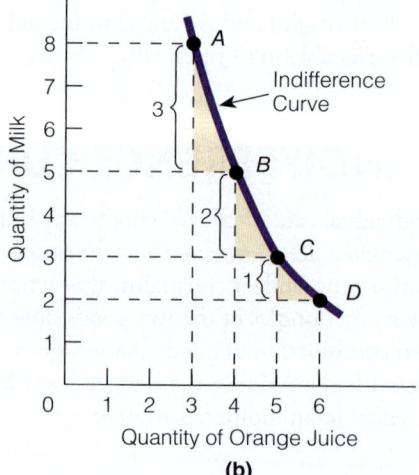

(b)

EXHIBIT 4

Indifference Curves for Goods Do Not Look Like This

(a) Bundle B has more milk and no less orange juice than bundle A, so an individual would prefer B to A and not be indifferent between them. (b) Bundle B has more orange juice and no less milk than bundle A, so an individual would prefer B to A and not be indifferent between them. (c) Bundle B has more milk and more orange juice than bundle A, so an individual would prefer B to A and not be indifferent between them.

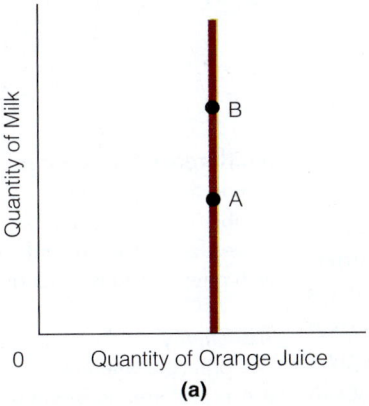

(a)

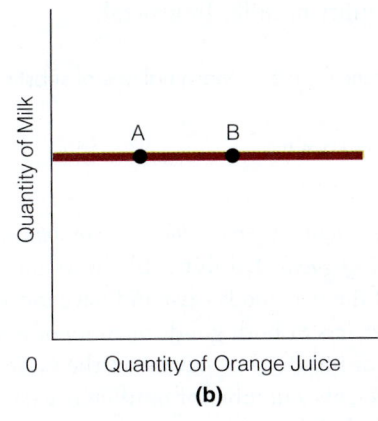

(b)

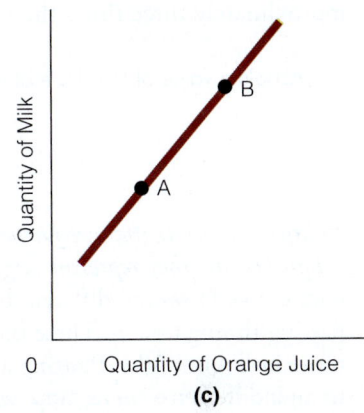

(c)

2. *Indifference curves are convex to the origin.* As we move down and to the right along the indifference curve, it becomes flatter. For example, at 8 units of milk [point *A* in Exhibit 3(b)], the individual is willing to give up 3 units of milk to get an additional unit of orange juice (and thus move to point *B*). At point *B*, where she has 5 units of milk, she is willing to give up only 2 units of milk to get an additional unit of orange juice (and thus move to point *C*). Finally, at point *C*, with 3 units of milk, she is now willing to give up only 1 unit of milk to get an additional unit of orange juice. Therefore, the more of one good that an individual has, the more units she will give up to get an additional unit of another good; the less of one good that an individual has, the fewer units she will give up to get an additional unit of another good.

What we have just described is reasonable: our observation is a reflection of diminishing marginal utility at work. As the quantity of a good consumed increases, the marginal utility of that good decreases; therefore, the more of one good an individual has, the more units he can (and will) sacrifice to get an additional unit of another good and still maintain total utility. Stated differently, if the law of diminishing marginal utility did not exist, saying that indifference curves of goods are convex to the origin would not make sense.

Another important point about marginal utilities is that *the absolute value of the slope of the indifference curve*—the **marginal rate of substitution**—*represents the ratio of the marginal utility of the good on the horizontal axis to the marginal utility of the good on the vertical axis:*

$$\frac{MU_{good\ on\ horizontal\ axis}}{MU_{good\ on\ vertical\ axis}}$$

Let's look carefully at the preceding assertion. First, the absolute value of the slope of the indifference curve is the marginal rate of substitution (*MRS*). The *MRS* is the amount of one good an individual is willing to give up to obtain an additional unit of another good and maintain equal total utility. For example, in Exhibit 3(b), we see that

Marginal Rate of Substitution
The amount of one good that an individual is willing to give up to obtain an additional unit of another good and maintain equal total utility.

moving from point *A* to point *B*, the individual is willing to give up 3 units of milk to get an additional unit of orange juice, with total utility between the two points remaining constant. The marginal rate of substitution is therefore 3 units of milk for 1 unit of orange juice in the area between points *A* and *B*. Further, the absolute value of the slope of the indifference curve (the *MRS*) is equal to the ratio of the *MU* of the good on the horizontal axis to the *MU* of the good on the vertical axis. How can this be? Well, if an individual giving up 3 units of milk and receiving 1 unit of orange juice maintains her total utility, then (in the area under consideration) the marginal utility of orange juice is approximately three times the marginal utility of milk. In general,

Absolute value of the slope of the indifference curve = Marginal rate of substitution

$$= \frac{MU_{good\ on\ horizontal\ axis}}{MU_{good\ on\ vertical\ axis}}$$

3. *Indifference curves that are farther from the origin are preferable to those that are nearer to the origin because they represent larger bundles of goods.* Exhibit 3(b) shows only one indifference curve. However, different bundles of the two goods exist and have indifference curves passing through them. These bundles have less of both goods or more of both goods than those in Exhibit 3(b). Plotting a number of indifference curves on the same diagram gives us an **indifference curve map**, which represents a number of indifference curves for a given individual with reference to two goods (see Exhibit 5).

In Exhibit 5, although only five indifference curves have been drawn, many more could have been added. For example, many indifference curves lie between I_1 and I_2. Also, the farther away from the origin an indifference curve lies, the higher the total utility is that it represents. To see why, compare point *A* on I_1 and point *B* on I_2. At point *B*, there is the same amount of orange juice as at point *A* but more milk. Point *B* is therefore preferable to point *A*, and, because *B* is on I_2 and *A* is on I_1, I_2 is preferable to I_1. The reason is simple: An individual receives more utility at any point on I_2 (because more goods are available) than at any point on I_1.

4. *Indifference curves do not cross (intersect).* Indifference curves do not cross because individuals' preferences exhibit **transitivity**, the logical principle whereby, if A is preferred to B and B is preferred to C, then A is preferred to C. For example, if Kristin prefers Coca-Cola to Pepsi-Cola and she also prefers Pepsi-Cola to root beer, then she must prefer Coca-Cola to root beer. If she said she preferred root beer to Coca-Cola, she would be contradicting her earlier preferences. To say that an individual has transitive preferences means that she maintains a logical order of preferences over a given period.

Indifference Curve Map
A map that represents a number of indifference curves for a given individual with reference to two goods.

Transitivity
The principle whereby, if A is preferred to B and B is preferred to C, then A is preferred to C.

EXHIBIT 5

An Indifference Map

A few of the many possible indifference curves are shown. Any point in the two-dimensional space is on an indifference curve. Indifference curves farther away from the origin represent greater total utility than those closer to the origin.

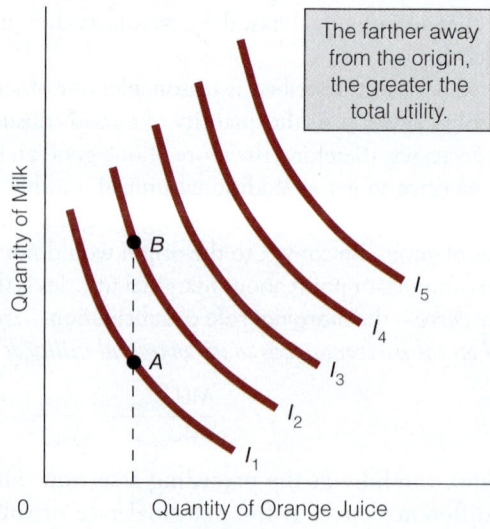

The farther away from the origin, the greater the total utility.

EXHIBIT 6

Intersecting Indifference Curves Are Inconsistent with Transitive Preferences

Point A lies on both indifference curves I_1 and I_2. This means that the individual is indifferent between A and B and between A and C, a pair of conditions that (supposedly) results in her being indifferent between B and C. But individuals prefer more to less (when it comes to goods) and thus would prefer C to B. We cannot have transitive preferences and make sense of intersecting indifference curves.

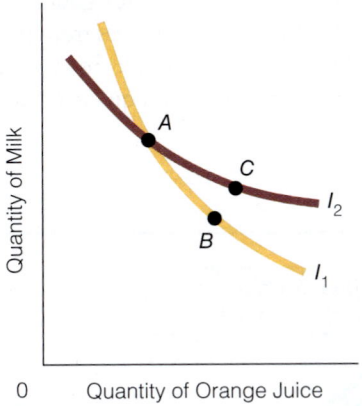

EXHIBIT 7

Consumer Equilibrium

Consumer equilibrium exists at the point where the slope of the budget constraint is equal to the slope of an indifference curve or where the budget constraint is tangent to an indifference curve. In the exhibit, this point is E. Here, $P_X/P_Y = MU_X/MU_Y$; or, rearranging, we have $MU_X/P_X = MU_Y/P_Y$.

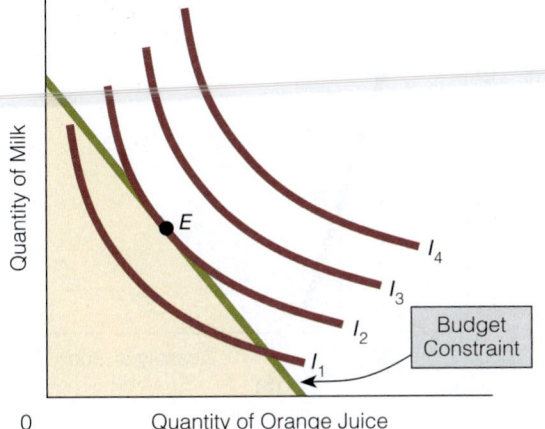

Consider what intersecting indifference curves would represent. In Exhibit 6, indifference curves I_1 and I_2 intersect at point A, which lies on both I_1 and I_2. Now, an individual must be indifferent between A and B, because they lie on the same indifference curve. The same holds for A and C. But if the individual is indifferent between A and B and between A and C, then she must be indifferent between B and C. But C has more of both goods than B, and thus the individual will *not* be indifferent between B and C; rather, she will prefer C to B. Thus, we cannot have transitive preferences and make sense of intersecting indifference curves. We can, however, have transitive preferences and make sense of *nonintersecting* indifference curves. Therefore, we go with the latter.

C-4 THE INDIFFERENCE MAP AND THE BUDGET CONSTRAINT COME TOGETHER

Together, the indifference map and the budget constraint illustrate consumer equilibrium. We have the following facts:

- The individual has a budget constraint.
- The absolute value of the slope of the budget constraint equals the relative prices of the two goods under consideration, say, P_X/P_Y.
- The individual has an indifference map.
- The absolute value of the slope of the indifference curve at any point is the marginal rate of substitution, which is equal to the marginal utility of one good divided by the marginal utility of another good, or MU_X/MU_Y.

The necessary condition for consumer equilibrium is obviously that the individual will try to reach a point on the highest indifference curve possible. This point is where the slope of the budget constraint is equal to the slope of an indifference curve (or where the budget constraint is tangent to an indifference curve). At that point, consumer equilibrium is established and the following condition holds:

$$\frac{P_X}{P_Y} = \frac{MU_X}{MU_Y}$$

In Exhibit 7, the preceding condition is met at point E. Note that the condition looks similar to that for consumer equilibrium described in this chapter. By rearranging the terms in the condition, we get[1]

$$\frac{MU_X}{P_X} = \frac{MU_Y}{P_Y}$$

C-5 FROM INDIFFERENCE CURVES TO A DEMAND CURVE

We can now derive a demand curve within a budget constraint–indifference curve framework. Exhibit 8(a) shows two budget constraints, one reflecting a $10 price for good X and the other reflecting a $5 price for good X. As the price of X falls, the consumer moves from point *A* to point *B*. At *B*, 35 units of X are consumed; at *A*, 30 units of X are consumed. So, a lower price for X results in greater consumption of X. By plotting the relevant price and quantity data, we derive a demand curve for good X in Exhibit 8(b).

EXHIBIT 8

From Indifference Curves to a Demand Curve

(a) At a price of $10 for good X, consumer equilibrium is at point *A*, with the individual consuming 30 units of X. As the price falls to $5, the budget constraint moves outward (away from the origin) and the consumer moves to point *B* and consumes 35 units of X. Plotting the price–quantity data for X gives a demand curve for X in (b).

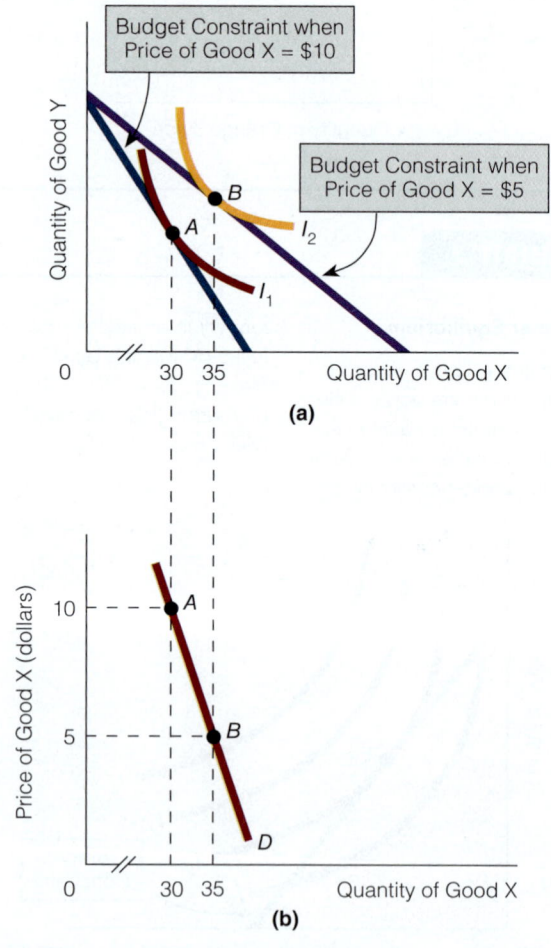

(a)

(b)

APPENDIX SUMMARY

- A budget constraint represents all combinations of bundles of two goods that a person can purchase, given a certain money income and prices for the two goods.
- An indifference curve shows all the combinations or bundles of two goods that give an individual equal total utility. Indifference curves are downward sloping, they are convex to the origin, and they do not cross. The farther away from the origin an indifference curve is, the greater total utility it represents for the individual.
- Consumer equilibrium is at the point where the slope of the budget constraint equals the slope of the in difference curve.
- A demand curve can be derived within a budget constraint–indifference curve framework.

KEY TERMS AND CONCEPTS

Budget Constraint
Indifference Set

Indifference Curve
Indifference Curve Map

Marginal Rate of Substitution
Transitivity

QUESTIONS AND PROBLEMS

1. Diagram the following budget constraints:
   a. Income = $4,000; $P_X = \$50$; $P_Y = \$100$
   b. Income = $3,000; $P_X = \$25$; $P_Y = \$200$
   c. Income = $2,000; $P_X = \$40$; $P_Y = \$150$

2. Explain why indifference curves
   a. are downward sloping.
   b. are convex to the origin.
   c. do not cross.

3. Explain why consumer equilibrium is the same under marginal utility analysis or indifference curve analysis.

4. Use indifference curve analysis to derive a demand curve.

8 PRODUCTION AND COSTS

INTRODUCTION

Everyone deals with business firms on a daily basis. People buy goods from firms: cars, clothes, food, books, entertainment, and other products. And people work for firms as accountants, truck drivers, secretaries, vice presidents, and editors. Our lives are constantly intermingled with business firms, as buyers of goods and as sellers of our labor services. Even though we deal with business firms daily, most of us probably know little about them. Why do they exist? What do they try to maximize? How do they go about producing the goods they produce? What concepts must firms concern themselves with? In this chapter, we answer many of these questions.

Monkey Business Images/Shutterstock.com

8-1 WHY FIRMS EXIST

Business Firm
An entity that employs factors of production (resources) to produce goods and services to be sold to consumers, other firms, or the government.

A **business firm** is an entity that employs resources, or factors of production, to produce goods and services to be sold to consumers, other firms, or the government. To understand why firms exist, we must explain worker behavior, markets, and the questions a firm must answer.

8-1a The Market and the Firm: Invisible Hand Versus Visible Hand

Through the forces of supply and demand, the market guides and coordinates individuals' actions, and it does so in an impersonal manner. No one orders buyers to reduce quantity demanded when price increases; they just do it. No one orders sellers to increase quantity supplied when price increases; they just do it. No one orders more resources to be moved into the production of personal computers when the demand and price for personal computers increase. The market guides individuals from the production of one good into the production of another. It coordinates individuals' actions so that suppliers and demanders find mutual satisfaction at equilibrium.

As economist Adam Smith observed, individuals in a market setting are "led by an invisible hand to promote an end which was no part of their intention."

Now, contrast the invisible hand of the market with the visible hand of a manager in a firm. The manager tells the employee on the assembly line to make more computer chips. The manager tells the employee to design a new engine, to paint the lamps green, to put steak and lobster on the menu. Thus, both the invisible hand of the market and the visible hand of the firm's manager guide and coordinate individuals' actions. There is, in other words, both **market coordination** and **managerial coordination**.

If the market is capable of guiding and coordinating individuals' actions, why did firms (and managers) arise in the first place? Why do firms exist?

8-1b The Alchian-and-Demsetz Answer

Economists Armen Alchian and Harold Demsetz suggest that firms are formed when benefits can be obtained from individuals working as a team.[1] Sometimes, the sum of what individuals can produce as a team is greater than the sum of what they can produce alone:

$$\text{Sum of team production} > \text{Sum of individual production}$$

Consider 11 individuals, all making shoe boxes. Each working alone produces 10 shoe boxes per day, for a total daily output of 110 shoe boxes. If they work as a team, however, the same 11 individuals can produce 140 shoe boxes. The added output (30 shoe boxes) may be reason enough for them to work together as a team and to create a firm.

8-1c Shirking on a Team

Although forming a firm can increase output, team production can have problems that do not occur in individual production. One problem of team production is **shirking**, which occurs when workers put forth less than the agreed-to effort. The amount of shirking increases on teams because the costs of shirking to individual team members are lower than when they work alone.

Consider five individuals—Alice, Bob, Carl, Denise, and Elizabeth—who form a team to produce lightbulbs because they realize that the sum of their team production will be more than the sum of their individual production. They agree to team-produce the lightbulbs, sell them, and split the proceeds five equal ways. On an average day, they produce 140 bulbs and sell each one for $2. Total revenue per day is $280, with each of the five team members receiving $56. Then Carl begins to shirk. Owing to his shirking, production falls to 135 lightbulbs per day and total revenue falls to $270 per day. Each person now receives $54. Notice that while Carl did all the shirking, his reduction in pay was only $2, one-fifth of the $10 drop in total revenue.

Economists predict that, in situations (such as team production) where one person receives all the benefits from shirking and pays only a part of the costs, there will be more shirking than when the person who shirks bears the full cost of shirking.

The Monitor (Manager): Taking Care of Shirking The **monitor** (or manager) plays an important role in the firm. The monitor reduces the amount of shirking by firing shirkers and rewarding the productive members of the firm. In carrying out this task, the monitor can preserve the benefits (increased output) that often come with team production and reduce, if not eliminate, the costs (increased shirking) associated with team production. But then the question is, who or what monitors the monitor? How can the monitor him- or herself be kept from shirking?

Market Coordination
The process in which individuals perform tasks, such as producing certain quantities of goods, on the basis of changes in market forces, such as supply, demand, and price.

Managerial Coordination
The process in which managers direct employees to perform certain tasks.

Shirking
The behavior of a worker who is putting forth less than the agreed-to effort.

Monitor
A person in a business firm who coordinates team production and reduces shirking.

[1] Armen Alchian and Harold Demsetz, "Production, Information Costs, and Economic Organization," *American Economic Review* 62 (December 1972): 777–795.

ECONOMICS 24/7

"He Never Showed Up"

College professors sometimes assign group projects to their students. They ask students to form groups of, say, five students each, and then they give each group a topic to research, write about, and present to the class. Moreover, the professors often assign the grade the group earns to each individual member of the group. In other words, if the group gets a "B" for its work, then each member of the group is assigned a "B."

Typically, at the beginning of the project, the group meets, assigns different members different tasks, and then arranges to meet later to put all their separate parts of the project together. Let's look at the group project from the perspective of one of the five members. He could very well think, "My grade is largely dependent on what others do, because I contribute only one-fifth of the work to the project. If I don't work very hard on the project, my grade will be a little lower. Therefore, there are certain costs to me of not doing my part, but there

Hero Images/Getty Images

are certain benefits too. In other words, there are both costs and benefits to my shirking. I have a lot of other things to do right now, so the benefits of shirking outweigh the costs. Consequently, I won't spend much time on the project."

In a group project, the costs of shirking are spread over five people and the benefits are received by one person. In an individual project, both the full costs and the full benefits accrue to the same person. The difference in the two projects will affect behavior. We would predict that there will be more shirking in a group project than in an individual project because the costs of shirking are relatively lower in the group project. Often, the professor will hear about this shirking. A member of the group, who does not shirk or shirks very little compared with others, says to the professor, "We were supposed to work on this project together, but Larry hasn't really been doing his part. In fact, we were supposed to meet at the library last night around seven, and he never showed up."

Residual Claimant
Persons who share in the profits of a business firm.

One possibility is to give the monitor an incentive not to shirk. This is often done by making the monitor a **residual claimant** of the firm. A residual claimant receives the excess of revenues over costs (profits) as income. If the monitor shirks, then profits are likely to be lower (or even zero or negative) and the monitor will receive less income.

8-1d Ronald Coase on Why Firms Exist

Ronald Coase, winner of the 1991 Nobel Prize in Economics, argued that "the main reason why it is profitable to establish a firm would seem to be that there is a cost of using the price mechanism."[2] Stated differently, firms exist either to economize on buying and selling everything or to reduce transaction costs.

For example, suppose it takes 20 different operations to produce good X. One way to produce good X, then, is to enter into a separate contract with everyone necessary to complete the 20 different operations. If we assume that one person completes one and only one operation, then we have 20 different contracts. Obviously, costs are associated with preparing and monitoring all these contracts. A firm is a recipe for reducing these costs, effectively replacing many contracts with one.

---

2. Ronald Coase, "The Nature of the Firm," *Economica*, November 1937.

Here is what Coase had to say:

The costs of negotiating and concluding a separate contract for each exchange transaction which takes place on a market must also be taken into account. … It is true that contracts are not eliminated when there is a firm, but they are greatly reduced. A factor of production (or the owner thereof) does not have to make a series of contracts as would be necessary, of course, if this cooperation were a direct result of the working of the price mechanism. For this series of contracts is substituted one. At this state, it is important to note the character of the contract into which a factor enters that is employed within a firm. The contract is one whereby the factor [the employee], for a certain remuneration (which may be fixed or fluctuating), agrees to obey the directions of an entrepreneur within certain limits.[3]

8-1e Markets: Outside and Inside the Firm

When we put the firm under the microeconomic microscope, what we see is a market of sorts at work. Economics is largely about trades or exchanges; it is about market transactions. In supply-and-demand analysis, the exchanges are between the buyers of goods and services and the sellers of goods and services. In the theory of the firm, the exchanges take place at two levels: (1) at the level of individuals coming together to form a team and (2) at the level of workers choosing a monitor.

Let's look at the theory of the firm in the context of exchange. Individuals initially come together because they realize that the sum of what they can produce as a team is greater than the sum of what they can produce as individuals. In essence, each individual trades working alone for working on a team. Later, after the team has been formed, the team members learn that shirking reduces the amount of the added output they came together to capture in the first place. Now the team members enter into another trade or market transaction: They trade some control over their daily behavior—specifically, they trade an environment in which the cost of shirking is low (teamwork without a monitor) for an environment in which the cost of shirking is high (teamwork with a monitor)—in order to receive a larger absolute amount of the potential benefits that drew them together. In effect, some individuals buy the monitoring services that other individuals sell.

As you continue your study of microeconomics, look for the markets that appear at different levels of analysis.

8-2 TWO SIDES TO EVERY BUSINESS FIRM

There are two sides to every market: a buying side (demand) and a selling side (supply). Similarly, there are two sides to every business firm: a revenue side and a cost side. We can see both sides of a firm by focusing on profit. The firm's objective is to maximize **profit**—the difference between total revenue and total cost:

Profit
The difference between total revenue and total cost.

$$\text{Profit} = \text{Total revenue} - \text{Total cost}$$

Looking at this profit equation, we can easily understand what any firm would like: its total revenue to be as high as possible and its total cost to be as low as possible. That way, its profit is as high as possible.

Total revenue is equal to the price of a good multiplied by the quantity of the good sold. For example, if a business firm sells 100 units of X at $10 per unit, its total revenue is $1,000. In the next chapter, we will begin our discussion of the firm's total revenue. In this chapter, we discuss

[3] Ibid.

the side of the firm that deals with total cost. Of course, the total cost that a firm incurs does not simply fall out of the sky: It is related to the production of the firm. Produce nothing, incur no costs; produce something, incur costs. So, this chapter is focused on production and costs.

8-2a More on Total Cost

Explicit Cost
A cost incurred when an actual (monetary) payment is made.

A disagreement sometimes arises as to what total cost should include. To illustrate, suppose Jill currently works as an attorney earning $80,000 a year. One day, dissatisfied with her career, Jill quits her job as an attorney and opens a pizzeria. After one year of operating the pizzeria, Jill sits down to compute her profit. She finds that she sold 20,000 pizzas at a price of $10 per pizza, so her total revenue (for the year) was $200,000. Jill computes her total costs by adding the dollar amounts she spent for everything she bought or rented to run the pizzeria. She spent $2,000 on plates, $3,000 on cheese, $4,000 on soda, $20,000 for rent in the mall where the pizzeria is located, $2,000 for electricity, and so on. The dollar payments Jill made for everything she bought or rented are called her *explicit costs*. An **explicit cost** is a cost that is incurred when an actual (monetary) payment is made. So Jill sums her explicit costs, which turn out to be $90,000. Then she computes her profit by subtracting $90,000 from $200,000, giving her a profit of $110,000.

A few days pass before Jill tells her friend Marian that she earned a $110,000 profit her first year of running the pizzeria. Marian asks, "Are you sure your profit is $110,000?" Jill assures her that it is. "Did you count the salary you earned as an attorney as a cost?" Marian asks. Jill tells Marian that she did not count the $80,000 salary as a cost of running the pizzeria because the $80,000 is not something she paid out to run the pizzeria. "I wrote a check to my suppliers for the pizza ingredients, soda, dishes, and so on," Jill says, "but I didn't write a check to anyone for the $80,000."

Marian says that, although Jill did not pay out $80,000 in salary to run the pizzeria, still she forfeited $80,000 to run it. "What you could have earned but didn't is a cost to you of running the pizzeria," says Marian.

Implicit Cost
A cost that represents the value of resources used in production for which no actual (monetary) payment is made.

Jill's $80,000 salary is what economists call an *implicit cost*. An **implicit cost** is a cost that represents the value of resources used in production for which no actual (monetary) payment is made. It is a cost incurred as a result of a firm's using resources that it owns or that the owners of the firm contribute to it.

If total cost is computed as explicit costs plus implicit costs, then Jill's total cost of running the pizzeria is $90,000 plus $80,000, or $170,000. Subtracting $170,000 from a total revenue of $200,000 leaves a profit of $30,000.

THINKING LIKE AN ECONOMIST

What Does the Person "Give Up"? The economist wants to know what a person gives up when she goes into business for herself. What she gives up isn't only the money she pays for resources (to run the business), but also the job she would have had (and the income she would have earned) had she not gone into business for herself.

8-2b Accounting Profit Versus Economic Profit

Accounting profit
The difference between total revenue and explicit costs.

Economists refer to the first profit that Jill calculated ($110,000) as *accounting profit*. **Accounting profit** is the difference between total revenue and total cost, where total cost equals explicit costs [see Exhibit 1(a)]:

$$\text{Accounting profit} = \text{Total revenue} - \text{Total cost (Explicit costs)}$$

EXHIBIT 1

Accounting Profit and Economic Profit

Accounting profit equals total revenue minus explicit costs. Economic profit equals total revenue minus the sum of explicit and implicit costs.

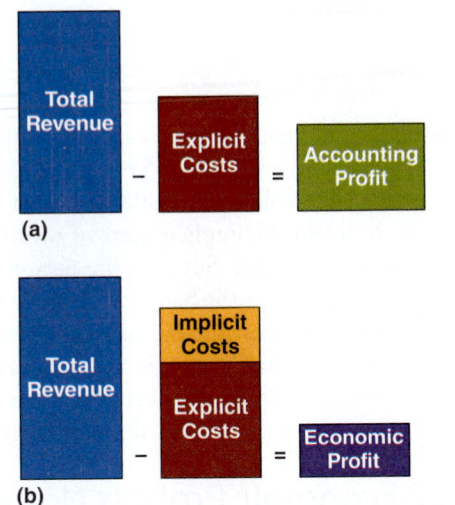

Does It Matter to You . . .
If You Think in Terms of Only Accounting Profit?

Wendy works as a software engineer in Santa Clara, California. Her annual salary is $130,000. While Wendy enjoys her work as a software engineer, she says that it has always been her wish to own a small business. Specifically, she has always wanted to own a restaurant. One day, she decides to quit her job as a software engineer and start her own restaurant.

In the first through third years of operation, she earns $50,000 in accounting profit each year. At the end of the third year of operation, Wendy is beginning to wonder if she should continue with the restaurant business. She admits that she is not making as much money as she hoped, and wonders if it would be better for her to return to work as a software engineer—she is fairly sure she could get a job as a software engineer earning $130,000—or to continue in the restaurant business.

Now consider this: Is Wendy's decision likely to be different if she only considers accounting profit than if she considers both accounting and economic profit? If she considers only accounting profit she realizes that, while she is earning an accounting profit in each of the three years of running her restaurant business, the dollar amount of accounting profit is not as great as what she earned as a software engineer.

Now suppose that besides considering her accounting profit, she also considers her economic profit. Once she considers her economic profit, she realizes that, while she earned an accounting profit of $50,000 in each year of operation, she actually earned a negative economic profit (or economic loss) of $80,000 in each year. If we subtract her implicit cost of $130,000 (her salary as a software engineer) from the $50,000 accounting profit, we are left with an economic loss of $80,000.

Now if Wendy is considering getting out of the restaurant business when earning an accounting profit of $50,000, would she be even more likely to get out of the restaurant business when she realizes that she actually took an economic loss of $80,000 in each year of operation?

There are three things for Wendy to consider when operating her restaurant business: total revenue, explicit costs, and implicit costs. When she considers accounting profit only, she considers total revenue and explicit costs, and ignores her implicit costs. Making a decision based on accounting profit alone, then, is basing a decision on less than the real and complete picture of what is happening. In contrast, making a decision based on economic profit is basing a decision on the real and complete picture of what is happening.

Taking the example of Wendy into consideration, does it matter to us whether we are aware of the real and complete picture of what is before us as opposed to not seeing it? Seeing the whole picture probably does matter.

Economic Profit
The difference between total revenue and total cost, including both explicit and implicit costs.

Economists refer to the second profit calculated ($30,000) as *economic profit*. **Economic profit** is the difference between total revenue and total cost, where total cost equals the sum of explicit and implicit costs [see Exhibit 1(b)]:

$$\text{Economic profit} = \text{Total revenue} - \text{Total cost (Explicit costs} + \text{Implicit costs)}$$

To illustrate the difference between explicit and implicit costs, suppose a person has $100,000 in the bank, earning an interest rate of 5 percent a year. This amounts to $5,000 in interest a year. Now suppose the person takes the $100,000 out of the bank to start a business. The $5,000 in *lost interest* is included in the implicit costs of owning and operating the firm. To see why, let's change the example somewhat. Suppose the person does not use her $100,000 in the bank to start a business but leaves it in the bank and instead takes out a $100,000 loan at an interest rate of 5 percent. Then the interest she has to pay on the loan—$5,000 a year—certainly would be an explicit cost and would take away from her overall profit. It just makes sense, then, to count the $5,000 interest that the owner doesn't earn if she uses her own $100,000 to start the business (instead of taking out a loan) as a cost, albeit implicit.

8-2c Zero Economic Profit Is Not as Bad as It Sounds

Economic profit is usually lower (never higher) than accounting profit. Whereas economic profit is the difference between total revenue and total cost (where total cost is the sum of explicit and implicit costs), accounting profit is the difference between total revenue and only explicit costs. Thus, a firm could earn both a positive accounting profit and a zero economic profit. In economics, a firm that makes a zero economic profit is said to be earning a **normal profit**:

Normal Profit
Zero economic profit, the level of profit necessary to keep resources employed in a firm. A firm that earns normal profit is earning revenue equal to its total costs (explicit plus implicit costs).

$$\text{Normal profit} = \text{Zero economic profit}$$

However, the owner of a firm should not be worried about making zero economic profit for the year just ending. A zero economic profit—as bad as it may sound—means that the owner has generated total revenue sufficient to cover total cost—that is, *both explicit and implicit costs*. If, for example, the owner's implicit cost is a (forfeited) $100,000 salary working for someone else, then earning a zero economic profit means that he has done as well as he could have done in his next-best (alternative) line of employment.

When we realize that zero economic profit (or normal profit) means doing as well as could have been done, we understand that it isn't bad to make zero economic profit. Zero accounting profit, however, is altogether different: It implies that some part of total cost has not been covered by total revenue.

FINDING ECONOMICS

In a Sports Bar Frank is sitting at the bar, watching the game on the nearby television set. The bartender asks him whether he wants another drink, and he says yes. The bartender and Frank start talking, and Frank learns that the bartender owns the bar. In fact, he opened up the bar 10 years ago. Is it more likely that, before the bartender opened up the bar, he was working at a high-paying job or a medium-paying job? Is there any economics here?

Think implicit costs. There are benefits to the bartender of owning and operating a sports bar, but there are costs too. Some costs are explicit (rent for the bar, pretzels, TV sets, beer, etc.), and some are implicit (specifically, the salary he earned in the job he had before he was the owner and bartender). The higher those implicit costs are, the less likely it is that the bartender would have quit the job to open a sports bar.

Hear What and How the Economist Thinks . . .
About Maximizing Revenue and Profit

The economist hears someone say:

Business firms are all about maximizing revenue. If a firm is currently earning $10 million in total revenue, and it can sell 10 more units of whatever it is that it sells—thus raising the total revenue to $10 million and $100—then it should do that: The more revenue, the better.

Hear what and how the economist thinks:

The person who thinks that firms want to maximize total revenue would be easily dissuaded of this once costs are brought into the picture. Suppose a firm could sell one more unit of what it produces for $400. Should it do this? The person would likely say yes. Then we could ask this person if the firm should do this if it cost the firm an additional $500 to produce the unit it sells for $400. Now the person would probably say no. It would be taking a loss of $100 on that item, and that is not advisable.

In short, it is not total revenue that the firm wants to maximize; instead, it is the difference between total revenue and total cost, or profit.

The economist says that when it comes to activities, there are usually benefits and costs, not just one or the other. When it comes to producing and selling goods and services, there are benefits to be derived, these are the revenues gained from producing and selling the goods, but there are costs too. To produce and sell a good is to derive a benefit, but it is to incur a cost too. If we focus only on the benefits or only on the costs, we only see part of the whole picture.

Think of a similar example that would likely generate different responses from an individual depending on the variables considered.

Suppose we were to ask someone if firms always hire the cheapest labor. We say to that person: The firm can hire labor in country X and pay $40 an hour for labor, or it can hire labor in country Y and pay $15 an hour for labor. In which country will the firm hire labor? My guess is that most people will say in country Y, where labor is $15 an hour. But there is something else to consider besides the wages paid to labor, and that is the productivity of labor. Suppose that in country Y a person receiving $15 an hour can produce 2 units of A an hour, but in country X a person receiving $40 an hour can produce 10 units of A an hour. Is it still in the firm's best interest to hire the $15-an-hour worker instead of the $40-an-hour labor? The $15-an-hour worker produces 2 units of A at a per-unit cost of $7.50, while the $40-an-hour worker produces 10 units of A at a per-unit cost of $4. Taking into account the productivity of the workers in the different countries, it now appears that the more expensive wage-earner in country X is really the cheaper worker to hire. We would have never come to this conclusion if we had focused on only one variable—the wage cost of workers. It was considering two variables at a time—the wage cost and the productivity of the workers—that led us to seeing the whole and true picture of what matters.

Questions to Think About:

1. A person tells us that it is important to get as much exercise as possible. Exercise comes with lots of benefits, she says. Would you agree that it is important to get as much exercise as possible? Explain your answer.

2. Can you identify the condition under which maximizing total revenue would be the same thing as maximizing profit?

SELF-TEST

(Answers to Self-Test questions are in Answers to Self-Test Questions at the back of the book.)

1. Will individuals form teams or firms in all settings?

2. Suppose everything about two people is the same except that currently one person earns a high salary and the other person earns a low salary. Which person is more likely to start his or her own business and why?

3. Is accounting profit or economic profit larger? Why?

4. When can a business owner be earning a profit but not covering costs?

8-3 PRODUCTION

Production is a transformation of resources or inputs into goods and services. You may think of production as you might think of making a cake. It takes certain ingredients to make a cake: sugar, flour, and so on. Similarly, it takes certain resources, or inputs, to produce a computer, a haircut, a piece of furniture, or a house.

Economists often talk about two types of inputs in the production process: fixed and variable. A **fixed input** is an input whose quantity cannot be changed as output changes. To illustrate, suppose the McMahon and McGee Bookshelf Company has rented a factory under a six-month lease: McMahon and McGee, the owners of the company, have contracted to pay the $16,000 monthly rent for six months, no matter what. Whether McMahon and McGee produce one bookshelf or 7,000, the $16,000 rent for the factory must be paid. The factory is a fixed input in the production process of bookshelves.

A **variable input** is an input whose quantity can be changed as output changes. Examples of variable inputs for the McMahon and McGee Bookshelf Company include wood, paint, nails, and so on. These inputs can (and most likely will) change as the production of bookshelves changes. As they produce more bookshelves, McMahon and McGee purchase more of these inputs; as they produce fewer bookshelves, they purchase fewer of these inputs. Labor might also be a variable input for McMahon and McGee. As they produce more bookshelves, they might hire more employees; as they produce fewer bookshelves, they might lay off some.

If any of the inputs of a firm are fixed inputs, then it is said to be producing in the *short run*. In other words, the **short run** is a period during which some inputs are fixed.

If none of the inputs of a firm is a fixed input—if all inputs are variable—then the firm is said to be producing in the *long run*. In other words, the **long run** is a period during which all inputs can be varied. (No inputs are fixed.)

When firms produce goods and services and then sell them, they necessarily incur costs. In this section, we discuss the production activities of the firm in the short run, leading to the law of diminishing marginal returns. In the next section, we tie the production of the firm to all the costs of production in the short run. We then turn to an analysis of production in the long run.

8-3a Common Misconception About the Short Run and Long Run

Individuals naturally think that the long run is a longer period than the short run. For example, if the short run is six months, then the long run is, say, 10 months. But this perspective is not the right way to differentiate the short run from the long run. Think of each as a period during which some condition exists. The short run is the period during which at least one input is fixed, and it could be a period of six months, two years, and so on. The long run is not necessarily longer in months and years than the short run; it is simply the period during which all inputs are variable (i.e., no input is fixed). In terms of days, weeks, and months, the short run could be a longer period than the long run.

8-3b Production in the Short Run

Suppose two inputs (or resources)—labor (L) and capital (C)—are used to produce some good. Furthermore, suppose one of those inputs—capital—is fixed. Obviously, because an input is fixed, the firm is producing in the short run.

In Exhibit 2, column 1 shows the units of the fixed input, capital (fixed at 1 unit). Column 2 shows different units of the variable input, labor. Notice that we go from 0 (no workers) through 10 units (10 workers). Column 3 shows the quantities of output produced with 1 unit of capital

---

Fixed Input
An input whose quantity cannot be changed as output changes.

Variable Input
An input whose quantity can be changed as output changes.

Short Run
A period during which some inputs in the production process are fixed.

Long Run
A period during which all inputs in the production process can be varied. (No inputs are fixed.)

EXHIBIT 2

Production in the Short Run and the Law of Diminishing Marginal Returns

In the short run, as additional units of a variable input are added to a fixed input, the marginal physical product of the variable input may increase at first. Eventually, the marginal physical product of the variable input decreases. The point at which marginal physical product decreases is the point at which diminishing marginal returns have set in.

(1) Capital (C), fixed input (units)	(2) Labor (L), variable input (number of workers)	(3) Quantity of Output, Q (units)	(4) Marginal Physical Product (MPP) of Labor, MPP of labor $= \Delta Q / \Delta L$, $\Delta(3)/\Delta(2)$ (units)
1	0	0	18
1	1	18	19
1	2	37	20
1	3	57	19
1	4	76	18
1	5	94	17
1	6	111	16
1	7	127	10
1	8	137	−4
1	9	133	−8
1	10	125	

and different amounts of labor. (The quantity of output is sometimes referred to as the *total physical product*, or *TPP*.) For example, 1 unit of capital and 0 units of labor produce 0 output; 1 unit of capital and 1 unit of labor produce 18 units of output; 1 unit of capital and 2 units of labor produce 37 units of output; 1 unit of capital and 3 units of labor produce 57 units of output; and so on.

Column 4 shows the marginal physical product of the variable input. The **marginal physical product (MPP)** of a variable input is equal to the change in output that results from changing the variable input by one unit while *holding all other inputs fixed*. Because, in our example, the variable input is labor, we are talking about the *MPP* of labor. Specifically, the *MPP* of labor is equal to the change in output Q that results from changing labor L by one unit while *holding all other inputs fixed*:

$$MPP \text{ of labor} = \Delta Q / \Delta L$$

Marginal Physical Product (MPP)
The change in output that results from changing the variable input by one unit, with all other inputs held fixed.

Notice that the marginal physical product of labor first rises (from 18 to 19 to 20), then falls (from 20 to 19 to 18 to 17 to 16 to 10), and then becomes negative (−4 and −8). When the *MPP* is rising, we say that there is increasing *MPP*; when it is falling, there is diminishing *MPP*; and when it is negative, there is negative *MPP*.

Now, focus on the point at which the *MPP* first begins to decline, namely, with the addition of the fourth worker. The point at which the *MPP* of labor first declines is the point at which diminishing marginal returns are said to have set in. Diminishing marginal returns are common in production—so common, in fact, that economists refer to the law of diminishing marginal returns (or the law of diminishing marginal product). The **law of diminishing marginal returns** states that *as ever larger amounts of a variable input are combined with fixed inputs, eventually the marginal physical product of the variable input will decline.*

Law of Diminishing Marginal Returns
As ever larger amounts of a variable input are combined with fixed inputs, eventually the marginal physical product of the variable input will decline.

The question is, why does the *MPP* of the variable input eventually decline? To answer this question, think of adding agricultural workers (variable input) to 10 acres of land (fixed input). The workers must clear the land, plant the crop, and then harvest the crop. In the early stages of adding labor to the land, perhaps the *MPP* rises or remains constant. But eventually, as we continue to add more workers to the land, it becomes overcrowded with workers. Workers are stepping around each other, stepping on the crops, and so on. Because of these problems, output growth begins to slow.

It may seem strange that the firm in Exhibit 2 would ever hire beyond the third worker. After all, the *MPP* of labor is at its highest (20) with the third worker. Why hire the fourth worker if the *MPP* of labor is going to fall to 19? The firm may hire the fourth worker because the worker adds output. It would be one thing if the quantity of output were 57 units with three workers and fell to 55 units with the addition of the fourth worker, but this isn't the case. With the addition of the fourth worker, output rises from 57 units to 76 units. The firm has to ask and answer two questions: (1) What can the additional 19 units of output be sold for? (2) What does it cost to hire the fourth worker? Suppose the additional 19 units can be sold for $100, and it costs the firm $70 to hire the fourth worker. In that case, hiring the fourth worker makes sense.

8-3c Whose Marginal Productivity Are We Talking About?

Look back at Exhibit 2, and note the data that follows the fourth worker. When the fourth worker is added, the quantity of output rises from 57 units to 76 units. Also, marginal productivity is 19 units. It is easy to fall into the trap of believing that 19 units is the marginal productivity of the fourth worker, but this is a misreading of the data. It's not as though the fourth worker walks through the door and we attach the number "19" to him. Instead, 19 is the marginal productivity of labor when there are four workers working with the one (fixed) unit of capital. The number can be as easily attached to the first, second, or third worker as it can be to the fourth worker.

THINKING LIKE AN ECONOMIST

Comparing One Thing with Another In economics, when making decisions, you usually compare one alternative with another. To illustrate, suppose you need to decide how much time to devote to studying. Would you consider just the additional *benefits* of spending more time studying, or would you consider the additional *costs* of spending more time studying too? You would want to consider both.

Similarly, when a firm has to decide how many workers to hire, it wouldn't consider only the additional benefits of hiring more workers (as measured by their additional output times the price the additional output could be sold for). Instead, it would consider the additional benefits against the additional costs of hiring more workers.

8-3d Marginal Physical Product and Marginal Cost

A firm's costs are tied to its production. Specifically, the *marginal cost (MC)* of producing a good is a reflection of the *MPP* of the variable input. Our objective in this section is to prove that this statement is true. Before doing so, however, we need to define and discuss some economic cost concepts.

Some Economic Cost Concepts Certainly, a cost is incurred whenever a fixed input or variable input is employed in the production process. The costs associated with fixed inputs are called **fixed costs**. The costs associated with variable inputs are called **variable costs**.

Because the quantity of a fixed input does not change as output changes, neither do fixed costs change with output. Payments for such things as fire insurance (the same amount every month),

Fixed Costs
Costs that do not vary with output; the costs associated with fixed inputs.

Variable Costs
Costs that vary with output; the costs associated with variable inputs.

liability insurance, and the rental of a factory and machinery are usually considered fixed costs. Whether the business produces 1, 10, 100, or 1,000 units of output, the rent for its factory is not likely to change. The rent is whatever amount was agreed to with the owner of the factory for the duration of the rental agreement.

Because the quantity of a variable input changes with output, so do variable costs. For example, it takes labor, wood, and glue to produce wooden bookshelves. The quantity of all these inputs (labor, wood, and glue) changes as the number of wooden bookshelves produced changes.

The sum of fixed costs and variable costs is **total cost (TC)**. If total fixed costs (*TFC*) are $100 and total variable costs (*TVC*) are $300, then total cost (*TC*) is $400:

$$TC = TFC + TVC$$

Given total cost, we can formally define marginal cost. **Marginal cost (MC)** is the change in total cost *TC* that results from a change in quantity of output *Q*:

$$MC = \frac{\Delta TC}{\Delta Q}$$

Total Cost (TC)
The sum of fixed costs and variable costs.

Marginal Cost (MC)
The change in total cost that results from a change in quantity of output: $MC = \Delta TC/\Delta Q$.

The Link Between *MPP* and *MC*   In Exhibit 3, we establish the link between the *MPP* of a variable input and *MC*. The first four columns present much of the same data first presented in Exhibit 2. Column 3 shows the different quantities of output produced by 1 unit of capital (fixed input) and various amounts of labor (variable input), and column 4 shows the *MPP* of labor. Exhibit 3(a) shows the *MPP* curve, which is based on the data in column 4. Notice that the *MPP* curve first rises and then falls.

In column 5, we have identified the total fixed cost (*TFC*) of production as $40. (Recall that fixed costs do not change as output changes.) For column 6, we have assumed that each worker is hired for $20; so, when there is only 1 worker, total variable cost (*TVC*) is $20; when there are 2 workers, total variable cost is $40; and so on. Column 7 shows total cost at various output levels; the figures in this column are simply the sum of the fixed costs in column 5 and the variable costs in column 6. Finally, in column 8, we compute marginal cost. Exhibit 3(b) shows the *MC* curve, which is based on the data in column 8.

Columns 4 and 8 show *MPP* and *MC*, respectively. Notice that when *MPP* is rising (from 18 to 19 to 20), *MC* is decreasing (from $1.11 to $1.05 to $1.00) and when *MPP* is falling (from 20 to 19, etc.), *MC* is increasing (from $1.00 to $1.05, etc.). In other words, *MPP* and *MC* move in opposite directions. You can also see this relationship by comparing the *MPP* curve with the *MC* curve. When the *MPP* curve is going up, the *MC* curve is moving down, and when the *MPP* curve is going down, the *MC* curve is going up. Of course, all this is common sense: As *MPP* rises—or, to put it differently, as the productivity of the variable input rises—we would expect costs to decline; and as the productivity of the variable input declines, we would expect costs to rise.

In conclusion, then, what the *MC* curve looks like depends on what the *MPP* curve looks like. Recall that the *MPP* curve must have a declining portion because of the law of diminishing marginal returns. So, if the *MPP* curve first rises and then (when diminishing marginal returns set in) falls, the *MC* curve must first fall and then rise.

Another Way to Look at the Relationship Between *MPP* and *MC*   An easy way to see that *MPP* and *MC* move in opposite directions is to reexamine the definition of *MC* (the change in total cost divided by the change in output). The change in total cost is the additional cost of an additional unit of the variable input. (See Exhibit 3.) The change in output is the *MPP* of the variable input. Thus, *MC* is equal to the additional cost of an additional unit of the variable input, divided by the input's *MPP*. In Exhibit 3, the variable input is labor, so $MC = W/MPP$, where MC = marginal cost, W = wage, and MPP = marginal physical product of labor.

EXHIBIT 3

Marginal Physical Product and Marginal Cost

(a) The marginal-physical-product-of-labor curve. The curve is derived by plotting the data from columns 2 and 4 in the table. (b) The marginal cost curve. The curve is derived by plotting the data from columns 3 and 8 in the table. Notice that as the *MPP* curve rises, the *MC* curve falls; and as the *MPP* curve falls, the *MC* curve rises.

(1) Capital (C), fixed input (units)	(2) Labor (L), variable input (workers)	(3) Quantity of Output, Q (units)	(4) Marginal Physical Product (MPP) of Labor, MPP of labor = $\Delta Q/\Delta L$ = $\Delta(3)/\Delta(2)$ (units)	(5) Total Fixed Cost (TFC)	(6) Total Variable Cost (TVC)	(7) Total Cost (TC), (5)+(6)	(8) Marginal Cost (MC), $\Delta TC/\Delta Q$, $\Delta(7)/\Delta(3)$
1	0	0		$40	$0	$40	
1	1	18	18	40	20	60	$1.11
1	2	37	19	40	40	80	$1.05
1	3	57	20	40	60	100	$1.00
1	4	76	19	40	80	120	$1.05
1	5	94	18	40	100	140	$1.11
1	6	111	17	40	120	160	$1.17
1	7	127	16	40	140	180	$1.25

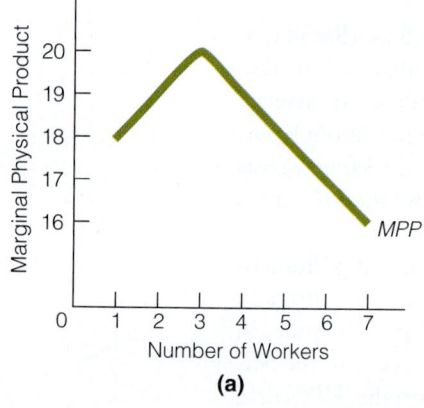

(a)

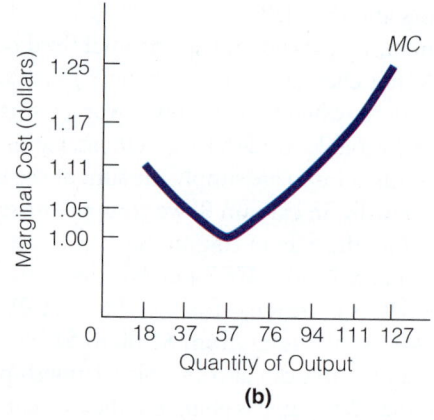

(b)

The following table reproduces column 4 from Exhibit 3, notes the wage, and uses the equation $MC = W/MPP$ to compute MC:

MPP	Variable Cost (W)	W/MPP = MC
18 units	$20	$20/18 = $1.11
19	20	20/19 = 1.05
20	20	20/20 = 1.00
19	20	20/19 = 1.05
18	20	20/18 = 1.11
17	20	20/17 = 1.17
16	20	20/16 = 1.25

Now compare the marginal cost figures in the last column in the table with the marginal cost figures in column 8 of Exhibit 3. Whether marginal cost is defined as equal to $\Delta TC/\Delta Q$ or as equal to W/MPP, the result is the same. The latter way of defining marginal cost, however, shows explicitly that as MPP rises, MC falls, and that as MPP falls, MC rises:

$$\frac{W}{MPP \uparrow} = MC \downarrow$$

$$\frac{W}{MPP \uparrow} = MC \downarrow$$

8-3e Average Productivity

When the press or laypersons use the word *productivity*, they are usually referring to *average physical product* instead of *marginal physical product*. To illustrate the difference, suppose 1 worker can produce 10 units of output a day and 2 workers can produce 18 units of output a day. Then *MPP* is 8 units (MPP of labor $= \Delta Q/\Delta L$). In contrast, average physical product, which is quantity of output divided by quantity of labor, is equal to 9 units.

$$AP \text{ of labor} = \frac{Q}{L}$$

Usually, when the term *labor productivity* is used in the newspaper and in government documents, it refers to the average hourly (physical) productivity of labor. By computing the average productivity of labor for different countries and noting the annual percentage changes, we can compare labor productivity between and within countries. Government statisticians have chosen 2009 as a benchmark year (a year against which we measure other years). They have also set a productivity index (a measure of productivity) of 100 for the year 2009. By computing a productivity index for other years and noting whether it is above, below, or equal to 100, the statisticians know whether productivity is rising, falling, or remaining constant, respectively. Finally, by computing the percentage change in productivity indexes from one year to the next, they know the rate at which productivity is changing.

Suppose the productivity index for the United States is 120 in year 1 and 125 in year 2. Because the productivity index is higher in year 2 than in year 1, labor productivity increased over the year; that is, output produced increased per hour of labor expended.

ECONOMICS 24/7

High School Students, Staying Out Late, and More

Can marginal cost affect a person's behavior? Let's analyze two different situations in which it might.

High School Students and Staying Out Late

A 16-year-old high school student asks her parents if she can have the car tonight. She says she plans to go with some friends to a concert. Her parents ask what time she will get home. She says that she plans to be back by midnight.

The girl's parents tell her that she can have the car and that they expect her home by midnight. If she's late, she will lose her driving privileges for a week.

Later that night, it is midnight and the 16-year-old is 15 minutes away from home. When she realizes she can't get home until 12:15

a.m., will she continue on home? She may not. The marginal cost of staying out later is now zero. In short, whether she arrives home at 12:15, 1:15, or 2:25, the punishment is the same: She will lose her driving privileges for a week. There is no additional cost for staying out an additional minute or an additional hour. There may, however, be additional benefits. The problem is that her punishment places a zero marginal cost on staying out after midnight: Once midnight has come and gone, the additional cost of staying out later is zero.

No doubt, her parents would prefer her to get home at, say, 12:01 rather than at 1:01 or even later. If so, however, then they should not have made the marginal cost of staying out after midnight zero. They should have increased the marginal cost of staying out late for every minute (or 15-minute period) that the 16-year-old was late. In other words, one of the parents might have said, "For the first 15 minutes you're late, you'll lose 1 hour of driving privileges, for the second 15 minutes you're late, you'll lose 2 hours of driving privileges, and so on." This punishment would have presented our teen with a rising marginal cost of staying out late. With a rising marginal cost, it is more likely that she will get home close to midnight.

Crime

Suppose that the sentence for murder in the first degree is life imprisonment, that the sentence for burglary is 10 years, and that the burglary rate has skyrocketed in the past few months. Many of the city residents have become alarmed and have called on the police and other local and state officials to do something about the rising burglary rate.

Someone proposes that the way to lower the burglary rate is to increase the punishment for it. Instead of having the offender

iStock.com/sturti

serve only 10 years in prison, make the punishment stiffer. In his zeal to reduce the burglary rate, a state legislator proposes that burglary carry the same punishment as first-degree murder: life in prison. That will certainly get the burglary rate down, he argues. After all, who will take the chance of committing a burglary knowing that, if he gets caught and convicted, he will spend the rest of his days in prison?

Unfortunately, by making the punishment for burglary and murder the same, the marginal cost of murdering someone while burglarizing a home falls to zero. To illustrate, suppose Smith is burglarizing a home and the residents walk in on him. Realizing that the residents can identify him as the burglar, Smith shoots and kills them. If he gets apprehended for burglary, the penalty is the same as it is for murder. Raising the cost of burglary from 10 years to life imprisonment may reduce the number of burglaries, but it may have the unintended effect of also raising the murder rate.

SELF-TEST

1. If the short run is six months, does it follow that the long run is longer than six months? Explain your answer.

2. "As we add more capital to more labor, eventually the law of diminishing marginal returns will set in." What is wrong with this statement?

3. Suppose an *MC* curve falls when output is in the range from 1 unit to 10 units. Then it flattens out and remains constant over an output range from 10 units to 20 units, after which it rises over a range from 20 units to 30 units. What does the curve's behavior have to say about the *MPP* of the variable input?

8-4 COSTS OF PRODUCTION: TOTAL, AVERAGE, MARGINAL

As we continue our discussion of the costs of production, the easiest way to see the relationships among the various costs is with the example in Exhibit 4.

Column 1 of Exhibit 4 shows the various quantities of output, ranging from 0 units to 10 units. Column 2 shows the total fixed costs of production (*TFC*), set at $100. Recall that fixed costs do not change as output changes. Therefore, *TFC* is $100 when output is 0 units, 1 unit, 2 units, and so on. Because *TFC* does not change as *Q* changes, the *TFC* curve in the exhibit is a horizontal line at $100.

In column 3, we have computed **average fixed cost (AFC)**, which is total fixed cost divided by quantity of output:

$$AFC = \frac{TFC}{Q}$$

For example, look at the fourth entry in column 3. To get a dollar amount of $33.33, we simply took *TFC* at 3 units of output, or $100, and divided by 3. Notice that the *AFC* curve in the exhibit continually declines.

In column 4, we have simply entered some hypothetical data for total variable cost (*TVC*). The *TVC* curve in the exhibit rises because variable costs are likely to increase as output increases.

In column 5, we have computed **average variable cost (AVC)**, which is total variable cost divided by quantity of output:

$$AVC = \frac{TVC}{Q}$$

For example, look at the third entry in column 5. To get a dollar amount of $40.00, we simply took *TVC* at 2 units of output, or $80, and divided by 2. Notice that the *AVC* curve declines and then rises.

Column 6 shows total cost (*TC*). Total cost is the sum of total variable cost and total fixed cost. Notice that the *TC* curve does not start at zero because, even when output is zero, there are some fixed costs. In this example, total fixed cost (*TFC*) at zero output is $100, so the total cost (*TC*) curve must start at $100 instead of at $0.

Column 7 shows **average total cost (ATC)**, which is total cost divided by quantity of output:

$$ATC = \frac{TC}{Q}$$

Average total cost is sometimes called *unit cost*.

Alternatively, we can say that *ATC* equals the sum of *AFC* and *AVC*:

$$ATC = AFC + AVC$$

To understand why this alternative formulation makes sense, remember that $TC = TFC + TVC$. Thus, if we divide all total magnitudes by quantity of output (*Q*), we necessarily get $ATC = AFC + AVC$. Notice that the *ATC* curve falls and then rises.

Column 8 shows marginal cost (*MC*), which is the change in total cost divided by the change in quantity of output:

$$MC = \frac{\Delta TC}{\Delta Q}$$

The *MC* curve has a declining portion and a rising portion. When *MC* is declining, *MPP* is rising. When *MC* is rising, the *MPP* of the variable input is falling. Obviously, the low point on the *MC* curve is when diminishing marginal returns set in.

Exhibit 5 brings together much of the material we have discussed relating to short-run production and costs.

Average Fixed Cost (AFC) Total fixed cost divided by quantity of output: $AVC = TVC/Q$.

Average Variable Cost (AVC) Total variable cost divided by quantity of output: $AVC = TVC/Q$.

Average Total Cost (ATC) Total cost divided by quantity of output: $ATC = TC/Q$

EXHIBIT 4

Total, Average, and Marginal Costs

TFC equals $100 (column 2 on the table) and TVC is as noted in column 4. From the data, we calculate AFC, AVC, TC, ATC, and MC. The curves associated with TFC, AFC, TVC, AVC, TC, ATC, and MC are shown in diagrams at the bottom of the corresponding columns. (*Note:* Scale is not the same for all diagrams.)

(1) Quantity of Output, Q (units)	(2) Total Fixed Cost (TFC)	(3) Average Fixed Cost (AFC) AFC = TFC/Q = (2)/(1)	(4) Total Variable Cost (TVC)	(5) Average Variable Cost (AVC) AVC = TVC/Q = (4)/(1)
0	$100	—	$0	—
1	100	$100.00	50	$50.00
2	100	50.00	80	40.00
3	100	33.33	100	33.33
4	100	25.00	110	27.50
5	100	20.00	130	26.00
6	100	16.67	160	26.67
7	100	14.28	200	28.57
8	100	12.50	250	31.25
9	100	11.11	310	34.44
10	100	10.00	380	38.00

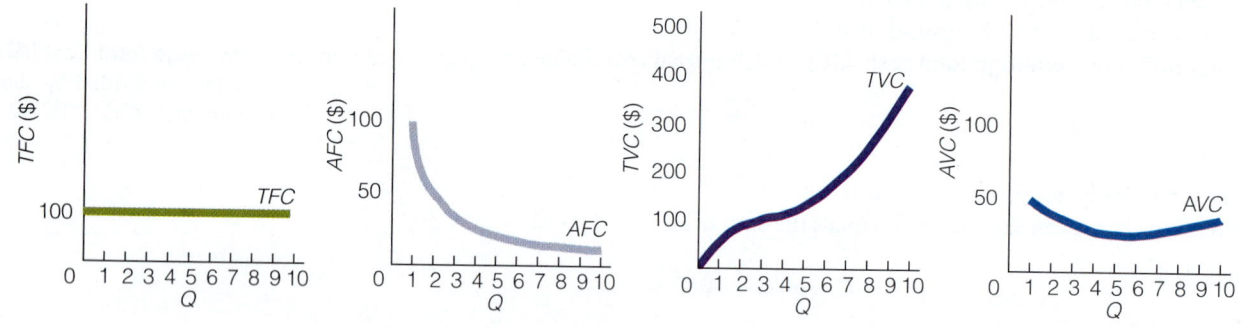

THINKING LIKE AN ECONOMIST

Deducing Things from What Is Known   Economists often deduce things from what they know, as we just did when discussing MPP and MC. Here is what we know: MPP and MC are inversely related; that is, as MPP rises, MC falls, and as MPP falls, MC rises. When diminishing marginal returns kick in, MPP begins to decline. We deduce, then, that when diminishing marginal returns kick in, MC begins to rise.

EXHIBIT 4

Continued

(6) Total Cost (TC) TC = TFC + TVC = (2) + (4)	(7) Average Total Cost (ATC) ATC = TC/Q = (6)/(1)	(8) Marginal Cost (MC) MC = ΔTC/ΔQ = Δ(6)/Δ(1)
$100.00	—	—
150.00	$150.00	$50.00
180.00	90.00	30.00
200.00	66.67	20.00
210.00	52.50	10.00
230.00	46.00	20.00
260.00	43.33	30.00
300.00	42.86	40.00
350.00	43.75	50.00
410.00	45.56	60.00
480.00	48.00	70.00

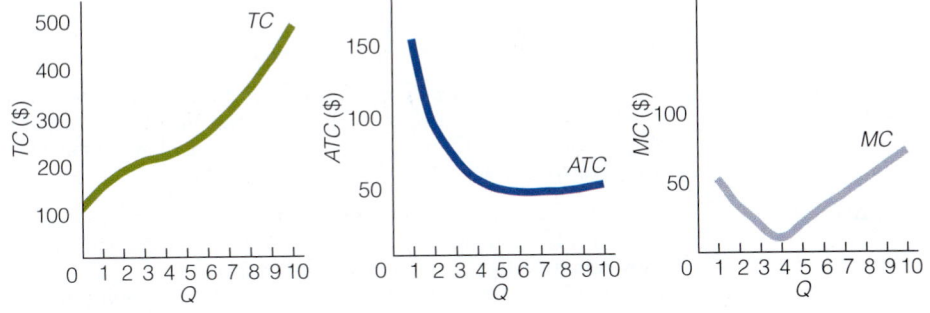

8-4a The *AVC* and *ATC* Curves in Relation to the *MC* Curve

What do the average total and average variable cost curves look like in relation to the *MC* curve? To explain, we need to discuss the **average–marginal rule**, which is best defined with an example.

average–marginal rule
When the marginal magnitude is above the average magnitude, the average magnitude rises; when the marginal magnitude is below the average magnitude, the average magnitude falls.

EXHIBIT 5

A Review of Production and Costs in the Short Run

Concept	Explanation	Example	Other Information (if relevant)
Production in the Short Run	Firm is producing with at least one input that is fixed.	Firm produces with capital and labor, where capital is the fixed input and labor is the variable input.	
Marginal Physical Product (MPP)	$MPP = \Delta Q / \Delta \text{Variable Input}$	If $\Delta Q = 40$ units, and ΔVariable Input $= 1$, then $MPP = 40$ units.	
Law of Diminishing Marginal Returns	The law of diminishing marginal returns states that, as ever larger amounts of a variable input are combined with a fixed input, eventually the MPP of the variable input declines.	See Exhibit 2. Diminishing marginal returns "kick in" with the addition of the fourth worker.	The law of diminishing marginal returns holds only in the short run, when at least one input is fixed.
Total Cost (TC)	$TC = TFC + TVC$	Let $TFC = \$10$, and $TVC = \$40$; it follows that $TC = \$50$.	
Total Fixed Cost (TFC)	$TFC = AFC \times Q$	Let $AFC = \$4$ and $Q = 40$ units; it follows that $TFC = \$160$.	TFC is constant over quantity of output. For example, TFC is, say, $100 when quantity of output is 10 units and also when quantity of output is 20 units.
Total Variable Cost (TVC)	$TVC = AVC \times Q$	Let $AVC = \$6$ and $Q = 40$ units; it follows that $TVC = \$240$.	TVC changes as quantity of output changes.
Average Fixed Cost (AFC)	$AFC = TFC / Q$	Let $TFC = \$50$ and $Q = 10$; it follows that $AFC = \$5$.	AFC declines as quantity of output rises.
Average Variable Cost (AVC)	$AVC = TVC / Q$	Let $TVC = \$120$ and $Q = 20$; it follows that $AVC = \$6$.	
Average Total Cost (ATC)	(1) $ATC = TC / Q$ (2) $ATC = AFC + AVC$	(1) Let $TC = \$50$ and $Q = \$5$; it follows that $ATC = \$10$. (2) Let $AFC = \$4$ and $AVC = \$1$; it follows that $ATC = \$5$.	ATC is the same as *unit cost*. Also, notice that ATC can be computed two ways, as we show at the left in the second column.
Marginal Cost (MC)	$MC = \Delta TC / \Delta Q$	Suppose that TC increases from $40 to $45 as quantity of output rises from 101 to 102 units. It follows that MC, which is the change in total cost divided by the change in quantity of output, is $5.	There is a second way of computing MC when the variable input is labor. Here it is: $MC = W / MPP$, where $W =$ wage rate and $MPP =$ marginal physical product of labor.

Suppose that 20 persons are in a room and that each person weighs 170 pounds. Your task is to calculate the average weight per person. The calculation is accomplished by adding the individual weights and dividing by 20. Obviously, this average weight will be 170 pounds. Now an additional person enters the room. We will refer to this additional person as the marginal (additional) person, and we will call the additional weight he brings into the room the marginal weight.

Let's suppose the weight of the marginal person is 275 pounds. Then, based on the 21 persons now in the room, the average weight per person is 175 pounds. The new average weight is greater than the old average weight because the average weight was pulled up by the weight of the additional person. In short, *when the marginal magnitude is above the average magnitude, the average magnitude rises*. This is one part of the average–marginal rule.

Now suppose the weight of the marginal person is *less than* the average weight of 170 pounds, such as 65 pounds. Then the new average is 165 pounds. In this case, the average weight was pulled *down* by the weight of the additional person. Thus, *when the marginal magnitude is below the average magnitude, the average magnitude falls*. This is the other part of the average–marginal rule. Putting the two parts together, we have

$$Marginal < Average \rightarrow Average \downarrow$$
$$Marginal > Average \rightarrow Average \uparrow$$

We can apply the average–marginal rule to find out what the *ATC* and *AVC* curves look like in relation to the *MC* curve. The following analysis holds for both the *ATC* curve and the *AVC* curve: We reason that

1. if marginal cost is below (less than) average variable cost, then average variable cost is falling; and

2. if marginal cost is above (greater than) average variable cost, then average variable cost is rising.

This reasoning implies that the relationship between the *AVC* curve and the *MC* curve must look like that in Exhibit 6(a). In region 1, marginal cost is below average variable cost and average variable cost is falling. In region 2, marginal cost is above average variable cost and average variable

EXHIBIT 6

Average and Marginal Cost Curves

(a) The relationship between *AVC* and *MC*. (b) The relationship between *ATC* and *MC*. The *MC* curve intersects both the *AVC* and *ATC* curves at their respective low points (*L*). This behavior is consistent with the average–marginal rule. (c) The *AFC* curve declines continuously.

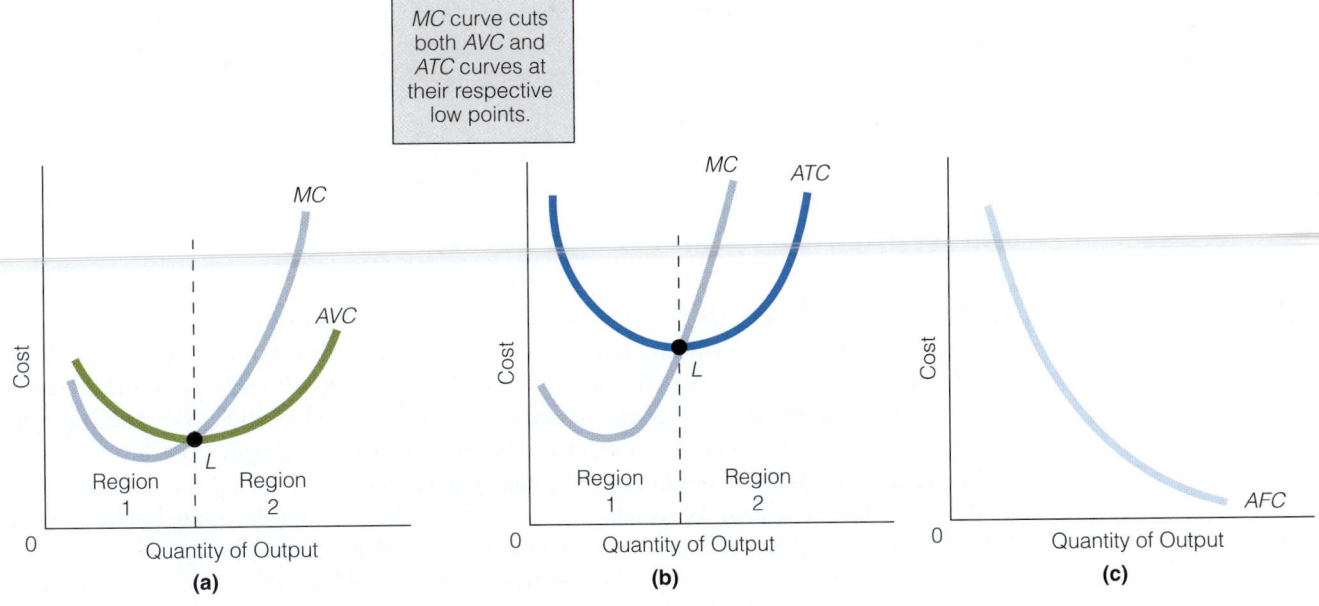

cost is rising. In sum, the relationship between the *AVC* curve and the *MC* curve, as shown in Exhibit 6(a), is consistent with the average–marginal rule.

In addition, because average variable cost is pulled down when marginal cost is below it and pulled up when marginal cost is above it, the *MC* curve must intersect the *AVC* curve at the latter's lowest point. This lowest point is point *L* in Exhibit 6(a).

The same relationship that exists between the *MC* and *AVC* curves also exists between the *MC* and *ATC* curves, as shown in Exhibit 6(b). In region 1, marginal cost is below average total cost and, consistent with the average–marginal rule, average total cost is falling. In region 2, marginal cost is above average total cost and average total cost is rising. The *MC* curve must therefore intersect the *ATC* curve at the latter's lowest point.

There is no relationship between the average fixed cost curve and the *MC* curve. We can indirectly see why by recalling that average fixed cost is simply total fixed cost (which is constant over output) divided by output ($AFC = TFC/Q$). As output (Q) increases and total fixed cost (TFC) remains constant, average fixed cost (TFC/Q) must decrease continuously. [See Exhibit 6(c).]

FINDING ECONOMICS

Why Doesn't Oliver Cheat?   Oliver is sitting in class taking a test, and his teacher is out of the class. He could easily look over at his neighbor's paper (which is uncovered) to see what the answer to question 25 is, but he doesn't. Why doesn't he cheat? Does it have anything to do with the average–marginal rule?

There may be a guilt cost to Oliver cheating, but let's ignore that reason for a moment. Even without a guilt cost and without the chance of being caught, Oliver may still not cheat, for a reason that could have something to do with the average–marginal rule. People usually cheat by copying the work of someone who they believe is smarter than they are. Suppose Oliver believes that his grade on the test will be 65 and that Ian (who is sitting next to him) will receive a grade of 60. Oliver's grade of 65 can be viewed as the average grade and Ian's as the marginal grade. Because the marginal grade is less than the average grade, the marginal will pull down the average. There's no need to cheat if copying someone else's work only lowers Oliver's grade. Oliver is more likely to cheat if he thinks that cheating will raise his grade, but that can occur only if he cheats off a person whose grade is likely to be higher than his (if he doesn't cheat).

8-4b Tying Short-Run Production to Costs

To see how costs are tied to production, let's summarize some of our earlier discussions. (See Exhibit 7.) We assume that production takes place in the short run, so there is at least one fixed input. Suppose we initially add units of a variable input to the fixed input and the *MPP* of the variable input (e.g., labor) rises. Then, as a result of *MPP* rising, MC falls. From the average–marginal rule, we know that, when *MC* has fallen enough to be below *AVC*, *AVC* will begin to decline. Also, when *MC* has fallen enough to be below *ATC*, *ATC* will begin to decline.

Eventually, though, the law of diminishing marginal returns will set in. When it does, the *MPP* of the variable input declines. As a result, *MC* rises. When *MC* has risen enough to be above *AVC*, *AVC* will rise. Also, when *MC* has risen enough to be above *ATC*, *ATC* will rise.

So, what happens in terms of production (rising or falling *MPP*) affects *MC*, which in turn eventually affects *AVC* and *ATC*. In short, the cost of a good is tied to its production.

EXHIBIT 7

Tying Production to Costs

What happens in terms of production (*MPP* rising or falling) affects *MC*, which in turn eventually affects *AVC* and *ATC*.

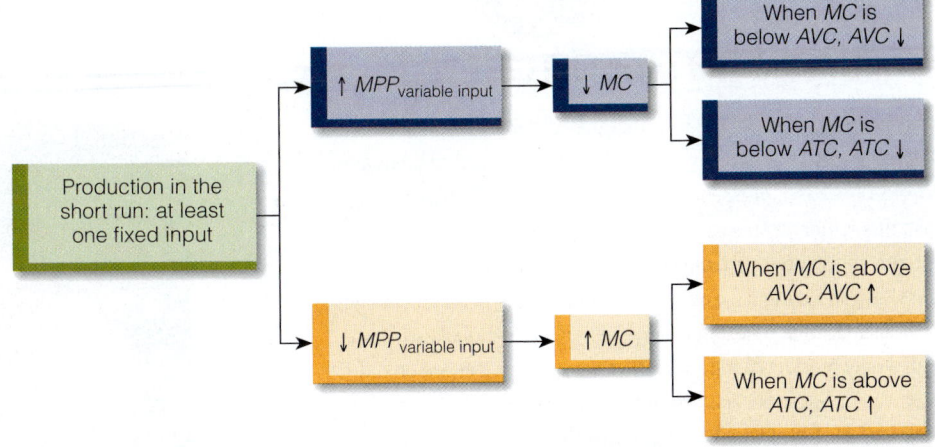

THINKING LIKE AN ECONOMIST

Seeing How Things Came to Be In economics, learning what comes before an event is important. To illustrate, suppose *ATC* is rising. Can you see the process that brought this event (*ATC* rising) at this particular moment?

Let's take one step back at a time. *ATC* is rising because (one step back) *MC* rose to a level above *ATC*. But why did *MC* rise to a level above *ATC*? Or, for that matter, why is *MC* rising at all? *MC* is rising because *MPP* (one step back) is declining. But why is *MPP* declining? *MPP* is declining because (one step back) the law of diminishing marginal returns set in.

Looking at a tree, you see its branches and leaves. If you look back, though, you can see the seed that was planted and that grew into the tree. You can do the same in economics. When looking at rising *ATC*, most of us simply see rising *ATC*. But if you look far enough back, you can see the law of diminishing marginal returns growing into rising *ATC*.

8-4c One More Cost Concept: Sunk Cost

Sunk cost is a cost incurred in the past that cannot be changed by current decisions and therefore cannot be recovered. For example, suppose that a firm must purchase a $10,000 government license before it can legally produce and sell lamp poles and that the government will not buy back the license or allow it to be resold. The $10,000 the firm spends to purchase the license is a sunk cost. It is a cost that, after it has been incurred (after the $10,000 was spent), cannot be changed by a current decision (the firm cannot go back into the past and undo what was done) and cannot be recovered (the government will neither buy back the license nor allow it to be resold).

Let's consider another example of a sunk cost. Suppose Jeremy buys a movie ticket, walks into the theater, and settles down to watch the movie. Thirty minutes into the movie, he realizes that he hates it. The money he paid for the ticket is a sunk cost. The cost was incurred in the past, it cannot be changed, and it cannot be recovered. (We are assuming that movie theaters do not give your money back if you dislike the movie.)

Sunk cost
A cost incurred in the past that cannot be changed by current decisions and therefore cannot be recovered.

ECONOMICS 24/7

Social Media and Marginal Cost

A key property of social media is that they allow someone to interact with a very large group of people across thousands of miles and various time zones *at essentially zero marginal cost*. Zero marginal cost: that is what is special about social media, and it is what differentiates social media in a big way from traditional media.

Using social media, a person can, for instance, send out a tweet to thousands of people, informing them of an earthquake in China or of a new product that performs well, or of what the person did in Hawaii on vacation. This property—their ability to reach large groups of people at very low, if any, marginal cost—is what makes social media unique.

Now, if talking, communicating, and interacting has become so cheap, what would you expect the consequences to be? First, you would expect there to be many more interactions between people at zero cost than at some positive cost. People who once could play games only with the person next door or with the friend invited over to the house, can now play games with people all over the world. It is commonplace to find someone in, say, Charleston, South Carolina, playing the video game "Halo" or "Call of Duty" with someone in Changsha, China. In other words, social media caused people who never would interact to interact. How so? Simply by lowering the cost of interacting with people over thousands of miles and various time zones.

By lowering the costs of interacting, social media have led to some groups being formed that otherwise could not, and therefore would not, have been formed. For example, think of the persons that come together on *Yelp*, a website that offers rating and review services.

By lowering the costs of "saying or writing something," social media have greatly increased the amount of things that are said and written. At one time, the only way the average person could

Christin Gilbert/age fotostoc /Superstock

comment on a political issue and have that comment reach large numbers of people was to write a letter to the editor of a newspaper. That is no longer the case. Today, anyone with a personal computer, tablet, or smartphone can read a news article on, say, Yahoo! and then post a comment at almost zero cost. We would expect that, at such low cost, there would be many more comments than when costs are higher. And with a greater number of comments, we would expect the average quality of a comment to decline—and some argue that it has. One can find all manner of comments on Yahoo! News items, from the insightful to the ordinary to the insubstantial.

Economists' Advice: Ignore Sunk Costs Economists advise individuals to ignore sunk costs. To illustrate, for Jeremy, who bought the movie ticket but dislikes the movie, the movie ticket is a sunk cost. Now, suppose Jeremy says the following to himself as he is watching the movie:

I paid to watch this movie, but I really hate it. Should I get up and walk out, or should I stay and watch the movie? I think I'll stay and watch the movie because, if I leave, I'll lose the money I paid for the ticket.

The error that Jeremy is making is believing that if he walks out of the theater he will lose the money he paid for the ticket. But he has already lost the money for the ticket. Whether he stays and watches the movie or leaves, the money is gone forever. It is a sunk cost.

An economist would advise Jeremy to ignore what has happened in the past and what can't be undone. In other words, ignore sunk costs. The question is not, What have I already lost? Nothing can be done about what has been lost. Instead, Jeremy should ask and answer these questions: What do I gain (what are my benefits) if I stay and watch the movie? What do I lose (what are my costs) if I stay and watch the movie? If what Jeremy expects to gain by staying and watching the movie is greater than what he expects to lose, he should stay and watch the movie. However, if what he expects to lose by staying and watching the movie is greater than what he expects to gain, he should leave.

To see this point more clearly, let's say that Jeremy has decided to stay and watch the movie because he doesn't want to lose the price of the movie ticket. Two minutes after he makes this decision, you walk up to him and offer him $200 to leave the theater. Do you think Jeremy will say, "I can't leave the movie theater, because, if I do, I will lose the price of the movie ticket?" Or do you think that he is more likely to take the money and leave? Most people will say that Jeremy will take the $200 and leave the movie theater simply because, if he doesn't leave, he loses the opportunity to receive $200.

However, wouldn't he have forfeited something—albeit not $200—if no one offered him $200 to leave? He might have given up at least $1 in benefits doing something else. In short, he must have had some opportunity cost of staying at the movie theater before the $200 was offered. The problem is that, somehow, by letting sunk cost influence his decision, Jeremy was willing to ignore this opportunity cost of staying at the theater. The $200 offer only made that cost obvious.

Consider another situation. Alicia purchases a pair of shoes on sale (no refunds), wears them for a few days, and then realizes that they are uncomfortable. An economist would recommend that Alicia simply not wear the shoes. To an economist, the cost of the shoes is a sunk cost because it (1) was incurred in the past, (2) cannot be changed by a current decision, and (3) cannot be recovered. An economist would advise Alicia not to base her current decision as to whether to wear the shoes on what has happened and what cannot be changed. If Alicia lets what she has done and can't undo influence her present decision, she runs the risk of compounding her mistake.

To illustrate, if Alicia decides to wear the uncomfortable shoes because she thinks that it is a waste of money not to, she may end up with an even bigger loss: certainly, less comfort and, possibly, a trip to the podiatrist. The relevant question she must ask herself is not "What did I give up by buying the shoes?" The right question is, "What will I give up by wearing the uncomfortable shoes?"

The message is that a present decision can affect only the future, never the past. Bygones are bygones; sunk costs are sunk costs.

ECONOMICS 24/7

Producing a Grade in a College Course

One way to think of your taking a college course is as a consumer. To illustrate, you might think of an economics lecture in the same way you would a movie. You sit in the classroom and watch the lecturer lecture. You sit in a theater and watch the movie on the screen.

Another (and perhaps "more nearly accurate") way to think of your taking a college course is as a producer. But if, by taking a course, you are a producer, what is it exactly that you are producing? The immediate answer is a grade. You work at producing an A, or a B, or a C, and so on.

If we dig below the surface of the grade, though, what you really are producing is knowledge for yourself. The grade is simply a reflection of the knowledge, in the sense that a higher grade reflects more knowledge produced by you for you and a lower grade reflects less knowledge produced by you for you.

Viktor Gladkov/Shutterstock.com

Now, one of the ways to understand what production and costs are about is to think through your actions as a producer. With this idea in mind, let's consider your producing a grade in a college course.

In your production of a grade, there are both fixed and variable costs. Your paper and pen (that you use to take notes) are largely fixed inputs. The cost of these items constitutes your fixed cost. No matter what grade you produce or how much knowledge you acquire, the cost of your paper and pen is not going to change. It is the same whether you end up producing an A, a B, or a C in the course.

Your variable costs relate to how carefully you listen, how carefully you take notes, and how many course assignments you complete. We would expect that the variable costs will rise as you listen more carefully, take more careful notes, and work on and turn in more assignments.

If we add your pen-and paper-costs (fixed costs) to your listening and note-taking costs (variable costs), we have the total cost of producing the grade.

Now consider marginal cost. Marginal cost is the change in total cost given a change in quantity of output. The "quantity of output" term here can be misleading, because rarely does a student sitting in class think of his or her producing so many units of a good,

the way a computer firm produces computers or a furniture firm produces furniture. Still, the student produces something, and that something can be roughly described as "units of knowledge." The more units of knowledge produced (by you for you), the higher the grade is likely to be. So, is there a positive marginal cost of producing a higher grade?

We expect that there would be, and you probably would agree if you have ever made a mental note of the "extra work" it takes you to move your current course grade up from an 89 (B+) to a 92 (A–). In other words, the marginal cost (to you) of producing a higher grade in the course, or acquiring more knowledge from the course, is positive and not zero. [As an aside, it could very well be that different students incur different marginal costs of moving their grade up from an 89 to a 92. In other words, it might be less costly (or easier) for some students to raise their grade 3 points than it is for other students.]

Let's compare the marginal cost of raising *your grade* in two courses, X and Y. The marginal cost of raising your grade by 3 points is $100 of extra effort in course X and $300 of extra effort in course Y. Many students may express the difference here by saying, "Course Y is a tougher course than course X." ("Econ 302 is a lot tougher than Sociology 270.") Will the difference in marginal cost in the two courses affect your behavior? Will it be the determining factor in which of the two courses you decide to enroll in (assuming that you don't have to take both courses)? It could be, if the benefits of taking the two courses are the same. All other things being equal, you will probably prefer to take course X than course Y.

Finally, do sunk costs exist in a college course? Suppose you took a midterm last week and received a low grade. Are the costs associated with taking the midterm a sunk cost? Well, a cost is sunk if it was (1) incurred in the past, (2) cannot be changed by current decisions, and therefore (3) cannot be recovered. The costs associated with taking the midterm (1) were incurred last week, (2) cannot be changed by a current decision (we are assuming that your professor will not let you retake the midterm, and therefore (3) cannot be recovered. Hence, the costs associated with taking the midterm are sunk costs.

Behavioral Economics and Sunk Cost   In a real-life experiment, two researchers randomly distributed discounts to buyers of subscriptions to Ohio University's 1982–1983 theater season.[4] One group of ticket buyers paid the normal ticket price of $15 per ticket, a second group received $2 off per ticket, and a third group received $7 off per ticket. In short, some buyers paid lower ticket prices than others.

4. Arkes and Catherine Blumer, "The Psychology of Sunk Cost," *Organizational Behavior and Human Decision Processes* 124 (1985).

The researchers found that people who paid more for their tickets attended the theater performances more often than those who paid less. Some people argue that the reason is that people who paid more for their tickets somehow wanted to attend the theater more than those who paid less. But this explanation isn't likely, because the discounts to buyers were distributed randomly. Instead, it seems to be that the more someone paid for the ticket (everyone paid for the ticket before the night of the performance), the greater was the sunk cost. And the greater the sunk cost, the more likely individuals were to attend the theater performance. In other words, at least some people were not ignoring sunk cost.

THINKING LIKE AN ECONOMIST

Viewing Sunk Cost as a Constraint Microeconomics emphasizes that all economic actors deal with objectives, constraints, and choices. Let's focus briefly on constraints. All economic actors would prefer to have fewer rather than more constraints and to have constraints that offer more rather than less latitude. For example, a firm would probably prefer to be constrained in having to buy its resources from five suppliers rather than from only one supplier. A consumer would rather have a budget constraint of $4,000 a month instead of $2,000 a month.

Now, suppose person A considers sunk cost when she makes a decision and person B ignores it when he makes a decision. Does one person face fewer constraints, *ceteris paribus*? The person who ignores sunk cost, person B, faces fewer constraints. Person A acts as if a constraint is there—the constraint of sunk cost, the constraint of having to rectify a past decision—when it really exists only in her mind.

In this sense, the fabricated constraint of sunk cost is very different from the real constraint of, say, scarcity. Whether a person believes it or not, scarcity exists. People are constrained by scarcity, just as they are by the force of gravity, whether they know it or not. But people are not constrained by sunk cost if they choose not to be. If you let bygones be bygones, if you realize that sunk cost is a cost that has been incurred and can't be changed, then it cannot constrain you when you are making a current decision.

Economists look at things this way: there are enough constraints in the world; you are not made better off by behaving as if there is one more than there actually is.

SELF-TEST

1. Identify two ways to compute average total cost (*ATC*).

2. Would a business ever sell its product for less than cost? Explain your answer.

3. What happens to unit costs as marginal costs rise? Explain your answer.

4. Do changes in *MPP* influence unit costs? Explain your answer.

8-5 PRODUCTION AND COSTS IN THE LONG RUN

This section discusses long-run production and costs. As noted earlier, there are no fixed inputs and no fixed costs in the long run. Consequently, the firm has *greater flexibility* in the long run than in the short run. (Because we discuss both short-run and long-run average total cost curves, we distinguish between them with prefixes: *SR* for short run and *LR* for long run.)

8-5a Long-Run Average Total Cost Curve

In the short run, because there are fixed costs and variable costs, total cost is the sum of the two. But in the long run, there are no fixed costs, so variable costs *are* total costs. This section focuses on (1) the long-run average total cost (*LRATC*) curve and (2) what it looks like.

Consider the manager of a firm that produces bedroom furniture. When all inputs are variable, the manager must decide what the situation of the firm should be in the upcoming short-run period. For example, he might need to determine the size of the plant: small, medium, or large. Once this decision is made, the firm is locked into a specific plant size for the short run. Associated with each of the three different plant sizes is a short-run average total cost (*SRATC*) curve, as illustrated in Exhibit 8 (a).

Suppose the manager of the firm wants to produce output level Q_1. Then, obviously, he will choose the plant size represented by $SRATC_1$. This size gives a lower unit cost of producing Q_1 than the plant size represented by $SRATC_2$, a size that has a higher unit cost of producing Q_1 ($6 as opposed to $5).

However, if the manager chooses to produce Q_2, he will choose the plant size represented by $SRATC_3$, because the unit cost of producing Q_2 is lower with that plant size than it is with the plant size represented by $SRATC_2$.

If we were to ask the same question for every (possible) output level, we would derive the **long-run average total cost (*LRATC*) curve**. The *LRATC* curve shows the lowest unit cost at which the firm can produce any given level of output. In Exhibit 8(a), the *LRATC* curve consists of the

Long-Run Average Total Cost (*LRATC*) Curve

A curve that shows the lowest (unit) cost at which a firm can produce any given level of output.

EXHIBIT 8

Long-Run Average Total Cost Curve (*LRATC*)

(a) There are three short-run average total cost curves, for three different plant sizes. If these are the only plant sizes, then the long-run average total cost curve is the heavily shaded, blue scalloped curve. (b) The long-run average total cost curve is the heavily shaded, blue smooth curve. The *LRATC* curve in (b) is not scalloped because it is assumed that there are so many plant sizes that the *LRATC* curve touches each *SRATC* curve at only one point.

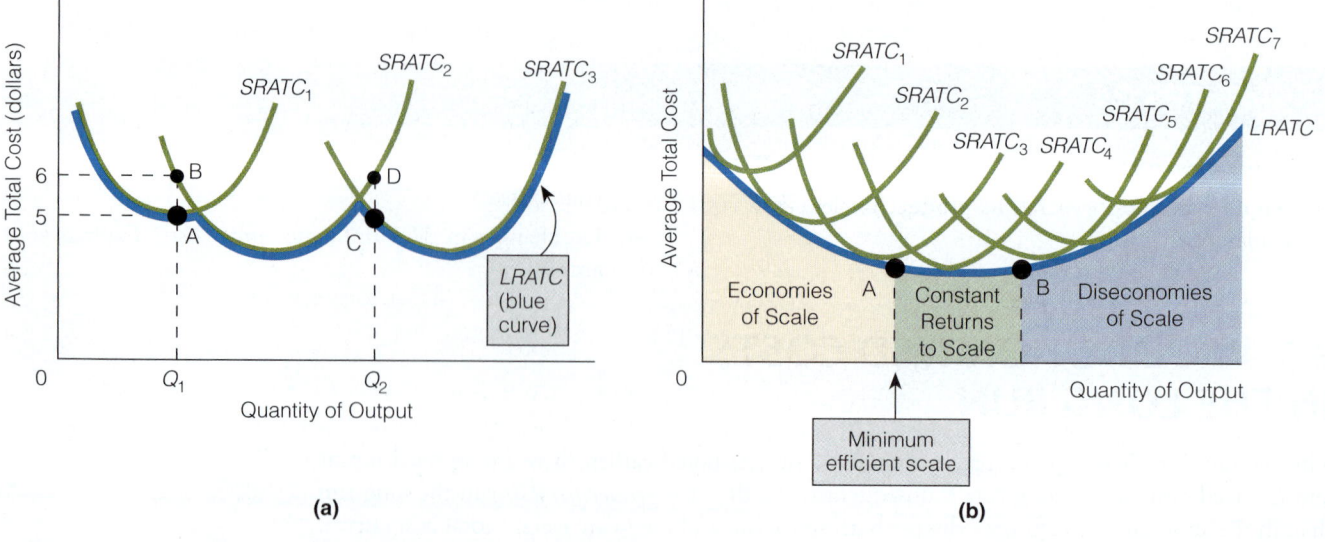

(a)

(b)

portions of the three *SRATC* curves that are tangential to the blue curve; it is the scalloped blue curve.

Exhibit 8(b) shows a host of *SRATC* curves and one *LRATC* curve. In this case, the *LRATC* curve is not scalloped, as it was in part (a). The *LRATC* curve is smooth in part (b) because we assume that there are many plant sizes in addition to the three represented in (a). In other words, although they have not been drawn, short-run average total cost curves representing different plant sizes exist in (b) between $SRATC_1$ and $SRATC_2$, between $SRATC_2$ and $SRATC_3$, and so on. In this case, the *LRATC* curve is smooth and touches each *SRATC* curve at one point.

8-5b   Economies of Scale, Diseconomies of Scale, and Constant Returns to Scale

Suppose two inputs—labor and capital—are used together to produce a good. If inputs are increased by some percentage (say, 100 percent) and if output increases by a greater percentage (more than 100 percent), then unit costs fall and **economies of scale** are said to exist.

For example, suppose that good X is made with two inputs, Y and Z, and it takes 20 Y and 10 Z to produce 5 units of X. Suppose also that the cost of each unit of input Y is $1 and the cost of each unit of input Z is $1. Thus, a total cost of $30 is required to produce 5 units of X. The unit cost (average total cost) of good X is $6 ($ATC = TC / Q$). Now, consider a doubling of inputs Y and Z, to 40 Y and 20 Z, and a more than doubling in output, say, to 15 units of X. Then a total cost of $60 is required to produce 15 units of X, and the unit cost (average total cost) of good X is $4.

An increase in inputs can have two other results. If inputs are increased by some percentage and output increases by an *equal* percentage, then unit costs remain constant and **constant returns to scale** are said to exist. If inputs are increased by some percentage and output increases by a *smaller* percentage, then unit costs rise and **diseconomies of scale** are said to exist.

The three conditions can easily be seen in the *LRATC* curve in Exhibit 8(b): if economies of scale are present, the *LRATC* curve is falling; if constant returns to scale are present, the curve is flat; if diseconomies of scale are present, the curve is rising. In sum,

Economies of scale → *LRATC* is falling

Constant returns to scale → *LRATC* is constant

Diseconomies of scale → *LRATC* is rising

If, in the production of a good, economies of scale give way to constant returns to scale or to diseconomies of scale, as in Exhibit 8(b), the point at which this transition occurs is referred to as the minimum efficient scale. The **minimum efficient scale** is the lowest output level at which average total costs are minimized. Point A represents the minimum efficient scale in Exhibit 8(b).

The significance of the minimum efficient scale of output can be seen by looking at the long-run average total cost curve between points A and B in Exhibit 8(b). Between these points, there are constant returns to scale: the average total cost is the same over the various output levels between the two points. This means that larger firms (firms producing greater output levels) within the range from point A to point B do not have a cost advantage over smaller firms that operate at the minimum efficient scale.

Keep in mind that economies of scale, diseconomies of scale, and constant returns to scale are relevant only in the long run. Implicit in the definition of these terms, and explicit in our examples, all inputs necessary to the production of a good are changeable (not fixed). Because no input is fixed, economies of scale, diseconomies of scale, and constant returns to scale are relevant only in the long run.

Exhibit 9 reviews some of the material we have discussed about long-run production and costs.

Economies of Scale
Economies that exist when inputs are increased by some percentage and output increases by a greater percentage, causing unit costs to fall.

Constant Returns to Scale
The condition when inputs are increased by some percentage and output increases by an equal percentage, causing unit costs to remain constant.

Diseconomies of Scale
The condition when inputs are increased by some percentage and output increases by a smaller percentage, causing unit costs to rise.

Minimum Efficient Scale
The lowest output level at which average total costs are minimized.

EXHIBIT 9

A Review of Production and Costs in the Long Run

Concept	Explanation	Example	Other Information (if relevant)
Production in the long run	There are no fixed inputs in the production process. All inputs are variable.	Firms use two inputs—capital (C) and labor (L)—and both are variable.	
Economies of scale	Percentage increase in output is greater than percentage increase in inputs.	Inputs increase by, say, 5 percent, and quantity of output increases by, say, 9 percent.	When the firm experiences economies of scale, its $LRATC$ (long-run average total cost) curve declines.
Diseconomies of scale	Percentage increase in output is less than percentage increase in inputs.	Inputs increase by, say, 5 percent, and quantity of output increases by, say, 2 percent.	When the firm experiences diseconomies of scale, its $LRATC$ (long-run average total cost) curve rises.
Constant returns to scale	Percentage increase in output is equal to percentage increase in inputs.	Inputs increase by, say, 5 percent, and quantity of output increases by 5 percent.	When the firm experiences constant returns to scale, its $LRATC$ curve is constant.

8-5c Why Economies of Scale?

Up to a certain point, long-run unit costs of production fall as a firm grows, for two main reasons: (1) Growing firms offer greater opportunities for employees to specialize. Individual workers can become highly proficient at narrowly defined tasks, often producing more output at lower unit costs. (2) Growing firms (especially, large growing firms) can take advantage of highly efficient mass production techniques and equipment that ordinarily require large setup costs and thus are economical only if they can be spread over a large number of units. For example, assembly-line techniques are usually relatively cheap when millions of units of a good are produced but are expensive when only a few thousand units are produced.

8-5d Why Diseconomies of Scale?

Diseconomies of scale usually arise at the point where a firm's size causes coordination, communication, and monitoring problems. In very large firms, managers often find it difficult to coordinate work activities, communicate their directives to the right persons in a timely way, and monitor personnel effectively. The business operation simply gets too big. There is, of course, a monetary incentive not to pass the point of operation at which diseconomies of scale exist, and firms usually find ways to do so, including reorganizing, dividing operations, hiring new managers, and more.

8-5e Minimum Efficient Scale and Number of Firms in an Industry

Some industries are composed of a smaller number of firms than other industries. Or we can say that there is a different degree of concentration in different industries.

The minimum efficient scale (*MES*) as a percentage of U.S. consumption or total sales is not the same for all industries. For example, in industry X, *MES* as a percentage of total sales might be 6.6, and in industry Y, it might be 2.3. In other words, firms in industry X reach the minimum efficient scale of plant and thus exhaust economies of scale at an output level of 6.6 percent of total industry sales, whereas firms in industry Y experience economies of scale only up to an output level of 2.3 percent of total industry sales.

Clearly, we would expect to find fewer firms in industry X. By dividing the *MES* as a percentage of total sales into 100, we can estimate the number of efficient firms it takes to satisfy total consumption for a particular product. For the product produced by industry X, it takes 15 firms (100/6.6 = 15). For the product produced by industry Y, it takes 43 firms.

8-6 SHIFTS IN COST CURVES

In discussing the shape of short- and long-run cost curves, we assumed that certain factors remained constant. We discuss a few of these factors now and describe how changes in them can shift cost curves.

8-6a Taxes

Consider a tax on each unit of a good produced. Suppose, for example, that a company has to pay a tax of $3 for each unit of X it produces. What effects will this tax have on the firm's cost curves? Well, the tax won't affect the firm's fixed costs, because the tax is paid only when output is produced—and fixed costs are present even if output is zero. (If the tax were a lump-sum tax—that is, if the company pays a lump sum no matter how many units of X it produces—then the tax *would* affect fixed costs.) So, given that the tax is not a lump-sum tax, we conclude that the tax does not affect fixed costs and therefore cannot affect average fixed cost.

The tax, however, will affect variable costs. As a consequence of the tax, the firm has to pay more for each unit of X it produces. Because variable costs rise, so does total cost. This relationship means that average variable cost and average total cost rise and that the representative cost curves shift upward. Finally, because marginal cost is the change in total cost divided by the change in output, marginal cost rises and the marginal cost curve shifts upward.

8-6b Input Prices

A rise or fall in variable input prices causes a corresponding change in the firm's average total, average variable, and marginal cost curves. For example, if the price of steel rises, the variable costs of building skyscrapers rise and so must average variable cost, average total cost, and marginal cost. The cost curves shift upward. If the price of steel falls, the opposite effects occur.

8-6c Technology

Technological changes often bring either (1) the capability of using fewer inputs to produce a good (e.g., the introduction of the personal computer reduced the hours necessary to key and edit a manuscript) or (2) lower input prices (e.g., technological improvements in transistors led to price reductions in the transistor components of calculators). In either case, technological changes of this variety lower variable costs and consequently lower average variable cost, average total cost, and marginal cost. The cost curves shift downward.

SELF-TEST

1. Give an arithmetical example to illustrate economies of scale.
2. What would the *LRATC* curve look like if there were always constant returns to scale? Explain your answer.
3. Firm A charged $4 per unit when it produced 100 units of good X, and it charged $3 per unit when it produced 200 units. Furthermore, the firm earned the same profit per unit in both cases. How can this happen?

OFFICE HOURS

"What Is the Difference Between the Law of Diminishing Marginal Returns and Diseconomies of Scale?"

STUDENT: I'm not sure I understand the difference between the law of diminishing marginal returns and diseconomies of scale. They sound similar to me.

INSTRUCTOR: The law of diminishing marginal returns holds in the short run when at least one input is fixed. In our example in class, we held capital constant (at one unit) and changed the units of labor. Diseconomies of scale are relevant to the long run, which is a period when all inputs are variable. In other words, no input is fixed.

STUDENT: But don't both the law of diminishing marginal returns and diseconomies of scale have something to do with less output per unit of input?

INSTRUCTOR: Let's define each and see. The law of diminishing marginal returns says that, as we add additional units of a variable input (such as labor) to a fixed input (such as capital), we get to a point where the *MPP* of the variable input (the *MPP* of labor) declines.

This decline has to do with less output per unit of input. Specifically, as we add additional units of the variable input to the fixed input, our output might rise, but it rises at a decreasing rate. To illustrate, adding the fourth worker to the production process might raise output from 100 units to 120 units (an increase of 20 units), but adding the fifth worker raises output from 120 units to 135 units (an increase of 15 units).

STUDENT: Okay, then, how is the law of diseconomies of scale different?

INSTRUCTOR: Here is an example of diseconomies of scale: The firm increases each of its inputs by, say, 10 percent, but its output rises by only 3 percent. In other words, its output rises less than the increase in its inputs. Also, notice that we don't hold any input fixed. We have assumed that there are two inputs the firm uses—labor and capital—and that it increases its usage of each input by 10 percent.

STUDENT: Are we getting less output per unit of input, as we did with respect to the law of diminishing marginal returns?

INSTRUCTOR: Yes and no. We are getting less output per unit of input if we compare diseconomies of scale with, say, economies of scale. To illustrate, with economies of scale, we might increase each input by 10 percent and end up with 20 percent more output. With diseconomies of scale, we increase each input by 10 percent and end up with, say, only 3 percent more output. Obviously, when diseconomies of scale exist, we get less output for each percentage increase in inputs than we do when economies of scale exist.

Points to Remember

1. The law of diminishing marginal returns holds in the short run when at least one input is fixed.

2. Diseconomies of scale are relevant to the long run, which is a period when all inputs are variable.

CHAPTER SUMMARY

THE FIRM

- Armen Alchian and Harold Demsetz argue that firms are formed when individuals derive benefits from working as a team—specifically, when the sum of what individuals can produce as a team is greater than the sum of what individuals can produce alone: Sum of team production > Sum of individual production.

- Team production has its advantages and disadvantages. The chief advantage (in many cases) is the positive difference between the output produced by the team and the sum of the output produced by individuals working alone. The chief disadvantage is the increased shirking that happens on teams. The role of the monitor (manager) in the firm is to preserve the increased output and to reduce or eliminate the increased

- shirking. The monitors have a monetary incentive not to shirk their monitoring duties when they are residual claimants.
- Ronald Coase argued that firms exist to reduce the "costs of negotiating and concluding a separate contract for each exchange transaction which takes place on a market." In short, firms exist to reduce transaction costs.

EXPLICIT COST AND IMPLICIT COST

- An explicit cost is incurred when an actual (monetary) payment is made. An implicit cost represents the value of resources used in production for which no actual (monetary) payment is made.

ECONOMIC PROFIT AND ACCOUNTING PROFIT

- Economic profit is the difference between total revenue and total cost, including both explicit and implicit costs. Accounting profit is the difference between total revenue and explicit costs. Economic profit is usually lower (never higher) than accounting profit. Economic profit (not accounting profit) motivates economic behavior.

PRODUCTION AND COSTS IN THE SHORT RUN

- The short run is a period in which some inputs are fixed. The long run is a period in which all inputs can be varied. The costs associated with fixed and variable inputs are referred to as fixed costs and variable costs, respectively.
- Marginal cost is the change in total cost that results from a change in quantity of output.
- The law of diminishing marginal returns states that, as ever larger amounts of a variable input are combined with fixed inputs, eventually the marginal physical product of the variable input will decline. When this decline happens, marginal cost rises.

- The average–marginal rule states that, if the marginal magnitude is above (below) the average magnitude, then the average magnitude rises (falls).
- The marginal cost curve intersects the average variable cost curve at its lowest point. The marginal cost curve intersects the average total cost curve at its lowest point. There is no relationship between marginal cost and average fixed cost.

PRODUCTION AND COSTS IN THE LONG RUN

- In the long run, because there are no fixed costs, variable costs equals total costs.
- The long-run average total cost curve is the envelope of the short-run average total cost curves. It shows the lowest unit cost at which a firm can produce a given level of output.
- If inputs are increased by some percentage and output increases by a greater percentage, then unit costs fall and economies of scale exist. If inputs are increased by some percentage and output increases by an equal percentage, then unit costs remain constant and constant returns to scale exist. If inputs are increased by some percentage and output increases by a smaller percentage, then unit costs rise and diseconomies of scale exist.
- The minimum efficient scale is the lowest output level at which average total costs are minimized.

SUNK COST

- Sunk cost is a cost incurred in the past that cannot be changed by current decisions and therefore cannot be recovered. A person or firm that wants to minimize losses will hold sunk costs to be irrelevant to present decisions.

SHIFTS IN COST CURVES

- A firm's cost curves will shift if there is a change in taxes, input prices, or technology.

KEY TERMS AND CONCEPTS

Business Firm
Market Coordination
Managerial Coordination
Shirking
Monitor
Residual Claimant
Profit
Explicit Cost
Implicit Cost
Accounting Profit

Economic Profit
Normal Profit
Fixed Input
Variable Input
Short Run
Long Run
Marginal Physical Product (*MPP*)
Law of Diminishing Marginal Returns

Fixed Costs
Variable Costs
Total Cost (*TC*)
Marginal Cost (*MC*)
Average Fixed Cost (*AFC*)
Average Variable Cost (*AVC*)
Average Total Cost (*ATC*), or Unit Cost
Average–Marginal Rule
Sunk Cost

Long-Run Average Total Cost (*LRATC*) Curve
Economies of Scale
Constant Returns to Scale
Diseconomies of Scale
Minimum Efficient Scale

QUESTIONS AND PROBLEMS

1. Explain the difference between managerial coordination and market coordination.

2. Is the managerial coordination that goes on within a business firm independent of market forces? Explain your answer.

3. Explain why even conscientious workers will shirk more when the cost of shirking falls.

4. Illustrate the average–marginal rule in a noncost setting.

5. "A firm that earns only normal profit is not covering all its costs." Do you agree or disagree? Explain your answer.

6. The average variable cost curve and the average total cost curve get closer to each other as output increases. What explains this convergence?

7. Explain why earning zero economic profit is not as bad as it sounds.

8. Why does the *AFC* curve continually decline (and get closer and closer to the quantity axis)?

9. What is the difference between diseconomies of scale and the law of diminishing marginal returns?

10. When would total costs equal fixed costs?

11. Is studying for an economics exam subject to the law of diminishing marginal returns? If so, what is the fixed input? What is the variable input?

12. Some individuals decry the decline of the small family farm and its replacement with the huge corporate megafarm.

Discuss the possibility that this shift is a consequence of economies of scale.

13. We know that there is a link between productivity and costs. For example, recall the link between the marginal physical product of the variable input and marginal cost. With this link in mind, what link might there be between productivity and prices?

14. Some people's everyday behavior suggests that they do not hold sunk costs irrelevant to present decisions. Give some examples different from those presented in this chapter.

15. Explain why a firm might want to produce its good even after diminishing marginal returns have set in and marginal cost is rising.

16. People often believe that large firms in an industry have cost advantages over small firms in the same industry. For example, they might think that a big oil company has a cost advantage over a small oil company. For this to be true, however, what condition must exist? Explain your answer.

17. The government says that firm X must pay $1,000 in taxes simply because it is in the business of producing a good. What cost curves, if any, does this tax affect?

18. On the basis of your answer to question 17, does *MC* change if *TC* changes?

19. Under what condition would a billionaire producer be rich yet earn zero economic profit?

WORKING WITH NUMBERS AND GRAPHS

1. For each lettered space in the following table, determine the appropriate dollar amount:

(1) Quantity of Output, Q (units)	(2) Total Fixed Cost ($)	(3) Average Fixed Cost (AFC)	(4) Total Variable Cost (TVC)	(5) Average Variable Cost (AVC)	(6) Total Cost (TC)	(7) Average Total Cost (ATC)	(8) Marginal Cost (MC)
0	$200	A	$0		V		
1	200	B	30	L	W	GG	QQ
2	200	C	50	M	X	HH	RR
3	200	D	60	N	Y	II	SS
4	200	E	65	O	Z	JJ	TT
5	200	F	75	P	AA	KK	UU
6	200	G	95	Q	BB	LL	VV
7	200	H	125	R	CC	MM	WW
8	200	I	165	S	DD	NN	XX
9	200	J	215	T	EE	OO	YY
10	200	K	275	U	FF	PP	ZZ

2. Give a numerical example to show that as marginal physical product (MPP) rises, marginal cost (MC) falls.

3. Price = $20, quantity = 400 units, unit cost = $15, implicit costs = $4,000. What does economic profit equal?

4. If economic profit equals accounting profit, what do implicit costs equal?

5. If accounting profit is $400,000 greater than economic profit, what do implicit costs equal?

6. If marginal physical product is continually declining, what does marginal cost look like? Explain your answer.

7. If the ATC curve is continually declining, what does this imply about the MC curve? Explain your answer.

8. When will total cost equal total variable cost?

9. Answer the following:

   a. If TVC = $80 and AVC = 4, then what does quantity (Q) equal?

   b. If total cost is $40 when Q = 2 and total cost is $45 when Q = 3, then what does marginal cost equal?

   c. What does average fixed cost equal at Q = 2 if total variable cost is $15 at Q = 2?

   d. Why does the AFC curve get continually closer to the horizontal axis in Exhibit 6(c) as quantity of output increases?

PERFECT COMPETITION

INTRODUCTION

Every firm shares two things with all other firms. First, every firm has to answer certain questions: (1) What price should the firm charge for the good it produces and sells? (2) How many units of the good should the firm produce? (3) How much of the resources that the firm needs to produce its good should it buy? Regardless of whether a firm sells shirts or cars, whether it is large or small, whether it is located in Georgia or Maine, it must answer all three of these questions. Period.

Second, every firm finds itself operating in a certain market structure. A **market structure** is a firm's environment or setting whose characteristics influence the firm's pricing and output decisions. This chapter focuses on a particular market structure: perfect competition.

9-1 THE THEORY OF PERFECT COMPETITION

Market Structure
The environment whose characteristics influence a firm's pricing and output decisions.

Perfect Competition
A theory of market structure based on four assumptions: (1) There are many sellers and buyers; (2) the sellers sell a homogeneous good; (3) buyers and sellers have all relevant information; (4) entry into, and exit from, the market is easy.

The theory of **perfect competition** is built on four assumptions:

1. *There are many sellers and many buyers, none of which is large in relation to total sales or purchases.* This assumption speaks to both demand (the number of buyers) and supply (the number of sellers). Given many buyers and sellers, each buyer and each seller may act independently of other buyers and sellers, respectively, and each is such a small part of the market as to have no influence on price.

2. *Each firm produces and sells a homogeneous product.* Each firm sells a product that is indistinguishable from all other firms' products in a given industry. (For example, a buyer of wheat cannot distinguish between Farmer Stone's wheat and Farmer Gray's wheat.) As a consequence, buyers are indifferent to the sellers.

3. *Buyers and sellers have all relevant information about prices, product quality, sources of supply, and so forth.* Buyers and sellers know who is selling what, at what prices, at what quality, and on what terms. In short, they know everything that relates to buying, producing, and selling the product.

4. *Firms have easy entry and exit.* New firms can enter the market easily, and existing firms can exit the market easily. There are no barriers to entry or exit.

Before discussing the perfectly competitive firm in the short and long run, we discuss some of the characteristics of the perfectly competitive firm that logically follow from these four assumptions.

9-1a A Perfectly Competitive Firm Is a Price Taker

A perfectly competitive firm is a **price taker**, which is a seller that does not have the ability to control the price of its product; in other words, such a firm "takes" the price determined in the market. For example, if Farmer Stone is a price taker, he can increase or decrease his output without significantly affecting the price of his product.

Why is a perfectly competitive firm a price taker? A firm is restrained from being anything but a price taker if it finds itself one among many firms whose supply is small relative to the total market supply (assumption 1 in the theory of perfect competition) and if it sells a homogeneous product (assumption 2) in an environment where buyers and sellers have all relevant information (assumption 3).

Some people suggest that the assumptions of the theory of perfect competition give economists what they want. In other words, economists want the perfectly competitive firm to be a price taker, so they choose the assumptions that make it so. But this isn't the case. Instead, economists start out with certain assumptions and then logically conclude that the firm for which these assumptions hold, or that behaves as if these assumptions hold, is a price taker; that is, it has no control over price. Afterward, economists test the theory by observing whether it accurately predicts and explains the real-world behavior of some firms. Then, until a counterexample is found, economists have good reason to believe what the theory states.

Price Taker
A seller that does not have the ability to control the price of the product it sells; the seller "takes" the price determined in the market.

9-1b The Demand Curve for a Perfectly Competitive Firm Is Horizontal

The perfectly competitive setting has many sellers and many buyers. Together, all buyers make up the market demand curve; together, all sellers make up the market supply curve. An equilibrium price is established at the intersection of the market demand and market supply curves [Exhibit 1(a)].

When the equilibrium price has been established, a single perfectly competitive firm faces a horizontal (flat, perfectly elastic) demand curve at the equilibrium price [Exhibit 1(b)]. In short, the firm takes the equilibrium price as given—hence the firm is a price taker—and sells all quantities of output at this price.[1]

Why Does a Perfectly Competitive Firm Sell at the Equilibrium Price? If a perfectly competitive firm tries to charge a price higher than the market-established equilibrium price, it won't sell any of its product. The reasons are that the firm sells a homogeneous product, its supply is small relative to the total market supply, and all buyers are informed about where they can obtain the product at the lower price.

If the firm wants to maximize profits, it does not offer to sell its good at a lower price than the equilibrium price. Why should it? It can sell all it wants at the market-established equilibrium price. The equilibrium price is the only relevant price for the perfectly competitive firm.

---

[1] The horizontal demand curve means not that the firm can sell an infinite amount at the equilibrium price, but that price will be virtually unaffected by the variations in output that the firm may find it practicable to make.

EXHIBIT 1

The Market Demand Curve and Firm Demand Curve in Perfect Competition

(a) The market, composed of all buyers and sellers, establishes the equilibrium price.
(b) A single perfectly competitive firm then faces a horizontal (flat, perfectly elastic) demand curve. We conclude that the firm is a price taker: it takes the equilibrium price established by the market and sells any and all quantities of output at this price. (The capital *D* represents the market demand curve; the lowercase *d* represents the single firm's demand curve.)

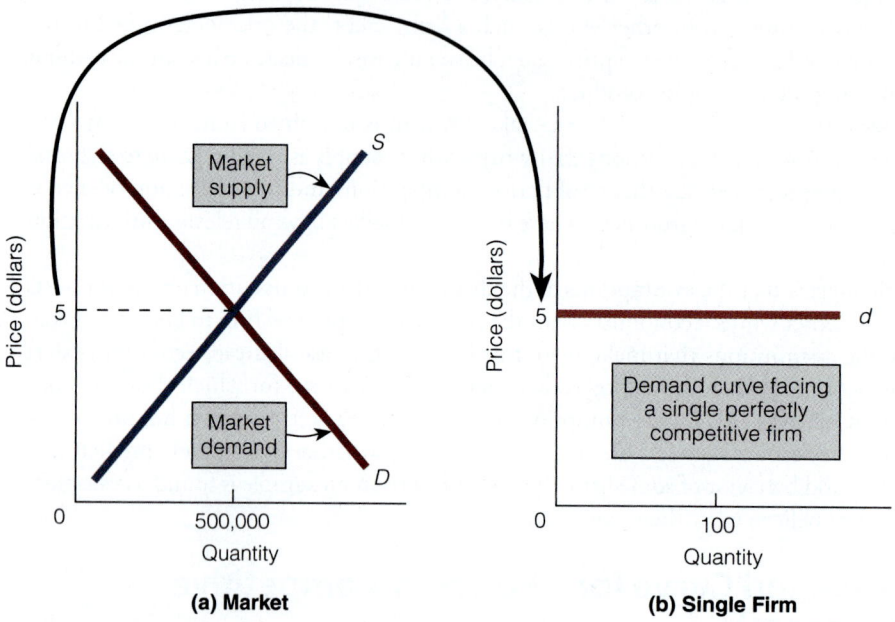

(a) Market

(b) Single Firm

FINDING ECONOMICS

When Selling Shares of Stock   Roberta wakes up in the morning and turns on her computer. She checks the prices of the stocks she owns. The price of stock X is selling at $35 per share. She had bought 200 shares of the stock when the price was only $11, and now she decides to sell. She places a sell order with her online broker, and in a matter of minutes she has sold her 200 shares of stock. Where is the economics? Does Roberta's sale of stock have anything to do with operating in a perfectly competitive market?

If Roberta wants to sell her shares of stock X, she must sell at the current market price. Roberta, as a seller of stock, is a price taker. She cannot sell her shares of stock at $2 over the current price, and she will not sell below the market price. Why should she sell her shares of stock at $33 when she can sell them at the current market price of $35?

9-1c Common Misconceptions about Demand Curves

The law of demand posits an inverse relationship between price and quantity demanded. So it follows that, if a demand curve is to represent the law of demand graphically, it must be downward sloping. A common misconception, though, is to think that *all* demand curves have to be downward sloping. Why this is not true can be explained by distinguishing the market demand curve from the demand curve faced by a single firm.

In Exhibit 1(a), the market demand curve is downward sloping, implying an inverse relationship between price and quantity demanded, *ceteris paribus*. The *single* perfectly competitive firm's demand curve does not contradict this relationship; the curve simply represents the pricing situation in which the *single* perfectly competitive firm finds itself. Recall from an earlier chapter that the more substitutes a good has, the higher the price elasticity of demand will be. In the perfectly competitive market setting, there are many substitutes for the firm's product—so many, in fact, that the firm's demand curve is perfectly elastic.

Intuitively, a single perfectly competitive firm's supply is such a *small percentage* of the total market supply that the firm cannot perceptibly influence price by changing its quantity of output. To put it differently, the firm's supply is so small, compared with the total market supply, that the inverse relationship between price and quantity demanded, although present, cannot be observed on the firm's level, although it is observable on the market level.

9-1d The Marginal Revenue Curve of a Perfectly Competitive Firm Is the Same as Its Demand Curve

Total revenue is the price of a good multiplied by the quantity sold. If the equilibrium price is $5, as in Exhibit 2(a), and the perfectly competitive firm sells 3 units of its good, its total revenue is $15. If the firm sells an additional unit, bringing the total number of units sold to 4, its total revenue is $20.

A firm's **marginal revenue (MR)** is the change in total revenue (TR) that results from selling one additional unit of output (Q):

$$MR = \frac{\Delta TR}{\Delta Q}$$

Marginal Revenue (MR)
The change in total revenue (TR) that results from selling one additional unit of output (Q).

EXHIBIT 2

The Demand Curve and the Marginal Revenue Curve for a Perfectly Competitive Firm

(a) By computing marginal revenue, we find that it is equal to price. (b) By plotting columns 1 and 2, we obtain the firm's demand curve; by plotting columns 2 and 4, we obtain the firm's marginal revenue curve. The two curves are the same.

(1) Price	(2) Quantity	(3) Total Revenue = (1) × (2)	(4) Marginal Revenue = $\Delta TR / \Delta Q$ = $\Delta(3)/\Delta(2)$
$5	1	$5	$5
5	2	10	5
5	3	15	5
5	4	20	5

(a)

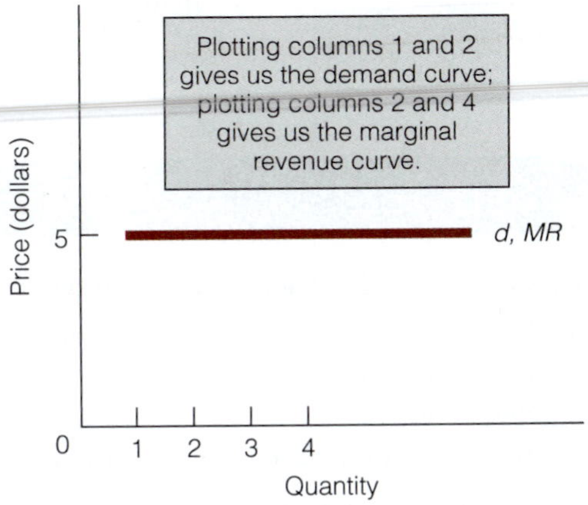

Plotting columns 1 and 2 gives us the demand curve; plotting columns 2 and 4 gives us the marginal revenue curve.

(b)

Column 4 in Exhibit 2(a) shows that the firm's marginal revenue ($5) at any output level is always equal to the equilibrium price ($5). For a perfectly competitive firm, therefore, price (P) is equal to marginal revenue:

$$\text{For a perfectly competitive firm, } P = MR$$

But if price is equal to marginal revenue, then *the marginal revenue curve for the perfectly competitive firm is the same as its demand curve.*

A demand curve plots price against quantity, whereas a marginal revenue curve plots marginal revenue against quantity. If price equals marginal revenue, then the demand curve and marginal revenue curve are the same [Exhibit 2(b)]:

$$\text{For a perfectly competitive firm, Demand curve} = \text{Marginal revenue curve}$$

9-1e   Theory and Real-World Markets

The theory of perfect competition describes how firms act in a market structure in which (1) there are many buyers and sellers, none of whom is large in relation to total sales or purchases; (2) sellers sell a homogeneous product; (3) buyers and sellers have all relevant information; and (4) market entry and exit are easy. These assumptions are closely met in some real-world markets, such as some agricultural markets and a small subset of the retail trade. The stock market, with its hundreds of thousands of buyers and sellers of stock, is also sometimes cited as an example of perfect competition.

The four assumptions of the theory of perfect competition are also *approximated* in some real-world markets. In such markets, the number of sellers may not be large enough for every firm to be a price taker, but the firm's control over price may be negligible. The amount of control may be so negligible, in fact, that the firm acts *as if* it were a perfectly competitive firm.

Similarly, buyers may not have all relevant information concerning price and quality. However, they may still have a great deal of information, and the information they do not have may not matter. The products that the firms in the industry sell may not be homogeneous, but the differences may be inconsequential.

In short, a market that does not *exactly* meet the assumptions of perfect competition may nonetheless *approximate* the assumptions to a degree that it behaves *as if* it were a perfectly competitive market. If so, then the theory of perfect competition can be used to predict that market's behavior.

SELF-TEST

(Answers to Self-Test questions are in Answers to Self-Test Questions at the back of the book.)

1. "If a firm is a price taker, it does not have the ability to control the price of the product it sells." What does this statement mean?

2. Why is a perfectly competitive firm a price taker?

3. The horizontal demand curve for the perfectly competitive firm signifies that it cannot sell any of its product for a price higher than the market equilibrium price. Why not?

4. Suppose the firms in a real-world market do not sell a homogeneous product. Does it necessarily follow that the market is not perfectly competitive?

9-2 PERFECT COMPETITION IN THE SHORT RUN

For the perfectly competitive firm, a price taker, price is equal to marginal revenue ($P = MR$), and therefore the firm's demand curve is the same as its marginal revenue curve. This section discusses the amount of output the firm will produce in the short run.

9-2a What Level of Output Does the Profit-Maximizing Firm Produce?

In Exhibit 3, the perfectly competitive firm's demand curve (d) and marginal revenue curve (MR, which is the same as d) are drawn at the equilibrium price of $5. The firm's marginal cost curve (MC) is also shown. On the basis of these curves, the firm will continue to increase its quantity of output as long as marginal revenue is greater than marginal cost. It will not produce units of output for which marginal revenue is less than marginal cost. Therefore, the firm will stop increasing its quantity of output when marginal revenue and marginal cost are equal. The **profit maximization rule** for a firm says, *produce the quantity of output at which MR = MC*.[2] In Exhibit 3, $MR = MC$ at 125 units of output.

For the perfectly competitive firm, the profit maximization rule can be written as $P = MC$ because, for that firm, $P = MR$. In other words, in perfect competition, profit is maximized when

$$P = MR = MC$$

Profit Maximization Rule
Profit is maximized by producing the quantity of output at which $MR = MC$.

9-2b The Perfectly Competitive Firm and Resource Allocative Efficiency

Resources (or inputs) are used to produce goods and services; for example, wood may be used to produce a chair. To the buyers of a good, the resources used in its production have an exchange value that is approximated by the price that people pay for the good. For example, when buying a chair for $100, Smith values the resources used to produce the chair as worth at least $100. Wood that is used to produce chairs cannot be used to produce desks. Hence, the opportunity cost of producing chairs is best measured by the marginal cost of producing the chairs.

Now, suppose that 100 chairs are produced and that, at this quantity, the price is greater than marginal cost; for example, suppose the price is $100 and the marginal cost is $75. Then, obviously, buyers place a higher value on wood when it is used to produce chairs than when it is used to produce an alternative good.

EXHIBIT 3

The Quantity of Output That the Perfectly Competitive Firm Will Produce

The firm's demand curve is horizontal at the equilibrium price. Its demand curve is its marginal revenue curve. The firm produces that quantity of output at which $MR = MC$.

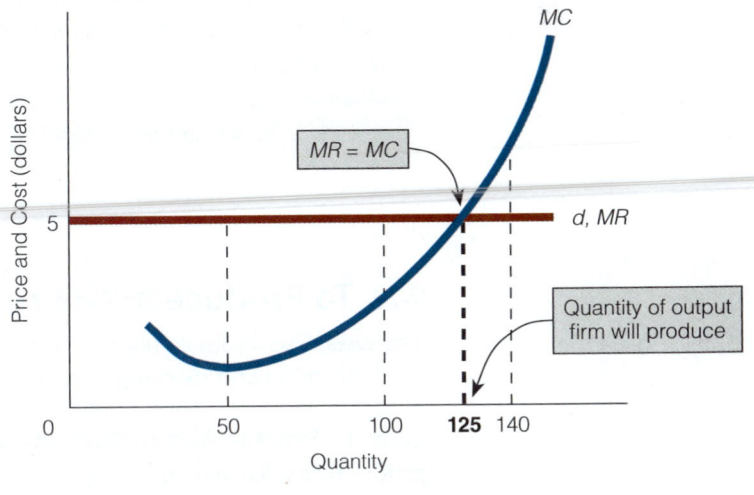

---

2. The profit maximization rule is the same as the loss minimization rule because maximizing profits is impossible without minimizing losses. The profit maximization rule holds for *all firms*, not just for perfectly competitive firms.

Resource Allocative Efficiency
The situation in which firms produce the quantity of output at which price equals marginal cost: $P = MC$.

Producing a good—any good—until price equals marginal cost ensures that all units of the good are produced that are of greater value to buyers than the alternative goods that might have been produced. In other words, a firm that produces the quantity of output at which price equals marginal cost $(P = MC)$ is said to exhibit **resource allocative efficiency**.

Does the perfectly competitive firm exhibit resource allocative efficiency? We know two things about this type of firm: First, the perfectly competitive firm produces the quantity of output at which $MR = MC$. Second, for such a firm, $P = MR$. If the perfectly competitive firm produces the output at which $MR = MC$ and if, for this firm, $P = MR$, then the firm produces the output at which $P = MC$. In short, the perfectly competitive firm *is* resource allocative efficient.

Also, for a perfectly competitive firm, profit maximization and resource allocative efficiency are not at odds. (Whether they might be for other market structures is discussed in the next two chapters.) The perfectly competitive firm seeks to maximize profit by producing the quantity of output at which $MR = MC$. Because, for that firm, $P = MR$, it automatically accomplishes resource allocative efficiency $(P = MC)$ when it maximizes profit $(MR = MC)$.

THINKING LIKE AN ECONOMIST

Profit Maximization Can Be Consistent with Consumer Welfare With good X, as with all goods, there is a right and a wrong quantity to produce. From the perspective of consumers, the right quantity is the efficient quantity. The consumer says to the manufacturers of X, "keep producing X as long as its price is greater than its marginal cost. Stop when $P = MC$." Let's say that $P = MC$ when the quantity of X is 10,000 a month.

The question now is whether the manufacturers of X want to produce 10,000 units of X a month. For manufacturers, the right quantity of X is the quantity at which $MR = MC$. In other words, manufacturers will continue making units of X as long as MR is greater than MC and they will stop when $MR = MC$.

For a perfectly competitive firm, we know that $P = MR$, so what consumers want (produce until $P = MC$) is really the same thing that manufacturers want (produce until $MR = MC$). Simply put, when manufacturers do what is in their best interest—produce until $MR = MC$—*they are automatically producing the efficient amount of the good—an amount that, in fact, consumers want. Who would have thought it?*

9-2c To Produce or Not to Produce: That Is the Question

The cases described next illustrate three applications of the profit maximization (loss minimization) rule by a perfectly competitive firm.

Case 1: Price Is Above Average Total Cost Exhibit 4(a) illustrates the perfectly competitive firm's demand and marginal revenue curves. If the firm follows the profit maximization rule and produces the quantity of output at which marginal revenue equals marginal cost, it will

EXHIBIT 4

Profit Maximization and Loss Minimization for the Perfectly Competitive Firm: Three Cases

(a) In case 1, $TR > TC$ and the firm earns profits. It continues to produce in the short run.

(b) In case 2, $TR < TC$ and the firm takes a loss. It shuts down in the short run because it minimizes its losses by doing so; it is better to lose $400 in fixed costs than to take a loss of $450. (c) In case 3, $TR < TC$ and the firm

takes a loss. It continues to produce in the short run because it minimizes its losses by doing so; it is better to lose $80 by producing than to lose $400 in fixed costs.

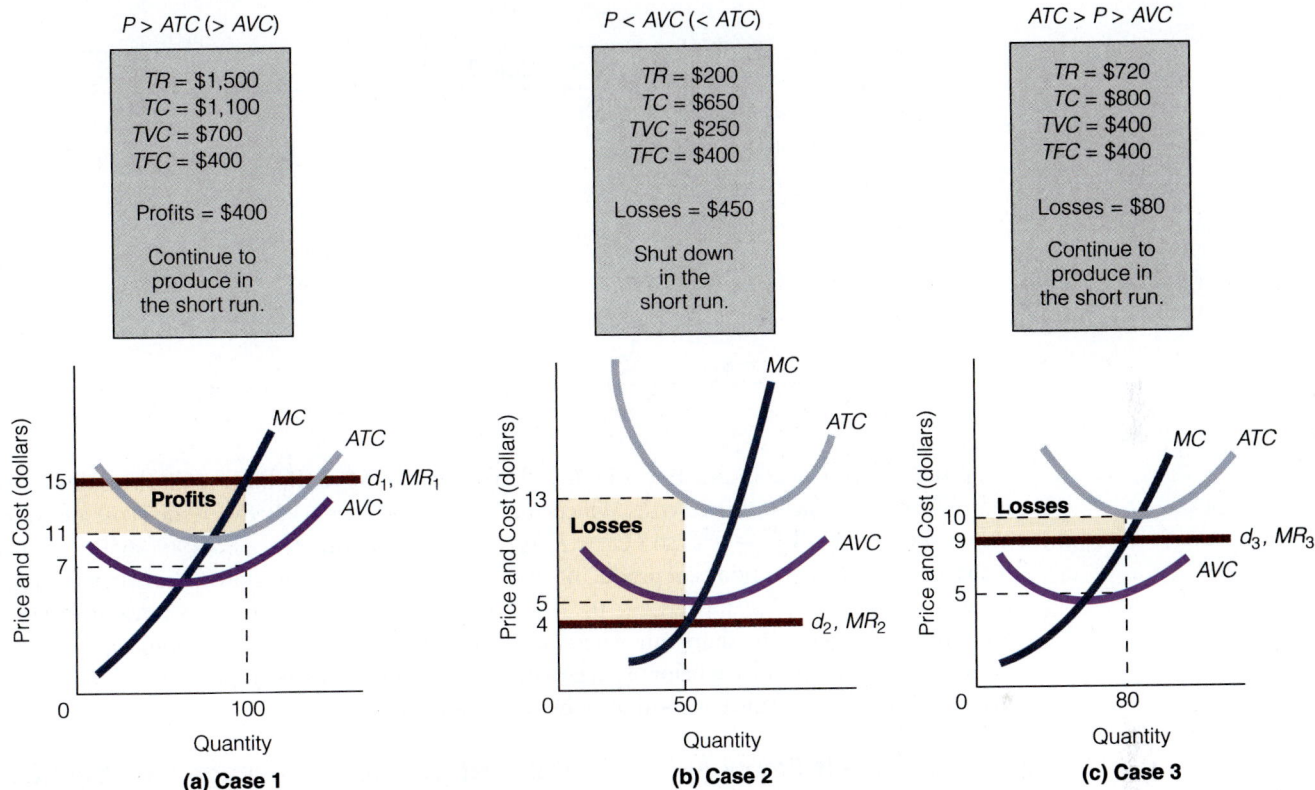

$P > ATC (> AVC)$	$P < AVC (< ATC)$	$ATC > P > AVC$
$TR = \$1,500$	$TR = \$200$	$TR = \$720$
$TC = \$1,100$	$TC = \$650$	$TC = \$800$
$TVC = \$700$	$TVC = \$250$	$TVC = \$400$
$TFC = \$400$	$TFC = \$400$	$TFC = \$400$
Profits = \$400	Losses = \$450	Losses = \$80
Continue to produce in the short run.	Shut down in the short run.	Continue to produce in the short run.

(a) Case 1　　**(b) Case 2**　　**(c) Case 3**

produce 100 units of output—the profit-maximizing quantity of output. At this quantity of output, price is above average total cost. Using the information in the exhibit, we can make the following calculations:

Case 1	
Equilibrium price (P)	= $15
Quantity of output produced (Q)	= 100 units
Total revenue ($P \times Q = \$15 \times 100$)	= $1,500
Total cost ($ATC \times Q = \$11 \times 100$)	= $1,100
Total variable cost ($AVC \times Q = \$7 \times 100$)	= $700
Total fixed cost ($TC - TVC = \$1,100 - \$700$)	= $400
Profits ($TR - TC = \$1,500 - \$1,100$)	= $400

Therefore, for the perfectly competitive firm, if price is above the average total cost, the firm maximizes profits by producing the quantity of output at which $MR = MC$.

Case 2: Price Is Below Average Variable Cost Exhibit 4(b) illustrates the case in which price is below the average variable cost. The equilibrium price at which the perfectly competitive firm sells its good is $4. At this price, total revenue is less than both total cost and total variable cost, as the following calculations indicate:

Case 2	
Equilibrium price (P)	= $4
Quantity of output produced (Q)	= 50 units
Total revenue ($P \times Q = \$4 \times 50$)	= $200
Total cost ($ATC \times Q = \$13 \times 50$)	= $650
Total variable cost ($AVC \times Q = \$5 \times 50$)	= $250
Total fixed cost ($TC - TVC = \$650 - \$250$)	= $400
Profits ($TR - TC = \$200 - \$650$)	= $-450

So, if the firm produces in the short run, it will take a loss of $450. If, however, it shuts down, its loss will be less, namely, its fixed costs, which amount to the difference between total cost and variable cost ($TFC + TVC = TC$, so $TC - TVC = TFC$). This difference is $400 ($650 – $250). Thus, between the two options of producing in the short run or shutting down, the firm will minimize its losses by shutting down ($Q = 0$). It will lose $400 by shutting down, whereas it will lose $450 by producing in the short run. Therefore, to minimize its loss, the firm should shut down.

In general, then, if price is below average variable cost, the perfectly competitive firm minimizes losses by choosing to shut down—that is, by not producing.

Case 3: Price Is Below Average Total Cost but Above Average Variable Cost
Exhibit 4(c) illustrates the case in which price is below average total cost but above average variable cost. The equilibrium price at which the perfectly competitive firm sells its good is $9. If the firm follows the profit maximization rule, it will produce 80 units of output. At this price and quantity of output, total revenue is less than total cost (hence, the firm will incur a loss), but total revenue is greater than total variable cost. The calculations are as follows:

Case 3	
Equilibrium price (P)	=$9
Quantity of output produced (Q)	=80 units
Total revenue ($P \times Q = \$9 \times 80$)	=$720
Total cost ($ATC \times Q = \$10 \times 80$)	=$800
Total variable cost ($AVC \times Q = \$5 \times 80$)	=$400
Total fixed cost ($TC - TVC = \$800 - \$400$)	=$400
Profits ($TR - TC = \$720 - \$800$)	=$-80

If the firm decides to produce in the short run, it will take a loss of $80. If it shuts down, it will lose its fixed costs, which, in this case, are $400 ($TC - TVC = \$800 - \$400$). Therefore, continuing to produce in the short run is better than shutting down. Losses are minimized by producing.

In general, then, if price is below average total cost but above average variable cost, the perfectly competitive firm minimizes its losses by continuing to produce in the short run instead of shutting down.

9-2d Common Misconceptions over the Shutdown Decision

Asked when a business firm should shut down (stop producing), the layperson is likely to say when the firm is no longer earning a profit. In economics, that is when price is lower than average total cost ($P < ATC$). But that could be the wrong way to go, as we have just shown. Even if price is below average total cost and a loss is being incurred, a firm should not necessarily shut down. The shutdown decision depends, in the short run, on whether the firm loses more by shutting down than by not shutting down. Even though price is below average total cost, it could still be above average variable cost, and if it is, the firm minimizes its losses (in the short run) by continuing to produce than by shutting down.

Summary of Cases 1–3 *A perfectly competitive firm produces in the short run as long as price is above average variable cost (cases 1 and 3):*

$$P > AVC \rightarrow \text{Firm produces}$$

A perfectly competitive firm shuts down in the short run if price is less than average variable cost (case 2):

$$P < AVC \rightarrow \text{Firm shuts down}$$

We can summarize the same information in terms of total revenue and total variable costs. *A perfectly competitive firm produces in the short run as long as total revenue is greater than total variable costs (cases 1 and 3):*

$$TR > TVC \rightarrow \text{Firm produces}$$

A perfectly competitive firm shuts down in the short run if total revenue is less than total variable costs (case 2):

$$TR < TVC \rightarrow \text{Firm shuts down}$$

Exhibit 5 reviews some of the material discussed in the previous section. Exhibit 6 reviews, in a question-and-answer format, some of the material discussed in the last few sections.

EXHIBIT 5

What Should a Perfectly Competitive Firm Do in the Short Run?

The firm should produce in the short run as long as price (P) is above average variable cost (AVC). It should shut down in the short run if price is below average variable cost.

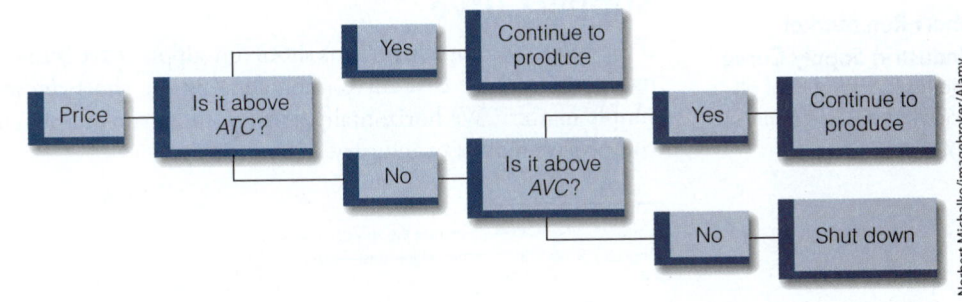

Norbert Michalke/imagebroker/Alamy

EXHIBIT 6

Q&A about Perfect Competition

Question	Answer
What four assumptions is the theory of perfect competition built on?	1. There are many buyers and many sellers. 2. Each firm produces and sells a homogeneous good. 3. Buyers and sellers have all relevant information about prices, product quality, sources of supply, and so forth. 4. Firms have easy entry into the market and easy exit out of the market.
What does it mean to say the perfectly competitive firm is a price taker?	The perfectly competitive firm *takes* the market-determined equilibrium price as the price at which it sells its product. The firm has no ability to control the price of the product it sells.
At what price does the perfectly competitive firm sell its product?	It sells at the price determined by the market. In other words, market demand and market supply determine the price of the good—say, $10—and then the firm takes this price as the price at which it will sell its product.
What quantity does the single perfectly competitive firm produce?	The quantity at which $MR = MC$.
How do we know if the perfectly competitive firm is earning profit or incurring a loss?	If $P > ATC$ for the firm, then it is earning profit. If $P < ATC$ for the firm, then it is incurring a loss.
What is resource allocative efficiency, and is the perfectly competitive firm resource allocative efficient?	Resource allocative efficiency exists if firms produce the quantity of output at which $P = MC$. The perfectly competitive firm is resource allocative efficient. Proof: (1) The firm produces the quantity of output at which $MR = MC$. (2) In perfect competition, $P = MR$. (3) Because $P = MR$ and the firm produces the quantity at which $MR = MC$, it follows that $P = MC$. Hence, the firm is resource allocative efficient.

9-2e The Perfectly Competitive Firm's Short-Run Supply Curve

Short-Run (Firm) Supply Curve

The portion of the firm's marginal cost curve that lies above the average variable cost curve.

The perfectly competitive firm produces (supplies output) in the short run if price is above average variable cost. It shuts down (does not supply output) if price is below average variable cost. Therefore, the **short-run (firm) supply curve** is the portion of the firm's marginal cost curve that lies above the average variable cost curve. Only a price above average variable cost will induce the firm to supply output. The short-run supply curve of the perfectly competitive firm is illustrated in Exhibit 7.

9-2f From Firm Supply Curve to Market (Industry) Supply Curve

Short-Run Market (Industry) Supply Curve

The horizontal sum of all existing firms' short-run supply curves.

If the perfectly competitive firm's short-run supply curve is the part of its marginal cost curve above its average variable cost curve, then deriving the **short-run market (industry) supply curve** is a simple matter:[3] We horizontally add the short-run supply curves for all firms in the perfectly competitive market or industry.

---

3. In discussing market structures, the words "industry" and "market" are often used interchangeably when a single-product industry is under consideration, which is the case here.

Consider, for simplicity, an industry made up of three firms: A, B, and C. [See Exhibit 8(a).] At a price P_1, firm A supplies 10 units, firm B supplies 8 units, and firm C supplies 18 units. One point on the market supply curve thus corresponds to P_1 on the price axis and 36 units $(10 + 8 + 18 = 36)$ on the quantity axis.[4] If we follow this procedure for all prices, we have the short-run market supply curve. This curve, shown in the market setting in part (b) of the exhibit, is used along with the market demand curve (derived in Chapter 3) to determine equilibrium price and quantity.

EXHIBIT 7

The Perfectly Competitive Firm's Short-Run Supply Curve

The short-run supply curve is that portion of the firm's marginal cost curve that lies above the average variable cost curve.

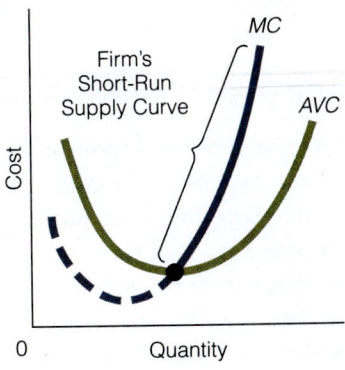

EXHIBIT 8

Deriving the Market (Industry) Supply Curve for a Perfectly Competitive Market

In (a), we add (horizontally) the quantity supplied by each firm to derive the market supply curve. The market supply curve and the market demand curve are shown in (b). Together, they determine equilibrium price and quantity.

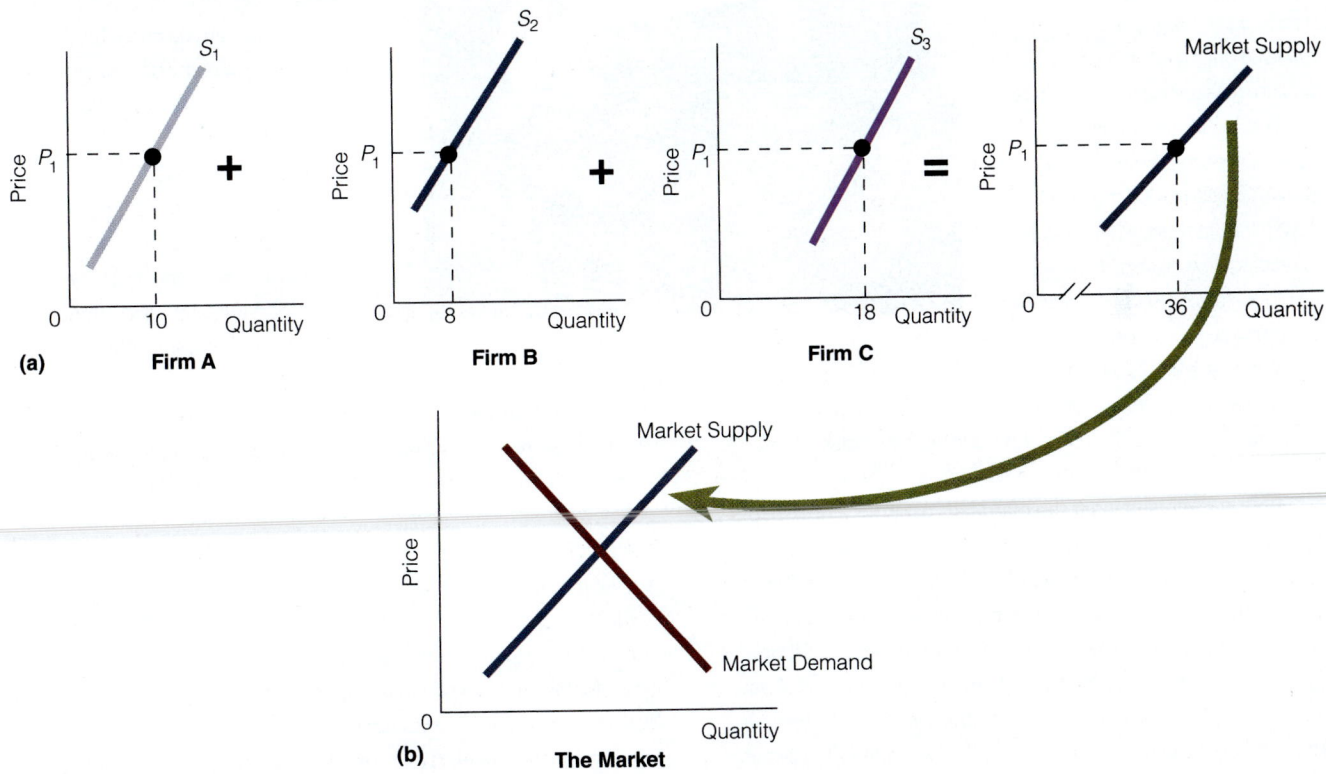

---

4. We add one qualification: Each firm's supply curve is drawn on the assumption that the prices of the variable inputs are constant.

ECONOMICS 24/7

The Digital Revolution, Price, and Marginal Cost

The digital revolution has had a big effect on the dollar price of many goods. In some cases, it has caused the dollar price to drop to zero. For example, consider newspapers, both print and online. Before the digital revolution, only printed newspapers existed. What did one have to give up to read a newspaper? First, there was the dollar price of the newspaper—say, $1—and whatever one could be doing, but wasn't, while one was reading the newspaper. Today, many newspapers are free (zero price) online. So what does a person today who reads the newspaper online (that she once read in its printed version) give up? No longer is there the $1 price, so one simply gives up whatever one could be doing, but isn't, while reading the online newspaper. In short, when it comes to reading newspapers, the digital revolution has caused the dollar price to drop to zero.

But why is that? Think back to our model of perfect competition. In that model, the price the customer paid for a good or service was equal to the marginal cost of producing the product ($P = MC$). So, if marginal cost was $4, then price was $4.

Now ask yourself what the marginal cost is for a newspaper company that wants an additional reader for its newspaper. Well, if it's a printed newspaper, there is the positive additional cost of producing an additional copy of the newspaper. But if it's an online newspaper, the marginal cost is zero. The newspaper has already been uploaded to the company website, and if, say, 10,000 people are reading the newspaper online, then there is really no additional cost incurred (by the newspaper publishing company) if one more person reads the newspaper online. In other words, the marginal cost here is zero and, in this case, the price (of the online newspaper) tends to gravitate toward zero.

Iain Masterton/age fotostock/Superstock

But, then, we notice that not all online newspapers come at zero price. Some online publications, such as *The Wall Street Journal* or *The Economist*, charge a fee if a reader chooses to read more than a small number of articles. For example, with some publications, two or three articles a week might be free, but if a person wants to read more, a subscription to the publication is required. Why do *The Wall Street Journal* and *The Economist* require readers (beyond a certain limit) to become subscribers while many other publications do not? It has to do with how many close or perfect substitutes there are for the publications.

Think of hundreds of local newspapers across the country. For the most part, they are close to identical (homogeneous): they often report the same sports stories, national news stories, weather across the country, and so on. What is different among local newspapers is, of course, the local news. In other words, only the local newspaper in Savannah, Georgia, has the local Savannah news and only the local newspaper in Topeka, Kansas, has the local Topeka news. But isn't the local news in each town newspaper enough to make local newspapers dissimilar ? Not so much if people can easily get the local news by searching on the Internet.

In the end, the reason that *The Wall Street Journal* and *The Economist* can charge for their online publications, and that it is so much harder for the local newspaper in Anytown, USA, to do so, is that *The Wall Street Journal* and *The Economist* are more nearly unique products. For example, some readers think that, when it comes to economic and financial news and analysis, there really are no close substitutes for *The Wall Street Journal*. And when it comes to economic and political reporting and analysis, there is no close substitute for *The Economist*.

9-2g Why Is the Market Supply Curve Upward Sloping?

When the demand and supply curves were introduced in Chapter 3, the supply curve was drawn upward sloping. To understand why, consider the following questions and answers:

- *Question 1:* Why do we draw market supply curves upward sloping?

- *Answer:* Because market supply curves are the horizontal sum of firms' supply curves and firms' supply curves are upward sloping.

- *Question 2:* But why are firms' supply curves upward sloping?

- *Answer:* Because the supply curve for each firm is the portion of its marginal cost (MC) curve that is *above* its average variable cost (AVC) curve—and this portion of the MC curve is upward sloping.

- *Question 3:* But why do MC curves have an upward-sloping portion?

- *Answer:* According to the law of diminishing marginal returns, the marginal physical product (MPP) of a variable input eventually declines. When that happens, the MC curve begins to rise.

  Conclusion: Because of the law of diminishing marginal returns, MC curves are upward sloping, and because MC curves are upward sloping, so are market supply curves.

FINDING ECONOMICS

In the Production of Air Conditioners Peter is willing to produce more air conditioners if the price of a unit is $800 than if it is $600. Where is the economics?

We can detect the law of supply in Peter's behavior—he produces more at a higher price than at a lower price—and we know that his supply curve is upward sloping. But is there more? As already explained, supply curves are upward sloping because a producer's supply curve is the portion of its MC curve above the AVC curve and that portion of the MC curve is upward sloping. Finally, at least a portion of an MC curve is upward sloping because of the law of diminishing marginal returns.

SELF-TEST

1. If a firm produces the quantity of output at which $MR = MC$, does it necessarily earn profits?

2. In the short run, if a firm finds that its price (P) is less than its average total cost (ATC), should it shut down its operation?

3. The layperson says that a firm maximizes profits when total revenue (TR) minus total cost (TC) is as large as possible and positive. The economist says that a firm maximizes profits when it produces the level of output at which $MR = MC$. Explain how the two ways of looking at profit maximization are consistent.

4. Why are market supply curves upward sloping?

9-3 PERFECT COMPETITION IN THE LONG RUN

The number of firms in a perfectly competitive market may not be the same in the short run as in the long run. For example, if the typical firm is making economic profits in the short run, new firms will be attracted to the industry and the number of firms will increase. If the typical firm is sustaining losses, some existing firms will exit the industry and the number of firms will decrease. The two processes are explained in greater detail later in this section. For now, we begin by outlining the conditions of long-run competitive equilibrium.

9-3a The Conditions of Long-Run Competitive Equilibrium

Long-Run Competitive Equilibrium
The condition in which $P = MC = SRATC = LRATC$. Economic profit is zero, firms are producing the quantity of output at which price is equal to marginal cost, and no firm has an incentive to change its plant size.

The following conditions characterize **long-run competitive equilibrium**:

1. *Economic profit is zero; that is, price (P) is equal to short-run average total cost (SRATC):*

$$P = SRATC$$

The logic of this condition is clear when we analyze what will happen if price is above or below short-run average total cost. If it is above, positive economic profits will attract firms to the industry in order to obtain the profits. If price is below, losses will result and some firms will want to exit the industry. Long-run competitive equilibrium cannot exist if firms have an incentive to enter or exit the industry in response to positive economic profits or losses. For long-run equilibrium to exist, there can be no incentive for firms to enter or exit. This condition is brought about by zero economic profit (normal profit), which is a consequence of the equilibrium price being equal to short-run average total cost.

2. *Firms are producing the quantity of output at which price (P) is equal to marginal cost (MC):*

$$P = MC$$

Perfectly competitive firms naturally move toward the output level at which marginal revenue (or price, because, for a perfectly competitive firm, $MR = P$) equals marginal cost.

3. *No firm has an incentive to change its plant size to produce its current output; that is, at the quantity of output at which P = MC, the following condition holds:*

$$SRATC = LRATC$$

To understand this condition, suppose $SRATC > LRATC$ at the quantity of output established in condition 2. Then the firm has an incentive to change its plant size in the long run because it wants to produce its product with the plant size that will give it the lowest average total cost (unit cost). It will have no incentive to change its plant size when it is producing the quantity of output at which price equals marginal cost and $SRATC$ equals $LRATC$.

The three conditions necessary for long-run competitive equilibrium can be stated as shown in Exhibit 9: long-run competitive equilibrium exists when $P = MC = SRATC = LRATC$.

In conclusion, long-run competitive equilibrium exists when firms have no incentive to make any changes—that is, when there is no incentive for firms to do any of the following:

1. enter or exit the industry.

2. produce more or less output.

3. change their plant size.

EXHIBIT 9

Long-Run Competitive Equilibrium

(a) Equilibrium in the market.
(b) Equilibrium for the firm. In (b), $P = MC$ (the firm has no incentive to move away from the quantity q_1 of output at which this equality occurs), $P = SRATC$ (there is no incentive for firms to enter or exit the industry), and $SRATC = LRATC$ (there is no incentive for the firm to change its plant size).

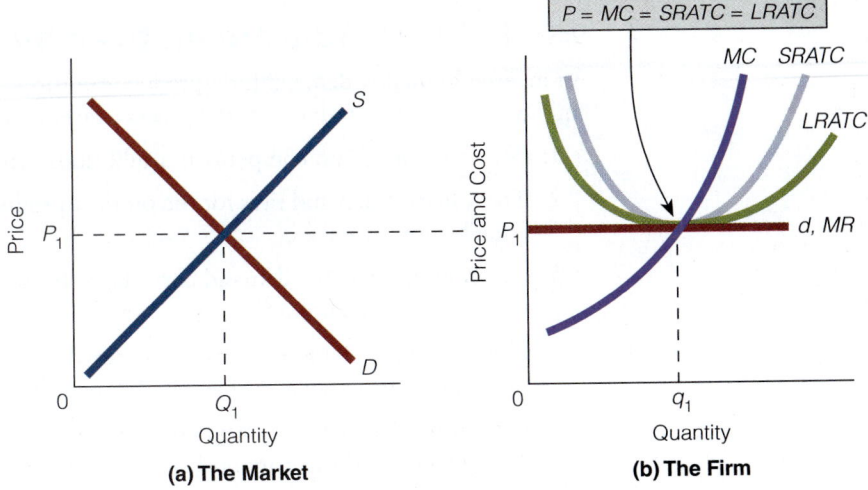

(a) The Market

(b) The Firm

THINKING LIKE AN ECONOMIST

Equilibrium Is Where Things Are Headed The concept of equilibrium is important in economics because equilibrium is where things are headed; in a way, it is the destination point. Suppose that firms in a perfectly competitive market are currently earning positive economic profit. At this point, say, 100 firms are in the market. But things are not likely to stay that way, and the number of firms is not likely to remain at 100. Firms are earning positive profits, so firms that are not currently in the market will join the market, pushing the number of participants upward from 100. Only when all firms are earning normal profit (zero economic profit) will the number of firms remain where it is. Only then will the market be in equilibrium.[5]

When you get on a plane in, say, Los Angeles that is headed for New York City, you are fairly sure that the trip is not over until you reach New York City. However, knowing when the trip is over in economics is not as easily determined. Theoretically, we know that the trip is over when equilibrium has been reached. But what conditions indicate that equilibrium has been reached?

9-3b The Perfectly Competitive Firm and Productive Efficiency

A firm that produces its output at the lowest possible per-unit cost (lowest ATC) is said to exhibit **productive efficiency**. The perfectly competitive firm is productively efficient in long-run equilibrium, as shown in Exhibit 9. Productive efficiency is desirable from society's standpoint because perfectly competitive firms are economizing on society's scarce resources and therefore not wasting them.

To illustrate, suppose the lowest unit cost at which good X can be produced is $3, the minimum ATC. If a firm produces 1,000 units of good X at this unit cost, then its total cost is $3,000. Now suppose the firm produces good X not at its lowest unit cost of $3, but at a slightly higher unit cost of $3.50. Then total cost now equals $3,500, and resources worth $500 were employed producing good X that could have been used to produce other goods had the firm exhibited

Productive Efficiency
The situation in which a firm produces its output at the lowest possible per-unit cost (lowest ATC).

[5.] We are assuming that our other long-run equilibrium conditions hold, such as that no firms want to change their plant size and that there is no incentive for any firm to produce any more or any less output.

productive efficiency. In other words, society could have been richer in goods and services, but because of the firm's decision to produce at $3.50, it isn't.

9-3c   Industry Adjustment to an Increase in Demand

An increase in market demand for a product can throw an industry out of long-run competitive equilibrium. Exhibit 10 describes the process, numbered in the exhibit as follows:

1. We start at long-run competitive equilibrium, where $P = MC = SRATC = LRATC$.

2. Then, market demand rises for the product produced by the firms in the industry, and the equilibrium price rises.

3. As a consequence, the demand curve faced by an individual firm (the firm's marginal revenue curve) shifts upward.

4. Next, *existing firms* in the industry increase the quantity of output because marginal revenue now intersects marginal cost at a higher quantity of output.

5. In the long run, new firms begin to enter the industry because price is currently above average total cost and there are positive economic profits.

6. As new firms enter the industry, the market (industry) supply curve shifts rightward.

7–8. As a consequence, equilibrium price falls until long-run competitive equilibrium is reestablished—that is, until economic profit is zero once again.

Now look at the process again, from the initial increase in market demand to the reestablishment of long-run competitive equilibrium: price increased in the short run (owing to the increase in demand) and then decreased in the long run (owing to the increase in supply). Also, profits increased (owing to the increase in demand and consequent increase in price) and then decreased (owing to the increase in supply and consequent decrease in price). They went from zero to some positive amount and then back to zero.

The *up-and-down* movements in both price and profits in response to an increase in demand are important. Too often, people see only the primary upward movements in both price and profits and they ignore or forget the secondary downward movements. However, the secondary effects in price and profits are as important as the primary effects.

The adjustment to an increase in demand brings up an important question: if price first rises owing to an increase in market demand and later falls owing to an increase in market supply, will the new equilibrium price be greater than, less than, or equal to the *original* equilibrium price? (In Exhibit 10, the new equilibrium price is shown as equal to the original equilibrium price, but this need not be the case.)

For example, if the equilibrium price is $10 before the increase in market demand, will the new equilibrium price (after market and firm adjustments) be greater than, less than, or equal to $10? The answer depends on whether cost is remaining constant, increasing, or decreasing in the industry.

Constant-Cost Industry In a constant-cost industry, average total costs (unit costs) do not change as output increases or decreases when firms enter or exit the industry. If market demand increases for a good produced by firms in a constant-cost industry, price will initially rise and then will finally fall to its original level, as shown in Exhibit 11(a). Point 1 represents long-run competitive equilibrium, at which economic profits are zero. Then demand increases, and price rises from P_1 to P_2. At P_2, there are positive economic profits, which cause the firms currently in the industry to increase output, so we move up the supply curve, S_1, from point 1 to point 2. Next, new firms, drawn by the profits, enter the industry, causing the supply curve to shift rightward (S_2).

EXHIBIT 10

The Process of Moving from One Long-Run Competitive Equilibrium Position to Another

This exhibit describes what happens on both the market level and the firm level when demand rises and throws an industry out of long-run competitive equilibrium.

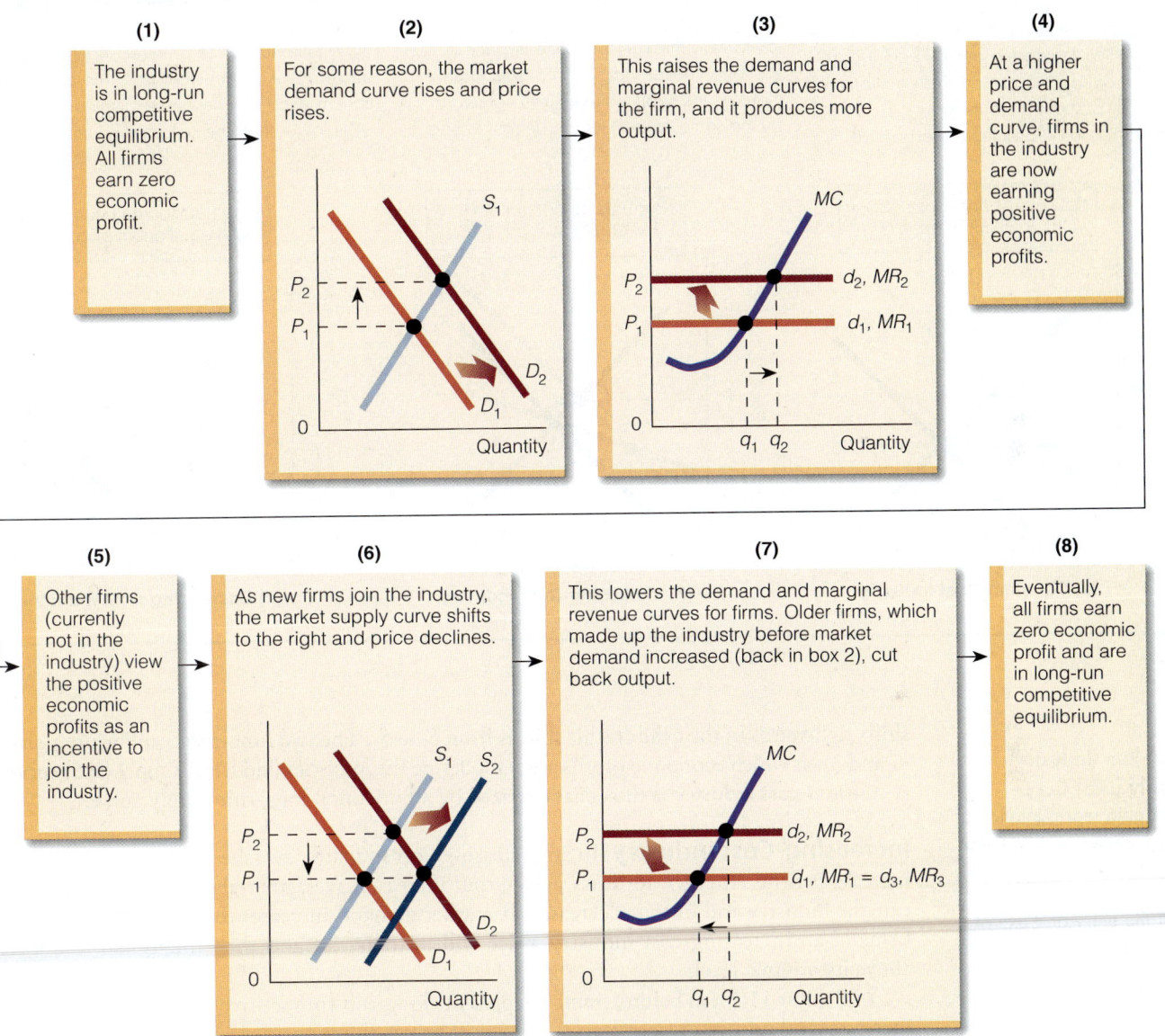

(1) The industry is in long-run competitive equilibrium. All firms earn zero economic profit.

(2) For some reason, the market demand curve rises and price rises.

(3) This raises the demand and marginal revenue curves for the firm, and it produces more output.

(4) At a higher price and demand curve, firms in the industry are now earning positive economic profits.

(5) Other firms (currently not in the industry) view the positive economic profits as an incentive to join the industry.

(6) As new firms join the industry, the market supply curve shifts to the right and price declines.

(7) This lowers the demand and marginal revenue curves for firms. Older firms, which made up the industry before market demand increased (back in box 2), cut back output.

(8) Eventually, all firms earn zero economic profit and are in long-run competitive equilibrium.

For a constant-cost industry, output is increased without a change in the price of inputs. Because of this situation, the firms' cost curves do not shift. But if costs do not rise to reduce the profits in the industry, then price must fall. (Profits can be reduced in two ways: through a rise in costs or a fall in price.) Price must fall to its original level P_1 before profits can be zero, implying that the supply curve shifts rightward by the same amount that the demand curve

EXHIBIT 11

Long-Run Industry Supply Curves

LRS = Long-run industry supply. Each part illustrates the same scenario but with different results, depending on whether the industry has (a) constant costs, (b) increasing costs, or (c) decreasing costs. In each part, we start at long-run competitive equilibrium (point 1). Demand then increases, price rises from P_1 to P_2, and there are positive

economic profits. Consequently, existing firms increase output and new firms are attracted to the industry. In (a), input costs remain constant as output increases, so the firms' cost curves do not shift. Profits fall to zero through a decline in price. This scenario implies that, in a constant-cost industry, the supply curve shifts rightward by the same amount as the demand curve

shifts rightward. In (b), input costs increase as output increases. Profits are squeezed by a combination of rising costs and falling prices. The new equilibrium price P_3 for an increasing-cost industry is higher than the old equilibrium price P_1. In (c), input costs decrease as output increases. The new equilibrium price P_3 for a decreasing-cost industry is lower than the old equilibrium price P_1.

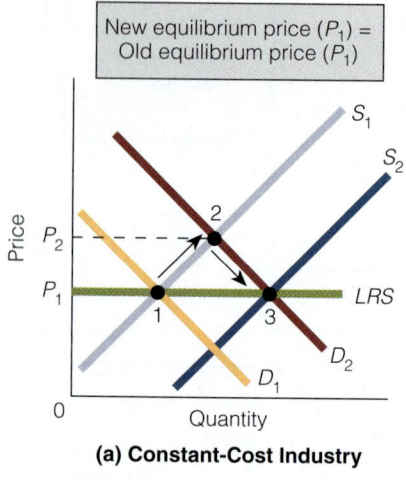

(a) Constant-Cost Industry

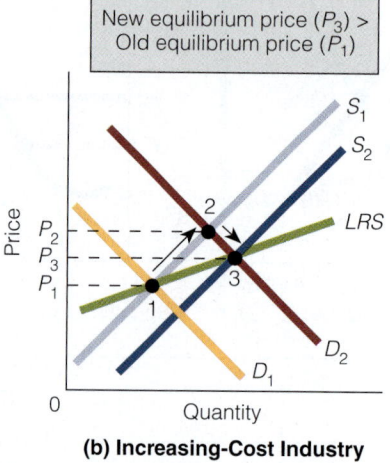

(b) Increasing-Cost Industry

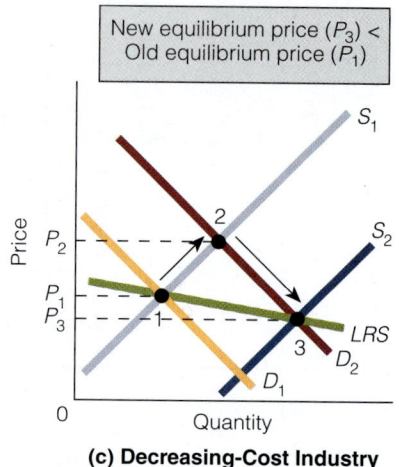

(c) Decreasing-Cost Industry

Long-Run (Industry) Supply (*LRS*) Curve

A graphic representation of the quantities of output that an industry is prepared to supply at different prices after the entry and exit of firms are completed.

Constant-Cost Industry

An industry in which average total costs do not change as (industry) output increases or decreases when firms enter or exit the industry, respectively.

shifts rightward. In the exhibit, this shift is from S_1 to S_2. The two long-run equilibrium points (1 and 3), at which economic profits are zero, define the **long-run (industry) supply (*LRS*) curve**. A **constant-cost industry** is thus characterized by a horizontal long-run supply curve.

Increasing-Cost Industry In an increasing-cost industry, average total costs (unit costs) increase as firms enter the industry and output increases; average total costs decrease as firms exit the industry and output decreases. If market demand increases for a good produced by firms in an increasing-cost industry, price will initially rise and then finally fall to a level above its original level.

In Exhibit 11(b), as before, point 1 represents long-run competitive equilibrium. Demand increases, and price rises from P_1 to P_2. This shift brings about positive economic profits, which cause firms in the industry to increase output and new firms to enter the industry. So far, the process is the same as that for a constant-cost industry. However, in an increasing-cost industry, as firms purchase more inputs to produce more output, some input prices rise and cost curves shift. In short, as industry output increases, profits are caught in a two-way squeeze: price is coming down, and costs are rising. If costs are rising as price is falling, then price will not have to fall to its original level before zero economic profits rule once again. Thus, in an increasing-cost industry, price will not have to fall as far to restore long-run competitive equilibrium as it will in a constant-cost industry. We would expect, then, that, when an increasing-cost industry experiences an increase in demand, the new equilibrium price will be higher than the old equilibrium price. Accordingly, the supply curve shifts rightward by less than the demand curve shifts rightward. An **increasing-cost industry** is characterized by an upward-sloping long-run supply curve.

Decreasing-Cost Industry

In a decreasing-cost industry, average total costs (unit costs) decrease as firms enter the industry and output increases; average total costs increase as firms exit the industry and output decreases. If market demand increases for a good produced by firms in a decreasing-cost industry, then price will initially rise and then finally fall to a level below its original level. In Exhibit 11(c), price moves from P_1 to P_2 and then to P_3. In such an industry, average total costs decrease as new firms enter the industry, so price must fall below its original level to eliminate profits. A **decreasing-cost industry** is characterized by a downward-sloping long-run supply curve.

> **Increasing-Cost Industry**
> An industry in which average total costs increase as output increases and decrease as output decreases when firms enter and exit the industry, respectively.

> **Decreasing-Cost Industry**
> An industry in which average total costs decrease as output increases and increase as output decreases when firms enter and exit the industry, respectively.

THINKING LIKE AN ECONOMIST

Common Misconceptions about Profits The layperson often views profits in much the same way as the English teacher views a period. Profits come at the end of a production process, and a period comes at the end of a sentence. In reality, profit is more like a comma, in that something comes after it. Profit is more like an ongoing process, as just explained: demand rises, causing price to rise, causing profits to rise. But things don't stop there: The higher profits encourage new firms to enter the market, causing the supply curve in the market to shift rightward, in turn causing price and profits to fall.

Think of how not knowing about the up-and-down movements in price and profits can lead to some unintended effects. The demand for a good rises, and with it both price and profits rise. Big profits are reported in the news, and politicians start talking about taxing those so-called high profits. However, might taxing those high profits stop the price–profits story from continuing? Without the profits, new firms don't enter the market. Without the new firms, supply doesn't increase. In other words, taxing the profits might have the unintended effect of reducing the supply of goods from what it would be if the profits weren't taxed.

9-3d Profit from Two Perspectives

From one perspective, profit serves as an *incentive* for individuals to produce. From another perspective, it serves as a *signal*.

Profit serves as an incentive by prompting or encouraging certain behavior. John produces furniture to sell because he hopes to earn a profit; Jackie opens up a hair salon because she hopes to earn a profit.

As a signal, profit acts a little like a neon sign, identifying where resources are most welcome. To illustrate, suppose company A produces good A' and company B produces good B'. Suppose also that, currently, company A is earning profits producing good A' and company B is incurring a loss producing good B'. To those viewing the profits and losses from the outside, it is as if the profits are signaling, "If you are thinking of producing either good A' or good B', choose A'. That is where the profit can be found." Stated differently, it is as if profit tells others where resources are best allocated: Allocate them toward producing good A'.

FINDING ECONOMICS

In the Computer Industry and Elsewhere   Years ago, the prices of a personal computer, calculator, DVD recorder, and LCD television set were higher than they are today. Where is the economics? Do higher prices have anything to do with what we have just discussed—prices and profits?

The early introduction of these goods often came with (what in hindsight appears to be) high prices and high profits. The high profits called forth new firms into the market. The new firms ended up increasing supply and reducing prices and profits. (Other changes were occurring at the same time, such as changes in technology.)

THINKING LIKE AN ECONOMIST

Easy Entry into a Market Matters   Once again, demand rises, price rises, and profits go from zero to positive. Yet, as explained, the increase in profits is not the end of the story, as long as new firms can enter the market. But suppose they can't. If something prevents firms from entering the market, the end of the story will not be the same, with price moving down and profit returning to zero. The different ending points out how important easy entry into the market is to the story. Without easy entry, the story is a different one altogether: Prices are more likely to stay high, and profits are more likely to stay positive.

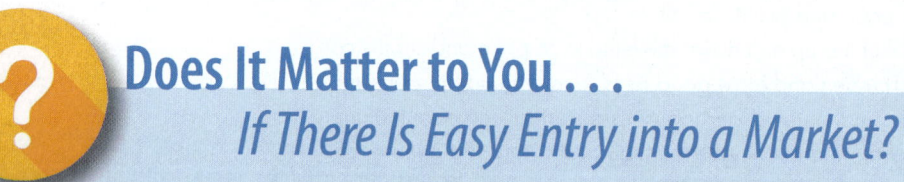

? Does It Matter to You . . .
If There Is Easy Entry into a Market?

The theory of perfect competition is built upon four assumptions, one of which is that it is easy to enter into the market. In other words, firms not currently in the market can easily gain entry into it.

Think of what easy entry means in terms of profit, output, and prices. Consider a perfectly competitive market that is in long-run (competitive) equilibrium. In long-run equilibrium, firms in the market are earning normal profit or zero economic profit. Now suppose that the demand for the good sold by these firms increases. What are buyers "saying" by increasing demand? They are saying that they are willing and able to buy more units of the good at each and every price—whereas previously they might have been willing and able to buy 20 units of the good at $1, they are now willing and able to buy 30 units at $1.

Are suppliers likely to give buyers more of what they want? In a perfectly competitive market, as market demand rises, so does market price. And as market price rises, the firm's demand curve rises too. This is visible in panels (2) and (3) of Exhibit 10. Current firms in the market end up producing more of the good that their buyers want to buy.

Not only do current firms start producing more, but new firms begin to enter the market to add to the supply of the good as well. This is because, as market price rises, firms in the perfectly competitive market no longer simply earn normal or zero economic profit but begin to earn positive economic profits, and it is the positive economic profits that the new firms entering the market are after.

Is easy entry into the market beneficial to you as a buyer? Or would you be better off if there was some kind of major obstacle preventing firms from entering the market? For you, as a buyer, it is much better if firms can easily enter the market because it increases the supply and lowers the price of the good you buy.

Returning to the original question: Does it matter to you if there is easy entry into a market? Without it, the buyers' call for more of a good, which is expressed through an increasing demand for the good, is likely not to be answered.

9-3e Industry Adjustment to a Decrease in Demand

Demand can decrease as well as increase. Suppose that, starting at long-run competitive equilibrium, market demand decreases. As a consequence, in the short run the equilibrium price falls, effectively shifting the firm's demand curve (marginal revenue curve) downward. Some firms in the industry then decrease production because marginal revenue intersects marginal cost at a lower level of output, and other firms shut down.

In the long run, some firms will leave the industry because price is below average total cost and they are suffering ongoing losses. As firms leave the industry, the market supply curve shifts leftward. As a consequence, the equilibrium price rises and continues to rise until long-run competitive equilibrium is reestablished—that is, until there are, once again, zero economic profits (instead of negative economic profits). Whether the new equilibrium price is greater than, less than, or equal to the original equilibrium price depends on whether cost is decreasing, increasing, or remaining constant, respectively, in the industry.

9-3f Differences in Costs, Differences in Profits: Now You See It, Now You Don't

Two farmers, Hancock and Cordero, produce wheat. Farmer Cordero grows his wheat on fertile land; farmer Hancock grows her wheat in poor soil. Both farmers sell their wheat for the same price, but because of the difference in the quality of their land, Cordero has lower average total costs than Hancock, as shown in Exhibit 12. Given the initial situations of the two farmers ATC_1, we notice that Cordero is earning profits and Hancock is not. Cordero is earning profits because he pays lower average total costs than Hancock as a consequence of farming higher quality land.

But Cordero is not likely to continue earning profits. Individuals will bid up the price of the fertile land that Cordero farms vis-à-vis the poor-quality land that Hancock farms. In other words, if Cordero is renting his farmland, the rent he pays will increase to reflect the superior quality of the land. The rent will increase by an amount equal to the profits earned per period—that is, an amount equal to the shaded portion in Exhibit 12(b). If Cordero owns the land, the superior quality of the land will have a higher implicit cost.

EXHIBIT 12

Differences in Costs, Differences in Profits: Now You See It, Then It's Gone

At ATC_1 for both farmers, Cordero earns profits and Hancock does not. Cordero earns profits because the land he farms is of higher quality (is more productive) than Hancock's land. Eventually, this fact is taken into account, by Cordero either paying higher rent for the land or incurring implicit costs for it. Either way, Cordero's ATC curve moves upward to the same level as Hancock's and Cordero earns zero economic profits. The profits have gone as payment (implicit or explicit) for the higher-quality, more productive land.

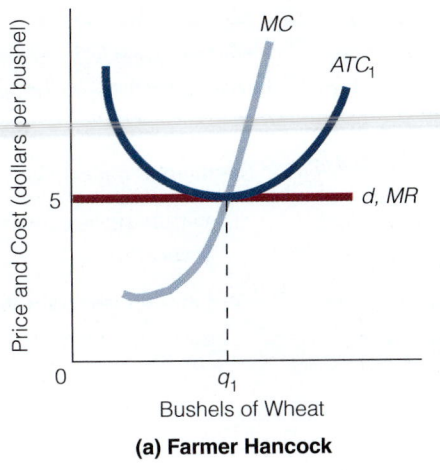

(a) Farmer Hancock

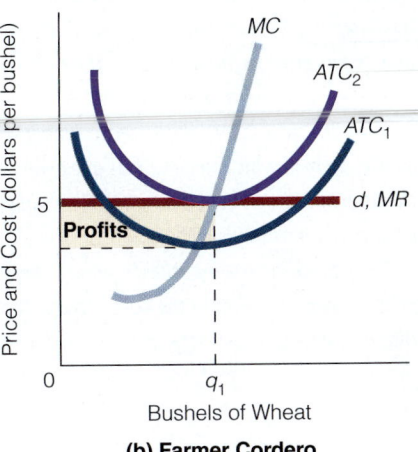

(b) Farmer Cordero

In Exhibit 12(b), ATC_2 reflects either the higher rent Cordero must pay for the superior land or the full implicit cost he incurs by farming the land he owns. In either case, when the average total cost curve reflects all costs, Cordero will be in the same situation as Hancock: he, too, will be earning zero economic profits.

The profit has gone as payment for the higher quality, more productive resource responsible for the lower average total costs in the first place. Consequently, average total costs are no longer relatively lower for the person or firm that employs the higher quality, more productive resource or input.

Hear What and How the Economist Thinks . . .
About Buyers and Sellers

The economist over hears the following conversation:

Person 1: When it comes to understanding markets, it is important to remember that, just as there are two teams in football that work against each other, there are two teams in markets. There are the sellers and the buyers. And what usually happens is that the sellers are working against the buyers.

Person 2: I agree with you. I would only add that when the sellers gain, the buyers lose; and when the buyers gain, the sellers lose.

Hear what and how the economist thinks:

I don't think the football analogy works in the case of sellers and buyers. It's not really the case that the sellers are on one team and the buyers are on the other, and they each have opposing goals. To understand this, consider what we've been looking at in this chapter. In a perfectly competitive market if price rises, profits rise, and new sellers enter the market. Now, the existing sellers will certainly be unhappy about the entry of new sellers into the market. This is because the new sellers will increase supply, and lower price. Here is a case, then, in which the interests of existing sellers are opposed to the interests of new sellers entering the market. In short, some sellers are against other sellers.

But do we have some sellers against buyers too? We do. The existing sellers are against the buyers in that the buyers would prefer that the new sellers enter the market and drive price down. But it is

the lower price that benefits buyers. So here we have existing sellers against buyers.

While the best interest of some sellers (existing sellers) is at odds with buyers, it is also the case that some sellers (new sellers) have their interests aligned with buyers. The new sellers want to enter the market in order to earn some of the profit that exists in it. It just so happens that entering the market also benefits buyers because the new sellers entering the market increases the supply of the good being produced and sold, thus lowering its price to buyers. In this instance, we have the interests of new sellers aligned with the interests of buyers.

Is a market like a football game with two opposing teams each pulling in the opposite direction and at odds with each other? Not really. Here we have shown that we can have sellers against sellers (existing sellers against new sellers entering the market), some sellers against buyers (existing sellers do not want the new sellers to enter the market and lower prices for buyers), and some sellers aligned with buyers (new sellers entering the market benefits these sellers and the buyers). In short, it is not always us (sellers) against them (buyers) in a market.

Questions to Think About:

1. Are the best interests of buyers always aligned with other buyers? Explain your answer.

2. Are the best interests of workers always aligned with that of other workers? Explain your answer.

ECONOMICS 24/7

How Is High-Quality Land Like a Genius Software Engineer?

In the example of two farmers who produce wheat, Cordero was earning profits and Hancock was not, because Cordero farmed higher-quality land. In time, though, Cordero's higher profits ended up going into higher rent for the higher-quality land. The profit therefore went as payment for the higher quality, more productive resource responsible for the lower average total costs in the first place.

In the field of designing and developing computer software applications, suppose there are two companies, A and B. Software engineers work at both companies, but one of company A's software engineers is considered a genius within the software industry. Currently, the genius earns the same salary as other software engineers in the software industry.

Because the genius works for company A, company A comes up with better software applications than other companies. As a result, company A not only sells more software applications, but also can charge higher prices for the software it sells. Thus, largely as a result of having hired the genius software engineer, company A currently earns higher profits than company B does.

If company A's higher profits are attributable to the genius software engineer, then other software companies will soon compete to hire him. He will find his salary being bid up. To keep the software genius, company A will have to turn over some of

lee khoai lang/Shutterstock.com

its profits to him in the form of salary. Profits on Wednesday turn into the genius's salary on Thursday.

High-quality land is like a genius software engineer in that both are the source of profits and eventually those profits get transformed into something else. In the farming example, high profits get turned into higher rent for the higher-quality land. In the software engineer example, high profits (for company A) get turned into a higher salary for our genius software engineer. Stated differently, the higher-quality land in our first example "is" the genius software engineer in the second.

9-3g Profit and Discrimination

A firm's discriminatory behavior can affect its profits in the context of the model of perfect competition. Suppose that, under the conditions of long-run competitive equilibrium, at which firms are earning zero economic profits, the owner of a firm chooses not to hire an excellent (i.e., above average) worker simply because of that worker's race, religion, or gender. What happens to the owner of the firm who discriminates in any way? If he chooses not to employ high-quality employees because of their race, religion, or gender, then his costs will rise above those of competitors who hire the best employees irrespective of race, religion, or gender. Because he is initially earning zero profit ($TR = TC$), the act of discrimination will raise TC and push the firm into taking economic losses. If the owner in the example is a manager, he may lose his job because the firm's owners may decide to replace managers earning subnormal profits. Thus, profit maximization by shareholders works to reduce discrimination.

Our conclusion is that, if a firm is in a perfectly competitive market structure, it will pay penalties if it chooses to discriminate. Discrimination will not necessarily disappear, but it comes with a price tag. And according to economic theory, the more something costs, the less of it there will be, *ceteris paribus*.

SELF-TEST

1. If firms in a perfectly competitive market are earning positive economic profits, what will happen?

2. If firms in a perfectly competitive market want to produce more output, is the market in long-run equilibrium?

3. If a perfectly competitive market in long-run equilibrium witnesses an increase in demand, what will happen to price?

4. Two firms produce computer software. Firm A employs a software genius at the same salary that firm B employs a mediocre software engineer. Will the firm that employs the software genius earn higher profits than the other firm, *ceteris paribus*?

9-4 TOPICS FOR ANALYSIS IN THE THEORY OF PERFECT COMPETITION

This section briefly analyzes three topics in the theory of perfect competition: higher costs and higher prices, advertising, and setting prices.

9-4a Do Higher Costs Mean Higher Prices?

Suppose that 600 firms are in an industry and that each firm sells the same product at the same price. Then one of these firms experiences a rise in its marginal costs of production. Someone immediately comments, "Higher costs for the firm today, higher prices for the consumer tomorrow," the assumption being that firms experiencing a rise in costs simply pass the higher costs on to consumers in the form of higher prices.

Passing along costs, however, cannot occur in a perfectly competitive market. In that kind of market, each firm in the industry is a price taker; furthermore, only one firm has experienced a rise in marginal costs. Because this firm supplies only a tiny percentage of the total market supply, the market supply curve is unlikely to undergo more than a negligible change. And if the market supply curve does not change, neither will the equilibrium price. In short, a rise in costs incurred by one of many firms does not mean that consumers will pay higher prices. Of course, if many of the firms in the industry experience a rise in costs, the market supply curve will be affected, along with price.

9-4b Will the Perfectly Competitive Firm Advertise?

Individual farmers don't advertise. You've never seen an advertisement for, say, farmer Johnson's milk, for a couple of reasons. First, farmer Johnson sells a homogeneous product, so advertising his milk is the same as advertising every dairy farmer's milk. Second, farmer Johnson is in a perfectly competitive market, so he can sell all the milk he wants at the going price. Why should he advertise? From his viewpoint, advertising has all cost and no benefits.

However, a perfectly competitive industry might advertise. For example, if farmer Johnson won't advertise his milk, the milk industry might advertise milk in general in the hope of shifting the market demand curve for milk to the right. Such a shift is actually what the milk industry hopes to bring about with its commercial message "Got milk?"

9-4c Supplier-Set Price Versus Market-Determined Price: Collusion or Competition?

Suppose the only thing you know about an industry is that all the firms in it sell their products at the same price. To explain this unanimity, some people argue that the firms are colluding—that is, they come together, pick a price, and stick to it. Collusion, of course, is one way for all firms to arrive at the same price for their products, but it is not the only way. Another way, as described in this chapter, is that all firms are price takers; that is, the firms are in a perfectly competitive market structure. In that case, there is no collusion.

THINKING LIKE AN ECONOMIST

A Reasonable-Sounding Argument Is Not Enough   Sometimes, two or more explanations may seem equally reasonable. For example, if all firms in an industry sell their products for the same price, two explanations seem equally plausible: (1) the firms collude on price and (2) the firms are price takers. But for the economist, a reasonable explanation is not sufficient; she wants the correct explanation. The economist is skeptical of any explanation that simply sounds reasonable. She needs evidence (often in the form of data) to support the explanation.

SELF-TEST

1. In a perfectly competitive market, do higher costs mean higher prices?

2. If you see a product advertised on television, does it follow that the product cannot be produced in a perfectly competitive market?

OFFICE HOURS

"Do You Have to Know the $MR = MC$ Condition in Order to Be Successful in Business?"

STUDENT: Something seems odd to me. Some people are successful in business without knowing any of the material in this chapter. Isn't it possible for a person to be successful in business without knowing the $MR = MC$ condition or the shutdown decision (shut down when P is less than AVC), and so on?

INSTRUCTOR: Yes, but keep in mind that someone doesn't have to know the $MR = MC$ condition to try to put it into operation. Most people don't know the physics behind the operation of a car, but they drive a car as if they do know the physics.

STUDENT: Are you saying that we can know and not know something at the same time? That sounds odd to me.

INSTRUCTOR: That's not exactly what I am saying. You can do something you don't know you're doing. Let me give you an example. Suppose Jack owns and operates his own business producing shoe boxes. He has never taken an economics course in his life, and he doesn't know the first thing about marginal revenue, marginal cost, average total cost, and so on. Not knowing these things doesn't mean that he doesn't have to figure out how many shoe boxes to produce. So how does he do it without a knowledge of marginal revenue and marginal cost? All Jack has to know is that it is a good idea to keep producing shoe boxes when more money is coming in the front door (in additional revenue) than is going out the back door (in additional costs). That's it. That basic, very elemental idea is behind the $MR = MC$ condition.

STUDENT: Does the same hold for things like knowing when to continue producing a good and knowing when to shut down?

INSTRUCTOR: Yes. The economist advises a business owner to shut down when $P < AVC$, but this is just a slightly more sophisticated way of expressing the idea that a firm should shut down when it would lose more from not shutting down. Consider Yvonne, who, like Jack, owns her own business. She is currently wondering whether she should stop producing a good. She may not know the first thing about the relationship between price and average variable cost, but certainly she can put some numbers down on paper and figure out how much money she loses if she shuts down and how much money she loses if she doesn't shut down.

STUDENT: I think I see what you are getting at. The economist seems only to be formalizing what people do if they are trying to maximize their profits or minimize their losses. The average Joe or Jane in business simply continues producing additional units of a good as long as more money comes into the firm by selling the additional unit than is going out by producing it. Then the economist simply says, "Produce as long as MR is greater than MC." Am I right?

INSTRUCTOR: Yes, you're right.

STUDENT: Looking at things that way makes the material in this chapter seem a little easier and a little more grounded in reality.

INSTRUCTOR: That's good to hear.

Points to Remember

1. Not knowing the $MR = MC$ condition doesn't mean that a real-world businessperson doesn't abide by it.

2. Many of the rules or conditions in this chapter (e.g., produce until $MR = MC$, shut down when $P < AVC$) are simply formalized ways of expressing what individuals in business settings do when they seek to maximize profits or minimize losses.

CHAPTER SUMMARY

THE THEORY OF PERFECT COMPETITION

- The theory of perfect competition is built on four assumptions: (1) There are many sellers and many buyers, none of whom is large in relation to total sales or purchases. (2) Each firm produces and sells a homogeneous product. (3) Buyers and sellers have all relevant information with respect to prices, product quality, sources of supply, and so on. (4) Entry into, and exit from, the industry is easy.

- The theory of perfect competition predicts the following: (1) Economic profits will be squeezed out of the industry in the long run by the entry of new firms; that is, zero economic profit exists in the long run. (2) In equilibrium, firms produce the quantity of output at which price equals marginal cost. (3) In the short run, firms will stay in business as long as price covers average variable costs. (4) In the long run, firms will stay in business as long as price covers average total costs. (5) In the short run, an increase in demand will lead to a rise in price; whether the price in the long run will be higher than, lower than, or equal to the original price depends on whether the firm is in an increasing-, decreasing-, or constant-cost industry.

THE PERFECTLY COMPETITIVE FIRM

- The perfectly competitive firm is a price taker. It sells its product only at the market-established equilibrium price.
- The perfectly competitive firm faces a horizontal (flat, perfectly elastic) demand curve. Its demand curve and its marginal revenue curve are the same.
- The perfectly competitive firm (as well as all other firms) maximizes profits (or minimizes losses) by producing the quantity of output at which $MR = MC$.
- For the perfectly competitive firm, price equals marginal revenue.
- The perfectly competitive firm is resource allocative efficient because it produces the quantity of output at which $P = MC$.

PRODUCTION IN THE SHORT RUN

- If $P > ATC (> AVC)$, the firm earns economic profits and will continue to operate in the short run.
- If $P < AVC (< ATC)$, the firm takes losses. It will shut down because the alternative (continuing to produce) increases the losses.
- If $ATC > P > AVC$, the firm takes losses. Nevertheless, it will continue to operate in the short run because the alternative (shutting down) increases the losses.
- The firm produces in the short run only when price is greater than average variable cost. Therefore, the portion of its marginal cost curve that lies above the average variable cost curve is the firm's short-run supply curve.

CONDITIONS OF LONG-RUN COMPETITIVE EQUILIBRIUM

- Long-run competitive equilibrium exists when there is no incentive for firms (1) to enter or exit the industry, (2) to produce more or less output, and (3) to change their plant size. We formalize these conditions as follows: (1) Economic profits are zero. Firms have no incentive to enter or exit the industry. (2) Firms are producing the quantity of output at which price is equal to marginal cost. (Firms have no incentive to produce more or less output. After all, when $P = MC$, it follows that $MR = MC$ for the perfectly competitive firm, and thus the firm is maximizing profits.) (3) $SRATC = LRATC$ at the quantity of output at which $P = MC$. (Firms do not have an incentive to change their plant size.)
- A perfectly competitive firm exhibits productive efficiency because, in the long run, it produces its output at the lowest possible per-unit cost (lowest ATC).

INDUSTRY ADJUSTMENT TO A CHANGE IN DEMAND

- In a constant-cost industry, an increase in demand will result in a new equilibrium price equal to the original equilibrium price (before demand increased). In an increasing-cost industry, an increase in demand will result in a new equilibrium price higher than the original one. In a decreasing-cost industry, an increase in demand will result in a new equilibrium price lower than the original one.
- The long-run supply curve for a constant-cost industry is horizontal (flat, perfectly elastic). The long-run supply curve for an increasing-cost industry is upward sloping. The long-run supply curve for a decreasing-cost industry is downward sloping.

KEY TERMS AND CONCEPTS

Market Structure
Perfect Competition
Price Taker
Marginal Revenue (*MR*)
Profit Maximization Rule

Resource Allocative Efficiency
Short-Run (Firm) Supply Curve
Short-Run Market (Industry) Supply Curve

Long-Run Competitive Equilibrium
Productive Efficiency
Long-Run (Industry) Supply (*LRS*) Curve

Constant-Cost Industry
Increasing-Cost Industry
Decreasing-Cost Industry

QUESTIONS AND PROBLEMS

1. "The firm's entire marginal cost curve is its short-run supply curve." Is the preceding statement true or false? Explain your answer.

2. In a perfectly competitive market, firms always operate at the lowest per-unit cost." Is the preceding statement true or false? Explain your answer.

3. "Firm A, one firm in a competitive industry, faces higher costs of production. As a result, consumers end up paying higher prices." Discuss.

4. Suppose all firms in a perfectly competitive market structure are in long-run equilibrium. Then demand for the firms' product increases. Initially, price and economic profits rise. Soon afterward, the government decides to tax most (but not all) of the economic profits, arguing that the firms in the industry did not earn the profits. Rather, the profits were simply the result of an increase in demand. What effect, if any, will the tax have on market adjustment?

5. Explain why one firm sometimes appears to be earning higher profits than another but, in reality, is not.

6. For a perfectly competitive firm, profit maximization does not conflict with resource allocative efficiency. Do you agree? Explain your answer.

7. The perfectly competitive firm does not increase its quantity of output without limit, even though it can sell all it wants at the going price. Why not?

8. You read in a business magazine that computer firms are reaping high profits. With the theory of perfect competition in mind, what do you expect to happen over time to each of the following?

   a. Computer prices
   b. The profits of computer firms
   c. The number of computers on the market
   d. The number of computer firms

9. In your own words, explain resource allocative efficiency.

10. The term "price taker" can apply to buyers as well as to sellers. A price-taking buyer is a buyer who cannot influence price by changing the amount she buys. What goods do you buy for which you are a price taker? What goods do you buy for which you are not a price taker?

11. Why study the theory of perfect competition if no real-world market completely satisfies all of the theory's assumptions?

12. Explain why a perfectly competitive firm will shut down in the short run if price is lower than average variable cost but will continue to produce if price is below average total cost but above average variable cost.

13. In long-run competitive equilibrium, $P = MC = SRATC = LRATC$. Because $P = MR$, we can write the preceding condition as $P = MR = MC = SRATC = LRATC$. The condition thus consists of four parts: (a) $P = MR$, (b) $MR = MC$, (c) $P = SRATC$, and (d) $SRATC = LRATC$. Part (b)—$MR = MC$—is true because the perfectly competitive firm attempts to maximize profits, and that equation represents how it does so. What are the explanations for parts (a), (c), and (d)?

14. Suppose the government imposes the following production tax on one perfectly competitive firm in an industry: For each unit the firm produces, it must pay $1 to the government. Will consumers in this market end up paying higher prices because of the tax? Why or why not?

15. Why is the marginal revenue curve for a perfectly competitive firm the same as its demand curve?

16. Many plumbers charge the same price for coming to your house to fix a kitchen sink. Is this because plumbers are colluding?

17. Do firms in a perfectly competitive market exhibit productive efficiency? Why or why not?

18. Profit serves as both an incentive and a signal. Explain.

WORKING WITH NUMBERS AND GRAPHS

1. Given the following information, state whether the perfectly competitive firm should shut down or continue to operate in the short run:

   a. $Q = 100$; $P = \$10$; $AFC = \$3$; $AVC = \$4$.
   b. $Q = 70$; $P = \$5$; $AFC = \$2$; $AVC = \$7$.
   c. $Q = 150$; $P = \$7$; $AFC = \$5$; $AVC = \$6$.

2. If total revenue increases at a constant rate, what does this condition imply about marginal revenue?

3. According to the accompanying table, what quantity of output should the firm produce? Explain your answer.

Q	TR	TC
0	$0	$0
1	100	50
2	200	110
3	300	180
4	400	260
5	500	360
6	600	480

4. Is the firm in question 3 a perfectly competitive firm? Explain your answer.

5. Explain how a market supply curve is derived.

6. Draw the relevant curves and the areas within them that show the following:

   a. A perfectly competitive firm that earns profits

   b. A perfectly competitive firm that incurs losses but that will continue operating in the short run

   c. A perfectly competitive firm that incurs losses and that will shut down in the short run

7. Why is the perfectly competitive firm's supply curve the portion of its marginal cost curve that is above its average variable cost curve?

8. In the accompanying figure, what area(s) represent(s) the following at Q_1?

   a. Total cost
   b. Total variable cost
   c. Total revenue
   d. Loss (negative profit)

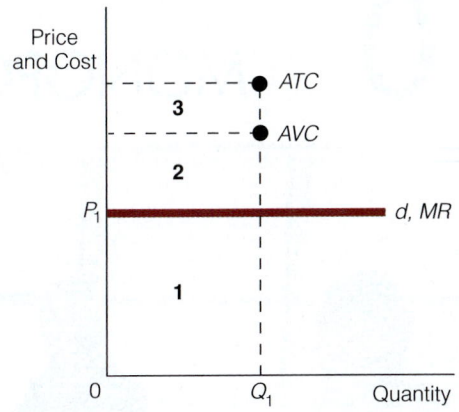

9. Why does the MC curve cut the ATC curve at the latter's lowest point?

10. Suppose all firms in a perfectly competitive market are in long-run equilibrium. Illustrate what a perfectly competitive firm will do if market demand rises.

10 MONOPOLY

INTRODUCTION

Monopoly is at the opposite end of the market structure spectrum from perfect competition. We begin our discussion of monopoly by outlining the assumptions on which the theory of monopoly is built. We then move on to talk about the quantity of output the monopolist wants to produce and the price (per unit) at which it sells that output. Much of this chapter focuses on the differences between the perfectly competitive firm and the monopoly firm.

ESB Professional/Shutterstock.com

10-1 THE THEORY OF MONOPOLY

Monopoly
A theory of market structure based on three assumptions: There is one seller, it sells a product that has no close substitutes, and the barriers to entry are extremely high.

The theory of **monopoly** is built on three assumptions:

1. *There is one seller.* In effect, the firm is the industry. Contrast this situation with perfect competition, where many firms make up the industry.

2. *The single seller sells a product that has no close substitutes.* Because there are no close substitutes for its product, the single seller—the monopolist or monopoly firm—faces little, if any, competition.

3. *The barriers to entry are extremely high.* In the theory of perfect competition, a firm can enter the industry easily. In the theory of monopoly, entering the industry is very hard (if not impossible). Extremely high barriers keep out new firms.

Examples of monopoly include many public utilities (local public utilities such as electricity, water, and gas companies) and the U.S. Postal Service (in the delivery of first-class mail).

10-1a Barriers to Entry: A Key to Understanding Monopoly

If a firm is a single seller of a product, why don't other firms enter the market and produce the same product? The answer is that legal barriers, economies of scale, or one firm's exclusive ownership of a scarce resource may make it difficult or impossible for new firms to enter the market.

Legal Barriers Legal barriers include public franchises, patents, and government licenses. A **public franchise** is a right that government grants to a firm and that permits the firm to provide a particular good or service and excludes all others from doing so (thus eliminating potential competition by law). For example, the U.S. Postal Service has been granted the exclusive franchise to deliver first-class mail. Many public utilities operate under state and local franchises, as do food and gas suppliers along many state turnpikes.

In the United States, patents are granted to inventors of a product or process for a period of 20 years. During that time, the patent holder is shielded from competitors: No one else can legally produce and sell the patented product or process. The rationale behind patents is that they encourage innovation in an economy. Few people will waste their time and money trying to invent a new product if their competitors can immediately copy and sell it.

Entry into some industries and occupations requires a government-granted license. For example, radio and television stations cannot operate without a license from the Federal Communications Commission (FCC). In most states, a person needs to be licensed to join the ranks of physicians, dentists, architects, nurses, embalmers, barbers, veterinarians, and lawyers, among others.

Economies of Scale In some industries, low average total costs (low unit costs) are obtained only through large-scale production. Thus, if new entrants are to compete in the industry, they must enter it on a large scale. But having to produce on this scale is risky and costly, and it therefore acts as a barrier to entry. If economies of scale are so pronounced that only one firm can survive in the industry, the firm is called a **natural monopoly**. Often-cited examples of natural monopoly include public utilities that provide gas, water, and electricity. A later chapter discusses government regulation of a natural monopoly.

Exclusive Ownership of a Necessary Resource Existing firms may be protected from the entry of new firms by the exclusive or nearly exclusive ownership of a resource needed to enter the industry. The classic example is the Aluminum Company of America (Alcoa), which, for a time, controlled almost all the sources of bauxite in the United States. Alcoa was the sole producer of aluminum in the country from the late nineteenth century until the 1940s. In a similar vein, many people today view the De Beers Company of South Africa as a monopoly because it controls such a large percentage of diamond production and sales. Strictly speaking, De Beers is more of a marketing cartel than a monopoly, although, as discussed in the next chapter, a successful cartel acts much like a monopolist.

10-1b What Is the Difference Between a Government Monopoly and a Market Monopoly?

Sometimes high barriers to entry exist because competition is legally prohibited, and sometimes barriers exist independently. When high barriers take the form of public franchises, patents, or government licenses, competition is *legally* prohibited. When high barriers take the form of economies of scale or exclusive ownership of a resource, competition is not legally prohibited. In the latter cases, nothing legally prohibits rival firms from entering the market and competing, even though they may choose not to do so; there is no sign on the industry entrance that reads, "No competition allowed."

Public Franchise
A firm's government-granted right that permits the firm to provide a particular good or service and that excludes all others from doing so.

Natural Monopoly
The condition in which economies of scale are so pronounced that only one firm can survive.

Some economists use the term "government monopoly" to refer to a monopoly that is legally protected from competition and the term "market monopoly" to refer to a monopoly that is not legally protected from competition. But these terms do not imply that one type is better or worse than the other.

ECONOMICS 24/7

Monopoly and the Boston Tea Party

The original meaning of the word "monopoly" was "an exclusive right to sell something." At one time, kings and queens granted monopolies to people whom they favored. The monopoly entitled the person to be the sole producer or seller of a particular good. If anyone dared to compete, the crown could have the offender fined or imprisoned.

SuperStock/SuperStock

The issue of monopoly came up in the early history of the America. In 1767, the British Parliament passed the Townshend Acts, which imposed taxes (or duties) on various products imported into the American colonies. The taxes were so hated in the colonies that they prompted protest and noncompliance, and they were repealed in 1770, except for one: the tax on tea. Some historians state that the British Parliament left the tax on tea to show the colonists that it had the right to raise tax revenue

without seeking colonial approval. To get around the tax, the colonists started to buy tea from Dutch traders.

Then, in 1773, the British East India Company was in financial trouble. To help solve its financial problems, it sought a special privilege—a monopoly—from the British Parliament. In response, Parliament passed the Tea Act, which granted the company the sole right to export tea to the colonies—a monopoly. The combination of the tax and the monopoly right given to the British East India Company angered the colonists and is said to have led to the Boston Tea Party on December 16, 1773. The colonists who took part in the Boston Tea Party threw overboard 342 chests of tea owned by the monopoly-wielding British East India Company.

SELF-TEST

(Answers to Self-Test questions are in Answers to Self-Test Questions at the back of the book.)

1. "There are always some close substitutes for the product any firm sells; therefore, the theory of monopoly (which assumes no close substitutes) cannot be useful." Comment.

2. How do economies of scale act as a barrier to entry?

3. How is a movie superstar like a monopolist?

10-2 MONOPOLY PRICING AND OUTPUT DECISIONS

Price Searcher
A seller that has the ability to control, to some degree, the price of the product it sells.

A monopolist is a **price searcher**—that is, a seller with the ability to control, to some degree, the price of the product it sells. In contrast to a price taker, a price searcher can raise its price and still sell its product—although it will not sell as many units as it would at the lower price. The pricing and output decisions of the monopolist are discussed in this section.

10-2a The Monopolist's Demand and Marginal Revenue

In the theory of monopoly, the monopoly firm is the industry, and the industry is the monopoly firm; they are one and the same. Thus, the demand curve for the monopoly firm *is* the market demand curve, which is downward sloping. Because a downward-sloping demand curve posits an inverse relationship between price and quantity demanded, more is sold at lower prices than at higher prices, *ceteris paribus*. Unlike the perfectly competitive firm, the monopolist can raise its price and still sell its product (though not as much).

Because it faces a downward-sloping demand curve, to sell an additional unit of its product, the monopolist must necessarily lower its price for the product. For example, suppose the monopoly seller originally planned to sell 2 units of X a day at $10 each and now wishes to sell 3 units a day. To sell more units, it must lower the price to, say, $9.75, and it sells the 3 units at $9.75 each.[1]

So, to sell an additional unit, a monopoly firm must lower its price on all previous units. Note that the terms "previous" and "additional" do not refer to an actual sequence of events. A firm doesn't sell 100 units of a good and then decide to sell one more unit. The firm is in an either–or situation: Either the firm sells 100 units over some length of time, or it sells 101 units over the same length of time. If the firm wants to sell 101 units, the price per unit must be lower than if it wants to sell 100 units.

A monopoly seller both gains and loses by lowering the price of its product. As Exhibit 1 shows, the monopolist in our example gains $9.75, the price of the additional unit sold, because the price was lowered. It loses 50¢: 25¢ on the first unit it used to sell at $10, plus 25¢ on the second unit it used to sell at $10.

EXHIBIT 1

The Dual Effects of a Price Reduction on Total Revenue

To sell an additional unit of its good, a monopolist needs to lower the price of the good. This price reduction both gains revenue and loses revenue for the monopolist. In the exhibit, the revenue gained and revenue lost are shaded and labeled. Marginal revenue is equal to the revenue gained (tan) minus the revenue lost (green).

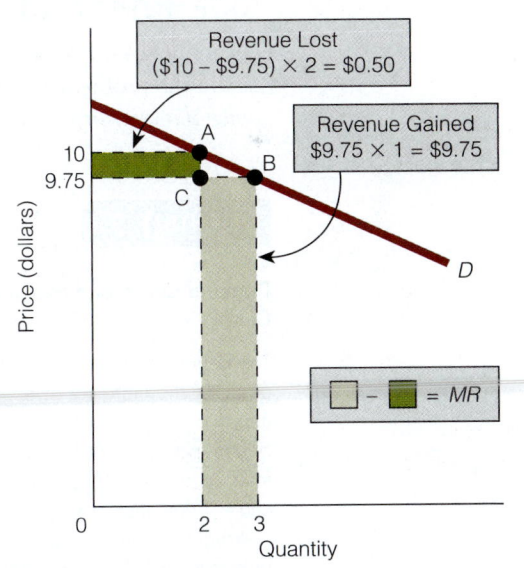

(1) P	(2) Q	(3) TR	(4) MR
$10.00	2	$20.00	___
9.75	3	29.25	$9.25

---

[1] This discussion is of the behavior of a single-price monopolist, which is a monopolist that sells all units of its product for the same price. Later, we discuss a price-discriminating monopolist.

Gains are greater than losses; the monopolist's net gain from selling the additional unit of output is $9.25 ($9.75 − $0.50 = $9.25). This is the monopolist's *marginal revenue*, the change in total revenue that results from selling one additional unit of output. (Total revenue is $20 when 2 units are sold at $10 each and $29.25 when 3 units are sold at $9.75 each. The change in total revenue that results from selling one additional unit of output is $9.25.)

Notice that the price of the good ($9.75) is greater than the marginal revenue ($9.25): $P > MR$. This is the case for a monopoly seller or any price searcher (recall that, for the firm in perfect competition, $P = MR$):

$$\text{For a monopolist, } P > MR$$

10-2b The Monopolist's Demand Curve and Marginal Revenue Curve Are Not the Same

In perfect competition, the firm's demand curve *is* the same as its marginal revenue curve. In monopoly, the firm's demand curve is not the same as its marginal revenue curve but rather lies *above* its marginal revenue curve.

The relationship between a monopolist's demand curve and marginal revenue curve is illustrated in Exhibit 2. The demand curve (D) plots price and quantity; the marginal revenue curve (MR) plots marginal revenue and quantity. Because price is greater than marginal revenue for a monopolist, its demand curve necessarily lies *above* its marginal revenue curve. (Note that price and marginal revenue are the same for the first unit of output, so the demand curve and the marginal revenue curve will share one point in common.)

10-2c Price and Output for a Profit-Maximizing Monopolist

The monopolist that seeks to maximize profit produces the quantity of output at which $MR = MC$ (as did the profit-maximizing perfectly competitive firm) and *charges the highest price per unit at which this quantity of output can be sold.*

EXHIBIT 2

Demand Curve and Marginal Revenue Curve

The demand curve plots price against quantity. The marginal revenue curve plots marginal revenue against quantity. For a monopolist, $P > MR$, so the marginal revenue curve must lie below the demand curve. (Note that, when a demand curve is a straight line, the marginal revenue curve bisects the horizontal axis halfway between the origin and the point where the demand curve intersects the horizontal axis.)

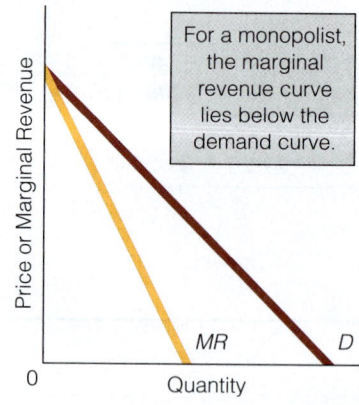

For a monopolist, the marginal revenue curve lies below the demand curve.

In Exhibit 3, the highest price at which Q_1, the quantity at which $MR = MC$, can be sold is P_1. At Q_1, the monopolist charges a price that is greater than its marginal cost ($P > MC$). Therefore, the monopolist is *not* resource allocative efficient.

EXHIBIT 3

The Monopolist's Profit-Maximizing Price and Quantity of Output

The monopolist produces the quantity of output (Q_1) at which $MR = MC$ and charges the highest price per unit (P_1) at which this quantity of output can be sold. Notice that, at the profit-maximizing quantity of output, price is greater than marginal cost ($P > MC$).

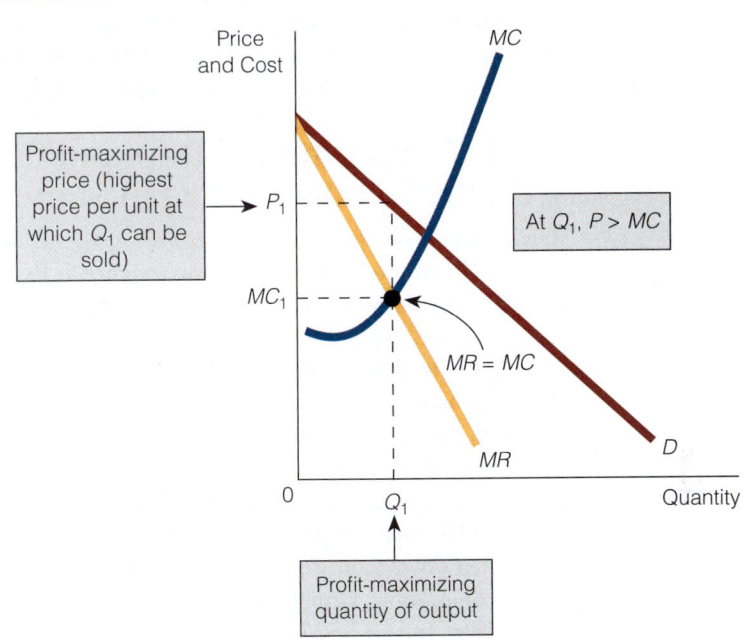

EXHIBIT 4

Monopoly Profits and Losses

A monopoly seller is not guaranteed any profits. In (a), price is above average total cost at Q_1, the quantity of output at which $MR = MC$. Therefore, TR (the area OP_1BQ_1) is greater than TC (the area $OCAQ_1$), and profits equal the area CP_1BA. In (b), price is below average total cost at Q_1. Therefore, TR (the area OP_1AQ_1) is less than TC (the area $OCBQ_1$), and losses equal the area P_1CBA.

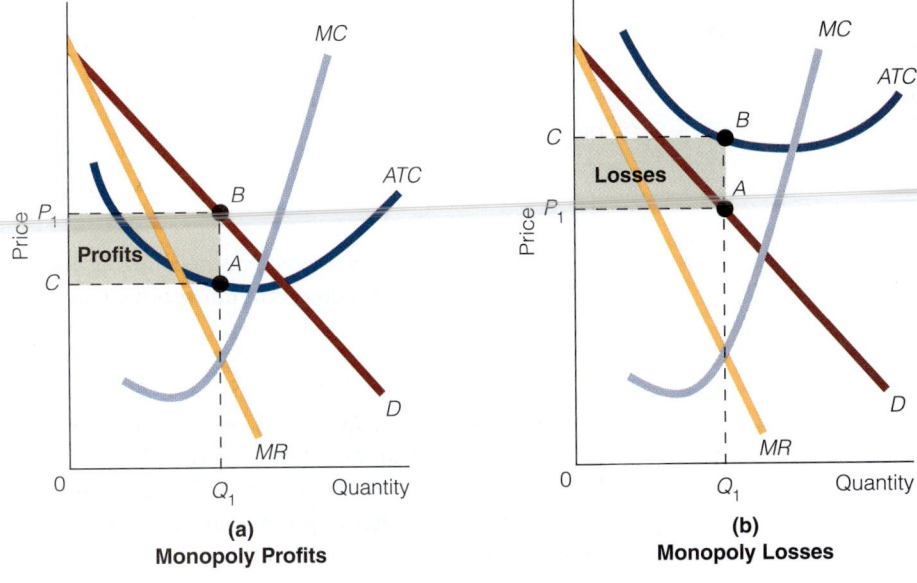

(a)
Monopoly Profits

(b)
Monopoly Losses

Whether profits are earned depends on whether P_1 is greater or less than average total cost at Q_1. In short, the profit-maximizing price may be the loss-minimizing price. Monopoly profits and monopoly losses are illustrated in Exhibit 4.

Some people argue that suggesting that a monopolist can take a loss is unrealistic. If the monopolist is the only seller in the industry, they maintain, it is guaranteed a profit. But even when a firm is the only seller of a product, it may not earn a profit. A monopolist cannot charge any price it wants for its good—only the highest price that the demand curve allows it to charge. In some instances, the highest price may be lower than the firm's average total costs (unit costs). If so, the monopolist incurs a loss, as shown in Exhibit 4(b).

10-2d Comparing the Demand Curve in Perfect Competition with the Demand Curve in Monopoly

The perfectly competitive firm is a *price taker*; it has no control over the price of the product it sells. The monopoly firm is a *price searcher*; it has some control over the price of the product it sells. Essentially, what determines whether a firm is a price taker or a price searcher is the demand curve that it faces. The perfectly competitive firm faces a horizontal demand curve. The monopoly firm faces a downward-sloping demand curve. If a firm faces a horizontal (or flat) demand curve, then it is a price taker. If a firm faces a downward-sloping demand curve, then it is a price searcher. Let's remind ourselves what each demand curve implies about the firm's ability to control price. A horizontal (or flat) demand curve implies that the firm can sell its good at only *one price*: the price determined by the market. In other words, if the market-determined price is $10, then the perfectly competitive firm's demand curve is a horizontal line at $10. In contrast, a downward-sloping demand curve implies that the firm can sell its good at *different prices*. For example, it might sell 100 units at $12 per unit and 150 units at $11 per unit. In short, it "searches" for the best price among the many possible prices.

10-2e If a Firm Maximizes Revenue, Does It Automatically Maximize Profit Too?

Profit is the difference of total revenue (TR) and total cost (TC):

$$\text{Profit} = TR - TC$$

Because TC is the sum of total fixed costs (TFC) and total variable costs (TVC), we can rewrite our profit equation as

$$\text{Profit} = TR - (TFC + TVC)$$

Maximizing profit is the same as maximizing total revenue under one condition: $TVC = 0$. When $TVC = 0$, TVC falls out of our profit equation and we are left with

$$\text{Profit} = TR - TFC$$

Because TFC is constant as output increases, a rise in TR will automatically increase profit by the same amount. To illustrate, if $TR = \$100$ and $TFC = \$40$, then profit is $60. If TR rises by $10, to $110, and TFC remains constant at $40, then profit rises to $70. The rise in TR is equal to the rise in profit: $10. Therefore, to maximize total revenue is to maximize profit.

Now change things a bit. Suppose TVC is not zero. We return to our profit equation:

$$\text{Profit} = TR - (TFC + TVC)$$

Again, let $TR = \$100$ and $TFC = \$40$. But this time $TVC = \$20$. It follows that profit is $40. Now, if TR rises to $110, will profit again rise by $10, as it did in the previous example? Perhaps not, because what happens to profit depends on what happens not only to TR, but to TVC too. Suppose TVC rises to $37 as TR rises by $110. Now profit is $33. In other words, total revenue increased (from $100 to $110), but profit decreased (from $40 to $33).

Therefore, profit maximization is the same as revenue maximization only when there are no variable costs (i.e., when $TVC = \$0$).

10-3 PERFECT COMPETITION AND MONOPOLY

Because perfect competition and monopoly are at opposite ends of the market structure spectrum, there are major differences between them. In this section, we discuss those differences.

10-3a Price, Marginal Revenue, and Marginal Cost

Here are two key differences between perfect competition and monopoly:

1. For the perfectly competitive firm, $P = MR$; for the monopolist, $P > MR$. The perfectly competitive firm's demand curve *is* its marginal revenue curve; the monopolist's demand curve lies *above* its marginal revenue curve.

2. The perfectly competitive firm charges a price equal to its marginal cost; the monopolist charges a price greater than its marginal cost. That is,

$$\text{Perfect competition: } P = MR \text{ and } P = MC$$
$$\text{Monopoly: } P > MR \text{ and } P > MC$$

10-3b Monopoly, Perfect Competition, and Consumers' Surplus

A monopoly firm differs from a perfectly competitive firm in terms of how much consumers' surplus buyers receive. To illustrate, Exhibit 5 shows a downward-sloping market demand curve D, a downward-sloping marginal revenue curve MR, and a horizontal marginal cost curve MC. Although you are used to seeing upward-sloping marginal cost curves, nothing prevents marginal cost from being constant over some range of output. A horizontal MC curve simply means that marginal cost is constant. Now, if the market in Exhibit 6 is perfectly competitive, the demand curve *is* the marginal revenue curve. Therefore, the profit-maximizing output is Q_{PC} and the buyer will pay P_{PC} per unit of the good. Recall that consumers' surplus is the area under the demand curve and above the price. For the perfectly competitive firm, consumers' surplus is the triangular area $P_{PC}AB$.[2]

---

[2] The demand curve is downward sloping because we are looking at the market demand curve, not the firm's demand curve. All market demand curves are downward sloping.

EXHIBIT 5

Monopoly, Perfect Competition, and Consumers' Surplus

If the market in the exhibit is perfectly competitive, the demand curve is the marginal revenue curve. The profit-maximizing output is Q_{PC} and price is P_{PC}. Consumers' surplus is the area $P_{PC}AB$. If the market is a monopoly market, the profit-maximizing output is Q_M and price is P_M. In this case, consumers' surplus is the area P_MAC. Consumers' surplus is greater by the area $P_{PC}P_MCB$ in perfect competition than in monopoly.

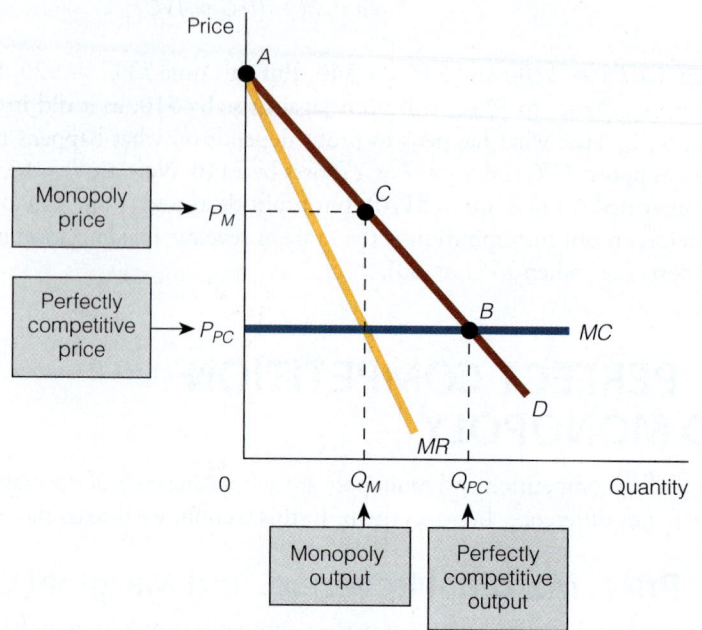

In a monopoly market, the demand curve and the marginal revenue curve are different. The profit-maximizing output is where the MR curve intersects the MC curve; thus, the profit-maximizing output is Q_M, and the price the buyer pays is P_M. In the case of monopoly, consumers' surplus is the area P_MAC.

EXHIBIT 6

Monopoly or Nothing?

We start with the demand and marginal revenue curves and with $MC_1 = ATC_1$. Because cost is "so high," no firm produces the good. Later, a single firm figures out how to lower cost to $MC_2 = ATC_2$. This firm produces Q_M and charges the monopoly price of P_M per unit. Is monopoly preferable to no firm producing the good? From a consumer's perspective, the answer is yes. Consumers' surplus is zero when no firm produces the good, and consumers' surplus is the area P_MAB when the monopoly firm produces the good.

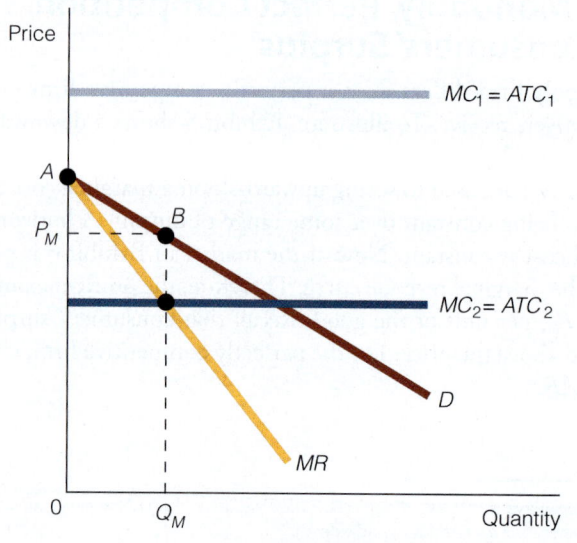

Obviously, consumers' surplus is greater in the perfectly competitive case than in the monopoly case by the area $P_{PC} P_M CB$. This area is the loss in consumers' surplus due to monopolization.

10-3c Monopoly or Nothing?

Suppose you could push one of two buttons to determine the conditions under which a particular good is produced. If you push the first button, the good is produced under the conditions of perfect competition. If you push the second button, the good is produced under the conditions of monopoly. Which button would you push?

From a consumer's perspective, perfect competition would seem to be the better choice because it provides more output and a lower price than monopoly does. In short, there is more consumers' surplus. Perfect competition would therefore seem to be superior to monopoly. But life doesn't always present a choice between perfect competition and monopoly. Sometimes it presents a choice between monopoly and nothing.

Exhibit 6 shows the demand curve (D) for a good, along with the relevant marginal revenue curve (MR) and two sets of MC and ATC curves. Assume that MC_1 and ATC_1 are the relevant cost curves. Because the MC_1 curve is so far above the MR curve, the two do not intersect. In other words, there is no profit-maximizing quantity of output for a firm to produce. Although there is demand for the particular good, the costs of producing it are so high that no firm will produce it. Consumers therefore receive no consumers' surplus from the purchase and consumption of the good.

But suppose a firm—a single firm—is able to lower costs to MC_2 and ATC_2. Now marginal cost is low enough for the firm to produce the good. The firm produces a quantity Q_M and charges a price P_M. The area $P_M AB$ is equal to consumers' surplus.

No doubt, the firm producing this good and charging a price P_M is a monopoly firm. However, consumers are better off having a monopoly firm produce the good than having no firm produce it: If no firm produces the good because costs are too high, consumers' surplus is zero, but when the monopoly firm produces the good, consumers' surplus is positive.

So under certain conditions, a monopoly may be created in a market because a firm figures out a way to lower the cost of producing a good enough to make producing it worthwhile. Of course, once the monopoly firm exists, consumers would prefer that the good be produced under perfect competition than under monopoly conditions. But that is not always the relevant choice. Sometimes, the choice is between monopoly and nothing, and when that is the choice, the consumers' surplus is greater with monopoly than it is with nothing.

SELF-TEST

1. Why does the monopolist's demand curve lie above its marginal revenue curve?

2. Is a monopolist guaranteed to earn profits?

3. Is a monopolist resource allocative efficient? Why or why not?

4. Why do you think a monopolist is called a price searcher? What is it searching for?

10-4 THE CASE AGAINST MONOPOLY

Monopoly is often said to be inefficient in comparison with perfect competition. This section examines some of the shortcomings of monopoly.

10-4a The Deadweight Loss of Monopoly

Exhibit 7 shows demand, marginal revenue, marginal cost, and average total cost curves. For simplicity's sake, assume that the product is produced under constant cost conditions, so that marginal cost equals long-run average total cost. If the product is produced under perfect competition, then output Q_{PC} is produced and is sold at price P_{PC}. At the competitive equilibrium output level, $P = MC$. If the product is produced under monopoly, output Q_M is produced and is sold at price P_M. At the monopoly equilibrium, $P > MC$.

As the exhibit shows, greater output is produced under perfect competition than under monopoly. The net value of the difference in these two output levels is said to be the **deadweight loss of monopoly**. In Exhibit 7, the value to buyers of increasing output from Q_M to Q_{PC} is equal to the maximum amount they would pay for this increase in output, designated by the trapezoidal area $Q_M CBQ_{PC}$. The costs that would have to be incurred to produce the additional output are designated by the rectangular area $Q_M DBQ_{PC}$. The difference between the two is the triangle DCB, *the amount buyers value the additional output over and above the costs of producing the additional output.* This triangular area is the loss attached to not producing the competitive quantity of output. The triangle DCB is referred to as the *deadweight loss triangle.*

Deadweight Loss of Monopoly

The net value (the value to buyers over and above the costs to suppliers) of the difference between the competitive quantity of output (where $P = MC$) and the monopoly quantity of output (where $P > MC$); the loss due to not producing the competitive quantity of output.

EXHIBIT 7

Deadweight Loss and Rent Seeking as Costs of Monopoly

The monopolist produces Q_M, and the perfectly competitive firm produces the higher output level Q_{PC}. The deadweight loss of monopoly is the triangle (DCB) between these two levels of output. Rent-seeking activity is directed to obtaining the monopoly profits, represented by the area $P_{PC} P_M CD$. Rent seeking is a socially wasteful activity because resources are expended to transfer income rather than to produce goods and services.

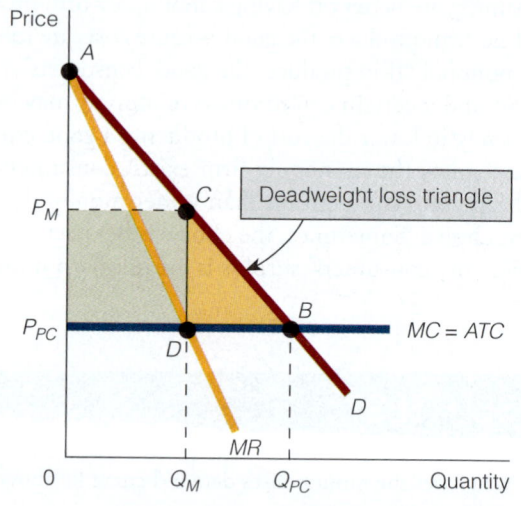

Therefore, monopoly produces a quantity of output that is too small in comparison to the quantity of output produced in perfect competition. This difference in output results in a welfare loss to society.

Arnold Harberger was the first economist who tried to determine the actual size of the deadweight loss cost of monopoly in the manufacturing sector of the U.S. economy. He estimated the loss to be a small percentage of the economy's total output. Additional empirical work by other economists puts the figure at approximately 1 percent of total output.

Does It Matter to You . . .
If There Is a Deadweight Loss of Monopoly Triangle?

Look at Exhibit 7. There you will see a triangle (*DCB*) that represents the deadweight loss of monopoly. Does that deadweight loss of monopoly matter to you?

To get the answer, consider that with a monopoly an output of Q_M is produced and offered for sale, whereas with perfect competition an output of Q_{PC} is produced and offered for sale (see Exhibit 7). Let's suppose that Q_{PC} equals 100 units and Q_M represents 55 units. This means that, under a monopoly, 45 fewer units are produced than would be produced under perfect competition.

Producing and selling 45 fewer units is a loss if people value those 45 units more than it costs to produce those 45 units. And this is the case, as we can see in Exhibit 7. We know that the value of those 45 units to buyers is greater than the costs to producers of producing those 45 units because we can see that the demand curve, which represents the value to buyers, lies above the *MC* curve, which represents the costs to producers, between the quantities of Q_{PC} and Q_M. The deadweight loss triangle represents how much, in terms of net benefits, is lost when 55 units (Q_M) is produced instead of 100 units (Q_{PC}).

Now suppose you wanted to buy an additional 45 units under monopoly conditions (as opposed to perfectly competitive conditions). You wouldn't be able to because they wouldn't exist. The manifestation of this loss is the deadweight loss triangle.

10-4b Rent Seeking

Sometimes, individuals and groups try to influence public policy in the hope of redistributing (transferring) income from others to themselves. In Exhibit 7, the market produces Q_{PC} output and charges a price P_{PC}. Suppose, however, that one of the, say, 100 firms currently producing some of Q_{PC} asks the government to grant it a monopoly; that is, firm A asks the government to prevent the 99 other firms from competing with it. Consider the benefit for firm A of becoming a monopolist (a single seller). Currently, it is earning zero economic profit because it is selling at a price that equals *ATC*. If it becomes a monopolist, though, it will earn profits equal to the area $P_{PC}P_MCD$ in Exhibit 7.

These profits are the result of a *transfer* from buyers to the monopolist. To see why, consider what happens to consumers' surplus. If the market in Exhibit 7 is perfectly competitive, consumers' surplus is equal to the triangular area $P_{PC}AB$; if the market is monopolized, consumers' surplus is equal to the smaller triangular area P_MAC. The difference is the area $P_{PC}P_MCB$, the area that represents the loss in consumers' surplus if the market is monopolized. Part of this area—the rectangular area $P_{PC}P_MCD$—is transferred to the monopolist in terms of profits. *In other words, if the market is monopolized, part of the consumers' surplus that is lost to buyers becomes profits for the monopolist.* (The other part is the deadweight loss of monopoly, identified by the deadweight loss triangle *DCB*.)

If firm A tries to get the government to transfer income in the form of consumers' surplus from buyers to itself, it is undertaking a *transfer-seeking activity*. In economics, such activities are usually called **rent seeking**. In other words, firm A is **rent seeking**.[3]

Rent Seeking
Actions of individuals and groups that spend resources to influence public policy in the hope of redistributing (transferring) income to themselves from others.

---

[3]. The word "rent" (used in this context) often confuses people. In everyday life, "rent" refers to the payment for an apartment. In economics, rent, or, more formally, economic rent, is a payment in excess of opportunity cost. The term "rent seeking" was introduced by economist Anne Krueger in her article "The Political Economy of the Rent-Seeking Society," *American Economic Review* 64 (June 1974): 291–303.

Economist Gordon Tullock has made the point that rent-seeking behavior is individually rational but socially wasteful. To see why, suppose the profits in Exhibit 7 (the area $P_{PC}P_{M}CD$) are equal to $10 million. Firm A wants the $10 million in profits, so it asks the government for a monopoly because it wants the government to prevent the 99 other firms from competing with it.

Firm A will not get its monopoly privilege simply by asking for it. The firm will have to spend money and time to convince government officials that it should give the firm this monopoly privilege. It will have to hire lobbyists, take politicians and other government officials to dinner, and perhaps make donations to some of them. Firm A will have to spend resources to get what it wants, and all the resources firm A uses to try to bring about a transfer from buyers to itself, says Tullock, are wasted. Those resources cannot be used to produce shoes, computers, television sets, and many other things that people would like to buy. The resources are instead used to try to transfer income from one party to another, not to produce more goods and services.

Society would be very different if no one produced anything but instead invested time and money in rent seeking. For example, Jones would try to get what is Matsui's, Matsui would try to get what is Kahn's, and Kahn would try to get what is Patel's. No one would produce anything; everyone would simply spend time and money trying to get what currently belongs to someone else. In such a world, no one would produce the food, the computers, and the cars that people would like to buy.

Tullock makes the point that the resource cost of rent seeking should be added to the dead-weight loss of monopoly. This addition, according to Tullock, makes the overall cost of monopoly to society higher than anyone initially thought.

THINKING LIKE AN ECONOMICS

No $10 Bills Here is a joke that tells us something about how economists think: Two economists are walking down the street. One sees a $10 bill on the sidewalk and asks the other, "Isn't that a $10 bill?" "Obviously not," says the other. "If it were, someone would have already picked it up." Specifically, economists believe that an opportunity for gain won't last long because someone will grab it—quickly. By the time you come along, it's gone.

Apply this thinking to what Gordon Tullock says about monopoly. As a seller, a monopolist is in a better position than a competitive firm. Like a $10 bill on the sidewalk, a monopoly position is worth something. Just as people will pick up a $10 bill on the sidewalk, they will try to become monopolists. In terms of rent seeking, to which Tullock first called our attention, just as people will bend down to pick up the $10 bill, so will they invest resources to capture the monopoly rents. No opportunity for gain is likely to be ignored.

10-4c X-Inefficiency

X-inefficiency
The increase in costs, due to the organizational slack in a monopoly, resulting from the absence of competitive pressure to push costs down to their lowest possible level.

Economist Harvey Leibenstein maintains that the monopolist is not under pressure to produce its good at the lowest possible cost; it can produce its good above the lowest possible unit cost and still survive. Certainly, the monopolist benefits if it can and does lower its costs, but it doesn't have to in order to survive (with the proviso that average total costs cannot be higher than price). Leibenstein refers to the organizational slack that is directly tied to the monopolist operating at a cost that is higher than the lowest possible as **X-inefficiency**.

Obtaining accurate estimates of X-inefficiency is difficult, but, whatever its magnitude, forces are at work to mitigate it. For example, if a market monopoly is being run inefficiently, other people, realizing this situation, may attempt to buy the monopoly and to lower costs in order to make higher profits.

ECONOMICS 24/7

Religion and Monopoly

Suppose a government were to prohibit certain firms from competing in a particular market—say, the personal computer market. As a consumer, you might think that this government-imposed restraint on competition would probably end up harming you. After all, if only firms A, B, and C could produce and sell personal computers, and firms D, E, and F were prohibited from doing so, you might expect to pay higher prices for personal computers of lower quality than would be the case if all firms were permitted to compete for your personal computer dollar.

Now suppose a government were to prohibit certain religions from competing in the religion market. For example, suppose that a particular government (in a particular country) permitted only religion A to exist. Other existing religions, as well as any new religions that might arise in the future, would be prohibited. If anyone were to practice a religion other than A, that person would be subject to fines and punishment and perhaps certain types of discrimination too.

Here, then, we would have a religion—religion A—that held a monopoly position in society. Religion A would be the only legal provider of religion in our hypothetical country. Moreover, the barriers to entry in the religion market would be extremely high, in that the government decreed that no other religions could compete with religion A.

If religions are analogous to firms, we would expect that the customers of religion (just like the customers of firms) would do better in an open, competitive religion market (with free entry and exit) than in a closed, monopolistic religion market (with high barriers to entry). Is there any empirical evidence that they do, in fact, do better?

Laurence Iannaccone is an economist at Chapman University and a pioneer in the field of the economics of religion. He has argued that, across countries in which a free and open market in religion exists, a larger percentage of the population considers themselves religious, attends religious worship, and generally exhibits a greater degree of religiosity than in countries where religion is heavily regulated or where the state prohibits competition in religion. He states,

Weekly church attendance rates range from 40 percent of the total population of the United States (where the Constitution guarantees religious competition), to less than 10 percent in Scandinavian countries (where a single, state-run Lutheran church dominates the market, runs on tax dollars, and pays its clergy as civil servants). Indeed, every available measure of piety, including frequency of prayer, belief in God, and confidence in religion, is greater in countries with numerous competing churches than in countries dominated by a single established church, and these relationships remain strong even after controlling for income, education or urbanization.[4]

[4.] Laurence R. Iannaccone, "Introduction to the Economics of Religion," *Journal of Economic Literature*, September 1998, p. 1486.

10-5 PRICE DISCRIMINATION

The monopoly seller may sell all units of its product for the same price; that is, it may be a single-price monopolist. However, under certain conditions, a monopolist could practice **price discrimination**, which occurs when the seller charges different prices for the product it sells and the price differences do not reflect cost differences.

Price Discrimination
A price structure in which the seller charges different prices for the product it sells and the price differences do not reflect cost differences.

10-5a Types of Price Discrimination

There are three types of price discrimination:

Perfect Price Discrimination

A price structure in which the seller charges the highest price that each consumer is willing to pay for the product rather than go without it.

- *Perfect price discrimination:* Suppose a monopolist produces and sells 1,000 units of good X. It sells each unit separately, charging the highest price that each consumer would be willing to pay for the product rather than go without it. This practice is **perfect price discrimination**, sometimes called *discrimination among units*.

Second-Degree Price Discrimination

A price structure in which the seller charges a uniform price per unit for one specific quantity, a lower price for an additional quantity, and so on.

- *Second-degree price discrimination:* If a monopolist charges a uniform price per unit for one specific quantity, a lower price for an additional quantity, and so on, then it is practicing **second-degree price discrimination**, sometimes called *discrimination among quantities*. For example, the monopolist might sell the first 10 units for $10 each, the next 20 units for $9 each, and so on.

Third-Degree Price Discrimination

A price structure in which the seller charges different prices in different markets or charges different prices to various segments of the buying population.

- *Third-degree price discrimination:* If a monopolist charges different prices in various markets or charges different prices to various segments of the buying population, then the monopolist is practicing **third-degree price discrimination**, sometimes called *discrimination among buyers*. For example, if your local pharmacy charges senior citizens lower prices for medicine than it charges non-senior citizens, then it is practicing **third-degree price discrimination**.

10-5b Why a Monopolist Wants to Price Discriminate

Suppose the following units of a product can be sold at varying maximum prices: first unit, $10; second unit, $9; third unit, $8; fourth unit, $7. If the monopolist wants to sell 4 units, and it charges the same price for each unit (suppose it is a single-price monopolist), its total revenue is $28 ($7 × 4). If the monopolist practices perfect price discrimination, it charges $10 for the first unit, $9 for the second unit, $8 for the third unit, and $7 for the fourth unit. Its total revenue is then $34 ($10 + $9 + $8 + $7). A comparison of total revenues with and without price discrimination explains why the monopolist would want to price discriminate. A perfectly price-discriminating monopolist receives the maximum price for each unit of the good it sells; a single-price monopolist does not.

For the monopolist who practices perfect price discrimination, price equals marginal revenue ($P = MR$). To illustrate, when the monopolist sells its second unit for $9 (having sold the first unit for $10), its total revenue is $19—or its marginal revenue is $9, which is equal to the price of the second unit.

10-5c Conditions of Price Discrimination

Why the monopolist would *want* to price discriminate is obvious. However, for it actually to price discriminate, the following conditions must hold:

1. *The seller must exercise some control over price; that is, it must be a price searcher.* If the seller is not a price searcher (if it is a price taker), it has no control over price and therefore cannot sell a good at different prices to different buyers.

2. *The seller must be able to distinguish among buyers who are willing to pay different prices.* Unless the seller can distinguish among buyers who would pay different prices, it cannot price discriminate. After all, how would it know whom to charge the higher or lower prices?

Arbitrage

Buying a good at a low price and selling it for a higher price.

3. *Reselling the good to other buyers must be impossible or too costly.* **Arbitrage**, or buying low and selling high, must not be possible. If a buyer can resell the good, price discrimination is not possible because buyers of the good at a lower price will simply resell it to other buyers for a price lower than the original seller's higher price. In time, no one will pay the higher price.

ECONOMICS 24/7

One for $40 or Two for $70

Sellers sometimes advertise one unit of their good for $X, but two units of the same good for less than $2X. For example, a clothing store might advertise one pair of men's trousers for $40, but two pairs for $70 (which is $10 less than double $40). At first sight, this might appear to be quite a deal. Whether it is or is not is a personal judgment. What it is for certain, however, is an act of price discrimination.

Look at the situation in terms of an individual's demand curve for trousers. For example, an individual's demand curve might tell us that he is willing to buy one pair of trousers at $40 a pair but that he will buy two pairs if the price is $30 a pair. In other words, one point on the demand curve represents $40 and one pair of trousers, and a second point on the demand curve (lower down) represents $30 and two pairs of trousers.

Now, suppose the store wishes to sell this person two pairs of trousers. How might it go about doing that? Well, it could price trousers at $30 a pair, and then the person would buy two pairs. Under this pricing scheme, total revenue for the store is $60. Or it could price the first pair at $40 and the second pair at $30, for a

iStock.com/tibor5

total of $70 for two. ("Buy one pair at full price and get the second pair for $10 off.") Will the individual be willing to pay $40 for the first pair and $30 for the second pair? From the person's demand curve, we realize that he would, because, as we stated earlier, one point on the person's demand curve represents $40 and one pair of trousers and another point represents $30 and two pairs of trousers.

Hear What and How the Economist Thinks . . .
About Price Discrimination

The economist reads the following:

Businesses often price discriminate, charging different customers different prices for the same good. It is usually the case that the customer who pays the higher price is subsidizing the customer who pays the lower price. One pays $100 for the good so that the other can only pay $80.

Hear what and how the economist thinks:

Think about this for a minute. From what this person has said, it sounds as if he believes that the person who pays $80 for the good is provided some sort of deal or discount because there is a person who pays $100

for the good. It's as if the seller thinks, "I can charge a high price ($100) to the first person, which means I can charge a lower price ($80) to the second person, so I might as well go ahead and do this, because all I really want to earn from the two buyers is $180."

Now why would the seller choose to sell the good at a lower price ($80) just because he or she charged a higher price ($100) to someone else? Wouldn't it be better for the seller to charge the highest price it could to each and every customer—assuming that it could price discriminate? To illustrate, suppose there are two individuals, A and B, and the highest price that A can be charged and still buy the good is $100, and the highest price that B can be charged and still buy the good is $99. Wouldn't the seller be better off charging A $100 and charging B $99 instead of charging A $100 and B $80? In short, wouldn't the seller be better off charging each customer the highest price he or she would be willing to pay instead of charging one person a higher price so that he can then charge another person a lower price?

The mistake that this person makes in thinking that one person pays $100 so that another can pay $80, is that he or she sees two prices, one higher than the other, and jumps to the conclusion that the person who pays the higher price somehow makes it possible for the seller to then charge a lower price to someone else. This leads to the reasoning that, somehow, the person who pays the higher price is "subsidizing" the person who pays the lower price.

But this story line doesn't make sense if we hold that sellers would want to earn as much total revenue as possible, all other things being the same. Yes, $80 is a lower price than $100, but still, it is likely that each of the two prices is the highest price that different buyers are willing and able to pay. The seller isn't saying: "Now that I have charged one buyer $100, I can now charge $80 to another buyer, even though that other buyer is willing and able to pay $99." Instead the seller is asking himself why he or she should give up the difference between $99 and $80 if there is no need to. Why leave the $19 difference for someone else if there is no need to?

Now think of the following. Suppose Smith owns a car dealership. Two people come in to the dealership to buy the same make and style of car. One person Smith does not know. The other person has been a lifelong friend of Smith. Let's suppose the highest price that each person is willing and able to pay for the car is $40,000. Smith ends up selling the car to the person he doesn't know for $39,500, and he ends up selling the car to his lifelong friend for $38,000, even though he is quite sure that the his lifelong friend was willing and able to pay $39,500. Is this a case where one customer pays more so that the other customer can pay less? The answer is still no. What we have here is Smith, the owner of the car dealership, giving his lifelong friend a gift, of sorts. Smith knows that his friend will pay $39,500 for the car, and that he will be giving up $1,500 in revenue if he sells the car to his friend for $38,000, but he is still willing to give this $1,500 gift to his friend.

Questions to Think About:

1. An adult and a child go to see the same movie in a theater. The theater charges the child $6 to see the movie and it charges the adult $12 to see the movie. Is it the case that the adult is paying a higher price so that the child can pay a lower price? Explain your answer.

2. A person aged 30 and a person aged 70 both order the same entrée at a restaurant. The younger person ends up paying full price for the entrée and the older person receives a 10 percent discount because he is a senior citizen. Is the younger person paying more so that the older person can pay less?

10-5e Moving to $P = MC$ Through Price Discrimination

We know that the perfectly competitive firm exhibits resource allocative efficiency; it produces the quantity of output at which $P = MC$. We also know that the single-price monopolist produces the quantity of output at which $P > MC$; that is, it produces an inefficient level of output. But does the perfectly price-discriminating monopolist also produce an inefficient level of output?

The answer is no. For a perfectly price-discriminating monopolist, $P = MR$ (as is the case for the perfectly competitive firm). It follows that, when the perfectly price-discriminating monopolist produces the quantity of output at which $MR = MC$, it automatically produces the quantity at which $P = MC$. In short, the perfectly price-discriminating monopolist and the perfectly competitive firm both exhibit resource allocative efficiency.

In part (a) of Exhibit 8, the perfectly competitive firm produces where $P = MC$. In part (b), the single-price monopolist produces where $P > MC$. In part (c), the perfectly price-discriminating monopolist produces where $P = MC$.

There is one important difference between the perfectly competitive firm and the perfectly price-discriminating monopolist. Although both produce where $P = MC$, the perfectly competitive firm charges the same price for each unit of the good it sells whereas the perfectly price-discriminating monopolist charges a different price for each unit it sells.

EXHIBIT 8

Comparison of a Perfectly Competitive Firm, a Single-Price Monopolist, and a Perfectly Price-Discriminating Monopolist

For both the perfectly competitive firm (a) and the perfectly price-discriminating monopolist

(c), $P = MR$ and the demand curve is the marginal revenue curve. Both produce where $P = MC$. The single-price monopolist (b), however, produces where $P > MC$, because for such a firm, $P > MR$ and its demand curve lies above its marginal revenue curve. One

difference between the perfectly competitive firm and the perfectly price-discriminating monopolist is that the former charges the same price for each unit of the good that it sells whereas the latter charges a different price for each unit of the good that it sells.

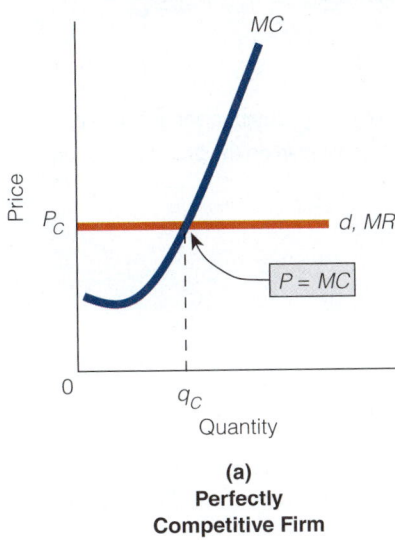

(a)
Perfectly
Competitive Firm

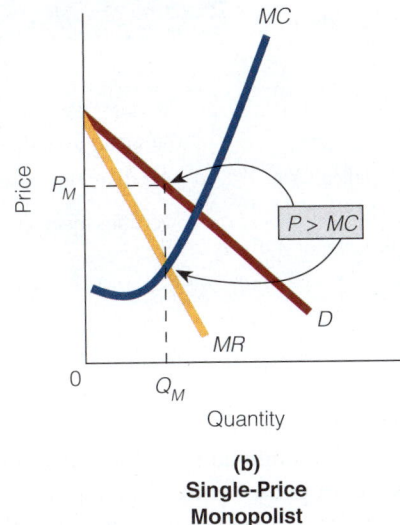

(b)
Single-Price
Monopolist

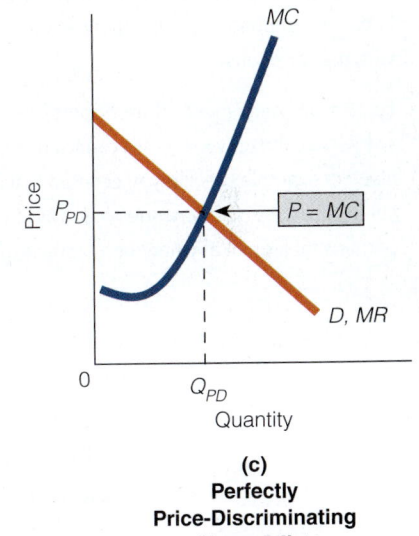

(c)
Perfectly
Price-Discriminating
Monopolist

ECONOMICS 24/7

Do Colleges and Universities Price Discriminate?

Many colleges and universities practice price discrimination. For example, consider the university that gives out student or financial aid. The student aid is nothing more than a reduction in the tuition a student pays. As an example, University X states that it will give a low-income student, if admitted, $10,000 in student aid. So, if the tuition at the university is, say, $15,000, the student ends up paying

only $5,000. The student with a high income does not get the student aid and therefore pays $15,000 upon admission. Even though the cost to the university to educate each student is the same, the students pay different tuition prices.

Another example is the university that offers a scholarship to an academic high achiever or to a star athlete (just coming out of high school). To either or both, the university offers a scholarship, which lowers the tuition the person pays.

If the universities price discriminate, they must meet all the conditions necessary for price discrimination:

- *The seller must be a price searcher.* First, universities are price searchers; they exercise some control over the tuition they charge. In other words, universities can lower tuition and sell more or raise tuition and sell less.

- *The seller must be able to distinguish among buyers who would be willing to pay different prices.* Universities can distinguish among students (customers) who would be willing to pay different prices. For example, the student with few universities seeking him would probably be willing to pay more than the student with many options.

- *Reselling the good to other buyers must be impossible or too costly.* The service the university sells cannot be resold to someone else. For example, reselling an economics lecture is difficult. You could, of course, tell someone what was covered in the lecture, perhaps for a small payment or a promise to do the same for you

iStock.com/abalcazar

at a later date. But this is like telling someone about a movie. Reselling something that is consumed on the premises is often difficult or impossible.

Universities meet all three requirements.

10-5f Coupons and Price Discrimination

Third-degree price discrimination, or discrimination among buyers, is sometimes employed by means of cents-off coupons. (Third-degree price discrimination exists if a seller sells the same product at different prices to different segments of the population.)

One of the conditions of price discrimination is that the seller has to be able to distinguish among customers who are willing to pay different prices. For example, some sellers think that people who value their time highly are willing to pay a higher price for a product than people who do not. These sellers argue that people who place a high value on their time want to economize on the shopping time connected with the purchase. If sellers want to price discriminate between these two types of customers—charging more to customers who value time more and charging less to customers who value time less—they must determine the category into which each of their customers falls.

If you were a seller, how would you go about finding out this information? Many real-world sellers place cents-off coupons in newspapers and magazines. They hypothesize that people who place a relatively low value on their time are willing to spend it clipping and sorting coupons. People who place a relatively high value on their time are not. In effect, price discrimination works much like the following scenario in, say, a grocery store:

1. The posted price for all products is the same for all customers.

2. Both Linda and Josh put product X in their shopping carts.

3. When Linda gets to the checkout counter, the clerk asks, "Do you have any coupons today?" Linda says no. She is therefore charged the posted price for all products, including X.

4. When Josh gets to the checkout counter, the clerk asks, "Do you have any coupons today?" Josh says yes and gives the clerk a coupon for product X. Josh pays a lower price for it than Linda pays.

Thus, one of the uses of the cents-off coupon is to enable the seller to charge a higher price to one group of customers than to another group. (We say *one* of the uses because cents-off coupons are also used to induce customers to try a product.)

ECONOMICS 24/7

Buying a Computer and Getting a Printer for $100 Less Than the Retail Price

Some computer companies offer a rebate on a printer if you first buy a computer. In other words, buy the computer for $1,400 and then get $100 off the price of a printer that sells for $250. Instead of paying $1,650 for a computer and a printer, you pay $1,550.

But at the time of purchase, you pay $1,650, not $1,550. Afterward, you can submit a rebate-request form online for the $100 rebate. So you pay $1,650, fill out the form, submit it, and get the $100 rebate.

Now, the computer company could do things differently. It could certainly discount the computer plus printer at the time of purchase; that is, it could ask you to pay only $1,550 at the time of purchase. That way, there would be no rebate form to fill out and to process and no rebate check to send to the customer. But the company does not do things this way. Why not?

The answer has to do with price discrimination. The company will end up charging some customers $1,550, and other customers $1,650, for the computer and printer. It charges the lower price to the customers who submit the rebate form. It charges the higher price to the customers who do not submit the form.

By offering the $100 rebate, the company is effectively separating customers according to the value they place on their time. (See the earlier section "Coupons and Price Discrimination.") Some sellers think that people who value their time more will pay a higher price for a product than those who value their time less. The company can separate those customers by offering a price reduction in the form of a rebate and then waiting to see who requests the rebate. To those who request it, the company gives the rebate. These customers are the ones who aren't as willing to pay as much for the product as others are.

SELF-TEST

1. What are some of the costs, or shortcomings, of monopoly?

2. What is the deadweight loss of monopoly?

3. Why must a seller be a price searcher (among other things) before he can price discriminate?

OFFICE HOURS

"Does the Single-Price Monopolist Lower Price Only on the Additional Unit?"

STUDENT: You said that a single-price monopolist has to lower its price to sell an additional unit of the good it produces. Does this statement mean that it can sell the first unit of a good for, say, $20, but that if it wants to sell a second unit, it has to lower the price to, say, $19?

INSTRUCTOR: I would say things a little differently. If the monopoly firm wants to sell one unit, it charges $20, but if it wants to sell two units, it must charge $19 for each of the two units.

STUDENT: How is what you said different from what I said?

INSTRUCTOR: I spoke of two units instead of the second unit.

STUDENT: I don't see the critical difference.

INSTRUCTOR: Your statement made it sound as though the monopolist earned $20 on the first unit and $19 on the second unit, but this is not how things work for a single-price monopolist. A single-price monopolist has to charge the same price for *every unit* of the good it sells. In other words, if it sells 100 units, it sells each of the 100 units for the same price. It doesn't sell the first unit for $20, the second unit for $19, and so on.

STUDENT: But I'm still confused. We know that a monopoly firm has to lower its price to sell an additional unit, so why can't we just say that it has to lower its price to sell the *second* unit?

INSTRUCTOR: Because it has to lower the price on the previous (the first) unit, too, if it wants to sell two units. To illustrate, suppose the price of a good is $20 and at this price the quantity demanded is 1 unit. At a price of $19, the quantity demanded rises to 2 units. What you said implied that the firm would sell the first unit for $20. Then, with that transaction done, it considers whether it wants to sell an additional unit (the second unit). If it does, it charges $19 for it. That's not the way things happen. The firm—from the beginning, before any units of the good have been sold—has to decide whether it wants to sell 1 unit or 2. If it wants to sell only 1 unit, it charges $20. If it wants to sell 2 units, it sells each unit for $19.

STUDENT: I think I understand now. That's what you must have meant in class when you said that the word "additional" doesn't refer to a sequence of events, as in "sell the first unit, then sell the additional unit (the second unit), and so on." Instead, the story is, "sell 1 unit at $4, *or* sell two units at $3 each, *or* sell three units at $2 each, and so on."

INSTRUCTOR: Yes, that's correct.

Points to Remember

1. A single-price monopolist must lower its price to sell an additional unit of the good it produces.

2. The lower price (necessary to sell an additional unit) applies to the additional unit and *to all units that preceded it*.

CHAPTER SUMMARY

THE THEORY OF MONOPOLY

- The theory of monopoly is built on three assumptions: (1) There is one seller. (2) The single seller sells a product for which there are no close substitutes. (3) The barriers to entry into the industry are extremely high.

- High barriers to entry may take the form of legal barriers (public franchises, patents, government licenses), economies of scale, or exclusive ownership of a scarce resource.

MONOPOLY PRICING AND OUTPUT

- The profit-maximizing monopolist produces the quantity of output at which $MR = MC$ and charges the highest price per unit at which this quantity of output can be sold.

- For the single-price monopolist, $P > MR$; therefore, its demand curve lies above its marginal revenue curve.

- The single-price monopolist sells its output at a price higher than its marginal cost ($P > MC$) and therefore is *not* resource allocative efficient.

- Consider a perfectly competitive market and a monopoly market, each with the same demand and marginal cost curves. Consumers' surplus is greater in the perfectly competitive market.

RENT SEEKING

- Activity directed at competing for and obtaining transfers is referred to as rent seeking. From society's perspective, rent seeking is a socially wasteful activity. People use resources to bring about a transfer of income from others to themselves instead of producing goods and services.

PRICE DISCRIMINATION

- Price discrimination occurs when a seller charges different prices for its product and the price differences are not due to cost differences.

- Before a seller can price discriminate, certain conditions must hold: (1) The seller must be a price searcher. (2) The seller must be able to distinguish among customers who are willing to pay different prices. (3) Reselling the good to others must be impossible or too costly for a buyer.

- A seller that practices perfect price discrimination (charges the maximum price for each unit of product sold) sells the quantity of output at which $P = MC$. This kind of seller exhibits resource allocative efficiency.

- The single-price monopolist is said to produce too little output because it produces less than would be produced under perfect competition. This is not the case for a perfectly price-discriminating monopolist.

KEY TERMS AND CONCEPTS

Monopoly	Deadweight Loss of	Price Discrimination	Third-Degree Price
Public Franchise	Monopoly	Perfect Price Discrimination	Discrimination
Natural Monopoly	Rent Seeking	Second-Degree Price	Arbitrage
Price Searcher	X-Inefficiency	Discrimination	

QUESTIONS AND PROBLEMS

1. The perfectly competitive firm exhibits resource allocative efficiency ($P = MC$), but the single-price monopolist does not. What is the reason for this difference?

2. Because the monopolist is a single seller of a product with no close substitutes, can it obtain any price for its good that it wants? Why or why not?

3. When a single-price monopolist maximizes profits, price is greater than marginal cost. In other words, buyers are willing to pay more for additional units of output than the units cost to produce. Given this situation, why doesn't the monopolist produce more?

4. Is there a deadweight loss if a firm produces the quantity of output at which price equals marginal cost? Explain.

5. Under what condition will a monopoly firm incur losses?

6. A perfectly competitive firm will produce more output and charge a lower (per-unit) price than a single-price monopoly firm. Do you agree or disagree with this statement? Explain your answer.

7. Rent seeking is individually rational but socially wasteful. Explain.

8. Occasionally, students accuse their instructors, rightly or wrongly, of practicing grade discrimination. These students claim that the instructor "charges" some students a higher price for a given grade than he or she charges other students (by requiring some students to do more or better work). Unlike price discrimination, grade discrimination involves no money. Discuss the similarities and differences between the two types of discrimination. Which do you prefer less or perhaps dislike more? Why?

9. Make a list of real-world price discrimination practices. Do they meet the conditions posited for price discrimination?

10. For many years in California, car washes would advertise Ladies' Day: On one day during the week, a woman could have her car washed for a price lower than what a man would pay. Some people argued that this was a form of sexual discrimination. A California court accepted the argument and ruled that car washes could no longer have a Ladies' Day. Do you think that this was a case of sexual discrimination or price discrimination? Explain your answer.

11. Make a list of market monopolies and a list of government monopolies. Which list is longer? Why do you think this is so?

12. Fast-food stores often charge higher prices for their products in high-crime areas than they charge in low-crime areas. Is this an act of price discrimination? Why or why not?

13. Coupons tend to be more common on small-ticket items than they are on big-ticket items. Explain why.

14. A firm maximizes its total revenue. Does it automatically maximize its profit too? Why or why not?

WORKING WITH NUMBERS AND GRAPHS

1. Draw a graph that shows a monopoly firm incurring losses.

2. A monopoly firm is currently earning positive economic profit, and the owner decides to sell it. He asks for a price that takes into account the economic profit. Explain and diagrammatically show what a price that takes into account economic profit does to the average total cost (ATC) curve of the firm.

3. Suppose a single-price monopolist sells its output Q_1 at P_1. Then it raises its price to P_2, and its output falls to Q_2. In terms of Ps and Qs, what does this monopolist's marginal revenue equal?

Use the accompanying figure to answer questions 4–6:

4. If the market is perfectly competitive, how much does profit equal?

5. If the market is a monopoly market, how much does profit equal?

6. Redraw the figure and label consumers' surplus when the market is perfectly competitive and when it is monopolized.

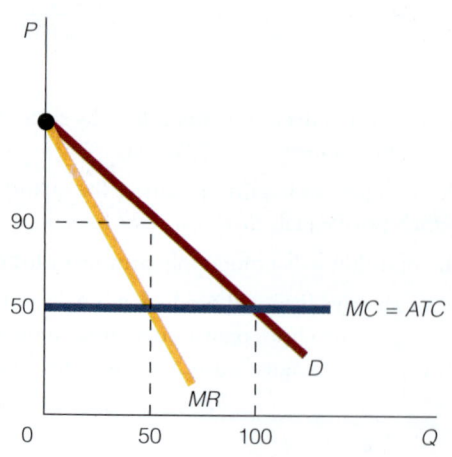

CHAPTER 11

MONOPOLISTIC COMPETITION, OLIGOPOLY, AND GAME THEORY

Stephen Bardens/Alamy Stock Photo

INTRODUCTION

How do firms in a market act toward one another? Are they fiercely competitive, much like runners in a race to the finish line, where only one can be the winner? Or do firms act like people strolling in a park on a warm spring day, without a care in the world and certainly without competition on their minds? As you read this chapter, keep these two images in mind. Also, keep two words in mind: *competition* and *collusion*. This chapter is about both.

11-1 THE THEORY OF MONOPOLISTIC COMPETITION

The theory of **monopolistic competition** is built on three assumptions:

1. *There are many sellers and buyers.* This assumption holds for perfect competition too. For that reason, you might think that the monopolistic competitor should be a price taker, but it is a price searcher, basically because of the next assumption.

2. *Each firm (in the industry) produces and sells a slightly differentiated product.* Differences among the products may be due to brand names, packaging, location, credit terms connected with the sale of the product, the friendliness of the salespeople, and so forth. Product differentiation may be real or imagined. For example, aspirin may be aspirin, but if some people view a name-brand aspirin (such as Bayer®) as better than a generic brand, product differentiation exists.

3. *Entry and exit are easy.* Monopolistic competition resembles perfect competition in this respect. There are no barriers to entry and exit, legal or otherwise. Examples of industries with monopolistic competition include retail clothing, computer software, restaurants, and service stations.

Monopolistic Competition
A theory of market structure based on three assumptions: many sellers and buyers, firms producing and selling slightly differentiated products, and easy entry and exit.

287

11-1a The Monopolistic Competitor's Demand Curve

The perfectly competitive firm has many rivals, all producing the same good, so the good that it produces has an endless number of substitutes. Accordingly, the elasticity of demand for its product is extremely high—so high, in fact, that the demand curve it faces is horizontal (for all practical purposes).

The monopoly firm has practically no rivals, and it produces a good that has no substitutes. The elasticity of demand for its product is low, as partly reflected by its downward-sloping demand curve.

The monopolistic competitor, like the perfectly competitive firm, has many rivals. But unlike the rivals of the perfectly competitive firm, the monopolistic competitor's rivals do not sell exactly the same product that the monopolistic competitor sells. Because its product has substitutes, but not perfect ones, the elasticity of demand for the monopolistic competitor's product is not as great as that of the perfectly competitive firm. Nor does its demand curve look like the one faced by the perfectly competitive firm. The monopolistic competitor's demand curve is not horizontal; it is downward sloping.

11-1b The Relationship between Price and Marginal Revenue for a Monopolistic Competitor

Because a monopolistic competitor faces a downward-sloping demand curve, it has to lower its price to sell an additional unit of the good it produces. (It is a price searcher.) For example, let's say that it can sell 3 units at $10 each but that it has to lower its price to $9 to sell 4 units. Its marginal revenue is therefore $6 (total revenue at 3 units is $30, and total revenue at 4 units is $36), which is below its price of $9. Thus, for the monopolistic competitor $P > MR$.

11-1c Output, Price, and Marginal Cost for the Monopolistic Competitor

The monopolistically competitive firm is the same as both the perfectly competitive firm and the monopoly firm in one regard: it produces the quantity of output at which $MR = MC$. In Exhibit 1, the firm produces q_1. For this quantity, the monopolistic competitor charges the highest price it can charge: P_1 in the exhibit.

For the monopolistic competitor, $P > MR$. Because the monopolistic competitor produces the quantity of output at which $MR = MC$, it must produce a level of output at which price is greater than marginal cost ($P > MC$), as is obvious in Exhibit 1.

11-1d Will There Be Profits in the Long Run?

If the firms in a monopolistically competitive market are currently earning profits, as is the firm in Exhibit 1, most likely they will not continue to earn profits in the long run. The assumption of easy entry and exit precludes this possibility. If firms in the industry are earning profits, new

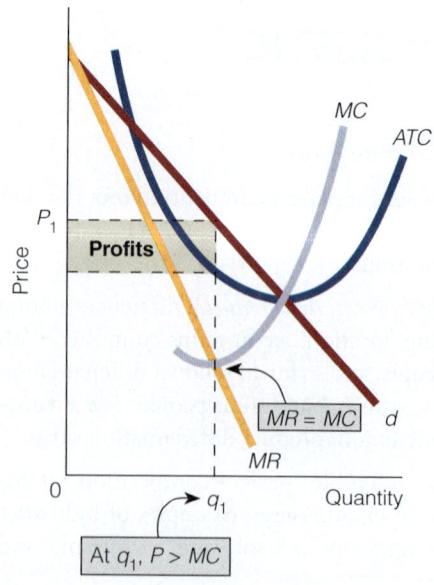

EXHIBIT 1

The Monopolistically Competitive Firm's Output and Price

The monopolistic competitor produces that quantity of output for which $MR = MC$. This quantity is q_1 in the exhibit. The monopolistic competitor charges the highest price consistent with q_1, namely, P_1.

Labels in figure: MC, ATC, P_1, Price, Profits, $MR = MC$, d, MR, q_1, Quantity, At q_1, $P > MC$

firms will enter the industry and reduce the demand that each firm faces. In other words, the demand curve for each firm may shift to the left. Eventually, in the long run, competition will reduce economic profits to zero, as is shown for the monopolistically competitive firm in Exhibit 2.

Note, however, that the answer to the question of whether firms will continue to earn profits in the long run was "most likely" they won't, instead of no. In monopolistic competition, new firms usually produce a *close substitute* for the product made by existing firms, not an *identical* one. In some instances, this difference may be enough to upset the zero economic profit condition in the long run. An existing firm may be able to differentiate its product sufficiently in the minds of buyers such that it continues to earn profits, even though new firms enter the industry and compete with it.

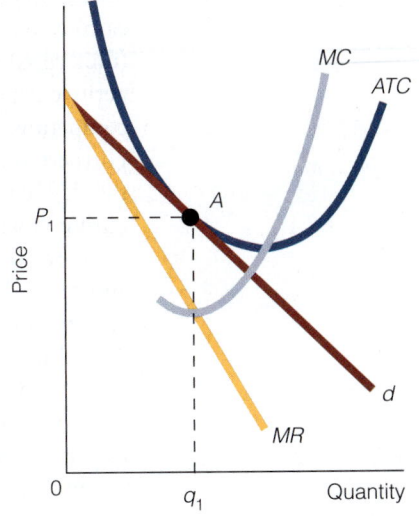

EXHIBIT 2

Monopolistic Competition in the Long Run

Because of easy entry into the industry, there are likely to be zero economic profits in the long run for a monopolistic competitor. In other words, $P = ATC$.

Firms that try to differentiate their products from those of other sellers in ways other than price are said to be engaged in *nonprice competition*. This type of competition may take the form of advertising or of trying to establish a well-respected brand name, among other efforts. For example, soft-drink companies' advertising often tries to stress the uniqueness of their product. In the past, Dr. Pepper has been advertised as "the unusual one" and 7-Up as "the uncola." In a similar vein, Wheaties has been promoted as the "breakfast of champions," and Budweiser as the "king of beers." Apple has a well-respected name in personal computers, Bayer in aspirin, and Marriott in hotels. Such well-respected names sometimes differentiate products sufficiently in the minds of buyers so that short-run profits are not easily or not completely eliminated by the entry of new firms into the industry.

FINDING ECONOMICS

In an Online Radio Service Abbie just found an online radio station that plays the songs and artists she wants to hear. She types in the title of the song or the name of the artist she would like to hear, and the service creates a virtual radio station just for her. Where is the economics?

Firms can compete in terms of price (price competition) or in areas other than price (nonprice competition). With respect to free radio (radio you do not pay to hear), radio stations cannot compete on price, so they must turn to nonprice competition. Customizing a radio station for a listener is a nonprice way of competing for listeners.

11-1e Excess Capacity: What Is It, and Is It "Good" or "Bad"?

The theory of monopolistic competition makes a major prediction, which is generally referred to as the **excess capacity theorem**: A monopolistic competitor will produce an output smaller than the one that would minimize its unit costs of production.

Excess Capacity Theorem
A monopolistic competitor in equilibrium produces an output smaller than the one that would minimize its costs of production.

At point A in Exhibit 3(a), the monopolistic competitor is in long-run equilibrium because profits are zero $(P = ATC)$. Point A is *not* the lowest point on the average total cost curve; the lowest point is point L. Therefore, in long-run equilibrium, when the monopolistic competitor earns zero economic profits, it is not producing the quantity of output at which average total costs (unit costs) are minimized, given the scale of the plant. Exhibit 3 contrasts the perfectly competitive firm and the monopolistic competitor in long-run equilibrium. In part (b), the perfectly competitive firm is earning zero economic profits and price (P_{C_1}) equals average total cost (ATC). Furthermore, the point at which price equals average total cost (point L) is the lowest point on the ATC curve. In long-run equilibrium, the perfectly competitive firm produces the quantity of output at which unit costs are minimized.

Now look back at part (a). The monopolistic competitor is earning zero economic profits, and price (P_{MC_1}) equals average total cost. If the monopolistic competitor produced the quantity of output at which unit costs were minimized, it would produce q_{MC_2}. For this reason, it has been argued that the monopolistic competitor produces too little output (q_{MC_1} instead of q_{MC_2}) and charges too high a price (P_{MC_1} instead of P_{MC_2}). With respect to output, too little translates into the monopolistic competitor's underutilizing its present plant size; it is said to have *excess capacity*. In part (a), the excess capacity is equal to the difference of q_{MC_2} and q_{MC_1}.

Some have argued that the monopolistic competitor operates at excess capacity because it faces a downward-sloping demand curve. In Exhibit 3(a), the only way the firm would not operate at excess capacity is if its demand curve were tangent to the ATC curve at point L—the lowest point on the ATC curve. But for tangency at L to occur, the demand curve *would have to be horizontal*, a condition that would require homogeneous products. A downward-sloping demand curve *cannot* be tangent to the ATC curve at point L.

EXHIBIT 3

A Comparison of Perfect Competition and Monopolistic Competition: The Issue of Excess Capacity

The perfectly competitive firm produces a quantity of output consistent with lowest unit costs. The monopolistic competitor does not. If it did, it would produce q_{MC_2} instead of q_{MC_1}. The monopolistic competitor is said to underutilize its plant size or to have excess capacity.

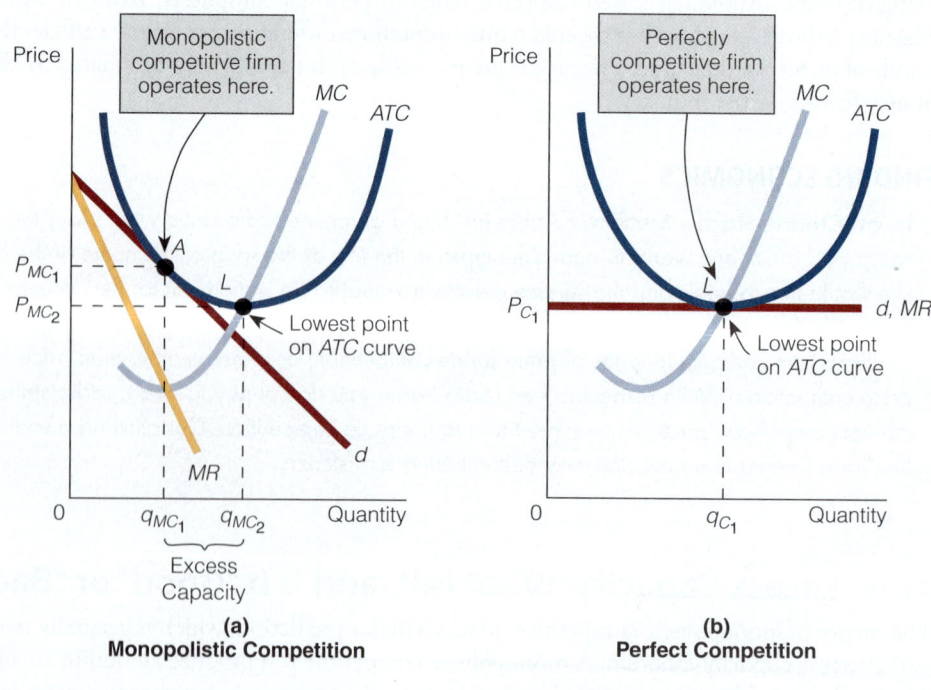

(a)
Monopolistic Competition

(b)
Perfect Competition

ECONOMICS 24/7

The People Wear Prada

Suppose you own a business that is considered a monopolistically competitive firm. Your business is one of many sellers, you sell a product slightly differentiated from the products of your competitors, and entry into and exit from the industry are easy. Would you rather your business were a monopoly firm? Wouldn't it be better for you to be the *only* seller of a product than to be one of many? Most business owners would answer yes, so we consider how monopolistic competitors may try to become monopolists.

One possibility is through a designer label. If a monopolistic competitor can, through the use of a designer label, persuade the buying public that her product is more than just slightly differentiated from those of her competitors, she stands a better chance of becoming a monopolist. (Remember that a monopolist produces a good that has *no* close substitutes.)

For example, many firms produce women's jeans, and, to many people, the jeans all look very much alike. To differentiate its product from the pack, a firm could add a designer label to the jeans to suggest uniqueness—that they are the only Calvin Klein Jeans, for example. For added impact, it could try to persuade the buying public through advertising that its jeans are "the" jeans worn by the most famous, best-looking people.

Think of a list of firms that have employed a designer label to try to outcompete their competitors: Gucci, Tommy Hilfiger, Perry Ellis, Liz Claiborne, Armani, Versace, Dolce & Gabbana, Prada, Valentino, Chanel, L. L. Bean, and many others.

Nata Sha/Shutterstock.com

In short, *the monopolistic competitor operates at excess capacity as a consequence of its downward-sloping demand curve*, and its downward-sloping demand curve is a consequence of differentiated products. A question that many economists ask, but not all answer in the same way, is this: *If excess capacity is the price we pay for differentiated products (more choice), is it too high a price?*

11-1f The Monopolistic Competitor and Two Types of Efficiency

We know that a firm is resource allocative efficient if it charges a price that is equal to its marginal cost—that is, if $P = MC$. Because the monopolistically competitive firm charges a price that is greater than marginal cost ($P > MC$), it is not resource allocative efficient.

We also know that a firm is productive efficient if it charges a price that is equal to its lowest ATC. Because the monopolistic competitor operates at excess capacity, it is not productive efficient.

SELF-TEST

(Answers to Self-Test questions are in Answers to Self-Test Questions at the back of the book.)

1. How is a monopolistic competitor like a monopolist? How is it like a perfect competitor?

2. Why do monopolistic competitors operate at excess capacity?

11-2 OLIGOPOLY: ASSUMPTIONS AND REAL-WORLD BEHAVIOR

Unlike perfect competition, monopoly, and monopolistic competition, there is no one accepted theory of **oligopoly**. However, the different theories of oligopoly have the following common assumptions:

1. *There are few sellers and many buyers.* The assumption is usually that the few firms of an oligopoly are interdependent; each one is aware that its actions influence the others and that the actions of the other firms affect it. This interdependence among firms is a key characteristic of oligopoly.

2. *Firms produce and sell either homogeneous or differentiated products.* Aluminum is a homogeneous product produced in an oligopolistic market; cars are a differentiated product produced in an oligopolistic market.

3. *The barriers to entry are significant.* Economies of scale constitute perhaps the most significant barrier to entry in an oligopoly, but patent rights, exclusive control of an essential resource, and legal obstacles also act as barriers to entry.

The oligopolist is a price searcher. Like all other firms, it produces the quantity of output at which $MR = MC$.

Oligopoly
A theory of market structure based on three assumptions: few sellers and many buyers, firms producing either homogeneous or differentiated products, and significant barriers to entry.

11-2a The Concentration Ratio

Which industries today are dominated by a small number of firms—that is, are oligopolistic? Economists have developed the *concentration ratio* to help answer this question. The **concentration ratio** is the percentage of industry sales (or assets, output, labor force, or some other factor) accounted for by x number of firms in the industry. The number x in the definition is usually four or eight, but it can be any number (although it is usually small):

Four-firm concentration ratio: CR_4 = Percentage of industry sales accounted for by four largest firms

Eight-firm concentration ratio: CR_8 = Percentage of industry sales accounted for by eight largest firms

Concentration Ratio
The percentage of industry sales (or assets, output, labor force, or some other factor) accounted for by x number of firms in the industry.

A high concentration ratio implies that few sellers make up the industry; a low concentration ratio implies that more than a few sellers make up the industry.

As an example, let's calculate a four-firm concentration ratio for industry Z. Suppose total industry sales for a given year are $5 million and the four largest firms in the industry account for $4.5 million in sales. The four-firm concentration ratio is 0.90, or 90 percent ($5 million × 0.90 = $4.5 million). Industries with high four- and eight-firm concentration ratios in recent years are cigarettes, cars, tires, cereal breakfast foods, farm machinery, and soap and other detergents, to name a few.

Although concentration ratios are often used to determine the extent (or degree) of oligopoly, they are not perfect guides to industry concentration. Most important, they do not take into account foreign competition and competition from substitute domestic goods. For example, the U.S. automobile industry is concentrated, but it still faces stiff competition from abroad. A more relevant concentration ratio for this particular industry might be one computed on a worldwide basis.

11-3 PRICE AND OUTPUT UNDER THE CARTEL THEORY

In this section we discuss why oligopoly firms might want to form a cartel and some of the problems they encounter in doing so.

11-3a The Cartel Theory

The key behavioral assumption of the **cartel theory** is that, within a given industry, oligopolists act as if there were only one firm. In short, they form a cartel to capture the benefits that would exist for a monopolist. A **cartel** is an organization of firms that reduces output and increases price in an effort to increase joint profits.

Forming and maintaining a cartel has its benefits. Exhibit 4 shows an industry in long-run competitive equilibrium. Price is P_1, and quantity of output is Q_1. The industry is producing the output at which price equals marginal cost, and economic profits are zero. Now, suppose the firms making up the industry form a cartel and reduce output to Q_C. Then the new price is P_C (the cartel price), and profits, which are equal to the area CP_CAB, can be shared among the members of the cartel. With no cartel, there are no profits; with a cartel, profits are earned. Thus, the firms have an incentive to form a cartel and to behave cooperatively rather than competitively.

However, firms may not be able to form a cartel, even though they have a profit incentive to do so. Also, even if they are able to form the cartel, the firms may not be able to maintain it. Firms that wish to form and maintain a cartel will encounter several problems, two of which are that legislation prohibits certain types

Cartel Theory
A theory of oligopoly in which oligopolistic firms act as if there were only one firm in the industry.

Cartel
An organization of firms that reduces output and increases price in an effort to increase joint profits.

EXHIBIT 4

The Benefits of a Cartel (to Cartel Members)

We assume that the industry is in long-run competitive equilibrium, producing Q_1 and charging P_1. There are no profits. A reduction in output to Q_C through the formation of a cartel raises prices to P_C and brings profits of CP_CAB. (*Note:* In an earlier chapter, a horizontal demand curve faces the *firm*. Here a downward-sloping demand curve faces the *industry*. Don't be misled by this difference. No matter what type of demand curve we use, long-run competitive equilibrium is where $P = MC = SRATC = LRATC$.)

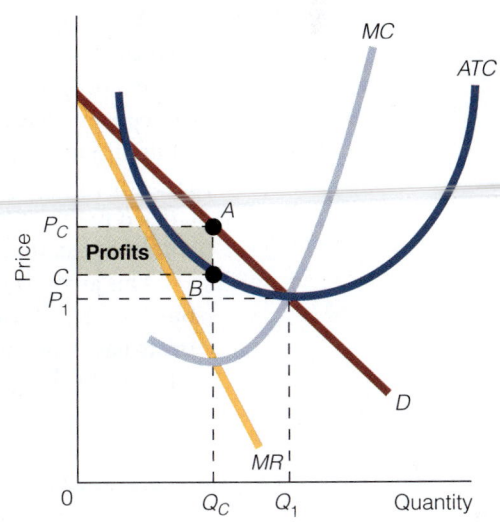

of cartels in the United States and organizing and forming a cartel involves costs as well as benefits.[1]

The Problem of Forming the Cartel   Even if it were legal, getting the sellers of an industry together to form a cartel can be costly, even when the number of sellers is small. Each potential cartel member may resist incurring the costs of forming the cartel because it stands to benefit more if other firms do the work. In other words, each potential member has an incentive to be a free rider—to stand by and take a free ride on the actions of others.

The Problem of Formulating Cartel Policy   Even if prospective firms form a cartel, the problem of formulating policy arises. For example, firm A might propose that each cartel member reduce output by 10 percent, and firm B might advocate that all bigger cartel members reduce output by 15 percent and all smaller members reduce output by 5 percent. In fact, there may be as many policy proposals as there are cartel members, and reaching agreement may be difficult. Such disagreements become harder to resolve as the differences among cartel members in costs, size, and so forth, grow.

The Problem of Entry into the Industry   Even if the cartel members manage to agree on a policy that generates high profits, those high profits will provide an incentive for firms outside the industry to join the industry. If current cartel members cannot keep new suppliers from entering, the cartel is likely to break up.

The Problem of Cheating   As paradoxical as it first appears, after the cartel agreement is made, members have an incentive to cheat on it. Exhibit 5 shows three situations for a *representative firm* of the cartel: (1) the situation before the cartel is formed, (2) the situation after the cartel is formed when all members adhere to the cartel price, and (3) the situation if the firm cheats on the cartel agreement but the other cartel members do not.

Before the cartel is formed, the firm in the exhibit is in long-run competitive equilibrium; it produces output q_1, charges price P_1, and earns zero economic profits. After the cartel is formed, the firm reduces its output to q_C, as directed by the cartel (the cartel has set a quota for each member), and it charges the cartel price of P_C. Now the firm earns profits equal to the area CP_CAB.

What happens if the firm cheats on the cartel agreement and produces q_{CC} instead of the stipulated q_C? As long as other firms do not cheat, this firm views its demand curve as horizontal at the cartel price (P_C). The reason is simple: Because it is one of a number of firms, our hypothetical representative firm cannot affect price by changing output. Therefore, it can produce and sell additional units of output without lowering its price. So, if the firm cheats on the cartel agreement and other firms do not, then the cheating firm can increase its profits from the smaller amount CP_CAB to the larger amount FP_CDE. Of course, if all the firms cheat, the cartel members are back where they started—with no cartel agreement and at price P_1.

This analysis illustrates a major theme of cartels: firms have an incentive to form a cartel, but once it is formed, they have an incentive to cheat. As a result of this flaw, some economists have concluded that, even if cartels are formed successfully, they are not likely to be effective for long.

---

[1] Sometimes, economists discuss the benefits and costs of organizing a cartel without specifying the market structure. We have followed suit here by broadening our discussion of cartel theory to include market structures other than oligopoly. This broadening of the discussion will be noticeable in places. For example, even though there are few sellers in oligopoly, we discuss cartel theory in the context of both few and many sellers.

EXHIBIT 5

The Benefits of Cheating on the Cartel Agreement

In the exhibit we see the situation for a representative firm of a cartel. In long-run competitive equilibrium, the firm produces q_1 and charges P_1, earning zero economic profits. As a consequence of the cartel agreement, it reduces its output to q_C and charges P_C. Its profits are the area CP_CAB. If the firm cheats on the cartel agreement and others do not, it will increase output to q_{CC} and reap profits of FP_CDE. Note, however, that if this firm can cheat on the cartel agreement, so can others. Given the monetary benefits gained by cheating, it is likely that the cartel will exist for only a short time.

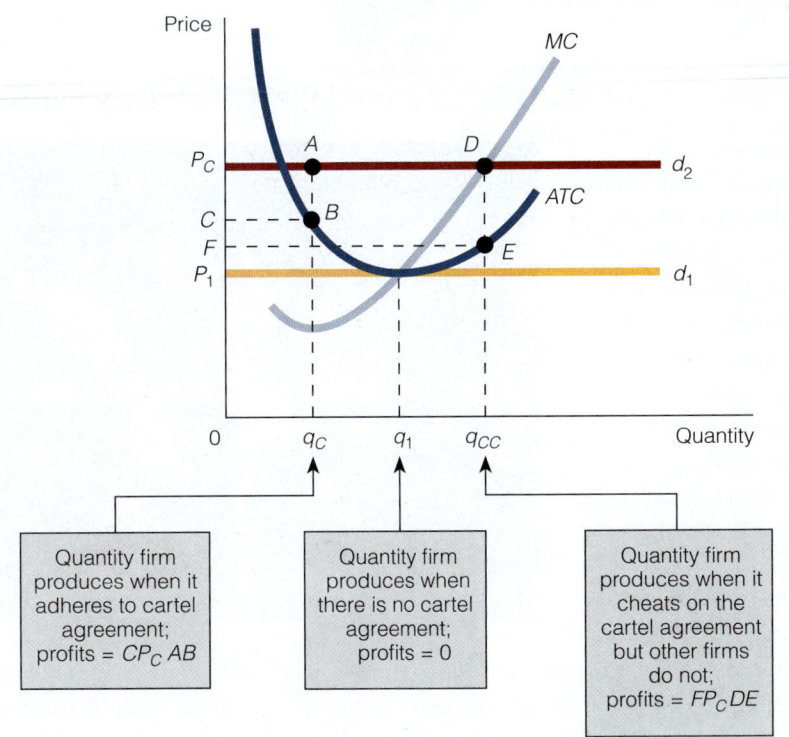

Quantity firm produces when it adheres to cartel agreement; profits = $CP_C AB$

Quantity firm produces when there is no cartel agreement; profits = 0

Quantity firm produces when it cheats on the cartel agreement but other firms do not; profits = $FP_C DE$

THINKING LIKE AN ECONOMIST

The Target Sometimes Moves In economics, there are moving targets. Consider the target of higher profits for the firms in an oligopolistic industry. After the firms form a cartel to capture the higher profits, the target moves to the point where a cartel member must cheat on the cartel to hit the target. But if all cartel members take aim at the target's new position, the target moves back to its original position—at which cartel members must agree to stop cheating.

The layperson may think that an economic objective, or economic target, is stationary. All an economic actor has to do to hit it is to take careful aim. But the economist knows that sometimes the target moves, and a careful aim is not always enough.

SELF-TEST

1. "Firms have an incentive to form a cartel, but once it is formed, they have an incentive to cheat." What is the specific incentive to form the cartel? What is the incentive to cheat on the cartel?

2. Is an oligopolistic firm a price taker or a price searcher? Explain your answer.

ECONOMICS 24/7

How Is a New Year's Resolution Like a Cartel Agreement?

In a cartel, one firm makes an agreement with another firm or other firms. In a New Year's resolution, you essentially make an agreement with yourself. So both cases—the cartel and the resolution—involve an agreement.

Both cases also raise the possibility of cheating on the agreement. Suppose your New Year's resolution is to exercise more, take better notes in class, and read one good book a month. You might set such objectives because you know you will be better off in the long run if you do these things. Then the short run enters into the picture. You have to decide between exercising today or plopping down in your favorite chair and watching television. You have to decide between starting to read *Moby Dick* or catching up on the latest entertainment news in *People* magazine. The part of you that wants to hold to the resolution is at odds with the part of you that wants to watch television or read *People*. Often, the television-watching, *People*-reading part wins out. Breaking a New Year's resolution—as you probably already know—is just too easy.

So is breaking a cartel agreement. For the firm that has entered into the agreement, the lure of higher profits is often too strong to resist. In addition, the firm is concerned that, if it doesn't break the agreement (and cheat), some other firm might,

Hero Images Inc./Alamy Stock Photo

and then it will have lost out completely.

In short, both resolutions and cartel agreements take a lot of willpower to hold them together. Willpower, however, seems to be in particularly short supply, and something is needed to take its place. Both a resolution and a cartel agreement need something if they are to endure: Something or someone has to exact a penalty from the party who breaks the resolution or cartel agreement. Government sometimes plays this role for firms. Family members and friends occasionally play the role for individuals by reminding or reprimanding them if they fail to live up to their resolutions. (Usually, though, family members and friends are not successful.)

So, we draw the following conclusions:

- First, an agreement is at the heart of both a New Year's resolution and a cartel.

- Second, both the resolution and the cartel are subject to cheating behavior.

- Third, if the resolution and the cartel are to have a long life, they often need someone or something to prevent each party from breaking the agreement.

11-4 GAME THEORY, OLIGOPOLY, AND CONTESTABLE MARKETS

Of the four market structures (perfect competition, monopoly, monopolistic competition, and oligopoly), oligopoly is often described as the most difficult to analyze. Analysis is difficult because of the interdependence among firms in such a market. Economists often use game theory to get a workable understanding of the interdependence of oligopoly firms.

Game theory is a mathematical technique used to analyze the behavior of decision makers who (1) try to reach an optimal position through game playing or the use of strategic behavior, (2) are fully aware of the interactive nature of the process at hand, and (3) anticipate the moves of other decision makers.

In this section, we describe a famous game and then use it to discuss oligopoly behavior. We also discuss the issue of contestable markets.

11-4a Prisoner's Dilemma

A well-known game in game theory, the prisoner's dilemma illustrates a case in which individually rational behavior leads to a jointly inefficient outcome. The lesson of the game has been described this way: "You do what is best for you, I'll do what is best for me, and somehow we end up in a situation that is not best for either of us." Here is how the game is played.

The Facts Two men, Bob and Nathan, are arrested and charged with jointly committing a crime. They are put into separate cells so that they cannot communicate with each other. The district attorney (DA) goes to each man separately and says the following:

- If you confess to the crime and agree to turn state's evidence and if your accomplice does not confess, I will let you off with a $500 fine.

- If your accomplice confesses to the crime and agrees to turn state's evidence and if you do not confess, I will fine you $5,000.

- If both you and your accomplice remain silent and refuse to confess to the crime, I will charge you with a lesser crime, which I can prove you committed, and you and your accomplice will pay fines of $2,000 each.

- If both you and your accomplice confess, I will fine each of you $3,000.

The Options and Consequences Each man has two choices: confess or not confess, as shown in the grid in Exhibit 6. The grid shows the following possibilities laid out by the district attorney:

- *Box 1*. If both men do not confess, each pays a fine of $2,000.

- *Box 2*. If Nathan confesses and Bob does not, then Nathan gets off with the light fine of $500 and Bob pays the stiff penalty of $5,000.

Game Theory
A mathematical technique used to analyze the behavior of decision makers who try to reach an optimal position for themselves through game playing or the use of strategic behavior, who are fully aware of the interactive nature of the process at hand, and who anticipate the moves of other decision makers.

EXHIBIT 6

Prisoner's Dilemma

Nathan and Bob each have two choices: confess or not confess. No matter what Bob does, it is always better for Nathan to confess. No matter what Nathan does, it is always better for Bob to confess. Both Nathan and Bob confess and end up in box 4, with each paying a $3,000 fine. Both men would have been better off had they not confessed. That way they would have ended up in box 1, paying a $2,000 fine.

	Nathan's Choices	
	Not Confess	Confess
Bob's Choices Not Confess	**1** Nathan pays $2,000. Bob pays $2,000.	**2** Nathan pays $500. Bob pays $5,000.
Bob's Choices Confess	**3** Nathan pays $5,000. Bob pays $500.	**4** Nathan pays $3,000. Bob pays $3,000.

- *Box 3*. If Nathan does not confess and Bob confesses, then Nathan pays the stiff penalty of $5,000 and Bob pays the light fine of $500.

- *Box 4*. Finally, if both men confess, each pays $3,000.

What Nathan Thinks Nathan considers his choices and their possible outcomes. He reasons to himself, "I have two options, confess or not confess, and Bob has the same two options. Let me ask myself two questions:

- "*If Bob chooses not to confess, what is the best thing for me to do?* The answer is to confess, because, if I do not confess, I will end up in box 1, paying $2,000, but if I confess, I will end up in box 2, paying only $500. No doubt about it: If Bob chooses not to confess, I should confess."

- "*If Bob chooses to confess, what is the best thing for me to do?* The answer is also to confess, because, if I do not confess, I will end up in box 3, paying $5,000, but if I confess, I will pay $3,000. No doubt about it: If Bob chooses to confess, I should confess."

Nathan's Conclusion Nathan concludes that, no matter what Bob chooses to do—not confess or confess—he (Nathan) is always better off if he confesses. Therefore, Nathan decides to confess to the crime.

The Situation Is the Same for Bob Bob goes through the same mental process that Nathan does. Asking himself the same two questions Nathan asked himself, Bob gets the same answers and draws the same conclusion. Therefore, Bob decides to confess to the crime.

The Outcome The DA goes to each man and asks him what he has decided. Both Nathan and Bob say, "I confess." The outcome is shown in box 4, with each man paying a fine of $3,000.

Now Look Where They Could Be Another outcome represented by one of the four boxes is better for both Nathan and Bob than the one whereby each pays $3,000: In box 1, both Nathan and Bob pay $2,000. To get to box 1, all the two men had to do was keep silent and not confess.

Changing the Game What would happen if the DA gave Nathan and Bob another chance? Suppose she tells them that she will not accept their confessions. Instead, she wants them to talk it over together for 10 minutes, after which time she will come back, place each man in a separate room, and ask for his decision. The second time, she will accept each man's decision, no matter what.

Will a second chance change the outcome? Most people will say yes, arguing that Nathan and Bob will now see that their best choice is to remain silent so that each ends up with a $2,000 fine instead of a $3,000 fine. Let's assume that they do see this and Nathan and Bob enter into an agreement to remain silent.

Nathan's Thoughts on the Way to His Room The DA returns and takes Nathan to a separate room. On the way, Nathan thinks to himself, "I'm not sure I can trust Bob. Suppose he goes back on our agreement and confesses. If I hold to the agreement and he doesn't, he'll end up with a $500 fine and I'll end up paying $5,000. Of course, if I break the agreement and confess and he holds to the agreement, then I'll reduce my fine to $500. Maybe the best thing for me to do is break the agreement and confess, hoping that he doesn't, and I'll pay only $500. If I'm not so lucky, at least I'll protect myself from paying $5,000."

Once in the room, the DA asks Nathan what his decision is. He says, "I confess."

The Situation Is the Same for Bob Bob sees the situation in the same way that Nathan does and again chooses to confess.

The Outcome Again Both men end up confessing a second time. Each pays $3,000, realizing that if they had been silent and kept to their agreement, their fine would be only $2,000 each.

11-4b Oligopoly Firms' Cartels and the Prisoner's Dilemma

When oligopoly firms enter into a cartel agreement, do they create a prisoner's dilemma? Most economists answer yes. To illustrate, suppose two firms, A and B, produce and sell the same product and are in stiff competition with each other. In fact, the competition is so stiff that each firm earns only $10,000 in profits. Soon the two firms decide to enter into a cartel agreement in which each agrees to raise prices and, after prices are raised, not to undercut the other. If they hold to the agreement, each firm will earn profits of $50,000. But if one firm holds to the cartel agreement and the other does not, the one that does not will earn profits of $100,000 and the one that does will earn $5,000 in profits. Of course, if neither holds to the agreement, then both will be back where they started, earning $10,000 in profits. The choices for the two firms and the possible outcomes are outlined in Exhibit 7.

Each firm is likely to behave as the two prisoners did in the prisoner's dilemma game. Each firm will see the chance to earn $100,000 by breaking the agreement (instead of $50,000 by holding to it); each will also realize that if it does not break the agreement and the other firm does, it will be in a worse situation than it was before entering into the cartel. Most economists predict that the two firms will end up in box 4 in Exhibit 7, earning the profits they did before they entered into the agreement. In sum, they will cheat on the cartel agreement and again be in competition—the very situation they wanted to escape.

EXHIBIT 7

Cartels and the Prisoner's Dilemma

Many economists suggest that firms trying to form a cartel are in a prisoner's dilemma situation. Both firms A and B earn higher profits holding to a (cartel) agreement than not, but each will earn even higher profits if it breaks the agreement while the other firm holds to it. We predict that, if cartel formation is a prisoner's dilemma situation, then cartels will be short-lived.

	Firm A's Choices	
	Hold to Agreement	Break Agreement
Firm B's Choices — Hold to Agreement	**1** A earns $50,000 profits. B earns $50,000 profits.	**2** A earns $100,000 profits. B earns $5,000 profits.
Firm B's Choices — Break Agreement	**3** A earns $5,000 profits. B earns $100,000 profits.	**4** A earns $10,000 profits. B earns $10,000 profits.

The only way out of the prisoner's dilemma for the two firms is to have some entity enforce the cartel agreement so that the two firms do not cheat. As odd as it may sound, sometimes government has played this role. Normally, we think of government as trying to break up cartel agreements because, after all, such agreements are illegal. Nevertheless, sometimes government acts as the enforcer, not the eliminator, of cartel agreements.

For example, the Civil Aeronautics Board (CAB) was created in the days of airline regulation to protect the airlines from so-called cutthroat competition. The CAB had the power to set airfares, allocate air routes, and prevent the entry of new carriers into the airline industry. In the days before deregulation, the federal government's General Accounting Office estimated that airline fares would have been, on average, as much as 52 percent lower if the CAB had not been regulating them. Clearly, the CAB was doing for the airlines what an airline cartel would have done: prevent price competition, allocate routes, and prevent new entries into the industry.

In a similar vein, Judge Richard Posner has observed that "the railroads supported the enactment of the first Interstate Commerce Act, which was designed to prevent railroads from price discrimination, because discrimination was undermining the railroad's cartels."[2]

11-4c Are Markets Contestable?

Market structures, from perfect competition to oligopoly, have been traditionally defined in terms of the *number of sellers*. In perfect competition, there are many sellers; in monopoly, there is only one; in monopolistic competition, there are many; in oligopoly, there are few. The message is that the number of sellers in a market influences their behavior. For example, the monopoly seller is more likely to restrict output and charge higher prices than is the perfect competitor.

Some economists have shifted the emphasis from the number of sellers in a market to the issue of *entry into and exit from an industry*. This shift brings us to a discussion of contestable markets. A **contestable market** is a market in which the following conditions are met:

Contestable Market
A market in which entry is easy and exit is costless, new firms can produce the product at the same cost as current firms, and exiting firms can easily dispose of their fixed assets by selling them.

1. *Entry into the market is easy, and exit from it is costless.*

2. *New firms entering the market can produce the product at the same cost that current firms produce it.*

3. *Firms exiting the market can easily dispose of their fixed assets by selling them elsewhere.* In other words, except for depreciation, fixed costs are not sunk but recoverable.

Suppose that eight firms are in an industry and that all of them are earning profits. Then, firms outside the industry notice the situation and decide to enter the industry. (By condition 1, nothing prevents their entry.) They acquire the necessary equipment and produce the product at the same cost that current producers do. Time passes, and the firms that entered the industry decide to exit it. They can either switch their machinery into another line of production or sell their equipment for what they paid for it, less depreciation.

Perhaps the most important element of a contestable market is so-called hit-and-run entry and exit. New entrants can enter (hit), produce the product, take profits from current firms, and then exit costlessly (run).

The theory of contestable markets has been criticized because of its assumptions—in particular, the assumption that entry into the industry is free and exit is costless. However, even though this theory, like most theories, does not describe the real world perfectly, it has its usefulness.

At a minimum, the contestable markets theory has rattled orthodox market structure theory. Here are a few of its conclusions:

1. Even if an industry is composed of a small number of firms—or even just one firm—the firms do not necessarily perform in a noncompetitive way. They might be extremely competitive if the market they are in is contestable.

2. Profits can be zero in an industry even if the number of sellers in the industry is small.

3. If a market is contestable, inefficient producers cannot survive. Cost inefficiencies invite lower cost producers into the market, driving price down to the minimum average total cost and forcing inefficient firms to change their ways or exit the industry.

---

[2] Richard A. Posner, "Theories of Regulation," *Bell Journal of Economics and Management Science* 5 (Autumn): 337.

4. If, as the previous conclusion suggests, a contestable market encourages firms to produce at their lowest possible average total cost and charge a price equal to average total cost, then they also will sell at a price equal to marginal cost. (The marginal cost curve intersects the average total cost curve at its minimum point.)

The theory of contestable markets has also led to a shift in policy perspectives. To some (but certainly not all) economists, the theory suggests a new way to encourage firms to act as perfect competitors. Rather than direct interference in the behavioral patterns of firms, efforts should perhaps be directed at lowering entry and exit costs.

11-4d Necessary and Sufficient Conditions and Efficiency

In the last few chapters, we have discussed various market structures. We started by discussing perfect competition, then moved on to discuss monopoly, and finally, in this chapter, we discussed monopolistic competition and oligopoly.

The only market structure (out of the four we discussed) that we labeled as resource allocative efficient was perfect competition. Recall that a firm is resource allocative efficient if it produces the level of output at which price equals marginal cost ($P = MC$). This condition holds for a perfectly competitive firm.

Also, when discussing a perfectly competitive firm, we said that in the long run it is productive efficient; that is, it produces its output at the lowest per-unit cost, or average total cost ($P = ATC$).

For the first-time student of economics, there is almost no way of coming away from a discussion of the four market structures without thinking that perfect competition is far and away the superior market structure because of its efficiency properties. But keep one thing in mind: the conditions that we specified for the theory of perfect competition (such as many sellers and many buyers, a homogeneous product, buyers having all relevant information, and easy entry and exit) are sufficient—not necessary—conditions for achieving efficiency. What this statement means is that, if these conditions hold, they are enough to give us the result of efficiency. It is similar to saying that, if A exists, then X will follow. In other words, A is sufficient to get X to follow.

But these (perfectly competitive) conditions are not *necessary* to achieve efficiency. That is, even if A does not exist, but C exists instead, X could follow. In terms of achieving efficiency, even if there is a market that does not satisfy all the conditions of perfect competition, efficiency can still be achieved.

With this idea of necessary and sufficient conditions in mind, think again of contestable markets. Just because a given contestable market does not satisfy all the conditions of a perfectly competitive market, it does not necessarily follow that the given contestable market will not achieve efficiency (resource allocative or productive). In fact, in laboratory experiments, the economist Vernon Smith, a founder of experimental economics, has found that participants who have significant price-setting power (which does not exist in perfect competition) and little or no information about their counterparts consistently produce efficient results, given certain trading institutions.

11-5 A REVIEW OF MARKET STRUCTURES

Exhibit 8 reviews some of the characteristics and consequences of the four different market structures: perfect competition, monopoly, monopolistic competition, and oligopoly. The first four columns of the exhibit summarize the characteristics. The last column notes the long-run market tendencies of price and average total cost. The relationship between price and *ATC* indicates whether long-run profits are possible. In the exhibit, three of the four market structures (monopoly, monopolistic competition, and oligopoly) have superscript letters beside the possible profits.

EXHIBIT 8

Characteristics and Consequences of Market Structures

Market Structure	Number of Sellers	Type of Product	Barriers to Entry	Long-Run Market Tendency of Price and *ATC*
Perfect competition	Many	Homogeneous	No	$P = ATC$ (zero economic profits)
Monopoly	One	Unique	Yes	$P > ATC$ (positive economic profits)[a],[c]
Monopolistic competition	Many	Slightly differentiated	No	$P = ATC$ (zero economic profits)[b]
Oligopoly	Few	Homogeneous or differentiated	Yes	$P > ATC$ (positive economic profits)[a],[c]

[a] It is possible for positive profits to turn into zero profits through the capitalization of profits or rent-seeking activities.

[b] It is possible for the firm to earn positive profits in the long run if it can differentiate its product sufficiently in the minds of the buying public.

[c] It is possible for positive profits to turn into zero profits if the market is contestable.

These letters refer to notes that describe alternative market tendencies given different conditions. For example, the market tendency in oligopoly is for $P > ATC$ and for profits to exist in the long run. Because oligopoly has significant barriers to entry, short-run profits cannot be reduced by competition from new firms entering the industry. However, the market tendency of price and average total cost may be different if the particular oligopolistic market is contestable.

11-6 APPLICATIONS OF GAME THEORY

Game theory, especially the prisoner's dilemma, is applicable to a number of real-world situations. In this section, we discuss a few of these applications.

11-6a Grades and Partying

Suppose your economics professor announces in class one day that on the next test she will give the top 10 percent of the students in the class A's, the next 15 percent B's, and so on. Because studying to get, say, a 60 takes less time than studying to get a 90 on the test, you hope that everyone studies only a little. If so, you can study only a little and earn a high letter grade. But, of course, everyone in the class is thinking the same thing.

Envision yourself entering into an agreement with your fellow students. You say the following to them one day:

There are 30 students in our class. Each of us can choose to study either two hours or four hours for the test. Our relative standing in the class will be the same whether we all study for two hours or all study for four hours. So why don't we all agree to study for only two hours. That way, we have two extra hours to do other things. I'd rather receive my B by studying for only two hours than studying for four.

Everyone agrees with the logic of the argument and agrees to study only two hours. Of course, once all the students have agreed to do this, they have an incentive to cheat on the agreement and study more. If everyone else in your class agrees to study two hours and you study four, you increase your relative standing in the class. You go from, say, a B to an A.

You and the other students in your class are in a prisoner's dilemma. Exhibit 9 shows the payoffs for you and for Jill, a representative other student. If both you and Jill study four hours, each receives

EXHIBIT 9

Studying and Grades

Suppose your letter grade in class depends on how well you do relative to others. In this setting, you and the other students are in a prisoner's dilemma, which is shown here. If you and Jill (a representative other student) each study 4 hours, each of you earns a point grade of 85, which is a B (box 4). If each of you studies 2 hours, each of you earns a point grade of 65, which is a B (box 1).

Box 1 is preferred over box 4 because you get the same letter grade in each box, but you study less in box 1 than in box 4.

If you study 4 hours while Jill studies 2 hours, your point grade rises to 85 and Jill's point grade remains at 65. In this case, 85 is an A and 65 is a C (box 2). You are better off and Jill is worse off.

If you study 2 hours while Jill studies 4 hours, Jill's point grade rises to 85 and

your point grade remains at 65. Jill earns a letter grade of A, and you earn a letter grade of C.

No matter what Jill decides to do—study 2 or 4 hours—it is always better for you to study 4 hours (assuming that the costs of studying additional hours are less than the benefits of studying additional hours). The same holds for Jill. Our outcome, then, is box 4, where both you and Jill study 4 hours.

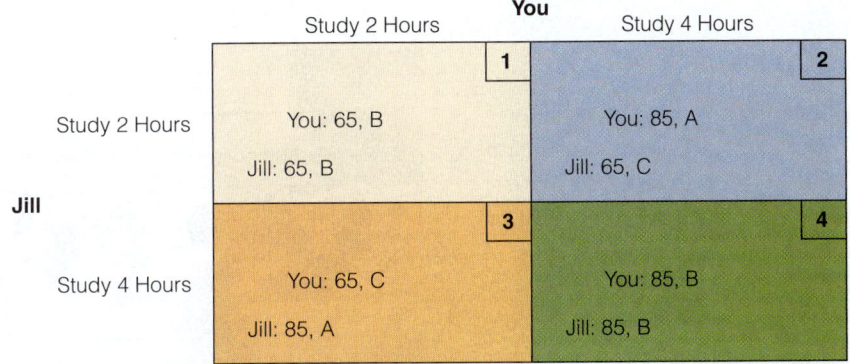

an 85, which is a B (box 4). With your professor's new relative grading plan, if you study two hours and Jill studies two hours, the grade for each of you falls to 65, but now 65 is a B (box 1). In other words, in comparison with box 4, box 1 is better because you receive the same letter grade (B) in both cases but spend less time studying.

Of course, once you and Jill agree to lower your study time from four hours to two, each of you has an incentive to cheat on the agreement. If you study four hours and Jill studies two, then you raise your grade to an 85, which is now an A, whereas Jill's grade is 65, which now becomes a C (box 2). Of course, if Jill studies four hours and you study two, then Jill raises her grade to an 85, which is now an A, and your grade is 65, which is now a C (box 3).

No matter what you think Jill is going to do, the best thing for you to do is study four hours.[3] The same holds for Jill with respect to whatever you choose to do. The outcome, then, is box 4, where both of you study four hours.

Ideally, what you and Jill need is a way to enforce your agreement not to study more than two hours. How might students do this? One way is to party. (That's right, party.) If you can get all the students in your class together and party, you can be fairly sure that no one is studying. In general, students in the same class understand (1) that some professors set aside some percentage of A's for the top students in the class (no matter how low the top is) and (2) that the students in the class are all in a prisoner's dilemma. They realize that it would be better for them to cooperate

___

[3.] We are assuming that the cost of studying two additional hours is lower than the benefits you receive by raising your grade one letter.

and study less than to compete and study more. Instead of actually entering into an agreement to study less (sign on the dotted line), they think up ways to keep the studying time down. One way to keep the studying time down—one way to enforce the implicit and unspoken agreement not to study too much—is to do things with others that do not entail studying. One such institution that satisfies all requirements is partying: everyone is together, not studying.

Hear What and How the Economist Thinks . . .
About Grade Inflation

The economist overhears a college student say the following:

You often hear that grade inflation exits in colleges today. Today's college students receive an A− or B+ for the same work that would have earned them a C+ or C, say, 25 years ago. But I'm not sure that is a bad thing. First, it looks a lot better for students who go out into the job market to have earned higher grades than lower grades. Employers look more favorably upon students with high grades than with low grades. Second, if college professors really wanted to end grade inflation, they could do so tomorrow. Just stop giving high grades out. It's as simple as that. The fact that they don't do this must mean that they prefer to give high grades to low grades.

iStock.com/skynesher

Hear what and how the economist thinks:

The student could be wrong on two counts. First, he says that if students receive high grades like an A or B instead of a C, they will look better to employers. But this isn't necessarily true if employers take the grade inflation into account. Consider two settings: In the first setting, the non-grade inflation setting, only 10 percent of college students have a grade point average of 3.8. In the second setting, the grade inflation setting, 32 percent of college students have a grade point average of 3.8. Now in which setting is an employer more likely to think that the grade point average is reflective of very special performance? It is likely to be in the non-grade inflation setting in which a smaller percentage of students receive the grade point average of 3.8. Consider the following dialog between two employers: The first employer says: "I am interviewing this college graduate today for a job. She earned a 3.8 GPA." The second employer responds: "Almost everyone I interview these days has that GPA, it is not as uncommon as it once was. I've had to figure out some other way to separate the true 3.8 GPA students

from those who only have a 3.8 due to grade inflation. For that reason, our company has recently started giving our interviewees a battery of tests. We want to see what they know before we hire them. In earlier years, we didn't have to do that."

The second thing that the student says that may not be true is that if college professors wanted to stop grade inflation, they could do so tomorrow. College professors may want to stop grade inflation, but it doesn't necessarily follow that they will be able to stop it. They could very well be in a prisoner's dilemma setting. To illustrate, suppose college professors on a particular college campus enter into an agreement with other college professors on the same campus to stop inflating grades. Each professor now has the choice of holding to the agreement or breaking it, continuing to inflate grades. If a professor wants to raise the grades of his or her students relative to other students, he or she may choose to inflate grades, thinking that other professors are not inflating grades. The result? All (or almost all) professors will end up inflating grades.

Questions to Think About:

1. A student's relative standing in a particular college class of 40 students may be the same regardless of whether there is grade inflation or not. Do you agree or disagree? Explain your answer.

2. Do you agree or disagree that a prisoner's dilemma setting of two parties can be described as: "You do what is best for you, and I will do what is best for me, but unfortunately, the outcome will not be the best for both of us." Explain your answer.

11-6b The Arms Race

During much of the Cold War, the United States and the Soviet Union engaged in an arms race. Each country was producing armaments directed at the other. Occasionally, representatives of the two countries would meet and try to slow down the race. The United States would agree to cut armaments production if the Soviet Union did, and vice versa. Many arms analysts generally agreed that the arms agreements between the United States and the Soviet Union were unsuccessful. In other words, representatives of the two countries would meet and enter into an agreement not to compete so heavily on arms production, but then the countries would just keep competing.

The two countries were in a prisoner's dilemma. When both the United States and the Soviet Union were competing on arms production, they were in box 4 of Exhibit 10, each receiving a utility level of 7. Their collective objective was to move from box 4 to box 1, with each cooperating with the other and reducing its production of armaments. In box 1, each country received a utility level of 10. The arms agreements that the United States and the Soviet Union entered into were attempts to get to box 1.

Of course, after the agreement was signed, each country had an incentive to cheat. Certainly, the United States would be better off if it increased its armaments production while the Soviet Union cut back its production. Then the United States could establish clear military superiority over the Soviet Union. The same held for the Soviet Union with respect to the United States.

The payoff matrix in Exhibit 10 makes it easy to see that the best strategy for both the United States and the Soviet Union was to compete. So the two countries ended up in box 4, racing to outproduce the other in arms.

11-6c Speed Limit Laws

Envision a world with no law against speeding. In such a world, you and everyone else speeds. With everyone speeding, a good number of accidents occur each day, some of which may involve you. In time, everyone decides that something has to be done about the speeding. It is just too dangerous, everyone admits, to let it continue.

Someone offers a proposal: "Let's agree that we will post signs on the road that state the maximum speed. Furthermore, let's agree here and now that we will all obey the speed limits." The proposal sounds like a good one, and everyone agrees to it.

Of course, as we know by now, once the agreement not to speed is made, we have a prisoner's dilemma. Each person will be better off if he (and he alone) speeds while everyone else obeys the speed limit. In the beginning, everyone agrees to the speed limit; in the end, however, everyone breaks it.

What is missing, of course, is an effective enforcement mechanism. To move the speeders out of the classic prisoner's dilemma box (box 4 in our earlier examples) to box 1, someone or something has to punish people who do not cooperate. A law against speeding—backed up by the police and the court system—solves the prisoner's dilemma. The law, the police, and the court system change the payoff for cheating on the agreement.

EXHIBIT 10

An Arms Race

In the days of the Cold War, the United States and the Soviet Union were said to be in an arms race. Actually, the arms race was a result of the two countries being in a prisoner's dilemma. Start with each country racing to produce more military goods than the other country; that is, each country is in box 4. In their attempt to move to box 1, they enter into an arms agreement (to reduce the rate at which they produce arms). But no matter what the Soviet Union does (hold to the arms agreement or break it), it is always better for the United States to break the agreement. The same holds for the Soviet Union with respect to the United States. The two countries end up in box 4. (*Note*: In the exhibit, the higher the number, the better the position is for the country.)

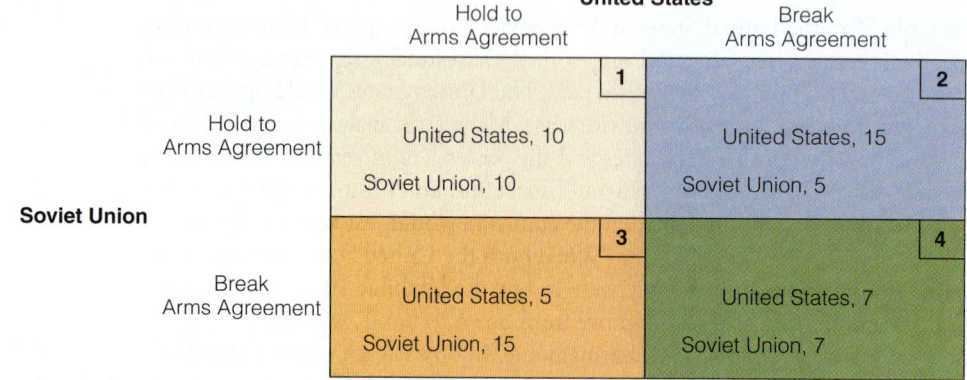

	United States	
	Hold to Arms Agreement	Break Arms Agreement
Soviet Union — Hold to Arms Agreement	**1** United States, 10 / Soviet Union, 10	**2** United States, 15 / Soviet Union, 5
Soviet Union — Break Arms Agreement	**3** United States, 5 / Soviet Union, 15	**4** United States, 7 / Soviet Union, 7

OFFICE HOURS

"Are Firms (as Sellers) Price Takers or Price Searchers?"

STUDENT: Now that I have studied four different market structures, I want to see whether I have some things correct. First, am I correct that all firms—no matter the market structure—will seek to produce that quantity of output at which $MR = MC$?

INSTRUCTOR: Yes, that's correct.

STUDENT: And is it correct that a firm either faces a horizontal demand curve and is a price taker or faces a downward-sloping demand curve and is a price searcher? In other words, is it true that a firm is either one of two things: a price taker or a price searcher? To put it differently, (1) perfectly competitive firms are price takers and (2) monopoly, monopolistically competitive, and oligopolistic firms are price searchers.

INSTRUCTOR: Yes, that's correct. To be more specific, if a firm is a price taker, it does not have to lower its price to sell additional units of a good. It can sell 100 units at $4 per unit, and it can sell 200 units at $4 a unit. But for a price searcher, the only way it can sell additional units of a good is by lowering its price. In other words, it can sell 100 units at $4 per unit, but if it wants to sell 101 units, it has to charge less than $4 per unit.

STUDENT: As for the issue of resource allocative efficiency ($P = MC$), am I right that a price taker is resource allocative efficient but a price searcher is not, unless it can and does practice perfect price discrimination?

INSTRUCTOR: Yes, that's correct.

Points to Remember

1. All firms seek to produce the quantity of output at which $MR = MC$.

2. A firm faces either a horizontal demand curve or a downward-sloping demand curve; that is, a firm is either a price taker or a price searcher, respectively.

3. Perfectly competitive firms are price takers, and monopoly, monopolistically competitive, and oligopolistic firms are price searchers.

4. A price taker is resource allocative efficient, and a price searcher is not, unless it can and does practice perfect price discrimination.

CHAPTER SUMMARY

MONOPOLISTIC COMPETITION

- The theory of monopolistic competition is built on three assumptions: (1) There are many sellers and buyers. (2) Each firm in the industry produces and sells a slightly differentiated product. (3) Entry and exit are easy.

- The monopolistic competitor is a price searcher.

- For the monopolistic competitor, $P > MR$ and the marginal revenue curve lies below the demand curve.

- The monopolistic competitor produces the quantity of output at which $MR = MC$. It charges the highest price per unit for this output.

- Unlike the perfectly competitive firm, the monopolistic competitor does not exhibit resource allocative efficiency.

- The monopolistically competitive firm does not earn profits in the long run (because of easy entry into the industry), unless it can successfully differentiate its product (e.g., by brand name) in the minds of buyers.

EXCESS CAPACITY THEOREM

- The excess capacity theorem states that a monopolistic competitor will, in equilibrium, produce an output smaller than that at which average total costs (unit costs) are minimized. Thus, the monopolistic competitor is not productive efficient.

OLIGOPOLY ASSUMPTIONS

- All of the many different oligopoly theories are built on the following assumptions: (1) There are few sellers and many buyers. (2) Firms produce and sell either homogeneous or differentiated products. (3) The barriers to entry are significant.

- One of the key characteristics of oligopolistic firms is their interdependence.

CARTEL THEORY

- The cartel theory assumes that firms in an oligopolistic industry act in a manner consistent with there being only one firm in the industry.

- Four problems are associated with cartels: (1) the problem of forming the cartel, (2) the problem of formulating policy, (3) the problem of entry into the industry, and (4) the problem of cheating.

- Firms that enter into a cartel agreement are in a prisoner's dilemma situation, where individually rational behavior leads to a jointly inefficient outcome.

THE THEORY OF CONTESTABLE MARKETS

- The conditions for a contestable market are as follows: (1) Entry into the market is easy, and exit from it is costless. (2) New firms entering the market can produce the product at the same cost as current firms. (3) Firms exiting the market can easily dispose of their fixed assets by selling them elsewhere (less depreciation).

- Compared with orthodox market structure theories, the theory of contestable markets places more emphasis on the issue of entry into and exit from an industry and less emphasis on the number of sellers in an industry.

GAME THEORY

- Game theory is a mathematical technique used to analyze the behavior of decision makers (1) who try to reach an optimal position through game playing or the use of strategic behavior, (2) who are fully aware of the interactive nature of the process at hand, and (3) who anticipate the moves of other decision makers.

- The prisoner's dilemma game illustrates individually rational behavior leading to a jointly inefficient outcome.

KEY TERMS AND CONCEPTS

Monopolistic Competition   Oligopoly   Cartel Theory   Game Theory
Excess Capacity Theorem   Concentration Ratio   Cartel   Contestable Market

QUESTIONS AND PROBLEMS

1. What, if anything, do all firms in all four market structures have in common?

2. "Excess capacity is the price we pay for product differentiation." Evaluate this statement in terms of monopolistic competition.

3. Why might a producer use a designer label to differentiate her product from that of another producer?

4. Will there be profits in the long run in a monopolistically competitive market? Explain your answer.

5. Would you expect cartel formation to be more likely in industries composed of a few firms or in those which include many firms? Explain your answer.

6. Does the theory of contestable markets shed any light on oligopoly pricing theories? Explain your answer.

7. There are 60 types or varieties of product X on the market. Is product X made in a monopolistically competitive market? Explain your answer.

8. Why does the interdependence of firms play a major role in oligopoly but not in perfect competition or monopolistic competition?

9. Concentration ratios have often been used to note the tightness of an oligopoly market. A high concentration ratio indicates a tight oligopoly market, and a low concentration ratio indicates a loose oligopoly market. Would you expect firms in tight markets to reap higher profits, on average, than firms in loose markets? Would it matter if the markets were contestable? Explain your answers.

10. Market theories are said to have the happy consequence of getting individuals to think in more focused and analytical ways. Is this effect true for you? Give examples to illustrate.

11. Give an example of a prisoner's dilemma situation other than the ones mentioned in this chapter.

12. How are oligopoly and monopolistic competition alike? How are they different?

WORKING WITH NUMBERS AND GRAPHS

1. Diagrammatically identify the quantity of output a monopolistic competitor produces and the price it charges.

2. Diagrammatically identify a monopolistic competitor that is incurring losses.

3. Total industry sales are $105 million. The top four firms account for sales of $10 million, $9 million, $8 million, and $5 million, respectively. What is the four-firm concentration ratio?

4. Refer to the accompanying figure. Because of a cartel agreement, a firm has been assigned a production quota of q_2 units. The cartel price is P_2. What do the firm's profits equal if it adheres to the cartel agreement? What do the firm's profits equal if it breaks the cartel agreement and produces q_3?

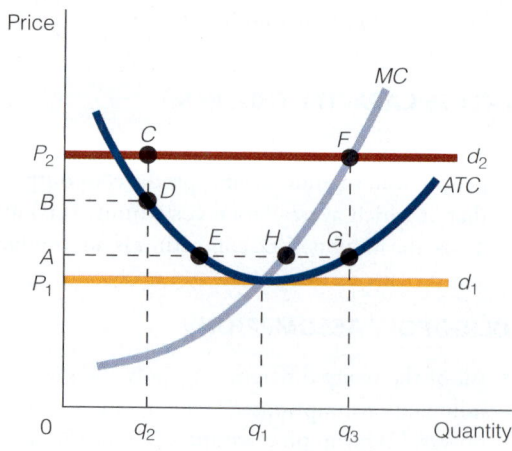

GOVERNMENT AND PRODUCT MARKETS: ANTITRUST AND REGULATION

GlowImages/Alamy Stock Photo

INTRODUCTION

In Washington, D.C., you may see the building that houses the Department of Justice. One of the many duties of the Justice Department is the enforcement of the country's antitrust laws, whose stated purpose is to control monopoly and to preserve and promote competition. Does it matter to your life whether the Justice Department does a good, bad, or mediocre job of controlling monopoly and preserving and promoting competition? It matters in more ways than you can imagine.

12-1 ANTITRUST

A monopoly (1) produces a smaller output than is produced by a perfectly competitive firm with the same revenue and cost considerations, (2) charges a higher price, and (3) causes a deadweight loss. Some economists argue that, on the basis of these facts, government should place restrictions on monopolies. In addition, government should restrict the activities of cartels because the objective of a cartel is to behave as if it were a monopoly.

Other economists argue that monopolies do not have as much market power as some people think: Witness the competition some monopolies face from broadly defined substitutes and imports. As for cartels, they usually contain the seeds of their own destruction, so it is only a matter of (a usually short) time before they fall apart naturally.

We are concerned, not with the debate about whether to restrict monopoly power, but rather with how government deals with it—specifically, through antitrust laws and regulation. We examine antitrust law in this section and regulation in the next. **Antitrust law** is legislation passed for the stated purpose of controlling monopoly power and preserving and promoting competition. Let's look at the uses and effects of a few of the major antitrust acts.

Antitrust Law
Legislation passed for the stated purpose of controlling monopoly power and preserving and promoting competition.

309

12-1a **Antitrust Acts**

Following are a few key acts whose provisions constitute U.S. antitrust policy:

- Sherman Act (1890).
- Clayton Act (1914).
- Federal Trade Commission Act (1914).
- Robinson–Patman Act (1936).
- Wheeler–Lea Act (1938).
- Celler–Kefauver Antimerger Act (1950).

Trust
A combination of firms that come together to act as a monopolist.

Sherman Act (1890) The Sherman Act was passed to deal with mergers of companies. (A *merger* occurs when two companies combine under single ownership of control.) At that time, the organization that companies formed by combining was called a **trust**; a term that gave us the word *antitrust*.

The Sherman Act contains two major provisions:

1. "Every contract, combination in the form of trust or otherwise, or conspiracy, in restraint of trade or commerce among the several states, or with foreign nations, is hereby declared to be illegal."

2. "Every person who shall monopolize, or attempt to monopolize, or combine or conspire with any other person or persons to monopolize any part of the trade or commerce . . . shall be guilty of a misdemeanor."

Some people have argued that the provisions of the Sherman Act are vague. For example, the act never explains which specific acts constitute a restraint of trade, although it declares such acts illegal.

Clayton Act (1914) The Clayton Act makes the following business practices illegal when their effects "may be to substantially lessen competition or tend to create a monopoly":

1. *Price discrimination.* An example is charging different customers different prices for the same product when the price differences are not related to cost differences.

2. *Exclusive dealing.* This is selling to a retailer on the condition that the retailer not carry any rival products.

3. *Tying contracts.* Arrangements made whereby the sale of one product is dependent on the purchase of some other product or products.

4. *The acquisition of competing companies' stock if the acquisition reduces competition.* Some say a major loophole of the act is that it does not ban the acquisition of competing companies' physical assets and therefore does not prevent anticompetitive mergers from doing what they are intended to do.

The Clayton Act also makes the following arrangement illegal at all times, not just when its effects "may be to substantially lessen competition. . . .":

5. *Interlocking directorates.* In this type of arrangement, the directors of one company sit on the board of another company in the same industry.

Federal Trade Commission Act (1914) The Federal Trade Commission Act contains the broadest and most general language of any antitrust act. It declares illegal "unfair methods of competition in commerce." In essence, it declares illegal acts that are judged to be "too aggressive" in competition. The problem is how to decide what is fair and what is unfair, what is aggressive but not too aggressive. This act also set up the Federal Trade Commission (FTC) to deal with "unfair methods of competition."

Robinson–Patman Act (1936) The Robinson–Patman Act was passed in an attempt to decrease the failure rate of small businesses by protecting them from the competition of large and growing chain stores. The large chain stores were receiving price discounts from suppliers and, in turn, passing the discounts on to their customers. As a result, small businesses had a difficult time competing, and many of them failed. The Robinson–Patman Act prohibits suppliers from offering special discounts to large chain stores unless they also offer the discounts to everyone else. Many economists believe that, rather than preserving and strengthening competition, the Robinson–Patman Act limits it. The act seems to be more concerned about a certain group of competitors than about the process of competition and the buying public as a whole.

Wheeler–Lea Act (1938) The Wheeler–Lea Act empowers the Federal Trade Commission to deal with false and deceptive acts or practices. Major moves in this area have been against advertising that the FTC has deemed false and deceptive.

Celler–Kefauver Antimerger Act (1950) The Celler–Kefauver Act was designed to close the merger loophole in the Clayton Act. (See point 4 in the earlier list discussing the Clayton Act.) The Celler–Kefauver Act bans anticompetitive mergers that occur as a result of one company's acquiring the physical assets of another company.

ECONOMICS 24/7

Thomas Edison and Hollywood

Thomas Alva Edison was born in 1847 and died in 1931. In his 84 years of life, Edison was granted 1,093 patents. Almost everyone knows the role Edison played in the development of electric light and power, but not everyone knows the role he played in indirectly and unwittingly making Hollywood the film capital of the world.

Our story begins with an Edison invention, a machine called the kinetophonograph, which showed a moving picture that was synchronized with a phonograph record. Later, Edison invented the kinetoscope, a device that allowed users to deposit a coin and watch a short motion picture through a small hole.

After inventing the kinetophonograph and kinetoscope, Edison went on to construct the first building that was used solely to make movies. A hole in the ceiling of the building allowed the sun to shine through and illuminate the stage. The entire building was placed on a set of tracks so that it could be moved around to follow the sun. The first film that Edison produced was a 15-minute movie called *The Great Train Robbery*. Over the years, he produced more than 2,000 short films.

turtix/Shutterstock.com

There is some evidence that Edison and a few other people tried to gain complete control over the movie industry in its early days. Edison played a critical role in putting together the Movie Trust, sometimes called the Edison Trust, a group of 10 film producers and distributors. The Movie Trust reportedly tried to eliminate its competition. First, it entered into an exclusive contract with Eastman Kodak Company, which manufactured film, to sell film only to it. Second, it refused to lease or sell equipment to certain filmmakers and theater owners. One of the independent movie producers whom the Movie Trust tried to run out of the industry was Carl Laemmle. Laemmle and some other movie producers decided to leave the East Coast, where the Movie Trust had the greatest control over the industry, and went to the West Coast, specifically to southern California. Others soon followed. The rush of independent filmmakers to southern California set the stage for the development of Hollywood as the film capital of the world. In 1917, the Movie Trust was dissolved by court order, but by then the movie industry had a new home. Laemmle, for example, founded Universal Studios in Hollywood in 1912.

Whether Hollywood would be the film capital of the world had it not been for the Movie Trust is doubtful. Without the exclusionary and anticompetitive tactics of the Movie Trust, the film capital of the world would probably be on the East Coast of the United States, very likely in or near New York City.

12-1b Unsettled Points in Antitrust Policy

Not always clear is where the lines should be drawn in implementing antitrust policy. Which firms should be allowed to enter into a merger and which prohibited? What constitutes restraint of trade? Which firms should be treated as monopolists and broken into smaller firms? Which firms should be left alone?

As you might guess, not everyone answers these questions the same way. In short, some points of antitrust policy are still unsettled.

Does the Definition of the Market Matter?

How a market is defined—broadly or narrowly—helps determine whether a firm is considered a monopoly. For example, in an important antitrust suit in 1945, a court ruled that Alcoa (Aluminum Company of America) was a monopoly because it had 90 percent of the virgin aluminum ingot market. If Alcoa's market had been broadened to include stainless steel, copper, tin, nickel, and zinc (some of the goods competing with aluminum), it is unlikely that Alcoa would have been ruled a monopoly.

Later court rulings have tended to define markets broadly rather than narrowly. For instance, in the DuPont case in 1956, the market relevant to DuPont was ruled to be the flexible wrapping materials market rather than the narrower cellophane market.

Concentration Ratios

Concentration ratios have often been used to gauge the amount of competition in an industry, but their use presents two major problems. First, concentration ratios do not address the issue of foreign competition. For example, the four-firm concentration ratio in an industry may be very high, but the four firms that make up the concentration ratio may still face stiff competition from abroad. Second, a four-firm concentration ratio can remain stable over time despite competition among the four major firms in the industry.

In 1982, the Justice Department replaced the four- and eight-firm concentration ratios with the Herfindahl index, although it, too, is subject to some of the same criticisms as the concentration ratios. The **Herfindahl index**, which measures the degree of concentration in an industry, is equal to the sum of the squares of the market shares of each firm in the industry. That is,

> **Herfindahl Index**
> An index that measures the degree of concentration in an industry, equal to the sum of the squares of the market shares of each firm in the industry.

$$\text{Herfindahl index} = (S_1)^2 + (S_2)^2 + \cdots + (S_n)^2$$

where S_1 through S_n are the respective market shares of firms 1 through n. For example, if 10 firms are in an industry and if each firm has a 10 percent market share, then the Herfindahl index is 1,000 $(10^2 + 10^2 + 10^2 + 10^2 + 10^2 + 10^2 + 10^2 + 10^2 + 10^2 + 10^2 = 1,000)$.

EXHIBIT 1

A Comparison of the Four-Firm Concentration Ratio and the Herfindahl Index

According to the old method (in this case, the four-firm concentration ratio), the top four firms in the industry shown have a 48 percent market share. The Justice Department would therefore likely frown on a proposed merger between any of the top four firms and any other firm (including another one of the top four firms). However, the Herfindahl index of 932 is representative of an unconcentrated industry.

Firms	Market Share (%)
A	15
B	12
C	11
D	10
E	8
F	7
G	7
H	6
I	6
J	6
K	6
L	6

Old Method: Four-Firm Concentration Ratio

$15\% + 2\% + 11\% + 10\% = 48\%$

New Method: Herfindahl Index

Square the market share of each firm and then add:

$(15)^2 + (12)^2 + (11)^2 + (10)^2 + (8)^2 + (7)^2 + (7)^2 + (6)^2 + (6)^2 + (6)^2 + (6)^2 + (6)^2 = 932$

Exhibit 1 compares the Herfindahl index with the four-firm concentration ratio. When the four-firm concentration ratio is used, the top four firms (A–D) have a 48 percent market share, which generally is thought to describe a concentrated industry. A merger between any of the top four firms and any other firm (e.g., between firm B and firm G in Exhibit 1) would give the newly merged firm a greater market share than any existing firm and usually incur frowns at the Justice Department.

The Herfindahl index for the industry is 932, however, and the Justice Department generally considers any number less than 1,000 representative of an *un*concentrated (or competitive) industry. An index between 1,500 and 2,500 is considered representative of a moderately concentrated industry, and an index greater than 2,500 is representative of a highly concentrated industry.

When is the Justice Department likely to take antitrust actions? Primarily when transactions increase the HHI [the Herfindahl-Hirschman Index, another name for the Herfindahl Index] by more than 200 points in highly concentrated markets [markets with an index greater than 2,500].

To illustrate, suppose seven firms are in an industry. Two of the firms, A and B, want to merge. The market share of firm A is 35 percent, and the market share of firm B is 34 percent. The market shares for the other five firms in the industry are 10 percent, 10 percent, 5 percent, 5 percent, and 1 percent, respectively. Then the Herfindahl index for this industry is 2,632 $(35^2 + 34^2 + 10^2 + 10^2 + 5^2 + 5^2 + 1^2)$.

If the merger is approved, there will be 6, not 7, firms in the industry. Moreover, the market share of the merged firm (when A and B form one firm) will be 69 percent. The Herfindahl index after the merger will be 5,012. In other words, the increase will be 2,380 points if the firms merge. With this substantial increase in the index, the proposed merger is likely to be blocked.

Innovation and Concentration Ratios Because innovation and technical change are so important to our economic well-being, some economists argue that concentration ratios should not play so large a role in determining a merger's approval. The merger's effect on innovation should also be taken into account. There is some evidence that antitrust authorities accept this line of thinking.

In the past, small firms in highly competitive markets with many rivals were thought to have a stronger incentive to innovate than firms in markets where only a few firms existed and where each firm had sizable market power. Increasingly, however, these small competitive firms seem often to face a greater risk of innovation than firms with substantial market power, and therefore they tend to innovate less.

To illustrate, consider a market with 100 firms, each of which supplies one-hundredth of the market. Suppose one of these firms invests heavily in research and develops a new product or process. It has to worry about any of its 99 rivals soon developing a similar innovation and therefore reducing the value of its innovation. In contrast, if a firm is one of four firms and has substantial market power, it doesn't face as much so-called innovative risk. It has only 3, not 99, rivals to worry about. And, of course, the less likely it is that competitors can render one's own innovations less valuable, the higher the expected return from innovating will be.

Today, antitrust authorities say that they consider the benefits of both competition and innovation when ruling on proposed mergers. On the one hand, increased competition lowers prices for consumers. On the other hand, monopoly power may yield more innovation. If it does, then the lower prices brought about through increased competition have to be weighed against the increased innovation that may come about through greater market concentration and monopoly power.

THINKING LIKE AN ECONOMIST

Different Roads to the Same Destination   If a firm has a large share of the market, the economist will ask, "Is there only one possible explanation for this, or are there many?" If there are many, then the economist will try to find out which is the correct explanation. As an analogy, suppose someone gets the highest grade in three of three courses. There may well be more than one explanation: The person could be studying more than anyone else. Or the student could be innately smarter than anyone else. Or the individual could be cheating. The economist knows that, usually, different roads end up at the same destination. Trying to figure out which road was taken to the destination is part of the task economists set for themselves.

12-1c Antitrust and Mergers

Horizontal Merger
A merger between firms that are selling similar products in the same market.

Vertical Merger
A merger between companies in the same industry but at different stages of the production process.

Conglomerate Merger
A merger between companies in different industries.

There are three basic types of mergers:

1. A **horizontal merger** is a merger between firms that are selling similar products in the same market. For example, suppose both companies A and B produce cars. If the two companies combine under single ownership of control, then the merger is horizontal.

2. A **vertical merger** is a merger between companies in the same industry but at different stages of the production process. A vertical merger occurs between companies, one of which buys (or sells) something from (or to) the other. For example, suppose company C, which produces cars, buys tires from company D. If the two companies combine under single ownership of control, then the merger is vertical.

3. A **conglomerate merger** is a merger between companies in different industries. For example, if company E, in the car industry, and company F, in the pharmaceutical industry, combine under single ownership of control, then the result is a conglomerate.

Of the three types of mergers—vertical, horizontal, and conglomerate—the federal government looks most carefully at proposed horizontal mergers. These mergers are the most likely to change the degree of concentration, or competition, in an industry. For example, if General Motors (manufacturer of cars) and Ford Motor Company (cars) were to merge horizontally, then competition in the car industry would be likely to decrease by more than if General Motors (cars) and BF Goodrich (tires) were to merge vertically. In the latter case, the competition among car companies and among tire companies is likely to be the same after the merger as it was before. (However, that is not necessarily the case, so the government does not always approve vertical mergers.)

12-1d Common Misconceptions about Antitrust Policy

Some people believe that all the big issues in antitrust policy have been settled. This belief is simply not true. For example, predatory pricing practices—such as selling a good for a low price in order to eliminate competitors—are deemed illegal. But difficult questions arise: How low must a price be before it is deemed predatory? How long must the low price persist before it is deemed predatory?

Also, in a monopoly case, the relevant market is not always obvious. For example, is the relevant market for soft drinks the soft-drink market? Or is it the much larger beverage market (which includes soft drinks, water, juices, etc.)?

Finally, mergers and tying arrangements are deemed illegal if they "substantially reduce competition," but how much competition has to be reduced before it is "substantial"?

12-1e Network Monopolies

A network connects things. A telephone network connects telephones; the Internet (which is a network of networks) connects computers; and a bank network connects, among other things, automated teller machines (ATMs).

A **network good** is a good whose value increases as the expected number of units sold increases. A telephone is a network good. You buy a telephone to network with other people. It has little value to you if you expect only 100 people to buy telephones, but its value increases for you if you expect thousands or millions of people to buy telephones. Software is also a network good, in the sense that if Smith and Jones both buy software X, they can then easily exchange documents. As new buyers buy a network good, the present owners of the good receive greater benefits because the network connects them to more people. For example, if Brown and Thompson also buy software X, Smith and Jones benefit more because they can exchange documents with two more people.

The production and sale of a network good can lead to monopoly. Suppose three companies (A, B, and C) make some version of network good X. Company A makes the most popular version, so its good is said to have the greatest network value. Consequently, people who are thinking of buying good X buy it from company A. As more people purchase good X from company A, the network value increases, prompting even more people to buy good X from company A rather than from the other two companies. Eventually, the customers of companies B and C may switch to company A, and at some point almost everyone buys good X from company A. Company A is then a network monopoly.

Antitrust Policy for Network Monopolies Currently, the antitrust authorities move against a network monopoly on the basis of how it behaves, not because of what it is. For example, the authorities would not issue a complaint against company A in our example unless it undertook predatory or exclusionary practices to *maintain* its monopoly position.

Network Good
A good whose value increases as the expected number of units sold increases.

Innovation and Network Monopolies Recall that economists are undecided as to whether market share helps or hinders innovation. For example, one firm among four firms may have less innovative risk than one firm among 100. Therefore, the firm with a larger market share would innovate more, *ceteris paribus*. Presumably, a network monopoly will have a large market share and therefore should be a major innovator.

Actually, the situation may be different for network monopolies because high switching costs sometimes accompany a network monopoly. To illustrate, suppose firm A produces network good A. Suppose further that network good A begins to sell quite well and, because it is a network good, its robust sales increase its value to potential customers. Then potential customers soon turn into actual customers, and before long, good A has set the market, or industry, standard.

Because network good A is now the industry standard and because network goods (especially those related to the high-tech industries) are sometimes difficult to learn, good A may have a lock on the market. Specifically, a **lock-in effect** increases the costs of switching from good A to another good. Because of the relatively high switching costs, good A has some staying power in the market. Firm A, the producer of good A, thus has staying power too, possibly causing firm A to rest on its laurels. Instead of innovating—instead of trying to outcompete its existing and future rivals with better production processes or better products—it may do very little. Firm A will realize that the high switching costs keep customers from changing to a different network good. Some economists suggest that, in this environment, the network monopoly may have little reason to innovate.

Lock-In Effect
The situation in which a product or technology becomes the standard and is difficult or impossible to dislodge from that role.

ECONOMICS 24/7

Why It May Be Hard to Dislodge People from Facebook

Consider two different reasons for purchasing a good. The first is the intrinsic value that one gets from the good. In other words, people might buy an apple because it tastes good to them, a computer because it helps them do their work, a television set because they can then watch their favorite television programs, and a watch because they want to know what time it is. The second reason is because the good is a *network good*. For example, the spreadsheet Excel and the word-processing program Word are both network goods in that some people may end up purchasing and using both Excel and Word because other people (before them) have purchased and used those programs. Why so? Because if you want to share computer files with people, you have a better chance of doing so if you use the same software program that they use.

Or consider the videotape format war of the 1970s and 1980s. Then, there were principally two video cartridge formats for use in a videocassette recorder (VCR): Betamax and VHS. At first, some customers decided to go with the Betamax format and others with the VHS format. In time, though, more people went with VHS, and as the numbers of VHS users rose, the remaining Betamax users found

AlesiaKan/Shutterstock.com

that it was less likely that they would be able to share tapes with others (because Betamax video tapes could not be played in VHS machines and VHS tapes could not be played in Betamax machines). In other words, VHS was becoming a network good, so some people chose to change over to VHS or to go with VHS for their first purchase, because doing so made it easier to share videos with people.

Now consider Facebook. There is some intrinsic value that the users of Facebook receive. Specifically, they get to post photos and comments, and so on. But suppose that tomorrow a company were to arise that wanted to compete with Facebook. Suppose the new company were to take out a full one-minute ad during the Super-Bowl, informing people that it has a platform that is as good as, if not better than, Facebook's and then invited people to leave Facebook and come to it.

First, is it possible for some company to provide as good a site as Facebook does? Certainly. Is it possible that, if you are currently on Facebook, you would do many of the same things on the new company's social networking site—such as put up a profile, post photos, and update your status—as you do on Facebook? Certainly. But, then, it is not the Facebook site itself that makes Facebook what it is; it is the fact that millions of people use Facebook. It is the fact that "Facebook is where everyone seems to be" when it comes to social networking. In short, Facebook is a network good. The company that wants to compete with Facebook is not. In a world where people want to network socially with others, Facebook, because of its millions of users, is unlikely to be outcompeted by a company that starts out with zero users. When it comes to network goods, it really seems to pay if a company is one of the early ones out with the good.

ECONOMICS 24/7

High-Priced Ink Cartridges and Expensive Minibars

Shopping for a printer for your computer, you see one priced at $169. "That's a good price," you think, so you buy it. Later, you learn that you have to pay $43 for an ink cartridge. The printer wasn't so well priced after all.

You spend the night at a hotel. Once in your room, you look in the minibar and decide to eat a small bag of almonds. You learn later, after looking at your bill, that the small bag of almonds came with a price tag of $6.

You sign up with a cell phone company, decide on a plan, and get a free cell phone. Later, you learn that for every minute you go over your allotted monthly number of minutes, you pay 33¢.

Because of such everyday occurrences, some economists today are talking about the hidden-fee economy—an economy in which many main items for sale (a printer, a hotel room, cell phone service) come with high hidden fees that you did not expect when you purchased the main item.

According to two economists, David Laibson and Xavier Gabaix, firms reap certain benefits through hidden fees. (There are certain costs, too, but sometimes the benefits are greater than the costs.) For example,[1] suppose that hotel X rents its rooms for $80 a night and has some hidden fees: $12 for parking, $6 for a small bag of almonds from the minibar, and $3 for a local call. Suppose also that hotel Y rents its rooms for $95 a night and has no high hidden fees. It does not charge

Berni/Shutterstock.com

for parking or for a local call, and the small bag of almonds comes at the price that it sells for at a grocery store. What are the major differences between the two hotels? On the basis of just the price of a room, hotel X is cheaper than hotel Y. Add in hidden and unexpectedly high fees, however, and hotel X is a culprit while hotel Y is not.

The natural question to ask is, Why doesn't hotel Y simply advertise the fact that its competitor, hotel X, is trying to dupe its customers by charging high hidden fees? (The ad might read, "Sure,

---

[1] The source of the material in this feature (and the source of the example) is Christopher Shea, "The Hidden Economy," *The Boston Globe*, June 27, 2006.

hotel X has cheaper rooms, but what about all the hidden fees?") According to Laibson and Gabaix, that strategy could backfire because of one of the two types of customers who frequent hotel X. One type of customer is unaware of the hidden fees and initially responds to the lower room rate of hotel X. With this customer, the strategy of pointing out the hidden fees of hotel X will be successful. Another type of customer is sophisticated when it comes to sellers' tactics. This customer realizes that, if she doesn't park at hotel X, doesn't eat anything from the minibar, and makes calls on her cell phone instead of on the hotel telephone, she can then get a lower priced room at hotel X. The ad by hotel Y simply notifies the sophisticated customer that she can get a good deal at the hotel with the hidden fees, as long as she doesn't purchase the goods or services that come with the high hidden fees.

So hotel Y both gains and loses with its ad pointing out the high hidden fees of hotel X. It gains the clueless customers ("Thanks for telling me about those hidden fees!"), but it may lose some sophisticated customers ("Thanks for telling me about the lower priced rooms your competitor is offering!"). If hotel Y thinks that it will lose more sophisticated customers than it will gain clueless ones, it will not run the ad. Instead, it may simply join the ranks of hotels like hotel X and lower its room rate and increase the use of high hidden fees.

But consider something else. Barry Nalebuff, a professor of business strategy, has noted that a firm which charges hidden fees incurs a cost and that cost comes in the form of customers getting angry at the hidden fees. Angry customers, Nalebuff says, often turn their backs on sellers they are angry with. In other words, they seek out other (perhaps more up-front and straightforward) sellers to buy from.

In the end, it becomes a matter of a seller having to consider both the benefits and the costs of a hidden-fees strategy. Perhaps initially the benefits outweigh the costs, but there is no guarantee that, in time, the costs won't rise above the benefits.

SELF-TEST

(Answers to Self-Test questions are in Answers to Self-Test Questions at the back of the book.)

1. Why does it matter whether a market is defined broadly or narrowly for purposes of antitrust policy?

2. Suppose that 20 firms are in an industry and that each firm has a 5 percent market share. What is the four-firm concentration ratio for this industry? What is the Herfindahl index?

3. What is the advantage of the Herfindahl index over the four- and eight-firm concentration ratios? Explain your answer.

12-2 REGULATION

This section examines the various types of regulation, theories of regulation, the stated objectives of regulatory agencies, and the effects of regulation on natural and other monopolies.

12-2a The Case of Natural Monopoly

We know that, if economies of scale are so pronounced or so large in an industry that only one firm can survive, that firm is a *natural monopoly*. Firms that supply local electricity, gas, and water service are usually considered natural monopolies.

In Exhibit 2, the market consists of one firm, which produces Q_1 units of output at an average total cost of ATC_1. (Q_1 is the output at which $MR = MC$; to simplify the diagram, the MR curve is not shown.) At Q_1, the allocation of resources is inefficient. Resource allocative efficiency exists when the marginal benefit to demanders of the resources used in the goods they buy equals the marginal cost to suppliers of the resources used in the production of the goods they sell. In Exhibit 2, resource allocative efficiency exists at Q_2, corresponding to the point where the demand curve intersects the MC curve.

There are two ways to reach the higher, efficient quantity of output, Q_2: (1) The firm currently producing Q_1 could increase its output to Q_2. (2) Another firm could enter the market and produce Q_3—the difference between Q_2 and Q_1. Each way has its associated costs. If the firm currently in the market increases its production to Q_2, it incurs average total costs of ATC_2. If, instead, a new firm enters the market and produces Q_3, it incurs an average total cost of ATC_3. In this way, both firms together produce Q_2, but the new firm incurs average total costs of ATC_3 whereas the existing firm incurs average total costs of ATC_1.

EXHIBIT 2

The Natural Monopoly Situation

The only existing firm produces Q_1 at an average total cost of ATC_1. (Q_1 is the output at which $MR = MC$; to simplify the diagram, the MR curve is not shown.) Resource allocative efficiency exists at Q_2. There are two ways to obtain this output level: (1) The only existing firm can increase its production to Q_2, or (2) a new firm can enter the market and produce Q_3, which is the difference between Q_2 and Q_1. The first way minimizes total cost; the second way does not. The graph shown, then, represents a natural monopoly situation: one firm can supply the entire output that is demanded at a lower cost than two or more firms can.

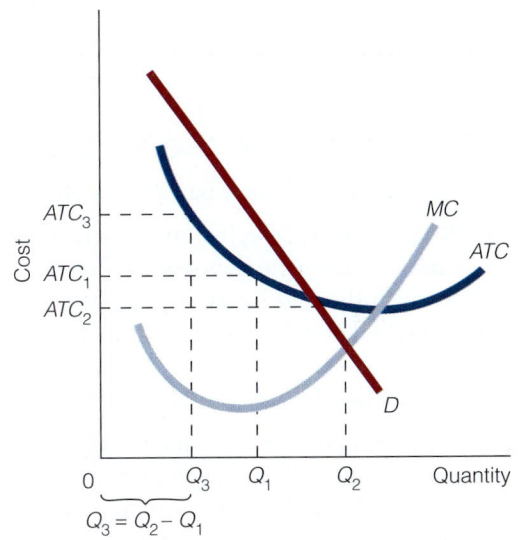

As long as the objective is to increase output to the level of resource allocative efficiency, it is cheaper (total costs are lower) to have the firm currently in the market increase its output to Q_2 than to have two firms together produce Q_2. So the situation in Exhibit 2 is a natural monopoly situation. A natural monopoly exists when one firm can supply the entire output demanded at lower cost than two or more firms can. A natural monopoly will evolve over time as the low-cost producer undercuts its competitors.

Some economists say that the natural monopolist will charge the monopoly price. In Exhibit 3, the natural monopoly firm produces quantity Q_1, at which marginal revenue equals marginal cost, and charges price P_1, which is the highest price per unit consistent with the output it produces. Because it charges the monopoly price, some people argue that the natural monopoly firm should be regulated. The form that the regulation should take is a question addressed in the next section.

EXHIBIT 3

The Profit-Maximizing Natural Monopoly

The natural monopoly that seeks to maximize profits will produce the quantity of output at which $MR = MC$ and charge the (monopoly) price P_1.

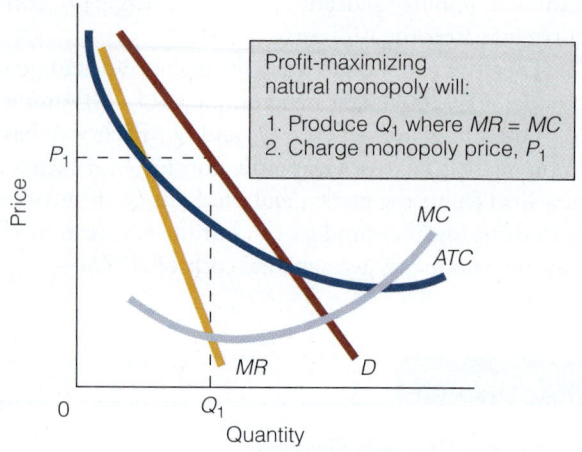

Profit-maximizing natural monopoly will:

1. Produce Q_1 where $MR = MC$
2. Charge monopoly price, P_1

12-2b Regulating the Natural Monopoly

The natural monopoly may be regulated through price, profit, or output regulation:

1. *Price regulation.* Marginal cost pricing is one form of price regulation. The objective is to set a price for the natural monopoly firm that equals its marginal cost at the quantity of output at which demand intersects marginal cost. In Exhibit 4, this price is P_1. At that price, the natural monopoly takes a loss: At Q_1, average total cost is greater than price and thus total cost is greater than total revenue. Obviously, the natural monopoly would rather go out of business than be subject to this type of regulation, unless it receives a subsidy for its operation.

2. *Profit regulation.* Government may want the natural monopoly to earn only zero economic profits. If so, government will require the natural monopoly to charge a price P_2 (because $P_2 = ATC$) and to supply the quantity demanded at that price (Q_2). This form of regulation is often called *average cost pricing*. Theoretically, it may seem like a good way to proceed, but in practice it often turns out differently. The problem is that, if the natural monopoly is always held to zero economic profits—and is not allowed to fall below or rise above this level—then it has an incentive to let costs rise. Higher costs—in the form of higher salaries or more luxurious offices—simply mean higher prices to cover the higher costs. In this case, average cost pricing is not likely to be an efficient way to proceed.

3. *Output regulation.* Government can mandate a quantity of output it wants the natural monopoly to produce. Suppose that quantity is Q_3 in Exhibit 4, so that there are positive economic profits because price is above average total cost. However, the natural monopoly could want even higher profits, and, at a fixed quantity of output, higher profits can be obtained by lowering costs. The natural monopolist might lower costs by reducing the quality of the good or service it sells, knowing that it faces no direct competition and that it is protected (by government) from competitors.

Government regulation of a natural monopoly does not always turn out the way it was intended. Regulation—whether it takes the form of price, profit, or output regulation—can distort the incentives of those who operate the natural monopoly. For example, if profit is regulated to the

EXHIBIT 4

Regulating a Natural Monopoly

The government can regulate a natural monopoly through (1) price regulation, (2) profit regulation, or (3) output regulation. Price regulation usually means marginal cost pricing, and profit regulation usually means average cost pricing.

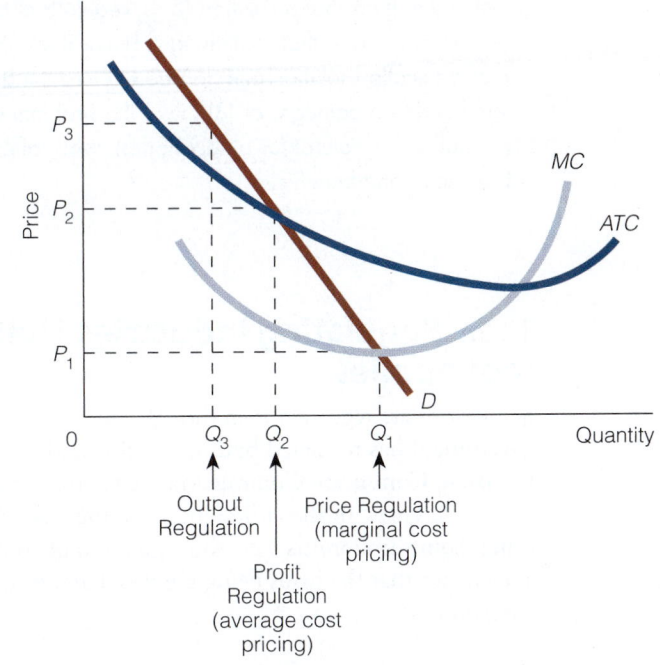

extent that zero economic profits are guaranteed, then the natural monopoly has little incentive to hold costs down. Furthermore, the owners of the natural monopoly have an incentive to try to influence the government officials or other persons who are regulating the firm.

In addition, each of the three types of regulation requires information. For example, if the government wishes to set price equal to marginal cost or average total cost for the natural monopoly, it must know the cost conditions of the firm.

Three problems arise in gathering information: (1) The cost information is not easy to determine, even for the natural monopoly itself. (2) The cost information can be rigged (to a degree) by the natural monopoly, and therefore the regulators will not get a true picture of the firm. (3) The regulators have little incentive to obtain accurate information, because they are likely to keep their jobs and prestige even if they work with less-than-accurate information. (This problem raises another question: Who will ensure that the regulators do a good job?)

Finally, the issue of *regulatory lag* is indirectly related to information. **Regulatory lag** is the period between the time that a natural monopoly's costs change and the time that the regulatory agency adjusts prices to account for the change. For example, suppose the local gas company rates are regulated. Subsequently, the gas company's costs rise, and it seeks a rate hike through the local regulatory body. The rate hike is not likely to be approved quickly. The gas company will probably have to submit an application for a rate hike, document its case, have a date set for a hearing, argue its case at the hearing, and then wait for the regulatory agency to decide on the merits of the application. Many months may pass between the beginning of the process and the end. During that time, the regulated firm will be operating in ways and under conditions that both the firm and the regulatory body might not have desired.

Regulatory Lag
The period between the time that a natural monopoly's costs change and the time that the regulatory agency adjusts prices to account for the change.

THINKING LIKE AN ECONOMIST

Something Is Not Always Better Than Nothing   The public is perhaps naturally inclined to think that a solution (e.g., regulation) to a problem (e.g., monopoly) is better than no solution at all—that something is better than nothing. The economist has learned, though, that a so-called solution can do one of three things: (1) solve a problem, (2) not solve a problem but do no damage, or (3) make the problem worse. Thinking through the entire range of possibilities is natural for an economist, who, after all, understands that solutions come with both costs and benefits.

12-2c Regulating Industries That Are Not Natural Monopolies

Some firms are regulated even though they are not natural monopolies. For instance, in the past, government has regulated both the airline and trucking industries. In the trucking industry, the Interstate Commerce Commission (ICC) fixed routes, set minimum freight rates, and erected barriers to entry. In the airline industry, the Civil Aeronautics Board (CAB) did much the same thing. Some economists view the regulation of competitive industries as unnecessary. They see it as evidence that the firms being regulated are, in turn, controlling the regulation to reduce their competition.

12-2d Theories of Regulation

The **capture theory of regulation** holds that, no matter what the motive is for the initial regulation and the establishment of the regulatory agency, eventually the agency will be captured (i.e., controlled) by the special interests of the industry being regulated. The following are a few of the interrelated points that have been put forth to support this theory:

Capture Theory of Regulation
A theory holding that, no matter what the motive is for the initial regulation and the establishment of the regulatory agency, eventually the agency will be captured (controlled) by the special interests of the industry being regulated.

1. In many cases, persons who have been in the industry are asked to regulate the industry because they know the most about it. Such regulators are likely to feel a bond with people in the industry, to see their side of the story more often than not, and thus to be inclined to cater to them.

2. At regulatory hearings, members of the industry attend in greater force than do taxpayers and consumers. The industry turns out in force because the regulatory hearing can affect it substantially and directly. In contrast, the effect on individual taxpayers and consumers is usually small and indirect. (The effect is spread over millions of people.) Thus, regulators are much more likely to hear and respond to the industry's side of the story.

3. Members of the regulated industry make a point of getting to know the members of the regulatory agency. They may talk frequently about business matters; perhaps they socialize. The bond between the two groups grows stronger over time, possibly having an impact on regulatory measures.

4. After they either retire or quit their jobs, regulators often go to work for the industries they once regulated.

Public Interest Theory of Regulation
A theory holding that regulators are seeking to do—and will do through regulation—what is in the best interest of the public or society at large.

The capture theory is markedly different from what has come to be called the **public interest theory of regulation**. This theory holds that regulators are seeking to do—and will do through regulation—what is in the best interest of the public or society at large.

An alternative to both theories is the **public choice theory of regulation**. This theory suggests that, to understand the decisions of regulatory bodies, we must first understand how the decisions

Public Choice Theory of Regulation
A theory holding that regulators are seeking to do—and will do through regulation—what is in their best interest (specifically, to enhance their power and the size and budget of their regulatory agencies).

affect the regulators themselves. For example, a regulation that increases the power, size, and budget of the regulatory agency should not be viewed in the same way as a regulation that decreases the agency's power and size. The theory predicts that the outcomes of the regulatory process will tend to favor the regulators instead of either business interests or the public.

These are three interesting, different, and, at first sight, believable theories of regulation, and economists have directed much effort to testing them. There is no clear consensus yet, but in the area of business regulation, the adherents of the capture and public choice theories have been increasing.

Hear What and How the Economist Thinks . . .
About Regulation

The economist overhears two people talking:

Person 1: "Business needs to be regulated. If business firms were not regulated, then prices would be higher, quality would be lower, employees would be treated poorly, and who knows what else."

Person 2: "But I've heard that regulations can end up doing more harm than good."

Hear what and how the economist thinks:

Where to begin? When it comes to regulation, there seems to be so much to discuss. Person 1 says that if business firms were not regulated, certain things would follow, such as higher prices, lower-quality goods, and so on. This isn't necessarily true. Economists often point out that competition between firms is often what keeps prices low, quality high, and so on. In short, firms often compete on price, quality, terms of service, location, and more. Think of firms producing computers for sale. Does one computer company care about the prices other computer companies are selling their computers for? Does it care what quality of computer is being offered by other computer companies? If it doesn't take into account where potential customers can buy their computers, then the company may find itself without any sales.

Regulation isn't guaranteed to give consumers the lowest price or highest quality goods. Suppose profit regulation is enacted, in which the government requires that the price be set equal to the average total cost so that economic profits are zero. But now the regulated firm can let its average costs rise, knowing that it will then be allowed by the government to raise its price. In other words, with profit regulation, sometimes called average cost pricing, we might see higher prices over time.

Finally, it also seems that person 1 believes that the regulations that government imposes on business firms are regulations that business firms would rather do without. In other words, business firms do not want the regulations that government foists upon them. But this isn't always true. To illustrate, suppose there are ten airline companies operating in the country. These ten airline companies may actually want government to impose certain regulations on the airline industry. For example, they may want a regulation that says that each of the airlines cannot compete on price. In other words, a trip between New York and Los Angeles is set at $500 and no firm can charge a lower price than $500. Or perhaps these airline companies want a regulation that restricts the number of airline companies that can travel the same route between cities. Or maybe the ten airline companies want a regulation that prevents new airline companies from entering the industry. Regulating price, routes, and entry into the existing airline industry serves the ten airline companies by preventing them from competing with each other in terms of price or routes, and by preventing new firms from entering the industry and competing with them.

Person 2 thinks like an economist by saying that regulations can end up doing more harm than good. This is not necessarily the case, of course. But the statement does show an understanding that there are both costs and benefits to regulation.

Questions to Think About:

1. "It is in the best interest of the consumer for government to regulate business." This is a somewhat broad statement. What do you think is missing from, or left unidentified, in this statement?

2. A person believes that government almost always benefits consumers instead of producers when it regulates business. Would an advocate of the capture theory of regulation agree? Why or why not?

12-2e The Costs and Benefits of Regulation

Suppose a business firm is polluting the air with smoke from its factories. The government then passes an environmental regulation requiring such firms to purchase antipollution devices that reduce the smoke emitted into the air.

Among the benefits of this kind of regulation is the obvious one of cleaner air, but cleaner air can lead to other benefits. For example, people may have fewer medical problems in the future. In some parts of the country, pollution from cars and factories causes people to cough, feel tired, and experience eye discomfort. More important, some people have chronic medical problems from constantly breathing dirty air. Government regulation that reduces the amount of pollution in the air clearly helps these people.

However, regulation usually comes with costs as well as with benefits. For example, when a business firm incurs the cost of antipollution devices, its overall costs of production rise. Simply put, making its product is costlier for the firm after the regulation is imposed. As a result, the business firm may produce fewer units of the product, raising its product price and causing some workers to lose their jobs.

If you are a worker who loses your job, you may view the government's insistence on antipollution devices differently than if, say, you are someone suffering from chronic lung disease. If you have asthma, less pollution may be the difference between feeling well and feeling sick. If you are a worker for the business firm, less pollution may cost you your job. Ideally, you prefer a little less pollution in your neighborhood, but perhaps not at the cost of losing your job.

Economists are neither for nor against such government regulation. The job of the economist is to make the point that regulation involves both benefits and costs. To the person who sees only the costs, the economist asks, what about the benefits? To the person who sees only the benefits, the economist asks, what about the costs? Then the economist goes on to identify the benefits and the costs as best as possible.

Does It Matter to You . . .

If People Are Aware of Both the Costs and the Benefits of Regulation?

Economists often make the point that there are both costs and benefits to most activities. Consider getting an education, buying a car, or taking a trip to South America. With all these, there are costs and benefits. To consider only one, and not the other, is to get a false view of things. To consider only the costs of getting an education, and not the benefits, is to underestimate how valuable an education can be. To consider only the benefits of buying a car and not the costs as well is to overestimate how valuable the car can be.

When it comes to some things, it is somewhat difficult not to consider both the costs and benefits. For example, since one actually pays for a car, it is difficult to forget the costs of buying the car and

consider only the benefits. The same probably also holds for education too. Since one has to pay for the education (in the form of paying tuition, buying books, etc.), it is somewhat difficult to ignore the costs of buying an education and consider only the benefits.

But when it comes to things that we do not explicitly pay for, it is much easier to ignore the costs and consider only the benefits. With this in mind, consider regulations. Often when the government regulates the individual is not explicitly paying for the regulation. For instance, individuals are not asked to explicitly pay $100 for safety regulation, or $1,000 for health regulation, and so on. The costs of regulations are often invisible to the average person. Given this, the average person often only sees the benefits of the regulation and not the costs. This can bias the average person into thinking that there are only benefits to regulation and no costs.

There are regulations that apply to a wide variety of things: the environment, safety issues, work-place behavior, health issues, pricing policy, and much more. Often, when it comes to these types of regulations, it is easy to see the benefits, but since no one explicitly asks individuals to directly pay for the regulation in the same way that a person may directly pay for a loaf of bread, a pair of shoes, or a trip to South America, the costs of the regulations are ignored.

Does it matter to you if people are aware of both the costs and the benefits of regulation? Think of how they may vote for regulations if they are not. It is much more likely that a person would be in favor of a regulation if she or he saw only the benefits and not the costs. And if this person is representative of others, then it is likely that many people will favor regulations, not so much because they have carefully considered both the benefits and the costs of those regulations, but because they have considered mainly the benefits and not the costs. What this means for you, then, is that you are likely to end up living in a world where there is much more regulating going on than there would be if people saw both the benefits and the costs of regulations.

SELF-TEST

1. State one criticism of average cost pricing.
2. State the essence of the capture theory of regulation.

3. What is the difference between the capture theory and the public choice theory of regulation?
4. Are economists for or against regulation?

OFFICE HOURS

"What Is the Advantage of the Herfindahl Index?"

STUDENT: In the last chapter, we learned about the four- and eight-firm concentration ratios. These ratios were used to compute the percentage of sales accounted for by the largest four and eight firms in an industry, respectively. In other words, the ratios were used to measure concentration in an industry. In this chapter, we learned about the Herfindahl index, which also measures concentration in an industry. Is the Herfindahl index better at measuring concentration than the other two ratios?

INSTRUCTOR: Many economists think so. The Herfindahl index provides some information that the four- and eight-firm concentration ratios don't. To illustrate, consider two settings: (1) Four firms together have a 50 percent market share, and there are only five other firms in the industry; (2) four firms together have a 50 percent market share, and there are 50 other firms in the industry. The four-firm concentration ratio is the same in both settings, but the Herfindahl index is not.

STUDENT: In other words, the four-firm concentration ratio is 50 percent in both settings, but the Herfindahl index in the first setting would be different from the Herfindahl index in the second setting because of how it is calculated. Is that correct?

INSTRUCTOR: Yes, that's correct.

STUDENT: This has me thinking. Something about the concentration ratios and Herfindahl index makes me a little uneasy. In the past, I haven't been able to figure out what it is, but now I think I can. There seems to be a little too much emphasis and importance on a single number. Is a high number for the Herfindahl index (say, above 2,500) always bad? It just seems to me that a high number doesn't always have to signify the same thing.

INSTRUCTOR: Others have made that very point. In fact, both the four- and eight-firm concentration ratios, as well as the Herfindahl index, have been criticized for implicitly arguing from firm size and industry concentration to market power. Both assume that firms with large market shares have market power which they are likely to be abusing, but perhaps they're not. Size could be a function of efficiency, and a firm with a large market share could be serving the buying public well.

STUDENT: Yes, that is what I was getting at. It seems to me that the process of how a firm got to be big matters.

INSTRUCTOR: I should say that the terms "process" and "behavior" have come to mean more in recent years, particularly with economists and with the Antitrust Division of the U.S. Justice Department. With respect to behavior, more emphasis these days is placed on how the firm behaves—no matter its size and market power. To illustrate, two firms of equal size relative to other firms

in their respective industries could behave differently. One firm may reduce output and charge higher prices, while the other firm may increase output and charge lower prices.

Points to Remember

1. In the two settings (four firms have 50 percent market share but the number of other firms in the industry is different), the four-firm concentration ratio is the same, but the Herfindahl index is not. The Herfindahl index supplies more information, specifically about the dispersion of firm size in an industry, than either the four- or eight-firm concentration ratio does.

2. In recent years, process (how did the firm get to be big?) and behavior (how does the firm act?) have come to mean more when firms are evaluated.

CHAPTER SUMMARY

DEALING WITH MONOPOLY POWER

- A monopoly produces less than a perfectly competitive firm produces (assuming the same revenue and cost conditions), charges a higher price, and causes a deadweight loss. These factors represent the monopoly power problem, and solving it is usually put forth as a reason for antitrust laws and/or government regulatory actions. Some economists note, though, that government antitrust and regulatory actions do not always have their intended effect. In addition, such actions are sometimes implemented when there is no monopoly power problem to solve.

ANTITRUST LAWS

- Two major criticisms have been directed at the antitrust acts. First, some argue that the language in the laws is vague; for example, even though the words "restraint of trade" are used in the Sherman Act, the act does not clearly explain what actions constitute a restraint of trade. Second, it has been argued that some antitrust acts appear to hinder, rather than promote, competition; an example is the Robinson–Patman Act.

- Antitrust policy has a few unsettled points. One centers on the proper definition of a market—specifically, whether it should

be defined narrowly or broadly. How this question is answered has an impact on which firms are considered monopolies. In addition, the use of concentration ratios for identifying monopolies or deciding whether to allow two firms to enter into a merger has been called into question. Recently, for purposes of implementing antitrust policy, concentration ratios have been largely replaced with the Herfindahl index, which is subject to some of the same criticisms as the concentration ratios. Antitrust authorities are also beginning to consider the benefits of innovation in ruling on proposed mergers.

REGULATION

- Even if we assume that the intent of regulation is to serve the public interest, we may not assume that it will in fact do so. To work as desired, regulation (1) must be based on complete information (e.g., the regulatory body must know the cost conditions of the regulated firm) and (2) must not distort incentives (e.g., to keep costs down). Many economists are quick to point out that neither condition is likely to be fully met.

- Government uses three basic types of regulation to regulate natural monopolies: price, profit, and output regulation. Price regulation usually means marginal cost price regulation—that is, setting $P = MC$. Profit regulation usually means zero economic profits. Output regulation specifies a particular quantity of output that the natural monopoly must produce.

- The capture theory of regulation holds that, no matter what the motive is for the initial regulation and the establishment of the regulatory agency, eventually the agency will be captured (controlled) by the special interests of the industry being regulated. The public interest theory holds that regulators are seeking to do—and will do through regulation—what is in the best interest of the public or society at large. The public choice theory holds that regulators are seeking to do—and will do through regulation—what is in their best interest (specifically, enhance their own power, size, and budget).

KEY TERMS AND CONCEPTS

Antitrust Law	Vertical Merger	Regulatory Lag	Public Choice Theory of
Trust	Conglomerate Merger	Capture Theory of Regulation	Regulation
Herfindahl Index	Network Good	Public Interest Theory of	
Horizontal Merger	Lock-In Effect	Regulation	

QUESTIONS AND PROBLEMS

1. Why was the Robinson–Patman Act passed? The Wheeler–Lea Act? the Celler–Kefauver Antimerger Act?

2. Explain why defining a market narrowly or broadly can make a difference in how antitrust policy is implemented.

3. What is one difference between the four-firm concentration ratio and the Herfindahl index?

4. How does a vertical merger differ from a horizontal merger? Why would the government look more carefully at one than at the other?

5. What is the implication of saying that regulation is likely to affect incentives?

6. Explain price regulation, profit regulation, and output regulation.

7. Why might profit regulation lead to rising costs for the regulated firm?

8. What is the major difference between the capture theory of regulation and the public interest theory of regulation?

9. George Stigler and Claire Friedland studied both unregulated and regulated electric utilities and found no difference in the rates they charged. One could draw the conclusion that regulation is ineffective when it comes to utility rates. What ideas or hypotheses presented in this chapter might have predicted this result?

10. The courts have ruled that it is a reasonable restraint of trade (and therefore permissible) for the owner of a business to sell his business and sign a contract with the new owner saying that he will not compete with her within a vicinity of, say, 100 miles, for a period of, say, 5 years. If this type of contract is a reasonable restraint of trade, can you give an example of what you would consider an unreasonable restraint of trade? Explain how you decide what is a reasonable restraint of trade and what isn't.

11. In your opinion, what is the best way to deal with the monopoly power problem? Do you advocate antitrust laws, regulation, or something not discussed in the chapter? Give reasons for your answer.

12. It is usually asserted that public utilities such as electric companies and gas companies are natural monopolies, but an assertion is not proof. How would you go about trying to prove (or disprove) that electric companies and the like are (or are not) natural monopolies? (*Hint:* Consider comparing the average total cost of a public utility that serves many customers with the average total cost of a public utility that serves relatively few customers.)

13. Discuss the advantages and disadvantages of regulation (as you see it).

14. Explain how the lock-in effect might make it less likely for a firm that benefits from it to innovate.

WORKING WITH NUMBERS AND GRAPHS

1. Calculate the Herfindahl index and the four-firm concentration ratio for the following industry:

Firms	Market Share (%)
A	17
B	15
C	14
D	14
E	12
F	10
G	9
H	9

Use the accompanying figure to answer questions 2–4.

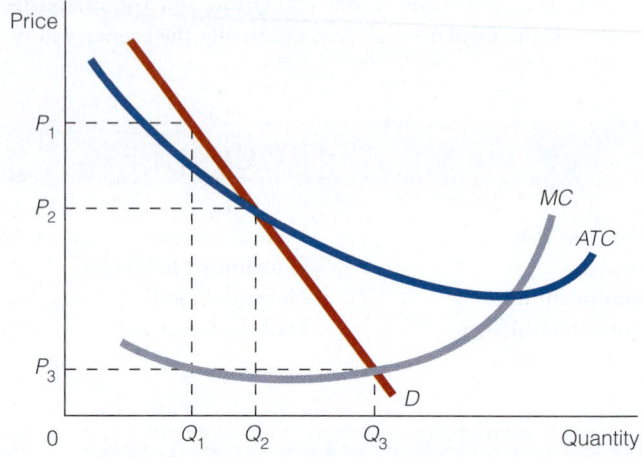

2. Is the firm in the figure a natural monopoly? Explain your answer.

3. Will the firm in the figure earn profits if it produces Q_3 and charges P_3? Explain your answer.

4. Which quantity in the figure is consistent with profit regulation? With price regulation? Explain your answers.

FACTOR MARKETS: WITH EMPHASIS ON THE LABOR MARKET

Monkey Business Images/Shutterstock.com

INTRODUCTION

Employees want to know why their salaries can't be higher: They would like to have more income for spending and saving. Employees might wonder, "Why am I not getting paid $10,000 more? Why not $20,000 more?" Of course, employers look at salaries differently: They would like to pay lower salaries. Employers may look at a salary and wonder, "Why couldn't I have paid $10,000 less? Why not $20,000 less?" Salaries are determined by economic forces. This chapter identifies the factors and the process affecting your pay. Without a doubt, this chapter is relevant to you.

13-1 FACTOR MARKETS

Just as there is a demand for and a supply of a product, there is a demand for and a supply of a factor, or resource, such as labor.

13-1a The Demand for a Factor

All firms—perfectly competitive firms, oligopolistic firms, or whatever—purchase factors in order to make products to sell. For example, farmers buy tractors and fertilizer in order to produce crops to sell. General Motors buys steel in order to build cars to sell.

The demand for factors is a **derived demand**; that is, it is derived from, and directly related to, the demand for the product that the resources go to produce. If the demand for the product rises, so does the demand for the factors that go into the making of the product. If the demand for the product falls, so does the demand for the factors. For example, if the demand for a university education falls, so does the demand for university professors. If the demand for computers rises, so does the demand for skilled computer workers.

When the demand for a seller's product rises, the seller needs to decide how much more of a factor to buy. Marginal revenue product and marginal factor cost are relevant to this decision.

Derived Demand
Demand that is the result of some other demand. For example, factor demand is derived from the demand for the products that the factors go to produce.

FINDING ECONOMICS

In a Restaurant Frank is sitting in a restaurant giving his order to the server. Where is the economics?

It is to be found in the server. The demand for servers is a derived demand—derived from the demand for eating out at restaurants. If the demand for eating out falls, we can expect the demand for servers to fall; if the demand for eating out rises, we can expect the demand for servers to rise.

13-1b Marginal Revenue Product: Two Ways to Calculate It

Marginal Revenue Product (MRP)

The additional revenue generated by employing an additional factor unit.

Marginal revenue product (MRP) is the additional revenue generated by employing an additional factor unit, such as one more unit of labor. For example, if a firm employs one more unit of a factor and its total revenue rises by $20, the *MRP* of the factor equals $20. Marginal revenue product can be calculated in two ways, either as

$$MRP = \frac{\Delta TR}{\Delta \text{Quantity of the factory}}$$

or as

$$MRP = MR \times MPP$$

where TR = total revenue, MR = marginal revenue, and MPP = marginal physical product. Exhibit 1 shows the two methods for calculating *MRP* for a hypothetical firm.

Method 1: $MRP = \Delta TR / \Delta$ Quantity of the Factor   Look at Exhibit 1(a):

- Column 1 shows the different quantities of factor X.
- Column 2 shows the quantity of output produced at the different quantities of factor X.
- Column 3 lists the price and the marginal revenue of the product that the factor goes to produce. We have assumed that the product's price (*P*) equals the product's marginal revenue (*MR*). So the seller in Exhibit 1 is a perfectly competitive firm, for which $P = MR$.
- In column 4, we calculate the total revenue, or price multiplied by quantity.
- In column 5, we calculate the marginal revenue product (*MRP*) by dividing the change in total revenue (from column 4) by the change in the quantity of the factor.

Method 2: $MRP = MR \times MPP$ Now look at Exhibit 1(b). Columns 1 and 2 are the same as in Exhibit 1(a), and the other columns show the corresponding calculations.

13-1c The *MRP* Curve Is the Firm's Factor Demand Curve

Value Marginal Product (VMP)

The price of a good multiplied by the marginal physical product of the factor: $VMP = P \times MPP$.

Look again at column 5 in part (a) of Exhibit 1. Column 5 shows the *MRP* for factor X. By plotting the data in column 5 against the quantity of the factor (in column 1), we derive the *MRP* curve for factor X. This curve is the same as the firm's demand curve for factor X (or, simply, the firm's factor demand curve; see Exhibit 2):

$$MRP \text{ curve} = \text{Factor demand curve}$$

EXHIBIT 1

Calculating Marginal Revenue Product (MRP)

There are two methods of calculating MRP. Part (a) shows one method ($MRP = \Delta TR / \Delta$ Quantity of the factor), and part (b) shows the other ($MRP = MR \times MPP$).

(1) Quantity of Factor X	(2) Quantity of Output, Q	(3) Product Price, Marginal Revenue ($P = MR$)	(4) Total Revenue $TR = P \times Q$ $= (3) \times (2)$	(5) Marginal Revenue Product of Factor X: $MRP = \Delta TR / \Delta$Quantity of Factor X $= \Delta(4)/\Delta(1)$
0	10*	$5	$50	—
1	19	5	95	$45
2	27	5	135	40
3	34	5	170	35
4	40	5	200	30
5	45	5	225	25

(a)

(1) Quantity of Factor X	(2) Quantity of Output, Q	(3) Marginal Physical Product $MPP = \Delta(2)/\Delta(1)$	(4) Product Price, Marginal Revenue ($P = MR$)	(5) Marginal Revenue Product of Factor X: $MRP = MR \times MPP$ $= (4) \times (3)$
0	10*	—	$5	—
1	19	9	5	$45
2	27	8	5	40
3	34	7	5	35
4	40	6	5	30
5	45	5	5	25

(b)

* Because the quantity of output is 10 at 0 units of factor X, other factors (not shown in the exhibit) must also be used to produce the good.

The *MRP* curve in Exhibit 2 is downward sloping. You can understand why when you recall that *MRP* can be calculated as $MRP = MR \times MPP$. With regard to *MPP*, the marginal physical product of a factor, you know that, according to the law of diminishing marginal returns, eventually the *MPP* of a factor will diminish. Because *MRP* is equal to $MR \times MPP$ and because *MPP* will eventually decline, *MRP* will eventually decline too.

13-1d Value Marginal Product

Value marginal product (VMP) is equal to the price of the product multiplied by the marginal physical product of the factor:

$$VMP = P \times MPP$$

EXHIBIT 2

The MRP Curve Is the Firm's Factor Demand Curve

The data in columns (1) and (5) in Exhibit 1 are plotted to derive the *MRP* curve. The curve shows the various quantities of the factor the firm is willing to buy at different prices, which is what a demand curve shows. The *MRP* curve is the firm's factor demand curve.

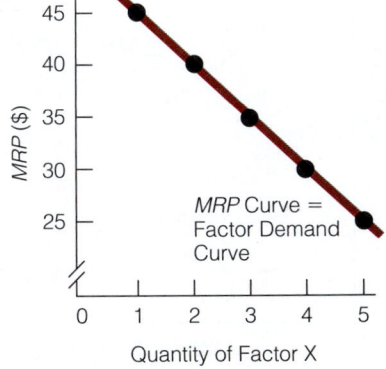

MRP Curve = Factor Demand Curve

Quantity of Factor X

For example, if $P = \$10$ and $MPP = 9$ units, then $VMP = \$90$. Think of VMP as a measure of the value that each factor unit adds to the firm's product or simply as MPP measured in dollars.

A firm wants to know the VMP of a factor because it helps in deciding how many units of the factor to hire. To illustrate, put yourself in the shoes of the owner of a firm that produces computers. One of the factors you need to produce computers is labor, and currently you are thinking of hiring an additional worker. Whether you actually hire the additional worker will depend on (1) how much better off you are—in dollars and cents—with the additional worker and (2) what you have to pay the new hire. Simply put, you want to know what the worker will do for you and what you will have to pay the worker. The VMP of a factor is a dollar measure of how much an additional unit of the factor will do for you.

13-1e An Important Question: Is $MRP = VMP$?

In the computations of MRP in Exhibit 1, price (P) was equal to marginal revenue (MR) because we assumed that the firm was perfectly competitive. Then, because $P = MR$ for a perfectly competitive firm, $MRP = VMP$ for a perfectly competitive firm. Given that

$$MRP = MR \times MPP$$

and

$$VMP = P \times MPP$$

it follows that

$$MRP = VMP \text{ for a perfectly competition firm}$$

because $P = MR$ for a perfectly competitive firm. [See Exhibit 3(a).]

EXHIBIT 3

MRP and VMP Curves

$MRP = MR \times MPP$ and $VMP = P \times MPP$. (a) The MRP (factor demand) curve and the VMP curve. These are the same for a price taker, or perfectly competitive firm, because $P = MR$. (b) The MRP (factor demand) curve and the VMP curve for a firm that is a price searcher (monopolist, monopolistic competitor, oligopolist). The MRP curve lies below the VMP curve because, for these firms, $P > MR$.

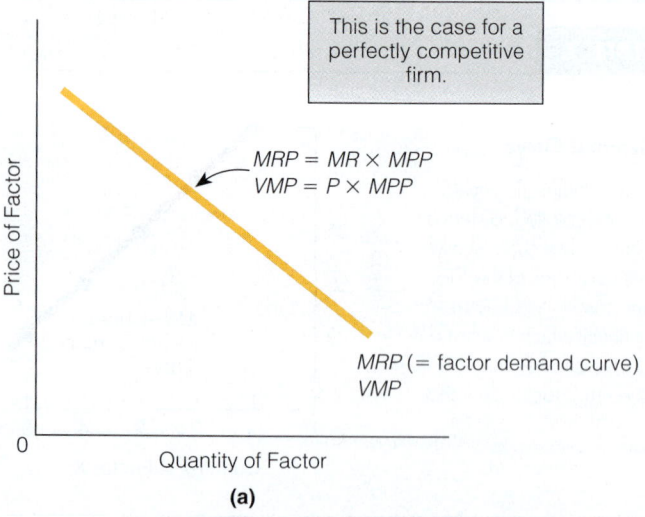

This is the case for a perfectly competitive firm.

$MRP = MR \times MPP$
$VMP = P \times MPP$

MRP (= factor demand curve)
VMP

Price of Factor

0   Quantity of Factor

(a)

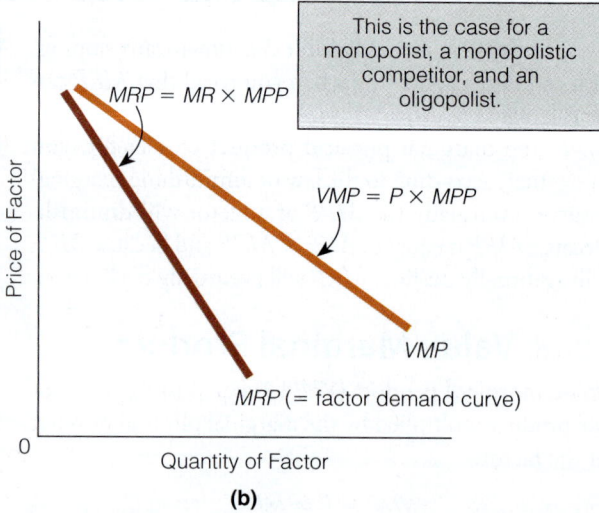

This is the case for a monopolist, a monopolistic competitor, and an oligopolist.

$MRP = MR \times MPP$

$VMP = P \times MPP$

VMP

MRP (= factor demand curve)

Price of Factor

0   Quantity of Factor

(b)

Although $MRP = VMP$ for perfectly competitive firms, this is not the case for firms that are price searchers (monopolist, monopolistically competitive, and oligopolistic firms). All these firms face downward-sloping demand curves for their products. For all of these firms, $P > MR$, so VMP (which is $P \times MPP$) is greater than MRP (which is $MR \times MPP$).[1] That is,

$VMP > MRP$ for monopolists, monopolistic competitors, and oligopolists

[See Exhibit 3(b).]

13-1f Marginal Factor Cost: The Firm's Factor Supply Curve

Marginal factor cost (MFC) is the additional cost incurred by employing an additional factor unit. It is calculated as

$$MFC = \frac{\Delta TC}{\Delta \text{Quantity of the factor}}$$

where TC = total costs.

Let's suppose a firm is a **factor price taker**: it can buy all it wants of a factor at the equilibrium price. For example, suppose the equilibrium price for factor X is $5. If a firm is a factor price taker, it can buy any quantity of factor X at $5 per factor unit. [See Exhibit 4(a).] For this kind of firm, the marginal factor cost (MFC) curve (the firm's factor supply curve) would be horizontal (flat, or perfectly elastic), as shown in Exhibit 4(b).[2]

Marginal Factor Cost (MFC)
The additional cost incurred by employing an additional factor unit.

Factor Price Taker
A firm that can buy all of a factor it wants at the equilibrium price. Such a firm faces a horizontal (flat, perfectly elastic) supply curve of factors.

EXHIBIT 4

Calculating MFC and Deriving the MFC Curve (the Firm's Factor Supply Curve)

In (a), MFC is calculated in column 4. Notice that the firm is a factor price taker because it can buy any quantity of factor X at a given price per factor unit ($5, as shown in column 2). In (b), the data from columns (1) and (4) are plotted to derive the MFC curve, which is the firm's factor supply curve.

(1) Quantity of Factor X	(2) Price of Factor X	(3) Total Cost $TC = (2) \times (1)$	(4) $MFC = \Delta TC/\Delta$ Quantity of the Factor $= \Delta(3)/\Delta(1)$
0	$5	$0	—
1	5	5	$5
2	5	10	5
3	5	15	5
4	5	20	5
5	5	25	5
6	5	30	5

(a)

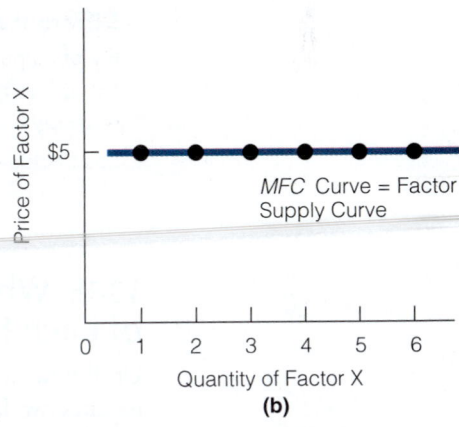

(b)

[1] An exception is the perfectly price-discriminating monopoly firm, for which $P = MR$.

[2] Although the MFC (factor supply curve) for the single-factor price taker is horizontal, the market supply curve is upward sloping. This situation is similar to the one for the perfectly competitive firm, where the firm's demand curve is horizontal but the market (or industry) demand curve is downward sloping. In factor markets, we are simply talking about the supply side of the market instead of the demand side. The firm's supply curve is flat because it can buy additional factor units without driving up the price of the factor; it buys a relatively small portion of the factor. For the industry, however, higher factor prices must be offered to entice factors (e.g., workers) from other industries. The difference in the two supply curves—the firm's and the industry's—is basically a reflection of the different sizes of each.

EXHIBIT 5

Equating *MRP* and *MFC*

The firm continues to purchase a factor as long as the factor's *MRP* exceeds its *MFC*. In the exhibit, the firm purchases Q_1.

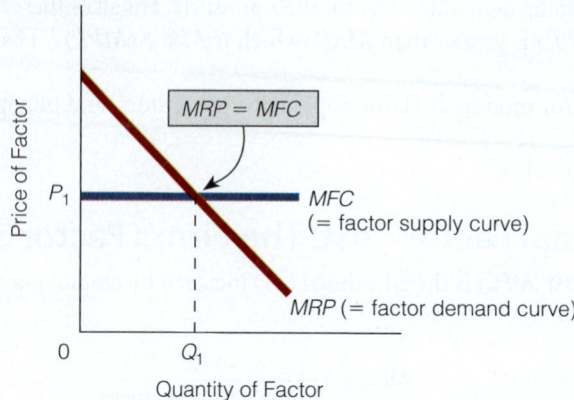

13-1g How Many Units of a Factor Should a Firm Buy?

Suppose you graduate with a BA in economics and go to work for a business firm. The first day on the job, you are involved in a discussion about factor X. Your employer asks you, "How many units of this factor should we buy?" What would you say?

Your response is based on marginal analysis. "Continue buying additional units of the factor," you say, "until the additional revenue generated by employing an additional factor unit is equal to the additional cost incurred by employing an additional factor unit." Simply stated, keep buying additional units of the factor until $MRP = MFC$. In Exhibit 5, MRP equals MFC at a factor quantity of Q_1.

THINKING LIKE AN ECONOMIST

Different Markets, Same Principles   In the product market, a firm produces that quantity of output at which marginal revenue equals marginal cost $(MR = MC)$. In the factor market, a firm buys the factor quantity at which marginal revenue product equals marginal factor cost $(MRP = MFC)$. The economic principle of equating additional benefits with additional costs holds in both markets.

13-1h When There Is More Than One Factor, How Much of Each Factor Should the Firm Buy?

Until now, we have discussed the purchase of only one factor. Suppose, however, that a firm requires two factors, labor (L) and capital (K), to produce its product. How does it combine these two factors to minimize costs? Does it combine, say, 20 units of labor with 5 units of capital or perhaps 15 units of labor with 8 units of capital?

The answer is that the firm purchases the two factors until the ratio of MPP to price for one factor equals the ratio of MPP to price for the other factor—in other words,

$$\frac{MPP_L}{P_L} = \frac{MPP_K}{P_K}$$

This is the **least-cost rule**. To understand its logic, consider an example. Suppose that, for a firm, (1) the price of labor is $5, (2) the price of capital is $10, (3) an extra unit of labor results in an increase in output of 25 units, and (4) an extra unit of capital results in an increase in output of 25 units. Notice that MPP_L/P_L is greater than MPP_K/P_K: 25/$5 > 25/$10. Thus, for this firm, $1 spent on labor is more effective at raising output than $1 spent on capital. In fact, it is twice as effective.

Now, suppose the firm currently spends an extra $5 on labor and an extra $10 on capital. With this purchase of the two factors, the firm *is not* minimizing costs. It spends an additional $15 and produces 50 additional units of output. If, instead, it spent an additional $10 on labor and $0 on capital, it could still have produced the 50 additional units of output and saved $5.

To minimize costs, the firm will rearrange its purchases of factors until the least-cost rule is met. To illustrate, if $MPP_L/P_L > MPP_K/P_K$, then the firm buys more labor and less capital. As a result, the MPP of labor falls and the MPP of capital rises, bringing the two ratios closer in line. The firm continues to buy more of the factor whose MPP-to-price ratio is larger. It stops when the two ratios are equal.

Least-Cost Rule
Rule that specifies the combination of factors that minimizes costs and so requires that the following condition be met:
$MPP_1/P_1 = MPP_2/P_2 = \cdots = MPP_N/P_N$
where the subscript numbers stand for the different factors.

THINKING LIKE AN ECONOMICS

Two Different Settings, Same Principles We can compare a firm's least-cost rule with how buyers allocate their consumption dollars. A buyer of goods in the product market chooses combinations of goods so that the marginal utility of good A divided by the price of good A is equal to the marginal utility of good B divided by the price of good B—that is, $MU_A/P_A = MU_B/P_B$.

A firm buying factors in the factor market chooses combinations of factors so that the marginal physical product of, say, labor, divided by the price of labor (the wage rate), is equal to the marginal physical product of capital, divided by the price of capital—that is, $MPP_L/P_L = MPP_K/P_K$.

Thus, consumers buy goods in the same way that firms buy factors. This similarity points out something that you may already have sensed: Although economic principles are few, they sometimes seem numerous because we find them in so many different settings.

The same economic principle lies behind equating the MU/P ratios for different goods in the product market and equating the MPP/P ratios for different resources in the resource market. In short, only one economic principle is at work in the two markets, not two different ones. That principle simply says that, in their attempt to meet their objectives, economic actors will arrange their purchases in such a way that they receive equal additional benefits per dollar of expenditure.

Seeing how a few economic principles operate in many different settings is part of the economic way of thinking.

SELF-TEST

(Answers to Self-Test questions are in Answers to Self-Test Questions at the back of the book.)

1. When a perfectly competitive firm employs one worker, it produces 20 units of output, and when it employs two workers, it produces 39 units of output. The firm sells its product for $10 per unit. What is the marginal revenue product connected with hiring the second worker?

2. What is the difference between marginal revenue product (*MRP*) and value marginal product (*VMP*)?

3. What is the distinguishing characteristic of a factor price taker?

4. How much labor should a firm purchase?

13-2 THE LABOR MARKET

Labor is a factor of special interest because, at one time or another, most people find themselves in the labor market. This section discusses first the demand for labor, then the supply of labor, and finally the two together. The section focuses on a firm that is a price taker both in the product market (i.e., a perfectly competitive firm) and in the factor market.[3] In this setting, the demand for and supply of labor determine wage rates.

13-2a Shifts in a Firm's *MRP*, or Factor Demand, Curve

As explained earlier, a firm's *MRP* curve is its factor demand curve and marginal revenue product equals marginal revenue multiplied by marginal physical product:

$$MRP = MR \times MPP \tag{1}$$

For a perfectly competitive firm, for which $P = MR$, we can write equation (1) as

$$MRP = P \times MPP \tag{2}$$

Now consider the demand for a specific factor input: labor. What will happen to the factor demand (*MRP*) curve for labor as the price of the product that the labor produces changes? In Exhibit 6, the initial product price is $10 and the initial factor demand curve is MRP_1. At wage rate W_1, the firm hires Q_1 labor. Suppose the product price rises to $12. As we can see from equation (2), *MRP* also rises. At each wage rate, the firm wants to hire more labor. For example, at W_1, it wants to hire Q_2 labor instead of Q_1. In short, a rise in product price shifts the firm's *MRP*, or factor demand, curve rightward. If product price falls from $10 to $8, then *MRP* falls. At each wage rate, the firm wants to hire less labor. For example, at W_1 it wants to hire Q_3 labor instead of Q_1. In short, a fall in product price shifts the firm's *MRP*, or factor demand, curve leftward.

EXHIBIT 6

Shifts in the Firm's *MRP*, or Factor Demand, Curve

It is always the case that $MRP = MR \times MPP$. For a perfectly competitive firm, for which $P = MR$, it follows that $MRP = P \times MPP$. If P changes, *MRP* will change. For example, if the product price rises, then *MRP* rises and the firm's *MRP* curve (factor demand curve) shifts rightward. If the product price falls, then *MRP* falls and the firm's *MRP* curve (factor demand curve) shifts leftward. If *MPP* rises (reflected in a shift in the *MPP* curve), then *MRP* rises and the firm's *MRP* curve shifts rightward. If *MPP* falls, then *MRP* falls and the firm's *MRP* curve shifts leftward.

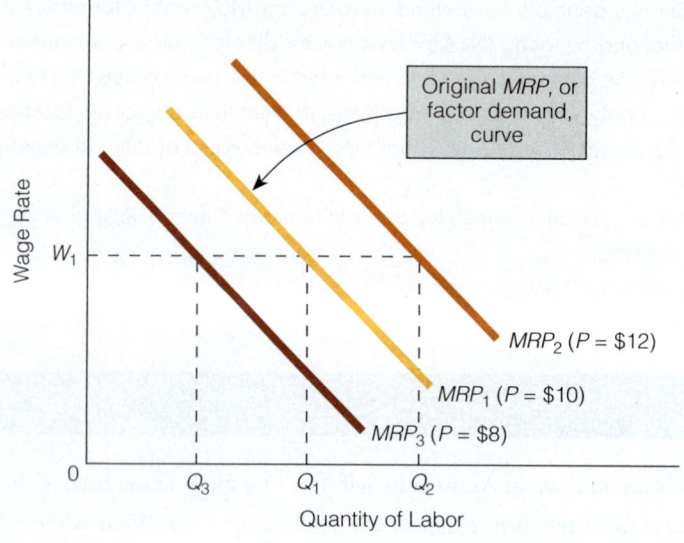

[3] Keep in mind that, in the labor market here, neither buyers nor sellers have any control over wage rates. Consequently, supply and demand are our analytical tools. In the next chapter, we modify this analysis.

Changes in the *MPP* of the factor—reflected in a shift in the *MPP* curve—also change the firm's *MRP* curve. As we can see from equation (2), an increase in, say, the *MPP* of labor will increase *MRP* and shift the *MRP*, or factor demand, curve rightward. A decrease in *MPP* will decrease *MRP* and shift the *MRP*, or factor demand, curve leftward.[4]

ECONOMICS 24/7

Why Jobs Don't Always Move to a Low-Wage Country

Some people think that tariffs are needed to protect U.S. workers. They argue that, without tariffs, U.S. companies will relocate to countries where wages are lower. They will produce their products there and then transport the products to the United States to sell them. Tariffs will make this scenario less likely because the gains the companies receive in lower wages will be offset by the tariffs imposed on their goods.

What this argument overlooks is that U.S. companies are interested not only in what they pay workers, but also in the marginal productivity of the workers. For example, suppose a U.S. worker earns $10 an hour and a Mexican worker earns $4 an hour. Say the marginal physical product (*MPP*) of the U.S. worker is 10 units of good X and the *MPP* of the Mexican worker is 2 units. Thus, we have lower wages in Mexico and higher productivity in the United States. Where will the company produce?

Golden Brown/Shutterstock.com

To answer this question, compare the output produced per $1 of cost in the two countries:

$$\text{Output produced per \$1 of cost} = \frac{\text{MPP of the factor}}{\text{Cost of the factor}}$$

In the United States, at an *MPP* of 10 units of good X and a wage rate of $10, workers produce 1 unit of good X for every $1 they are paid:

$$\frac{\text{MPP of U.S. labor}}{\text{Wage rate of U.S. labor}} = \frac{10 \text{ units of good X}}{\$10}$$

$$= 1 \text{ unit of good X per \$1}$$

In Mexico, at an *MPP* of 2 units and a wage rate of $4, workers produce half a unit of good X for every $1 they are paid:

$$\frac{\text{MPP of Mexican labor}}{\text{Wage rate of Mexican labor}} = \frac{2 \text{ units of good X}}{\$4}$$

$$= 1/2 \text{ unit of good X per \$1}$$

Thus, the company gets more output per $1 of cost by using U.S. labor and will produce good X in the United States. It is cheaper to produce the good in the United States than it is in Mexico, even though wages are lower in Mexico.

In other words, U.S. companies look at the following ratios:

(1)

$$\frac{\text{MPP of labor in U.S.}}{\text{Wage rate in U.S.}}$$

(2)

$$\frac{\text{MPP of labor in country X}}{\text{Wage rate in country X}}$$

If ratio (1) is greater than ratio (2), U.S. companies will hire labor in the United States. As they do so, the *MPP* of labor in the United States will decline (according to the law of diminishing marginal returns). Companies will continue to hire labor in the United States until ratio (1) is equal to ratio (2).

---

[4] We are talking about a change in MPP that is reflected in a shift in the *MPP* curve, not a movement along a given *MPP* curve.

13-2b **Market Demand for Labor**

We would expect the market demand curve for labor to be the horizontal addition of the firm's demand curves (*MRP* curves) for labor. However, this expectation is not met, as Exhibit 7 illustrates. Two firms, A and B, make up the buying side of the factor market, and the product price for both firms is P_1. Parts (a) and (b) in the exhibit show the *MRP* curves for the two firms, based on this product price.

The Derivation of the Market Demand Curve for Labor Units

Two firms, A and B, make up the buying side of the market for labor. At a wage rate of W_1, firm A purchases 100 units of labor and firm B purchases 150 units. Together, they purchase

250 units, as illustrated in (c). Then the wage rate rises to W_2, and the amount of labor purchased by both firms initially falls to 180 units, as shown in (c). Higher wage rates translate into higher costs, a fall in product supply, and a rise in product price from P_1 to P_2. Finally, an

increased price raises *MRP*, and each firm has a new *MRP* curve. The horizontal addition of the new *MRP* curves shows that the two firms together purchase 210 units of labor. Connecting the units of labor purchased by both firms at W_1 and W_2 gives the market demand curve.

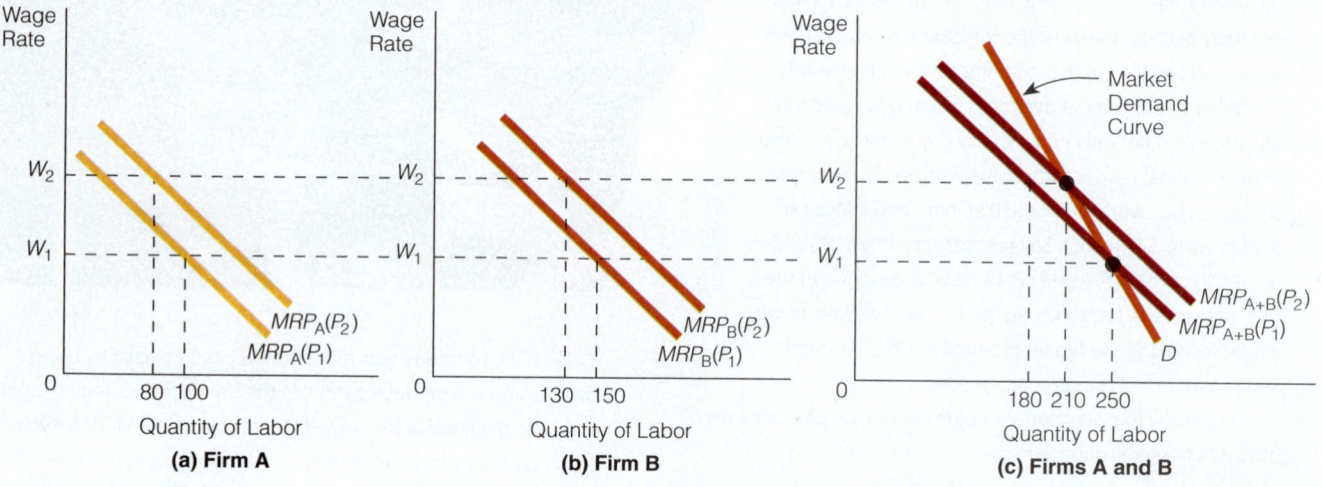

(a) Firm A   **(b) Firm B**   **(c) Firms A and B**

At a wage rate of W_1, firm A purchases 100 units of labor, the amount of labor at which its marginal revenue product equals marginal factor cost (or the wage). At this same wage rate, firm B purchases 150 units of labor. If we add the *MRP* curves of firms A and B horizontally, we get the curve $MRP_{A+B}(P_1)$ in part (c), in which the two firms together purchase 250 units of labor at W_1.

Now assume that the wage rate increases to W_2. In part (c), firms A and B move up the given MRP_{A+B} curve and purchase 180 units of labor. The process may seem to end here, but of course it does not, because a higher wage rate increases each firm's costs and thus shifts its supply curve leftward. This shift, in turn, leads to an increase in product price, to P_2.

Recall that the firm's marginal revenue product is equal to marginal revenue (or price if the firm is perfectly competitive) times marginal physical product: $MRP = MR \times MPP = P \times MPP$. So, if price rises (which it did), so does *MRP*, and therefore each firm faces a new *MRP* curve at the wage rate W_2. Parts (a) and (b) in Exhibit 7 illustrate these new *MRP* curves for firms A and B, and part (c) shows the horizontal addition of the *new MRP* curves. Now the firms together purchase 210 units of labor at W_2.

After all adjustments have been made, connecting the units of labor purchased by both firms at W_1 and W_2 gives the market demand curve in part (c).

13-2c The Elasticity of Demand for Labor

If the wage rate rises, firms will cut back on the labor they hire. How much they cut back depends on the **elasticity of demand for labor**, which is the percentage change in the quantity demanded of labor divided by the percentage change in the price of labor (the wage rate). That is,

$$E_L = \frac{\text{Percentage change in quantity demanded of labor}}{\text{Percentage change in wage rate}}$$

where $E_L =$ coefficient of elasticity of demand for labor or, simply, the elasticity coefficient.

For example, when the wage rate changes by 20 percent, the quantity demanded of a particular type of labor changes by 40 percent. The elasticity of demand for this type of labor is, then, 2 (40 percent ÷ 20 percent), and the demand between the old wage rate and the new wage rate is elastic. There are three main determinants of elasticity of demand for labor:

- The elasticity of demand for the product that labor produces

- The ratio of labor costs to total costs

- The number of substitute factors

Elasticity of Demand for Labor
The percentage change in the quantity demanded of labor divided by the percentage change in the wage rate.

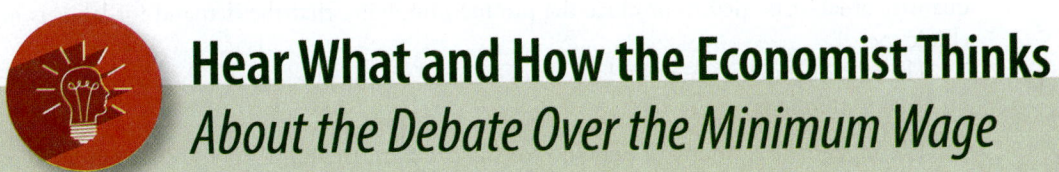

Hear What and How the Economist Thinks . . .
About the Debate Over the Minimum Wage

The economist is watching the news on television. A reporter says: "The debate is heating up over the proposed increase in the minimum wage. We asked people at random if they thought a rise in the minimum wage would lower employment, profits, or both. Nine out of ten said profits. The argument we heard most often was that companies would not lay off people who earned the minimum wage just because it was increased. Instead, the companies would simply see their costs rise, and their profits decline."

Hear what and how the economist thinks:

When it comes to proposals to raise the minimum wage, it seems as if you hear from two groups of people. First, there are those who claim an increase in the minimum wage will not affect the number of persons employed. In other words, if there are 400,000 employees earning a wage rate of $10 an hour, these same 400,000 will still be employed when the wage rate is raised to $15 an hour.

Then there are those who often claim that an increase in the minimum wage will reduce employment quite substantially. For instance, if there are 400,000 employees earning $10 an hour, and then the wage

rate changes to $15 an hour, this increase will cause employment to fall precipitously, say, to 200,000.

What each of the two groups is predicting can be viewed in terms of the formula for the elasticity of labor demand, which is the percentage change in the quantity demanded of labor divided by the percentage change in the wage rate:

Elasticity of labor demand = Percentage change in quantity demanded of labor / Percentage change in wage rate

The first group we mentioned holds that as the denominator in the elasticity formula changes, the numerator does not. In other words, if there is a percentage rise in the wage rate, the percentage change in the quantity demanded of labor will be zero.

The second group we mentioned holds that, as the denominator changes, the numerator will change by a much greater percentage than the denominator. In other words, if the denominator rises by 10 percent, then the numerator will change by 40 percent.

In reality, how many people actually end up losing their minimum-wage jobs as the minimum wage rises depends upon the elasticity of demand for labor. If the demand for labor that is paid the minimum wage is inelastic, then the percentage change in the quantity demanded of labor will be less than the percentage rise in the wage rate. If it is elastic, then the percentage change in the quantity demanded of labor will be greater than the percentage rise in the wage rate. Simply put, it might be the case that as the minimum wage is increased, the cutback in the quantity demanded of labor is very small. But it might also be the case that as the minimum wage is increased, the cutback in the quantity demanded of labor is very large. Again, whether there are large, small, or no reductions in the quantity demanded of labor depends upon the elasticity of labor demand.

Questions to Think About:

1. A person says, "Even if there is a little rain tomorrow, I still think there will be a lot of people going to the beach." How is this similar to the person who says, "Even if the price of the good rises, I still think people will buy as much of the good as they bought before."

2. Person 1 says, "A rise in the minimum wage will not lead to a cutback in the number of persons employed." Person 2 says, "That is not true if the demand curve for labor is downward sloping." Does person 2's comment have any relevance to what person 1 says? Explain your answer.

Elasticity of Demand for the Product That Labor Produces   If the demand for the product that labor produces is highly elastic, a small percentage increase in price (e.g., owing to a wage increase that shifts the supply curve for the product leftward) will decrease the quantity demanded of the product by a relatively large percentage. In turn, this will greatly reduce the quantity of labor needed to produce the product, implying that the demand for labor is highly elastic too.

The relationship between the elasticity of demand for the product and the elasticity of demand for labor is as follows:

- The higher the elasticity of demand for the product, the higher is the elasticity of demand for the labor that produces the product.

- The lower the elasticity of demand for the product, the lower is the elasticity of demand for the labor that produces the product.

Ratio of Labor Costs to Total Costs   Labor costs are a part of total costs. Consider two situations: in one, labor costs are 90 percent of total costs; in the other, labor costs are only 5 percent of total costs. Suppose wages increase by $2 per hour. Then total costs are affected more when labor costs are 90 percent of total costs (the $2-per-hour wage increase is being applied to 90 percent of all costs) than when labor costs are only 5 percent of total costs. Thus, price rises more when labor costs are a larger percentage of total costs. And, of course, the more price rises, the more the quantity demanded of the product falls. Therefore, labor, being a derived demand, is affected more. In short, for a $2-per-hour wage increase, the decline in the quantity demanded of labor is greater when labor costs are 90 percent of total costs than when labor costs are 5 percent of total costs.

The relationship between the ratio of labor cost to total cost and the elasticity of demand for labor is as follows:

- The higher the ratio of labor cost to total cost, the higher is the elasticity of demand for labor (i.e., the greater is the cutback in labor for any given wage increase).

- The lower the ratio of labor cost to total cost, the lower is the elasticity of demand for labor (i.e., the less is the cutback in labor for any given wage increase).

Number of Substitute Factors The more substitutes labor has, the more sensitive buyers of labor will be to a change in its price. This principle was established in the discussion of price elasticity of demand. The more factors that can be substituted for labor, the more likely it is that firms will cut back on their use of labor if its price rises. In sum,

- The more substitutes there are for labor, the higher will be the elasticity of demand for labor.

- The fewer substitutes there are for labor, the lower will be the elasticity of demand for labor.

Does It Matter to You . . .
If the Elasticity of Demand for the Good or Service You Produce Is High or Low?

Consider two individuals: Smith and Jones. Smith works for a company that produces good X, and the elasticity of demand for good X is 3.43.[5] This means that for a 1 percent increase in the price of X, the quantity demanded of X will decline by 3.43 times that 1 percent or −3.43 percent. In other words, for a 10 percent increase in the price of X, quantity demanded of X will decline by 3.43 times 10 percent or −34.3 percent.

Now, if there is a −34.3 percent decline in the quantity demanded of X, then there is not going to be as much need for labor that produces good X. If Smith works for a company that produces X, then there is a chance that he is going to lose his job. The chance of his losing his job is greater when the elasticity of demand for good X is 3.43, than if it were 0.25.

To illustrate, suppose that Jones works for a company that produces good Y and the elasticity of demand for good Y is 0.25. This means that for a 1 percent increase in the price of good Y, the quantity demanded of Y will decline by 0.25 times that 1 percent or −0.25

percent (1/4 of 1 percent). So, in other words, for a 10 percent increase in the price of Y, quantity demanded of Y will decline by 0.25 times 10 percent or −2.5 percent.

Now if there is a −2.5 percent decline in the quantity demanded of Y, there won't be as much a need for labor that produces good Y, so Jones could lose his job. But Jones is not as likely to lose his job as Smith is. Why? Because Smith produces a good that has a much higher price elasticity of demand (3.43) than Jones (0.25).

Does it matter to you if you produce a good or service that has a high or low elasticity of demand? It probably does, because the higher the elasticity of demand for the product that you produce, the less likely you will end up losing your job if the price of the product rises.

---

[5] We are staying with the standard practice here of identifying the coefficient of the price elasticity of demand as an absolute number instead of as a negative number.

13-2d Market Supply of Labor

As the wage rate rises, the quantity supplied of labor rises, *ceteris paribus*. The upward-sloping labor supply curve in Exhibit 8 illustrates this relationship. At a wage rate of W_1, individuals are willing to supply 100 labor units. At the higher wage rate of W_2, individuals are willing to supply 200 labor units. Some individuals who were not willing to work at a wage rate of W_1 are willing to work at a wage rate of W_2, and some individuals who were working at W_1 will be willing to supply more labor units at W_2. At the even higher wage rate of W_3, individuals are willing to supply 280 labor units.

13-2e An Individual's Supply of Labor

Exhibit 8 shows an upward-sloping *market* supply curve of labor. Let's consider an *individual's* supply curve of labor—specifically, whether John's supply curve of labor is upward sloping. The answer depends on the relative strengths of the substitution and income effects.

Suppose John currently earns $10 an hour and works 40 hours a week. If John's wage rate rises to, say, $15 an hour, he will feel two effects, pulling him in opposite directions:

1.   *Substitution effect.* As his wage rate rises, John recognizes that his monetary reward from working has increased. As a result, John will want to work more—say, 45 hours a week instead of 40 hours (an additional 5 hours).

2.   *Income effect.* As his wage rate rises, John knows that he can earn $600 a week (40 hours at $15 an hour) instead of $400 a week (40 hours at $10 an hour). If leisure is a normal good (the demand for which increases as income increases), then John will want to consume more leisure as his income rises. But the only way to consume more leisure is to work fewer hours. Consequently, John might want to decrease his work hours per week from 40 to 37 (3 fewer hours).

Clearly, then, the substitution effect pulls John in one direction (toward working 5 more hours), and the income effect pulls him in the opposite direction (toward working 3 fewer hours). Which effect is stronger? In our numerical example, the substitution effect is stronger, so, on net, John wants to work 2 more hours a week as his wage rate rises. This means that John's supply curve of labor is upward sloping between a wage rate of $10 and $15 per hour.

EXHIBIT 8

The Market Supply of Labor

A direct relationship exists between the wage rate and the quantity of labor supplied.

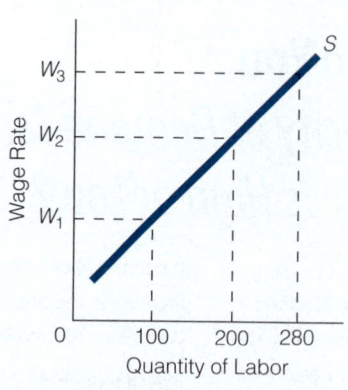

FINDING ECONOMICS

In the Number of Hours a Person Works   Larry works at a job where it is easy to get overtime. He has been earning $20 an hour for the last year, and most weeks he works 45 hours. He recently got a raise to $23 an hour. Since getting his $3-an-hour raise, he has been working about 40 hours a week. Where is the economics?

The economics can be found in the substitution and income effects. As a result of the higher wage, part of Larry wants to work more; this is the substitution effect at work. But part of Larry wants to work less; this is the income effect at work. In the end, Larry works fewer hours (40 instead of 45), showing that his income effect was stronger than his substitution effect.

ECONOMICS 24/7

Adam Smith's Philosopher and Street Porter

In modern economic life, two things are noticeable. First, people specialize in their work: the division of labor is extensive. One is an accountant, not an accountant–painter–teacher. Second, individuals seem to have a strong inclination to trade with each other. How many trades a day do you enter into?

Now, along with the division of labor and the inclination to trade, something else appears: differences in the talents or abilities of people. The surgeon appears to have talents and abilities different from those of the house builder; the architect appears to have talents and abilities different from those of the accountant.

But keep this in mind when we compare the talents and abilities of the surgeon with those of the house builder: Both are adults. In other words, we see a difference between two adults. One wonders, Could we have seen the difference in the talents and abilities between the surgeon and the house builder when they were children?

The father of modern economics, Adam Smith, thought not. In his monumental work *An Inquiry into the Causes and Nature of the Wealth of Nations*, he argued that it was the division of labor and the inclination of individuals to want to trade that, to a large degree,

Library of Congress Prints and Photographs Division [LC-USZ62-17407]

caused the differences in talents and abilities. In the following excerpt, he talks about the differences between a philosopher and a street porter:

The difference of natural talents in different men is, in reality, much less than we are aware of; and the very different genius which appears to distinguish men of different professions, when grown up to maturity, is not upon many occasions so much the cause, as the effect of the division of labour. The difference between the most dissimilar characters, between a philosopher and a common street porter, for example, seems to arise not so much from nature, as from habit, custom, and education. When they came into the world, and for the first six or eight years of their existence, they were perhaps, very much alike, and neither their parents nor playfellows could perceive any remarkable difference. About that age, or soon after, they come to be employed in very different occupations. The difference of talents comes then to be taken notice of, and widens by degrees, till at last the vanity of the philosopher is willing to acknowledge scarce any resemblance. But without the disposition to truck, barter, and exchange, every man must have procured to himself every necessary and conveniency of life which he wanted. All must have had the same duties to perform, and the same work to do, and there could have been no such difference of employment as could alone give occasion to any great difference of talents.

13-2f Shifts in the Labor Supply Curve

Changes in the wage rate change the quantity supplied of labor units; that is, they cause a *movement* along a given supply curve. Two factors of major importance, however, can *shift* the entire labor supply curve: wage rates in other labor markets and the nonmoney, or nonpecuniary, aspects of a job.

Wage Rates in Other Labor Markets Suppose Deborah works as a technician in a television-manufacturing plant but she has skills suitable for a number of jobs. One day, she learns that the computer-manufacturing plant on the other side of town is offering 33 percent more pay per hour. Deborah is also trained to work as a computer operator, so she decides to leave her current job and apply for work at the computer-manufacturing plant. In short, the wage rate offered in other labor markets can bring about a shift of the supply curve in a particular labor market.

Nonmoney, or Nonpecuniary, Aspects of a Job Other things held constant, people prefer to avoid dirty, heavy, dangerous work in cold climates. An increase in the overall unpleasantness of a job (e.g., an increased probability of contracting lung cancer by working in a coal mine) will cause a decrease in the supply of labor to the associated firm or industry and a leftward shift in its labor supply curve. An increase in the overall pleasantness of a job (e.g., employees are now entitled to a longer lunch break and use of the company gym) will cause an increase in the supply of labor to the associated firm or industry and a rightward shift in its labor supply curve.

13-2g Putting Supply and Demand Together

Exhibit 9 illustrates a labor market. The equilibrium wage rate and quantity of labor are established by the forces of supply and demand. At a wage rate of W_2, there is a surplus of labor. Some people who want to work at this wage rate will not be able to find jobs and will begin to offer their services for a lower wage rate. The wage rate will move down until it reaches W_1.

At a wage rate of W_3, there is a shortage of labor. Some demanders of labor will begin to bid up the wage rate until it reaches W_1. At the equilibrium wage rate, W_1, the quantity supplied of labor equals the quantity demanded of labor.

EXHIBIT 9

Equilibrium in a Particular Labor Market

The forces of supply and demand bring about the equilibrium wage rate and quantity of labor. At the equilibrium wage rate, the quantity demanded of labor equals the quantity supplied. At any other wage rate, there is either a surplus or a shortage of labor.

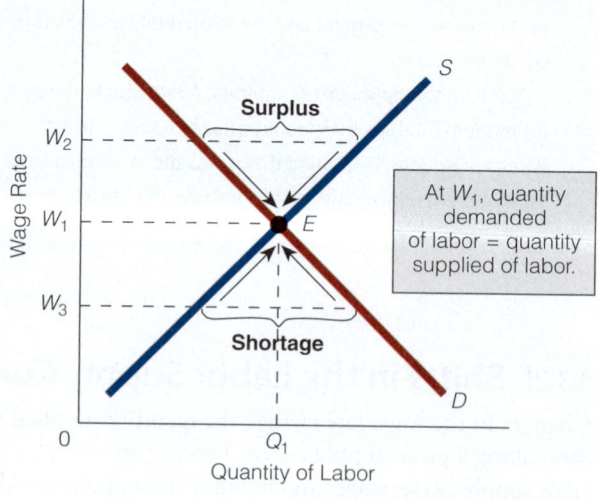

13-2h Why Do Wage Rates Differ?

To discover why wage rates differ, we must determine what conditions are necessary for everyone to receive the same pay. Assume the following conditions:

1. The demand for every type of labor is the same. (Throughout our analysis, any wage differentials caused by demand are short-run phenomena.)

2. The jobs have no special nonpecuniary aspects.

3. All labor is ultimately homogeneous, and laborers can be trained at no cost (costlessly) for different types of employment.

4. All labor is mobile at zero cost.

Given these conditions, there would be no difference in wage rates in the long run. Exhibit 10 shows two labor markets, A and B. Initially, the supply conditions are different, with a greater supply of workers in labor market B (S_B) than in labor market A (S_A). Because of the different supply conditions, more labor is employed in labor market B (Q_B) than in labor market A (Q_A) and the equilibrium wage rate in labor market B ($10) is lower than it is in labor market A ($30).

EXHIBIT 10

Wage Rate Equalization Across Labor Markets

Given the four necessary conditions (noted in the text), there will be no wage rate differences across labor markets. We start with a wage rate of $30 in labor market A and a wage rate of $10 in labor market B. Soon, some individuals in B relocate to A. This shift increases the supply in one market (A), driving down the wage rate, and decreases the supply in the other market (B), driving up the wage rate. Equilibrium comes when the same wage rate is paid in both labor markets. This outcome critically depends on the necessary conditions holding.

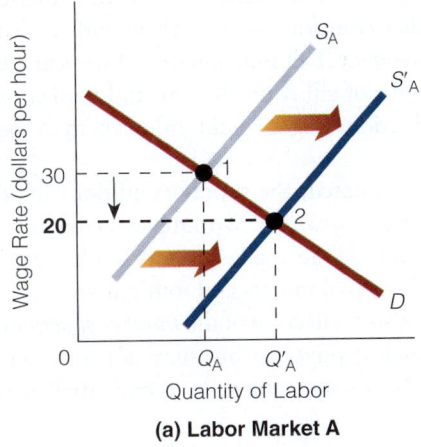

(a) Labor Market A

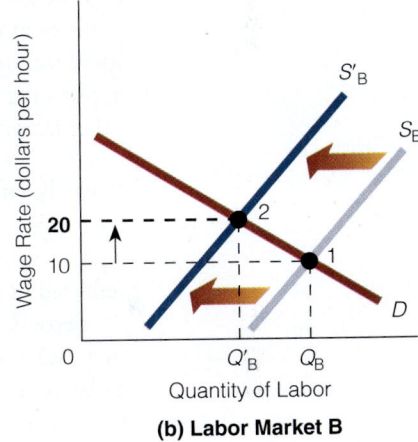

(b) Labor Market B

The differences in the wage rates between the two labor markets will not last. We have assumed that (1) labor can move costlessly from one labor market to another (so labor moves from the lower paying job to the higher paying job); (2) the jobs have no special nonpecuniary aspects (there are no nonpecuniary reasons for not moving); (3) labor is ultimately homogeneous (workers who work in labor market B can work in labor market A); and (4) if workers need training to move from one labor market to another, they not only are capable of being trained but also can acquire the training costlessly.

As a result, some workers in labor market B will relocate to labor market A, decreasing the supply of workers to the level S'_B in labor market B and increasing the supply to the level S'_A in market A. The relocation of workers ends when the equilibrium wage rate in both markets is the same, at $20. Therefore, wage rates will not differ in the long run if our four conditions hold.

Given the conditions under which wage rates will not differ, we now know why wage rates do differ. Obviously, they differ because demand conditions are not the same in all labor markets (a factor that explains only short-run wage differentials) and because supply conditions are not the same in all markets. Jobs *do have* nonpecuniary aspects, labor is *not* homogeneous, labor *cannot* be retrained without cost, and labor is *not* costlessly mobile.

13-2i Why Demand and Supply Differ among Labor Markets

If wage rates differ because demand and supply conditions differ from one market to another, the next question is why. Let's consider the factors that affect the demand for, and the supply of, labor.

Demand for Labor The market demand curve for labor is based on the *MRP* curves for labor of the individual firms in the market. So we need to look at what affects the components of *MRP*, namely, *MR* and *MPP*.

Marginal revenue, *MR*, is indirectly affected by product supply and demand conditions because these conditions determine price ($MR = \Delta TR/\Delta Q$ and $TR = P \times Q$). Thus, product demand and supply conditions affect factor demand. In short, because the supply and demand conditions in product markets are different, the demand for labor in labor markets will be different too.

The second factor, the marginal physical product of labor, is affected by individual workers' *own abilities and skills* (both innate and learned), the *degree of effort* they put forth on the job, and the *other factors of production* available to them. (American workers are more productive than workers in many other countries because they work with many more capital goods and much more technical know-how.) If all individuals had the same innate and learned skills and abilities, applied the same degree of effort on the job, and worked with the same amount and quality of other factors of production, wages would differ less than they currently do.

Supply of Labor As noted, the supply conditions in labor markets are different. First, jobs have *different nonpecuniary qualities*. Working as a coal miner in West Virginia is not as attractive a job as working as a tour guide at a lush resort in Hawaii. We would expect this difference to be reflected in the supply of coal miners and tour guides.

Second, supply is also a reflection of the *number of persons who can actually do a job*. Williamson may want to be a nuclear physicist but may not have the ability in science and mathematics to become one. Johnson may want to be a basketball player but may not have the ability to become one.

Third, even if individuals have the ability to work at a certain job, they may perceive the *training costs as too high* (relative to the perceived benefits) to train for it. For example, Tyler may have the ability to be a brain surgeon but views the years of schooling required to be too high a price to pay.

Fourth, sometimes the supply in different labor markets reflects a difference in the *cost of moving* across markets. Thus, wage rates might be higher in Alaska than in Alabama for comparable labor because the workers in Alabama find the cost of relocating to Alaska too high relative to the benefits of receiving a higher wage.

In conclusion, because the wage rate is determined by supply-and-demand forces, the factors that affect these forces indirectly affect wage rates. Exhibit 11 summarizes these factors.

13-2j Why Did You Choose Your Major?

What happens in the labor market sometimes influences our lives. Consider a college student who is trying to decide whether to major in accounting or English. The student believes that English is more fun and interesting but that accounting, on average, will earn her enough additional

EXHIBIT 11

The Wage Rate

A step-by-step framework that describes the factors that affect the wage rate.

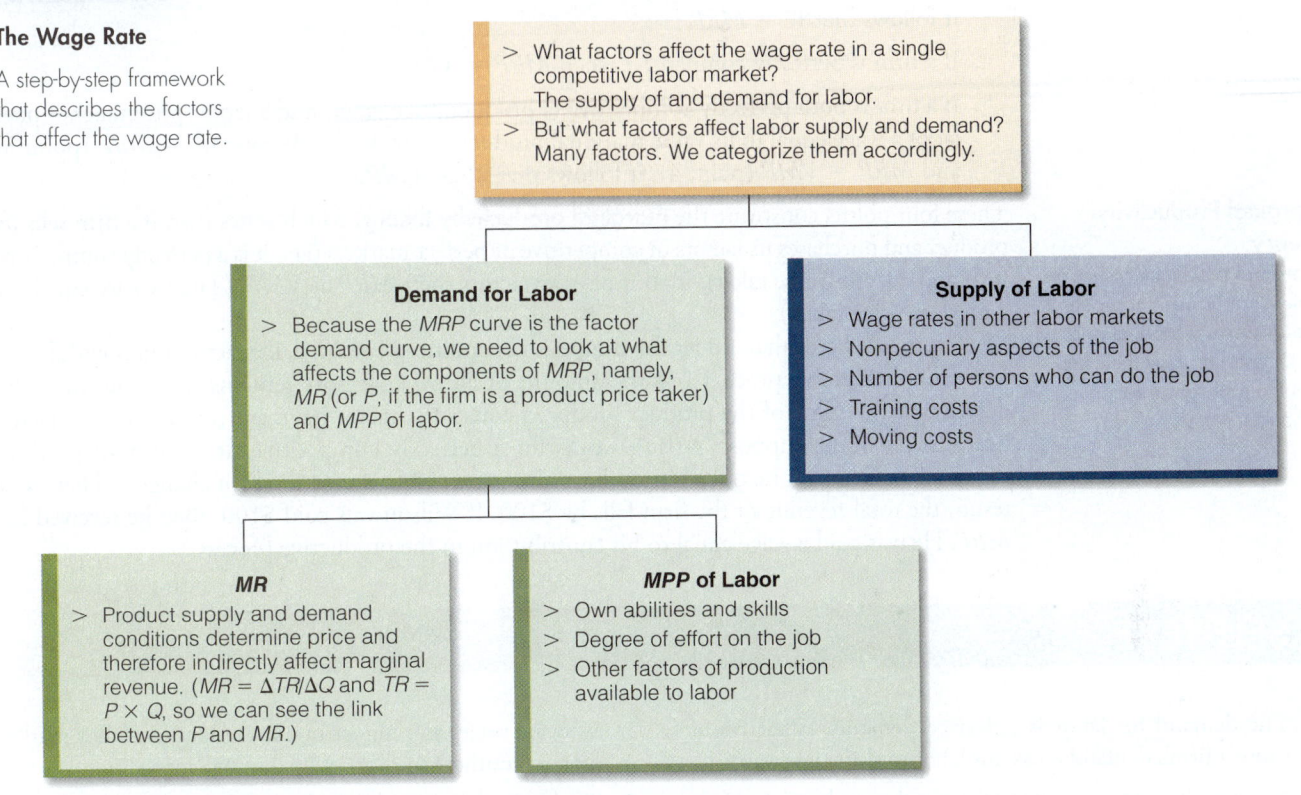

> What factors affect the wage rate in a single competitive labor market?
> The supply of and demand for labor.
> But what factors affect labor supply and demand? Many factors. We categorize them accordingly.

Demand for Labor
> Because the *MRP* curve is the factor demand curve, we need to look at what affects the components of *MRP*, namely, *MR* (or *P*, if the firm is a product price taker) and *MPP* of labor.

Supply of Labor
> Wage rates in other labor markets
> Nonpecuniary aspects of the job
> Number of persons who can do the job
> Training costs
> Moving costs

MR
> Product supply and demand conditions determine price and therefore indirectly affect marginal revenue. ($MR = \Delta TR/\Delta Q$ and $TR = P \times Q$, so we can see the link between P and MR.)

MPP of Labor
> Own abilities and skills
> Degree of effort on the job
> Other factors of production available to labor

income to compensate for the lack of fun in accounting. Specifically, at a $55,000 annual salary for accounting and a $39,000 annual salary for teaching English, the student is indifferent between accounting and English. But at a $56,000 annual salary for accounting and a $39,000 annual salary for teaching English, accounting moves ahead.

Of course, what accounting pays is determined by the demand for and supply of accountants. Given that fact, we see that other people influenced the student's decision to become an accountant. To illustrate, suppose Congress passes more intricate tax laws that require more accountants to figure them out. The change in the law increases the demand for accountants, which in turn raises the wage rate for them. And an increase in the wage rate for accountants increases the probability that more people—perhaps you—will major in accounting, not in English, philosophy, or history.

As you can see, economics—in which markets play a major role—helps explain why part of your life is the way it is.

13-2k Marginal Productivity Theory

An analysis of some of the things we know from this chapter leads us to the following conclusions:

1. If a firm is a factor price taker, then its marginal factor cost is constant and equal to its factor price ($MFC = P$). If the factor price taker hires labor, then, for the firm, $MFC = W$, where W is the wage rate.

2. Firms hire the factor quantity at which $MRP = MFC$.

3. Given points 1 and 2 together, a factor price taker pays labor a wage equal to its marginal revenue product: $W = MRP$. Because $MFC = W$ (point 1) and $MRP = MFC$ (point 2), it follows that $W = MRP$.

4. If a firm is perfectly competitive, then $MRP = VMP$.

5. If a firm is both perfectly competitive (a product price taker) and a factor price taker, it pays labor a wage equal to its value marginal product: $W = VMP$. Because $W = MRP$ (point 3) and $MRP = VMP$ (point 4), it follows that $W = VMP$.

Marginal Productivity Theory

Marginal productivity theory states that firms in competitive or perfect product and factor markets pay their factors their marginal revenue products.

These four points constitute the **marginal productivity theory**, which states that, if a firm sells its product and purchases its factors in competitive or perfect markets (i.e., it is a perfectly competitive firm and a factor price taker), then it pays its factors their MRP or VMP. (The two are equal for a product price taker.)

The theory holds that, under the competitive conditions specified, if a factor unit is withdrawn from the productive process and the amount of all other factors remains the same, then the decrease in the value of the product produced equals the factor payment received by the factor unit. To illustrate, suppose Wilson works for a perfectly competitive firm (firm X) producing good X. One day, he quits his job (but nothing else relevant to the firm changes). Then, as a result, the total revenue of the firm falls by $100. If Wilson was paid $100, then he received his MRP. He was paid a wage equal to his contribution to the productive process.[5]

SELF-TEST

1. The demand for labor is a derived demand. What could cause a firm's demand curve for labor to shift rightward?

2. Suppose the coefficient of elasticity of demand for labor is 3. What does this mean?

3. Why are wage rates higher in one competitive labor market than in another? In short, why do wage rates differ?

4. Workers in labor market X do the same work as workers in labor market Y, but they earn $10 less per hour. Why?

ECONOMICS 24/7

Who Pays the Social Security Tax?

When Congress established the Social Security system, it instituted Social Security taxes and split the tax between the employer and the employee. By doing so, it intended to split the cost of the system. But economists know that taxes *placed* on one group of persons can be actually *paid* for by another group. To a large extent, that is so with the Social Security tax: Although half of the tax is placed on the employer and half is placed on the employee, the employee ends up paying almost all of the tax.

Exhibit 12 shows an approximation of this statement. We say "approximation" because most economists believe that the supply curve for labor *in the aggregate is extremely inelastic*. For simplicity, the supply curve is drawn as perfectly inelastic.

When no Social Security tax is placed on the employer, D_1 is the relevant demand curve for labor. The equilibrium wage rate is $19; that is, employers are willing to pay a maximum of $19 per hour (per worker) for Q_1 workers.

---

[5] Recall that MRP can be calculated in two ways: $MRP = \Delta TR / \Delta$ Quantity of the factor and $MRP = MR \times MPP$. In this example, we use the first method. When Wilson quits his job, the change in the denominator is 1 factor unit. If, as a result, TR falls by $100, then the change in the numerator must be $100.

Now, instead of placing half the Social Security tax on the employer and half on the employee, let's take an extreme position and place the *entire tax on the employer*. Suppose employers calculate the Social Security tax on an hourly basis and find that they have to pay $1 per hour for every employee they hire. If $19 was the equilibrium wage rate *before the tax*, then employers are not willing to pay any more for the same number of workers *after the tax*. Employers are willing to pay labor only $19 per hour *minus* the hourly computed tax. In short, from the employer's perspective, the demand curve for labor falls by $1 for each alternative quantity of labor. In other words, the demand curve shifts leftward and down from D_1 to D_2. Given our vertical supply curve of labor, the new equilibrium wage rate is now $18 per worker for Q_1 workers.

So, if the supply curve is perfectly inelastic, and if the Social Security tax is *placed* wholly on employers, employees will end up *paying* the full tax in the form of lower wages.

EXHIBIT 12

Who Pays the Social Security Tax?

With no Social Security tax, the equilibrium wage rate is $19 per hour; that is, employers are willing to pay a maximum of $19 per hour (per worker) for Q_1 workers. With the Social Security tax fully placed on the employer and computed on an hourly basis, employers are willing to pay $19 per hour *minus* the hourly computed tax for Q_1 workers. Because we have assumed that the hourly tax is $1 per employee and that the supply curve for labor is perfectly inelastic in the aggregate, the new equilibrium wage rate is $18. Under the conditions stated, the employee ends up paying the full Social Security tax in the form of lower wages.

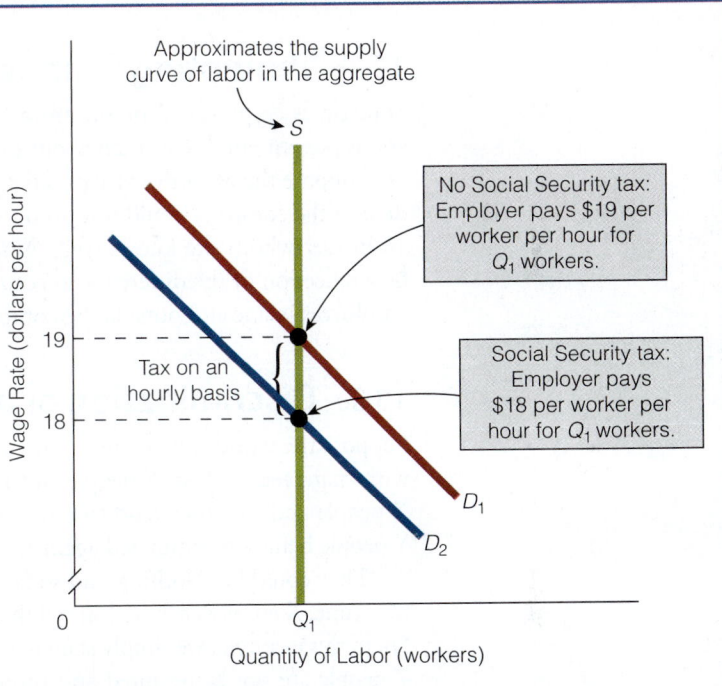

13-3 LABOR MARKETS AND INFORMATION

This section looks at job hiring, employment practices, and employment discrimination, as well as how information or the lack of it affects these considerations.

13-3a Screening Potential Employees

Employers typically do not know exactly how productive a prospective employee will be. What the employer wants, but lacks, is complete information about the employee's future job performance. This need raises two questions:

1. *Why would an employer want complete information about a potential employee's future job performance?* The answer is obvious: Employers have a strong monetary incentive to hire good,

stable, quick-learning, responsible, hardworking, punctual employees. One study found that corporate spending on training employees reached $40 billion annually. Obviously, corporations want to see the highest return possible for their training expenditures, so they try to hire employees who will make the training worthwhile.

2. *What does the employer do in the absence of such complete information?* This is where screening comes in.

Screening is the process employers use to increase the probability of choosing good employees on the basis of certain criteria. For example, as a step in the screening mechanism, an employer might ask a young college graduate searching for a job what his or her GPA was in college. The employer might know from past experience that persons with high GPAs turn out to be better employees, on average, than persons with low GPAs. Screening is one thing an employer does in the absence of complete information.

Screening
The process employers use to increase the probability of choosing good employees on the basis of certain criteria.

13-3b Promoting from Within

Sometimes employers promote from within the company because they have more information about present employees than about prospective employees.

Suppose the executive vice president in charge of sales is retiring from Trideck, Inc. The president of the company could hire an outsider to replace the vice president, but often she will select an insider whom she knows well. What may look like discrimination to outsiders may simply be a reflection of the difference in costs to the employer of acquiring relevant information about employees inside and outside the company.

13-3c Discrimination or an Information Problem?

Suppose the world is made up of just two kinds of people: those with characteristic X and those with characteristic Y, or X people and Y people. Over time, it so happens that most employers are X people and that they tend to hire and promote proportionally more X than Y people. Are the Y people being discriminated against?

They could be. Nothing said so far rules out this possibility. But another explanation is that, over time, X employers have learned that Y people, on average, do not perform as well as X people. So, in this example, we simply state that X people are not discriminating against Y people. Instead, Y people are not being hired and promoted as often as X people because, for whatever reason, Y people, on average, are not as productive.

Suppose that, in this environment, an extremely productive Y person applies for a job with an X employer. The problem is that the X employer does not know—that is, lacks complete information about—the full abilities of the Y person. Furthermore, acquiring complete information is costly. The employer bases her decision to reject the Y person's job application on what she knows about Y people, which is that, on average, they are not as productive as X people. She makes this decision not because she has something against Y people but because acquiring complete information on every potential employee—X or Y—is simply too costly.

Legislation mandating equal employment opportunities requires employers to absorb some information costs to open the labor markets to all. All but the smallest of firms are required to search for qualified Y persons who can perform the job even if the employer believes that the average Y person cannot. Requiring employers to forgo the use of a screening mechanism typically increases firm costs and raises prices to consumers, but the premise of the legislation is that the social benefits of having more Y persons in the mainstream of society more than outweigh such costs.

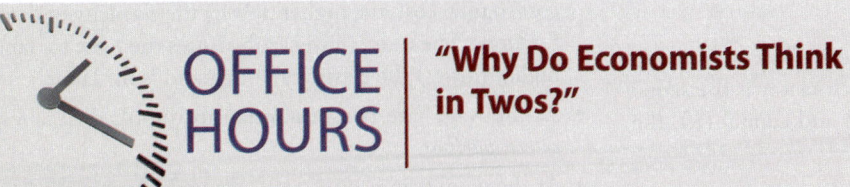

OFFICE HOURS | "Why Do Economists Think in Twos?"

STUDENT: Before I read this chapter, I had thought that U.S. firms would rather pay low wages in other countries than pay high wages in the United States. Now I realize that wages aren't the only thing that matters to a firm: The productivity of labor matters too.

INSTRUCTOR: Does this ring a bell?

STUDENT: What do you mean?

INSTRUCTOR: Well, one of the things emphasized in the "Thinking Like an Economist" feature in various chapters is that economists often compare one thing with another when trying to determine what economic actors will do. To illustrate, when a firm decides where to hire labor, it compares wage rates against productivity in various countries. The firm compares marginal revenue with marginal cost when it decides how much of a good to produce. Marginal revenue product is compared with marginal factor cost when a firm decides how much of a factor to hire or buy. A consumer who decides to buy more or less of various goods compares marginal utility with price.

STUDENT: So, what's the lesson? Why do economists seem to think in twos?

INSTRUCTOR: The lesson goes back to something explained in Chapter 1: Usually, our activities have costs and benefits. Producing goods in the United States has a cost (paying high wages) and a benefit too (high productivity). Producing an additional unit of a good has a cost (*MC*) but an additional benefit too (*MR*). Hiring an additional unit of labor comes with a cost (the wage rate) but with a benefit too (higher *VMP* or *MRP*). In the end, what matters is not the costs alone, or the benefits alone, but the benefits relative to the costs.

Points to Remember

1. When firms are trying to decide where to hire workers (the United States or Mexico), wages are not the only factor that matters. Productivity matters too.

2. Economists often think in twos. They often compare the benefits and costs of doing X, where X can stand for various actions (e.g., hiring workers in various countries, producing an additional unit of a good, and so on).

CHAPTER SUMMARY

DERIVED DEMAND

• The demand for a factor is derived; hence, it is called a *derived demand*. Specifically, it is derived from, and directly related to, the demand for the product that the factor goes to produce; for example, the demand for auto workers is derived from the demand for autos.

MRP, MFC, VMP

• Marginal revenue product (*MRP*) is the additional revenue generated by employing an additional factor unit. Marginal factor cost (*MFC*) is the additional cost incurred by employing

an additional factor unit. The profit-maximizing firm buys the factor quantity at which $MRP = MFC$.

• The *MRP* curve is the firm's factor demand curve; it shows how much of a given factor the firm buys at different prices.

• Value marginal product (*VMP*) is a measure of the value that each factor unit adds to the firm's product. Whereas $MRP = MR \times MPP$, $VMP = P \times MPP$. For a perfectly competitive firm, $P = MR$, so $MRP = VMP$. For a monopolist, a monopolistic competitor, or an oligopolist, $P > MR$, so $VMP > MRP$.

THE LEAST-COST RULE

- A firm minimizes costs by buying factors in the combination at which the MPP-to-price ratio for each factor is the same. For example, for two factors, labor (L) and capital (K), the least-cost rule is $MPP_L / P_L = MPP_K / P_K$.

LABOR AND WAGES

- A change in the price of the product that labor produces or a change in the marginal physical product of labor (reflected in a shift in the MPP curve) will shift the demand curve for labor.

- The higher (lower) the elasticity of demand is for the product that labor produces, the higher (lower) the elasticity of demand is for labor. The higher (lower) the ratio is of labor cost to total cost, the higher (lower) the elasticity of demand is for labor. The more (fewer) substitutes there are for labor, the higher (lower) the elasticity of demand is for labor.

- As the wage rate rises, the quantity supplied of labor rises, *ceteris paribus*.

- At the equilibrium wage rate, the quantity supplied of labor equals the quantity demanded of labor.

DEMAND FOR AND SUPPLY OF LABOR

- The demand for labor is affected by (1) marginal revenue and (2) marginal physical product. The supply of labor is affected by (1) wage rates in other labor markets, (2) the nonpecuniary aspects of the job, (3) the number of persons who can do the job, (4) training costs, and (5) moving costs.

KEY TERMS AND CONCEPTS

Derived Demand
Marginal Revenue Product
   (MRP)

Value Marginal Product (VMP)
Marginal Factor Cost (MFC)
Factor Price Taker

Least-Cost Rule
Elasticity of Demand for
   Labor

Marginal Productivity
   Theory
Screening

QUESTIONS AND PROBLEMS

1. What does it mean to say that the demand for a factor is a derived demand?

2. Why is the MRP curve a firm's factor demand curve?

3. "$VMP = MRP$ for a price taker but not for a price searcher." Do you agree or disagree with this statement? Explain your answer.

4. Compare the firm's least-cost rule with how buyers allocate their consumption dollars.

5. The supply curve is horizontal for a factor price taker; however, the industry supply curve is upward sloping. Explain why this occurs.

6. What forces and factors determine the wage rate for a particular type of labor?

7. What is the relationship between labor productivity and wage rates?

8. What might be one effect of government legislating wage rates?

9. Using the theory developed in this chapter, explain the following:

  a. Why a worker in Ethiopia is likely to earn much less than a worker in Japan

  b. Why the army expects recruitment to rise during economic recessions

  c. Why basketball stars earn relatively large incomes

  d. Why jobs that carry a health risk offer higher pay than jobs that do not, *ceteris paribus*

10. Discuss the factors that might prevent the equalization of wage rates for identical or comparable jobs across labor markets.

11. Prepare a list of questions that an interviewer is likely to ask an interviewee in a job interview. Try to identify which of the questions are part of the interviewer's screening process.

12. Explain why the market demand curve for labor is not simply the horizontal addition of the firms' demand curves for labor.

13. Discuss the firm's objective, its constraints, and how it makes choices in its role as a buyer of resources.

14. Explain the relationship between each of the following pairs of concepts:

   a. The elasticity of demand for a product and the elasticity of demand for the labor that produces the product

   b. The ratio of labor cost to total cost and the elasticity of demand for labor

   c. The number of substitutes for labor and the elasticity of demand for labor

15. How might you go about determining whether a person is worth the salary he or she is paid?

16. What do substitution and income effects have to do with the supply curve of labor?

WORKING WITH NUMBERS AND GRAPHS

1. Determine the appropriate numbers for the lettered spaces:

(1) Units of Factor X	(2) Quantity of Output	(3) Marginal Physical Product of X (MPP_X)	(4) Product Price, Marginal Revenue ($P = MR$)	(5) Total Revenue	(6) Marginal Revenue Product of X (MRP_X)
0	15	0	$8	F	L
1	24	A	8	G	M
2	32	B	8	H	N
3	39	C	8	I	O
4	45	D	8	J	P
5	50	E	8	K	Q

2. On the basis of the preceding table, if the price of a factor is constant at $48, how many units of the factor will the firm buy?

3. In one diagram, draw the *VMP* curve and the *MRP* curve for an oligopolist. Explain why the curves look the way you drew them.

4. Explain why the factor supply curve is horizontal for a factor price taker.

5. Look at the two factor demand curves in the accompanying figure. Is the price of the product that labor goes to produce higher for MRP_2 than for MRP_1? Explain your answer.

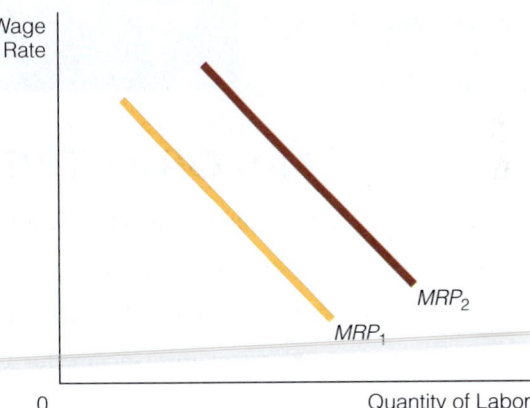

CHAPTER
14

WAGES, UNIONS, AND LABOR

INTRODUCTION

Certain organizations seem to engender controversy. Labor unions are such organizations. Some people are strongly prounion; others are strongly antiunion. Moreover, many millions of people between these extremes don't have a strong opinion on labor unions. In this chapter, we discuss the objectives, practices, and effects of unions.

14-1 OBJECTIVES OF LABOR UNIONS

Labor unions usually seek at least one of three objectives:

- to employ all their members,
- to maximize the total wage bill, or
- to maximize income for a limited number of union members.

14-1a Employment for All Members

Suppose the demand curve in Exhibit 1 represents the demand for labor in a given union and the total membership of the union is Q_1. If the objective of the union is to have its total membership employed, then the wage rate that must exist in the market is W_1. At W_1, firms want to hire the total union membership.

EXHIBIT 1

Labor Union Objectives

If total membership in the union is Q_1 and the union's objective is employment for all of its members, it chooses W_1. If the objective is to maximize the total wage bill, it chooses W_2, the wage at which the elasticity of demand for labor equals 1. If the union's objective is to maximize the income of a limited number of union workers (represented by Q_3), it chooses W_3.

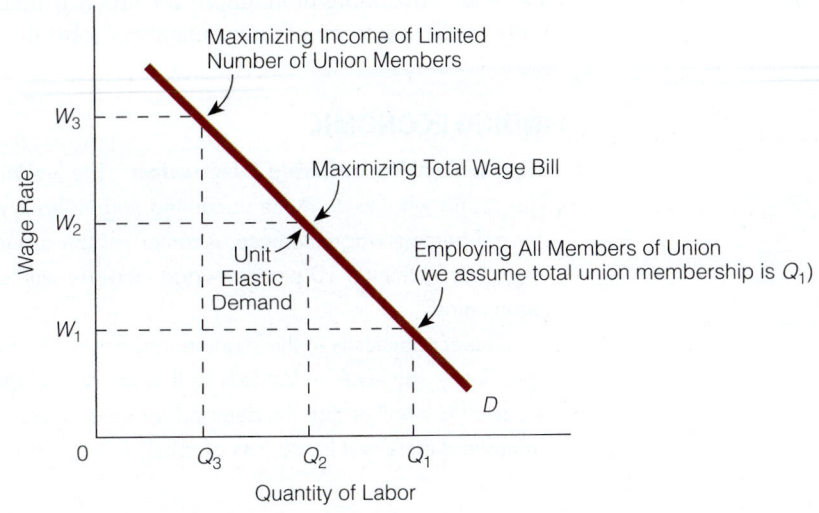

14-1b **Maximizing the Total Wage Bill**

The total wage bill paid to the membership of a union is equal to the wage rate multiplied by the number of labor hours worked. One objective of a labor union is to maximize this dollar amount—that is, to maximize the number of dollars coming *from* the employer *to* union members.

In Exhibit 1, the wage rate that maximizes the total wage bill is W_2. At W_2, the quantity of labor is Q_2 and the elasticity of demand for labor is equal to 1. Recall that total revenue (or total expenditure) is maximized when the price elasticity of demand is equal to 1—in other words, when demand has unit elasticity. So the total wage bill is maximized at that point where the demand for labor is unit elastic. However, less union labor is working at W_2 than at W_1, indicating that there is a trade-off between higher wages and the employment of union members.

14-1c **Maximizing Income for a Limited Number of Union Members**

Some economists have suggested that a labor union might want neither total employment of its membership nor maximization of the total wage bill. Instead, it might prefer to maximize income for a *limited number* of union members, perhaps those with the most influence or seniority in the union. Suppose this group is represented by Q_3 in Exhibit 1. The highest wage at which this group can be employed is W_3; thus, the union might seek this wage rate instead of any lower rate.

14-1d **Wage–Employment Trade-Off**

Exhibit 1 suggests that a union can get higher wage rates, but some of the union members will lose their jobs in the process. Hence, the wage–employment trade-off depends on the *elasticity of demand for labor*.

To illustrate, consider the demand for labor in two unions, A and B, shown in Exhibit 2. Suppose both unions bargain for a wage increase from W_1 to W_2. Then the quantity of labor drops much more in union B, where the demand for labor is elastic between the two wage rates, than in union A, where the demand for labor is inelastic between the two wage rates. Thus, union B is less likely than union A to push for higher wages, *ceteris paribus*. The reason is that the wage–employment trade-off is more pronounced for union B than for union A. Pushing for higher wages is simply costlier (in terms of union members' jobs) for union B than it is for union A.

FINDING ECONOMIC

In a Union Roundtable Discussion The leaders of a union are sitting around the table discussing what to do in the upcoming negotiations with management. One person argues for a 7-percent wage increase. Another person argues for a 10-percent wage increase, saying, "I don't think a 10 percent wage increase will lose us many jobs—if any." Where is the economics?

The economics is in the statement about the 10-percent wage increase. Believing that few, if any, jobs will be lost tells us that the person believes either that the wage–employment trade-off is small or that the demand for union labor is highly inelastic (maybe even perfectly inelastic if there will be no loss of jobs).

14-2 PRACTICES OF LABOR UNIONS

This section explains how labor unions try to meet their objectives by influencing one or more of the following factors:

- The elasticity of demand for labor

- The demand for labor

- The supply of labor

We also discuss how unions can directly affect wages.

14-2a Affecting the Elasticity of Demand for Union Labor

Exhibit 2 shows that, the lower the elasticity of demand is for labor, the smaller will be the cutback in labor for any given wage increase. Obviously, the smaller the cutback in labor for a given wage increase, the better it is for the labor union. Given a choice between losing either 200 jobs or 50 jobs because of a wage rate increase of $2, the labor union prefers to lose the smaller number of jobs. Thus, a labor union looks for ways to lower the elasticity of demand for its labor, and it does so mainly by attempting to reduce the availability of substitutes.

Availability of Substitute Products Consider the United Automobile Workers union, whose members produce American automobiles. We know that the lower the elasticity of demand is for American automobiles, the lower the elasticity of demand will be for the labor that produces automobiles. So unions might attempt to reduce the availability of substitutes for the products they produce by such means as restrictions on imports.

Availability of Substitute Factors The fewer the substitute factors there are for union labor, the lower the elasticity of demand will be for union labor. Union labor has two general substitutes: nonunion labor and certain types of machines. For example, a musical synthesizer (which can sound like many different instruments) is a substitute for a group of musicians playing different instruments. Labor unions have often attempted to reduce the availability of

EXHIBIT 2

The Wage-Employment Trade-Off: Two Cases

For union A, which has an inelastic demand for its labor between W_1 and W_2, a higher wage rate brings about a smaller cutback in the quantity of labor than for union B, which has an elastic demand for its labor between W_1 and W_2. Accordingly, we predict that union B will be less likely to push for higher wages than union A because its wage–employment trade-off is more pronounced.

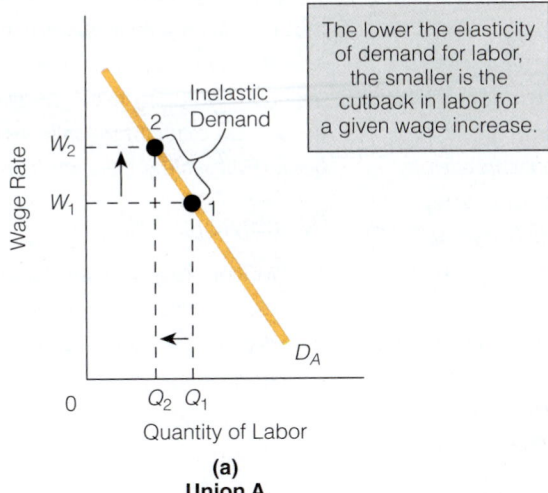

The lower the elasticity of demand for labor, the smaller is the cutback in labor for a given wage increase.

(a)
Union A

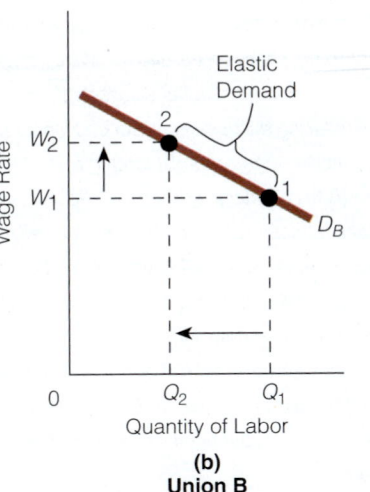

(b)
Union B

substitute factors—both nonunion and nonhuman. Thus, labor unions sometimes oppose the relaxation of immigration laws, they generally are in favor of a high minimum wage (which increases the relative price of nonunion labor vis-à-vis union labor), and they usually oppose machines that can be substituted for their labor. In addition, in the area of construction, unions usually specify that certain jobs are done by, say, electricians only (thus prohibiting substitute factors from being employed on those jobs).

Hear What and How the Economist Thinks . . .
About Unions and Wages

The economist overhears someone say:

The objective of labor unions is to obtain higher wages for their members. They just keep pushing wages up, up, and up.

What and how the economist thinks:

This statement makes me think about a seller of a good. Many people agree that the seller wants to keep pushing the price higher. But if the seller was to do this, he or she wouldn't sell anything. Imagine that there is a downward-sloping demand curve that intersects the price (vertical) axis at $40 per unit. Now think of the seller charging a price of $20 per unit. Can he sell some units of the good? Yes. Can he sell

some units of the good at $30 per unit? Yes. What about at $40 per unit? No. At $40, the quantity demanded of the good is zero. So, the seller who wanted to keep pushing price continually up would find that at some point, no one would want to buy the good.

Now consider a labor union. The labor union faces a downward-sloping demand curve for its members' labor. Now suppose the demand curve for this labor intersects the wage rate (vertical) axis at $50 an hour. Will some union labor be demanded at a wage rate of $20 an hour? Yes. What about at $30 an hour? Yes, again, and the same holds for $40 an hour. But once the wage rate rises to $50 an hour, the quantity demanded of labor falls to zero. No employer will be willing to hire members of the labor union once wages reach $50 an hour.

Let's reconsider the statement that the person made: "The objective of labor unions is to obtain higher wages for their members. They just keep pushing wages up, up, and up." Well, it might be the objective of labor unions to obtain higher wages for their members, but not at the cost of reducing the number of working labor union members to zero.

What the non-economist often forgets is that there are often trade-offs to consider in economics. The seller wants higher prices, but not if higher prices mean that he can't sell his goods anymore. The labor union wants higher wage rates, but not if higher wage rates mean that no firm is willing and able to hire its labor.

Think of other trade-offs. A person might say that she wants to get into better shape and eat better, but not if it means that she has to give up everything that is enjoyable in life. A person may say that she wants a high-paying job, but not if it means she has to work 80 hours a week, 50 weeks a year.

Economists do not often talk in terms of extremes. An economist wouldn't say, for instance, it is important to become as physically strong as you can. Nor would an economist say that it is important for society to achieve zero pollution. Moreover, why doesn't the economist talk in terms of extremes? This is simply because she realizes there are often trade-offs to consider.

Questions to Think About:

1. "You should always study as hard as you can, eat as well as you can, and exercise as much as you can." Would the economist agree with the sentiments expressed in this statement? Explain your answer.

2. Sometimes you hear people say that if it weren't for labor unions, firms would pay their employees a very low wage. Is this true? Explain your answer.

14-2b Affecting the Demand for Union Labor

Labor unions can try to meet their objectives by increasing the demand for union labor. All other things held constant, this approach leads to higher wage rates and more union labor employed. Labor unions can increase the demand for their labor in a number of ways.

Increasing Product Demand Unions occasionally urge the buying public to buy the products produced by union labor. Union advertisements urge people to "look for the union label" or to look for the label that reads "Made in the U.S.A." As mentioned, unions sometimes also support legislation that either keeps out imports altogether or makes them more expensive.

Increasing Substitute Factor Prices If union action leads to a rise in the relative price of factors that are substitutes for union labor, the demand for union labor rises. For this reason, unions have often lobbied for an increase in the minimum wage—the wage received mostly by unskilled labor, which is a substitute for skilled union labor. The first minimum-wage legislation was passed in 1938, when many companies were moving from the unionized North to the nonunionized South. The minimum wage made the nonunionized, relatively unskilled labor in the South more expensive and is said to have slowed the movement of companies to the South.

Increasing Marginal Physical Product If unions can increase the productivity of their members, the demand for their labor will rise. With this idea in mind, unions prefer to add skilled labor to their ranks, and they sometimes undertake training programs for new entrants.

14-2c Affecting the Supply of Union Labor

Labor unions also try to meet their objectives by decreasing the supply of labor, because a decreased supply translates into higher wage rates. One way to lower the supply below what it might be if the union did not exist is to control the supply of labor in a market.

Craft unions, in particular, have been moderately successful in getting employers to hire only union labor. In the past, they were successful at turning some businesses into closed shops. A **closed shop** is an organization in which an employee must belong to the union before being able to work. (In contrast, in an *open shop*, an employer may hire union or nonunion workers.) When unions can determine, or at least control in some way, the supply of labor in a given market, they can decrease it from what it would be otherwise. They can do this by restricting membership, by requiring long apprenticeships, or by imposing rigid certification requirements. In 1947, the Taft–Hartley Act prohibited the closed shop.

The **union shop**, however, is legal in many states today. A union shop is an organization that does not require individuals to be union members to be hired but does require them to join the union within a certain time after becoming employed.

Today, unions typically argue for union shops, against open shops, and against the prohibition of closed shops. They also typically argue against state right-to-work laws (which some, but not all, states have), which make it illegal to require union membership for purposes of employment. (The Taft–Hartley Act allowed states to pass right-to-work laws and thus to override federal legislation that legalized union shops.) In short, the union shop is illegal in right-to-work states.

14-2d Affecting Wages Directly: Collective Bargaining

Besides increasing wage rates indirectly by influencing the demand for and supply of their labor, unions can directly affect wage rates through collective bargaining. **Collective bargaining** is the process whereby unions bargain with management on behalf of union members to determine wage rates. In collective bargaining, union members act together as a single unit to increase their bargaining power with management. On the other side of the market, employers of labor may also band together and act as one unit, with the same objective: to increase *their* bargaining power.

From the viewpoint of the labor union, collective bargaining is unlikely to be successful unless the union can strike. A **strike** occurs when unionized employees refuse to work at a certain wage or under certain conditions.

Exhibit 3 illustrates the effects of successful union collective bargaining. Suppose the initial wage rate that exists in the labor market is the competitive wage rate W_1. This is the wage rate that would exist if each employee were to bargain separately with management. The equilibrium quantity of labor is Q_1.

Management and the union now sit down at a collective-bargaining session. The union specifies that it wants a wage rate of W_2 and says that *none*

Closed Shop
An organization in which an employee must belong to the union before he or she can be hired.

Union Shop
An organization in which a worker is not required to be a member of the union in order to be hired but must become a member within a certain time after being employed.

Collective Bargaining
The process whereby wage rates and other issues are determined by a union bargaining with management on behalf of all union members.

Strike
The union employees' refusal to work at a certain wage or under certain conditions.

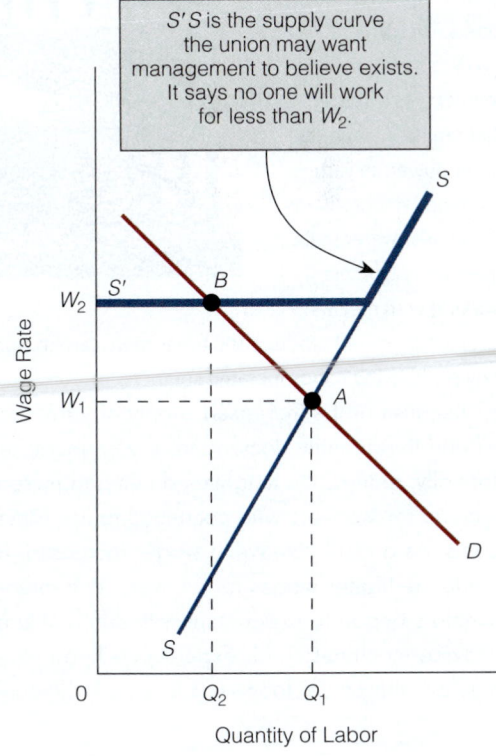

EXHIBIT 3

Successful Collective Bargaining by the Union

We start at a wage rate of W_1. The union's objective is to increase the wage rate to W_2. Such a wage rate means that the union holds that the new supply curve of labor is $S'S$—the heavy supply curve. To convince management that the new supply curve looks as the union says it does, the union will have to either threaten a strike or call one. We assume that the union is successful at raising the wage rate to W_2. As a consequence, the quantity of labor employed is less than it would have been at W_1.

$S'S$ is the supply curve the union may want management to believe exists. It says no one will work for less than W_2.

Wage Rate

Quantity of Labor

of its members will work at a lower wage rate. Thus, the union holds that the new supply curve is $S'S$—the heavy supply curve in Exhibit 3. In effect, the union is telling management that it cannot hire anyone for a wage rate lower than W_2.

Whether the union can bring about this higher wage rate (W_2) depends on whether it can prevent labor from working at less than that wage. That is, if management does not initially agree to W_2, the union will have to call a strike and show management that it cannot hire any labor for a wage rate lower than W_2. It has to convince management that the new supply curve looks the way the union says it looks. (We assume that the strike threat, or actual strike, is successful for the union and that management agrees to the higher wage rate of W_2.) As a result, the quantity of labor employed, Q_2, is less than it would have been at W_1. The new equilibrium is at point B instead of point A.

ECONOMICS 24/7

Technology, the Price of Competing Factors, and Displaced Workers[1]

For most of the eighteenth century in England, spinners and weavers worked on hand-operated spinning wheels and looms. Then, in the 1770s, a mechanical spinner was invented that required steam or water power, so yarn-spinning factories were set up near water mills. The factory workers, working with mechanical spinners, could produce 100 times more yarn in a day than they could using hand-operated spinners.

North Wind Picture Archives/Alamy Stock Photo

Because of the increased supply of yarn, the price fell and the quantity demanded of yarn increased substantially. In turn, the heightened demand increased the demand for weavers who continued to use hand-operated looms. As a result, weavers' wages increased. In reaction to the higher wages for weavers, entrepreneurs and inventors began to experiment with different kinds of weaving machines. Their experiments began to pay off: in 1787, the power loom was invented, although it was not perfected until the 1820s. By the 1830s, two workers using a power loom could produce in one day 20 times what a weaver could produce on a hand-operated loom.

Soon, the weavers who used hand-operated looms found themselves without jobs, displaced by the power loom. Some of the displaced workers showed their frustration and anger at their predicament by burning power looms and factories.

The story of spinners and weavers in eighteenth-century England helps us realize two important points about technology. First, as long as technology advances, some workers will be temporarily displaced. Second, an advance in technology often has an identifiable cause; it doesn't simply fall out of the sky. If it had not been for the higher weavers' wages, the power loom might not have been invented.

[1] This feature is based on Elizabeth Hoffman, "How Can Displaced Workers Find Better Jobs?" in *Second Thoughts: Myths and Morals of U.S. Economic History*, ed. by Donald McCloskey (Oxford: Oxford University Press, 1993).

14-2e Strikes

The purpose of a strike is to convince management that the supply curve is what the union says it is. Often, success depends on the ability of striking union employees to prevent nonstriking and nonunion employees from working for management at a lower wage rate than the union is seeking through collective bargaining. For example, if management can easily hire individuals at a wage rate lower than W_2 in Exhibit 3, it will not be convinced that the heavy supply curve is the relevant supply curve.

SELF-TEST

(Answers to Self-Test questions are in Answers to Self-Test Questions at the back of the book.)

1. What will lower the demand for union labor?

2. What is the difference between a closed shop and a union shop?

3. What is the objective of a strike?

14-3 EFFECTS OF LABOR UNIONS

This section addresses two questions:

- What are the effects of labor unions on wage rates?

- Are the effects the same in all labor markets?

14-3a The Case of Monopsony

A single buyer in a factor market is known as a **monopsony**. Some economists refer to a monopsony as a buyer's monopoly; that is, whereas a monopoly is a single *seller* of a product, a monopsony is a single *buyer*.

Monopsony
A single buyer in a factor market.

For example, if a firm in a small town is the only buyer of labor because there are no other firms for miles around, the firm is a monopsony. Because it is a monopsony, it cannot buy additional units of a factor without increasing the price it pays for it (in much the same way that a monopolist in the product market cannot sell an additional unit of its good without lowering the price.) The reason is that the supply of labor the monopsonist faces is the market supply of labor.

Marginal factor cost (*MFC*) increases as the monopsonist buys additional units of a factor, and the supply curve of the factor *is not the same* as the firm's *MFC* curve. [For a price taker in the factor market, *MFC* is constant and the *MFC* curve is the same as the supply curve for the factor. A monopsonist is not a price taker in the factor market: *MFC* rises as the monopsonist buys additional units of a factor, and its *MFC* curve and supply curve (for the factor) are not the same.]

As shown in Exhibit 4, *MFC* increases as additional units of the factor are purchased. Notice in part (a) that, as workers are added, the wage rate rises. For example, for the monopsonist to employ two workers, the wage rate must rise from $6.00 per hour to $6.05. To employ three workers, the monopsonist must offer to pay $6.10. Comparing column 2 with column 4, we notice that the *MFC* for a monopsonist is greater than the wage rate (in the same way that for a monopolist in a product market, price is greater than marginal revenue). Plotting columns

EXHIBIT 4

The Labor Union and the Monopsonist

(a) For the monopsonist, $MFC >$ wage rate. This relationship implies that the supply curve the monopsonist faces lies below its MFC curve. (b) The monopsonist purchases quantity Q_1 of labor and pays a wage rate W_1, which is less than MRP. (In other words, labor is being paid less than its MRP.) (c) If the labor union succeeds in increasing the wage rate from W_1 to W_2 through collective bargaining, then the firm will also hire more labor (Q_2 instead of Q_1). We conclude that, in the case of monopsony, higher wage rates (over a given range) do not imply fewer persons working.

(1) Workers	(2) Wage Rate	(3) Total Labor Cost (1) × (2)	(4) Marginal Factor Cost $\dfrac{\Delta(3)}{\Delta(1)}$
0	—	—	—
1	$6.00	$6.00	$6.00
2	6.05	12.10	6.10
3	6.10	18.30	6.20
4	6.15	24.60	6.30
5	6.20	31.00	6.40

(a)

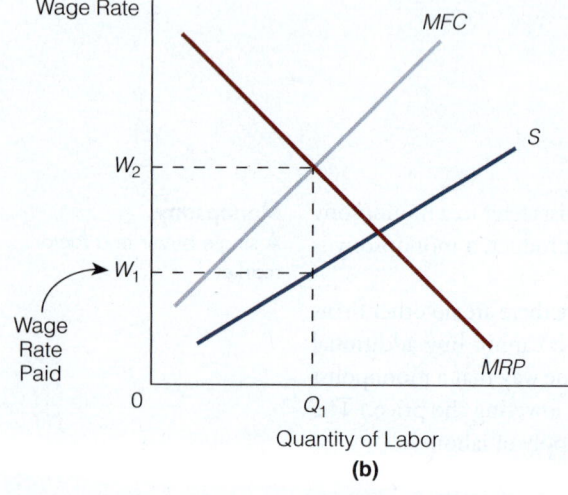

(b)

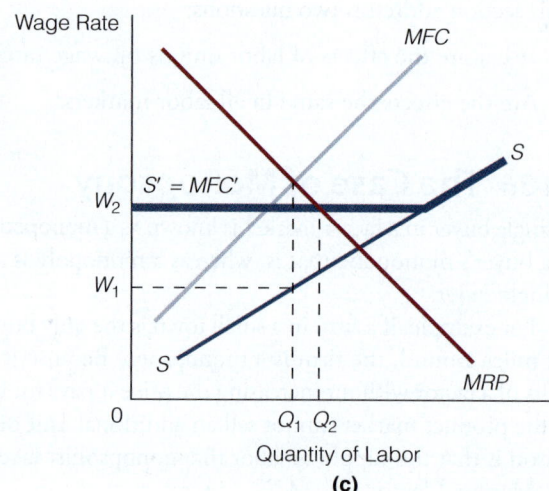

(c)

1 and 2 gives the supply curve for the monopsonist [see Exhibit 4(b)]; plotting columns 1 and 4 gives the monopsonist's MFC curve. Because MFC is greater than the wage rate, the supply curve lies below the MFC curve.

Exhibit 4(b) shows that the monopsonist chooses to purchase Q_1 units of labor (where $MRP = MFC$) and that it pays a wage rate of W_1 (the wage rate necessary to get Q_1 workers to offer their services).

If the monopsonist were to pay workers what their services were worth to it (as represented by the MRP curve), it would pay a higher wage. Some persons contend that labor unions and collective bargaining are necessary when labor is paid less than its marginal revenue product. Furthermore, they argue that successful collective bargaining on the part of the labor union in this setting is not subject to the wage–employment trade-off it encounters in other settings, as illustrated in Exhibit 4(c).

In Exhibit 4(c), successful collective bargaining by the labor union moves the wage rate from W_1 to W_2. The labor union is essentially saying to the monopsonist that it cannot hire any labor below W_2. If the labor union is right, then the monopsonist's MFC curve changes from MFC to MFC', which corresponds to the new supply curve the monopsonist faces, $S'S$. The monopsonist once again purchases the quantity of labor at which marginal revenue product equals MFC. But now, because the MFC curve is MFC', equality is at Q_2 workers and a wage rate of W_2. Therefore, over a range, there is no wage–employment trade-off for the labor union when it faces a monopsonist. It can raise both the wage rate and the number of workers employed.

14-3b Unions' Effects on Wages

Most studies show that some unions have increased their members' wages substantially whereas other unions have not done so at all. Work by H. Gregg Lewis concludes that, during the period 1920–1979, the average wage of union members was 10–15 percent higher than that of comparable nonunion labor. (Keep in mind, though, that the union–nonunion wage differential can differ quite a bit in different years and among industries; for data on this subject, see Exhibit 5.)

The Union–Nonunion Wage Gap Exhibit 6 illustrates the theoretical basis of the observation that higher union wages lead to lower nonunion wages (a union–nonunion wage gap). Two sectors of the labor market are shown: the unionized sector in part (a) and the nonunionized sector in part (b). Assume that labor is homogeneous and that the wage rate is $15 an hour in both sectors.

EXHIBIT 5

Median Weekly Earnings in the Union and Nonunion Sectors, Selected Industries, 2016

In four of the five (selected) industries shown, union workers earned a higher weekly salary in 2016 than did nonunion workers.

Source: Bureau of Labor Statistics

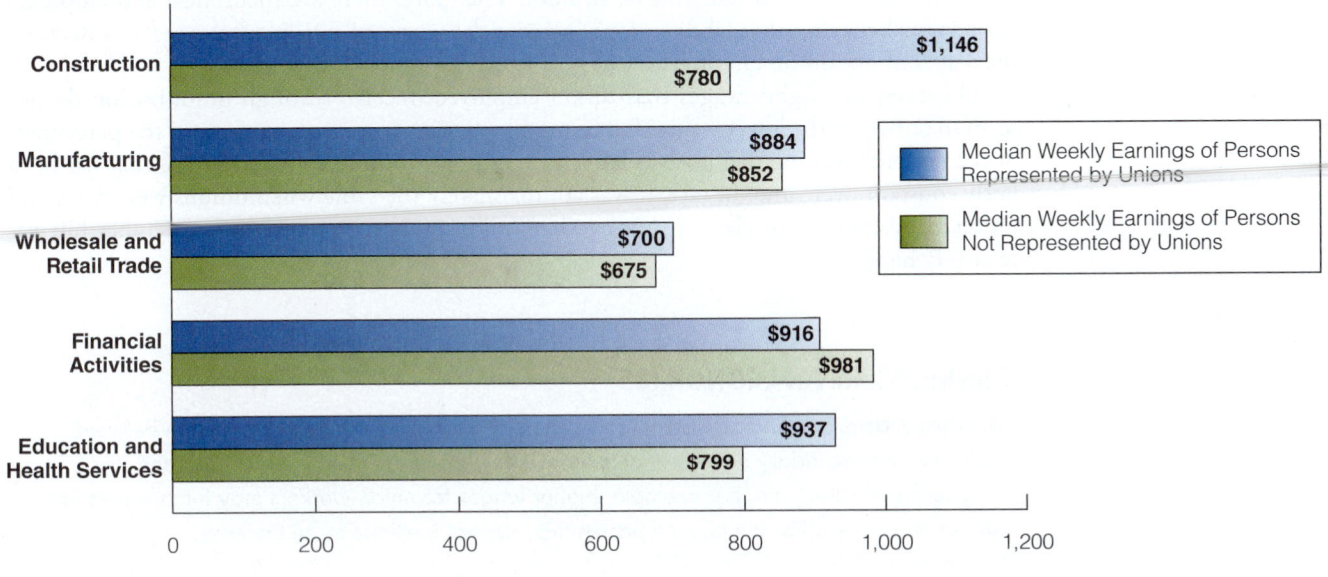

Industry	Median Weekly Earnings of Persons Represented by Unions	Median Weekly Earnings of Persons Not Represented by Unions
Construction	$1,146	$780
Manufacturing	$884	$852
Wholesale and Retail Trade	$700	$675
Financial Activities	$916	$981
Education and Health Services	$937	$799

EXHIBIT 6

The Effect of Labor Unions on Union and Nonunion Wages

We begin at a wage rate of $15 in both the unionized sector (a), and the nonunionized sector (b). Next, the union manages to increase its wage rate to $18, either through collective bargaining or by decreasing the supply of labor in the unionized sector (shown). Fewer persons now work in the unionized sector, and we assume that those persons who lose their jobs move to the non-unionized sector. Consequently, the supply of labor in the nonunionized sector rises and the wage rate falls.

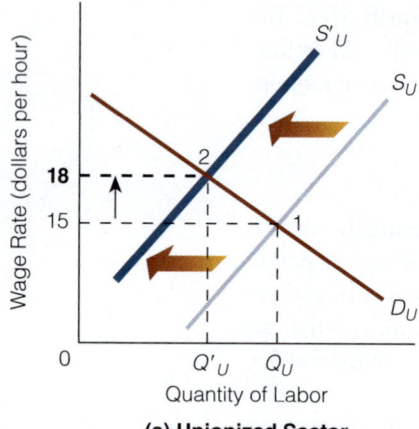

(a) Unionized Sector

Changes in supply conditions and wage rates in the unionized sector can cause changes in supply conditions and wage rates in the nonunionized sector.

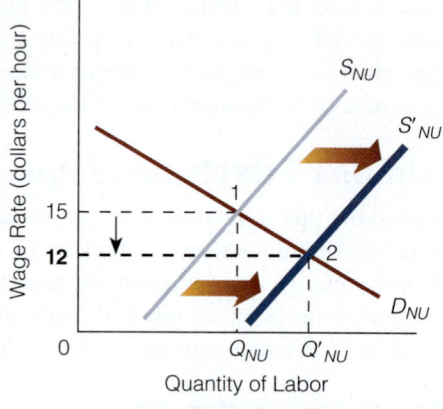

(b) Nonunionized Sector

The labor union either collectively bargains to a higher wage rate of, say, $18 an hour or manages to reduce supply so that the higher wage rate comes about. (The exhibit shows a decrease in supply.) As a consequence, less labor is employed in the unionized sector. If those now not working in the unionized sector can work in the nonunionized sector, then the supply of labor in the nonunionized sector increases from S_{NU} to S'_{NU} and the wage rate in the nonunionized sector falls to $12 an hour. Therefore, there are theoretical and empirical reasons for believing that labor unions increase the wages of union employees and decrease the wages of nonunion employees.

However, the higher wages that union employees receive through unionization do not seem to outweigh the lower wages that nonunion employees receive in terms of the percentage of the national income that goes to labor (union plus nonunion), a percentage that has been fairly constant over time. In fact, it was approximately the same when unions were weak and union membership was relatively low as when unions were strong and union membership was relatively high.

THINKING LIKE AN ECONOMICS

Primary and Secondary Effects   Economists make the important distinction between primary and secondary effects—that is, between what happens in the short run and what happens in the long run. For example, higher wages for union workers may initially come at the expense of profits, but as time passes this may not continue to be the case.

Does It Matter to You . . .
If Things Are Different in the Short-Run Than in the Long Run?

Sometimes, the effects of an action are different in the short run than in the long run. With this in mind, consider the layperson's view of labor unions, which is that labor unions obtain higher wages for their members at the expense of the owners of the firm and not at the expense of other workers. But this view may be built upon only the short-run effect of higher wages and not the long-run effect.

To explain, consider that, in the theory of perfect competition, if short-run profits exist, new firms will enter the industry, the industry supply curve will shift rightward, and profits are competed away. Conversely, given short-run losses, firms exit the industry; the industry supply curve shifts leftward, prices increase, and losses finally disappear. So, in the long run, there is zero economic profit in the perfectly competitive market.

Now in this market structure, consider a labor union that manages to obtain higher wages for its members. In the short run, these higher wages can diminish profits, as any cost increase would diminish profits, *ceteris paribus*. But in the long run, adjustments are made as firms exit the industry, supply curves shift, less is produced, some people may lose their jobs, and prices rise. In the long run, zero economic profit will exist. Therefore, in the short run, higher wages may come out of profits, but in the long run they probably do not.

Does this matter to you? It very well might if you are the union worker who got a higher wage in the short run, only to lose your job in the long run.

14-3c Unions' Effects on Prices

One effect of labor unions is that union wages are relatively high and nonunion wages are relatively low. The higher union wages mean higher costs for the firms that employ union labor, and higher costs affect supply curves, which in turn affect product prices. Therefore, higher union wages will cause higher prices for the products that the union labor produces. Conversely, lower nonunion wages mean lower costs for the firms that employ nonunion labor and thus lower prices for the products produced by nonunion labor.

14-3d Unions' Effects on Productivity and Efficiency: Two Views

There are two major views of the effects that labor unions have on productivity and efficiency.

The Traditional (or Orthodox) View The traditional view holds that labor unions have a negative impact on productivity and efficiency. Its proponents make the following arguments:

- Labor unions often have unnecessary staffing requirements and insist that only certain persons be allowed to do certain jobs. Because of these considerations, the economy operates below its potential—that is, inefficiently.

- Strikes disrupt production and prevent the economy from realizing its productive potential.

- Labor unions drive an artificial wedge between the wages of comparable labor in the union and nonunion sectors of the labor market.

This last point warrants elaboration. In Exhibit 6, labor is homogeneous and the wage rate is initially the same in both sectors of the labor market. Union efforts then increase the wage rate in the union sector and decrease the wage rate in the nonunion sector. At this point, the marginal revenue product of persons who work in the union sector is higher than the marginal revenue product of individuals who work in the nonunion sector. [We are farther up the factor demand (*MRP*) curve in the union than in the nonunion sector.] If labor could move from the nonunionized sector to the unionized sector, it would be moving from where it is worth less to where it is worth more, but it cannot do so because of the supply-restraining efforts of the union. Economists call this state of affairs a misallocation of labor: Not all labor is employed where it is the most valuable.

The Labor Union as a Collective Voice   There is evidence that, in some industries, union firms have a higher rate of productivity than nonunion firms. Some economists believe that this effect is a result of the labor union's role as a collective voice mechanism for its members. Without a labor union, workers who are disgruntled with their jobs, who feel taken advantage of by their employers, or who feel unsafe in their work will leave their jobs and seek work elsewhere. Job exiting comes at a cost: It raises the turnover rate, results in lengthy job searches during which individuals are not producing goods and services, and raises training costs. Such costs can be reduced, it is argued, when a labor union acts as a collective voice for its members. Instead of individual employees having personally to discuss ticklish matters with their employer, the labor union does so for them. Overall, the labor union makes employees feel more confident, less intimidated, and more secure in their work. Such positive feelings usually mean happier, more productive employees. Some proponents of this view also hold that employees are less likely to quit their jobs. In fact, there is evidence that unionism does indeed reduce job quits.

Critics have contended, though, that the reduced job quits are less a function of the labor union's collective voice than of the labor union's institutional capability of increasing its members' wages. Also, the productivity-increasing aspects of the labor union, which are linked to its role as a collective voice mechanism, are independent of the productivity-decreasing aspects of the labor union in its role as a monopolizer of labor.

ECONOMICS 24/7

Are You Ready for Some Football?

Sometimes, firms that sell a similar good try to form a cartel so that they can act as a monopoly. Can firms that buy a factor do the same—that is, form a cartel so that they can act as a monopsony? Students know such a "firm." Many universities and colleges have banded together to buy the services of college-bound athletes. In other words, they have entered into a cartel agreement to reduce the monetary competition among themselves for college-bound athletes. The National Collegiate Athletic Association (NCAA) is the cartel, or monopsony, enforcer.

Here's how it works: The NCAA sets certain rules and regulations by which its member universities and colleges

must abide or else face punishment and fines. For example, universities and colleges are prohibited from offering salaries to athletes to play on their teams. They are prohibited from creating jobs for them at the university or paying them relatively high wage rates for a job that usually pays much less, such as paying athletes $60 an hour to reshelve books in the university library. Universities and colleges are also prohibited from offering inducements to attract athletes, such as cars, clothes, and trips.

The stated objectives of these NCAA regulations are to maintain the amateur standing of college athletes, to prevent the rich schools from getting all the good players, and to enhance the competitiveness of college sports. Some economists suggest that some schools may have other objectives. They note that college athletics can be a revenue-raising activity for schools and that these institutions would rather pay college athletes less than their marginal revenue products (as a monopsony does) to play sports. Currently, universities and colleges openly compete for athletes by offering scholarships, free room and board, and school jobs. They also compete in terms of their academic reputations and the reputations of their sports programs. (Obviously, some find it easier to do than others.)

LOOK-foto/LOOK-foto/Superstock

Although the practice is prohibited, some universities and colleges compete for athletes in ways not sanctioned by the NCAA; that is, they compete, as it is said, under the table. Such practices are evidence, some economists maintain, that certain schools are cheating on the cartel agreement. Such cheating usually benefits the college athletes, who receive a payment for their athletic abilities that is closer to their marginal revenue products. For example, some college athletes, many of whom come from families of modest means, drive flashy, expensive cars, which often come from community friends of the university or boosters of its sports program. The NCAA may prohibit such payments to college athletes, but, as we have seen, members of cartels (of the monopoly or monopsony variety) usually find ways of evading the rules.

Not all economists agree that the NCAA is a cartel. Some argue that paying college athletes would diminish the reputation of college athletics, thus decreasing public demand for college sports programs. They conclude that the NCAA imposes its rules and regulations—one of which is that college athletes should not be paid to play sports—in order to keep college sports nonprofessional and in relatively high demand, not to suppress players' wages.

SELF-TEST

1. What is a major difference between a monopsonist and a factor price taker?

2. Under what conditions will the minimum wage increase the number of people working?

3. How could a collectively bargained higher wage rate in the unionized sector of the economy lead to a lower wage rate in the nonunionized sector of the economy?

OFFICE HOURS | "Don't Higher Wages Reduce Profits?"

STUDENT: I'm beginning to find that many things in economics are counterintuitive. Things I expect to be true turn out to be false, and things that I think are false turn out to be true.

INSTRUCTOR: Are you thinking of something in particular?

STUDENT: I had thought that labor unions obtained higher wages at the expense of the firm owners by reducing the owners' profits. Now I know that this is not necessarily true in the long run, especially in a perfectly competitive market.

INSTRUCTOR: Any thoughts on why economics is full of the counterintuitive?

STUDENT: I'm not sure.

INSTRUCTOR: Well, part of the answer might have to do with how far we take the analysis. To illustrate, consider your example dealing with the labor union and profits. You had thought that the labor union obtained higher wages at the expense of the firm owners. That can be true in the short run. In other words, your intuition was correct for the short run. But when we extended the analysis beyond the immediate effects of higher wages, things began to turn out differently than you thought.

STUDENT: So, is there a lesson here?

INSTRUCTOR: Don't stop analyzing things too soon. The problem, though, is that we don't always know that we're stopping too soon.

STUDENT: In other words, I saw the story this way: Wages for members of labor unions rise, causing profits to fall for owners of firms. But I should have seen it this way: Wages for members of labor unions rise, profits fall for owners of firms, some firms leave the industry, the market supply curve shifts leftward, and price rises.

Of course, my problem, as you imply, was that I didn't know that I should have gone beyond steps 1 and 2. I didn't know steps 3 through 5 were there. So, I guess my question now is, how do you get to those steps if you don't know they exist?

INSTRUCTOR: That's a good question. What you need is a device to use that can propel you onward. That device comes in the form of the question, is there anything else? To illustrate, go back to the way you initially saw the story: Wages for members of labor unions rise, causing profits to fall for owners of firms.

Now, instead of putting a period at the end of that, ask a question: If profits fall for the owners of firms, what, if anything, do falling profits lead to? This question—a form of the question "Is-there-anything-else?"—propels you forward and reduces the probability that you will stop before you have tried to figure out the full story.

Points to Remember

1. Do higher wages lead to lower profits—end of story? Our answer depends on how far we take the analysis.
2. To propel our analysis forward, we often need to ask whether there is anything else.

CHAPTER SUMMARY

OBJECTIVES OF A UNION

- Objectives of a union include (1) employment for all its members, (2) maximization of the total wage bill, and (3) maximization of the income for a limited number of union members. A labor union faces a wage–employment trade-off: Higher wage rates mean lower labor union employment. An exception is when a labor union faces a monopsonist; then the union can raise both wage rates and employment of its members (over a given range). Exhibit 4(c) illustrates this possibility.

PRACTICES OF A LABOR UNION

- To soften the wage–employment trade-off, a labor union seeks to lower the elasticity of demand for its labor. Ways of doing this are (1) reducing the availability of substitute products and (2) reducing the availability of substitute factors for labor.

- Union wage rates can be increased indirectly by increasing the demand for union labor or by reducing the supply of union labor, or they can be increased directly by collective bargaining. To increase demand for its labor, a union might try to (1) increase demand for the good it produces, (2) substitute factor prices, or (3) increase its marginal physical product. To decrease the supply of its labor, a union might argue for closed and union shops and against right-to-work laws.

- In a way, successful collective bargaining by a labor union changes the supply curve of labor that the employer faces. The labor union is successful if, through its collective-bargaining efforts, it can prevent the employer from hiring labor at a wage rate below a union-determined level. In this case, the supply curve of labor becomes horizontal at the union-determined wage rate. (see Exhibit 3).

MONOPSONY

- For a monopsonist, MFC rises as it buys additional units of a factor. Also, the monopsonist's supply curve lies below its MFC curve. The monopsonist buys the factor quantity at which $MRP = MFC$. The price of the factor is less than the monopsonist's MFC, so the monopsonist pays the factor less than its marginal revenue product.

EFFECTS OF UNIONS

- There is evidence that labor unions generally have the effect of increasing their members' wage rates (over what they would be without the union) and of lowering the wage rates of nonunion labor.

- The traditional view of labor unions holds that unions negatively affect productivity and efficiency by (1) arguing for, and often obtaining, unnecessary staffing requirements, (2) calling strikes that disrupt production, and (3) driving an artificial wedge between the wages of comparable labor in the union and nonunion sectors.

- The new view of labor unions holds that labor unions act as a collective voice mechanism for individual union employees and cause them to feel more confident in their jobs and less intimidated by their employers. This effort leads to more productive employees, who are less likely to quit.

KEY TERMS AND CONCEPTS

Closed Shop
Union Shop

Collective Bargaining
Strike

Monopsony

QUESTIONS AND PROBLEMS

1. Will a union behave differently if it wants to get all of its members employed instead of maximizing the total wage bill? Explain your answer.

2. What does the elasticity of demand for labor have to do with the wage–employment trade-off?

3. Identify one practice of labor unions that is consistent with the following:

   a. Affecting the elasticity of demand for union labor
   b. Increasing the demand for union labor
   c. Decreasing the supply of labor union workers

4. What view is a labor union likely to hold on each of the following issues?

   a. A quota on imported products
   b. Free trade
   c. A decrease in the minimum wage

5. Most actions or practices of labor unions are attempts to affect one of three factors. What are they?

6. Explain why the monopsonist pays a wage rate less than labor's marginal revenue product.

7. Organizing labor unions may be easier in some industries than in others. What industry characteristics make unionization easier?

8. What is the effect of labor unions on nonunion wage rates?

9. Some persons argue that a monopsony firm exploits its workers if it pays them less than their marginal revenue products. Others disagree. They say that, as long as the firm pays the workers their opportunity costs (which must be the case, or else the workers would not stay with the firm), the workers are not being exploited. This view suggests that there are two definitions of exploitation:

   a. Paying workers below their marginal revenue products (even if wages equal the workers' opportunity costs)
   b. Paying workers below their opportunity costs

   Keeping in mind that your answer may be a subjective judgment, which definition of exploitation do you think is more descriptive of the process and why?

10. A discussion of labor unions usually evokes strong feelings. Some people argue vigorously against labor unions; others argue with equal vigor for them. Some people see labor unions as the reason the workers in this country enjoy as high a standard of living as they do; others see labor unions as the reason the country is not so well off economically as it might be. Speculate on why the topic of labor unions generates such strong feelings and emotions—often with little analysis.

11. What forces may lead to the breakup of an employer (monopsony) cartel?

12. Unions can affect (a) a firm's profits, (b) the price consumers pay for a good, and (c) the wages received by nonunion workers. Do you agree or disagree? Explain your answer.

13. Contrast the traditional (or orthodox) and new views of labor unions.

WORKING WITH NUMBERS AND GRAPHS

1. Determine the appropriate numbers for the lettered spaces:

(1) Workers	(2) Wage Rate	(3) Total Labor Cost	(4) Marginal Factor Cost
1	A	$12.00	$12.00
2	$12.10	24.20	E
3	12.20	C	F
4	B	D	12.60

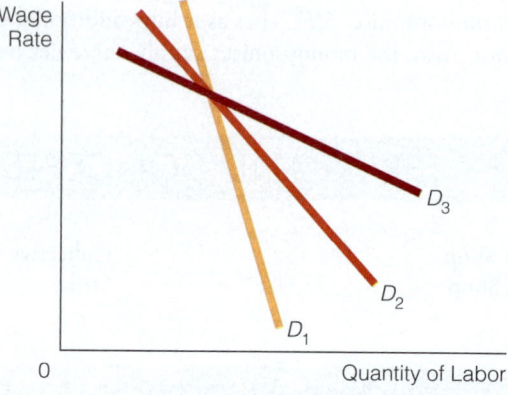

2. Which demand curve for labor in the accompanying figure exhibits the most pronounced wage–employment trade-off? Explain your answer.

3. Diagrammatically explain how changes in supply conditions and wage rates in the unionized sector can cause changes in supply conditions and wage rates in the nonunionized sector.

THE DISTRIBUTION OF INCOME AND POVERTY

INTRODUCTION

A random sample of people from the general population will have various incomes. Some people will be in the top 20 percent of income earners, some in the lowest 20 percent, and many others between these two extremes. In other words, some people earn high incomes, some earn low incomes, and many earn middle incomes. What factors influence the amount of income a person earns? Why are some people more likely than others to be poor? Why are some people more likely to be rich? You'll find the answers to these questions and to many other questions about the distribution of income and poverty in this chapter.

15-1 SOME FACTS ABOUT INCOME DISTRIBUTION

In discussing public policy issues, people sometimes talk about a single fact when they should talk about a collection of facts. A single fact is usually not as informative as a collection of facts, in much the same way that a single snapshot does not tell as much of a story as a moving picture—a succession of snapshots—does. This section presents a collection of a few facts about the distribution of income in the United States.

15-1a Who Are the Rich and How Rich Are They?

By many interpretations, the lowest fifth (the lowest quintile) of households in the United States is considered poor, the top fifth is considered rich, and the middle three-fifths are considered middle income.[1]

---

[1] A household consists of all people who occupy a housing unit. It includes the related family members and all unrelated people living in the unit.

Susan Montgomery/Shutterstock.com

EXHIBIT 1

Distribution of Household Income Shares, 2015

The annual income shares for different quintiles of households is shown here.

Source: U.S. Bureau of the Census.

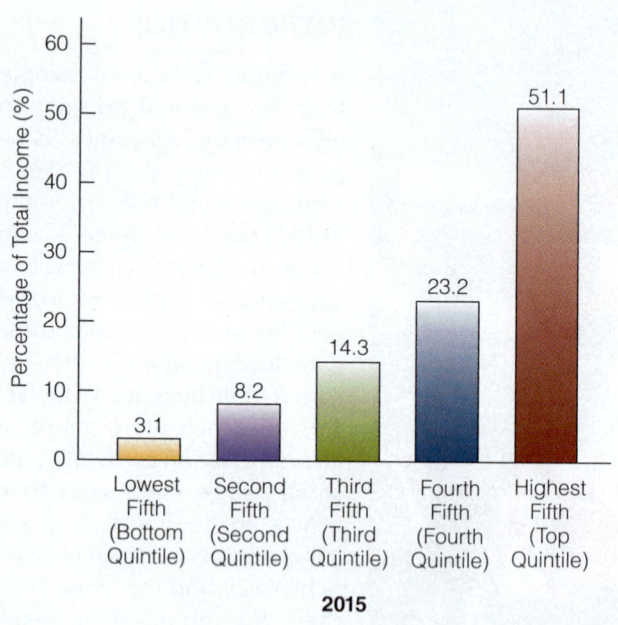

2015

In 2015, the lowest fifth (the poor) in the United States received 3.1 percent of the total money income, the second fifth received 8.2 percent, the third fifth received 14.3 percent, the fourth fifth received 23.2 percent, and the top fifth (the rich) received 51.1 percent (see Exhibit 1).[2]

Has the income distribution become more or less equal over time? Exhibit 2 shows the income shares of households in 1967 and 2015. In 1967, the highest fifth (top) of households accounted for 43.8 percent of all income; in 2015, the percentage had risen to 51.1 percent.

At the other end of the income spectrum, in 1967 the lowest fifth received 4.0 percent of all income; in 2015, the percentage had fallen to 3.1 percent. The middle groups—the three-fifths of income recipients between the lowest fifth and the highest fifth—accounted for 52.3 percent of all income in 1967 and 45.7 percent in 2015.

Many people implicitly assume that the quintiles (the fifths) in the income distribution contain an equal number of persons, but they do not. Instead, each quintile contains an equal percentage (20 percent) of households. But a household can contain any number of people. For example, in the United States, high-income households tend to be married couples with many members and earners. Low-income households tend to be single persons with little or no earnings. In 2015, the average household in the top quintile consisted of 3.2 persons while the average household in the bottom quintile comprised 1.8 persons.

Some economists have argued that the unequal quintile populations skew the Census Bureau's measure of the income distribution. For example, in 2002 the top quintile contained 24.6 percent of the population and the bottom quintile contained 14.3 percent of the population. In terms of a head count, 69.4 million persons were in the highest fifth and 40.3 million persons were in the lowest fifth.

15-1b   The Effect of Age on the Income Distribution

In analyzing the income distribution, we have to distinguish between people who are poor for long periods (sometimes their entire lives) and people who are poor temporarily. Consider Sherri Holmer, who attends college and works part time as a server at a nearby restaurant. Currently, her income is so low that she falls into the lowest quintile of income earners, but she isn't likely always to be in this quintile. After she graduates from college, Sherri's income will probably rise. If she is like most people, her income will rise during her twenties, thirties, and forties. In her late forties or early fifties, her income will take a slight downturn and then level off.

---

[2] Because of rounding, percentages in this chapter do not always sum to 100 percent.

EXHIBIT 2

Income Distribution, 1967 and 2015

Note that income shares have not been adjusted for such things as taxes and in-kind transfer payments, which are transfer payments made in terms of a specific good or service rather than in cash.

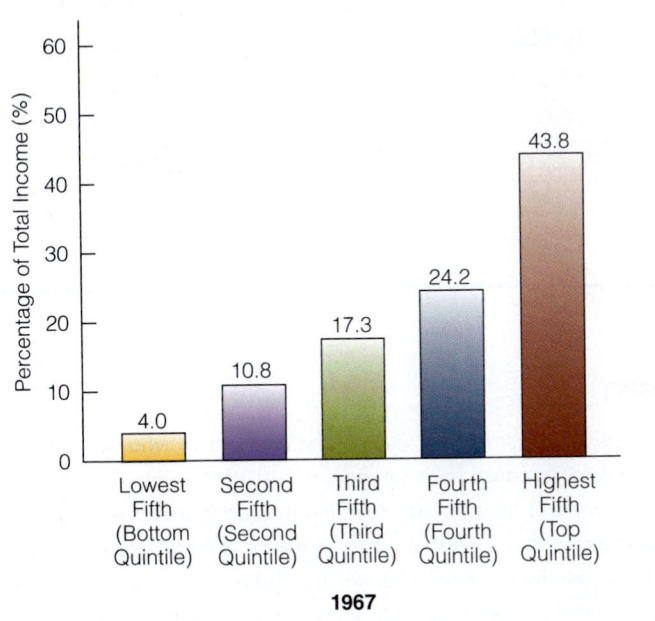

1967

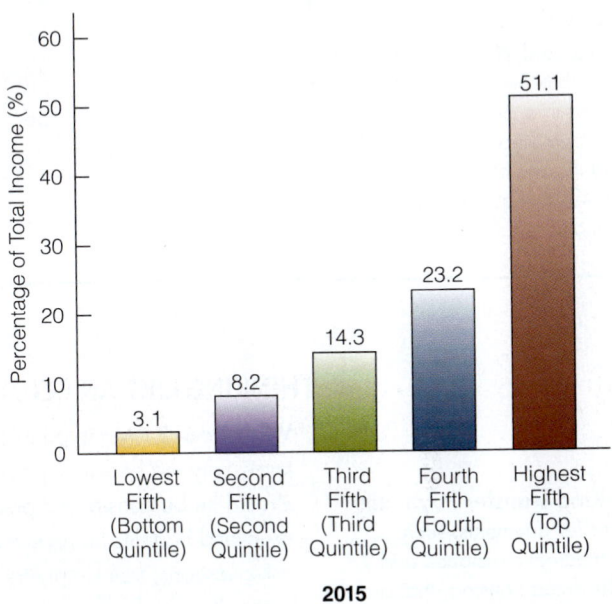

2015

Possibly—in fact, very likely—a person in her late twenties, thirties, or forties will have a higher income than a person in his early twenties or a person in her sixties, even though their total lifetime incomes will be identical. If we view each person over time, income equality is greater than if we view each person at a particular point in time (say, when one person is 58 years old and another is 68).

Exhibit 3 shows the incomes of John and Stephanie over a span of years. In 2000, John is 18 years old and earning $10,000 per year and Stephanie is 28 years old and earning $30,000 a year. The income distribution between John and Stephanie is unequal in 2000. Ten years later, the income distribution is still unequal, with Stephanie earning $45,000 and John earning $35,000. In fact, the income distribution is unequal in every year shown in the exhibit. However, the total income earned by each person is $236,000, giving a perfectly equal income distribution over time.

In the United States, people seem to experience quite a bit of upward income mobility over time. The University of Michigan's Panel Survey on Dynamics tracked 50,000 Americans for 17 years. Of the people in the lowest fifth of the income distribution in 1975, only 5.1 percent were still there in 1991—and 29 percent of them had reached the highest fifth!

EXHIBIT 3

Income Distribution at One Point in Time and Over Time

In each year, the income distribution between John and Stephanie is unequal, with Stephanie earning more than John in 2000, 2010, 2020, and 2030 and John earning more than Stephanie in 2040. In the five years specified, however, both John and Stephanie earned the same total income of $236,000, giving a perfectly equal income distribution over time.

Year	John's Age (years)	John's Income	Stephanie's Age (years)	Stephanie's Income
2000	18	$10,000	28	$30,000
2010	28	35,000	38	45,000
2020	38	52,000	48	60,000
2030	48	64,000	58	75,000
2040	58	75,000	68	26,000
Total		$236,000		$236,000

THINKING LIKE AN ECONOMIST

Why Poor? Many people believe that poor is poor, but not the economist, who wants to know why the person is poor. Is he poor because he is young and just starting out in life? Would he be considered poor if we were to take into account the **in-kind transfer payments** or in-kind benefits he receives? Some people argue that when someone is poor, you do not ask questions; you simply try to help. But the economist knows that not everyone is in the same situation for the same reason and that the reason may determine whether you proceed with help and, if you do proceed, how to do so. Both the elderly person with a disability and the young, smart college student may earn the same low income, but you may feel more obliged to help the elderly person with a disability than the college student.

In-Kind Transfer Payments
Transfer payments, such as medical assistance and subsidized housing, that are made in a specific good or service rather than in cash.

15-1c A Simple Equation

The following simple equation combines four of the factors that determine a person's income:

$$\text{Individual income} = \text{Labor income} + \text{Asset income} + \text{Transfer payments} - \text{Taxes}$$

- *Labor income* is equal to the wage rate an individual receives, multiplied by the number of hours worked.

- *Asset income* consists of such things as the return to saving, the return to capital investment, and the return to land.

- *Transfer payments* are payments to persons that are not made in return for goods and services currently supplied (e.g., Social Security payments and cash welfare assistance are government transfer payments).

- Finally, from the sum of labor income, asset income, and **transfer payments**, we subtract *taxes* to see what an individual is left with (i.e., individual income).

Transfer Payments
Payments to persons that are not made in return for goods and services currently supplied.

The preceding equation provides a quick way of focusing on the direct and indirect factors affecting an individual's income and on the degree of income inequality in society. The next section examines the conventional ways that income inequality is measured.

ECONOMICS 24/7

Statistics Can Mislead If You Don't Know How They Are Made

If you read that U.S. household income has not grown in the last 20 years, would you conclude that incomes in the United States are stagnant? Many people might think so, but it may not be true. A household consists of all the people who occupy a housing unit. Individual incomes can rise while household incomes remain unchanged if households become smaller over time.

To illustrate, suppose 10 households have four persons in each. Each person in each household earns $30,000 a year. So each household earns an income of $120,000 a year. Some years pass, each person's income in each household rises to $60,000, but two of every four persons in each household leave to set up a new household. In other words, we now have 20 households with two persons in each, and the total income of each of the 20 households is still $120,000. On an individual basis, certainly all 40 persons are better off earning $60,000 each than earning $30,000 each. But on the basis of household income, we get a very different picture.

Lesson: Individual income can rise while household income remains unchanged because households could be getting smaller as individual incomes rise.

Consider another assertion: "The middle class in this country is getting smaller and smaller." On the surface, this statement sounds fairly ominous. Where is the middle class going? Is it disappearing because it is becoming poorer or because it is becoming richer?

The problem is that, if we have a fixed definition of the middle class—say, persons who earn between $40,000 and $50,000 a year—then a changing income distribution can cause the number of persons in that (middle-class) income range to fall. Suppose that, of 10 people, the lowest-earning person earns $10,000 a year, the next-lowest-earning person earns $20,000

a year, and so on up to the highest-earning person, who earns $100,000 a year.

Incomes for various persons ($000)

10, 20, 30, 40, 50, 60, 70, 80, 90, 100

Let's say that the middle class consists of persons in the middle of the income distribution: those who earn between $40,000 and $70,000 a year. In other words, the middle class consists of four persons. These four persons' incomes are enclosed in brackets in the following sequence:

10, 20, 30, [40, 50, 60, 70], 80, 90, 100

Years pass, and now everyone earns $50,000 more than before. So, now the lowest-earning person earns $60,000 a year and the highest-earning person earns $150,000:

Incomes for various persons ($000)

60, 70, 80, 100, 110, 120, 130, 140, 150

The income distribution has become skewed toward higher incomes. The middle class has been cut in half if we continue to define it as persons earning between $40,000 and $70,000 a year. Now only two persons fall within this category: the person who once earned $10,000 and now earns $60,000 and the person who once earned $20,000 and now earns $70,000.

Lesson: As individual incomes rise, the middle class can get smaller (and disappear altogether) if it is defined by a fixed-dollar income range. Contrary to what some people believe, a disappearing middle class does not necessarily connote a world of only the rich and the poor.

Does It Matter to You . . .
What Your Educational Attainment Level Is?

Does the level of your educational attainment matter to you? Does it matter if you if you have only a high school education as opposed to a college education? There are data that show that one's weekly income and chances of becoming unemployed do depend upon one's level of educational attainment.

To illustrate, in 2015, the median (usual) weekly earnings for a person with less than a high school diploma was $493, and the unemployment rate for persons with less than a high school diploma was 8 percent. In contrast, the median weekly earnings for a person with a high school diploma was $678 and the unemployment rate was 5.4 percent.[3]

Let's go even higher on the educational attainment scale. If a person had some college, but no degree, median weekly earnings rose to $738 and the unemployment rate fell to 5.0 percent. Going even

iStock.com/PeopleImages

higher, if a person had a bachelor's degree the median weekly earnings rose to $1,137 and the unemployment rate fell to 2.8 percent. And moving even higher, to a person with a master's degree, the median weekly earnings increased to $1,341 and the unemployment rate fell to 2.4 percent.

Does it matter what your educational attainment level is? It seems to matter when it comes to both one's weekly earnings (the higher one's educational attainment, the higher one's weekly earnings) and to the chances of one becoming unemployed (the higher one's educational attainment level, the less likely one is to be unemployed).

_____

[3] The source for all data is the Bureau of Labor Statistics and the Current Population Survey.

SELF-TEST

(Answers to Self-Test questions are in Answers to Self-Test Questions at the back of the book.)

1. How can government change the distribution of income?

2. "Income inequality at one point in time is sometimes consistent with income equality over time." Comment.

3. Smith and Jones have the same income this year: $40,000. Does it follow that their income came from the same sources? Explain your answer.

Lorenz Curve
A graph of the income distribution that expresses the relationship between the cumulative percentage of households and the cumulative percentage of income.

15-2 MEASURING INCOME EQUALITY

Two commonly used measures of income inequality are the Lorenz curve and the Gini coefficient.

15-2a The Lorenz Curve

The **Lorenz curve** represents the distribution of income; it expresses the relationship between the cumulative percentage of households and the cumulative percentage of income.

Exhibit 4 shows a hypothetical Lorenz curve. The data in part (a) are used to plot the Lorenz curve in part (b). According to (a), the lowest fifth of households has an income share of 10 percent, the second fifth has an income share of 15 percent, and so on. The Lorenz curve in (b) is derived by plotting five points:

- Point *A* represents the cumulative income share of the lowest fifth of households (10 percent of income goes to the lowest fifth of households).

- Point *B* represents the cumulative income share of the lowest fifth plus the second fifth (25 percent of income goes to two-fifths, or 40 percent, of the income recipients).

- Point *C* represents the cumulative income share of the lowest fifth, plus the second fifth, plus the third fifth (45 percent of income goes to three-fifths, or 60 percent, of the income recipients).

Points *D* and *E* are calculated in the same way as points *A*, *B*, and *C*.

Connecting the five points gives the Lorenz curve that represents the data in (a); the Lorenz curve is another way of depicting the income distribution in (a). Exhibit 5 illustrates the Lorenz curve for the United States based on the (money) income shares in Exhibit 1.

What would the Lorenz curve look like if there were perfect income equality among all households? It would be the line of perfect income equality illustrated in Exhibit 4(b). At any point on this 45-degree line, the cumulative percentage of income (on the vertical axis) equals the cumulative percentage of households (on the horizontal axis). For example, at point *F*, 60 percent of the households receive 60 percent of the total income.

EXHIBIT 4

A Hypothetical Lorenz Curve

The data in (a) were used to derive the Lorenz curve in (b). The bowed Lorenz curve shows an unequal distribution of income. The more bowed the Lorenz curve, the more unequal is the distribution of income.

Quintile	Income Share (%)	Cumulative Income Share (%)
Lowest fifth	10	10
Second fifth	15	25
Third fifth	20	45
Fourth fifth	25	70
Highest fifth	30	100

(a)

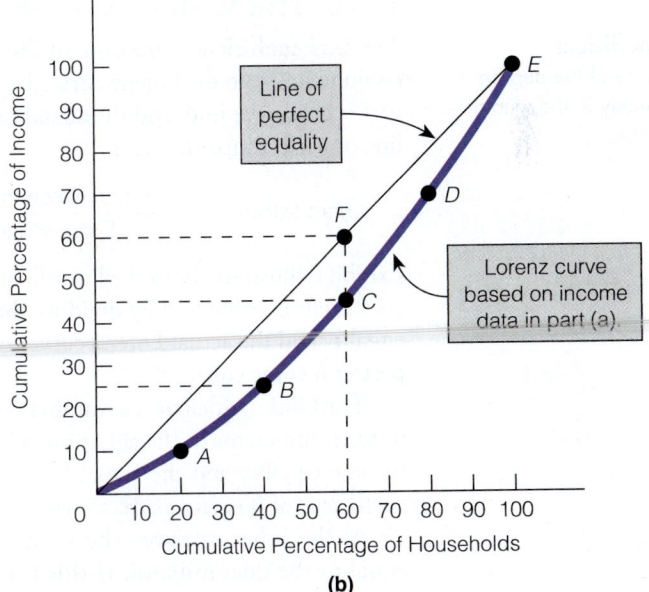

(b)

EXHIBIT 5

Lorenz Curve for the United States, 2015   This Lorenz curve is based on the 2015 income shares for the United States.

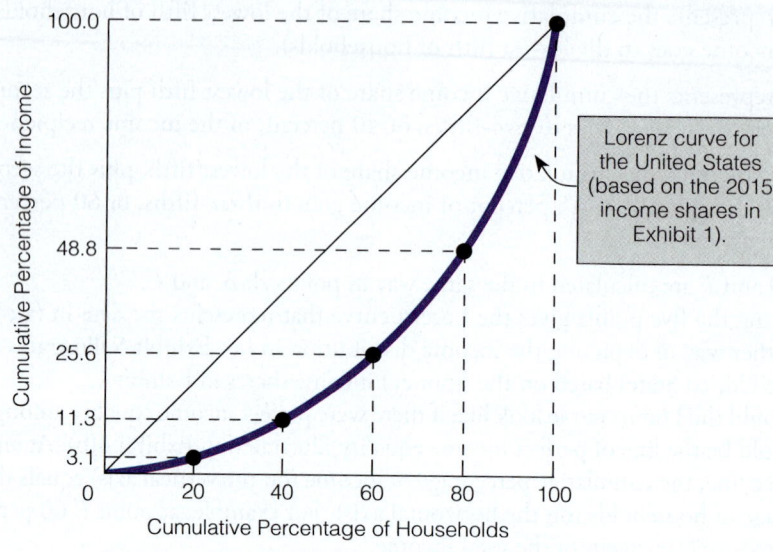

Lorenz curve for the United States (based on the 2015 income shares in Exhibit 1).

15-2b The Gini Coefficient

Gini Coefficient
A measure of the degree of inequality in the income distribution.

The **Gini coefficient**, a measure of the degree of inequality in the income distribution, is used in conjunction with the Lorenz curve. It is equal to the area between the line of perfect income equality (or 45-degree line) and the actual Lorenz curve, divided by the entire triangular area under the line of perfect income equality:

$$\text{Gini coefficient} = \frac{\text{Area between the line of perfect income equality and actual Lorenz curve}}{\text{Entire triangular area under the line of perfect income equality}}$$

Exhibit 6 illustrates both the line of perfect income equality and an actual Lorenz curve. The Gini coefficient is computed by dividing the shaded area (the area between the line of perfect income equality and the actual Lorenz curve) by the area $0AB$ (the entire triangular area under the line of perfect income equality).

The Gini coefficient is a number between 0 and 1. At one extreme, the Gini coefficient equals 0 if the numerator in the equation is 0, meaning that there is no area between the line of perfect income equality and the actual Lorenz curve. In that case, the lines are the same. Thus, a Gini coefficient of 0 means perfect income equality.

At the other extreme, the Gini coefficient equals 1 if the numerator in the equation is equal to the denominator. If this is the case, the actual Lorenz curve is as far away from the line of perfect income equality as is possible. Thus, a Gini coefficient of 1 means complete income inequality. (In this situation, in terms of the actual Lorenz curve, one person would have all the income there is and no one else would have any. In Exhibit 6, a Lorenz curve representing complete income inequality would lie along the horizontal axis from 0 to A and then move from A to B.)

EXHIBIT 6

The Gini Coefficient

The Gini coefficient is a measure of the degree of income inequality. It is equal to the area between the line of perfect income equality and the actual Lorenz curve, divided by the entire triangular area under the line of perfect income equality. In the diagram, the area representing the Gini coefficient is equal to the shaded portion divided by the triangular area OAB. A Gini coefficient of 0 means perfect income equality; a Gini coefficient of 1 means complete income inequality. The larger the Gini coefficient, the greater is the income inequality; the smaller the Gini coefficient, the lower is the income inequality

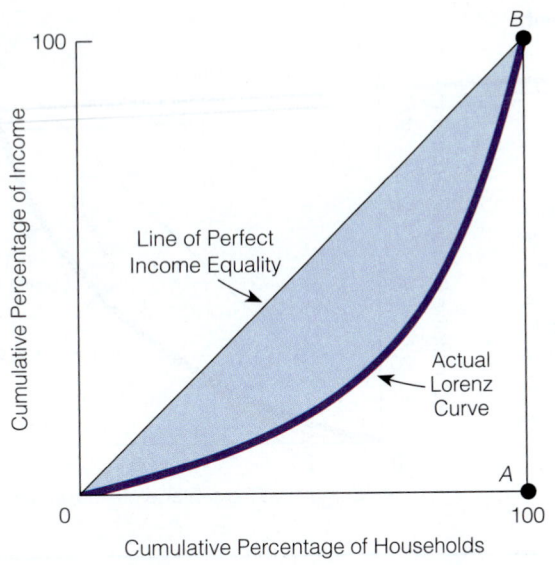

If a Gini coefficient of 0 represents perfect income equality and a Gini coefficient of 1 represents complete income inequality, then the larger the Gini coefficient is, the higher the degree of income inequality will be. Conversely, the smaller the Gini coefficient is, the lower the degree of income inequality. In 2007, the Gini coefficient in the United States was 0.450; in 1947, it was 0.376. By way of comparison, here are the Gini coefficients for some other countries: Russia, 0.423 (2008); Argentina, 0.49 (2007); Mexico 0.483 (2008); the United Kingdom, 0.34 (2005); Spain, 0.32 (2005), Sweden, 0.23 (2005).

15-2c A Limitation of the Gini Coefficient

Although the Gini coefficient indicates a lot about the degree of inequality in income distribution, we have to be careful not to misinterpret it. For example, if the Gini coefficient is 0.33 in country 1 and 0.25 in country 2, we know that the income distribution is more nearly equal in country 2 than in country 1. But in which country does the lowest fifth of households receive the larger percentage of income? The natural inclination is to answer, "in the country with the more nearly equal income distribution: country 2."

However, this answer may not be true. Exhibit 7 shows two Lorenz curves. Overall, Lorenz curve 2 is closer to the line of perfect income equality than Lorenz curve 1 is; thus, the Gini coefficient is smaller for Lorenz curve 2 than for Lorenz curve 1. But the lowest 20 percent of households has a smaller percentage of total income with Lorenz curve 2 than with Lorenz curve 1.

Therefore, the Gini coefficient cannot tell us what is happening in different quintiles. If the Gini coefficient is lower in country 2 than in country 1, it does not necessarily follow that the lowest fifth of households has a greater percentage of total income in country 2 compared with country 1.

15-2d Common Misconceptions about Income Inequality

Some people suggest that, in a country where income inequality is rising, individuals cannot become better off. Suppose a society is made up of five individuals, A–E. Let the yearly income for each individual be as follows: A earns $20,000, B earns $10,000, C earns $5,000, D earns

EXHIBIT 7

Limitation of the Gini Coefficient

By itself, the Gini coefficient cannot tell us anything about the income share of a particular quintile. Although there is a tendency to believe that the bottom quintile receives a larger percentage of total income the lower the Gini coefficient, that need not be the case. In the diagram, the Gini coefficient for Lorenz curve 2 is lower than the Gini coefficient for Lorenz curve 1 but the bottom 20 percent of households obtains a smaller percentage of total income in the case of Lorenz curve 2, the curve with a lower Gini coefficient.

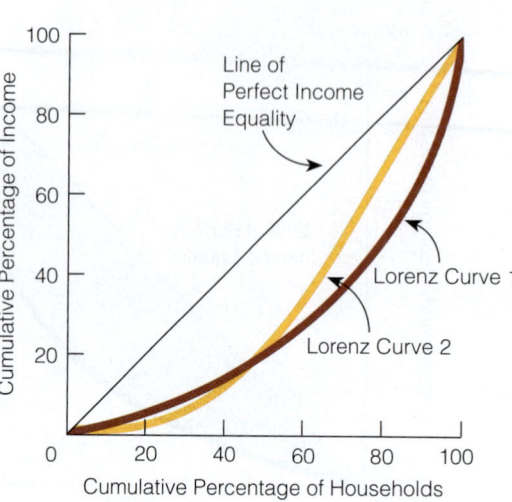

$2,500, and E earns $1,250. Then the total yearly income in this society is $38,750, and the distribution of income is certainly unequal: A earns 51.61 percent of the income, B earns 25.81 percent, C earns 12.90 percent, D earns 6.45 percent, and E earns only 3.23 percent.

Now suppose each person earns additional real income. A earns $10,000 more real income, for a total of $30,000; B earns $3,000 more real income, for a total of $13,000; C earns $2,000 more real income, for a total of $7,000; D earns $1,000 more real income, for a total of $3,500; and E earns $200 more real income, for a total of $1,450. In terms of real income, each of the five persons is better off, but the income distribution has become even more unequal. For example, A (at the top fifth of income earners) now receives 54.60 percent of all income instead of 51.61 percent, and E (at the bottom fifth of income earners) now receives 2.64 percent instead of 3.23 percent. A newspaper headline might read, "The rich get richer as the poor get poorer." People reading this headline might naturally think that the poor in society are worse off. But we know that they are not worse off in terms of the goods and services they can purchase. They have more real income than they had when the income distribution was less unequal. In short, everyone can be better off even if the income distribution becomes more unequal.

SELF-TEST

1. Starting with the top fifth of income earners and proceeding to the lowest fifth, suppose the income share of each group is 40 percent, 30 percent, 20 percent, 10 percent, and 5 percent. Can these percentages be right?

2. Country A has a Gini coefficient of 0.45. What does that statement mean?

15-3 WHY INCOME INEQUALITY EXISTS

The question of why income inequality exists can be answered by focusing on our earlier simple equation:

Individual income = Labor income + Asset income + Transfer payments − Taxes

Generally, income inequality exists because people do not receive the same labor income, asset income, and transfer payments, and/or because they do not pay the same taxes. By focusing on factors that often contribute to differences, this section discusses some of the specific reasons that people don't receive, say, the same labor income and asset income.

15-3a   Factors Contributing to Income Inequality

Six factors that contribute to income inequality are innate abilities and attributes, work and leisure, education and other training, risk taking, luck, and wage discrimination.

Innate Abilities and Attributes   Individuals are not all born with the same innate abilities and attributes. People vary in their degrees of intelligence, in their appearance, and in their levels of creativity. Some individuals have more marketable innate abilities and attributes than others. For example, the man or woman born with exceptionally good looks, the natural athlete, or the person who is musically gifted or mathematically adept is more likely to earn a higher income than someone with lesser abilities or attributes.

Work and Leisure   There is a trade-off between work and leisure: more work means less leisure, and less work means more leisure. Some individuals will choose to work more hours (or take a second job) and thus have less leisure, and this choice will be reflected in their labor income: They will earn a larger income than persons who choose not to work more, *ceteris paribus*.

Education and Other Training   Economists usually refer to schooling and other types of training as an investment in human capital. To buy or to invest in a capital good, a person has to give up present consumption and does so in the hope that the capital good will increase future consumption.

Schooling can be looked on as capital. First, one must give up present consumption to obtain it. Second, by providing individuals with certain skills and knowledge, schooling can increase their future consumption over what it would be without schooling. Schooling, then, is human capital. In general, **human capital** includes education, the development of skills, and any other improvements that are particular to the individual and that increase productivity.

Contrast a person who has obtained an education with a person who has not. The educated person is likely to have certain skills, abilities, and knowledge that the uneducated person lacks. Consequently, the educated person is likely to be worth more to an employer. Most college students know this truth; it is one of the reasons they attend college.

Human Capital
Education, development of skills, and anything else that is particular to the individual and that increases personal productivity.

Risk Taking   Individuals have different attitudes toward risk. Some individuals are more willing to take on risk than others. Some of the individuals who are willing to take on risk will do well and rise to the top of the income distribution, and others will fall to the bottom. Individuals who prefer to play it safe aren't as likely to reach the top of the income distribution or to hit bottom.

Luck   When individuals can't explain why something has happened to them, they often say it was the result of good or bad luck. At times, the good or bad luck explanation makes sense; at other times, it is more of a rationalization than an explanation.

Good and bad luck may influence incomes. For example, the college student who studies biology, only to find out in her senior year that the bottom has fallen out of the biology market, has experienced bad luck. The farmer who hits oil while digging a well has experienced good luck. An automobile worker who is unemployed during a recession is experiencing bad luck. A person who trains for a profession in which there is an unexpected increase in demand experiences good luck.

Although luck can and does influence incomes, it is not likely to have (on average) a great or long-run effect. The person who experiences good luck today and whose income reflects this fact isn't likely to experience luck-boosting income increases time after time. In the long run, such factors as innate ability and attributes, education, and personal decisions (e.g., how much work versus how much leisure) are more likely to have a greater, more sustained effect on income than luck does.

Wage Discrimination
The situation in which individuals of equal ability and productivity (as measured by their contribution to output) are paid different wage rates.

Wage Discrimination **Wage discrimination** exists when an employer pays different wages to individuals of equal ability and productivity, as measured by their marginal revenue products. For example, in 2010, females working full time earned approximately 81 percent of the male median income. In the same year, African Americans had a median income approximately 60 percent that of whites. These differences between white and black incomes and between male and female incomes are not due wholly to discrimination. Most empirical studies show that approximately half the differences are due to variations in education, productivity, and job training (although one may ask whether discrimination has anything to do with the education, productivity, and job training differences). The remainder of the wage differential is due to other factors, one of which is hypothesized to be discrimination.

Most people agree that discrimination exists, although they differ on how much they think it affects income. Also, discrimination is not always directed at employees by employers. For example, consumers may practice discrimination: Some white consumers may wish to deal only with white physicians and lawyers; some Asian Americans may wish to deal only with Asian American physicians and lawyers.

15-3b Income Differences: Some Are Voluntary, Some Are Not

Even in a world with no discrimination, differences in income would exist because of other factors. Some individuals would have more marketable skills than others, some individuals would decide to work harder and longer hours than others, some individuals would take on more risk than others, and some individuals would undertake more schooling and training than others. Thus, some degree of income inequality occurs because individuals are innately different and make different choices. However, some degree of income inequality is also due to factors unrelated to innate ability or choices—such as discrimination or luck.

In an ongoing and interesting debate on the topic of discrimination-based income inequality, the opposing sides weight various factors differently. Some people argue that wage discrimination would be reduced if markets were allowed to be more competitive, more open, and freer. They believe that, in an open and competitive market with few barriers to entry and with no government protection of privileged groups, discrimination would have a high price. Firms that didn't hire the best and the brightest—regardless of race, religion, or gender—would suffer. They would ultimately pay for their act of discrimination by having higher labor costs and lower profits. Individuals holding this view usually propose that government deregulate markets, reduce legal barriers to entry, and, in general, not interfere with the workings of the free-market mechanism.

Others contend that, even if the government were to follow this script, much wage discrimination would still exist. They think that government should play an active legislative role in reducing both wage discrimination and other types of discrimination that they believe ultimately result in wage discrimination, such as discrimination in education and in on-the-job training. Proponents of an active role for government usually believe that such policy programs as affirmative action, equal pay for equal work, and comparable worth (equal pay for comparable work) are beneficial in reducing both the amount of wage discrimination in the economy and the degree of income inequality.

SELF-TEST

1. Jack and Harry work for the same company, but Jack earns more than Harry. Is this evidence of wage discrimination? Explain your answer.

2. A person decides to assume a lot of risk in earning an income. How could this decision affect her income?

15-4 POVERTY

This section presents some facts about poverty and examines its causes.

15-4a What Is Poverty?

There are principally two views on poverty:

- *Poverty should be defined in absolute terms.* In absolute terms, poverty might be defined as follows: poverty exists when the income of a family of four is less than $10,000 per year.

- *Poverty should be defined in relative terms.* In relative terms, poverty might be defined as follows: poverty exists when the income of a family of four places it in the lowest 10 percent of income recipients.

Viewing poverty in relative terms means that poverty will always exist—unless, of course, income equality is absolute. Given any unequal income distribution, some individuals will always occupy the bottom rung of the income ladder; thus, there will always be poverty. This assertion holds no matter how high the absolute standard of living is of the members of the society. For example, in a society of 10 persons in which 9 earn $1 million per year and 1 earns $400,000 per year, the person earning $400,000 per year is in the bottom 10 percent of the income distribution. If poverty is defined in relative terms, this person is considered to be living in poverty.

The U.S. government defines poverty in absolute terms. The absolute poverty measure was developed in 1964 by the Social Security Administration on the basis of findings of the Department of Agriculture. Called the **poverty income threshold** or **poverty line**, this measure refers to the income below which people are considered to be living in poverty. Individuals or families with incomes below the poverty income threshold, or poverty line, are considered poor.

The poverty threshold is updated yearly to reflect changes in the consumer price index. In 2015, the poverty income threshold was $24,257 for a family of four and $12,331 for an individual (under 65 years old). In 2015, 43.1 million people, or 13.5 percent of the U.S. population, were living below the poverty line.

Poverty Income Threshold (Poverty Line)
The income level below which people are considered to be living in poverty.

15-4b Limitations of the Official Poverty Income Statistics

The official poverty income statistics have certain limitations and shortcomings:

- Poverty figures are based solely on money incomes. Many money-poor persons receive in-kind benefits. For example, a family of four with a money income of $24,257 in 2015 was defined as poor, although it might have received in-kind benefits worth, say, $4,000. If the poverty figures are adjusted for in-kind benefits, the percentage of persons living in poverty drops.

- Poverty figures are not adjusted for unreported income, leading to an overestimate of poverty.

- Poverty figures are not adjusted for regional differences in the cost of living, leading to both overestimates and underestimates of poverty.

- Government counters are unable to find some poor persons—such as some of the homeless—a circumstance that leads to an underestimate of poverty.

15-4c Who Are the Poor?

Although the poor are persons of all religions, colors, genders, ages, and ethnic backgrounds, some groups are represented much more prominently in the poverty figures than others. For example, a greater percentage of African Americans and Hispanics than whites are poor. In 2015, 24.1 percent of African Americans, 21.4 percent of Hispanics, and 11.6 percent of whites lived below the poverty line. If we look at poverty in terms of absolute numbers instead of percentages, then more poor persons are white. In 2015, 17.7 million whites, 10.1 million African Americans, and 12.1 million Hispanics lived below the poverty line.

A greater percentage of families headed by females than families headed by males are poor, and families with seven or more persons are much more likely to be poor than are families with fewer than seven. In addition, a greater percentage of young persons than other age groups are poor, and the uneducated and poorly educated are more likely to be poor than are the educated.

15-4d What Is the Justification for Government Redistributing Income?

Some individuals say that there is no justification for government welfare assistance—that is, redistributing income. In their view, playing Robin Hood is not a proper role of government. Persons who make this argument say they are not against helping the poor (e.g., they are usually in favor of private charitable organizations), but they are against government using its powers to take from some to give to others.

Those who believe in government welfare assistance usually present the *public good-free rider* justification or the *social-insurance* justification. Proponents of the public good-free rider position make the following arguments: Most individuals in society would feel better if there were little or no poverty. Witnessing the signs of poverty, such as slums, hungry and poorly clothed people, and the homeless, is distressing. Therefore, there is a demand for reducing or eliminating poverty.

The reduction or elimination of poverty is a *nonexcludable public* good—a good that, if consumed by one person, can be consumed by other persons to the same degree and the consumption of which cannot be denied to anyone. That is, when poverty is reduced or eliminated, everyone will benefit from no longer viewing the ugly and upsetting sights of poverty, and no one can be excluded from such benefits. If no one can be excluded from experiencing the benefits of a reduction in, or the elimination of, poverty, then individuals will not have any incentive to pay for what they can get for free. Thus, they will become free riders. Economist Milton Friedman sums up the force of the argument this way:

> I am distressed by the sight of poverty. I am benefited by its alleviation; but I am benefited equally whether I or someone else pays for its alleviation; the benefits of other people's charity therefore partly accrue to me. To put it differently, we might all of us be willing to contribute to the relief of poverty, provided everyone else did it. We might not be willing to contribute the same amount without such assurance.[4]

[4] Milton Friedman, *Capitalism and Freedom* (Chicago: University of Chicago Press, 1962), p. 91.

Accepting the public good-free rider argument means that government is justified in taxing all persons to pay for the welfare assistance of some.

The social-insurance justification is a different type of justification for government welfare assistance. It holds that individuals not currently receiving welfare think that they might one day need it and thus are willing to take out a form of insurance for themselves by supporting welfare programs with their tax dollars and votes.

SELF-TEST

1. "Poor people will always exist." Comment.

2. What percentage of the U.S. population was living in poverty in 2015?

3. What is the general description of a disproportionate percentage of the poor?

OFFICE HOURS

"Are the Number of Persons in Each Fifth the Same?"

STUDENT: Earlier you said that in 2015 the lowest fifth of household income earners in the United States received 3.1 percent of the total money income, the second fifth received 8.2 percent, the third fifth received 14.3 percent, the fourth fifth received 23.2 percent, and the top fifth received 51.1 percent. Am I right that each fifth contains the same number of individuals? In other words, if there are 100 individuals in the lowest fifth, it follows that there are 100 individuals in the top fifth too.

INSTRUCTOR: No, you're not right. The quintiles (the fifths) are unequal in size because they are based on a count of households rather than persons and not every household has the same number of persons in it. For example, one household can have two persons in it, and another has four.

STUDENT: Well, then, are more persons in the top fifth of income earners than in the lowest fifth of income earners?

INSTRUCTOR: Yes. For example, in 2002 the top fifth contained 24.6 percent of the population whereas the lowest fifth contained 14.3 percent of the population. Stated differently, the top fifth contained 69.4 million persons and the lowest fifth contained 40.3 million persons.

STUDENT: What happens to the income distribution if we adjust each fifth so that it contains an equal number of

persons? In other words, what happens if we adjust every fifth so that it contains 20 percent of the population?

INSTRUCTOR: The income distribution becomes less unequal. To illustrate, if you look at the data for 2002 and deal with households instead of persons, you'd conclude that the lowest fifth received 3.5 percent of the total money income and the top fifth received 49.7 percent. Now, if you adjust the fifths so that each has 20 percent of the population, then you'll find that the lowest fifth received 9.4 percent (instead of 3.5 percent) of the total money income and the top fifth received 39.6 percent (instead of 49.7 percent).[5]

STUDENT: Can income distribution be adjusted for other things?

INSTRUCTOR: Yes. For one thing, persons in each fifth do not all work the same number of hours. For example, in 2002, individuals in the lowest fifth performed 4.3 percent of all work in the U.S. economy and those in the highest fifth performed 33.9 percent. To be fair, though, the low levels of paid employment in the lowest fifth reflect the

---

[5] The adjusted income distributions in this feature come from Census Bureau data and a publication by Robert Rector and Rea Hederman, Jr., *Two Americas: One Rich, One Poor? Understanding Income Inequality in the United States* (August 24, 2004), http://www.heritage.org/Research/Taxes/bg1791.cfm

low numbers of working-age people in this group. In 2002, the lowest fifth contained only 11.2 percent of all working-age adults whereas the highest fifth contained 27.6 percent. However, when we compare working-age adults in the lowest fifth with working-age adults in the highest fifth, we learn that the average working-age adult in the lowest fifth worked about half as many hours a year as the working-age adult in the highest fifth.

Now, if we adjust the income distribution to show us what it would be like if the average working-age adult in the lowest fifth worked as many hours as the average working-age adult in the top fifth, the income distribution becomes less unequal. In 2002, the lowest fifth would have received 12.3 percent (instead of 3.5 percent) of the total money income and the top fifth would have received 35.8 percent (instead of 49.7 percent).

STUDENT: The income distribution seems as though it can be portrayed in different ways. We can choose to adjust for taxes and transfer payments or choose not to; we can choose to adjust for the number of persons or

choose not to; we can choose to adjust for the number of hours worked or choose not to.

INSTRUCTOR: You're right about that. And that is part of the reason for such heated debate over income distribution. Person A might think it's better to view the income distribution after having adjusted for something (such as taxes, transfer payments, the number of persons, and the like), and Person B might think it better to view the income distribution before adjusting.

Points to Remember

1. The bottom fifth of household income earners does not contain the same number of persons as the top fifth of household income earners. For example, in 2002 the top fifth contained 69.4 million persons whereas the lowest fifth contained 40.3 million persons.

2. The income distribution (or distribution of income) can be adjusted for various factors. Such adjustments often change the degree of income equality or inequality of the income distribution.

CHAPTER SUMMARY

THE DISTRIBUTION OF INCOME

- In 2015, the lowest fifth of households received 3.1 percent of the total money income, the second fifth received 8.2 percent, the third fifth received 14.3 percent, the fourth fifth received 23.2 percent, and the top fifth received 51.1 percent.

- The government can change the distribution of income through taxes and transfer payments. Individual income = Labor income + Asset income + Transfer payments − Taxes. Government directly affects transfer payments and taxes.

- The Lorenz curve represents the income distribution. The Gini coefficient is a measure of the degree of inequality in the distribution of income. A Gini coefficient of 0 means perfect income equality; a Gini coefficient of 1 means complete income inequality.

- Income inequality exists because individuals differ in their innate abilities and attributes, their choices regarding work and leisure, their education and other training, their attitudes about risk taking, the luck they experience, and the amount

of wage discrimination directed against them. Some income inequality is the result of voluntary choices, and some is not.

POVERTY

- The income poverty threshold, or poverty line, is the income level below which a family or person is considered poor and living in poverty.

- Poverty income statistics have their limitations. The statistics are usually not adjusted for (1) in-kind benefits, (2) unreported and illegal income, and (3) regional differences in the cost of living. Furthermore, the statistics do not count the poor who exist but who are out of sight, such as some of the homeless.

- People who believe government should redistribute income from the rich to the poor usually base their argument on the public good–free rider justification or the social-insurance justification. The public good–free rider justification holds that many people are in favor of redistributing income from the rich to the poor and that the elimination of poverty is a public good. Unfortunately, individuals cannot create a public good, because of the incentive that everyone has to free ride on the contributions of others. Consequently, government is justified in taxing all persons to pay for the welfare assistance of some. The social-insurance justification holds that individuals not currently receiving redistributed

monies may one day find themselves in a position where they will need to, so they are willing to take out a form of insurance. In essence, they are willing to support redistribution programs today so that the programs exist if they should need them in the future.

KEY TERMS AND CONCEPTS

In-Kind Transfer Payments
Transfer Payments
Lorenz Curve

Gini Coefficient
Human Capital
Wage Discrimination

Poverty Income Threshold
(Poverty Line)

QUESTIONS AND PROBLEMS

1. What percentage of total money income did the lowest fifth of households receive in 2015? The fourth fifth?

2. "The Gini coefficient for country A is 0.35, and for country B it is 0.22. Therefore, the bottom 10 percent of income recipients in country B have a greater percentage of the total income than the bottom 10 percent of the income recipients in country A." Do you agree or disagree? Why?

3. Would you expect greater income inequality in country A, where there is a large disparity in age, or in country B, where there is a small disparity in age? Explain your answer.

4. Compare the U.S. income distribution in 1967 with the income distribution in 2015. Has the U.S. income inequality increased or decreased? What percentage of total money income did the top fifth of U.S. households receive in 2015?

5. What role might each of the following play in contributing to income inequality?
   a. Risk taking
   b. Education
   c. Innate abilities and attributes

6. Welfare recipients would rather receive cash benefits than in-kind benefits, but much of the welfare system provides in-kind benefits. Is there any reason for not giving recipients their welfare benefits the way they want to receive them? Would it be better to move to a welfare system that provides benefits only in cash?

7. What is the effect of age on the income distribution?

8. Can more people live in poverty at the same time that a smaller percentage of people live in poverty? Explain your answer.

9. How would you determine whether the wage difference between two individuals is due to wage discrimination?

10. Define each of the following:
    a. In-kind transfer payment
    b. Lorenz curve
    c. Wage discrimination

WORKING WITH NUMBERS AND GRAPHS

1. The lowest fifth of income earners have a 10 percent income share; the second fifth, a 17 percent income share; the third fifth, a 22 percent income share; the fourth fifth, a 24 percent income share; and the highest fifth, a 27 percent income share. Draw the Lorenz curve.

2. In Exhibit 7, using Lorenz curve 2, calculate the approximate percentage of income that goes to the second-highest 20 percent of households.

3. Is it possible for everyone's real income to rise even though the income distribution in a society has become more unequal? Prove your answer with a numerical example.

16

INTEREST, RENT, AND PROFIT

INTRODUCTION

The time between when individuals decide to start a business and the day they open their door for the first time can seem like forever. Starting up a business involves decisions and payments. Most likely, the entrepreneurs will need to obtain a loan, on which they will pay interest. They will need to find a suitable location and may need to pay rent on a piece of land. Finally, the grand-opening day arrives, and the new owners can look forward to earning a profit.

Interest, rent, and profit are the payments to capital, land, and entrepreneurship, respectively. A knowledge of these three payments is critical to understanding how markets operate and how economies function.

iStock.com/LdF

16-1 INTEREST

The word "interest" is used in two ways in economics. Sometimes, it refers to the price for credit, or **loanable funds**. For example, Lars borrows $100 from Rebecca and pays her back $110 a year later. The interest, obviously, is $10. "Interest" can also refer to the return that capital earns as an input in the production process. A person who buys a machine (a capital good) for $1,000 and earns $100 a year by using the productive services of the machine is said to earn $100 interest, or a 10 percent interest rate, on the capital.

Economists refer to both the price for loanable funds and the return on capital goods as interest because the two tend to become equal, as discussed later in this section.

Loanable Funds
Funds that someone borrows and another person lends, for which the borrower pays an interest rate to the lender.

16-1a Loanable Funds: Demand and Supply

The equilibrium interest rate, or the price for loanable funds (or credit), is determined by the demand for and supply of loanable funds (or credit). The demand for loanable funds is composed of the demand for consumption loans, the demand for investment loans, and government's demand for loanable funds. [The U.S. Treasury may need to finance budget deficits by borrowing (demanding) loanable funds in the loanable funds market.] This chapter focuses on the demand for consumption loans and the demand for investment loans. The supply of loanable funds comes from people's savings and from newly created money. The chapter discusses only people's savings.

So, in this chapter, the demand for loanable funds is taken to be composed of the demand for (1) consumption loans and (2) investment loans. The supply of loanable funds is taken to be composed entirely of people's savings.

The Supply of Loanable Funds   Savers are people who consume less than their current income. Without savers, there would be no supply of loanable funds. Savers receive an interest rate for the use of their funds, and the amount of funds saved and loaned is directly related to the interest rate.[1] Specifically, the supply curve of loanable funds is upward sloping: The higher the interest rate is, the greater the quantity supplied of loanable funds will be; the lower the interest rate, the less the quantity supplied of loanable funds will be.

The Demand for Loanable Funds: Consumption Loans   Consumers demand loanable funds because they have a **positive rate of time preference**; that is, consumers prefer earlier availability of goods to later availability. For example, most people would prefer to have a car today than to have one five years from today.

> **Positive Rate of Time Preference**
> A preference for earlier over later availability of goods.

There is nothing irrational about a positive rate of time preference; most, if not all, people have it. People differ, though, as to the *degree* of their preference for earlier availability. Some people have a high rate of time preference, signifying that they greatly prefer present to future consumption. ("I *must* have that new car today.") Other people have a low rate, signifying that they prefer present to future consumption only slightly. People with a high rate of time preference are less likely to postpone consumption than people with a low rate. People with a high rate of time preference feel that they need to have things now.

Consumers' positive rate of time preference is the reason for a demand for consumption loans. Consumers borrow today to buy today; they will pay back the borrowed amount plus interest tomorrow. The interest payment is the price consumers pay for the earlier availability of goods.

The Demand for Loanable Funds: Investment Loans   Investors (or firms) demand loanable funds (or credit) so that they can invest in capital goods and finance roundabout methods of production. A firm using a **roundabout method of production** first produces capital goods and then uses those goods to produce consumer goods.

> **Roundabout Method of Production**
> The production of capital goods that enhance productive capabilities.

Compare the direct method and the roundabout method for catching fish. In the direct method, a person uses his hands to catch fish. In the roundabout method, the person weaves a net (which is a capital good) and then uses the net to catch fish. Using the direct method, Charlie can catch 4 fish per day. Using the roundabout method, he can catch 10 fish per day. Suppose Charlie takes 10 days to weave a net. If Charlie does not weave a net and instead catches fish by hand, he can catch 1,460 fish per year (4 fish per day times 365 days). If, however, Charlie spends 10 days weaving a net (during which time he catches no fish), he can catch 3,550 fish the first year (10 fish per day times 355 days). Thus, the capital-intensive roundabout method of production is highly productive.

Because roundabout methods of production are so productive, investors are willing to borrow funds to finance them. For example, Charlie might reason, "I'm more productive if I use a fishing net, but I'll need to take 10 days off from catching fish and devote all my

---

[1] Because a higher interest rate may have both a substitution effect and an income effect, many economists argue that a higher interest rate can lead to either more saving or less saving, depending on which effect is stronger. We ignore these complications at this level of analysis and hold that the supply curve of loanable funds (from savers) is upward sloping.

energies to weaving a net. What will I eat during the 10 days? Perhaps I can borrow some fish from my neighbor. I'll need to borrow 40 fish for the next 10 days. But I must make it worthwhile for my neighbor to enter into this arrangement, so I will promise to pay her back 50 fish at the end of the year. Thus, my neighbor will lend me 40 fish today in exchange for 50 fish at the end of the year. I realize I'm paying an interest rate of 25 percent [the interest payment of 10 fish is 25 percent of the number of fish borrowed, 40], but it will be worth it." The highly productive nature of the capital-intensive roundabout method of production is what makes the loan worthwhile.

The reasoning in the fish example is repeated whenever a firm makes a capital investment. Producing computers on an assembly line is a roundabout method of production compared with producing them one by one by hand. Making copies on a copying machine is a roundabout method of production compared with copying by hand. In both cases, firms are willing to borrow now, use the borrowed funds to invest in capital goods in order to finance roundabout methods of production, and pay back the loan with interest later. If roundabout methods of production were not productive, firms would not be willing to borrow.

The Loanable Funds Market   The sum of the demand for consumption loans and the demand for investment loans is the total demand for loanable funds. The demand curve for loanable funds is downward sloping: As interest rates rise, consumers' cost of earlier availability of goods rises and they curtail their borrowing. Also, as interest rates rise, some investment projects that would be profitable at a lower interest rate will no longer be profitable. Therefore, the interest rate and the quantity demanded of loanable funds are inversely related.

Exhibit 1 illustrates the demand for and supply of loanable funds. The equilibrium interest rate occurs where the quantity demanded of loanable funds equals the quantity supplied of loanable funds.

16-1b The Price for Loanable Funds and the Return on Capital Goods Tend to Equality

As already explained, both the price for loanable funds and the return on capital are referred to as interest because they tend to become equal. To illustrate, suppose the return on capital is 10 percent and the price for loanable funds is 8 percent. Then, in this setting, firms will borrow in the loanable funds market and invest in capital goods. As they do so, the quantity of capital increases and its return falls (capital is subject to diminishing marginal returns). In short, the return on capital and the price for loanable funds begin to approach each other.

Now suppose instead that the percentages are reversed: the price for loanable funds is 10 percent and the return on capital is 8 percent. In this situation, no one will borrow loanable funds at 10 percent to invest at 8 percent. Over time, the capital stock will decrease (capital depreciates over time; it doesn't last forever), its marginal physical product will rise, and the return on capital and the price for loanable funds will eventually equal each other.

EXHIBIT 1

Loanable Funds Market

The demand curve shows the different quantities of loanable funds demanded at different interest rates. The supply curve shows the different quantities of loanable funds supplied at different interest rates. Through the forces of supply and demand, the equilibrium interest rate and the quantity of loanable funds at that rate are established as i_1 and Q_1, respectively.

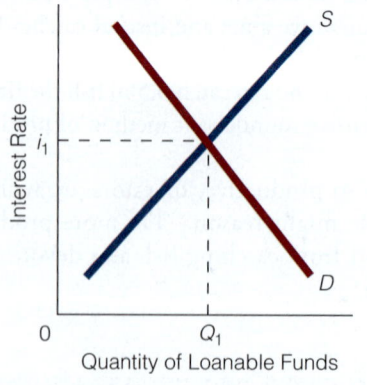

16-1c Why Do Interest Rates Differ?

The supply-and-demand analysis in Exhibit 1 suggests that the economy has only one interest rate. In reality, it has many. For example, a major business is not likely to pay the same interest rate for an investment loan to purchase new machinery as the person next door pays for a consumption loan to buy a car. Some of the factors that affect interest rates are discussed next. In each case, the *ceteris paribus* condition holds.

Risk Any time a lender makes a loan, there is a possibility that the borrower will not repay it. Some borrowers are better credit risks than others. A major corporation with a long and established history is probably a better credit risk than a person who has been unemployed three times in the last seven years. The more risk associated with a loan, the higher the interest rate will be; the less risk associated with a loan, the lower the interest rate will be.

Term of the Loan In general, the longer the term of the loan is, the higher the interest rate will be; the shorter the term of the loan, the lower the interest rate will be. Borrowers are usually more willing to pay higher interest rates for long-term loans because the longer term gives them greater flexibility. Lenders require higher interest rates to part with their funds for extended periods.

Cost of Making the Loan A loan for $1,000 and a loan for $100,000 may require the same amount of record keeping, making the larger loan cheaper (per dollar) to process than the smaller loan. In addition, some loans require frequent payments (e.g., payments for a car loan), whereas others do not. This difference is likely to be reflected in higher administrative costs for loans with more frequent payments. Therefore, loans that cost more to process and administer will have higher interest rates than loans that cost less to process and administer.

THINKING LIKE AN ECONOMIST

Tending to Equality In economics, factors typically converge. For example, in supply-and-demand analysis, the quantity demanded and the quantity supplied of a good tend to equality (through the equilibrating process). In consumer theory, the marginal utility–price ratios for different goods tend to equality. And, as just discussed, the price of loanable funds and the return on capital tend to equality (become equal).

In economics, many things tend to equality because equality is often representative of equilibrium. When quantity demanded equals quantity supplied, a market is said to be in equilibrium. When the marginal utility–price ratio for all goods is the same, the consumer is said to be in equilibrium. *In*equality therefore often signifies *dis*equilibrium. When the price of loanable funds is greater than the return on capital, there is disequilibrium.

The economist, knowing that equality often signifies equilibrium, looks for inequalities and then asks, "So what happens now?"

16-1d Nominal and Real Interest Rates

The **nominal interest rate** is the interest rate determined by the forces of supply and demand in the loanable funds market; it is the interest rate in current dollars. The nominal interest rate will change if the demand for or supply of loanable funds changes.

Individuals' expectations of inflation are one of the factors that can change both the demand for and supply of loanable funds. (Inflation occurs when the money prices of goods, on average,

Nominal Interest Rate
The interest rate determined by the forces of supply and demand in the loanable funds market.

EXHIBIT 2

Expected Inflation and Interest Rates

We start at an 8 percent interest rate and an actual and expected inflation rate of 0 percent. Later, both borrowers and lenders expect an inflation rate of 4 percent. Borrowers are willing to pay a higher interest rate because they will be paying off their loans with cheaper dollars. Lenders require a higher interest rate because they will be paid back in cheaper dollars. The demand and supply curves shift such that, at Q_1, borrowers are willing to pay, and lenders require, a 4 percent higher interest rate. The nominal interest rate is now 12 percent. The real interest rate is 8 percent. (Real interest rate = Nominal interest rate − Expected inflation rate)

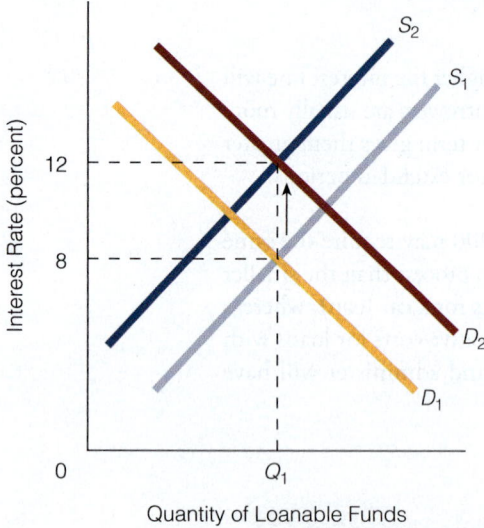

increase over time.) Exhibit 2 shows how inflation can affect the nominal interest rate. The current interest rate shown is 8 percent, and the actual and expected inflation rates are zero (Actual inflation rate = Expected inflation rate = 0 percent). Later, both the demanders and suppliers of loanable funds expect a 4 percent inflation rate. In anticipation of this expected rise in the inflation rate, borrowers (demanders of loanable funds) are willing to pay 4 percent more interest for their loans because they expect to be paying back the loans with dollars that have 4 percent less buying power than the dollars they are being lent. In other words, if they wait to buy the goods, the prices will have risen by 4 percent. To beat the price increase, they are willing to pay up to 4 percent more to borrow funds in order to purchase the goods now. In effect, the demand curve for loanable funds shifts rightward, so that, at Q_1, borrowers are willing to pay a 4 percent higher interest rate.

At the same time, the lenders (the suppliers of loanable funds) require a 4 percent higher interest rate (i.e., 12 percent) to compensate them for the 4 percent less valuable dollars in which the loan will be repaid. In effect, the supply curve of loanable funds shifts leftward, so that, at Q_1, lenders will receive an interest rate of 12 percent.

Thus, an expected inflation rate of 4 percent increases the demand for loanable funds and decreases their supply, so that the interest rate is 4 percent higher than it was when the inflation rate was expected to be zero. In this example, 12 percent is the nominal interest rate—the interest rate in current dollars—and it includes the expected inflation rate.

Real Interest Rate

The nominal interest rate adjusted for expected inflation; that is, the nominal interest rate minus the expected inflation rate.

If we adjust for the expected inflation rate, we have the **real interest rate**: the nominal interest rate minus the expected inflation rate (Real interest rate = Nominal interest rate − Expected inflation rate). In our example, the real interest rate is 8 percent (12 percent − 4 percent).

The real interest rate, not the nominal interest rate, matters to borrowers and lenders. Consider a lender who grants a $1,000 loan to a borrower at a 20 percent nominal interest rate at a time when the actual inflation rate is 15 percent. The amount repaid to the lender is $1,200, but $1,200 with a 15 percent inflation rate does not have the buying power that $1,200 with a zero inflation rate has. The 15 percent inflation rate wipes out much of the gain, and the lender's real return on the loan is not 20 percent, but only 5 percent. Thus, the rate lenders receive and borrowers pay (and therefore the rate they care about) is the real interest rate.

16-1e Present Value: What Is Something Tomorrow Worth Today?

Because of people's positive rate of time preference, $100 today is worth more than $100 a year from now. (Wouldn't you prefer to have $100 today to having $100 in a year?) Thus, $100 a year from now must be worth less than $100 today. The question is *how much* $100 a year from now is worth today. This question involves the concept of **present value**, which is the current worth of some future dollar amount (of receipts or income). In our example, "present value" refers to what $100 a year from now is worth today.

Present Value
The current worth of some future dollar amount of income or receipts.

Present value (PV) is computed with the formula

$$PV = \frac{A_n}{(1 + i)^n}$$

where A_n is the actual amount of income or receipts in some future year, i is the interest rate (expressed as a decimal), and n is the number of years in the future. Thus, the present value of $100 one year in the future at a 10 percent interest rate is $90.91:

$$PV = \frac{\$100}{(1 + 0.10)^1}$$
$$= \$90.91$$

That is, the right to receive $100 a year from now is worth $90.91 today. In other words, if $90.91 is put into a savings account paying a 10 percent interest rate, it would equal $100 in a year.

Suppose we wanted to know what a future income stream, instead of a future dollar amount, is worth today. The general formula is

$$PV = \sum_{i=0}^{n} \frac{A_n}{(1 + i)^n}$$

where the Greek letter $\sum$ stands for "sum of."

To see how the formula works, suppose a firm buys a machine that will earn $100 a year for the next three years. What is this future income stream, at $100 per year for three years, worth today? That is, what is the present value of that future income stream? At a 10 percent interest rate, it has a present value of $248.68:

$$PV = \frac{A_1}{(1 + 0.10)^1} + \frac{A_2}{(1 + 0.10)^2} + \frac{A_3}{(1 + 0.10)^3}$$
$$= \frac{\$100}{1.10} + \frac{\$100}{1.21} + \frac{\$100}{1.331}$$
$$= \$90.91 + \$82.64 + \$75.13 = \$248.68$$

FINDING ECONOMICS

In Living Longer Suppose that, because of an advancement in medical science, people start living longer. Can living longer affect the price of antique cars, famous paintings, and fine jewelry? Where is the economics?

The economics can be found in the concept of present value. Suppose that you are considering the purchase of a painting and that you would receive $2,000 worth of benefits a year from owning and viewing the painting. The dollar price you would be willing to pay for the painting is based partly on the present value of the benefits you would receive over the number of years you plan to enjoy the painting. The number of years could be higher because you expect to live longer. At a given interest rate, the longer you expect to live, the greater will be the present value of the benefits you receive from the painting, and the more you would be willing to pay for the painting.

ECONOMICS 24/7

Is the Car Worth Buying?

Business firms often compute present values in deciding whether to buy capital goods. Should consumers do the same when they are thinking about buying a durable good (i.e., a good that will last for a few years), such as a car?

Suppose you're thinking about buying a car. The market price of the car is $15,500, and you anticipate that you will receive $2,000 worth of services from the car each year for the next 10 years, after which time the car will have to be scrapped and will have no salvage value.

Now ask yourself the same type of question that the business firm asks when it considers buying a capital good: Is the present value of the car more than, less than, or equal to the present market price of the car?

To answer this question, you need to calculate the present value of the car. A car that yields $2,000 worth of benefits each year for 10 years at a 4 percent interest rate has a present value of approximately $16,223:

$$PV = \frac{\$2,000}{(1 + 0.04)^1} + \frac{\$2,000}{(1 + 0.04)^2} + \dots + \frac{\$2,000}{(1 + 0.04)^{10}}$$
$$= \$16{,}223 \text{ (approximately)}$$

The market price of the car ($15,500) is less than its present value ($16,223), so purchasing the car is worthwhile.

You should also be attentive to the interest rate. All other things remaining constant, an increase in the interest rate will lower the present value of the car. For example, at a 7 percent interest rate, the present value of the car is approximately $15,377. Now the market price of the car ($15,500) is *greater than* the present value of the car ($15,377), so the purchase is not worthwhile.

Thus, we would expect fewer cars to be sold when the interest rate rises and more cars to be sold when the interest rate falls, because a change in the interest rate changes the present value of cars.

Kzenon/Shutterstock.com

ECONOMICS 24/7

Investment, Present Value, and Interest Rates

Firms will often increase their level of investment (e.g., purchase more capital goods) as interest rates fall. Suppose a firm is thinking of purchasing a capital good that costs $1,000. The firm expects that the capital good will add to its revenue in each of two years. In year 1, the capital good is expected to add $600 and in year 2, $500. Should the firm purchase the capital good?

One way to decide whether to purchase the capital good is to compare its cost ($1,000) against the additional revenue it is expected to generate ($1,100). Because the additional revenue is greater than the cost, the inclination to say that the firm should buy the capital good is strong. But not all the additional revenue is generated in the first year of the life of the good: Some of that additional revenue—$500—comes in year 2.

So, we need to compute the present value of a stream of revenue to be realized over two years. Here is the calculation:

$$PV = \frac{\$600}{(1 + i)^1} + \frac{\$500}{(1 + i)^2}$$

What the present value (*PV*) turns out to be depends, of course, on the interest rate. At the assumed interest rate of 10 percent, the present value is $958.67. Now we see that, because the cost of the capital good ($1,000) is greater than the present value of the additional revenue generated by its use, the capital good is not worth purchasing.

But suppose the interest rate falls to 5 percent. Now the present value is $1,024.93. At the lower interest rate, the capital good is worth purchasing, because the present value of the additional revenue generated by its use (or $1,024.93) is greater than its purchase price.

The point is simple: Lower interest rates raise present values, and higher present values that are connected with the purchase of capital goods lead firms to buy more capital goods (i.e., increase their investing).

SELF-TEST

(Answers to Self-Test questions are in Answers to Self-Test Questions at the back of the book.)

1. Why does the price for loanable funds tend to equal the return on capital goods?

2. Why does the real interest rate, not the nominal interest rate, matter to borrowers and lenders?

3. What is the present value of $1,000 two years from today if the interest rate is 5 percent?

4. A business firm is thinking of buying a capital good, which will earn $2,000 a year for the next four years and cost $7,000. The interest rate is 8 percent. Should the firm buy the capital good? Explain your answer.

16-2 RENT

Mention the word "rent," and people naturally think of someone living in an apartment and making monthly payments to a landlord. That is not the type of rent discussed in this chapter. To an economist, rent means **economic rent**—that is, a payment in excess of opportunity costs (as discussed in an earlier chapter). A subset of economic rent, called **pure economic rent**, is a payment in excess of opportunity costs when opportunity costs are zero. Historically, the term "pure economic rent" was first used to describe the payment to the factor land, which is perfectly inelastic in supply.

In Exhibit 3, the total supply of land is fixed at Q_1 acres; there can be no more and no less than this amount of land. The payment for land (R_1) is determined by the forces of supply and demand. R_1 is more than sufficient to bring Q_1 acres into supply. In fact, by reason of the fixed supply of land (the supply curve is perfectly inelastic), the Q_1 acres would have been forthcoming at a payment of $0. In short, this land has zero opportunity costs. Therefore, the full payment—all of R_1—is referred to as pure economic rent.

Economic Rent
Payment in excess of opportunity costs.

Pure Economic Rent
A category of economic rent such that the payment is to a factor that is in fixed supply, implying that the factor has zero opportunity costs.

16-2a David Ricardo, the Price of Grain, and Land Rent

In nineteenth-century England, people were concerned about the rising price of grains, which were a staple in many English diets. Some argued that grain prices were rising because land rents were going up rapidly. People began pointing fingers at the landowners, maintaining that the high rents the landowners received for their land made it more and more costly for farmers to raise grains. These higher costs, in turn, were passed on to consumers in the form of higher prices. According to this argument, the solution was to lower rents, which would lead to lower costs for farmers and, eventually, to lower prices for consumers.

EXHIBIT 3

Pure Economic Rent and the Total Supply of Land

The total supply of land is fixed at Q_1. The payment for the services of this land is determined by the forces of supply and demand. Because the payment is for a factor in fixed supply, the payment is referred to as pure economic rent.

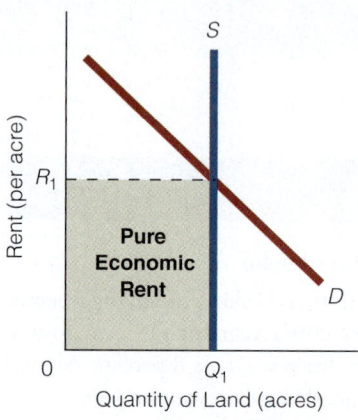

English economist David Ricardo thought that this line of argument stood logic on its head. He contended that it wasn't that grain prices were high because rents were high (as most individuals thought) but, conversely, that rents were high because grain prices were high. In current economic terminology, his argument was as follows: land is a factor of production; therefore, the demand for it is derived. Land is also in fixed supply; therefore, the only thing that will change the payment made to land is a change in the demand for it. (The supply curve isn't going to shift, and thus the only thing that can change price is a shift in the demand curve.) Landowners have no control over the demand for land, which comes from other persons who want to use it.

In nineteenth-century England, the demand came from farmers who were raising grains and other foodstuffs. Landowners could not have pushed up land rents, because they had no control over the demand for their land. Therefore, rents were high because the demand for land was high, and the demand for land was high because grain prices were high. Economists put it this way: *Land rents are price determined, not price determining.*

ECONOMICS 24/7

Grain Prices and Land Rent

David Ricardo argued that high grain prices cause high land rents. For example, suppose that there are three grades of land: excellent, good, and poor. Suppose also that grain can be produced on each grade of land. The excellent land can produce 10 bushels of grain, the good land can produce 5 bushels of grain, and the poor land can produce 2 bushels of grain. Further, it costs $10 to farm each grade of land, and the price of grain is currently $1.50 a bushel.

Mykola Mazuryk/Shutterstock.com

Under these circumstances, not all three grades of land will be farmed. Only the excellent grade of land will be farmed, because it can produce 10 bushels of grain, which can then be sold at $1.50 a bushel for a total revenue of $15. At a cost of $10 to farm this land, the farmer is then left with a $5 profit.

No one will farm the good or the poor land, though, because neither grade of land will earn the farmer any profit. The good land will cost $10 to farm but will generate only 5 bushels of grain, for a total revenue of $7.50. The poor land will cost $10 to farm but will generate only 2 bushels of grain, for a total revenue of $3.

So, the excellent land is the only grade that will be farmed if the price of grain is $1.50 a bushel, because that land earns the farmer $5 in profit. But the $5 profit may not last. If the farmer leases the land, the profit of $5 will soon become $5 in land rent for the owner of the land. Farmers will compete among themselves to lease the land from its owner. With $5 profit, the first farmer says that he is willing to pay $1 rent for the land, but the second farmer says $2, and the third farmer says $3, and so on. So, the profit on the land will soon turn into land rent received by the owner of the land. The land rent will eventually go up to $5. In other words, the excellent land—given the price of grain at $1.50 a bushel—will fetch a rent of $5.

Now suppose the price of grain rises from $1.50 a bushel to $2.10 a bushel. Two things will happen at this higher price. First, the good land, which wasn't farmed when the price of grain was $1.50, will now be farmed. The good land generates 5 bushels of grain

that, when sold at $2.10 a bushel, will generate $10.50 in revenue. Because the cost of farming the land is $10, this sale leaves the farmer with a profit of 50¢. Farming the good land is now profitable.

Second, the land rent on the excellent land will rise from $5. At a grain price of $2.10 a bushel, the excellent land now generates $21 in revenue. Given a cost of $10 for farming the excellent land, this amount of revenue generates $11 in profit, or only $6 in profit if we assume that the farmer is paying the owner of the excellent land $5 in land rent. Either way, we can expect land rent to rise soon, as farmers compete for the land that is generating the additional profits. We expect the land rent ultimately to rise to $11.

So, higher grain prices initially increase the profit on farming high-quality, or excellent, land. But higher profit ends up as higher land rent as farmers compete for the land. In short, high grain prices cause high land rents, and rising grain prices cause rising rents.

FINDING ECONOMICS

In a Sandwich and a Soft Drink in New York City During a visit to New York City, Rachel ordered a sandwich and a soft drink for lunch in a restaurant. Her bill was $21. She complained to a friend later in the day, saying, "I don't know why everything is so expensive in New York. I paid $21 for a sandwich and drink today." Her friend replied, "Sandwich prices are high because the owner of the restaurant has to pay such high rent for his place." Where is the economics?

Here is the same misperception about rents and prices that Ricardo found in the nineteenth century. Many people today complain that the prices in stores, hotels, and restaurants in New York City are high. When they notice the steep land rents, they reason that prices are high because land rents are high. But, as Ricardo pointed out, the reverse is true: Land rents are high because prices are high. If the demand for living, visiting, and shopping in New York City were not as high as it is, the prices for goods would not be as high. In turn, the demand for land would not be as high, and therefore the payments to land would not be as high.

16-2b The Supply Curve of Land Can Be Upward Sloping

Exhibit 3 depicts the supply of land as fixed—the case when the total supply of land is in question. For example, this country has only so many acres of land, and that amount is not likely to change.

Most subparcels of land, however, have competing uses. Consider 25 acres of land on the periphery of a major city. That parcel can be used for farmland, a shopping mall, or a road. If a parcel of land (as opposed to all land, or the total supply of land) has competing uses (the land can be used one way or another), then it has opportunity costs. Land that is used for farming could be used for a shopping mall. To reflect the opportunity cost of that land, the supply curve is upward sloping. The upward slope implies that, if individuals

EXHIBIT 4

Economic Rent and the Supply of Land (Competing Uses)

A particular parcel of land, as opposed to the total supply of land, has competing uses, or positive opportunity costs. For example, to obtain land to build a shopping mall, the developers must bid high enough to attract existing land away from competing uses. The supply curve is upward sloping. At a payment of R_1, economic rent is identified as the payment in excess of (positive) opportunity costs.

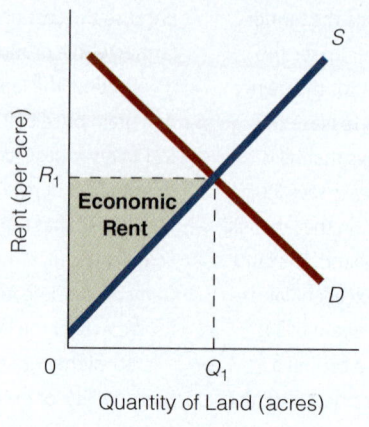

want more land for a specific purpose—say, for a shopping mall—they must bid high enough to attract existing land away from other uses (e.g., farming). Exhibit 4 illustrates this phenomenon, in which the equilibrium payment to land is R_1. The shaded area indicates the economic rent.

16-2c Economic Rent and Other Factors of Production

The concept of economic rent applies to economic factors besides land. For example, it applies to labor. Suppose Hanson works for company X and is paid $60,000 a year. suppose further that in his next-best alternative job he would be earning $57,000. Then Hanson is receiving economic rent by working for company X, in that he is receiving a payment in excess of his opportunity costs. That excess is his economic rent.

Or consider the local McDonald's that hires teenagers. It pays all its beginning employees the same wage, but not all beginning employees have the same opportunity cost. Suppose two teenagers, Tracy and Paul, sign on to work at McDonald's for $8.00 an hour. Tracy's next-best alternative wage is $8.00 an hour, working for her mother's business, and Paul's is $7.25 an hour, working in another store. Then Tracy receives no economic rent in her McDonald's job, but Paul receives 75¢ an hour economic rent in that same job.

Over time, teenagers and other beginning employees usually find that their opportunity costs rise (owing to continued schooling and job experience) and that the McDonald's wage no longer covers their opportunity costs. When this happens, they quit.

16-2d Economic Rent and Baseball Players: Perspective Matters

Economic rent varies with the perspective from which the factor is viewed. If a baseball star who earns $1 million a year playing baseball weren't playing the sport, he would be a coach at a high school. Therefore, the difference between what he is currently paid ($1 million a year) and what he would earn as a coach (say, $40,000 a year) is economic rent in the amount of $960,000. Thus, in this case economic rent is determined by identifying the alternative to the baseball star's playing major league ball.

However, a different alternative would be identified by asking what the alternative is to the baseball star's playing baseball *for his present team*. The answer is that he probably can play for another team. For example, if he weren't playing for the Boston Red Sox, he might be playing for the Pittsburgh Pirates, earning $950,000 a year. His economic rent in this instance is only $50,000. So, the player's economic rent as *a player for the Boston Red Sox* is $50,000 a year, and his next-best alternative is earning $950,000 a year playing for the Pittsburgh Pirates. But his economic rent as *a baseball player* is $960,000, and his next-best alternative is being a high school coach earning $40,000 a year.

16-2e Competing for Artificial and Real Rents

Individuals and firms compete for both *artificial rents* and *real rents*. An artificial rent is an economic rent that is artificially contrived by government; that is, it would not exist without government. Suppose government decides to award a monopoly right to one firm to produce good X. In so doing, it legally prohibits all other firms from producing good X. If the firm with the monopoly right receives a price for good X in excess of its opportunity costs, it receives a rent or monopoly profit because of government's restraint on supply.

Firms that compete for the monopoly right to produce good X expend resources in a socially wasteful manner. They use resources to lobby politicians in the hope of getting the monopoly, and those resources (from society's perspective) could be better used to produce goods and services.

Competing for real rents is different, however. If the rent is real (not artificially created) and if there are no barriers to competing for it, resources are used in a way that is socially productive. For example, suppose firm Z currently receives economic rent in the production of good Z. Suppose also that government does not prohibit other firms from competing with firm Z, so some do. Then the other firms also produce good Z, thus increasing its supply and lowering its price. The lower price reduces the rent firm Z receives in its production of good Z. In the end, firm Z has less rent and society has more of good Z and pays a lower price for it.

Does It Matter to You . . .
If People Compete for Artificial Rents as Opposed to Real Rents?

Individuals and firms compete for both *artificial rents* and *real rents*. An artificial rent is an economic rent that is artificially contrived by the government, that is, it would not exist without government. Suppose the government decides to award a monopoly to a firm to produce good X. In so doing, it legally prohibits all other firms from producing good X. If the firm with the monopoly right receives a price for good X in excess of its opportunity costs, it receives a rent or monopoly profit because of the government's restraint on supply.

Firms that compete for the monopoly right to produce good X expend resources in a socially wasteful manner.[2] They use resources to lobby politicians in the hope of getting the monopoly, and those resources (from society's perspective) could be better used to produce goods and services.

Competing for real rents is different, however. If the rent is real (not artificially created) and there are no barriers in competing for it, resources are used in a way that is socially productive. For example, suppose firm Z currently receives economic rent in the production of good Z. Also suppose that the government does not prohibit other firms from competing with firm Z. Then other firms could also produce good Z, thus increasing its supply and lowering its price. Do you see how you might gain from this as a consumer? The lower price reduces the rent firm Z receives in its production of good Z. In the end, firm Z has less rent and society has more of good Z and pays a lower price for it.

---

[2] This statement may sound familiar. The process whereby individuals expend resources by lobbying government for a special privilege was described as rent seeking in an earlier chapter.

SELF-TEST

1. Give an example to illustrate that economic rent varies with the perspective from which a factor is viewed.

2. Nick's salary is pure economic rent. What does this statement imply about Nick's next-best alternative salary?

3. What are the social consequences of firms competing for artificial rents, as opposed to competing for real rents (in an environment in which there are no barriers to competing for real rents)?

16-3 PROFIT

The profits that appear in newspaper headlines are *accounting profits*, not economic profits. Economic profit is the difference between total revenue and total cost, and both explicit and implicit costs are included in total cost. Economists emphasize economic profit over accounting profit because economic profit determines entry into and exit from an industry. For the most part, all this is how economic profit figured in the discussion of market structures in previous chapters.

In this section, we discuss profit as the payment to a resource. Recall the four resources, or factors of production: land, labor, capital, and entrepreneurship. Firms make payments to each of these resources: wages are the payment to labor, interest is the payment to capital, rent is the payment to land, and profit is the payment to entrepreneurship. Understanding the source of profits enables us to find out why economic profit exists.

16-3a Theories of Profit

Several different theories address the question of where profit comes from—that is, the source of profit. One theory holds that profit would not exist in a world of certainty; hence, uncertainty is the source of profit. Another theory is that profit is the return for alertness to broadly defined arbitrage opportunities. A third theory posits that profit is the return to the entrepreneur for innovation.

Profit and Uncertainty Uncertainty exists when the probability of something occurring is so unpredictable that it cannot be estimated. (For example, what is the probability that the United States will enter a world war in 2025?) Risk, which many people mistake for uncertainty, exists when the probability of a given event can be estimated. (For example, a coin toss has a 50–50 chance of coming up heads.) Therefore, risks can be insured against, but uncertainties cannot.

Anything that can be insured against can be treated as just another cost of doing business, and thus insurance coverage is an input in the production process. Only uncertain events can cause a firm's revenues to diverge from costs (including insurance costs). The investor/decision maker who is adept at making business decisions under conditions of uncertainty earns a profit. For example, on the basis of experience and some insights, an entrepreneur may believe that 75 percent of all college students will buy personal computers next year. This assessment, followed by investing in a chain of retail computer stores near college campuses, will ultimately prove to be right or wrong. The essential point is that the entrepreneur's judgment cannot be insured against. If it is correct, the entrepreneur will earn a profit; if it is incorrect, the entrepreneur will suffer a loss.

Profit and Arbitrage Opportunities The way to make a profit, the advice goes, is to buy low and sell high (usually the same item). For example, someone might buy good X in New York for $10 and sell good X in London for $11. We might say that the person is alert to where she can buy low and sell high, and thereby earn a profit. She is alert to what is called an *arbitrage opportunity*.

Sometimes, "buying low and selling high" does not refer to the same item. The phrase can refer to buying factors in one set of markets at the lowest possible prices, combining the factors into a finished product, and then selling the product in another market for the highest possible price. An example is buying oranges and sugar (in the orange and sugar markets, respectively), combining the two factors, and selling an orange soft drink (in the soft-drink market). If doing so results in profit, the person who undertook the act is considered alert to a (broadly defined) arbitrage opportunity. He saw that oranges and sugar together, in the form of an orange soft drink, would fetch more than the sum of oranges and sugar separately.

Profit and Innovation In this theory, profit is the return to the entrepreneur as innovator—the person who creates new profit opportunities by devising a new product, production process, or marketing strategy. Viewed in this way, profit is the return to innovative genius. People such as Thomas Edison, Henry Ford, Richard Sears, and Steve Jobs are said to have had innovative genius.

THINKING LIKE AN ECONOMIST

About Interest, Land Rent, and Profits Throughout history, interest, land rent, and profits have often been attacked. For example, Henry George (1839–1897), who wrote the influential book *Progress and Poverty*, believed that all land rents were pure economic rents and should be heavily taxed. Landowners benefited simply because they had the good fortune to own land. In George's view, landowners did nothing productive. He maintained that the early owners of land in the American West reaped high land rents not because they had made their land more productive but because individuals from the East began to move West, driving up the price of land. In arguing for a heavy tax on land rents, George said there would be no supply response in land owing to the tax because land was in fixed supply.

Profits have also frequently come under attack. High profits are somehow thought to be evidence of corruption or manipulation. Those who earn profits are sometimes considered no better than thieves. The economist thinks of interest, land rent, and profits differently from how many laypersons think of them.

The economist understands that all are returns to resources, or factors of production. Most people find it easy to understand that labor is a factor of production and that wages are the return to this factor. But understanding that land, capital, and entrepreneurship are also genuine factors of production, with returns that flow to them, seems more difficult.

Another overlooked point is that interest exists largely because individuals naturally have a positive rate of time preference. Those who dislike interest are in fact criticizing a natural characteristic of individuals. If the critics could change this natural trait and make individuals stop weighting present consumption higher than future consumption, interest would diminish.

A similar point can be made about profit. Some say that profit is the consequence of living in a world of uncertainty. If those who do not like profit could bring certainty to the world, or at least make the world less uncertain, then profit would disappear.

16-3b Profit and Loss as Signals

Although profit and loss are often viewed in terms of the benefit or harm they bring to persons, they also signal how a market may be changing. On the one hand, when a firm earns a profit, entrepreneurs in other industries view the profit as a signal that the firm is producing and selling a good that buyers value more than the factors that go into making the good. (The firm would not earn a profit unless its product had more value than the total of the payments to the other three factors of production.) The profit causes entrepreneurs to move resources into the production of the profit-linked good. In short, resources follow profit.

On the other hand, if a firm is taking a loss, the loss is a signal to the entrepreneur that the firm is producing and selling a good that buyers value less than the factors that go into making the good. The loss causes resources to move out of the production of the loss-linked good. Resources turn away from losses.

Hear What and How the Economist Thinks . . .[3]
About Profit

The economist reads about a survey of people picked at random who were asked the question: What percent profit on each dollar of sales do you think the average company earns after taxes? The average response was 36 percent.

Hear What and How the Economist Thinks:

Thirty-six percent is not even close to reality. When the economist Mark Perry checked the Yahoo! Finance database for 212 industries, he found that the "average profit margin for the most recent quarter was 7.5 percent and the median profit margin was 6.5 percent." He did not find a single industry out of 212 with a profit margin as high as 36 percent.

What about those companies that many members of the public seem to think earn higher profits, such as so-called Big Oil companies? They had a below-average profit margin of 5.1 percent in the most recent quarter. Wal-Mart's profit margin was 3.1 percent in the most recent quarter.

If the public believes that the profit margin is 36 percent (for companies) and the median profit margin is 6.5 percent, then we have a situation in which the profit margin is lower than what the public thinks it is.

Now, if the public's perception of the actual profit margin is off by a large percentage this may explain why many members of the public

think that it would be easy for most companies to pay higher wages, pay out greater benefits, and so on. But if the profit margins are not as hefty as the public thinks they are, if they are sometimes as low as 3.1 percent, then a rise in costs is likely to be viewed differently.

So why is there such a common misunderstanding? Economists have an answer for this: for every activity there are costs and benefits. To become more informed about economics has a cost—time, energy, and so on—which may not outweigh the benefits of what people perceive themselves to stand to gain from learning economics.

Questions to Think About:

1. On September 30, 2011, the CDFI Fund (Community Development Financial Institutions Fund, which is an organization within the U.S. Department of the Treasury) published the report "Understanding the Grocery Industry." In the report, the profit margin for the grocery store industry was identified. Do you think it was between 5 and 10 percent, 11 and 15 percent, or neither?

2. Did you think the profit margin for the grocery store industry, identified in the answer to question 1, would have been higher or lower than it was?

---

[3] This feature is based on the Carpe Diem blog entry "The public thinks the average company makes a 36% profit margin, which is about 5X too high" by Mark Perry on April 2, 2015. The blog entry can be found at https://www.aei.org/publication/the-public-thinks-the-average-company-makes-a-36-profit-margin-which-is-about-5x-too-high/.

16-4 THE ENTREPRENEUR

Back in Chapter 1, we identified four resources, or factors of production: land, labor, capital, and entrepreneurship. We know that land, labor, capital, and entrepreneurship go together to produce goods and services. When you think of land (natural resources), labor, and capital, it is fairly easy to envision someone taking these resources and putting them together to produce, say, a house or a car. Entrepreneurship, however, leaves us wondering. What is it exactly that entrepreneurship entails? We know what labor and capital look like, and we know what oil as a resource looks like, but what does entrepreneurship look like? How will we know it if we see it? What specifically is it that the entrepreneur does? In this section, we answer that question.

16-4a A Market

The role of the entrepreneur is closely tied to what happens in a market. A market is a place where individuals come together to exchange or trade: I will trade you $50 for a shirt; I will trade you $100 for a pair of shoes. We know that individuals will agree to a trade only if they expect to be made better off through the trade. In other words, Stephanie trades her $100 for the shoes, and the shoe salesman trades the shoes for the $100, only if each expect to be made better off by the trade.

Entrepreneurs operate within markets. Specifically, their actions are directed toward increasing the number of trades. Think of the situation strictly in numerical terms. Suppose 1,000 individuals are making 500 trades a week (among themselves). The entrepreneur will try to figure out a way to increase that number to 600 trades. What does the entrepreneur do? The entrepreneur devises ways to increase trade.

16-4b How Can the Entrepreneur Increase Trade?

There are two major ways of increasing trade. The first is to produce a good or service that satisfies an unmet demand. Think of Steve Jobs, the cofounder of Apple, Inc. Jobs was instrumental in the development of such products as the personal computer, the iPad, the iPhone, and the iPod. Focus for a minute on the iPod. Here is a product, small in size, that allows a person to compile and then listen to a large number of songs. Certainly, there was a time before the iPod existed. If we go back to that time—say, 1986—and ask the question whether people have a demand for a product that is easy to carry and that can hold thousands of songs that people want to listen to, what do you think would be the answer? Our guess is that the answer would be yes. But back in 1986, that demand would have been unmet. It was a demand for a good that simply did not exist yet.

What Steve Jobs did was satisfy that unmet demand. In that he did, he increased trade. After the introduction of the iPod, people were willing to trade dollars for iPods. Both the people who traded those dollars for iPods and the people who traded iPods for dollars were made better off through the trades.

So, in virtue of the fact that Steve Jobs came out with a good that increased trade by satisfying an unmet demand (for that good), he was an entrepreneur.

Now let's turn to the second major way of increasing trade: by reducing the transaction costs of making trades. With this idea in mind, consider the people behind the creation of eBay. Go back to a time before eBay, and consider two people, on opposite sides of the world, who might want to trade with each other. More specifically, consider a person living in London who wants to sell an old Beatles album. Suppose someone in Topeka, Kansas, wants to buy an old Beatles album. The problem here is that the two people—buyer and seller of the Beatles album—can't find each other. The transaction costs of their getting together and consummating a trade are just too high for them to overcome. Enter eBay, which lowers those transaction costs. What eBay essentially does is to tell everyone in the world the following: If you have something you want to sell, come to us and we will introduce you to a buyer; if you have something you want to buy, come to us and we will introduce you to a seller. In other words, what eBay has done is make it easier for buyers and sellers to find each other. The easier it became, the more likely a trade would occur.

By lowering the transaction costs of making certain kinds of trades, the people behind eBay increased the number of trades. Inasmuch as they increased the number of trades, they were acting as entrepreneurs.

16-4c Turning Potential Trades into Actual Trades

One way to describe entrepreneurs is to say that they turn potential trades into actual trades. That is exactly what both Steve Jobs and eBay did. Jobs took an unmet demand and satisfied it; eBay took trades that couldn't be realized because of high transaction costs, lowered the transaction costs, and thus turned potential trades into actual trades.

16-4d A Necessary Condition: Turn Potential Trades into Actual Trades in a Way Acceptable to Consumers

The way the entrepreneur turns a potential trade into an actual trade is important. Not all roads the entrepreneur may travel down to accomplish the feat will meet with success. For example, suppose there were 15 different ways to develop, produce, and sell the iPod. The most expensive way would give us a $100,000 price tag. Would the iPod then have been a product consumers would have run to the stores to purchase? Probably not. The point is that, while the entrepreneur seeks to turn potential trades into actual trades, he or she has to do so in a way that is acceptable to consumers.

16-4e Can Increasing Trades in One Area Reduce Trades in Another?

So far, we have talked about the entrepreneur as a person who promotes trade. In the example of Steve Jobs, the entrepreneur produced a good that satisfied a (theretofore) unmet demand. In the example of eBay, the entrepreneur lowered transaction costs and promoted trade. In the arbitrage example, the entrepreneur bought in one location and sold in another. But couldn't it very well be that in all these three cases, while trade blossomed in one place, it declined in another?

Could it be that, because of the iPod, there are now fewer trades for radios, or tape recorders, or stereos? In other words, didn't the iPod displace some products that consumers earlier had traded money for? Didn't the personal computer displace the typewriter? Didn't the car displace the horse?

Or consider the eBay in which the person in London sold the old Beatles album to the person in Topeka, Kansas. Mightn't it have been the case that, if there were no eBay, the person in London could have put an ad in the newspaper and eventually found a person who would buy his old Beatles album?

There are cases in which the entrepreneur actually does increase the number of trades. In other words, trades may rise from 500 to 600. There are also cases in which the entrepreneur does *not* increase the number of trades, but instead changes the nature of the trade (500 trades of dollars for X instead of 500 trades of dollars for Y). Finally, there are cases in which the entrepreneur does a little of both: he or she increases the number *and* nature of trades (600 trades of dollars for X instead of 500 trades of dollars for Y).

16-4f Uncertainty and the Entrepreneur

All entrepreneurs do something in the present that they hope will turn out well for them in the future. But no one knows exactly what the future will hold. It follows, then, that all entrepreneurs bear some degree of uncertainty. They operate with a cloud of uncertainty hanging over them.

Steve Jobs didn't know for sure if the iPod would be a success. He only thought it could be. The people who created eBay didn't know for sure if their company would be a success. They only thought it could be.

All entrepreneurs look for the $10 bill on the sidewalk, so to speak. But they can't be sure that the $10 bill is not a counterfeit bill or play money—so to speak. All entrepreneurs might think that they have discovered an economic opportunity that others remain blind to, but they can't be sure how things will turn out for them if they seize it. The landscape is littered with entrepreneurs who tried and failed.

SELF-TEST

1. What is the difference between risk and uncertainty?

2. Why does profit exist?

3. "Profit is not simply a dollar amount; it is a signal." Comment.

4. What are two majors ways of increasing trade?

OFFICE HOURS

"How Is Present Value Used in the Courtroom?"

STUDENT: I've heard that present value is sometimes used in law cases. Is this true? And if so, how?

INSTRUCTOR: Yes, it's true. It could be used in a divorce case. For example, suppose Jack and Carol are getting a divorce. Carol worked during the time Jack went to medical school. In the divorce, Carol and Jack agree to split the assets they own together: the house, the paintings, the jewelry, the cars, and so on. Carol claims that Jack's medical degree is an asset that she should have part of. "After all," she says, "I helped pay for Jack's medical education."

STUDENT: So, is the objective now to find out what the medical degree is worth?

INSTRUCTOR: Yes. And this is where present value comes in. Suppose Jack will earn $100,000 more each year for the next 25 years because he went to medical school. Carol's attorney needs to find the present value of this dollar amount, which turns out to be approximately $1.57 million.

Now the court has to decide whether the medical degree is an asset whose proceeds should be divided between Carol and Jack.

STUDENT: Does present value come up in any other cases?

INSTRUCTOR: Yes. Present value is sometimes used in injury cases. For example, suppose Yvonne gets hit by a drunk driver and can't work any longer. She might ask to be compensated for the injury plus the loss in her earning power. Her lawyer will need to find the present value of her lost earnings (over, say, the next 10 years).

Points to Remember

1. Present value can be used to determine today's worth of a medical education.

2. Present value can be used to determine today's worth of a loss in earning power.

CHAPTER SUMMARY

INTEREST

- Interest is (1) the price paid by borrowers for loanable funds and (2) the return on capital in the production process. These two things tend to become equal.

- The equilibrium interest rate (in terms of the price for loanable funds) is determined by the demand for and supply of loanable funds. The supply of loanable funds comes from savers, people who consume less than their current incomes. The demand for loanable funds comes from the demand for consumption loans and the demand for investment loans.

- Consumers demand loanable funds because they have a positive rate of time preference: they prefer earlier, rather than later, availability of goods. Investors (or firms) demand loanable funds so that they can finance roundabout methods of production.

- The nominal interest rate is the interest rate determined by the forces of supply and demand in the loanable funds market; it is the interest rate in current dollars. The real interest rate is the nominal interest rate adjusted for expected inflation. Specifically, Real interest rate = Nominal interest rate − Expected inflation rate (or Nominal interest rate = Real interest rate + Expected inflation rate).

RENT

- Economic rent is a payment in excess of opportunity costs. A subset of economic rent is pure economic rent, which is a payment in excess of opportunity costs when opportunity costs are zero. Historically, the term *pure economic rent* was used to describe the payment to the factor land, because land (in total) was assumed to be fixed in supply (perfectly inelastic).

Today, the terms "economic rent" and "pure economic rent" are also used in speaking about economic factors other than land.

- David Ricardo argued that high land rents were an effect of high grain prices, not a cause of them (in contrast to many of his contemporaries who thought high rents caused the high grain prices). In other words, land rents are price determined, not price determining.

- The amount of economic rent that a factor receives depends on the perspective from which the factor is viewed. For example, a university librarian earning $50,000 a year receives $2,000 in economic rent if his next-best alternative income at another university is $48,000. His economic rent is $10,000 if his next-best alternative is in a nonuniversity (nonlibrarian) position that pays $40,000.

PROFIT

- Several theories address the question of the source of profit. One theory holds that profit would not exist in a world of certainty; hence, uncertainty is the source of profit. Another theory holds that profit is the return for alertness to arbitrage opportunities. A third theory states that profit is the return to the entrepreneur for innovation.

THE ENTREPRENEUR

- Entrepreneurs operate within markets; specifically, their actions are directed toward increasing the number of trades.

- There are two major ways of increasing trade. The first is to produce a good or service that satisfies an unmet demand. The second is to reduce the transaction costs of making trades.

KEY TERMS AND CONCEPTS

Loanable Funds	Nominal Interest Rate	Economic Rent
Positive Rate of Time Preference	Real Interest Rate	Pure Economic Rent
Roundabout Method of Production	Present Value	

QUESTIONS AND PROBLEMS

1. What does it mean to say that an individual has a positive rate of time preference?

2. What does having a positive rate of time preference have to do with positive interest rates?

3. How would the interest rate change as a result of the following?

   a. A rise in the demand for consumption loans

   b. A decline in the supply of loanable funds

   c. A rise in the demand for investment loans

4. The interest rate on loan X is higher than the interest rate on loan Y. What might explain the difference in interest rates between the two loans?

5. The real interest rate can remain unchanged as the nominal interest rate rises. Do you agree or disagree with this statement? Explain your answer.

6. What type of person is most willing to pay high interest rates?

7. Some people have argued that, in a moneyless (or barter) economy, interest would not exist. Would it? Explain your answer.

8. In what ways are a baseball star who can do nothing but play baseball and a parcel of land similar?

9. What does it mean to say that land rent is price determined, not price determining?

10. What is the link between profit and uncertainty?

11. What is the overall economic function of profits?

12. "The more economic rent a person receives in his job, the less likely he is to leave the job and the more content he will be on the job." Do you agree or disagree? Explain your answer.

13. It has been said that a society with a high savings rate is a society with a high standard of living. What is the link (if any) between saving and a relatively high standard of living?

14. Make an attempt to calculate the present value of your future income.

15. Describe the effect of each of the following events on individuals' rate of time preference and thus on interest rates:

   a. A technological advance that increases longevity

   b. An increased threat of war

   c. Growing older

16. "As the interest rate falls, firms are more inclined to buy capital goods." Do you agree or disagree? Explain your answer.

17. What is it that the entrepreneur does?

WORKING WITH NUMBERS AND GRAPHS

1. Compute the following:

   a. The present value of $25,000 each year for 4 years at a 7 percent interest rate

   b. The present value of $152,000 each year for 5 years at a 6 percent interest rate

   c. The present value of $60,000 each year for 10 years at a 6.5 percent interest rate

2. Bobby is a baseball player who earns $1 million a year playing for team X. If he weren't playing baseball for team X, he would be playing baseball for team Y and earning $800,000 a year. If he weren't playing baseball at all, he would be working as an accountant earning $120,000 a year. What is his economic rent as a baseball player playing for team X? What is his economic rent as a baseball player?

3. Diagrammatically represent pure economic rent.

MARKET FAILURE: EXTERNALITIES, PUBLIC GOODS, AND ASYMMETRIC INFORMATION

INTRODUCTION

Markets are a major topic in this book. We have analyzed how markets work, beginning with the simple supply-and-demand model, as well as various market structures: perfect competition, monopoly, and others. Goods and services are produced in markets. For example, cars are produced in car markets, houses are produced in housing markets, and computers are produced in computer markets. We now ask: Do these markets produce the right amount (the optimal or ideal amount) of these various goods? What are the right amounts? For example, what is the ideal or optimal amount of houses to produce, and does the housing market actually produce that amount?

When a market produces more or less than the ideal or optimal amount of a particular good, economists say there is **market failure**. Economists want to know under what conditions market failure may occur. This chapter presents three topics in which market failure is a prominent part of the discussion: externalities, public goods, and asymmetric information.

James Morgan/Shutterstock.com

17-1 EXTERNALITIES

Sometimes, when goods are produced and consumed, side effects (spillover or third-party effects) are felt by people who are not directly involved in the market exchanges. In general, these side effects are called **externalities**, because the costs or benefits are external to the persons who caused them. In this section, we discuss the various costs and benefits of activities and describe how and when activities cause externalities. We then explain graphically how externalities can result in market failure.

17-1a Costs and Benefits of Activities

Most activities in life have both costs and benefits. For example, when Jim sits down to read a book, reading has some benefits for Jim and some costs. These benefits and costs are private to him—they affect only him; hence, we call them *private benefits* and *private costs*.

Jim can also undertake an activity that has benefits and costs not only for him but also for others. Suppose he decides to smoke a cigarette in the general vicinity of Angelica. For Jim, smoking the cigarette has both benefits and costs—his private benefits and costs. But Jim's smoking

Market Failure

A situation in which the market does not provide the ideal or optimal amount of a good.

might also affect Angelica: for example, she may react to cigarette smoke by coughing. In this case, Jim's smoking might impose a cost on Angelica. Because the cost Jim imposes on her is external to him, we call it an *external cost*. Jim's activity imposes a *negative externality* on Angelica, for which she incurs an external cost. A **negative externality** exists when a person's or group's actions impose a cost (or adverse side effect) on others.

In another example, suppose Jim lives across the street from Yvonne and beautifies his front yard (which Yvonne can clearly see from her house) by planting trees, flowers, and a new lawn. Obviously, Jim receives some benefits and costs by beautifying his yard, but Yvonne enjoys some benefits too: Not only does she have a pretty yard to look at (in much the same way that someone might benefit by gazing at a beautiful painting), but Jim's beautification efforts may also raise the market value of Yvonne's property.

Because the benefit that Jim generates for Yvonne is external to him, it is an *external benefit*. Jim's activity generates a *positive externality* for Yvonne, for which she receives an external benefit. A **positive externality** exists when a person's or group's actions create a benefit (or beneficial side effect) for others.

Externality
A side effect of an action that affects the well-being of third parties.

Negative Externality
The condition in which a person's or group's actions impose a cost (an adverse side effect) on others.

Positive Externality
The condition in which a person's or group's actions create a benefit (a beneficial side effect) for others.

FINDING ECONOMICS

In Students Talking in Class Blake sits near the back of the room in his biology class. Two students who sit near Blake often talk to each other while the class is in session. They usually whisper, but still, their talking disturbs Blake. Where is the economics?

As far as Blake is concerned, the two talking students are doing something (talking during the class) that adversely affects him. For Blake, their talking is a negative externality.

17-1b Marginal Costs and Benefits of Activities

When considering activities that have different degrees or amounts of costs and benefits (smoking one cigarette an hour or two, planting three trees or four), economists speak in terms of marginal benefits and costs. More specifically, for Jim, various activities have marginal private benefits (*MPB*) and marginal private costs (*MPC*). If Jim's activities generate external benefits or costs for others, then it makes sense to speak in terms of marginal external benefits (*MEB*) and marginal external costs (*MEC*).

To analyze the effects of an activity, we need to know the total marginal costs and benefits, so we sum them. The sum of marginal private costs (*MPC*) and marginal external costs (*MEC*) is referred to as **marginal social costs (MSC)**:

$$MSC = MPC + MEC$$

In our example, Jim's smoking a cigarette imposed an external cost on Angelica. Suppose Jim's *MPC* of smoking a cigarette is $1 and Angelica's *MEC* of Jim's smoking a cigarette is $2. Therefore, the *MSC* of Jim smoking a cigarette (taking into account both Jim's private costs and Angelica's external costs) is $3.

The sum of marginal private benefits (*MPB*) and marginal external benefits (*MEB*) is called **marginal social benefits (MSB)**:

$$MSB = MPB + MEB$$

Jim's beautifying his yard created an external benefit for Yvonne. Suppose Jim's *MPB* of beautifying his yard is $5 and Yvonne's *MEB* is $3. Then the *MSB* of Jim's beautifying his yard (at a given level of beautification) is $8.

Marginal Social Costs (MSC)
The sum of marginal private costs (*MPC*) and marginal external costs (*MEC*):
$MSC = MPC + MEC$.

Marginal Social Benefits (MSB)
The sum of marginal private benefits (*MPB*) and marginal external benefits (*MEB*):
$MSB = MPB + MEB$.

17-1c Social Optimality, or Efficiency, Conditions

Socially Optimal Amount (Output)
An amount that takes into account and adjusts for all benefits (external and private) and all costs (external and private); the amount at which $MSB = MSC$. Sometimes referred to as the efficient amount.

For an economist, there is always a right amount of something. There is a right amount of time to study for a test, a right amount of exercise, and a right number of cars to be produced. The right amount, for an economist, is the **socially optimal amount (output)**, or the efficient amount (output): the amount at which $MSB = MSC$. In other words, the right amount of anything is the amount at which the MSB (of that thing) equals the MSC (of that thing). Later in this section, we illustrate this condition graphically.

17-1d Three Categories of Activities

For the person who engages in an activity (whether it is producing a computer or studying for an exam), the activity almost always brings benefits and costs. It is hard to think of any activities in life in which private benefits and private costs do not exist.

Not so hard, however, is thinking of activities in life in which external benefits and external costs do not exist. For example, when reading a book, a person incurs benefits and costs, but probably no one else does. We can characterize this effect in the following way: $MPB > 0$, $MPC > 0$, $MEB = 0$, $MEC = 0$. Marginal private benefits and costs are both positive (greater than zero), but there are no marginal external benefits or costs. In other words, the activity has no positive or negative externalities.

Therefore, activities may be categorized according to whether negative or positive externalities exist, as shown in the following table:[1]

Category	Definition	Meaning in Terms of Marginal Benefits and Costs
1	No negative or positive externality	$MEC = 0$ and $MEB = 0$; it follows that $MSC = MPC$ and $MSB = MPB$.
2	Negative externality but no positive externality	$MEC > 0$ and $MEB = 0$; it follows that $MSC > MPC$ and $MSB = MPB$.
3	Positive externality but no negative externality	$MEB > 0$ and $MEC = 0$; it follows that $MSB > MPB$ and $MSC = MPC$.

17-1e Externalities in Consumption and in Production

Externalities can arise because someone *consumes* something that has an external benefit or cost for others or because someone *produces* something that has an external benefit or cost for others. Consider two examples of negative externalities. Barbara plays the radio in her car loudly, adversely affecting drivers around her at the stoplight. In this situation, Barbara is consuming music and creating a negative externality for others. John produces cars in his factory. As a result of the production process, he emits pollution into the air that adversely affects some people who live downwind from the factory. In this situation, the negative externality is the result of John's producing a good.

17-1f Diagram of a Negative Externality

Exhibit 1 shows the downward-sloping demand curve, D, for some good. Because the demand curve represents the marginal private benefits received by the buyers of the good, it is the same as the MPB curve. Because there are no positive externalities in this case, $MPB = MSB$, so the

---

[1] Theoretically, there is a fourth category—in which both a positive externality and a negative externality exist—but one would reasonably assume that this category has little, if any, practical relevance. For example, suppose Jim smokes a cigarette and cigarette smoke is a negative externality for Angelica but a positive externality for Bobby. It is possible that what is a bad for Angelica is a good for Bobby, but little is added to the discussion (at this time) by considering such cases.

demand curve is also the *MSB* curve. The supply curve, *S*, represents the marginal private costs (*MPC*) of the producers of the good. Equilibrium in this market setting is at E_1; Q_1 is the output—specifically, the market output.

Assume that negative externalities arise as a result of the production of the good. For example, suppose the good happens to be cars, whose production in a factory causes the emission of some air pollution. Because of the negative externalities, external costs associated with the production of the good exist; these costs are not taken into account at the market output. Still, by adding them (as best we can) to the marginal private costs, we can take into account the marginal external costs linked to the negative externalities. The result is the marginal social cost (*MSC*) curve shown in Exhibit 1. If all costs (both external and private) are taken into account, then equilibrium becomes E_2, where $MSB = MSC$. The quantity Q_2 produced at E_2 is the socially optimal, or efficient, output.

When negative externalities exist, the market output (Q_1) is greater than the socially optimal output (Q_2). The market is said to fail (hence the term "market failure") because it *overproduces* the good connected with the negative externality. The shaded triangle in Exhibit 1 is the visible manifestation of the market failure. It represents the net social cost of producing the market output (Q_1) instead of the socially optimal output (Q_2) or of moving from the socially optimal output to the market output.

EXHIBIT 1

The Negative Externality Case

Because of a negative externality, marginal social costs (*MSC*) are greater than marginal private costs (*MPC*) and the market output is greater than the socially optimal output. The market is said to fail in that it overproduces the good.

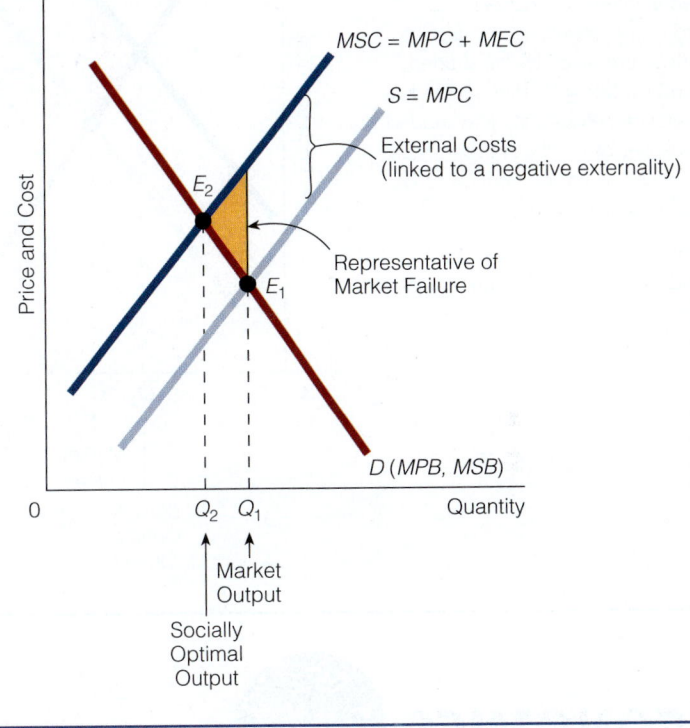

To understand exactly how the triangle in Exhibit 1 represents the net social cost of moving from the socially optimal output to the market output, look at Exhibit 2, in which, as in Exhibit 1, Q_2 is the socially optimal output and Q_1 is the market output. If society moves from Q_2 to Q_1, who specifically benefits and how do we represent the benefits? Buyers benefit (they are a part of society) because they will be able to buy more output at prices they are willing to pay. Thus, the area under the demand curve between Q_2 and Q_1 represents the benefits to society of moving from Q_2 to Q_1. (See the shaded area in window 1 of Exhibit 2.)

Next, if society moves from Q_2 to Q_1, both sellers and third parties incur costs. Sellers incur private costs, and third parties incur external costs. The area under *S* (the *MPC* curve) between Q_2 and Q_1 takes into account only part of society—sellers—and ignores third parties. The area under the *MSC* curve between Q_2 and Q_1 represents the full costs to society of moving from Q_2 to Q_1. (See the shaded area in window 2.)

The shaded area in window 2 is larger than the one in window 1, so the costs to sellers and third parties of moving from Q_2 to Q_1 outweigh the benefits to buyers of moving from Q_2 to Q_1. The difference between the shaded areas is the triangle shown in the main diagram. Thus, the costs to society outweigh the benefits to society by the area of the triangle. In short, the triangle in this example represents the net social cost of moving from Q_2 to Q_1, or of producing Q_1 instead of Q_2.

EXHIBIT 2

The Triangle

Q_2 is the socially optimal output; Q_1 is the market output. If society moves from Q_2 to Q_1, buyers benefit by an amount represented by the shaded area in window 1 but sellers and third parties together incur greater costs, represented by the shaded area in window 2. The triangle (the difference between the two shaded areas) represents the net social cost to society of moving from Q_2 to Q_1, or of producing Q_1 instead of Q_2.

(Note: On the vertical axis in windows 1 and 2, P = price and C = cost.)

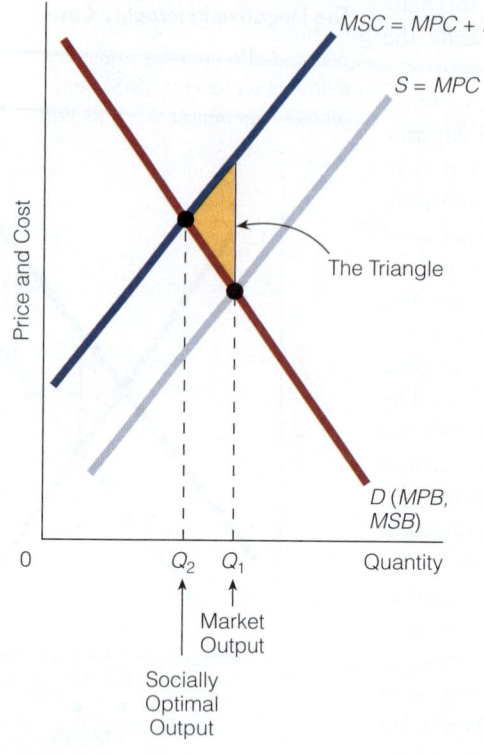

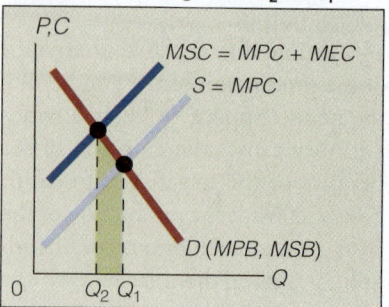

Window 1
Benefits of moving from Q_2 to Q_1

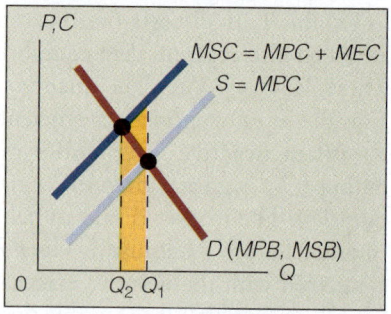

Window 2
Costs of moving from Q_2 to Q_1

ECONOMICS 24/7

An Unintended Effect of Social Media

A negative externality exists when a person's or group's actions impose a cost (an adverse side effect) on others. Are there any negative externalities connected with social media? Suppose Rob is in his car driving home. Before he reaches his destination, he hears the "ping" on his cell phone letting him know that a text message has arrived. He looks at the cars around him and concludes that it is safe for him to look down at his phone and read the message. He does so. No problem. Then, he decides to continue to drive while he responds to the text message. As he is texting, his eyes aren't on the

iStock.com/Geber86

road or the cars and pedestrians around him. He ends up running into the back of the car in front of him, and that car then pushes the car ahead of it into the crosswalk where people are walking. Two pedestrians are struck and hurt. As far as it goes for the driver of the car two cars in front of Rob (and maybe of the driver of the car in front of him) and the two pedestrians, Rob has undertaken an action—texting while driving—that has adversely affected them. Rob's direct action of texting created an unintended and negative effect on some others.

17-1g Diagram of a Positive Externality

Exhibit 3 shows the downward-sloping demand curve, D, for some good. This curve represents the marginal private benefits received by the buyers of the good, so it is the same as the MPB curve. The supply curve, S, represents the marginal private costs (MPC) of the producers of the good. The marginal social costs (MSC) are the same as the marginal private costs—$MPC = MSC$—because there are no negative externalities in this case. Equilibrium in this market setting is at E_1; Q_1 is the output—specifically, the market output.

EXHIBIT 3

The Positive Externality Case

Because of a positive externality, marginal social benefits (MSB) are greater than marginal private benefits (MPB) and the market output is less than the socially optimal output. The market is said to fail in that it underproduces the good.

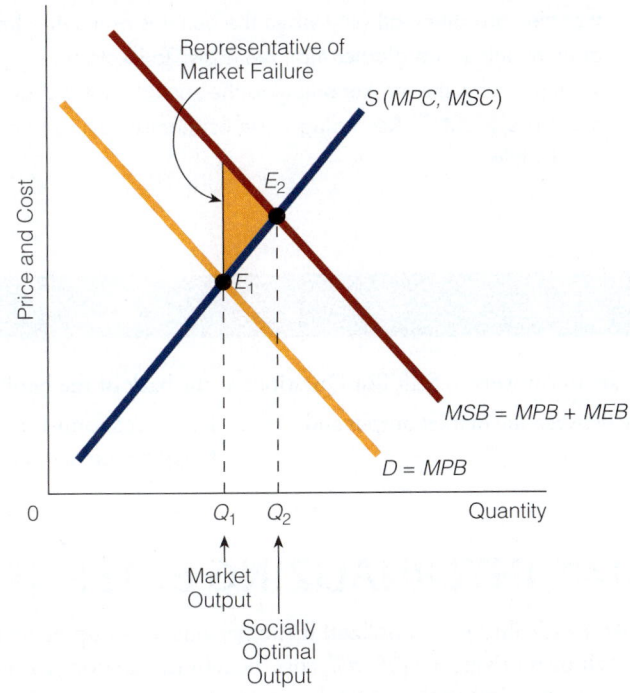

Assume that positive externalities arise as a result of the production of the good. For example, suppose Erica is a beekeeper who produces honey. The hives are near an apple orchard, and her bees occasionally fly over to the orchard and pollinate the blossoms, in the process making the orchard more productive. The orchard owner thus benefits from Erica's bees.

Because positive externalities exist, the production of the good has external benefits; these benefits are not taken into account at the market output. Still, by adding them (as best we can) to the marginal private benefits, we can take into account the marginal external benefits linked to the positive externalities. The result is the marginal social benefit (MSB) curve shown in Exhibit 3. If all benefits (both external and private) are taken into account, then equilibrium becomes E_2, where $MSB = MSC$. The quantity Q_2 produced at E_2 (is the socially optimal, or efficient, output).

The market output (Q_1) is less than the socially optimal output (Q_2) when positive externalities exist (just the opposite of when negative externalities exist). The market is said to fail (hence the term "market failure") because it *underproduces* the good connected with the positive externality.

The shaded triangle in Exhibit 3 is the visible manifestation of the market failure. It represents the net social benefit *that is lost* by producing the market output (Q_1) instead of the socially optimal output (Q_2). Stated differently, at the socially optimal output (Q_2), society realizes greater benefits than at the market output (Q_1). So, by being at Q_1, society loses out on some net benefits that it could obtain if it were at Q_2.

THINKING LIKE AN ECONOMIST

The Benefits and the Costs of Making the Move   An economist may seem to prefer the socially optimal output (according to which all benefits and costs are taken into account) to the market output (in which only private benefits and costs are taken into account), but not necessarily. An economist prefers the socially optimal output to the market output (assuming that they are different) only when the benefits of moving from the market output to the socially optimal output are greater than the costs. To illustrate, suppose $400 in benefits exists if we move from the market output to the socially optimal output but the costs of making the move are $1,000. According to an economist, trying to make the adjustment would not be worthwhile.

SELF-TEST

(Answers to Self-Test questions are in Answers to Self-Test Questions at the back of the book.)

1. What is the major difference between the market output and the socially optimal output?

2. For an economist, is the socially optimal output always preferred to the market output?

17-2   INTERNALIZING EXTERNALITIES

Internalizing Externalities
An externality is internalized if the persons or group that generated the externality incorporate into their own private or internal cost–benefit calculations the external benefits (in the case of a positive externality) or the external costs (in the case of a negative externality).

An externality is **internalized** if the persons or group generating the externality incorporate into their own private, or *internal*, cost–benefit calculations the external benefits (in the case of a positive externality) or the external costs (in the case of a negative externality). Simply put, internalizing externalities is the same as adjusting for externalities. An externality has been internalized, or adjusted for, *completely* if, as a result, the socially optimal or efficient output emerges. A few of the numerous ways to adjust for, or internalize, externalities are presented in this section.

17-2a   Persuasion

Many negative externalities arise partly because persons or groups do not consider other individuals when they decide to undertake an action. An example is the person who plays his CD player loudly at 3 o'clock in the morning. Perhaps if he considered the external cost of his action to his neighbors, he either would not play the CD player at all or would tune it down.

Trying to persuade those who impose external costs on us to take these costs into account is one way to make the imposers adjust for—or internalize—externalities. In today's world, such slogans as "Don't Drink and Drive" and "Don't Litter" are attempts to persuade individuals to consider the effects of their actions on others. The golden rule of ethical conduct, in one form or another—for example, "Do unto others as you would have them do unto you"—makes the same point.

17-2b **Taxes and Subsidies**

Taxes and subsidies are sometimes used as corrective devices for a market failure. A tax adjusts for a negative externality; a subsidy adjusts for a positive externality.

Consider the negative externality case in Exhibit 1. The objective of a corrective tax would be to move the supply curve S to the MSC curve (recall that a tax can shift a supply curve) and therefore move from the market-determined output, Q_1, to the socially optimal output, Q_2.

In the case of a positive externality, illustrated in Exhibit 3, the objective would be to subsidize the demand side of the market so that the demand curve D moves to the MSB curve and output moves from Q_1 to the socially optimal output, Q_2.

However, taxes and subsidies also involve costs and consequences. For example, suppose, as illustrated in Exhibit 4, that government misjudges the external costs when it imposes a tax on the supplier of a good. Then, instead of the supply S_1 moving to S_2 (the MSC curve), it moves to S_3. As a result, the output level will be farther away from the socially optimal output than it was before the "corrective" tax was applied.

EXHIBIT 4

A Corrective Tax Gone Wrong

Government may miscalculate external costs and impose a tax that moves the supply curve from S_1 to S_3 instead of from S_1 to S_2. As a result, the output level will be farther away from the socially optimal output than before the "corrective" tax was applied. (Q_3 is farther away from Q_2 than Q_1 is from Q_2.) For a corrective tax to bring about the socially optimal output, the tax would have to be set such that the S_1 curve shifts leftward to S_2.

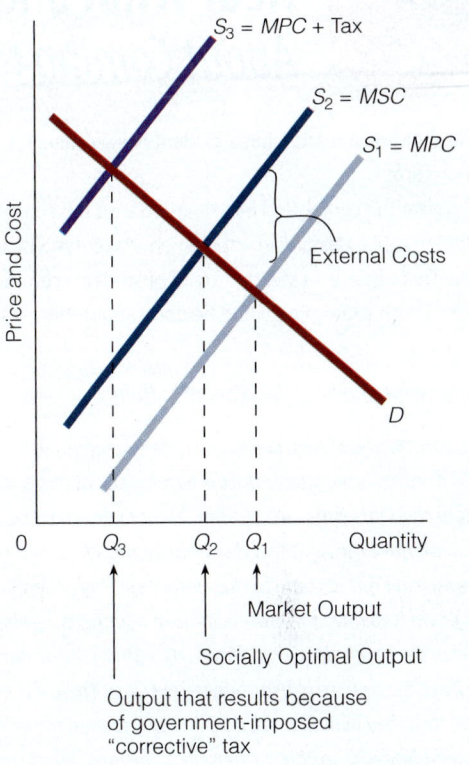

17-2c **Assigning Property Rights**

Consider the idea that air pollution and ocean pollution—both of which are examples of negative externalities—are the result of the air and oceans being unowned. No one owns the air, and no one owns the oceans. Because no one does, many individuals feel free to emit wastes into them. If private property, or ownership, rights in air and oceans could be established, the negative externalities would likely decrease. If someone owns a resource, then actions that damage it have a price, namely, the damages that the resource owner can sue for.

For example, in the early West, when grazing lands were open and unowned (common property), many cattle ranchers allowed their herds to overgraze. The reason was simple: No one owned the land, so no one could stop the overgrazing to preserve the value of the land. Even if one rancher decided not to allow his herd to graze, all he did was leave more grazing land for other ranchers. As a consequence of overgrazing, a future generation inherited barren, wasted land. From the point of view of future generations, the cattle ranchers who allowed their herds to overgraze were generating negative externalities.

If the Western lands had been privately owned, overgrazing would not have occurred because the monetary interests of the landowner would not have permitted it. The landowner would have charged ranchers a fee to graze their cattle, and more grazing would have entailed additional fees. There would have been less grazing at a positive fee than at a zero fee (the case when the lands were open and unowned). In other words, the externalities would have been internalized.

Hear What and How the Economist Thinks . . .
About Coming to Class Late

The economist reads what a student has written on a course evaluation form:

I like the course and have learned a lot this semester. However, I find myself getting distracted when students come into the class late. There is often a steady stream of students coming in late to class. I wish something could be done about this.

Hear what and how the economist thinks:

So, what we have here are some students coming to class late and this disturbs other students. One way to look at this is in terms of a property rights issue. Who has the right to do what? Does the on-time student have the right to a disturbance-free class, or do the latecomers have a right to come to class late? One way of dealing with the problem is to have the professor make a property rights assignment. The professor could give the property right to the on-time students to have the right to a disturbance-free class. Then, if the latecomers find that they benefit more from being late than the on-time students benefit from a disturbance-free class, the latecomers can purchase the property right from the on-time students. Let's say that the latecomers value being late by $4 and the on-time students value a disturbance-free class by $2. The latecomers can buy the right to be late for, say, $3 and both the latecomers and the students who come to class on time will be made better off. Of course, the transactions costs for the two groups of students getting together to effect the transaction at hand is probably high enough that they won't get together and work out an agreement.

Of course, if the professor thinks that the latecomers are not taking into account the cost they impose on the on-time students when

kristian sekulic/Getty Images

they decide to be late to class, he could try to make their marginal private cost (MPC) increase by the amount of the marginal external cost incurred by the on-time students. The way to do this is to impose a "tax" on the latecomers. The tax might be a one-point reduction in their final course grade for every time they come into class late. In other words, come to class late, pay a tax of a 1-point reduction in your course grade.

Questions to Think About:

1. Do you think persuasion or a tax would be more likely to get latecomers to reduce their lateness to class? Explain your answer. (Note: Persuasion would come in the form of the professor telling the latecomers that their lateness imposes a cost on the on-time students.)

2. How is a speeding ticket similar to a tax that is used as a corrective device for a market failure?

17-2d Voluntary Agreements

Externalities can sometimes be internalized through individual voluntary agreements. Suppose Pete and Sean live alone on a tiny island. They have agreed, between themselves, that Pete owns the northern part of the island and Sean owns the southern part. Pete occasionally plays his drums in the morning, and the sound awakens Sean, causing a negative externality problem. Pete wants to be free to play his drums in the morning, and Sean would like to sleep.

Suppose Sean values his sleep in the morning by a maximum of six oranges; that is, he would give up six oranges to be able to sleep without Pete playing his drums. On the other hand, Pete values drum playing in the morning by three oranges. He would give up a maximum of three oranges to be able to play his drums in the morning. Because Sean values his sleep by more than Pete values playing his drums, they have an opportunity to strike a deal. Sean can offer Pete some number of oranges greater than three, but fewer than six, to refrain from playing his drums in the morning. The deal will make both Pete and Sean better off.

In this example, the negative externality problem is successfully addressed through the individuals' voluntarily entering into an agreement. The condition for this output is that the *transaction costs*, or costs associated with making and reaching the agreement, must be low relative to the expected benefits of the agreement.

17-2e Combining Property Rights Assignments and Voluntary Agreements

The last two ways of internalizing externalities—property rights assignments and voluntary agreements—can be combined, as in the following example:[2] Suppose a rancher's cattle occasionally stray onto the adjacent farm and damage or eat some of the farmer's crops. The court assigns liability to the cattle rancher and orders him to prevent his cattle from straying; thus, a property rights assignment solves the externality problem. As a result, the rancher puts up a strong fence to prevent his cattle from damaging his neighbor's crops.

But the court's property rights assignment may be undone by the farmer and the cattle rancher if they find that doing so is in their mutual interest. Suppose the rancher is willing to pay $100 a month to the farmer for permission to allow his cattle to stray onto the farmer's land and the farmer is willing to give permission for $70 a month. Then, if the transaction costs are trivial or zero, the farmer and the rancher will undo the court's property rights assignment. For a payment of $70 or more a month, the farmer will allow the rancher's cattle to stray onto his land.

Coase Theorem

Suppose, in our example, that instead of assigning liability to the cattle rancher, the court had given him the property right to allow his cattle to stray. What would the resource allocative outcome have been in this case? With the opposite property rights assignment, the cattle would have been allowed to stray (exactly the outcome of the previous property rights assignment after the cattle rancher and farmer voluntarily agreed to undo the court's decision).

The **Coase theorem** can be expressed in various ways, two of which are as follows: (1) In the case of trivial or zero transaction costs, a property rights assignment will be undone (exchanged) if it benefits the relevant parties to undo it. (2) In the case of trivial or zero transaction costs, the resource allocative outcome will be efficient.

The Coase theorem is significant for two reasons: (1) It shows that, under certain conditions, the market can internalize externalities. (2) It provides a benchmark for analyzing externality problems; that is, it shows what will happen if transaction costs are trivial or zero.

Coase Theorem
The proposition that private negotiations between people will lead to an efficient resolution of externalities, as long as property rights are well defined and transaction costs are trivial or zero.

Pigou Versus Coase

The first editor of the *Journal of Law and Economics* was Aaron Director. In 1959, Director published an article by Ronald Coase entitled "The Federal Communications Commission." In the article, Coase took issue with economist A. C. Pigou, a trailblazer in the area of externalities and market failure, who had argued that government should use taxes and subsidies to adjust for negative and positive externalities, respectively. Coase argued that, in the case of negative externalities, whether the state should tax the person imposing the negative externality is not clear. First, Coase stressed the reciprocal nature of externalities, pointing out that it takes two to make a negative externality. (Who is harming whom is not always clear.) Second, Coase proposed a market solution to externality problems that was not implicit in Pigou's work.

---

[2] See Ronald Coase, "The Problem of Social Cost," *Journal of Law and Economics* 3 (October 1960): 1–44.

Director and others believed that Coase was wrong and Pigou was right. Coase, who was teaching at the University of Virginia at the time, was invited to discuss his thesis with Director and a handful of well-known economists. The group included Martin Bailey, Milton Friedman, Arnold Harberger, Reuben Kessel, Gregg Lewis, John McGee, Lloyd Mints, George Stigler, and, of course, Director.

The group met at Director's house one night. Before Coase began to outline his thesis, the group took a vote and found that everyone (with the exception of Coase) sided with Pigou. Then the sparks began to fly, with Friedman, it is reported, opening fire on Coase. Coase answered the intellectual attacks of his colleagues, and, at the end of the debate, another vote was taken. This time, everyone sided with Coase against Pigou. It is reported that, as the members of the group left Director's home that night, they said to one another that they had witnessed history in the making. The Coase theorem had taken hold in economics.

17-2f Beyond Internalizing: Setting Regulations

One way to deal with externalities—in particular, with negative externalities—is for government to apply regulations directly to the activities that generate the externalities. For example, factories producing goods also produce smoke, which is often seen as a negative externality. Government may decide that the factory must install pollution-reducing equipment, that it can emit only a certain amount of smoke into the air per day, or that it must be moved to a less populated area.

Critics of this approach often note that regulations, once instituted, are difficult to remove, even if conditions warrant their removal. Also, regulations are often applied across the board when individual circumstances dictate otherwise. For example, factories in relatively pollution-free cities might be required to install the same pollution control equipment as factories in smoggy, pollution-ridden cities.

Finally, regulation entails costs. If government imposes regulations, it needs regulators (whose salaries must be paid), offices (to house the regulators), word processors (to produce the regulations), and more. As noted earlier, dealing with externalities successfully may offer benefits, but the costs need to be considered as well.

ECONOMICS 24/7

Tribes, Transaction Costs, and Social Media

At one time in human history, it was common for humans to be members of tribes. Which tribe was dictated by where a person lived. If the only mode of transportation is walking by foot, it would make sense that people would stay near the group into which they were born. So, if you were born into group X in location X, you spent much of your life in group X. Group X was your tribe, so to speak. It was also common, long ago, for the individuals within a group or tribe to share a race or ethnicity. In short, we can speak of an ethnic or racial tribe.

As methods of transportation improved (from walking, to riding a horse, to driving a car, to flying in an airplane), the locale in which one was born became less of a constraint to movement. And because it became easier for people to travel, it would naturally become easier for a person who was born into one tribe to travel outside his particular tribe. It also became easier for a person who perhaps shared the same race as others within his tribe to find other tribes with whose members he had more in common than simply race and with whom he had common interests.

Think of the idea of tribes and social media today. What social media has largely done is make it more likely that people will form social tribes, no matter what race or ethnicity they may be. To illustrate, Meetup is an online social networking portal that helps facilitate off-line group meetings in different localities. Group members share a common interest, such as health, pets, hobbies, politics, and books. Essentially, Meetup lowers the transaction costs of forming groups. Picking a city at random reveals just a few of the many groups identified on Meetup that were getting together: active singles; active-lifestyle nerds; cheap-movie-night group; French-speaking group; mountain/trail and road biking group; sailing group; geek girls group; corgi Meetup group; baby playgroup; yoga group; book divas; and drink, dives, and darts group.

Think of how someone living 100,000 years ago, stuck in his tribe identified by race or ethnicity, might have reacted if, magically, he could get together with those in other tribes with whom he shared a nonethnic or nonracial attribute. There might have been the "counting-stars group," or the "run-among-the-trees group."

What the social networking portal Meetup has allowed people to do—perhaps more than anything else—is allow people who didn't have a "group" (because there were not enough people in the group in which they lived and worked who shared their interests) to find each other. To illustrate, if your home and work group, or "tribe," consists of no one who seems to enjoy reading books by author Neil Gaiman, and that is a passion for you, then you might feel somewhat "left out." Everyone wants to talk football, you think, but I can't find anyone who wants to talk about Neil Gaiman books.

So, what were some of the first groups to sign up on Meetup when it came into existence? They weren't Episcopalian groups, because Episcopalians already have a place where they meet up. Here were some of the topics of interest that were most often

Lenscap Photography/Shutterstock.com

identified for groups on Meetup: witches, Slashdot, Xena, pagans, ex-Jehovah's Witness, *Star Trek*, and vampires.[3]

It could very well be that people have always preferred to organize or group themselves in terms of their interests than in terms of their race or ethnicity, but that it was just so hard to do before transportation and communication became easy and cheap. What a social medium like Meetup does is make it very easy and cheap for individuals to group themselves in terms of what is of great importance to their personal and social lives. As an aside, there are over 125,000 groups listed on Meetup!

[3]. See Clay Shirky, *Here Comes Everybody: The Power of Organizing without Organizations* (New York: Penguin Press, 2008).

SELF-TEST

1. What does it mean to internalize an externality?

2. Are the transaction costs of buying a house higher or lower than those of buying a hamburger at a fast-food restaurant? Explain your answer.

3. Does the property rights assignment a court makes matter to the resource-allocative outcome?

4. What condition must be satisfied for a tax to adjust correctly for a negative externality?

17-3 ENVIRONMENTAL POLICY

In an earlier section, we discussed how the presence of (negative or positive) externalities can lead us away from social optimality or efficiency. In this section, we consider different approaches to dealing with negative environmental externalities, which we will address under the general term of "pollution." We discuss the specifics of three types of policies: (1) government regulation, or command and control, (2) emission taxes, and (3) tradable pollution permits (also known as cap and trade).

17-3a Method 1: Government Regulation, or Command and Control

Suppose that 10 tons of pollution (say, from factories) are emitted into the air over a given area during a certain period. One command-and-control policy that government might enact is to specify a certain type of pollution control technology to be used by factory owners. In other words, government mandates that factory owners must use technology X instead of technology Y because technology X causes less pollution to be emitted into the air than technology Y. As a result, pollution emission might fall, say, from 10 tons of pollution to 7 tons.

Another possible command-and-control policy might be to simply set a quantitative goal that is applied to the factories emitting pollution. In other words, simply specify that no factory can emit more than, say, 2 tons of pollution into the air over some time frame.

Generally, economists do not favor command-and-control policies as a means of reducing pollution. One reason is that mandating certain technologies to be used reduces the incentive to discover new, sometimes lower cost methods of reducing pollution. Also, mandating that all factories must eliminate, say, 3 tons of pollution fails to take into account that it is less costly for some factories to eliminate pollution than for others to do so. To illustrate, consider Exhibit 5, which shows the cost to each of three firms of eliminating various amounts of pollution.

Suppose that, currently, each firm is emitting 3 tons of pollution, for a total of 9 tons emitted. Suppose also that the government wants to reduce pollution by 6 tons (and thus bring the overall pollution level down from 9 tons to 3 tons). Thus, the government mandates that each firm must eliminate 2 tons of pollution. The cost to firm X of eliminating its first 2 tons of pollution is $125($50 + $75 = $125); the cost to firm Y of eliminating its first 2 tons is $155; and the cost to firm Z of eliminating its first 2 tons of pollution is $1,500. The total cost of eliminating 6 tons of pollution is $1,780($125 + $155 + $1,500 = $1,780). Is there a cheaper way of eliminating 6 tons of pollution? Yes, firms X and Y could have eliminated 3 tons of pollution each, for a total cost of $580($50 + $75 + $100 + $70 + $85 + $200 = $580).

EXHIBIT 5

The Cost of Reducing Pollution for Three Firms

These are hypothetical data showing the cost of reducing pollution for firms X, Y, and Z:

	Firm X	Firm Y	Firm Z
Cost of Eliminating:			
First ton of pollution	$50	$70	$500
Second ton of pollution	75	85	1,000
Third ton of pollution	100	200	2,000

17-3b Method 2: Emission Taxes

As we discussed earlier, a tax can be used to deal with a negative externality and the ideal corrective tax is equal to the marginal external cost associated with the negative externality. Economists generally prefer a corrective tax to command and control because such a tax can achieve the same reduction in pollution as a command-and-control policy, but in an efficient manner. The reason is that a tax effectively places a price on the right to pollute. The firm then has to weigh its cost of eliminating pollution against the tax it would pay if it didn't eliminate pollution. For example, suppose there is a $40 emission tax for each ton of pollution emitted. Then a firm that is emitting pollution would have to consider how much it would have to pay to eliminate a given amount of pollution and how much of a tax it would have to pay if it didn't.

Let's return to Exhibit 5 to see how a tax might work at eliminating 6 tons of pollution (the same quantity of pollution eliminated through the command-and-control policy). Suppose the tax were set at $330 per ton of pollution. Under this tax, firms X and Y would each reduce all 3 tons of their pollution, for a total of 6 tons of pollution eliminated. Firm Z would not eliminate any of its pollution, because, for each ton of pollution it emits, the cost of eliminating that amount of pollution is greater than the tax. The total cost to firms X and Y of eliminating their pollution would be $580, which again is much less than the total cost of $1,780 under the command-and-control system whereby each firm was mandated to eliminate 3 tons of pollution. Also, under an emission tax, firms have an incentive to find cleaner (less polluting) ways of producing their goods, because a cleaner way of producing goods means less pollution and a lower tax bill for polluting.

17-3c Method 3: Tradable Pollution Permits (Cap and Trade)

Under a system of tradable pollution permits, or cap and trade, a "cap," or ceiling, is placed on how much pollution can be emitted. Permits to pollute are then allocated to polluters (or auctioned off to the highest bidder), after which the polluters can trade (buy and sell) the permits. With this idea in mind, turn again to Exhibit 5. As before, the objective of the government is to eliminate 6 tons of pollution so that the total amount of pollution will fall from 9 tons to 3 tons. Toward that end, the government issues three pollution permits, one to each of the three firms. A single pollution permit allows the holder (of the permit) to emit 1 ton of pollution.

Currently, firm X has one pollution permit in its possession, so it can emit 1 ton of pollution and must eliminate the other 2. But firm X does not have to keep its pollution permit. It can sell its permit and then take measures to eliminate all 3 tons of its pollution. Might firm X be better off selling the permit and eliminating all 3 tons of pollution? We can ask the same question about firms Y and Z too? The answer for all of the firms depends on the price of a pollution permit.

A market for pollution permits emerges. The owners of the three firms get together, and the owner of firm Z says to the owners of the other two firms that he has to pay $500 to eliminate the first ton of pollution, so if anyone would be willing to sell him a permit for less than $500, he will buy it. Firms X and Y sell their permits because, for each of them, the cost of eliminating its third ton of pollution is less than $500. Suppose that, in the end, a price of $330 is agreed to as the price for a permit. As a result, firms X and Y each sell their permits to firm Z for $330 a permit. Then, firms X and Y eliminate 3 tons of pollution each, for a total of 6 tons eliminated, and firm Z, now holding 3 pollution permits, eliminates no pollution.

What is the cost of using tradable permits to eliminate pollution? Again, it is $580, which is the cost to firm X of eliminating all three units of pollution ($225) plus the cost to firm Y of eliminating all three units of pollution ($355).

You may wonder why we are not counting the cost to firm Z of buying the permits from firms X and Y. After all, firm Z paid $660 to buy two pollution permits. Although the $660 is a real cost of doing business for firm Z, it is not a cost to society of eliminating pollution. The $660 was not actually used to eliminate pollution; it was simply a transfer from firm Z to firms X and Y. The distinction is between a resource cost, which signifies an expenditure of resources, and a transfer, which does not.

Finally, instead of simply handing out pollution permits to firms, the government could auction off the permits. Under an auction, the government collects the revenue from the permits instead of letting it go to private firms.

17-3d Similarities and Differences Between Emission Taxes and Tradable Pollution Permits

One similarity between emission taxes and tradable permits is that both place a price on pollution. In both cases, one has *to pay* to pollute. With emission taxes, firms have to pay a tax to the government; with tradable permits, either firms have to pay each other to pollute (firm Z has to buy the permit from firm X), or they have to pay government at the permit auction. With auctioned permits, the government gets revenue in the same way that it gets revenue from an emission tax.

One way to clearly see the similarity between emission taxes and tradable pollution permits is in terms of Exhibit 6. Panels (a) and (b) each show the demand to pollute. In both panels, the demand is the same. In panel (a), an excise (corrective) tax is set at $50. At this tax, the quantity demanded of pollution (how much pollution polluters are willing to purchase) is 100 tons.

In panel (b), under a system of tradable pollution permits, government sets 100 tons of pollution as the permissible amount of pollution. In effect, it sets the supply curve of pollution permits at 100 tons. Then, this supply, combined with the demand to pollute, determines the price of a pollution permit as $50.

Under our scenario, the emission tax equals the price of the pollution permit. That's because we used the quantity demanded of 100 units of pollution in panel (a) as the permissible amount of pollution in panel (b). If we had, for example, set the permissible amount of pollution in panel (b) as 200 units, the price of the pollution permit would have been lower than the emission tax.

EXHIBIT 6

Emission Taxes and Tradable Pollution Permits

In panel (a), the emission tax is $50 and the quantity demanded of pollution is 100 units.

In panel (b), the government supplies 100 pollution permits (thus allowing 100 tons of pollution) and then supply and demand end up determining the price of a pollution

permit at $50. Here we have a case where the price to pollute (in the form of a tax or the price of a pollution permit) and the quantity of pollution are the same in both cases.

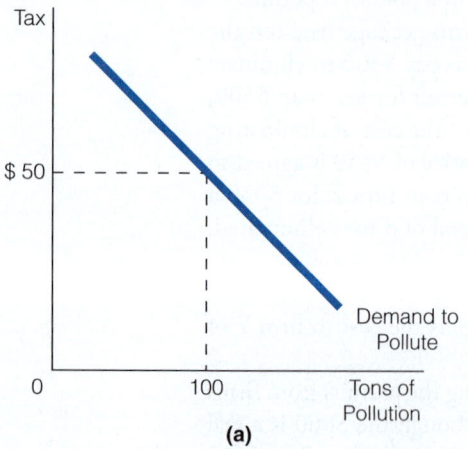

(a)

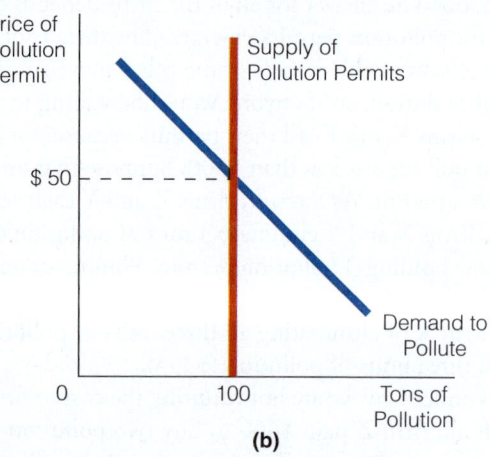

(b)

Under an emission tax, a price (a tax) is set and then the quantity of pollution is determined. Under a tradable pollution permits system, the quantity of permissible pollution is set and then the price of the pollution permit is determined. Under the specific conditions we specified (the quantity of pollution is the same in both cases), the emission tax equals the price of the pollution permit.

One of the things that government can't know with an emission tax is what the quantity demanded of pollution will be, given any specific tax. For example, if government sets the emission tax at $50, it can't be sure whether the quantity demanded of pollution at that tax will be 100 tons, more than 100 tons, or less than 100 tons. That's because it can't be sure what the demand is for pollution. So, if government sets as its objective to have only 100 tons of pollution, it can't be sure what emission tax will generate 100 tons as the quantity demanded of pollution.

This problem does not exist under a system of tradable permits. If government wants to permit only 100 tons of pollution, it will allocate only 100 permits. The equilibrium price of a pollution permit will then end up being a price that equates quantity demanded with the quantity supplied of 100.

Simply put, emission taxes and tradable pollution permits end up creating different kinds of uncertainty. Under an emission tax, polluters know what price they have to pay to pollute, but government doesn't know how much pollution will be generated. Under a tradable pollution permits system (cap and trade), government knows the amount of pollution, but polluters don't immediately know what the price to pollute will be. These uncertainties can be important, but they don't change the fundamental similarities between emission taxes and tradable permit systems.

SELF-TEST

1. Why is it likely that tradable pollution permits will eliminate a given level of pollution at lower cost than a command-and-control system which mandates that each polluter eliminate the same amount of pollution?

2. Emission taxes and tradable pollution permits create different kinds of uncertainty. Explain.

3. Under both emission taxes and tradable pollution permits, polluters must pay to pollute. Explain.

17-4 PUBLIC GOODS: EXCLUDABLE AND NONEXCLUDABLE

Many economists maintain that the market fails to produce nonexcludable public goods. In this section, we discuss public goods in general and nonexcludable public goods in particular.

17-4a Goods

Economists talk about two kinds of goods: private and public. A *private good* is a good whose consumption by one person reduces its consumption for another person. For example, a sweater, an apple, and a computer are all private goods. If one person is wearing a sweater, another person cannot wear (consume) it. If one person takes a bite of an apple, there is less apple for someone else to consume. If someone is using a computer, someone else can't use it. A private good is said to be **rivalrous in consumption**.

A **public good**, in contrast, is a good whose consumption by one person does not reduce its consumption by another. For example, a movie in a movie theater is a public good. If there are 200 seats in the theater, then 200 people can see the movie at the same time and no one person's viewing of it detracts from another's. An economics lecture is also a public good. If there are

Rivalrous in Consumption
Said of a good whose consumption by one person reduces its consumption by others.

Public Good
A good whose consumption by one person does not reduce its consumption by another person—that is, it is nonrivalrous in consumption.

Nonrivalrous in Consumption
Said of a good whose consumption by one person does not reduce its consumption by others.

Excludable
A characteristic of a good whereby it is possible or not prohibitively costly to exclude someone from receiving the benefits of the good after it has been produced.

Nonexcludable
A characteristic of a good whereby it is impossible or prohibitively costly to exclude someone from receiving the benefits of the good after it has been produced.

30 seats in the classroom, then 30 people can consume the economics lecture at the same time and one person's consumption does not detract from any other's. The chief characteristic of a public good is that it is **nonrivalrous in consumption**, which means that its consumption by one person does not reduce its consumption by others.

All public goods are nonrivalrous in consumption, but they are not all the same. Some public goods are **excludable** and some are nonexcludable. A public good is excludable if it is possible, or not prohibitively costly, to exclude someone from obtaining the benefits of it after it has been produced. For example, a movie in a movie theater is excludable in that persons who do not pay for admission can be excluded from seeing it. The same holds for an economics lecture. Someone who does not pay the tuition to attend the lecture can be excluded from consuming it. So both movies in movie theaters and economics lectures in classrooms are *excludable public goods*.

A public good is **nonexcludable** if it is impossible, or prohibitively costly, to exclude someone from obtaining the benefits of the good after it has been produced. National defense is a public good in that it is nonrivalrous in consumption. For example, if the U.S. national defense system is protecting people in New Jersey from incoming missiles, then it is automatically protecting people in New York as well. And just as important, protecting people in New Jersey does not reduce the degree of protection for the people in New York. Second, once national defense has been produced, excluding someone from consuming its services is impossible (or prohibitively costly). Thus, national defense is a *nonexcludable public good*. The same holds for flood control or large-scale pest control. After the dam has been built or the pest spray has been sprayed, excluding persons from benefiting from it is impossible.

17-4b The Free Rider

When a (private or public) good is excludable, individuals can obtain the benefits of it only if they pay for it. For example, no one can consume an apple (a private good) or a movie in a movie theater (a public good) without first paying for it. This is not the case with a nonexcludable public good, though. Individuals *can* obtain the benefits of a nonexcludable public good without paying for it. Persons who do so are referred to as **free riders**. Because of the so-called *free-rider problem*, most economists hold that the market will fail to produce nonexcludable public goods or at least fail to produce them at a desired level.

Free Rider
Anyone who receives the benefits of a good without paying for it.

To illustrate, consider someone contemplating the production of nonexcludable public good X, which, because it is a public good, is also nonrivalrous in consumption. After good X has been produced and provided to one person, others have no incentive to pay for it (even if they demand it), because they can receive all of its benefits without paying. No one is likely to supply a good that people can consume without paying for it. The market, it is argued, will not produce nonexcludable public goods. The door is then opened to government involvement in the production of nonexcludable public goods. Many argue that, if the market will not produce nonexcludable public goods, even though they are demanded, then the government must.

The free-rider argument is the basis for accepting government's (the public's, or taxpayers') provision of nonexcludable public goods. However, a nonexcludable public good is not the same as a government-provided good. A nonexcludable public good is a good that is nonrivalrous in consumption and nonexcludable. A government-provided good is self-defined: a good that government provides. In some instances, a government-provided good is a nonexcludable public good, such as national defense. However, it need not be: The government furnishes mail delivery and education, two goods that are also provided privately but are excludable and thus not subject to free riding.

Does It Matter to You . . .
If There Is a Free-Rider Problem?

Does it matter to you if there is a free-rider problem? As we know, a free-rider problem exists if individuals receive benefits from consuming a good without paying anything for the benefits they receive. The person who receives the benefits of a dam (less flooding), of national defense (security), or mosquito abatement (fewer mosquito bites or, in some cases, less disease) without paying something for these services is a free rider.

But, of course, if free riders exist, then benefits like the dam, national defense, or mosquito abatement would not be provided. That *is* the free-rider problem: because of free riders, certain goods that people may demand will not be provided.

No private company is going to produce a dam, and then, afterward, ask people who benefit from the dam to pay for it. This is because the company knows that once the dam is produced, no one is likely to pay anything for it because it can't be taken away from anyone.

Why, then, doesn't the private company ask people who are likely to benefit from the dam to pay for it before building the dam? Why not

say, "We are thinking about building a dam. If the dam is built, you will certainly benefit from it. So, we are asking that you pay something for the dam now, before we build it. If you and others who will benefit from the dam choose not to pay for the dam before it is built, then we won't build it, and you will not receive any benefits from the dam. Your choice."

This strategy could work, but it is probably unlikely to. This is because each person who would benefit from the dam could think that if he or she doesn't pay, and others do, the dam will still be built. To illustrate, suppose there are 20,000 people who could benefit from the dam being built. What if each one of the 20,000 people thinks that his or her contribution to building the dam is so small that it doesn't really matter if he or she contributes or not? Then no one would pay for the dam. Thus, the monetary payments are not forthcoming and the dam doesn't get built.

We return to our question: Does it matter to you if the free-rider problem exists? It could very well matter to you if you have a demand for a good that doesn't get provided because of the free-rider problem.

17-4c Nonexcludable Versus Nonrivalrous

The reason the market fails to produce a demanded good only when the good is nonexcludable is that the free-rider problem arises only if the good is nonexcludable. The rivalry-versus-nonrivalry issue is not relevant to the issue of market failure; that is, a good can be rivalrous or nonrivalrous in consumption and still be produced by the market. For example, a movie may be nonrivalrous in consumption but excludable too. And the market has no problem producing movies and movie theaters. The free-rider problem occurs only with goods that are nonexcludable.

The lighthouse makes for a good metaphor. For a long time, a lighthouse was thought to have the two characteristics of a nonexcludable public good: (1) It is nonrivalrous in consumption; any ship can use the light from the lighthouse, and one ship's use of it does not detract from another's. (2) It is nonexcludable; excluding any nonpaying ships from using the light is difficult. The lighthouse seemed to be a perfect good for government provision.

However, economist Ronald Coase found that in the eighteenth and early nineteenth centuries many lighthouses were privately owned; the market had not failed to provide lighthouses. Economists were left to conclude either that the market could provide nonexcludable public goods or that the lighthouse was not a nonexcludable public good, as had been thought. Closer examination showed that, although the lighthouse was nonrivalrous in consumption (it was a public good), the costs of excluding others from using it were fairly low (so it was an excludable public good). Lighthouse owners knew that usually only one ship was near the lighthouse at a time and that they could turn off the light if a ship did not fly the flag of a paying vessel.

ECONOMICS 24/7

"They Paved Paradise and Put Up a Parking Lot"

Don't it always seem to go
That you don't know what you've got
'Til it's gone,
They paved paradise
And put up a parking lot

From *Big Yellow Taxi* by Joni Mitchell

Andrey Khrolenok/Shutterstock.com

Suppose Smith owns 5 acres of land in the middle of a large city. One day, he is contacted by a man who wants to buy the land for $5 million. Smith asks the person what he plans to do with the land; the man says he represents a company that wants to "put up a parking lot." Smith is seriously thinking about selling the land to the man.

In time, the people who live and work in the area find out that Smith is contemplating selling the land to someone who wants to put up a parking lot. They urge Smith not to sell. They say that they like looking at Smith's land the way it is: natural and green. They tell Smith that his land is a green space in the city and that thousands of people enjoy passing by it every day. Smith tells the people that he is happy about that, but that he needs to pay his bills, so he has to sell the land. Smith tells the people that they can buy the land themselves if they want to—assuming that they are willing and able to pay $5 million for it.

So, of two groups of people, the first is represented by the man who wants to buy the land to put up a parking lot. This group includes the buyer, the company he represents, and all the people who would like to park their cars at the parking lot. Smith's land has a certain value to these people. Call these people "group P" (for "parking lot").

The second group consists of the people who benefit from the land in its natural state. These might be the people who live or work by Smith's land or who pass by it regularly. They like seeing the land in its natural state, especially because so few green places are left in the city. We'll call these people "group G" (for "green").

Which group, P or G, values the land more? There are three possibilities: (1) group P values the land more than group G, (2) group G values the land more than group P, and (3) each group values the land as much as the other.

So far, we know that group P values the land at (at least) $5 million, because this price is what they have agreed to pay for it. Suppose that group G values the land at $8 million. Group G, however,

is probably not as able to express how much they value the land as group P is. The members of group G face high transaction costs to find out how much each values the land and would be willing to pay to keep the land in its natural state. In contrast, the company that wants to put up a parking lot on the land can figure out relatively easily what persons are likely to pay for parking in the city. Other parking lots in the city are already charging *x* dollars per hour for parking.

Also, the land in its natural state is a nonexcludable public good. Everyone in the area around the land can see it, enjoy it, walk near it, and so on. If these people are asked to donate money to buy it so that it can stay in its natural state, many are likely to assume the role of free riders.

So, the combination of high transaction costs and the likelihood of free riders is a difficult problem to overcome. In other words, the $8 million value that group G places on the land might never be realized. And if isn't realized, then group G is not going to be able to bid for the land against group P.

Of course, things could be different. Maybe group P values the land much more than group G does, but that isn't the point. *Even if* group G values the land more than group P, group G might find it harder to express their greater value for the land than group P does. The "$8 million value of the land" is never heard, but the "$5 million value" is heard loud and clear in the form of a specific dollar offer to purchase. Not hearing the $8 million bid then leads Smith to believe that the high bid is $5 million. In this case, putting up a parking lot is really not the most valuable thing to do with the land.

1. Why does the market fail to produce nonexcludable public goods?

2. Identify each of the following goods as a nonexcludable public good, an excludable public good, or a private good:

   a. A composition notebook used for writing

   b. A Shakespearean play performed in a summer theater

   c. An apple

   d. A telephone in service

   e. Sunshine

3. Give an example, other than a movie in a movie theater or a play in a theater, of a good that is nonrivalrous and excludable.

17-5   ASYMMETRIC INFORMATION

In market failure, the market does not provide the efficient or optimal amount of a good. This chapter has shown that both externalities and nonexcludable public goods can lead to market failure. Specifically, in the presence of externalities, the market output is different from the socially optimal output. (In the case of negative externalities, the market produces too much; in the case of positive externalities, the market produces too little.) In the case of nonexcludable public goods, some economists maintain that the market produces zero output. Assuming that there is a demand for the nonexcludable public good, zero output is definitely too little.

This section looks at another possible cause of market failure: asymmetric information. **Asymmetric information** is information that either the buyer or the seller in a market exchange has and that the other does not have. In other words, some information is hidden. For example, the seller of a house may have information about the house that the buyer does not have, such as that the roof leaks during heavy rainfall.

Analyzing the effects of asymmetric information is similar to analyzing externalities—with one important difference: Externalities involve buyers, sellers, and third parties. The discussion that follows considers only buyers and sellers.

Asymmetric Information
Information that either the buyer or the seller in a market exchange has and that the other does not have.

17-5a   Asymmetric Information in a Product Market

In the discussion of externalities, the demand for a good represents marginal private benefits and the supply of a good represents marginal private costs. This is also the case for the asymmetric information situation shown in Exhibit 7; that is, the demand curve D_1 represents marginal private benefits (MPB), and the supply curve, S_1, represents marginal private costs (MPC). In the exhibit, D_1 and S_1 are the relevant curves when the seller has some information that the buyer does not have. Therefore, Q_1 is the market output when there is asymmetric information.

Suppose the buyer acquires the information that she previously did not have (but that the seller did have). With the new information, the buyer concludes that purchasing this particular good does not seem as appealing. The information she has acquired causes the buyer to lower her demand for the good. The relevant demand curve is now D_2. With symmetric information, the market output will be Q_2, which is less than Q_1.

As an example, the suppliers of cigarettes know that cigarette consumption can cause cancer but do not release that information to potential buyers. Under this condition, suppliers of cigarettes have certain information about cigarettes that buyers don't have; there is asymmetric information. If buyers do not have this information, the demand for cigarettes may be higher than it would be if buyers had it. In Exhibit 7, demand is D_1 instead of D_2. So, more cigarettes will be purchased and consumed (Q_1) when there is asymmetric information than when there is symmetric information (Q_2).

EXHIBIT 7

Asymmetric Information in a Product Market

Initially, the seller has some information that the buyer does not have; there is asymmetric information. As a result, D_1 represents the demand for the good and Q_1 is the equilibrium quantity. Then the buyer acquires the information that she did not have earlier, and there is symmetric information. The information causes the buyer to lower her demand for the good, so D_2 is now the relevant demand curve and Q_2 is the equilibrium quantity. Conclusion: Fewer units of the good are bought and sold when there is symmetric information than when there is asymmetric information.

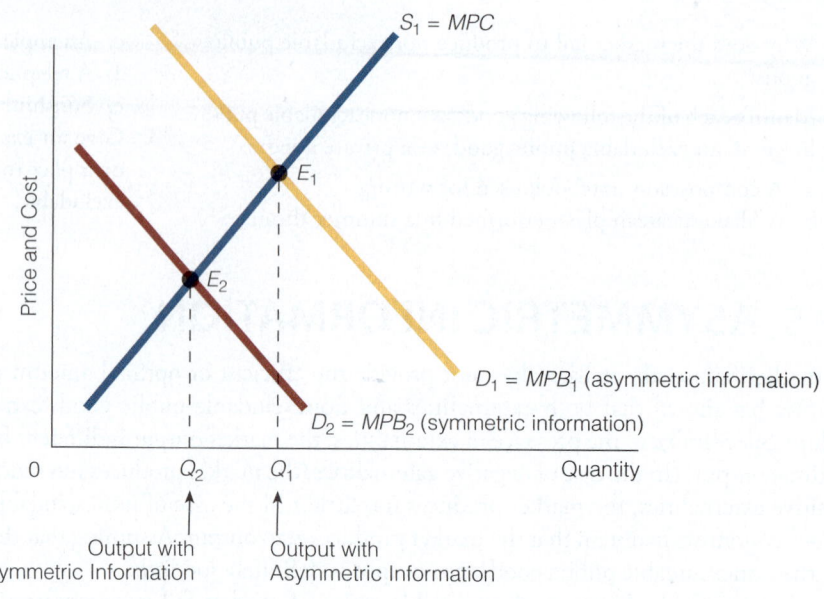

17-5b Asymmetric Information in a Factor Market

Suppose that, in a resource or factor market, such as the labor market shown in Exhibit 8, the buyer has information that the seller does not have. The employing firm knows that its workers will be using a possibly toxic substance that may cause health problems in 20–30 years. Further, the company does not release this information to workers but hides it from them. Without this information, the supply curve of labor is represented by S_1 and the quantity of labor will be Q_1 at a wage rate of W_1. With the information, though, not as many people will be willing to work at the firm at the current wage. The supply curve of labor will shift left to S_2. The new equilibrium position shows that the quantity of labor falls to Q_2 and the wage rate rises to W_2.

17-5c Is There Market Failure?

Does asymmetric information cause markets to fail? In other words, does it create a situation in which the market does not provide the optimal output of a particular good? Certainly, in our examples, the output level of a good and the quantity of labor were lower with symmetric information than with asymmetric information. Stated differently, asymmetric information seemingly resulted in too much or too many of something—either too much of a good being consumed or too many workers employed at a particular firm.

Some people argue that asymmetric information exists in nearly all exchanges. Rarely do buyers and sellers have the same information; each usually knows something the other doesn't. However, this argument misses the point, which is whether the asymmetric information fundamentally changes the outcome from what it would be if there were symmetric information. For example, the argument goes, a seller may know something that a buyer doesn't know, but even if the buyer knew what the seller knows, the outcome would be the same.

To illustrate, suppose a person buys a medication to relieve a severe headache. The person does not know that one side effect of the medication is sleepiness. In this case, asymmetric information may

EXHIBIT 8

Asymmetric Information in a Factor Market

Initially, the buyer (of the factor labor), or the firm, has some information that the seller (of the factor) does not have; there is asymmetric information. Consequently, S_1 is the relevant supply curve, W_1 is the equilibrium wage, and Q_1 is the equilibrium quantity of labor. Then, sellers acquire information that they did not have earlier, and there is symmetric information. The information causes the sellers to reduce their supply of the factor, and now S_2 is the relevant supply curve, W_2 is the equilibrium wage, and Q_2 is the equilibrium quantity of labor. Conclusion: Fewer factor units are bought and sold, and wages are higher, when there is symmetric information than when there is asymmetric information.

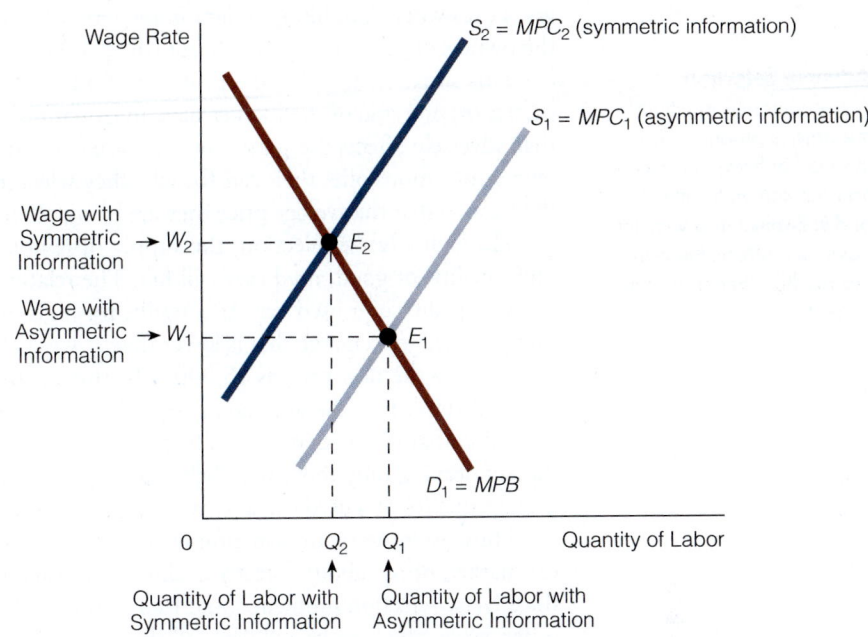

not matter. Possibly, the buyer would not have changed her behavior even if she had known that the medication caused sleepiness. So there is asymmetric information, but it may not change the outcome.

In another setting, however, the result may be different. Suppose the seller of a used car knows that the car is a lemon but the buyer doesn't know. The person buys the car because he doesn't have the information the seller has. Asymmetric information matters here in that the buyer would not have bought the car—or would not have bought the car at a given price—had he known what the seller knew. In this setting, asymmetric information changes the outcome.

Therefore, although the presence of asymmetric information does not guarantee that the market fails, if the asymmetric information brings about a different outcome than if there were symmetric information, then the case for market failure can be made.

17-5d Adverse Selection

Some economists argue that, under certain conditions, information problems can eliminate markets (i.e., create *missing markets*) or change the composition of markets (i.e., bring about *incomplete markets*). In the used-car market of our previous example,[4] sellers know more than buyers about the cars they are offering to sell; there is asymmetric information. For example, a seller knows whether the car requires a lot of maintenance. Because most buyers find it difficult to tell the difference between good used cars and lemons, suppose that a single used-car price that reflects both lemons and good cars emerges for a given model, make, and year of car.

Suppose this price is $10,000. Then, on the one hand, an owner of a lemon will think that that is a good price because she will receive an average price for a below-average car that she is selling.

---

4. The material that follows is based on the classic article by George Akerlof, "The Market for Lemons," *Quarterly Journal of Economics* (August 1970): 488–500.

But on the other hand, a person who owns an above-average car will find that price too low; he won't want to sell his car for an average price. So, as a result of lemon owners' liking the price and good car owners' not liking it, lemon owners will offer their cars for sale (the price is great), and the owners of good used cars will not (the price is too low).

Adverse Selection

A phenomenon in which the parties on one side of the market have information not known to others and self-select in a way that adversely affects the parties on the other side of the market.

This situation is called the problem of adverse selection. **Adverse selection** exists when the parties on one side of the market have information not known to others and self-select in a way that adversely affects the parties on the other side of the market. In the example presented, the owners of lemons offer their cars for sale; they select to sell their cars because they know (and only they know) that the average price they are being offered for their below-average cars is a good deal.

Through adverse selection, the supply of lemons on the market will rise and the supply of high-quality, or good, used cars will fall. The relatively greater number of lemons will lower the average quality of a used car. As a result, for a given make, model, and year of used car, a new average price will emerge that is lower than it was before.

Let's say the new price is $8,000. The process then repeats itself: People with above-average cars will think that the average price of $8,000 is too low, and people with below-average cars will think that it is a good price. The people with above-average cars will drop out of the used car market, leaving only those with below-average used cars. Again, this will lead to a decline in the average quality of a used car, and eventually the average price of a used car will drop once more.

Thus, asymmetric information leads to adverse selection, which, in the example of the used-car market, brings about a steady decline in the quality of used cars offered for sale. Theoretically, the adverse selection problem could lead to the total elimination of the good used-car market. In other words, the lemons will drive all the good cars out of the market.

Still, this type of ultimate adverse selection would not happen in the used-car market, for several possible reasons. For example, a buyer could hire his own mechanic to check the car he is thinking about buying. By doing so, he would acquire almost as much, if not as much, information about the car as the seller has. Thus, there would no longer be asymmetric information. Or the seller of a high-quality used car could offer a warranty on her car. Essentially, she could offer to fix any problems with the used car for a certain length of time after she sells it. The warranty offer would likely increase both the demand for the car and its price. (Owners of lemons would not be likely to offer warranties, so their cars would sell for less than cars with warranties.)

In some cases, government has played a role in dealing with adverse selection problems. State governments can pass, and in some situations have passed, lemon laws, stating that car dealers must take back any defective cars. In addition, many states now require car dealers to openly state whether a used car is offered with a warranty or as is.

17-5e Moral Hazard

In the preceding used-car example illustrating adverse selection, asymmetric information existed *prior* to an exchange. Before dollars changed hands, the seller of the used car had information about the car that the potential buyer did not have.

Moral Hazard

A condition that exists when one party to a transaction changes his or her behavior in a way that is hidden from and costly to the other party.

Asymmetric information can also exist *after* a transaction has been made. If it does, it can cause a moral hazard problem. **Moral hazard** occurs when one party to a transaction changes his behavior in a way that is hidden from, and costly to, the other party. For example, suppose Smith buys a health insurance policy. After she has the insurance, she may be less careful to maintain good health because the cost to her of future health problems is not as high as it would have been without the insurance. Smith does not set out to make herself ill so that she can collect on the insurance, but her incentive to be as careful about her health and physical well-being is not as strong as it once was. As another example, a person with automobile collision insurance may be more likely to drive on an icy road in December in Minneapolis than if he didn't have the insurance. Or a person who has earthquake insurance may be more likely to forget to do a few things that will minimize damage during an earthquake, such as attaching bookcases to the walls. In these examples, the moral hazard problem causes people to take too few precautionary actions.

Insurance companies try to control for moral hazard in different ways. One way is by specifying certain precautions that an insured person must take. For example, a company that insures your house from fire may require you to have smoke detectors and a fire extinguisher. The insurance company may also set a deductible so that you pay part of the loss in case of a fire, thereby increasing your cost in the event of a fire and providing you with an added incentive to be careful.

ECONOMICS 24/7

Arriving Late to Class, Grading on a Curve, and Studying Together for the Midterm

A series of young children's books titled *Where's Waldo?* present the character Waldo drawn among hundreds of people and things. Although the objective, finding Waldo, may seem easy, finding him is roughly similar to finding a needle in a haystack. If you look long and hard, you'll eventually find him; if you simply glance at the page, you won't.

Finding economics is like finding Waldo. If you simply glance at your daily life, you will miss the economics; if you look long and hard, you will often find it. With this idea in mind, consider your life as a college student. On a typical day, you walk into a college classroom, sit down, listen to a lecture and take notes, enter into discussions, ask questions, answer questions, and then leave. Can you find the economics in this daily experience? Following are some places you might find economics lurking.

Lucky Business/Shutterstock.com

Arriving Late to Class

Class started five minutes ago. You are sitting at your desk, listening to the professor and taking notes. The professor is discussing an unusually challenging topic today, and you are listening attentively. Then the classroom door opens. You turn at the sound and see two of your classmates arriving late to class. For a few seconds, your attention is diverted from the lecture. When you refocus your attention on the professor, you realize that you have missed an essential point and you become mildly frustrated.

This scenario illustrates a negative externality. Your two classmates undertook an action—arriving late—and you incurred a cost because of their action. Your two classmates considered only their private benefits and costs of arriving late to class. They did not consider your cost—the external cost—of their action.

To get students to internalize the cost to others of their being late, the professor could try to persuade students not to be late. She

could say that lateness imposes a cost on those who arrive on time and who are listening attentively to the lecture. Alternatively, the professor could impose a corrective tax on tardy students. In other words, she could set a tax equal to the external cost, perhaps taking one-half to one point off a student's test grade for each lateness.

Grading on a Curve

Alex is currently taking a sociology course. He would like to get an A or a B in the class but believes that he is likely to receive a C or a D. Alex's situation is similar to that of a person who would like to be healthy every day for the rest of his life but who knows that he probably won't be. When a person knows that he probably won't be healthy for his entire life, he buys health insurance. And, as explained in this chapter, after a person purchases health insurance, a moral hazard problem may arise: The person may not have so strong an incentive to remain healthy when he has health insurance as when he doesn't.

Would Alex react the same way if he could buy grade insurance? Suppose his sociology professor promises Alex that she will grade on a curve and that no one in the class will receive a grade lower than a C. With this assurance from his professor, will Alex have as strong an incentive to work hard to learn sociology? Does a moral hazard now arise? An economist is likely to answer no to the first question and yes to the second.

Studying Together for the Midterm

Students usually study together if they think that doing so will be mutually beneficial. That is, when two people agree to study together (say, for a midterm), they are usually entering into an exchange: "I will help you learn more of the material so that you can get a better grade, if you do the same for me."

Consider two types of colleges: (1) a dormitory-based college in which many of the students live on campus in dormitories and (2) a commuter college in which the entire student body lives off campus. Students tend to study together more on dormitory-based campuses than on commuter campuses because the transaction costs of studying together—of entering into the exchange—are lower on a dormitory-based campus. If you live in a dormitory on campus, you incur relatively low transaction costs by studying with someone who also lives on campus (maybe a person living down the hall from you). But if everyone lives off campus, you incur relatively high transaction costs by studying with a fellow student. One of you has to drive to the other's house or apartment, or you have to meet at a local coffee bar.

SELF-TEST

1. Give an example that illustrates how asymmetric information can lead to more of a good being consumed than if there is symmetric information.

2. Adverse selection has the potential to eliminate some markets. How so?

3. Give an example of moral hazard that is not used in the text.

OFFICE HOURS

"Doesn't It Seem Wrong to Let Some Business Firms Pay to Pollute?"

STUDENT: In our discussion, I know that pollution permits proved to be less costly at reducing pollution than setting pollution standards, but letting a business firm get away with polluting if it can pay enough money seems wrong. It seems as if it is paying to do something wrong.

INSTRUCTOR: There's a different way to look at things. The firm is not paying to pollute; instead, it is paying to have some other business firm reduce *its* pollution. Suppose firm A can eliminate its pollution at a lower cost than firm B can. Firm B now pays firm A to eliminate its own (firm A's) pollution. Instead of saying that firm B is "paying to pollute," why not say that "firm B is paying firm A not to pollute."

STUDENT: Putting it that way makes firm B sound like the good guy—the firm that pays other firms not to pollute.

INSTRUCTOR: My point is that you cast firm B as the bad guy—the firm that pays to pollute. What I did was simply bring out another aspect of what is happening. Firm B *pays firm A not to pollute* (that is my part of the story) so that, in turn, *it can pollute* (that is your part of the story). Also, keep in mind that at the end of the process, pollution is reduced, not increased. Instead of having the pollution from firms A and B, we have less (or no) pollution from firm A and perhaps the same amount of pollution from firm B.

STUDENT: I see your point, but wouldn't it still be fairer if no money changed hands and both firms A and B were told that they had to eliminate *x* amount of pollution? In other words, wouldn't it be fairer to treat each firm the same way?

INSTRUCTOR: Let's divide the world up into the two firms, A and B, and everyone else. Now, as far as A and B are concerned, each of these two firms would prefer a system of pollution permits to a system of standards. We know this because a pollution permits program can always be turned into a command and control program if doing so is preferable to buying and selling permits. To illustrate, suppose firms A and B are each emitting 3 units of pollution. Government now gives each firm 1 pollution permit, allowing it to emit 1 unit of pollution. If neither firm buys or sells its 1 permit, then what we essentially have is a standards system for eliminating (some) pollution. Each firm reduces its pollution from 3 units to 1 unit. End of story. But if the two firms start trading permits for money, we can conclude that each firm is better off with a pollution permits system than with a standards system. And this is what we usually see: firms buying and selling permits.

STUDENT: So the point is that firms A and B prefer a pollution permits system to a standards system?

INSTRUCTOR: Yes. But now we are left with what we call an "everyone else": Is everyone else better off with a pollution permits system than with a standards system? The answer is yes, because it is less costly to eliminate a given amount of pollution with a pollution permits system than with standards. "Less costly" here means "fewer resources used." If fewer resources are used to eliminate pollution, then more resources are left over for other things. As a member of the Everyone Else Group, I am better off with more resources left over, than with fewer resources, to produce things that I want to buy.

So, let's now return to your original question: Wouldn't it be fairer if no money changed hands and both firms A and B were told that they had to eliminate *x* amount of pollution? To whom would that be fairer? It's not fairer to firms A and B, because they prefer pollution permits to standards. And it's not really fairer to everyone else, because we suspect that everyone else prefers to have more instead of fewer resources left over after *x* amount of pollution has been emitted.

Points to Remember

1. Saying that "firms are paying to pollute" leaves out some of what is happening with a pollution permits system. Some firms are paying other firms not to pollute so that they can pollute. Firm B is paying firm A to not pollute so that it (firm B) can pollute.

2. Pollution permits (that can be bought and sold) can eliminate a given amount of pollution with a lower resource cost than can a command and control system.

CHAPTER SUMMARY

EXTERNALITIES

- An externality is a side effect of an action that affects the well-being of third parties. There are two types of externalities: negative and positive. A negative externality exists when an individual's or group's actions impose a cost (an adverse side effect) on others. A positive externality exists when an individual's or group's actions cause a benefit (a beneficial side effect) for others.

- When either negative or positive externalities exist, the market output is different from the socially optimal output. In the case of a negative externality, the market is said to overproduce the good connected with the negative externality. (The socially optimal output is less than the market output; see Exhibit 1.) In the case of a positive externality, the market is said to underproduce the good connected with the positive externality. (The socially optimal output is greater than the market output; see Exhibit 3.)

- Negative and positive externalities can be internalized, or adjusted for, in a number of different ways, including persuasion, the assignment of property rights, voluntary agreements, and taxes and subsidies. Also, regulations may be used to adjust for externalities directly.

THE COASE THEOREM

- The Coase theorem is the proposition that private negotiations between people will lead to an efficient resolution of externalities, as long as property rights are well defined and transaction costs are trivial or zero. The Coase theorem is significant for two reasons: (1) It shows that, under certain conditions, the market can internalize externalities. (2) It provides a benchmark for analyzing externality problems; that is, it shows what would happen if transaction costs are trivial or zero.

THE ENVIRONMENT

- Under government regulation, or command and control, government might specify a certain type of pollution control technology to be utilized by polluters or simply set a quantitative goal that is applied to polluters with respect to emitting pollution.

- Generally, economists do not favor command-and-control policies as a means of reducing pollution. One reason is that mandating certain technologies to be used reduces the incentive to discover new, lower cost methods of reducing pollution. Another reason is that it is often costlier to eliminate a given quantity of pollution by mandating that each polluter eliminate the same amount of pollution than by implementing emission taxes or tradable pollution permits.

- Under an emission tax, the tax is set and then the quantity demanded of pollution is determined by the demand for pollution.

- Under tradable pollution permits, government sets the quantity of pollution that is permissible and then issues or auctions off pollution permits that can be bought and sold.

- Emission taxes and tradable pollution permits end up creating different kinds of uncertainty. Under an emission tax, polluters know what price they have to pay to pollute but government doesn't know how much pollution will be generated. Under a tradable pollution permits system (cap and trade), government knows the amount of pollution but polluters don't immediately know what the price to pollute will be.

PUBLIC GOODS

- A public good is a good characterized by nonrivalry in consumption.

- A public good can be excludable or nonexcludable. Excludable public goods are goods that, while nonrivalrous in consumption, can be denied to people if they do not pay for them. Nonexcludable public goods are goods that are nonrivalrous in consumption and cannot be denied to people who do not pay for them.

- The market is said to fail in the provision of nonexcludable public goods because of the free-rider problem; that is, a supplier of the good is not able to extract payment for the good because its benefits can be received without payment.

ASYMMETRIC INFORMATION

- Asymmetric information exists when either the buyer or the seller in a market exchange has some information that the other does not have. Outcomes based on asymmetric information may be different from outcomes based on symmetric information.

- Adverse selection exists when the parties on one side of the market have information not known to others and self-select in a way that adversely affects the parties on the other side of the market. Adverse selection can lead to missing or incomplete markets.

- Moral hazard occurs when one party to a transaction changes his or her behavior in a way that is hidden from, and costly to, the other party.

KEY TERMS AND CONCEPTS

Market Failure	Marginal Social Benefits	Rivalrous in Consumption	Free Rider
Externality	(*MSB*)	Public Good	Asymmetric Information
Negative Externality	Socially Optimal Amount	Nonrivalrous in	Adverse Selection
Positive Externality	(Output)	Consumption	Moral Hazard
Marginal Social Costs	Internalizing Externalities	Excludable	
(*MSC*)	Coase Theorem	Nonexcludable	

QUESTIONS AND PROBLEMS

1. Under what condition will $MSC = MPC$? When will $MSB = MPB$?

2. Suppose there is a negative externality. If a tax is used to correct for the negative externality, what condition must be satisfied? What must the tax equal?

3. Explain why the shaded triangle in Exhibit 3 is representative of a market failure.

4. When will asymmetric information in a product market not cause market failure?

5. Give an example that illustrates the difference between private costs and social costs.

6. Consider two types of divorce laws. Law A allows either the husband or the wife to obtain a divorce without the other person's consent. Law B permits a divorce only if both parties agree to it. Will there be more divorces under law A or law B, or will there be the same number of divorces under both laws? Why?

7. People have a demand for sweaters, and the market provides sweaters. There is evidence that people also have a demand for national defense, but the market does not provide it. Why doesn't the market provide national defense? Is it because government is providing national defense and therefore there is no need for the market to do so? Or is it because the market can't provide it?

8. Identify three activities that generate negative externalities and three activities that generate positive externalities. Explain why each activity you identified generates the type of externality you specified.

9. Give an example of each of the following:

   a. A good that is rivalrous in consumption and is excludable.

   b. A good that is nonrivalrous in consumption and is excludable.

   c. A good that is rivalrous in consumption and is nonexcludable.

   d. A good that is nonrivalrous in consumption and is nonexcludable.

10. Some individuals argue that, with increased population growth, negative externalities will become more common and that there will be more instances of market failure and more need for government to solve externality problems. Other individuals believe that, as time passes, technological advances will be used to solve negative externality problems and that there will be fewer instances of market failure and less need for government to deal with externality problems. What do you believe will happen? Give reasons to support your position.

11. Name at least five government-provided goods that are excludable public goods.

12. There is a view that life is one big externality: Just about everything someone does affects someone else either positively or negatively. To permit government to deal with externality problems is to permit government to tamper with everything in life. No clear line divides externalities in which government should become involved from those it should not. Do you support this position? Why or why not?

13. Economists sometimes shock noneconomists by stating that they do not favor the complete elimination of pollution. Explain the rationale for this position.

14. Explain how both an emission tax and a tradable pollution permits system can reduce pollution.

15. Identify each of the following as an adverse selection or a moral hazard problem:

   a. A person with car insurance fails to lock his car doors when he shops at a mall.

   b. A person with a family history of cancer purchases the most complete health coverage available.

   c. A person with health insurance takes more risks on the ski slopes of Aspen than he would without health insurance.

   d. A college professor receives tenure (assurance of permanent employment) from her employer.

   e. A patient pays his surgeon before she performs the surgery.

WORKING WITH NUMBERS AND GRAPHS

1. Graphically portray the following:

   a. A negative externality
   b. A positive externality

2. Graphically represent the following:

   a. A corrective tax that achieves the socially optimal output
   b. A corrective tax that moves the market output farther away from the socially optimal output than was the case before the tax was applied

3. Using the following data, prove that pollution permits that can be bought and sold can reduce pollution from 12 tons to 6 tons at a lower cost than a regulation which specifies that each of the three firms must cut its pollution in half.

	Firm X	Firm Y	Firm Z
Cost of eliminating:			
First ton of pollution	$200	$500	$1,000
Second ton of pollution	300	700	2,000
Third ton of pollution	400	800	2,900
Fourth ton of pollution	500	900	3,400

PUBLIC CHOICE AND SPECIAL-INTEREST GROUP POLITICS

REUTERS/Alamy Stock Photo

INTRODUCTION

Economics is a powerful analytical tool. As you have seen, it can be used to analyze how markets and the economy work. In this chapter, we use economics to analyze the behavior of politicians, voters, and members of special-interest groups. Specifically, we analyze **public choice**, the branch of economics in which economic principles and tools are applied to public sector decision making. Public choice is, in a sense, economics applied to politics.

18-1 PUBLIC CHOICE THEORY

Public choice theorists reject the notion that people are like Dr. Jekyll and Mr. Hyde—that is, that they exhibit greed and selfishness in their transactions in the private (market) sector and altruism and public spirit in their actions in the public sector. The same people who are the employers, employees, and consumers in the market sector are the politicians, bureaucrats, members of special-interest groups, and voters in the public sector. According to public choice theorists, people in the market sector and people in the public sector behave differently not because they have different motives (or are different types of people) but because the two sectors have different institutional arrangements.

As a simple example, Erin Bloom works for a private, profit-seeking firm that makes radio components. Erin is cost conscious, does her work on time, and generally works hard. She knows that she must exhibit this type of work behavior if she wants to keep her job, get a raise, and be promoted. Suppose now that Erin leaves her job at the radio components company and takes a job with the Department of Health and Human Services (HHS) in Washington, D.C. Public choice theorists maintain that Erin is the same person (with different motives), whether working for HHS or for the radio components company.

Public Choice
The branch of economics in which economic principles and tools are applied to public sector decision making.

437

However, even though Erin is the same person in and out of government, she will not necessarily exhibit the same work behavior. The costs and benefits of certain actions may be substantially different at HHS than at the radio components company. For example, perhaps the cost of being late for work is less in Erin's new job at HHS than it was at her old job. In her former job, she had to work overtime if she came in late; in her new job, her boss doesn't say anything. Erin is therefore more likely to be late in her new job than she was in her old one. She is simply responding to costs and benefits as they exist in her new work environment.

18-2   THE POLITICAL MARKET

Economists who practice positive economics want to understand their world. They want to understand not only the production and pricing of goods, unemployment, inflation, and the firm, but also political outcomes and political behavior. This section is an introduction to the political market.

18-2a   Moving Toward the Middle: The Median Voter Model

During political elections, voters often complain that the candidates for office are too much alike. Some find the similarities frustrating, saying they would prefer to have more choice. However, as you will see, two candidates running for the same office often sound alike because they are competing for votes.

In Exhibit 1, parts (a), (b), and (c) all show a normal distribution of voters in which the political spectrum goes from the far left to the far right. Relatively few voters hold positions in either of the two extreme wings. Assuming, then, that voters will vote for the candidate who comes closest to matching their ideological or political views, people whose views are in the far left of the political spectrum will vote for the candidate closest to the far left, and so on.

EXHIBIT 1

The Move Toward the Middle

Given the voter distribution shown here, political candidates tend to move toward the middle of the political spectrum. Starting with (a), the Republican receives more votes than the Democrat and would win the election if it were held today. To offset this advantage, as shown in (b), the Democrat moves inward toward the middle of the political spectrum. The Republican tries to offset the Democrat's movement inward by also moving inward. As a result, both candidates move toward the political middle, getting closer to each other over time, as shown in (c).

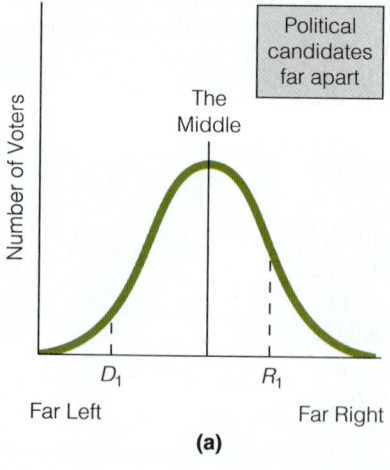

(a)

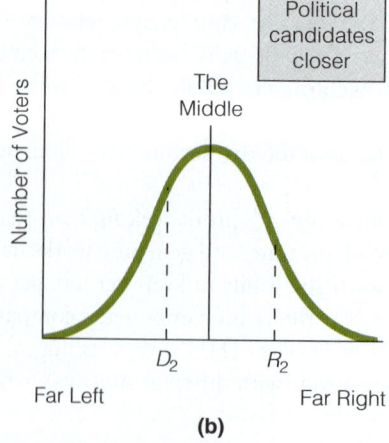

(b)

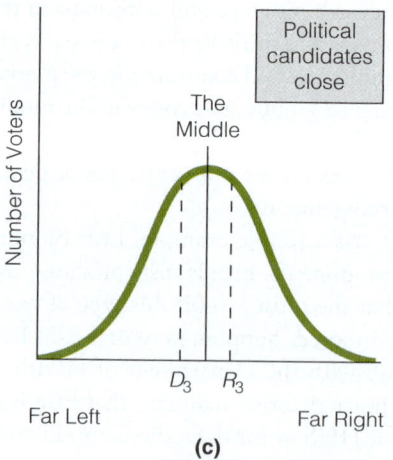

(c)

Our election process begins with two candidates, a Democrat and a Republican, occupying the positions D_1 and R_1 respectively, in part (a) of the exhibit. The Republican would receive all the votes of the voters who position themselves to the right of R_1, the Democrat would receive all the votes of the voters who position themselves to the left of D_1, and the voters between R_1 and D_1 would divide their votes between the two candidates. Thus, as shown, the Republican would receive more votes than the Democrat if the election were held today.

If, however, the election were not held today, the Democrat would likely notice (through polls and other sources) that her opponent was doing better than she was. To offset this advantage, she would move toward the center, or middle, of the political spectrum to pick up some votes. Part (b) in Exhibit 1 illustrates this move by the Democrat. Now voters to the left of D_2 would vote for the Democrat, voters to the right of R_2 would vote for the Republican, and the voters between the two positions would divide their votes between the two candidates. If the election were held at this time, the Democrat would win.

In part (c), each candidate, in an attempt to get more votes than his or her opponent, has moved closer to the middle. Thus, at election time, the two candidates are likely to be positioned side by side at the political center, or middle (D_3 and R_3).

The tendency of political candidates to move toward the center of the voter distribution—captured in the **median voter model**—is what causes many voters to complain that there is not much difference between candidates.

18-2b What Does the Theory Predict?

Although the median voter model explains why politicians running for the same office often sound alike, what does the model predict? Here are a few of the theory's predictions:

1. *Candidates will label their opponent as being either too far to the right or too far to the left.* The candidates know that whoever is closer to the middle of the political spectrum (in a two-person race) will win more votes and thus the election. Therefore, to win, they will move toward the political middle, at the same time saying that their opponent is a member of the political fringe (i.e., a person far from the center). A Democrat may argue that his Republican opponent is too conservative; a Republican may argue that her Democratic opponent is too liberal.

2. *Candidates will call themselves middle-of-the-roaders, not right- or left-wingers.* In their move toward the political middle, candidates will try to portray themselves as moderates. In their speeches, they will assert that they represent the majority of voters and that they are practical, not ideological. They will not be likely to refer to themselves as ultraliberal or ultraconservative or as right- or left-wingers because to do so would send a self-defeating message to the voters.

3. *Candidates will take polls, and, if they are not doing well in the polls and their opponents are, they will modify their positions to become more like their opponents.* Polls tell candidates who the likely winner of the election will be. A candidate who finds that she will lose the election (she is "down in the polls") is not likely to sit back and do nothing. The candidate will change her positions. Often, she will become more like the winner of the poll—that is, more like her political opponent.

4. *Candidates will speak in general, instead of specific, terms.* Voters agree more on ends than on the means of accomplishing those ends. For example, voters of the left, right, and middle believe that a strong economy is better than a weak economy. However, they do not all agree on the best way to make the economy strong. The person on the right might advocate less government intervention as one way, whereas the person on the left might advocate more government intervention. Most political candidates soon

Median Voter Model
A model suggesting that candidates in a two-person political race will attempt to match the preferences of the median voter.

learn that addressing the issues specifically requires them to discuss means and that doing so increases the probability of their having an extreme-wing label attached to them. For example, a candidate who advocates more government intervention in the economy is more likely to be labeled "too far left" than a candidate who simply calls for a stronger national economy without discussing any specific means. In the candidate's desire to be perceived as a middle-of-the-roader, he is much more likely to talk about ends, on which voters agree, than about means, on which voters disagree.

FINDING ECONOMICS

In a Presidential Election Debate During a presidential election debate, one candidate is asked what his plan is for health care in the country. He says that his plan would make health care more affordable and responsive to peoples' needs. He then goes on to say that health care has been a problem in the United States for a long time and that it is about time for a solution. Where is the economics?

The median voter model predicts that candidates will speak in general, not specific, terms. That is exactly what our hypothetical candidate has done. He did not get into any specifics about his plan. For example, he probably will not specifically address how much the health care plan will cost, whom it will serve, and so on.

THINKING LIKE AN ECONOMIST

Testing Theories An economist thinks about theories and then tests them. She is not content to accept a theory—such as the one which says that candidates in a two-person political race will gravitate toward the center of the political distribution—simply because it sounds right. The economist asks, "If the theory is right, what should I expect to see in the real world? If the theory is wrong, what should I expect to see in the real world?" Such questions direct the economist to look at effects to see whether the theory has explanatory and predictive power. If the four predictions of the median voter theory occur in the real world—candidates labeling themselves one way, speaking in general terms, and so on—then the economist can conclude that the evidence supports the theory. But if candidates en masse do not behave as the model predicts, then the economist must reject the theory.

ECONOMICS 24/7

A Simple-Majority Voting Rule: The Case of the Statue in the Public Square

Public questions are often decided by the simple-majority decision rule. Although most people think that this is the fair and democratic way to do things, in certain instances a simple majority vote leads to undertaking a project whose costs are greater than its benefits.

Consider a community of 10 people, whose names are listed in column 1 of Exhibit 2. The community is considering whether to

purchase a statue to put in the center of the public square. The cost of the statue is $1,000, and the community has previously agreed that if the statue is purchased, the 10 individuals will share the cost equally; that is, each will pay $100 in taxes (see column 3).

Column 2 shows the dollar value of the benefits that each individual will receive from the statue. For example, Applebaum places a dollar value of $150 on the statue, Browning places a dollar value of $140 on the statue, and so on. Column 4 notes the net benefit or net cost of the statue to each individual. A net benefit occurs if the dollar value an individual places on the statue is greater than the tax (cost) incurred. A net cost results if the reverse is true. Finally, column 5 indicates how each member of the community would vote. An individual who believes that the statue has a net benefit will vote for it, and an individual who believes that the statue has a net cost will vote against it. Thus, six individuals vote for the statue, and four individuals vote against it. The majority rules, and the statue is purchased and placed in the center of the public square.

However, the total dollar value of benefits to the community ($812) is less than the total tax cost to the community ($1,000).

Accordingly, using the simple-majority decision rule has resulted in the purchase of the statue even though the benefits of the statue to the community are less than its costs.

This outcome is not surprising when you understand that the simple-majority decision rule does not take into account the intensity of individuals' preferences. No matter how strongly a person feels about an issue, he or she registers only one vote. For example, even though Emerson places a net benefit of $1 on the statue and Isley places a net cost of $90 on the statue, each individual has only one vote. Isley has no way to register the fact that he does not want the statue more than Emerson wants it.

EXHIBIT 2

Simple-Majority Voting and Inefficiency

The simple-majority decision rule sometimes generates inefficient results. Here, a statue is purchased even though the total dollar value of the benefits of the statue is less than the total dollar costs.

(1) Individuals	(2) Dollar Value of Benefits to Individual	(3) Tax Levied on Individual	(4) Net Benefit or Net Cost	(5) Vote for or Against
Applebaum	$150	$100	+$50	For
Browning	140	100	+40	For
Carson	130	100	+30	For
Davidson	110	100	+10	For
Emerson	101	100	+1	For
Finley	101	100	+1	For
Gunter	50	100	−50	Against
Harris	10	100	−90	Against
Isley	10	100	−90	Against
Janowitz	10	100	−90	Against
Total	$812	$1,000		

18-3 VOTERS AND RATIONAL IGNORANCE

The preceding section explains something about the behavior of politicians, especially near or at election time. We turn now to voters.

18-3a The Costs and Benefits of Voting

Political commentators often remark that the voter turnout for this or that election was low: "Only 54 percent of registered voters actually voted." Are voter turnouts low because Americans are apathetic? Are they uninterested in political issues?

Public choice economists often explain low voter turnouts in terms of the costs and benefits of voting. As an example, Mark Quincy is thinking about voting in a presidential election. Mark may receive many benefits from voting: He may feel more involved in public affairs or think that he has met his civic responsibility. He may see himself as patriotic, or he may believe he has a greater right to criticize government if he takes an active part in it. In short, he may benefit by seeing himself as a doer instead of a talker. Ultimately, however, he will weigh these positive benefits against the costs of voting, which include driving to the polls, standing in line, and so on. If, in the end, Mark perceives the benefits of voting as greater than the costs, he will vote.

But suppose Mark believes that he receives only one benefit from voting: determining the outcome of the election. His benefits-of-voting equation may look like this:

$$\text{Mark's benefits of voting} = \text{Probability of Mark's vote determining the election outcome} \times$$
$$\text{Additional benefits Mark receives if his candidate wins}$$

Now, suppose two candidates, A and B, are running for office. If Mark votes, he will vote for A because he estimates that he benefits by $100 if A is elected but only by $40 if B is elected. The difference, $60, represents the additional benefits Mark receives if his candidate wins.

However, the probability that Mark's vote will determine the outcome is minuscule. With many potential voters, such as there are in a presidential election, the probability that one person's vote will determine the outcome is close to zero. To recognize this fact on an intuitive level, suppose A and B are the two major candidates in a presidential campaign. If you, as an individual voter, vote for A, the outcome of the election is likely to be the same as if you had voted for B or not voted at all. In other words, whether you vote at all, vote for A, or vote for B, the outcome is likely to be the same. In Mark's benefits-of-voting equation, $60 is multiplied by a probability so small that it might as well be 0. So, $60 times 0 is 0. In short, Mark receives no benefits from voting.

But Mark may face certain costs. His costs-of-voting equation may look like this:

$$\text{Mark's cost of voting} = \text{Cost of driving to the polls}$$
$$+ \text{Cost of standing in line}$$
$$+ \text{Cost of filling out the ballot}$$

Obviously, Mark faces some positive costs of voting. Because his benefits of voting are 0 and his costs of voting are positive, Mark makes the rational choice if he decides not to vote.

Clearly, not everyone behaves this way—that is, chooses not to vote. Many people do vote in elections. Probably what separates the Marks in the world from the people who vote is that the voters receive some benefits that Mark does not. They might receive benefits simply by being part of the excitement of election day, by doing what they perceive as their civic duty, or for some other reason.

The point public choice economists make is that, if many individual voters will vote only if they perceive their vote as making a difference, then they probably will not vote, because their vote is unlikely to make a difference. Thus, the low turnouts that appear to be a result of voter apathy may instead be a result of cost–benefit calculations.

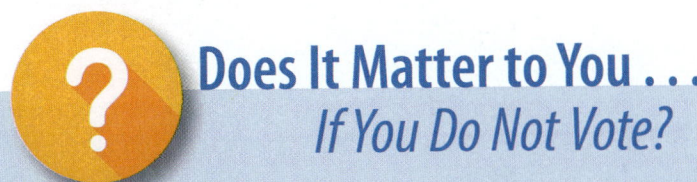

Does It Matter to You . . .
If You Do Not Vote?

Does it matter to you if you choose to vote or not in an election? That, of course, is a different question than asking if your vote determines the outcome of an election. To the second question, the answer is likely to be no: your vote does not determine the outcome of an election. Whether or not you voted in the last presidential election, the same person would have been elected president.

Even if you know that your one vote will not determine the outcome of an election, it still could matter to you if you vote or not. This is because you may get some sense of satisfaction if you vote and some sense of dissatisfaction if you do not vote. If you think that it is the right thing to vote, then it probably will matter to you

if you choose not to vote. Perhaps you will feel that you have done something wrong, or that you haven't met your obligation, duty, or responsibility to vote. This feeling could cause you some sense of uneasiness—some disutility.

Or perhaps, after many months of candidates campaigning for votes, you feel that your vote is like the period at the end of a sentence. It brings closure for you, and you feel that can't have closure unless you vote.

There is, of course, nothing wrong with feeling this way. If you vote—even if you know that your vote will not determine the election outcome—then you are doing so because, for whatever reason, you feel that it is better for you to vote than not vote.

18-3b Rational Ignorance

How often have you heard an opinion like this one? "Democracy would be better served if voters would take more of an interest in, and become better informed about, politics and government. Voters don't know much about the issues."

The problem, however, is not that voters are too stupid to learn about the issues. Many citizens who know little about politics and government are quite capable of learning about both, but they choose not to make the effort. The reason is perhaps predictable: The costs of becoming informed often outweigh the benefits. In short, many persons believe that becoming informed is simply not worth the effort. Hence, on an individual basis, it makes sense to be uninformed about politics and government—that is, to be in a state of **rational ignorance**.

As an example, Shonia Tyler has many things she can do with her leisure time. She could read a good novel, watch a television program, go out with friends, or become better informed about the candidates and the issues in the upcoming U.S. Senate race. Becoming informed, however, has costs. If Shonia stays home and reads about the issues, she can't go out with her friends. If she stays up late to watch a news program, she might be too tired to work efficiently the next day. These costs have to be weighed against the benefits of becoming better informed about the candidates and the issues. For Shonia, as for many people, the benefits are unlikely to be greater than the costs.

Many people see little personal benefit in becoming more knowledgeable about political candidates and issues. As with voting, the decision to remain uninformed may be linked to the small impact that any single individual can have in a large-numbers setting.

Rational Ignorance
The state of not acquiring information because the costs of acquiring it are greater than the benefits.

ECONOMICS 24/7

Economic Illiteracy and Democracy

Citizens can vote even if they have no idea what they are doing. If enough voters fit that description, democratic governments are bound to make foolish decisions.

—Bryan Caplan,
Straight Talk About Economic Literacy

Blend Images - Hill Street Studios/Getty Images

Economist Bryan Caplan argues that a large percentage of the American public is economically illiterate. The result is that a lot of foolishness gets turned into national economic policy.[1]

Although determining whether someone is illiterate may be easy, not so easy is ascertaining whether someone is economically illiterate. To determine illiteracy, you can just ask people to read or write something. If they can read and write, they are not illiterate. If they can't read or write, they are illiterate.

Unfortunately, there is no such simple test to determine economic illiteracy. Instead, Caplan points to a survey that compared the responses of 1,510 average Americans with those of 250 professional economists to the same set of questions concerning economics and the economy. Here is one question from the survey: "Which do you think is more responsible for the recent increase in gasoline prices: the normal law of supply and demand, oil companies are trying to increase profits, both, or neither?" Although only 8 percent of economists said that recent increases in gas prices were due to oil companies trying to increase profits, 78 percent of the noneconomists polled explained high gas prices in that way. The explanation for high gas prices chosen by 83 percent of economists was supply and demand.

Indirectly, Caplan uses the economists' overwhelming response to the question as a benchmark by which to measure the economic illiteracy of the public. The closer the public's responses are to the economists' responses, the less economically illiterate the public is; the farther away the public's responses are from the economists' responses, the more economically illiterate the public is.

According to Caplan, who looked at responses to numerous questions, the American public is largely economically illiterate. Caplan argues that such a great degree of economic illiteracy has to do with the price one pays for it. In fact, the price is rather low, and when the price is low, you would expect a higher degree of economic illiteracy than when the price is high. In a phrase, false beliefs about economics are cheap. As Caplan says, if you underestimate the costs of excessive drinking, you can ruin your life, but if you underestimate the economic benefits of, say, free international trade, nothing really bad happens to you. Whatever happens to you is what would have happened if you didn't underestimate the economic benefits of free international trade. In other words, when being wrong really has no cost, a lot of people will be wrong—especially if one receives a personal psychological lift from holding an erroneous belief or position. Caplan puts it succinctly: "In a sense, then, there is a method to the average voter's madness. Even when his views are completely wrong, he gets the psychological benefit of emotionally appealing political beliefs at a bargain price. No wonder he buys in bulk."[2] In other words, x might be the wrong answer to the question, but if x is emotionally appealing to the respondent and if having the wrong answer doesn't adversely affect the respondent, then x it is.

But if many people choose x, perhaps at a national level x gets turned into policy. In other words, if the majority of voting Americans believe that placing tariffs on foreign imports is desirable (when economists largely disagree), then, in a political system in

---

[1] Bryan Caplan, *The Myth of the Rational Voter: Why Democracies Choose Bad Policies* (Princeton, NJ: Princeton University Press, 2007).

[2] Bryan Caplan, "The Myth of the Rational Voter," *Cato Unbound,* November 6, 2006, http://www.cato-unbound.org/2006/11/06/bryan-caplan/the-myth-of-the-rational-voter.

which politicians compete for votes, the public's erroneous belief is likely to find its way into international trade policy.

If one person's erroneous belief adversely affects only him, that is one thing. But it is quite another thing, Caplan argues, when the erroneous beliefs of many people adversely affect those who do not hold that belief. Yet this outcome is what we often get in a representative democracy. Economically erroneous beliefs, chosen on an individual level because they are cheap to choose, often add up to democracies' choosing bad economic policies.

Hear What and How the Economist Thinks . . .
About Rational Ignorance

The economist reads the following:

A national survey poll found that two-thirds of Americans polled could not name all three branches of the United States government nor a single Supreme Court justice. Another poll found that 91 percent of the persons polled could not name the Chief Justice of the Supreme Court. When responders were asked if they could name any of the rights guaranteed by the First Amendment, a majority could only name free speech and only 40 percent knew that there were 100 senators in the U.S. Congress.

Hear what and how the economist thinks:

When the results of such polls are cited, usually people become shocked that their fellow citizens seem to know so little. Sometimes the people who do know the answers to the questions claim that their fellow citizens are just ignorant. But there is a big difference between ignorance and rational ignorance. Ignorance has the connotation of a person being unable to learn something; rational ignorance does not. It is important to realize that persons who are capable of knowing something may choose not to know it.

My guess is that if we asked college professors a few basic questions on economics and politics, many of them would have a hard time giving a correct answer. This is not because they are incapable of learning about what they don't know; instead, it is more likely that they have quickly calculated that it is not worth their knowing. Consider the following questions:

1. *What was the dollar amount of federal government expenditures last year?*
2. *Who is the current chair of the House Appropriations Committee?*
3. *What percentage of total income is earned by the top 10 percent of income earners in the country?*
4. *What percentage of federal income taxes is paid by the top 10 percent of income earners?*
5. *How many members of the House of Representatives come from your state?*
6. *What is the current dollar amount of the national debt and how much has the debt increased (in billions of dollars) in the last five years?*
7. *How did either of the two U.S. senators from your state vote on the last agricultural bill that came before Congress?*

There are probably millions of people who could know the answers to these questions, but don't. In other words, it is not a matter of their not having the ability to find the answers to these questions; it is a matter of their choosing not to find the answers to these questions. And so we need to ask the question: Why would they choose to not find the answers to these questions? Instead of answering the question directly, consider two settings.

In the first setting, a person is thinking of buying a car. In the second setting, a person is planning to vote in a presidential election. In the first setting, if the person doesn't find out about the car she is thinking of buying, and something is wrong with the car, then she is going to have to suffer the consequences in terms of lost time and money. Knowing this, she will likely take the time to learn about the car she is thinking of buying. In the second case, if she doesn't know much about whom she votes for, the election is likely to turn out the same way than if she had known a lot about whom she votes for. Economists would then expect that individuals would be more careful to acquire the necessary information to buy a car than to vote in a presidential election. Yes, who is president of the United States is more important than the type of car an individual buys, but it doesn't follow that individuals will invest more time, energy, and money in deciding for whom they will vote than in deciding which car to purchase.

SELF-TEST

(Answers to Self-Test questions are in Answers to Self-Test Questions at the back of the book.)

1. If a politician running for office does not speak in general terms, does not try to move to the middle of the political spectrum, and does not take polls, is the median voter model therefore wrong?

2. Voters often criticize politicians running for office who do not speak in specific terms (i.e., who do not specify which spending programs will be cut, whose taxes will be raised, etc.). If voters want politicians running for office to speak in specific terms, why don't politicians do so?

3. Would bad weather be something that could affect voter turnout? Explain your answer.

18-4   MORE ABOUT VOTING

Voting is often the method used to make decisions in the public sector. In this section, we discuss two examples to describe some of the effects (some might say problems) of voting as a decision-making method.

18-4a   Example 1: Voting for a Nonexcludable Public Good

Suppose a community of 7 persons, A–G, wants to produce or purchase nonexcludable public good X. Each person in the community wants a different number of units of X, as shown in the following table:

Person	Number of Units of X Desired
A	1
B	2
C	3
D	4
E	5
F	6
G	7

If the community of 7 persons holds a simple majority vote, then all 7 will vote to produce or purchase at least 1 unit of X. Six people (B–G) will vote for at least 2 units; five people (C–G), for at least 3 units; four people (D–G), for at least 4 units; three people (E–G), for at least 5 units; and two people (F–G), for at least 6 units. Only one person (G) will vote for 7 units.

The largest number of units that receives a simple majority vote (half the total number of voters plus 1, or 4 votes) is 4 units. In other words, the community will vote to produce or purchase 4 units of X. Interestingly, 4 units is the most preferred outcome of only one of the seven members of the community, person D, who is the median voter. Half the voters (A, B, and C) prefer fewer than 4 units, and half the voters (E, F, and G) prefer more. Thus, our voting process has resulted in only the median voter obtaining his most preferred outcome.

The outcome would have been the same even if the numbers had looked as they do in the following table:

Person	Number of Units of X Desired
A	0
B	0
C	0
D	4
E	7
F	7
G	7

In this case, four people (D–G) would have voted for at least 4 units and only three people would have voted for anything less than 4 units. Again, 4 units would have been the outcome of the vote, and only the median voter would have obtained his most preferred outcome.

18-4b Example 2: Voting and Efficiency

Suppose three individuals have the marginal private benefits (*MPB*) shown in the following table for various units of the nonexcludable public good Y:

Person	MPB of First Unit of Y	MPB of Second Unit of Y	MPB of Third Unit of Y
A	$400	$380	$190
B	150	110	90
C	100	90	80

If the cost of providing a unit of good Y is $360, what is the socially optimal, or efficient, amount of good Y? To answer this question, recall a few of the relationships from the last chapter:

1. The socially optimal, or efficient, amount of anything is the amount at which the marginal social benefits (*MSB*) equal the marginal social costs (*MSC*).

2. The sum of the marginal private benefits (*MPB*) and the marginal external benefits (*MEB*) equals the marginal social benefits (*MSB*): $MPB + MEB = MSB$.

3. The sum of the marginal private costs (*MPC*) and the marginal external costs (*MEC*) equals the marginal social costs (*MSC*): $MPC + MEC = MSC$.

In our example, the MSC for each unit of Y is given as $360. We calculate the *MSB* for each unit by summing the *MPBs* shown in the relevant column of the table. For the first unit, the

MSB is $650 ($400 + $150 + $100); for the second unit, it is $580; and for the third unit, it is $360. The socially optimal, or efficient, amount of good Y is 3 units because, at that amount, $MSB = MSC$.

Whether voting will give us efficiency depends largely on what tax each person, A–C, expects to pay. Suppose each person must pay an equal share of the price of a unit of good Y. In other words, the tax for each person is $120 ($360 per unit ÷ 3 persons = $120 per person per unit).

Person A will vote for 3 units because his *MPB* for each unit is greater than his tax of $120 per unit. Person B will vote for only 1 unit because his *MPB* for the first unit is greater than his tax of $120 per unit but his *MPB* is not greater for the second or third unit. Person C will not vote for any units because his *MPB* for each unit is less than his tax of $120 per unit. Thus, the outcome from using a simple-majority vote is only 1 unit, and a process of voting in which each voter pays an equal tax results in an inefficient outcome.

Now suppose that, instead of paying an equal tax (of $120), each person pays a tax equal to his *MPB* at the socially optimal, or efficient, outcome. The socially optimal, or efficient, outcome is 3 units of good Y, so person A would pay a tax of $190 (his *MPB* for the third unit is $190), person B would pay a tax of $90, and person C would pay a tax of $80. (The sum of the taxes paid is equal to the cost of the unit, or $360.)

With this different tax structure, will voting generate efficiency? If each person casts a truthful vote, the answer is yes: Each person will vote for 3 units.[3] In other words, if everyone casts a truthful vote and everyone pays a tax equal to his or her *MPB* at the efficient outcome, then voting will generate efficiency.

Comparing the two tax structures—one in which each person pays an equal tax and one in which each person pays a tax equal to his *MPB*—we see that the tax structure makes the difference. In the case of equal tax shares, voting did not lead to efficiency; in the case of unequal tax shares, it did.

SELF-TEST

1. If the *MSC* in Example 2 had been $580 instead of $360, what would the socially optimal, or efficient, outcome have been?

2. In Example 2 with equal taxes, did the outcome of the vote make anyone worse off? If so, whom and by how much?

18-5 SPECIAL-INTEREST GROUPS

Special-Interest Groups
Subsets of the general population that hold (usually) intense preferences for or against a particular government service, activity, or policy and that often gain from public policies that may not be in accord with the interests of the general public.

Special-interest groups are subsets of the general population that hold (usually) intense preferences for or against a particular government service, activity, or policy. Often, special-interest groups gain from public policies that may not be in accord with the interests of the general public. In recent decades, they have played a major role in government.

18-5a Information and Lobbying

Whereas the general voter is usually uninformed about issues, members of a special-interest group are very well informed, at least about the issues they are interested in. For example, teachers are likely to know a lot about government education policies, farmers about government agriculture

---

[3] Look at the situation for person A: His *MPB* for the first unit is $400 and his tax is $190, so he votes for the first unit. His *MPB* for the second unit is $380 and his tax is $190, so he votes for the second unit. His *MPB* for the third unit is $190 and his tax is $190, so he votes for the third unit. With respect to the last unit for person A, we are assuming that if his *MPB* is equal to the tax, he will vote in favor of the unit. The same holds for the analysis of voting for persons B and C.

policies, and union members about government union policies. The reason for their greater awareness is simple: The more directly and intensely issues affect them, the greater the incentive is for individuals to become informed about them.

Given an electorate composed of uninformed general voters and informed members of special-interest groups, the groups are often able to sway politicians in their favor. This effect occurs even when the general public is made worse off by such actions (which, of course, is not always the case).

Suppose special-interest group A, composed of 5,000 individuals, favors a policy that will result in the redistribution of $50 million from 100 million general taxpayers to the group. Then the dollar benefit for each member of the special-interest group is $10,000. Given the substantial dollar amount involved, members of the special-interest group are likely to (1) sponsor or propose legislation to redistribute the money and (2) lobby the politicians who will decide the issue.

Further, the politicians will probably not hear from the general voter (i.e., the general taxpayer). The general voters–taxpayers will be less informed about the legislation than the members of the special-interest group, and anyway, even if they were adequately informed, each person would have to calculate the benefits and the costs of lobbying against the proposed legislation. If the legislation passes, the average taxpayer will pay approximately 50¢ and the benefits of lobbying against the legislation are probably not greater than 50¢. Therefore, even if they are informed about the legislation, the general taxpayers would not be likely to argue against it. The benefits just wouldn't be worth the time and effort. Special-interest bills therefore have a good chance of being passed in our legislatures.

18-5b Congressional Districts as Special-Interest Groups

Most people do not ordinarily think of congressional districts as special-interest groups. Instead, special-interest groups are commonly thought to include the ranks of public school teachers, steel manufacturers, automobile manufacturers, farmers, environmentalists, bankers, truck drivers, doctors, and the like. On some issues, however, a congressional district may be a special-interest group.

Suppose an air force base is located in a Texas congressional district. Then, a Pentagon study determines that the base is not needed and that Congress should shut it down. The Pentagon study demonstrates that the cost to the taxpayers of keeping the base open is greater than the benefits to the country of maintaining it. But closing the air force base will hurt the pocketbooks of the people in the congressional district housing the base. Their congressional representative knows not only as much, but also that if she can't keep the base open, she isn't as likely to be reelected to office.

Therefore, she speaks to other members of Congress about the proposed closing. In a way, she acts as a lobbyist for her congressional district. Most members of Congress are probably willing to go along with the Texas representative, even though they know that their constituents will be paying more in taxes than, according to the Pentagon, is necessary to ensure the national security of the country. If they don't go along with her, when they need a vote on one of their own special-interest projects (sometimes the term "pork barrel" is used), the representative from Texas may not be so cooperative. In short, members of Congress sometimes trade votes: my vote on your air force base for your vote on subsidies to dairy farmers in my district. This type of vote trading—the exchange of votes to gain support for legislation—is commonly referred to as **logrolling**.

Logrolling
The exchange of votes to gain support for legislation.

18-5c Public-Interest Talk, Special-Interest Legislation

Special-interest groups lobbying for special-interest legislation usually don't use that phrase, but rather something like "legislation in the best interest of the general public." A couple of examples, past and present, come to mind.

In the early nineteenth century, the British Parliament passed the Factory Acts, which put restrictions on women and children working. Those who lobbied for the restrictions said they did so for humanitarian reasons: to protect young children and women from difficult and hazardous work in the cotton mills. There is evidence, however, that the men working in the factories were the main lobbyists for the Factory Acts and that a reduced supply of women and children directly benefited them by raising their wages. The male factory workers appealed to individuals' higher sensibilities instead of letting it be known that they would benefit at the expense of others.

Today, people calling for, say, economic protection from foreign competitors or greater federal subsidies rarely explain that they favor the measure because the legislation will make them better off while someone else pays the bill. Instead, they usually voice the public-interest argument. Economic protectionism isn't necessary to protect industry X (they say), but it is necessary to protect American jobs and the domestic economy. The special-interest message often is, "Help yourself by helping us."

Sometimes this message is sincere, but other times it is not. In either case, it is likely to be as forcefully voiced.

18-5d Rent Seeking

Rent Seeking
Actions of individuals and groups who spend resources to influence public policy in the hope of redistributing (transferring) income to themselves from others.

Rent seeking consists of the actions of individuals and groups who spend resources to influence public policy in the hope of redistributing (transferring) income to themselves from others. To illustrate, suppose Smith is one of many producers of shoes, and suppose he realizes that he would be better off if he were the only one who produces shoes. With less competition from other shoe producers, the supply of shoes would fall and the price would rise. Smith would then end up selling shoes at $200 a pair instead of $80 a pair.

In pursuit of his aim, suppose Smith hires a law firm that specializes in lobbying government for its clients. Members of the law firm go to members of Congress and ask them to pass a law prohibiting all companies other than the Smith Shoe Company from producing shoes. The attorneys representing Smith promise to donate money to the political campaigns of the congressional members with whom they speak. They also promise that Smith of Smith Shoe Company will try to persuade his workers that their work interests are best served by voting for specific members of Congress.

In this scenario, Smith is using resources to effect a transfer. Smith has spent money to influence Congress to give him a special privilege: the right to be the only producer of shoes. In essence, Smith is trying to bring about a transfer from shoe consumers to himself. He wants consumers to end up paying more for shoes so that he earns more from producing them. He is spending money to try to bring about this transfer from others to him. Smith is a *rent seeker*: he is using resources (the money he spends goes for resources) in order to bring about a transfer from others to him.

Let's say that Smith spends a total of $100,000 to bring about the transfer. This is the cost of his rent seeking. From Smith's perspective, the decision to spend $100,000 to bring about a transfer, of, say, $1 million is rational. But from society's perspective, all the resources that Smith uses to effect a transfer are wasted. The $100,000 is wasted because money spent trying to effect a transfer cannot be used to produce goods and services.

To see the negative effects rent seeking has on society even more clearly, consider an extreme example. Let's say that today 1,000 individuals are all producing goods and services. Together, they produce about $2 million worth of output a day. Tomorrow, all 1,000 individuals decide to spend their time and money trying to bring about a transfer. In other words, instead of producing, they spend their time rent seeking. At the end of the day, the cost to society of these 1,000 individuals' rent seeking instead of producing is obviously $2 million worth of output. Society is poorer by $2 million because the 1,000 individuals turned away from producing and toward rent seeking. In short, rent seeking is a socially wasteful activity.

18-5e Bringing About Transfers

In Exhibit 3, the market equilibrium price of a certain good is P_1. At this price, identifying both consumers' surplus and producers' surplus is easy. Consumers' surplus is the area under the demand curve and above the equilibrium price, out to the equilibrium quantity, Q_1: the triangular area $A + B + C$. Producers' surplus is the area under the equilibrium price and above the supply curve, out to the equilibrium quantity, Q_1: the triangular area $D + E$.

Now, suppose the producers of the good lobby government for a price floor, P_2. If government grants this floor, then the new price in the market is P_2 and consumers' surplus ends up being only area A. Consumers lose area $B + C$ in consumers' surplus. At the new price P_2, producers lose area E in producers' surplus and they gain area B. As long as area E (what they lose) is smaller than area B (what they gain), producers are better off selling at price P_2 than P_1. In Exhibit 3, area E is clearly smaller than B, so producers are better off.

The price floor has thus created a transfer. Area B, which was once con-

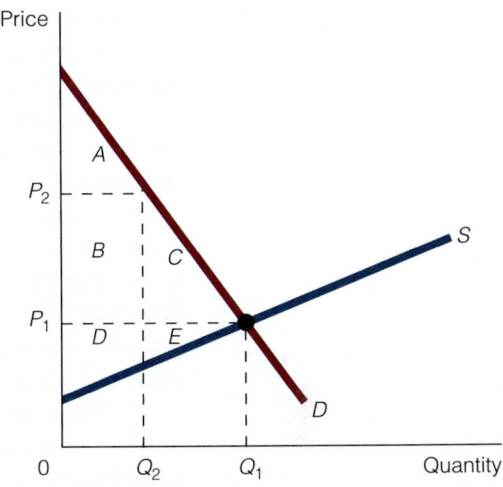

EXHIBIT 3

A Price Floor and a Transfer from Consumers to Producers

The market equilibrium price of the good is P_1. Consumers' surplus is the area $A + B + C$. Producers' surplus is the area $D + E$. If producers of the good lobby for and receive a price floor of P_2, then consumers' surplus ends up being only area A. Consumers lose areas $B + C$ in consumers' surplus, and producers gain area B in producers' surplus. By obtaining the price floor through government, producers of the good were able to take some consumers' surplus away from consumers and turn it into producers' surplus for themselves.

sumers' surplus, is now producers' surplus. By getting the price floor, the producers of the good were able to take some consumers' surplus away from consumers and turn it into producers' surplus. If area B is equivalent to, say, $1,000$, then producers have been able to transfer $1,000$ from consumers to themselves. All the resources that the producers expended to get that transfer of $1,000$ are referred to as the *rent-seeking costs*—that is, the costs of trying to bring about the transfer. Again, from society's perspective, the resources expended to effect the transfer are wasted in that they cannot be used to produce goods and services. Society as a whole is just a little bit poorer because of the rent-seeking behavior of the producers.

18-5f Information, Rational Ignorance, and Seeking Transfers

Will rent seekers tell the truth about their rent-seeking efforts (assuming that they know the truth)? Suppose Smith knows that his rent seeking will lead to greater producers' surplus for him and less consumers' surplus and that the losses to consumers will be greater than his gains. (If you look back at Exhibit 3, you will notice that the losses to consumers from the price floor—areas $B + C$—are greater than the gain of area B to the producer.) Will he advertise this information? Will he, for instance, lobby government by saying, "I would like a price floor for what I sell. I know that this will end up hurting consumers more than it benefits me, but so be it. As long as I am made better off, I don't really care how much consumers are made worse off. Can I have the transfer?"

He is unlikely to say this. For one thing, making such a barefaced request draws attention to the fact that he gains at consumers' expense and that his gain is smaller than what consumers lose.

Smith wouldn't draw attention to this fact. Instead, he might try to argue that what is good for him is good (not bad) for others.

Can such rent-seeking efforts be successful? Won't the politicians turn Smith down because moving from an equilibrium price to a price floor hurts consumers more than it helps producers? (Yet there are price floors in the real world.) Won't consumers rally against Smith because they know that they are being hurt by his actions? Moreover, aren't consumers greater in number than Smith (who is only one), and don't politicians care about votes (which means that they must then care about the number of voters)?

First, consumers may not rally against Smith, because they may not even know that he is lobbying government for a price floor. Recall the issue of rational ignorance—that is, not acquiring information because the costs of acquiring it are greater than the benefits.

Most individuals are rationally ignorant of many issues. If you know less about French literature than you could know, then you are rationally ignorant of the subject. If you know less about computers than you could know, then you are rationally ignorant of computers.

Similarly, many people are rationally ignorant of politics and government; that is, they know less than they could know—and that is largely because the marginal benefits of acquiring this kind of information are so low. And the benefits are low because an individual's one vote matters so little in the determination of an election, as we discussed earlier. In other words, the probability that your one vote will break a tie and decide who wins and who loses in an election—especially when millions of people are eligible to vote—is infinitesimally small.

So, if your vote is not going to determine the outcome of an election, what does it matter how much or how little information you have about the candidates, the issues, and the events? The answer to that question is perhaps best framed in terms of your options. Let's say two major candidates, A and B, are running for U.S. senator from your state. Then you have the following options:

- *Option 1:* Be fully informed (on the Senate election issues) and vote for A.

- *Option 2:* Be fully informed and vote for B.

- *Option 3:* Be rationally ignorant and vote for A.

- *Option 4:* Be rationally ignorant and vote for B.

- *Option 5:* Be fully informed and not vote.

- *Option 6:* Be rationally ignorant and not vote.

No matter which option you choose, the outcome of the election will be what it will be. Your vote will likely not break a tie; your vote will not determine the outcome of the election. Therefore, the least-cost option is obviously option 6, to be rationally ignorant and not vote.

Of course, not everyone chooses this option. In the last presidential election, approximately 138 million persons voted, although millions of other eligible voters chose not to vote. Of the approximately 138 million who did vote, probably very many were rationally ignorant. Being otherwise would have been just too costly for them, especially given the fact that very few of them were under the delusion that their single vote would determine outcome of the election.

So, if producers seek a transfer that ends up hurting consumers, consumers are not likely to know about it if they are rationally ignorant, and the incentive for them to be rationally ignorant is huge. Thus, when a producer lobbies members of Congress for a price floor that helps him and hurts consumers, the consumers may not even know about the rent seeking. And even if they do, do they also know that a price floor leads to a greater loss in consumers' surplus than an increase in producers' surplus, especially when the producer has an incentive not to state the details of the transfer? Instead, the producer will probably wrap his special-interest legislation in "public-interest talk." Perhaps he will argue that, without a price floor for his good, few producers will produce it and that if few producers produce the good, people will lose their jobs, communities will lose tax revenue, and so forth. None of this has to be true, of course, but trying to figure out whether it might be true may be too costly an effort for most individuals to undertake.

But suppose that rational ignorance does not exist: Everyone knows everything about everything. Then, when the producer lobbies government for a price floor, consumers immediately know about his activities; furthermore, they know that the loss of consumers' surplus (as a result of the price floor) will be greater than the gain in producers' surplus. Even so, consumers may still not fight the producers because, simply put, the loss to each individual consumer might be so small that it is not worth fighting to stop the price floor.

As an example, suppose 100 producers will benefit a total of $10 million if the price floor replaces the equilibrium price in the market. That amount is an average of $100,000 per producer. But suppose consumers will lose $15 million as a result of the price floor. If there are 100 million consumers, the average consumer loses only 15¢. A consumer will probably not spend $1 to fight a policy that costs him or her only 15¢.

The key in seeking transfers is to spread the loss from the transfer over as many people as possible so that, on a per-person basis, the loss is very small. The loss should be small enough that the individual will have little reason to argue against the policy that inflicts the loss.

18-6 CONSTITUTIONAL ECONOMICS

Most of economics deals with behavior within a certain set of constraints. For example, consider that your decisions as to what and how much to buy take place within income and price constraints. If your income is $1,000 a month and the price of all goods is $1, then you can purchase only 1,000 units of various goods a month.

Sometimes the constraints within which we choose are given, as in the example presented in the previous paragraph. But sometimes we *choose* to place ourselves within certain constraints. Consider a person who has decided that he wants to lose 15 pounds. To help himself lose the weight, he never keeps any snacks (potato chips, ice cream, or cookies) in his house. By this action, he has deliberately chosen to constrain himself (from eating snacks late at night when he knows that he is generally inclined to).

On a collective level, think of a group of people choosing to constrain their driving behavior by opting for speed limit laws. Each person reasons that, without such laws, he can drive as fast he wants to—but then, so can everyone else. But if everyone can drive as fast as he wants, there may be more accidents (and deaths) than if everyone had to obey a speed limit. Each person then opts to constrain his and everyone else's behavior by opting for speed limit laws.

In this chapter, we have discussed behavior within a political or government context. That behavior occurred within certain constraints. For example, voters could not vote more than once, elections were held every two or four years, and so on.

Might individuals living within a particular political setting seek to constrain themselves or others in some way in order to obtain better results than could be obtained in an environment without constraints or with different constraints? For example, at the current moment there is no constraint as to how much the federal government can spend. Some people argue that, as a result of this absence of a limit, the federal government is likely to spend too much—as is manifest by the nation's large budget deficits. Suppose the federal government were to opt for a constraint on itself? Suppose the Congress were to pass a law which stated that it could not spend more in any given year than the projected tax revenues in that year. For example, if projected tax revenues were $2.2 trillion, then spending had to be $2.2 trillion or less. Passing such a law would constrain the Congress; it would place a ceiling on how much the Congress could spend in a given year.

There is a branch of economics called constitutional economics or constitutional political economy in which economists study the types of constraints that individuals might place upon themselves in order to achieve some objective that doesn't seem achievable in an environment that lacks constraints.

In fact, constitutional economists sometimes argue that better outcomes are more readily forthcoming out of government by changing institutions, constraints, laws, and rules than by changing people. In other words, within a given set of institutions, constraints, laws and rules, outcomes might be the same no matter who is elected to office. For example, whether Republicans or Democrats are overwhelmingly elected to political office, big budget deficits might be the order of the day unless there is some constraint placed on government against running a budget deficit.

SELF-TEST

1. The average farmer is likely to be better informed about federal agricultural policy than the average food consumer is. Why?

2. Consider special-interest legislation that will transfer $40 million from group A to group B, a group with 10,000 persons. Is this legislation more likely to pass when group A consists of (a) 10,000 persons or (b) 10 million persons? Explain your answer.

3. Give an example of public-interest talk spoken by a special-interest group.

4. Why is rent-seeking activity socially wasteful?

OFFICE HOURS

"Doesn't Public Choice Paint a Bleak Picture of Politics and Government?"

STUDENT: In a way, public choice paints a rather bleak picture of politics and government.

INSTRUCTOR: How so?

STUDENT: Politicians don't seem to care about what is right or wrong. They just move to the middle of the voter distribution. People don't always vote, because voting is sometimes too costly. People aren't always well informed on issues, because accessing the information is too costly. And to top it off, special interests are engaged in rent seeking. Doesn't all this sound dismal to you?

INSTRUCTOR: It sounds as if you want things to work differently. Well, unfortunately, as the Rolling Stones told us, "You can't always get what you want."

STUDENT: I have to confess that I would like it if things worked differently. I want politicians to do the right thing, and I want people to be informed on issues and to cast intelligent votes.

INSTRUCTOR: Probably, many people want the same thing. My guess is that public choice economists want the same thing. But we can't let what we want color how we see the world.

STUDENT: But who is to say that public choice economists analyze the world in the right way? Maybe they are an overly cynical bunch of economists.

INSTRUCTOR: What they are doesn't matter. What matters is what they say and what they predict. We don't judge an economic theory by how it sounds to us or by how we feel about it; we judge it by how well it explains and predicts what we see in the world. If politicians move to the center of the voter distribution, if people are rationally ignorant, and if special interests sometimes engage in rent seeking, then that's the way things are whether we like it or not.

STUDENT: But aren't. economists supposed to be trying to make the world better?

INSTRUCTOR: Let's assume that they are. Then isn't a good understanding of the world critical to doing this? For example, if the world is X, and I think it is Y, then I might make mistakes when I try to make the world a better place. Basing what I do on how things are has to be better than basing them on how I might want them to be.

STUDENT: I see your point. It's sort of like a doctor who wants to know your true condition before she prescribes any therapy. She may not like the fact that you have a particular disease, but it's important that she know about it so that she can prescribe the right medicine.

INSTRUCTOR: I think that captures the spirit of what I'm talking about.

STUDENT: Does it follow, then, that everything in public choice theory is right?

INSTRUCTOR: No, it doesn't follow. Public choice theory—just like any theory in economics—has to be judged on how well it explains and predicts.

Points to Remember

1. Theories should be judged on how well they explain and predict (not on how they sound or feel).

2. Good economics seeks to know what exists, no matter how pleasant or unpleasant that is.

CHAPTER SUMMARY

POLITICIANS AND THE MIDDLE: THE MEDIAN VOTER MODEL

- In a two-person race, candidates for the same office will gravitate toward the median voter. If a candidate does not do so and her opponent does, the opponent will win the election.

- Candidates usually pick labels for themselves that represent the middle of the political spectrum, they speak in general terms, and they take polls and adjust their positions accordingly.

VOTING AND RATIONAL IGNORANCE

- Voting has both costs and benefits. Many potential voters will not vote because the costs of voting—in terms of time spent going to the polls and so on—outweigh the benefits of voting, measured as the probability of their single vote determining the election outcome.

- Being unable to learn certain information is different from choosing not to learn it. Many voters choose not to be informed about political and government issues because the costs of becoming informed outweigh the benefits of becoming informed. They choose to be rationally ignorant.

MORE ABOUT VOTING

- In a simple-majority vote, given several options to choose from, the voting outcome is the same as the most preferred outcome of the median voter.

- Simple-majority voting together with equal tax shares can generate a different result from simple-majority voting together with unequal tax shares.

SPECIAL-INTEREST GROUPS

- Special-interest groups are usually well informed about their issues because individuals have a greater incentive to become informed about issues that directly and intensely affect them.

- Legislation that concentrates benefits on a few and disperses costs over many is likely to pass because the beneficiaries will have an incentive to lobby for it whereas those who pay the bill will not lobby against it because each of them pays such a small part of the bill.

- Special-interest groups often engage in rent seeking, which is the expenditure of scarce resources to capture a pure transfer. Rent seeking is a socially wasteful activity because the resources used to effect transfers are not used to produce goods and services.

CONSTITUTIONAL ECONOMICS

- The subject matter of constitutional economics is choosing rules or constraints within which collective choices are made.

- Constitutional economists often argue that governmental outcomes will be more readily forthcoming by changing institutions, constraints, laws, and rules than by changing people. In other words, within a given set of institutions, constraints, laws, and rules, outcomes might be the same no matter who is elected to office.

KEY TERMS AND CONCEPTS

Public Choice
Median Voter Model

Rational Ignorance
Special-Interest Groups

Logrolling
Rent Seeking

QUESTIONS AND PROBLEMS

1. Some observers maintain that not all politicians move toward the middle of the political spectrum in order to obtain votes. They often cite Barry Goldwater in the 1964 presidential election and George McGovern in the 1972 presidential election as examples. Goldwater was viewed as occupying the right end of the political spectrum and McGovern the left end. Would these two examples necessarily be evidence that does not support the median voter model? Are they exceptions to the theory explained in this chapter?

2. The economist James Buchanan said, "If men should cease and desist from their talk about and their search for evil men and commence to look instead at the institutions manned by ordinary people, wide avenues for genuine social reform might appear." What did he mean?

3. Would voters have a greater incentive to vote in an election involving only a few registered voters or in one that has many? Why? Why might a Republican label her opponent too far left and a Democrat label his opponent too far right?

4. Many individuals learn more about the car they are thinking of buying than about the candidates running for president of the United States. Explain why.

5. If the model of politics and government presented in this chapter is true, what are some of the things we would expect to see?

6. It has often been said that Democratic candidates are more liberal in Democratic primaries and Republican candidates are more conservative in Republican primaries than either is in the general election. Explain why.

7. What are some ways of reducing the cost of voting to voters?

8. Provide a numerical example which shows that simple-majority voting may be consistent with efficiency. Next, provide a numerical example which shows that simple-majority voting may be inconsistent with efficiency.

9. John chooses not to vote in the presidential election. Does it follow that he is apathetic when it comes to presidential politics? Explain your answer.

10. Some individuals see national defense spending as benefiting special interests—in particular, the defense industry. Others see it as directly benefiting not only the defense industry but the general public as well. Does this same difference between viewpoints apply to issues other than national defense? Name a few.

11. Evaluate each of the following proposals for reform in terms of the material discussed in this chapter:

    a. Linking all spending programs to visible tax hikes

    b. A balanced-budget amendment stipulating that Congress cannot spend more than total tax revenues

    c. A budgetary referendum process whereby the voters actually vote on the distribution of federal dollars to the different categories of spending (x percentage to agriculture, y percentage to national defense, etc.) instead of letting elected representatives decide.

12. "Rent seeking may be rational from the individual's perspective, but it is not rational from society's perspective." Do you agree or disagree? Explain your answer.

WORKING WITH NUMBERS AND GRAPHS

1. Suppose that three major candidates—A, B, and C—are running for president of the United States and that the distribution of voters is that shown in Exhibit 1. Two of the candidates—A and B—are currently viewed as right of the median voter, and C is viewed as left of the median voter. Is it possible to predict which candidate is the most likely to win?

2. Look back at Exhibit 2. Suppose that the net benefits and net costs for each person are known a week before election day and that it is legal to buy and sell votes. Furthermore, suppose that neither buying nor selling votes has any conscience

cost (i.e., one does not feel guilty buying or selling votes). Would the outcome of the election be the same? Explain your answer.

3. In part (a) of the accompanying figure, the distribution of voters is skewed to the left; in part (b), the distribution is skewed neither left nor right; and in part (c), it is skewed right. Assuming a two-person race for each distribution, will the candidate who wins the election in (a) hold different positions from the candidates who win the elections in (b) and (c)? Explain your answer.

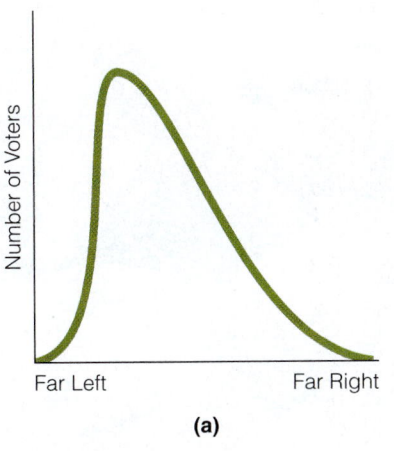

(a)

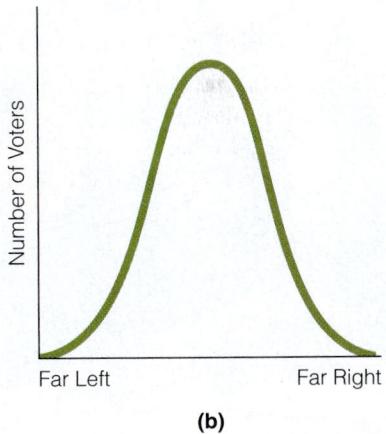

(b)

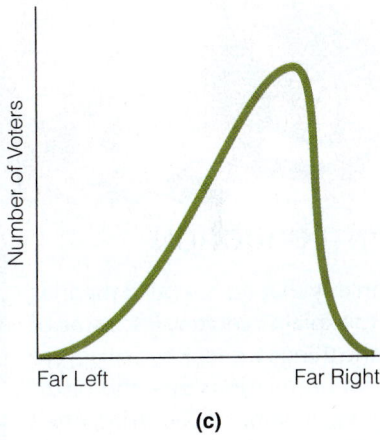

(c)

19

BUILDING THEORIES TO EXPLAIN EVERYDAY LIFE: FROM OBSERVATIONS TO QUESTIONS TO THEORIES TO PREDICTIONS

INTRODUCTION

In this chapter, we build theories to explain everyday life. Some of the things we seek to explain are dating relationships, the birthrates in various countries, one's ethical code, burglary, segregated neighborhoods, cheating on an exam, house prices, and school districts, and more.

Belushi/Shutterstock.com

19-1 A DIFFERENT KIND OF CHAPTER

This chapter differs from others in this text in two fundamental ways: in your experience and in its content.

First, the chapter offers a different experience. Think about a new house that took eight months to build. You see the house for the first time on the day it is completed. You look at the outside, then walk into the house, go into every room, and touch the various surfaces—the freshly painted walls, the granite countertop in the kitchen, the shiny new hardwood floor.

How different would it be to watch the house being built from day to day? You would see the land being cleared, the excavation dug, the concrete laid, the house framed, plumbing and wiring put in, and the walls painted.

These are two very different experiences: the view of a completed house and the building of the house. Which experience is more like yours in reading this text so far? It is probably like the first—viewing the completed house. The text has presented various complete theories, such as the theory of supply and demand. Then we discussed certain things within those theories. That is how the material in most texts about economics principles is presented, and it is an important part of your economic education.

Also important, however, is another part of your economic education: seeing the process that leads to the completed theory—seeing how the house is built. If contractors build houses, economists build theories. It is time for you to see the nitty-gritty process of how economists go about doing what they do. That is the experience of this chapter.

Building an economic theory is a five-step process:

1. It starts with economists making an observation or having a thought.

2. The observation or thought leads to a question.

3. The economist then builds a theory to try to answer the question.

4. Next, if the theory has been built correctly, predictions based on the theory pour forth.

5. Finally, data are gathered and analyzed, and the theory's predictions are tested against reality: Either they are borne out, or they are shown to be false.

In this chapter, we present only the first four steps. We leave the last step—testing the theory—to a course you might take in statistics or econometrics.

This chapter also differs from others in its content. Most of the other chapters in the text have contained discussions of fairly standard economic topics: supply and demand, market structures, labor markets, and the like. In this chapter, we include more everyday topics: dating relationships, the ethical code in small towns and large cities, punctuality and office hours, family size, and so on. We chose these topics for three reasons, two of which are that most people are familiar with them from their own everyday life experiences and no specialized knowledge is needed to discuss them.

The third reason is to show that economic thinking, concepts, and theorizing can often extend to places to which most people would not have guessed that they are applicable. To noneconomists, economic thinking and concepts can be readily applied to business firms, inflation, unemployment, markets, interest rates, and monetary policy. But rarely do they think that economic thinking and concepts can be applied to topics such as dating, ethical codes, or family size. Why are economists extending themselves into the domains of the sociologist, psychologist, and anthropologist? It's sort of like a baseball player telling a football player how to play football. Stick to baseball!

It's been said that economics is becoming an imperialist social science; that is, it is spreading out into other fields. With apologies to William Shatner of *Star Trek* fame, it is boldly going where it has never gone before: into sociology, history, political science, anthropology, psychology, and law. In any of these fields today, you will see the imprint of economists. For economic imperialists (those who venture into other fields), economics isn't so much a field of study as it is a method of analysis. Economics is not just a list of topics (unemployment, inflation, firms, monetary policy, and so on) but rather is a set of tools that can be applied to a whole host of phenomena. This set of tools is relevant not only to studying markets and the economy but also to social and political environments. That is the viewpoint taken in this chapter. In that sense, the chapter presents a different perspective of the practitioners of economics today from that given in the other chapters of the text.

19-2 THE PROCESS

As explained, the process of economics consists of five steps. Here are the first four, stated in slightly more formal terms:

1. Making an observation or having a thought

2. Formulating a question based on the observation or thought

Dragon Images/Shutterstock.com

3. Building a theory to answer the question

4. Making predictions based on the theory

We begin with our first of many observations.

19-3 OBSERVATION/ THOUGHT 1: THE BIRTH-RATES IN VARIOUS COUNTRIES ARE DIFFERENT

You observe that the birthrate is not the same in all countries. In some countries it is 1.4 children per couple, and in other countries it is 2.7.

19-3a The Question

Why are the birthrates different in various countries?

19-3b The Theory

The theory proposed to answer the question is based on a woman's opportunity cost of having a child. To illustrate, consider two women, A and B. Woman A lives in a rather poor country and has few opportunities to earn income. If she were to work, she would earn $10 a day. Woman B lives in a relatively rich country and has numerous opportunities to earn income. If she were to work, she would earn $400 a day.

Each woman is considering having a child. Each woman intends to take off two years from work to care for the child if she has one. For woman A, the opportunity cost of having the child is $10 a day for two years: $5,200. For woman B, the opportunity cost of having the child is $400 a day for two years: $208,000.[1]

19-3c The Predictions

Prediction 1 Our first prediction is a general one: The higher a woman's opportunity cost to have a child, the fewer children she will have.

Prediction 2 If women in rich countries have greater opportunities to earn income and women in poorer countries have fewer, then women in rich countries will have fewer children than women in poor countries will.

Prediction 3 Within a rich country, women who have the greatest opportunity to earn income will have fewer children than those who have poor opportunities to earn income. A more specific prediction is that a woman who goes to medical school and becomes a physician will have fewer children than a woman who becomes a schoolteacher. Stated slightly differently, women physicians are predicted to have fewer children, on average, than women schoolteachers have.

---

[1] To put things on an even more solid basis, after computing the two dollar amounts, we could adjust each for the cost of living in each country. For instance, the cost of living may be lower in the poor country than in the rich country, so that $1 buys more in the poor country than in the rich country. Still, it would probably be the case that one woman's opportunity cost of having children was different from another's. It is this relative relationship that matters for our example

19-3d A Detour: The Issue of Falsifiability (Refutability)

A good theory should have the virtue of falsifiability, or refutability. In other words, not only must a theory predict things that we should observe *if it is right*, but it should also predict things that we should observe *if it is wrong*. Consider, for example, the part of prediction 3 about women physicians and women schoolteachers: Women physicians will have fewer children, on average, than women schoolteachers will. If we collect data on women having children and find that women physicians, on average, have *more* children or *the same number of children* as women schoolteachers have, then we know that the theory is false (refuted). That is what we want in a theory: the ability to know not only when it is right, but also when it is wrong.

A theory can also be not falsifiable, or not refutable. Consider this theory: Everything that happens to you happens because of the specific time and day you were born. In other words, if a person was born on September 21, 1992, at 9:01:33 a.m. Eastern time, then everything that happens to the person happens because of his or her being born at that specific time. So, if the person goes to a specific college, takes a specific major, and eats a bologna sandwich for lunch one day—all this happens because of the person's being born at that specific time.

We cannot falsify or refute this model. No matter what a person does or doesn't do—go to college X or go to college Y, eat a bologna sandwich or eat a BLT sandwich—whatever it is is supposedly a consequence of being born on a certain day and time. The theory predicts nothing that, if it happens, can falsify or refute the model, so there is no way to know whether the theory is true or false. There is no way to judge or evaluate the theory. In effect, the theory is saying, "Accept what I say as true because I say it is true."

Instead, it would be better if the theory were to say, "Don't accept what I say as true just because I say it is true. Here is what I propose: I predict X, Y, and Z, so if you see X, Y, or Z, then that is evidence that what I have said is true. If you see not-X, not-Y, or not-Z, then what I have said is clearly false." Scientists strive to build theories that can be falsified or refuted. They seek to build theories that are capable of telling them not only when they are right, but also when they are wrong.

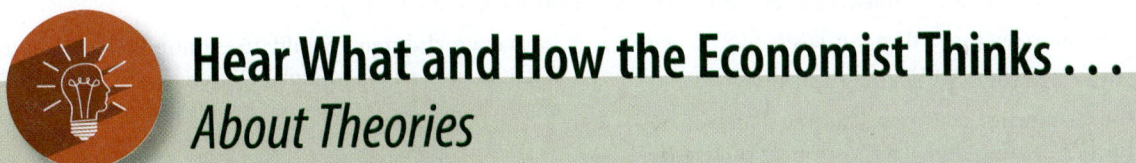

Hear What and How the Economist Thinks . . .
About Theories

The economist hears one person say to another:

I've heard that economists build a lot of theories. That's why I think that economics might be too abstract a course of study. Theories come with a lot of mathematics, diagrams, and complex terms. I prefer courses that are more reality based, more practical, and more descriptive.

Hear what and how the economist thinks:

Often, when people hear the word "theory" or "model" they think mathematics and diagrams with curves; they think that anyone who deals with theory deals with something that is naturally very difficult to work with. What many people seem to not be aware of is that they work with theories all the time.

To illustrate, suppose there are two friends, Bob and Jake. Usually, Bob and Jake are extremely friendly toward each other. But one day, Jake starts acting a little differently. He seems moody, a little upset, and somewhat angry. Bob begins to wonder why Jake is acting differently than usual. Bob wonders if it has something to do with something he said the other day, if Jake is just feeling out of sorts today, or if Jake had something go wrong at work. Notice that Bob has made an observation (Jake is acting differently today); he has formulated a question based on the observation (Why is Jake acting differently today?); and he is now trying to build a theory to answer the question. But where is the math? It is nowhere to be found. Bob's theory comes in the form of a story. One story has to do with something happening at Jake's work. Another story has to do with something that Bob might have said earlier. In a way, a theory is really no more than a story, which a theorist believes helps to explain things.

Now consider another setting. Karen and Melissa take a college course in economics together. Until today, their economics instructor has always come to class very neatly dressed. But today he came to class looking different from his usual self: his trousers were wrinkled, he wore a wrinkled T-shirt instead of an ironed shirt, his hair wasn't combed, and he hadn't shaved. When the instructor enters the class, Karen turns to Melissa and asks what she thinks is up with the instructor today? Why the change in appearance? Melissa tells a story (builds a theory). She says that she thinks the instructor got up late this morning and didn't have time to shave or comb his hair. He just picked up the first clothes he saw—an old T-shirt and a pair of wrinkled trousers—threw them on, and rushed to class. Karen tells a different story (builds a different theory). She says that she thinks the instructor has decided to make a change in his appearance. He wants to be more casual, and not so concerned with his appearance.

Does each person's theory come with a prediction? It does. Melissa's theory predicts that in the next class the instructor should be back to his old ways: hair combed, shaven, ironed shirt, and unwrinkled trousers. Karen's theory predicts that in the next class the instructor should look the same as he does in the current class.

Theories are not something to be afraid of. And it is not just economists, chemists, biologists, and others in the sciences that build theories. Everyday people build theories all the time. True, some theories come with mathematics and diagrams, but those are simply tools that some theorists use to construct their theories, and formalize things precisely.

Questions to Think About:

1. In this text you have learned about the theory of supply and demand. There were curves drawn, equilibrium points identified, and more. State the theory of supply and demand in story form.

2. Were both Melissa's and Karen's theories (or predictions based on their theories) falsifiable or refutable? Explain your answer.

SELF-TEST

(Answers to Self-Test questions are in Answer to Self-Test Questions at the back of the book.)

1. What does it mean to say that a theory is falsifiable?

2. What is the five-step process to building a theory?

3. Women in some countries have more children than women in other countries because they have a stronger preference for having children. Would an economist be likely to use different preferences to explain differences in behavior? Why or why not?

19-4 OBSERVATION/THOUGHT 2: THE ETHICAL CODE OF PEOPLE WHO LIVE IN A SMALL TOWN IS DIFFERENT FROM THAT OF PEOPLE WHO LIVE IN A LARGE CITY

Bob lives and works in New York City but recently visited a small town in the Midwest for two weeks. When he returned to New York City, he told all his friends and coworkers how friendly, decent, and honest the people seemed to be in the small town. Bob suspects that, on the basis of his limited observation, the people in small towns might have a slightly better ethical code than those who live in large cities.

19-4a The Question

Do small-town people have a somewhat different (better?) ethical code than big-city people have?

19-4b The Theory

The theory has to do with what percentage of the population an individual represents. If a person lives in a town of 1,000 persons, she is one one-thousandth of the population. If the person lives in a city of 5 million persons, she is one five-millionth of the population. According to the theory, the larger a percentage of the population that a person is, the more likely it is that the person will treat others as he or she wants to be treated. Why? The larger a percentage of the population a person is, the more likely it is that the person will keep meeting those he initially gets to know.

Songquan Deng/Shutterstock.com

For example, if John lives in a town of 200 people, he can be fairly sure of knowing most, if not all, of the town folk. He also knows that he has a good chance of running into the same people over and over again; after all, that's what happens in a small town. He might see Melanie in the grocery store, or at the post office, or getting her car fixed. He might run into Kevin at the park or at a restaurant. In other words, the probability of running into the same people over and over again is higher in a small town than in a large city.

The latter fact makes it fairly costly to treat people poorly—to lie to them, to cheat them, to take advantage of them. If you treat them poorly one day (i.e., not treat them as you yourself want to be treated), you could very well run into them the next day (and they will probably have a few choice words for you). Of course, even if you don't run into them the next day, word gets around in a small town. If you cheat Jack on Saturday and he tells Joanne on Sunday, then Joanne might be wary of you on Monday.

Things might be different in a big city, where one person is a smaller percentage of the population. In a big city, you don't have as great a chance of meeting the same people over and over again. You might cheat Jack on Saturday and he might tell Joanne on Sunday, but are you really going to run into Joanne on Monday? After all, it's a big city. Simply put, treating someone poorly in a big city may come with lower costs (fewer negative consequences) than treating someone poorly in a small town.

19-4c The Predictions

Prediction 1 The owner of a car repair shop in a small town will be more careful not to overcharge customers than the owner of a car repair shop in a large city.

Prediction 2 No matter the size of the town or city, people are more likely to treat others as they want to be treated in a small-numbers setting that they frequent often than in a large-numbers setting that they show up at rarely. Again, consider John, who lives and works in New York City. He works in lower Manhattan at a small office with 10 people. In his work life, it is as if he works in a very small town. It is as if he is back in that small town in the Midwest, except that the town is even smaller. He is a larger percentage of the office population than he is of the city. The theory predicts that he will more likely adopt the treat-others-as-you-want-to-be-treated principle in the office than he will outside the office. Generalizing the prediction, we say that people will have a higher ethical code toward those with whom they work (and see every day) than with those they rarely meet or with whom they are only mildly acquainted.

Prediction 3 If a person treats coworkers (whom she sees every day) poorly, then she will treat others (i.e., those whom she doesn't see regularly or have as much chance of running into later) worse.

ECONOMICS 24/7

Can Social Media Affect Whom a Person Dates?

Tyler meets Alicia through a mutual friend. Tyler and Alicia start talking, and before long, Tyler realizes that he would like to ask Alicia for a date. He does so; Alicia accepts. Later that day, Alicia goes online and reads the news on Yahoo! She happens to see an ad for a criminal-reporting service. It turns out that, for a certain fee, you can learn if a person has a criminal record. Alicia pays for the service and puts in Tyler's full name. She learns that Tyler does have a criminal record: He was convicted of home burglary five years ago. She calls up the friend who introduced her to Tyler and asks if she knew about Tyler's criminal record. The friend says that she has known Tyler for only a year and knows nothing of a criminal record. After some thought, Alicia decides that she doesn't want to go out with Tyler. She sends him a text message which states that her plans have changed and that, unfortunately, she will not be able to go out with him. Tyler texts her back, asking for a date "some other time," but Alicia ends up not responding to Tyler's text message.

The digital revolution has provided some services that did not exist previously. Being able to easily check whether someone has a criminal record is one such service. The story of Alicia and Tyler is fictional, but representative of what can and does happen every day.

karelnoppe/Shutterstock.com

People check on other people for a host of reasons: for dating purposes, business purposes, employment purposes, and so on. This kind of checking has become so much easier and less costly because of the Internet. Thus, we can expect more of it. In a way, the Internet has made every town and city in the United States a "small town." In a small town, before the days of the Internet, it was often said that "everyone knows everyone else's business." In fact, that very thing is what some people didn't like about small towns. Still, when "everyone knows everyone else's business," it would be hard for Alicia not to know that Tyler had been convicted of burglary. What online services that supply database searches of once-private information offer is the ability to change what locale one lives in into a "small town." Today, not only can one learn whether someone has a criminal record, but one can also learn how much someone paid for his house (if the home address is known), what his house looks like from the outside (via Google Earth), how many people live in the home, in some cases the person's religious affiliation, and so on. If, in the past, one of the reasons for moving from a small town was to get away from "everyone knowing everyone else's business," the Internet has made that reason less significant today.

19-5 OBSERVATION/THOUGHT 3: THE CLOSER THE DOLLAR TUITION THE STUDENT PAYS IS TO THE EQUILIBRIUM TUITION, THE MORE ON TIME AND RESPONSIVE UNIVERSITY INSTRUCTORS WILL BE FOR OFFICE HOURS

19-5a The Question

At universities where the gap between student tuition and the equilibrium tuition is small, will instructors be on time more often for, and more responsive in, office hours than instructors who teach at universities where the gap is large?

19-5b The Theory

At most four-year traditional universities (both private and public), the tuition the student is charged is not the same as the equilibrium tuition. Often, the student tuition is below the equilibrium tuition. For example, the equilibrium tuition at a private university might be $60,000 a year and the student is charged $40,000. Or, the equilibrium tuition at a public university might be $55,000 a year and the student is charged $20,000. Openings in universities (for first-year students) are not fully rationed by dollar price (tuition). Instead, they are rationed by a combination of dollar price, grades in high school, standardized test scores, and so on. In other words, to be admitted to a university, a student may need a GPA of at least 3.00 and an SAT score of at least 1200.

If most four-year traditional universities are charging students less than the equilibrium tuition, then a dollar gap must exist between what a student pays and the equilibrium tuition. If the equilibrium tuition is $60,000 and the student tuition is $40,000, the gap is $20,000. Does this gap matter to the behavior of university instructors when holding their office hours? According to our theory, it does.

Exhibit 1 shows the demand to attend two universities, A and B. The supply of openings at each university is assumed to be the same: 3,000. Because the demand to attend university A is higher than it is to attend university B, the equilibrium tuitions are $50,000 at university A and $40,000 at university B. However, the tuition charged students at each university is the same: $30,000. At this tuition, the gap (between the equilibrium tuition and student tuition) and the shortage (between the number of students applying and the number of openings) are both greater at university A than B. The shortage at university A at the $30,000 tuition is 2,200 students because, at this tuition, 5,200 students want to attend the university but only 3,000 can be admitted. At the same tuition, the shortage at university B is 1,000 students: 4,000 students want to attend but only 3,000 can be admitted.

Will the size of the gap and of the shortage affect how punctual an instructor will be for, and how responsive the instructor will be during, office hours?

The theory predicts that it will: The bigger the gap, the more the demand (to attend the university) has to fall before there is no shortage. In Exhibit 1, the demand curve to attend

iStock.com/amriphoto

EXHIBIT 1

The Gap between Equilibrium Tuition and Student Tuition

The supply of openings at each of two universities, A and B. The demand to attend university A is higher than the demand to attend university B, as shown by the respective demand curves. The equilibrium tuitions are $50,000 at university A and $40,000 at B. However, at each university the student pays $30,000. The gap between the equilibrium tuition at university A and the student tuition is $20,000; at B, the gap is $10,000. At university A, the shortage of openings at the student tuition ($30,000) is 2,200 students: 5,200 students want to be admitted but only 3,000 will be admitted. At university B, the shortage at the student tuition ($30,000) is 1,000: 4,000 students want to be admitted, but only 3,000 will be admitted. The demand to attend university A has to fall more to go through point X (where there is no shortage of openings at the student tuition) than the demand to attend university B has to fall. This fact gives the instructors at A more room to engage in demand-reducing behavior than the instructors at B.

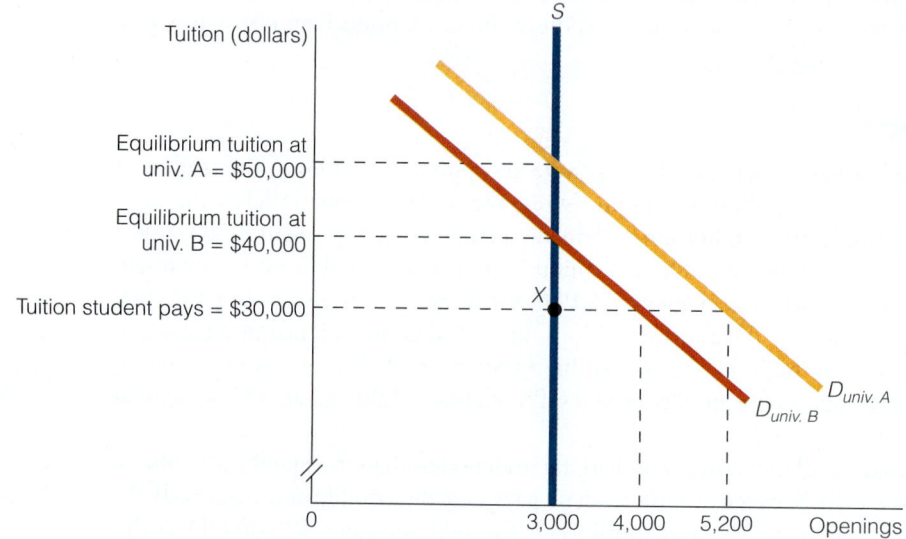

university A would have to shift leftward by enough to go through point X before there is no shortage of openings. The demand curve to attend university B would also have to shift leftward to go through point X, but *not as much*, because the demand curve to attend university B is closer to point X than the demand curve to attend university A is to point X.

What does this situation mean for the instructors at each university? The instructors at university A have more room to take *demand-reducing actions* than the instructors at university B have. Such actions might include showing up late for office hours and not being responsive during office hours, things that students (as customers of the university) do not like. If word gets around that instructors don't regularly meet their office hours at a given university, demand to attend that university may decrease. (Books and websites address students' experiences at various colleges in the country.)

Of course, why would an instructor not be punctual for office hours and not be responsive during them? We doubt that any instructor plans to be this way. Still, instructors might be on the other side of the university campus just before office hours and/or might be feeling a little hurried or overwhelmed on a particular day. The theory simply states that the cost of not hurrying to office hours or of being less responsive during office hours is lower for the instructor at a university with a big demand gap than for the instructor at a university with a small demand gap. At the big-gap university, many other students are willing to take the place of a student who leaves; at the small-gap college, there aren't as many.

19-5c The Predictions

Prediction 1 University instructors who work at big-gap universities will be less nearly punctual for office hours and less responsive during office hours than university instructors who work at small-gap or no-gap universities.

Prediction 2 The bigger the gap, the more flexibility instructors have to teach their courses the way they want to teach it. To illustrate, suppose an instructor wants to do X, Y, and Z in the course but students prefer the instructor to do A, B, and C. How will the course be taught? The bigger the gap, the more likely it is that the instructor will teach X, Y, and Z (even if it isn't what the students want) and not be adversely affected by the students who leave. That's because with a big gap between equilibrium and student tuition, there is a big shortage of openings at the university. Having students go elsewhere because they don't like how the instructor teaches the course (the papers he assigns, the material she goes over, the large number of readings she assigns) doesn't adversely affect the instructor because so many other students want to take their places.

19-6 OBSERVATION/THOUGHT 4: CRIMINALS ARE NOT RATIONAL

Some people say that criminals are not rational. They are not like regular people, who think in terms of the costs and benefits of their actions. Who, in their right mind, would commit a crime—whether it is burglary, kidnapping, arson, or murder?

19-6a The Question

Are criminals rational? Does their behavior respond to changes in costs and benefits?

19-6b The Theory

We build a theory, based on a rational criminal, holding that criminals think and act in terms of costs and benefits. The theory posits that criminals have two equations in mind (and might not be aware of them). The first equation relates to the benefits of committing a criminal act—let's say a burglary. The benefit equation is

$$EB = P_S \times \text{Loot}$$

where EB is the expected benefits of burglary, P_S is the probability of successfully burglarizing a house (getting into and out of a house with the goods), and Loot is the dollar take.

The cost equation is

$$EC = [P_P \times (I + F)] + AC$$

where EC is the expected costs of burglary, P_P is the probability of imprisonment, I is the income the criminal gives up if caught and imprisoned, F is the dollar value the criminal puts on freedom (how much the person would pay to stay out of prison), and AC is the anguish cost of committing a burglary.

An economist would say that criminals simply substitute various values into the equations and then determine whether the expected benefits of the intended criminal act are greater than, less than, or equal to the expected costs. If the expected benefits are greater than the expected costs, they commit the crime. If the expected benefits are less, they do not commit the crime. And if the expected benefits equal the expected costs, they flip a coin: heads, commit the crime; tails, don't commit the crime.

Suppose the values are as follows:

$$P_s = 80 \text{ percent}$$
$$Loot = \$400,000$$
$$P_p = 30 \text{ percent}$$
$$I = \$80,000$$
$$F = \$42,000$$
$$AC = \$3,000$$

Substituting these numbers for the variables into our two equations, we find that the expected benefits equal \$320,000 and the expected costs equal \$39,600. With these numbers, the person goes ahead and commits the crime.

19-6c The Predictions

Prediction 1 If people put more locks on their doors and install more security devices in their homes, the probability of success (P_s) will fall, lowering the benefits of burglary. Moreover, lowering the benefits of burglary will lead to fewer burglaries.

Prediction 2 If more police are on the streets, the probability of being arrested after committing a crime will rise and the probability of being imprisoned (P_p) will likely rise too. Thus, the costs of committing a burglary will rise, and fewer burglaries will be committed.

Prediction 3 During a recession, incomes usually fall and unemployment usually rises. Thus, the income one forfeits is usually lower during a recession than during boom times. Lower foregone income (I) will lower the cost of burglary and thus will lead to more burglaries.

Prediction 4 If prison became more severe (e.g., if burglars who were apprehended were uniformly sentenced to hard labor), a person would pay more to stay out of prison (F). Paying more to stay out of prison will raise the cost of burglary, and fewer burglaries will be committed.

19-6d A Detour: Does Evidence Prove a Theory Correct?

Suppose a theory predicts that all swans are white. You and others go out into the field to test the theory, looking for swans. So far, you and others have found and counted 4,324 swans—all white. Does your finding prove that the theory predicting that all swans are white is correct? No. The reason is simple: We can't be sure that all the existing swans have been found and counted. Perhaps there are 5,000 swans in total, and only 4,324 have been found, have been counted, and are white.

So, even if every swan we've found is white, that evidence does not prove the swan theory correct. The best that evidence can do is give us a reason not to reject a theory. We cannot say, "The evidence proves the theory correct." It is more accurate to say, "The evidence fails to reject the theory." In other words, given the evidence amassed so far, none of it is inconsistent with the predictions of the theory. In contrast, any piece of evidence that is inconsistent with the theory—such as finding a black swan—is reason enough to say, "The evidence rejects the theory." (As a matter of empirical fact, there are black swans in the world—in Australia.)

19-6e Another Detour: After You Have One Theory That Explains and Predicts, Search for Another

Suppose another planet, somewhere in the universe, has living beings that resemble human beings on Earth. These beings speak a language, they read and write, they do mathematics, they raise families—in short, they do all the things we do. However, half the beings on the planet are blue in color and half are green. In the neighborhoods on the planet, blue beings live only with blue beings and green beings live only with green beings. Asked to explain why only completely segregated neighborhoods exist on the planet, you think the explanation has something to do with color discrimination. You put forth a discrimination theory holding that the beings of one color (either green or blue) are discriminating against the beings of the other color. Perhaps green beings have gotten into positions of power and passed laws that prevent blue beings from living in neighborhoods where green beings reside.

You test your theory by seeking out evidence of discrimination. You find that green beings have, in fact, passed laws prohibiting blue persons from living in the same neighborhoods with green persons. Does it follow, then, that discrimination—and discrimination alone—explains the completely segregated neighborhoods? Perhaps not. To illustrate, suppose we advance a nondiscrimination theory of the segregated neighborhoods. This theory is based on the work of Thomas Schelling, cowinner of the Nobel Memorial Prize in Economic Science in 2005.[2]

We start with 200 persons, 100 of whom are blue and 100 of whom are green. Each person (no matter which color) prefers to live in an integrated neighborhood. However, no person wants to live in a neighborhood where he or she is a minority of less than 30 percent.

Now suppose that there are two neighborhoods, A and B, and that their populations are as follows:

Neighborhood A	Neighborhood B
70 blue persons	70 green persons
30 green persons	30 blue persons

Obviously, the two neighborhoods are integrated: Blue people and green people live in each. Also, the two neighborhoods are satisfactory to everyone living in them. No person in either neighborhood falls into a minority that is less than 30 percent of the population.

Then, for work-related reasons, one green person moves from A to B and one blue person moves from B to A. The neighborhoods now look this way:

Neighborhood A	Neighborhood B
71 blue persons	71 green persons
29 green persons	29 blue persons

Green persons have fallen to a 29 percent minority in A, and blue persons have fallen to a 29 percent minority in B. Although both green and blue persons prefer integrated neighborhoods to

2. See Thomas C. Schelling, Micromotives and Macrobehavior (New York: W.W. Norton & Company, 1978).

segregated neighborhoods, they do not want to become a minority of less than 30 percent. So, green persons are likely to move from A to B and blue persons are likely to move from B to A.

If another green person and another blue person move, we get the following configuration:

Neighborhood A	Neighborhood B
72 blue persons	72 green persons
28 green persons	28 blue persons

In neighborhood A, blue persons are becoming a bigger majority and green persons are becoming a smaller minority. In neighborhood B, green persons are becoming a bigger majority and blue persons are becoming a smaller minority.

Where will the movement end? The neighborhoods will be in equilibrium when things look like this:

Neighborhood A	Neighborhood B
100 blue persons	100 green persons

The neighborhoods are now completely segregated. Blue people live with other blue people, and green people live with other green people. There are no blue-green neighborhoods at all.

Although this is an equilibrium setting, all blue and green persons would prefer to live in integrated neighborhoods. But no one wants to live in an integrated neighborhood as a minority of less than 30 percent. Therefore, after a move by one green person and one blue person, we ultimately end up with complete segregation.

Now, as the creator of the color discrimination theory, you had no idea of this process that ended with the segregated neighborhoods. What would you think if you came across the two segregated neighborhoods, not knowing how they came to be that way? You might think that color discrimination was the cause.

Does it follow that segregated neighborhoods can be caused only by one thing or another, but never by two? No. Sometimes multiple causes are behind what we observe, and each cause, by itself, is sufficient to bring about what we see. When trying to explain why neighborhoods are segregated, color discrimination, encased in law, could be enough to explain the segregated neighborhoods. But even in the absence of discrimination, segregated neighborhoods could arise—even when, paradoxically, everyone prefers to live in an integrated neighborhood.

The lesson is that a single-cause theory that predicts well (i.e., accurately) does not necessarily rule out other possible causes. Specifically, the lesson for the theory builder is that, after you have developed one theory to explain something (segregated neighborhoods, dating relationships, ethical codes, inflation, or unemployment), try to build another theory to explain the very same effect. If it, too, predicts well, and the predictions of one theory are not the opposite of the predictions of the other, then we probably have a multiple-cause explanation.

19-6f A Final Detour: Why Prediction Is so Important, or Why Good-Sounding Stories Are Not Enough

Sometimes we want to believe some theories over others, especially when the theory seems to confirm what we already believe. The theory seems to say, "See, you were right all along." Accepting a theory that tells us we were right all along is easier than accepting one that says, "You were wrong all along."

To illustrate, suppose Smith has always believed that people who are on welfare are lazy and unmotivated. Contrary to Smith, Jones believes that people who are on welfare have had unfortunate things happen: They've lost a job or gotten sick and were unable to work, and so on.

Two economists then present two different theories of welfare. The first theory seems to confirm the description of welfare recipients as lazy and unmotivated. The second theory describes welfare recipients in terms of job loss, sickness, and other causes beyond their control. Smith ends up believing the first theory because it seems to confirm what she has always believed. Jones ends up believing the second theory because it seems to confirm what he has always believed.

Do we accept theories because they seem to confirm what we have always believed or want to believe? Sure, people do it all the time. But what both Smith and Jones should be asking of the economists is, "What are your predictions? Do the data support your predictions? What are the predictions of the lazy-unmotivated-person theory of welfare?" If the predictions are X, Y, and Z, then the question is whether the evidence is consistent with X, Y, and Z. If it is, then we now have reason to accept the lazy-unmotivated-person theory of welfare, no matter what you might have believed before. The same goes for the beyond-their-control theory of welfare. If that theory predicts A, B, and C, then the question is whether the evidence is consistent with A, B, and C. If so, then there is now reason to accept that theory, no matter what you might have believed before.

By accepting theories simply because they confirm our beliefs, or because they sound right, or because we want them to be right, we do ourselves a disservice. We need to push theories and theorists to the limit and ask them for more than a "good" or "believable" story or explanation. We need to ask for the predictions. If the theory has no predictions, then it might be nothing more than a fictional account of what someone thinks explains something. Then we must ask for the evidence that leads us to say one of two things: (1) The evidence fails to reject the theory or (2) the evidence rejects the theory.

SELF-TEST

1. Consider Jack who attends both his son's high school football games and a few professional football games too. At which games is Jack more likely to be well behaved? Why?

2. Kidnappers can't be rational because no rational person would be a kidnapper. Comment.

3. Can evidence prove that a theory is correct?

19-7 OBSERVATION/THOUGHT 5: MORE STUDENTS WEAR BASEBALL CAPS IN CLASS ON EXAM DAYS THAN ON OTHER DAYS

19-7a The Question

What purpose does wearing a baseball cap in class on exam days serve that it doesn't serve on other days?

19-7b The Theory

A baseball cap can shield your eyes. A student may want to shield his eyes from the view of the instructor who is administering an exam if the student plans to glance over at his neighbor's test. Therefore, on exam day, wearing a baseball cap in class serves a purpose it doesn't serve any other

ESB Professional/Shutterstock.com

day: It helps a student pick up answers from his neighbors without anyone seeing. It makes one's cheating less visible to others.

19-7c The Predictions

Prediction 1 A smaller percentage of students will be wearing baseball caps when those students are taking an essay exam than when taking a multiple-choice exam.

Prediction 2 A smaller percentage of students will be wearing baseball caps when a lecture is being given than when an exam is being taken.

Prediction 3 Instructors are likely to notice anything that stands out on exam day as being different from other days. In nonclassroom environments, more males than females seem to wear baseball caps. This practice gives males a better chance than females of wearing a baseball cap in class without tipping the instructor into thinking that something is out of the ordinary. Thus, males wearing baseball caps on exam day are less likely to be noticed than females wearing them. Females, then, have one fewer thing they can use to help them cheat than males have, so we can expect females to cheat less. Specific prediction: On a multiple-choice exam, a larger percentage of the cheaters in the class will be male than female.

Prediction 4 Sooner or later, instructors figure out that a baseball cap can be used for shielding one's eyes when looking at another person's exam paper. At that time, they will either tell students that they can't wear baseball caps in class on exam days or perhaps closely watch students who are wearing baseball caps. After all, when instructors figure out the purpose of the cap on exam day, it becomes a signal to the instructor that the wearer may try to cheat on the exam. The baseball cap is then like a neon sign that reads, "Watch me. I am about to cheat on this exam." Specific prediction: On exam day, instructors will look more often at students who are wearing baseball caps than at other students. They will also patrol the class on exam day by walking more often near students who are wearing baseball caps than near other students.

Prediction 5 When the instructor is giving a lecture in class, a student who is wearing a baseball cap will often have to look down to write notes. When the student looks down, the bill of the baseball cap is pointed downward at a certain angle. On exam day, the student who is wearing a baseball cap always has to look downward in order to write answers, and, again, the bill of the cap will be at a certain angle. However, if the student intends to cheat, the angle is likely to be greater on exam day than on a lecture day, when the student is taking notes. That's because the student has more of a reason to shield his or her eyes on exam day. The greater slope (greater angle) of the bill on exam day is indicative that the student is doing something more than just writing: It is indicative that the student is writing and glancing left

ECONOMICS 24 / 7

Talking on a Cell Phone in Public

It appears that people are less likely to talk on their cell phone in some public locales than others. Here are some places that people don't seem to mind talking on their cell phone in public: in an airport while they are waiting to board a plane, in a restaurant, and anywhere in public when they are walking. But here is one place that people do seem to mind talking on their cell phone in public: in the waiting room of their doctor's office. Now, why the difference? Why would the person who is inclined to talk on her cell phone at a restaurant not talk on her cell phone in her doctor's office? Because we would expect the benefits of talking on the cell phone in public to be the same in both locales, it must be that the costs of talking on the cell phone in both locales are not the same. Obviously, the cost is higher in one's doctor's office.

iStock.com/nyul

The difference between a restaurant and one's doctor's office is that in the restaurant the people around you are talking to each other. In other words, two things go on in a restaurant: eating food and talking. People go out to eat and talk to each other. It is generally accepted, then, that one can go to a restaurant and talk. Therefore, talking on the cell phone (except when the server is trying to take your order) is not as disruptive as it would be in some other public settings, such as your doctor's office. In a doctor's office, the patients waiting to be called do not know each other, so there is really no reason for them to talk to each other. Instead, what they do is sit there and read a magazine while waiting to be called. In this setting, talking on one's cell phone would be jarring. First, there is quiet, and individuals are reading their magazines. Then, all of a sudden, we hear, "Hello," then a pause, then "I don't know what he is thinking about, but I told him that we weren't going that way. Did he get those sales numbers from you or Karen? No matter. . . ." In a public space where everyone is silent except the person on the cell phone, the person on the phone is very noticeable. That is the case in the doctor's office. But in a public space where everyone is talking, including the person on the cell phone, the person on the phone doesn't stand out (nearly as much). That is the case in the restaurant.

We would expect that, for most people, the cost of talking on their cell phones would be higher in their doctor's office than in a restaurant—even if in neither place is there a sign stating that people should not talk on cell phones. The cost is, specifically, in terms of "other people judging one's behavior as rude." We predict, then, that we will see more people talking on the cell phone in public places where other people are talking than in public places where other people are not talking. Or look at it this way: If the only person in the doctor's office other than you is a family of four, and they are talking to each other (which is likely to be the case, because they know each other), then you'd feel more at ease talking on your cell phone than you would be if four unrelated persons were in the office besides you.

and right. Therefore, specific prediction: Students with baseball caps in class on exam days and on lecture days will likely be cheating if the bill of their baseball caps is more sloped (at a greater angle) on exam days.

Prediction 6 Students who wear baseball caps backward on lecture days but frontward on exam days are probably cheating on exam days.

19-8 OBSERVATION/THOUGHT 6: HOUSES IN "GOOD" SCHOOL DISTRICTS ARE OFTEN MORE EXPENSIVE THAN COMPARABLE HOUSES IN "BAD" SCHOOL DISTRICTS

19-8a The Question

Why are comparable houses (same square footage, size of lot, etc.) often priced differently?

19-8b The Theory

Suppose school districts could be ranked on a scale from 1 to 10, with 10 being the best and 1 the worst. Two houses, A and B, are alike in every way except that house A is located in a school district ranked 5 and house B is in a school district ranked 10. Currently, the prices of both houses are the same. Which one would you buy if you had children starting school soon? Most people would choose the house in the number-10 school district: house B.

Why? Well, being in a higher ranked school district is something that people with children consider to be a good (something from which they derive utility), so a utility-maximizing couple would prefer to get more rather than less utility for a given amount of money spent on a house. Better to spend $250,000 for a house and get 10,000 utils of utility than to spend $250,000 for a house and get 9,000 utils of utility.

But the real question is, If people get more utility from house B than from house A (because it's located in a better school district), would the prices of the houses really be the same? The answer is no. If house B has something that people value that house A does not have, then the demand for house B will be higher. And a higher demand in the face of a given supply means a higher price. In other words, the house with something more—in this case, a higher ranked school district—will end up priced higher than the house with less—a lower ranked school district.

The conclusion: When a person buys a house in a higher ranked school district, part of the purchase price represents what one must pay to be in that school district. In other words, the benefits of being in the higher ranked school district are incorporated into the price of the house. You might be able to break down the price of the house this way: (1) land = $100,000; (2) materials and labor to build the house = $200,000; (3) price paid to be located in a higher ranked school district = $70,000. Total price = $370,000.

19-8c The Predictions

Prediction 1 Houses with ocean views will sell for higher prices than comparable houses with no view. You will pay for the view.

Prediction 2 Houses located in major metropolitan areas (where there are many things to do) can sell for higher prices than comparable houses in small towns. You will pay for having the opportunity to do a lot of things.

Prediction 3 Houses located in cities with clean air will sell for higher prices than comparable houses located in cities with dirty air. You will pay for the cleaner air.

Prediction 4 If a major professional sports team were to move to a city that previously did not have a major professional sports team, house prices in the city would rise. You will pay for the sports team. (This prediction is similar to prediction 2, except that it is more specific.)

Prediction 5 People will pay (donate money) to meet the president of the United States. Think of the president first as a human being and second as a unique human being. Of the billions of human beings, there is only one president at a time. Now think of the president of the United States and other human beings as you would think of two houses that were comparable in every way except that one had an ocean view and the other didn't. People will pay more for the house with the view. The president is similar to a house with an ocean view, whereas most people are similar to a house without a view. The president has something—the presidency—that all others do not. Although people might not be willing to pay to meet just an average, everyday human being, they would be willing to pay to meet a unique human being (the one and only president of the United States).

19-9 OBSERVATION/THOUGHT 7: ARE PEOPLE BETTER OFF WITH OR WITHOUT HEALTH CARE VOUCHERS?

Suppose 100,000 persons do not have health insurance of any kind. Then Congress passes legislation that mandates a $200 health care voucher per month for each person. With the vouchers, which can be used only to purchase health care, each person can have up to $200 worth of health care a month, or $2,400 of health care a year. For example, Jack doesn't have any health insurance. If he were to get hurt and need medical attention, he could simply go to a doctor or hospital, get the attention he needs, and pay for the services rendered (up to $200 a month, or $2,400 a year) with the vouchers.

19-9a The Question

Will the 100,000 persons purchase more health care with the vouchers than without them? The obvious answer to this question seems to be yes, but is it necessarily correct?

19-9b The Theory

Jack is one of the 100,000 persons currently without health insurance. He earns $3,200 a month and spends each month's income in the following way:

- Food = $1,000
- Rent = $2,000
- Savings for future health care expenses = $200

Now suppose Jack receives the $200-a-month health care voucher. Then he can reorder his expenditures in this way:

- Food = $1,000
- Rent = $2,000
- Health care voucher = $200
- Entertainment = $200

Because of the voucher, $200 is freed up for Jack to do other things—if he wants to. He decides to spend the $200 that he had been saving each month on entertainment.

Of course, he doesn't have to spend the money on entertainment. He could spend it on books, clothes, more food, more health care, a higher rent, or even cocaine, gambling, or alcohol. Fact is, we know some things about him but don't know other things about him. We don't know how he will spend the freed-up $200. What we do know is that he will spend it on whatever is *next* on his list of things to buy. If more health care is next on his list, then, instead of buying only $200 worth of health care a month (when he didn't have the voucher), he can now buy $400 worth. But if what is next on his list is, say, clothes, then the health care voucher is not financing more health care for Jack, but rather more clothes.

Essentially, our theory says this: A monetary gift (of, say, $200 in cash) or an in-kind gift (a $200 voucher that can be used only to purchase health care) will end up going for whatever is next on the recipient's list of desired purchases.

19-9c The Predictions

Prediction 1 A mother has two children. She gives each of them gifts of money and in-kind gifts. The theory predicts that she will give more gifts to the child whose next-on-the-list purchase is more acceptable to her. Here is an example: A mother says that child 1 is more trustworthy when it comes to spending money than child 2 is. In the eyes of the mother, what's next on child 1's list is superior to what's next on child 2's list. (Starkly, suppose that what's next on child 1's list are more books and DVDs and that what's next on child 2's list are more cigarettes.)

Prediction 2 If each of two candidates running for office says that she will do X, Y, and Z if elected, people will be more willing to vote for the candidate they more nearly agree with in terms of what comes next. To illustrate, suppose A and B are running against each other for U.S. senator from some state. Both say that they will vote for reduced taxes, more spending on education, and strong pollution standards. How does a voter who wants all three things decide whom to vote for? If the voter is equally convinced that both candidates are true to their word, she will think in terms of what's next: what will the candidate do if elected? If, for the voter, A's next-on-the-list purchase is thought to be better than B's next-on-the-list purchase, then the voter votes for A.

How could we test to see whether this prediction is correct? Perhaps the voter who speaks of a candidate as "trustworthy" is thinking in terms of what's next: The more the voter agrees with the candidate's next thing to do, the more trustworthy the voter believes the candidate is. We would predict, then, that the voter will vote for the candidate who seems more trustworthy.

19-10 OBSERVATION/THOUGHT 8: PEOPLE WHO GIVE TO OTHERS OFTEN COMPLAIN THAT THEY END UP GIVING TOO MUCH

19-10a The Question

Why don't people simply stop giving at the efficient point of giving—when the marginal benefits of giving equal the marginal costs?

19-10b The Theory[3]

Suppose person G is a gift giver (he gives gifts to person R) and person R is the gift recipient. The G's utility is specified as

$$U_G = f(\text{Goods A} - Z, U_R)$$

where U_G represents the utility that person G places on giving, goods A–Z are various goods that give person G utility, and U_R is the gift recipient's utility (stemming from receiving G's gifts). Because U_R is included in person G's utility function in a positive way, every time R's utility rises, so does G's utility. In other words, when G gives a gift to R, the gift benefits not only R, but also G. Person G likes seeing R happy and benefits more as R becomes happier. To make this point more concrete, think of a mother giving gifts to her children (the recipients). Giving the gifts to her children makes them happy, and when the mother sees her children happy, she gains some utility. She says, "I am happy when my children are happy."

Next, consider R's utility function:

$$U_R = f(\text{Goods A} - Z)$$

In this case, U_G is not included in the utility function of the gift recipient. Person R is unaffected by the utility that G receives.

Now consider what we mean by a gift. According to this theory, a gift is anything that one person gives (without seeking payment in return) to another person that benefits the other person. It could be money, a specific good (such as a computer, a car, or an item of clothing), or something as simple as a back rub. It could be doing the dishes for someone, going to the store to pick up something, and so on. Simply put, we define a gift broadly. Don't think only in terms of a birthday or holiday gift; think in terms of anything that someone wants and that gives the person utility or satisfaction.

Exhibit 2(a) shows the marginal benefits and marginal costs to person G of giving gifts to person R. The marginal benefits (MB) curve is downward sloping, indicating that the law of diminishing marginal utility (benefits) holds for gift giving. The marginal costs (MC) curve is horizontal, indicating the constant marginal cost of gift giving. Obviously, the efficient (or optimum) number of gifts, according to G, is 10, where $MB = MC$. The area under the MB curve and above the MC curve out to 10 gifts represents the net gains to G of giving gifts. This area is shaded in blue.

Now, it would be preferable for R to receive 11 gifts, rather than 10, but how can R get G to give 11 gifts if 10 is the efficient number of gifts for G to give? As shown in Exhibit 2(b), moving from the 10th to the 11th gift presents G with a net loss because, for the 11th gift, the marginal benefits are less than the marginal costs. The green area represents the net loss of utility with the 11th gift.

Perhaps R can get G to give 11 instead of 10 gifts by presenting G with an *all-or-nothing deal* that takes the efficient option (10 gifts) off the table. In other words, suppose R suggests to G that only two options are available for choosing: either zero gifts or 11 gifts. That is to say, instead of letting G choose from three options—0, 10, and 11—R makes G think that he must choose between only two options: 0 or 11. In other words, R is saying to G, "Either give me 11 gifts, or I will not accept any gifts from you."

Will limiting G to only two options—0 or 11—force G to give R 11 gifts? Yes. G now has to calculate what he receives in net gains by giving zero gifts with what he receives in net gains if he gives 11 gifts. Obviously, if he gives zero gifts, he receives no net gains. But if he gives 11 gifts,

---

3. This theory is based on a theory first put forth by Wilson E. Schmidt in "Charitable Exploitation," *Public Choice 10* (Spring 1969), pp. 103–104. The theory is also discussed in Richard B. McKenzie and Gordon Tullock, *The New World of Economics*, 5th ed. (New York: McGraw-Hill, 1994).

he receives net gains on the first 10 gifts and a net loss on the 11th. If the net gains on gifts 1–10 are greater than the net loss on the 11th gift, then it is better to give 11 gifts than to give none.

In dollar terms, let's say that the blue area in Exhibit 2(b) is worth $500 and the green area is worth $20. Subtracting the net loss on the 11th gift from the net gain of $500 on the first 10 gifts, we are left with $480 in net gains. Person G must therefore compare the $480 in net gains of giving 11 gifts to R against the net gains (zero) he would receive if he gives R zero gifts. In other words, because the blue area (the gains) is greater than the green area (the losses), it is better for G to go with 11 gifts than with zero. Conclusion: By presenting G with an all-or-nothing deal (all = 11 and nothing = 0), R is able to push G beyond his efficient level of gift giving and benefit by receiving more gifts.

EXHIBIT 2

Giving and Receiving Gifts

(a) The marginal benefits and marginal cost for a gift giver (person G) of giving gifts to a gift recipient (person R). The efficient or optimum number of gifts for G to give is 10, the point at which the marginal benefits of giving gifts equals the marginal costs of giving gifts. (b) G's net gain of giving 10 gifts (blue area) and G's net loss of giving an 11th gift

(green area). If person R presents G with an all-or-nothing deal ("Give me 11 gifts or give me nothing"), person G will likely give 11 gifts because the net gain on gifts 1–10 is greater than the net loss on the 11th gift. (c) How far can person R push G into giving more than the efficient number of gifts (10)? The answer is 20 gifts, at which point the net gain on gifts 1–10 for G equals the net loss

on gifts 11–20. G will not give R a 21st gift. (d) Unless R makes the all-or-nothing request of G in a subtle, nonconfrontational way, R is not likely to benefit. That's because G could find that he receives fewer benefits per gift in giving to R. In that case, the MB curve of giving gifts shifts to the left, from MB_1 to MB_2, and the new efficient number of gifts is 5 instead of 10.

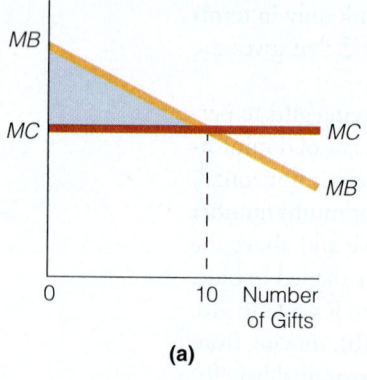

(a)

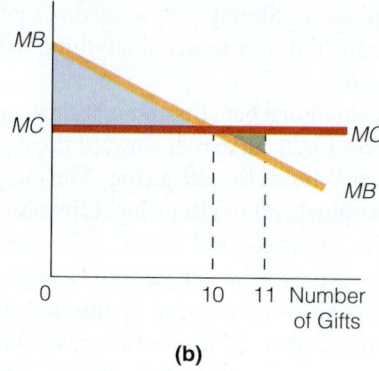

(b)

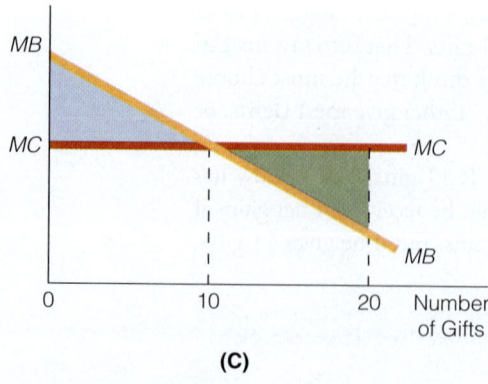

(C)

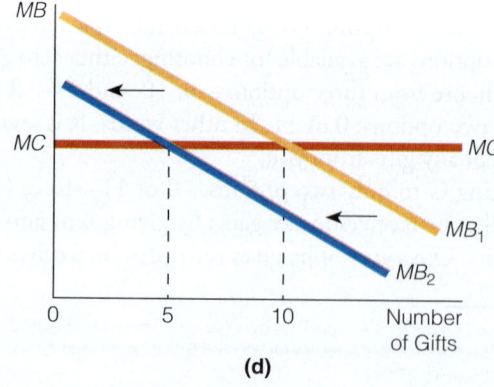

(d)

In the extreme, how far can R push G? A quick glance at Exhibit 2(c) shows the answer. When the blue area (gains) equals the green area (losses), G will become indifferent between giving R 20 gifts and giving R zero gifts. In other words, the most gifts R can get G to give is 20. Given the option of giving, say, 21 or zero gifts, G will choose zero gifts.

A question arises: Suppose R makes the all-or-nothing deal to G in a rude, demanding way. Might this approach cause G to rethink giving gifts to R at all? Person R would have to be wary of this effect because, if G reacts too negatively to the all-or-nothing deal, G's marginal benefits curve (of giving gifts to R) may shift leftward by enough to decrease the efficient number of gifts. This effect is shown in Exhibit 2(d) by a leftward shift in the marginal benefits curve from MB_1 to MB_2. As a result, G will now want to give fewer gifts to R than before the all-or-nothing stipulation. The new efficient number of gifts is 5 instead of 10.

19-10c The Predictions

Prediction 1 Gift givers will have less reason to move beyond their efficient number of gifts as the number of persons they can give gifts to increases. In other words, an all-or-nothing deal (from a gift recipient to a gift giver) has less chance of working if the gift giver can substitute one recipient for another. To illustrate, suppose G gives gifts to person R_1, who then tries to get G to give more gifts than the efficient number by presenting G with an all-or-nothing deal. But G has potential recipients waiting in the wings and simply replaces R_1 with R_2, to whom he gives the efficient number of gifts. Specific prediction: A recipient (an R person) who has few substitutes is more likely to push G beyond the efficient number of gifts than a recipient who has many substitutes.

To illustrate, consider two relationships:

1. A mother–daughter relationship in which the mother has only the one daughter

2. A relationship between two friends

In each relationship are two persons: an R and a G. In the mother–daughter relationship, the mother is the gift giver (G) and the daughter is the gift recipient. The mother (G) gives the efficient number of gifts to the daughter. The daughter tries to push the mother to give more gifts. The daughter gives the mother an all-or-nothing deal. Can the mother replace the daughter with another daughter? No, she has only the one daughter.

Now consider the relationship between two friends, G and R. G gives R the efficient number of gifts. R tries to push G beyond the efficient number. G can more easily find another friend to give gifts to than the mother can find another daughter. Specific prediction: A G person will give more gifts, beyond the efficient number of gifts, to an R person who cannot be replaced than to an R person who can be replaced. In short, the mother is more likely to give in to the daughter's requests than the G friend will give in to the R-friend's requests.

Prediction 2 Smith wants to buy goods X, Y, and Z from a company. Buying X, Y, and Z maximizes Smith's net gains. The company presents Smith with an all-or-nothing deal: Either buy W, X, Y, and Z or buy nothing. In other words, it's a package deal or nothing. Smith takes a net loss on buying W, but the net loss on W is smaller than the sum of the net gains on X, Y, and Z. Therefore, Smith chooses to buy the company's package. Specific prediction: Package deals often contain something that the customer would have preferred not to have purchased. For example, Smith buys a package of 40 cable channels from his cable television provider, but he says that he would have preferred buying only 30 because he never watches anything on 10 of the 40 channels.

Does It Matter to You . . .
If and How You Are in Someone Else's Utility Function?

In our discussion of gift givers and gift recipients, we held that the gift giver had the gift recipient in his utility function in a positive way. In other words, if the gift recipient's utility increased, this then caused the gift giver's utility to increase. Also, if the gift recipient's utility decreased, this then caused the gift giver's utility to decrease.

Does it matter to you if, and how, you are in someone else's utility function? Ideally, we all might like to be in other peoples' utility function the exact same way the gift recipient was in the gift giver's utility function. If everyone got utility if our utility increased, then we could expect everyone to try to make us better off, that is raise our utility, so that they could then be better off as a result. In other words, if Joe can raise his utility by first raising Kelly's utility, then you would think that Joe is going to work at trying to raise Kelly's utility, which is something you would certainly benefit from if you are Kelly.

Of course, it is not likely that we would be in everyone's utility function in a positive way. But we would certainly want to be in the utility functions (in a positive way) of those people we care about: friends, family, husband, or wife. To illustrate, consider Tyler and his father, Larry. Larry has Tyler in his utility function in a positive way. When things go well for Tyler (and Tyler gains utility), Larry feels good too. When things go poorly for Tyler (and Tyler suffers some disutility), Larry feels bad too.

Now Larry would probably prefer that Tyler feel the same way about him as he feels about Tyler. Larry would probably hope that, just as Tyler is in his utility function in a positive way, he is in Tyler's utility function in a positive way. This is because the alternatives are somewhat disappointing: either Larry is not in Tyler's utility function or he is in his utility function in a negative way.

Not being in someone's utility function means that no matter what happens to you—good or bad—it does not have any affect on the other person. Whether you are happy or sad, sick or well, it does not matter. This sends the message that the person really doesn't care one way or the other about you.

To be in someone's utility function in a negative way means that when good things happen to you (and your utility rises), the other person feels bad (and suffers disutility); and when bad things happen to you (and your disutility rises), the other person feels good (and gains utility). This sends the message that the person is better off when you are worse off, and is worse off when you are better off.

We return to our question: Does it matter to you if, and how, you are in someone else's utility function? Yes it does. Ideally, we would all want to be in everyone's utility function in a positive way. Knowing that this is impossible, we certainly prefer to be in the utility function of those we care about in a positive way, than either of the alternatives: not at all or in a negative way.

SELF-TEST

1. Identify two observations that are inconsistent with the baseball-cap-wearing theory of cheating on an exam.

2. Ocean views (from a house) are not free. Do you agree or disagree? Explain your answer.

3. What does it mean if you are included in another person's utility function in a positive way?

OFFICE HOURS | "Can Anyone Build a Theory?"

STUDENT: I always thought that building theories was the purview of people who are well educated in a particular subject. For example, only those with a PhD in economics should build economic theories, and only those with a doctorate in sociology should build sociological theories. Am I wrong about this?

INSTRUCTOR: There is no clear line of demarcation between who should and who should not try to build a theory. The purpose of this chapter is to give you the details of how to build and evaluate a theory. On this subject, consider what Richard Feynman (1918–1988), a Nobel laureate in physics, said about how theorists start to build theories. He said that the first step of building a theory is to "guess" how things work.

STUDENT: But anyone can guess why things are as they are. Isn't there a big difference between my guessing about physical laws and Richard Feynman guessing about laws? Aren't his guesses more likely to turn out right than mine?

INSTRUCTOR: Yes, probably so, but that's not the point. The point is that theory building starts with a guess—albeit sometimes an educated guess—as to the way things are. Then, from the guess, we "unravel," in Feynman's words, the consequences of the guess. And finally, we compare those consequences against experience. In other words, the evaluation part of the scientific method comes at the end of the process, when we compare the consequences of the guess, or the predictions of the theory, that we have built with real-world experience, observation, or data.

STUDENT: In other words, anyone can build a theory, but not everyone's theory is going to be consistent with experience–observation–data. Many theories will be rejected by the evidence.

INSTRUCTOR: Yes, that's correct. But if you want to get a feel for theorizing, try to build your own theories to explain something you are interested in. Once you have done so, be sure to logically deduce the theory's predictions. Then ask yourself whether the theory's predictions are accurate. Do you actually observe those things which are consistent with the theory?

Points to Remember

1. At the heart of building a theory is the motivation to explain something. (In this chapter, we've tried to explain why the birthrate is higher in some countries than in others, what might explain the burglary rate, why neighborhoods might be segregated, and so on.)

2. Building a theory differs from evaluating a theory. Guesswork plays a part in building a theory; in evaluating a theory, evidence matters. Simply put, the evidence either rejects or fails to reject the predictions of the theory.

CHAPTER SUMMARY

WHAT A THEORY IS AND IS NOT

- A theory is not perfectly descriptive of reality.
- Theories should not be judged by how they sound or by whether they say the things we want to hear. Theories should be judged according to how well they explain things and how consistently and accurately they predict.

THE BIRTHRATES IN VARIOUS COUNTRIES

- The question was, why do birthrates differ in various countries?
- A key part of answering the question was to consider a woman's opportunity cost of having a child. The higher the opportunity cost of having children (in terms of the wage

the woman would not earn if she took time off to have and raise a child), the fewer children she would have; the lower the opportunity cost of having children, the more children she would have.

THE ISSUE OF FALSIFIABILITY (REFUTABILITY)

- A good theory should have the virtue of falsifiability; that is, a theory must not only predict things that you should observe if it is right, but should also predict things that you should observe if it is wrong.

- Scientists strive to build theories that can be falsified or refuted. They seek to build theories that are capable of telling them not only when they are right, but also when they are wrong.

ETHICAL CODES AND TOWN SIZE

- The question was, Do people who live in small towns have a somewhat different (better?) ethical code than those who live in large cities?

- The theory argues that the larger a percentage of the population that a person is, the more likely it is that the person will treat others as he or she wants to be treated. That's because, as a larger percentage of the population, the person is more likely to have to meet again and again with people he or she initially meets.

STUDENT TUITION AND EQUILIBRIUM TUITION

- The question was, Will instructors who teach at universities with a small gap between student tuition and the equilibrium tuition be on time more often for office hours and more responsive during those hours than instructors at universities with a larger gap?

- At most four-year traditional public and private universities, the tuition the student pays is below the equilibrium tuition. The larger the gap between the student tuition and the equilibrium tuition, the greater is the shortage of spots at the university and the more it is that demand for the university can fall without completely eliminating the shortage at the university. Therefore, the larger the gap, the more room instructors have to take demand-reducing actions at the university without suffering any consequences. One of these demand-reducing actions might be not being on time for office hours or not being as responsive as possible during office hours.

CRIMINALS AND RATIONALITY

- The questions were, Are criminals rational? and Does their behavior respond to changes in costs and benefits?

- We built a simple theory based on two equations: one related to the expected benefits of committing a criminal act (specifically, burglary) and one related to the expected costs of committing the criminal act. We hypothesized that individuals would commit criminal acts only when the expected benefits outweighed the expected costs. Variables on the cost side and on the benefits side of the theory were then changed, and predictions materialized as to whether the crime rate (burglary rate) would rise or fall.

- If the predictions are consistent with reality, then we can argue that criminals are rational.

DOES EVIDENCE PROVE A THEORY IS CORRECT?

- If evidence is consistent with a theory's predictions, we state that the evidence fails to reject the theory. We do not say that the evidence proves that the theory is correct.

- If evidence is inconsistent with a theory's predictions, we state that the evidence rejects the theory.

BASEBALL CAPS IN CLASS AND EXAM DAYS

- The question was, What purpose does wearing a baseball cap in class on exam days serve that it doesn't serve on other days?

- One of the things that a baseball cap can do is shield one's eyes. If students want to cheat on a multiple-choice test, it is a good idea to shield their eyes from the view of the instructor. A baseball cap can help meet this objective.

HOUSE PRICES AND SCHOOL DISTRICTS

- The question was, Why are comparable houses often priced differently?

- If two houses are alike in every way, except that one is located in a good school district and the other in a bad school district, we would expect that the one located in a good school district would be priced higher. Individuals pay for the good school district in terms of house prices.

HEALTH CARE AND VOUCHERS

- The question was, Will individuals purchase more health care with health care vouchers than without them?

- A monetary or in-kind gift will end up going for whatever is next on the recipient's list of desired purchases. For example, suppose Smith is currently spending $200 on X and $300 on Y. Then, someone gives Smith $100. Smith may spend the $100 on X, on Y, or on a combination of the two, or he may spend it on Z. The monetary gift goes for whatever is next on his list of desired purchases.

GIVING

- The question was, Will a person who is giving gifts to another person stop giving gifts at the point at which the marginal benefits of giving gifts equals the marginal costs of giving gifts?
- Both marginal benefits and marginal costs accompany each gift a gift giver gives to a gift recipient. The efficient number of gifts that the gift giver wants to give is the number at which the marginal benefits of giving a gift equal the marginal costs. However, if the gift recipient presents the gift giver with an all-or-nothing demand that takes the efficient number of gifts off the table, the gift giver could end up giving the gift recipient more than the efficient number of gifts. How many more depends on net gains on the efficient number of gifts compared with net losses on the gifts beyond the efficient number.

QUESTIONS AND PROBLEMS

1. Why is it better for theories to be judged by how accurately they predict than by how they sound to us?

2. What role does opportunity cost play in the theory that birthrates are likely to be higher in some countries than others?

3. What does it mean to say that a theory is falsifiable or refutable?

4. A person is more likely to lose his temper with a friend than with his boss. Do you agree or disagree? Explain your answer.

5. One prediction made in the chapter was that "the owner of a car repair shop in a small town will be more careful not to overcharge customers than the owner of a car repair shop in a large city." Why?

6. Put forth two observations that are inconsistent with the cost–benefit theory of burglary discussed in the chapter.

7. What does the difference between the equilibrium tuition and the student tuition have to do with instructors holding office hours?

8. For an economist, is it preferable to assume that criminals are rational than to build a theory based on a rational criminal and then check the evidence? Explain your answer.

9. Segregated neighborhoods of blue and green people can be the result of the people of each color preferring a certain type of integration over segregation. What specifically is the certain type of integration?

10. The quality of the school district can affect house prices in that district. If this statement is true, what should we observe?

11. A man asks his brother for $400 to buy a television set. His brother gives him the money, and the man buys a television set. Is it guaranteed that the brother's $400 went to buy the television set? Why or why not?

12. People will often make charitable donations to religious organizations but not to gangs. Why?

13. Under what condition might persons buy more of something than the efficient amount for them to buy?

14. Do the following: (1) make an observation; (2) identify a question based on the observation; (3) put forth a theory to answer the question; and (4) identify at least two predictions based on the theory.

WORKING WITH NUMBERS AND GRAPHS

1. Diagrammatically represent what happens to the efficient number of gifts that a gift giver wants to give to a gift recipient as the marginal cost of giving gifts declines.

2. Diagrammatically represent what happens to the efficient number of gifts that a gift giver wants to give to a gift recipient as the marginal benefits of giving gifts decline.

20

INTERNATIONAL TRADE

INTRODUCTION

Economics is about trade, and trade crosses boundaries. People trade not only with people who live in their city, state, or country, but also with people in other countries. Many of the goods you consume are undoubtedly produced in other countries. This chapter examines international trade and the prohibitions sometimes placed on it.

20-1 INTERNATIONAL TRADE THEORY

International trade takes place for the same reasons that trade at any level and anywhere exists. Individuals trade to make themselves better off. Pat and Zach, both of whom live in Cincinnati, Ohio, trade because they both value something the other has more than they value some of their own possessions. On an international scale, Elaine in the United States trades with Cho in China because Cho has something that Elaine wants and Elaine has something that Cho wants.

Obviously, the countries of the world have different terrains, climates, resources, worker skills, and so on. Therefore, some countries will be able to produce goods that other countries cannot produce or can produce only at extremely high costs. For example, Hong Kong has no oil, and Saudi Arabia has a large supply of it. Bananas do not grow easily in the United States, but they flourish in Honduras. Americans could grow bananas if they used hothouses, but it is cheaper for Americans to buy bananas from Hondurans than to produce bananas themselves.

Major U.S. exports include automobiles, computers, aircraft, corn, wheat, soybeans, scientific instruments, coal, and plastic materials. Major imports include petroleum, automobiles, clothing, iron and steel, office machines, footwear, fish, coffee, and diamonds. Some of the major exporting countries of the world are the United States, China, Germany, Japan, France, and the United Kingdom. These same countries are also among the major importers in the world.

cdrin/Shutterstock.com

20-1a How Countries Know What to Trade

Recall the economic concept of **comparative advantage**, a concept discussed in Chapter 2. In this section, we discuss comparative advantage in terms of countries rather than in terms of individuals.

Comparative Advantage Assume a two-country, two-good world. Suppose the countries are the United States and Japan, and the goods are food and clothing. Both countries can produce the two goods in the four different combinations listed in Exhibit 1. For example, the United States can produce 90 units of food and 0 units of clothing, 60 units of food and 10 units of clothing, or either of the other two combinations shown. Japan can produce 15 units of food and 0 units of clothing, 10 units of food and 5 units of clothing, or two other combinations.

Now, suppose the United States is producing and consuming the two goods in the combination represented by point *B* on its production possibilities frontier (PPF) and Japan is producing and consuming the combination of the two goods represented by point *F* on its PPF. In this case, neither of the two countries is specializing in the production of one of the two goods, nor are the two countries trading with each other. We call this situation the *no-specialization–no-trade (NS–NT) case* (column 1 of Exhibit 2).

Suppose further that the United States and Japan decide to specialize in the production of a specific good and to trade with each other. We call this situation the *specialization–trade (S–T) case*.

> **Comparative Advantage**
> The advantage a country has when it can produce a good at lower opportunity cost than another country can.

EXHIBIT 1

Production Possibilities in Two Countries

The United States and Japan can produce the two goods in the combinations shown. Initially, the United States is at point *B* on its PPF and Japan is at point *F* on its PPF. Both countries can be made better off by specializing in and trading the good in which each has a comparative advantage.

United States				Japan		
Points on Production Possibilities Frontier	Food	Clothing		Points on Production Possibilities Frontier	Food	Clothing
A	90	0		E	15	0
B	60	10		F	10	5
C	30	20		G	5	10
D	0	30		H	0	15

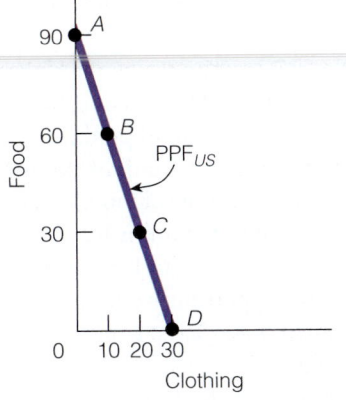

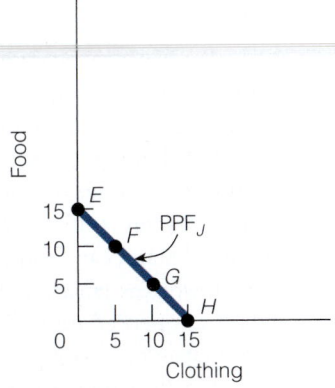

EXHIBIT 2

Both Countries Gain from Specialization and Trade

Column 1: Both the United States and Japan operate independently of each other. The United States produces and consumes 60 units of food and 10 units of clothing. Japan produces and consumes 10 units of

food and 5 units of clothing. Column 2: The United States specializes in the production of food; Japan specializes in the production of clothing. Column 3: The United States and Japan agree to terms of trade of 2 units of food for 1 unit of clothing. They go on to trade 20 units of food for 10 units

of clothing. Column 4: Overall, the United States consumes 70 units of food and 10 units of clothing; Japan consumes 20 units of food and 5 units of clothing. Column 5: Consumption levels are higher for both the United States and Japan in the S−T case than in the NS−NT case.

	No-Specialization−No-Trade (NS−NT) Case		Specialization−Trade (S−T) Case			
Country	(1) Production and Consumption in the NS−NT Case		(2) Production in the S−T Case	(3) Exports (−) Imports (+) Terms of Trade Are 2F = 1C	(4) Consumption in the S−T Case (2) + (3)	(5) Gains from Specialization and Trade (4) − (1)
United States						
Food	60 }	Point B in	90 }	−20	70	10
Clothing	10	Exhibit 1	0	+10	10	0
Japan						
Food	10 }	Point F in	0 }	+20	20	10
Clothing	5	Exhibit 1	15	−10	5	0

Whether the two countries will be better off through specialization and trade is best explained by means of a numerical example, but first we need to find the answers to two other questions: What good should the United States specialize in producing? and What good should Japan specialize in producing? The general answer to both questions is the same: *Countries specialize in the production of the good in which they have a comparative advantage.* A country has a comparative advantage with respect to another country in the production of a good when the one country can produce the good at a lower opportunity cost than the other country can.

For instance, in our hypothetical example, the opportunity cost to the United States of producing 1 unit of clothing (C) is 3 units of food (F): for every 10 units of clothing the United States produces, it forfeits 30 units of food. Thus, the opportunity cost of producing 1 unit of food is 1/3 unit of clothing. In Japan, the opportunity cost of producing 1 unit of clothing is 1 unit of food. (For every 5 units of clothing Japan produces, it forfeits 5 units of food.) So, in the United States, the situation is $1C = 3F$, or $1F = 1/3C$; in Japan, the situation is $1C = 1F$, or $1F = 1C$. The United States can produce food at a lower opportunity cost than Japan can ($1/3C$, as opposed to $1C$), whereas Japan can produce clothing at a lower opportunity cost than the United States can ($1F$, as opposed to $3F$). In other words, the United States has a comparative advantage in food and Japan has a comparative advantage in clothing.

Finally, suppose that the two countries specialize in the production of the goods in which they have a comparative advantage. The United States specializes in the production of food (producing 90 units), and Japan specializes in the production of clothing (producing 15 units). In Exhibit 1, the United States locates at point *A* on its PPF and Japan locates at point H on its PPF. (The two points are listed in column 2 of Exhibit 2.)

Settling on the Terms of Trade   After they have determined which goods they will specialize in producing, the two countries must settle on the terms of trade—that is, how much food to trade for how much clothing. The United States faces the following situation: For every 30 units of food it does not produce, it can produce 10 units of clothing, as shown in Exhibit 1. Thus, 3 units of food have an opportunity cost of 1 unit of clothing $(3F = 1C)$, or 1 unit of food has a cost of 1/3 unit of clothing $(1F = \frac{1}{3}C)$. Japan faces the following situation: For every 5 units of food it does not produce, it can produce 5 units of clothing. Thus, 1 unit of food has an opportunity cost of 1 unit of clothing $(1F = 1C)$. For the United States, $3F = 1C$, and for Japan, $1F = 1C$.

With these cost ratios, both countries should be able to agree on terms of trade which specify that $2F = 1C$. The United States would benefit by giving up 2 units of food, instead of 3 units, for 1 unit of clothing, whereas Japan would benefit by getting 2 units of food, instead of only 1 unit, for 1 unit of clothing. So, if the two countries agree to the terms of trade $2F = 1C$, and if they do trade—in absolute amounts, 20 units of food for 10 units of clothing (column 3 of Exhibit 2)—will they make themselves better off? We'll soon see that they will.

Results of the Specialization–Trade (S–T) Case   Now the United States produces 90 units of food and trades 20 units to Japan, receiving 10 units of clothing in exchange. The United States consumes 70 units of food and 10 units of clothing. Japan produces 15 units of clothing and trades 10 units to the United States, receiving 20 units of food in exchange. Japan consumes 5 units of clothing and 20 units of food. (The two sets of numbers are shown in column 4 of Exhibit 2.)

Column 5 of Exhibit 2 shows both countries' gains from specialization and trade: the United States and Japan each consume 10 more units of food and no less clothing in the specialization–trade case than in the no-specialization–no–trade case. Apparently, then, a country gains by specializing in producing and trading the good in which it has a comparative advantage.

Does It Matter to You . . .
If There Is Always Someone Who Can Do Something Better Than You?

Suppose there are 100 things that people can do: sing, dance, play basketball, build houses, pave streets, cut trees, cut hair, build furniture, provide dental care or legal services, teach, and so on. Now let's suppose that there are 10 million people in the world, each of whom can do each of these 100 things. Finally, let's suppose that there is always someone who can do one of those 100 things better than you can, so that you are not the best at doing anything. The fact is you may not even be the second, third, fourth, or even nine millionth best at doing anything. Does this matter to you?

Well, it could if you wanted to be the best at something, or even the tenth best, or even the hundredth best. But if you think that not being the best at something means that you won't work, or that you won't be able to earn an income, you should think again. It is very likely that you will work, and earn an income, even if you aren't the best at anything. This is the lesson that the law of comparative advantage teaches.

The law of comparative advantage teaches us that if there are two people, A and B, and A can produce more of two goods, X and

Y, than B can, it still may be better for A to produce only one of the two goods, and then trade it for the other good. This is, of course, what we showed in Exhibits 1 and 2 with respect to the United States and Japan. The United States was better at producing both food and clothing than Japan, but it still benefitted the United States to produce only one good (food) and then trade that good to Japan for another good (clothing). Although the United States was better at producing food and clothing than Japan, the United States ended up producing food and Japan ended up producing clothing.

Does it follow that, because you are not the best at anything, you will end up not working or earning an income? This would be unlikely.

20-1b A Common Misconception about How Much We Can Consume

No country can consume beyond its PPF if it doesn't specialize and trade with other countries. But, as we have just seen, it can do so when there is specialization and trade. Look at the PPF for the United States in Exhibit 1. In the NS–NT case, the United States consumes 60 units of food and 10 units of clothing; that is, the United States consumes at point B on its PPF. In the S–T case, however, it consumes 70 units of food and 10 units of clothing. A point that represents this combination of the two goods is beyond the country's PPF.

20-1c How Countries Know When They Have a Comparative Advantage

Government officials of a country do not analyze pages of cost data to determine what their country should specialize in producing and then trade. Bureaucrats do not plot production possibilities frontiers on graph paper or calculate opportunity costs. Instead, the individual's desire to earn a dollar, a peso, or a euro determines the pattern of international trade. The desire to earn a profit determines what a country specializes in and trades.

To illustrate, suppose Henri, an enterprising Frenchman, visits the United States and observes that beef is relatively cheap (compared with the price in France) and that perfume is relatively expensive. Noticing the price differences for beef and perfume between his country and the United States, he decides to buy some perfume in France, bring it to the United States, and sell it there for the relatively higher U.S. price. With his profits from the perfume transaction, he buys beef in the United States, ships it to France, and sells it there for the relatively higher French price. Obviously, Henri is buying low and selling high. He buys a good in the country where it is cheap and sells it in the country where it is expensive.

Henri's activities have a couple of consequences. First, he is earning a profit. The larger the price differences are between the two countries and the more he shuffles goods between countries, the more profit Henri earns.

Second, Henri's activities are moving each country toward its comparative advantage. The United States ends up exporting beef to France, and France ends up exporting perfume to the United States. Just as the pure theory predicts, individuals in the two countries specialize in and trade the good in which they have a comparative advantage. The outcome is brought about spontaneously through the actions of individuals trying to make themselves better off; they are simply trying to gain through trade.

THINKING LIKE AN ECONOMIST

The Benefits of Searching for Profit   Is the desire to earn profit useful to society at large? Henri's desire for profit moved both the United States and France toward specializing in and trading the good in which each had a comparative advantage. And when countries specialize and trade, they are better off than when they do neither.

ECONOMICS 24/7

Dividing the Work

John and Veronica, husband and wife, have divided their household tasks: John usually does all the lawn work, fixes the cars, and does the dinner dishes, and Veronica cleans the house, cooks the meals, and does the laundry. Some sociologists might suggest that John and Veronica divided the household tasks along gender lines: Men have done the lawn work, fixed the cars, and so on for years, and women have cleaned the house, cooked the meals, and so on for years. In other words, John is doing man's work, and Veronica is doing woman's work.

Maybe they have followed gender lines, but the question remains why certain tasks became man's work and others became woman's work. Moreover, their arrangement doesn't explain why John and Veronica don't split every task evenly. In other words, why doesn't John clean half the house and Veronica clean half the house? Why doesn't Veronica mow the lawn on the second and fourth week of every month and John mow the lawn every first and third week of the month?

The law of comparative advantage may be the answer to all these questions. Consider two tasks: cleaning the house and mowing the lawn. The following table shows how long John and Veronica take to complete the two tasks individually:

Person	Time Taken to Clean the House	Time Taken to Mow the Lawn
John	120 minutes	50 minutes
Veronica	60 minutes	100 minutes

Here is the opportunity cost of each task for each person:

Person	Opportunity Cost of Cleaning the House	Opportunity Cost of Mowing the Lawn
John	2.40 mowed lawns	0.42 clean house
Veronica	0.60 mowed lawn	1.67 clean houses

In other words, John has a comparative advantage in mowing the lawn and Veronica has a comparative advantage in cleaning the house.

Now let's compare two settings. In setting 1, John and Veronica each do half of each task. In setting 2, John only mows the lawn and Veronica only cleans the house.

In setting 1, John spends 60 minutes cleaning half of the house and 25 minutes mowing half of the lawn, for a total of 85 minutes; Veronica spends 30 minutes cleaning half of the house and 50 minutes mowing half of the lawn, for a total of 80 minutes. The total time spent by Veronica and John cleaning the house and mowing the lawn is 165 minutes.

In setting 2, John spends 50 minutes mowing the lawn, and Veronica spends 60 minutes cleaning the house. The total time spent by Veronica and John cleaning the house and mowing the lawn is 110 minutes.

In which setting are Veronica and John better off? John works 85 minutes in setting 1 and 50 minutes in setting 2, so he is better off in setting 2. Veronica works 80 minutes in setting 1 and 60 minutes in setting 2, so she is also better off in setting 2. Together, John and Veronica spend 55 fewer minutes in setting 2 than in setting 1. Getting the job done in 55 fewer minutes is the benefit of specializing in various duties around the house. Given those numbers, we would expect that John will mow the lawn (and do nothing else) and Veronica will clean the house (and do nothing else).

Comstock Images/Jupiter Images

SELF-TEST

(Answers to Self-Test questions are in Answers to Self-Test Questions at the back of the book.)

1. Suppose the United States can produce 120 units of X at an opportunity cost of 20 units of Y and the United Kingdom can produce 40 units of X at an opportunity cost of 80 units of Y. Identify favorable terms of trade for the two countries.

2. If a country can produce more of all of its goods than any other country can, would it benefit from specializing and trading? Explain your answer.

3. Do government officials analyze data to determine what their country can produce at a comparative advantage?

Hear What and How the Economist Thinks . . .
About Common Sense

The economist hears a person say:

Good economics turns out to be no more than common sense. If an economic doctrine doesn't make common sense, then it can't be good economics.

Hear what and how the economist thinks:

This is a widely held view, I think. If something goes against common sense, it can't be right. Sometimes, in economics, though, we need more than common sense. We sometimes need more than "what just seems right or wrong to us."

Take the previous example of the United States and Japan each producing two goods. We showed the data for the two countries in Exhibit 1 in which we saw that the United States was better at producing both food and clothing than Japan. In other words, the United States could produce both goods in greater quantities than Japan. Now suppose we were to ask a person unfamiliar with economics if there is any benefit to the United States of trading with Japan. He or she might say that it is "just common sense that if the United States is better at producing both goods, then there is no reason for it to trade with Japan." After all, just look at the numbers: The United States can produce 90, 60, or 30 units of food and Japan can only produce 15, 10,

or 5 units of food. The United States can produce 10, 20, or 30 units of clothing and Japan can only produce 5, 10, or 15 units of clothing. But as we have shown, the United States is better off if it specializes in producing one good (the good for which it has a comparative advantage) and then trading that good to Japan. In short, common sense doesn't always lead you to the right answer.

Take another example. In an earlier chapter, we talked about Adam Smith's diamond-water paradox. Diamonds are something you do not need for life, water is. Diamonds have very little use value; water has very high use value. Common sense might lead you to conclude that the good that has the higher use value (such as water) would have the greater exchange value (or price), but this is not the case. It takes an understanding of the difference between total utility and marginal utility to unravel the diamond-water paradox. Common sense, by itself, is not enough.

Questions to Think About:

1. Provide two examples, in which a common sense answer to a question turned out to be wrong.

2. Person 1 is better at being an attorney and at gardening than person 2. Does it follow that person 1 ought to be both an attorney and do his own gardening?

20-2   TRADE RESTRICTIONS

International trade theory holds that countries gain from free international trade—that is, from specializing in the production of the goods in which they have a comparative advantage and trading them for other goods. In the real world, however, numerous types of trade restrictions imposed by many countries give rise to the following question: If countries gain from international trade, why are there trade restrictions? The answer requires an analysis of costs and benefits; specifically, we need to determine who benefits and who loses when trade is restricted. First, we need to explain some pertinent background information.

20-2a The Distributional Effects of International Trade

The previous section explained that specialization and international trade benefit individuals in different countries, but the benefit is a *net* benefit. Not every individual person may gain.

To illustrate, suppose Pam Dickson lives and works in the United States and makes clock radios. She produces and sells 12,000 clock radios per year at a price of $40 each. Currently, clock radios are not traded internationally. Individuals in other countries who make clock radios do not sell them in the United States.

Then, one day, the U.S. market is opened to clock radios from China. Chinese manufacturers seem to have a comparative advantage in the production of clock radios because they sell theirs in the United States for $25 each. Pam realizes that she cannot compete at this price. Her sales drop to such a degree that she goes out of business. Thus, the introduction of international trade in this instance has harmed Pam personally.

20-2b Consumers' and Producers' Surpluses

The preceding example raises the issue of the distributional effects of free trade. The benefits of international trade are not equally distributed to all individuals in the population. Therefore, the topics of consumers' and producers' surpluses (Chapter 3) are relevant to our discussion of international trade.

Recall that *consumers' surplus* is the difference between the maximum price a buyer is willing and able to pay for a good or service and the price actually paid for the good or service:

$$\text{Consumers' surplus} = \text{Maximum buying price} - \text{Price paid}$$

Consumers' surplus is a dollar measure of the benefit gained by being able to purchase a unit of a good for less than one is willing to pay for it. For example, if Yakov would have paid $10 to see the movie at the Cinemax but paid only $4, his consumers' surplus is $6. Consumers' surplus is the consumers' net gain from trade.

Producers' surplus (or sellers' surplus) is the difference between the price sellers receive for a good and the minimum or lowest price for which they would have sold the good:

$$\text{Producers' surplus} = \text{Price received} - \text{Minimum selling price}$$

Producers' surplus is a dollar measure of the benefit gained by being able to sell a unit of output for more than one is willing to sell it. For example, if Joan sold her knit sweaters for $24 each but would have sold them for as low as (but no lower than) $14 each, her producer surplus is $10 per sweater. Producers' surplus is the producers' net gain from trade.

Both consumers' and producers' surplus are represented in Exhibit 3. In part (a), the shaded triangle represents consumers' surplus. This triangle comprises the area under the demand curve and above the equilibrium price. In part (b), the shaded triangle represents producers' surplus. This triangle comprises the area above the supply curve and under the equilibrium price.

EXHIBIT 3

Consumers' and Producers' Surplus

(a) Consumers' surplus. As the shaded area indicates, the difference between the maximum or highest amount consumers would be willing to pay and the price they actually pay is consumers' surplus. (b) Producers' surplus. As the shaded area indicates, the difference between the price sellers receive for the good and the minimum or lowest price they would be willing to sell the good for is producers' surplus.

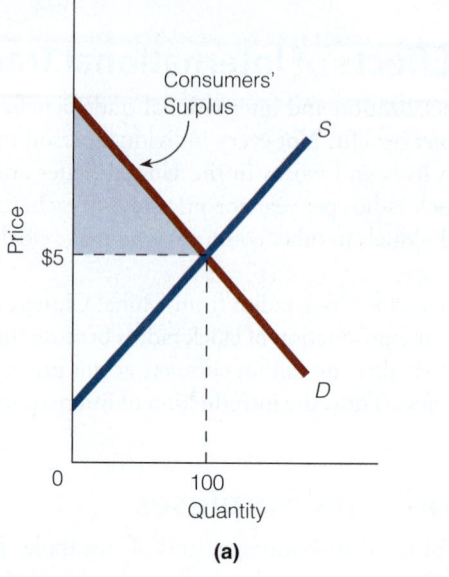

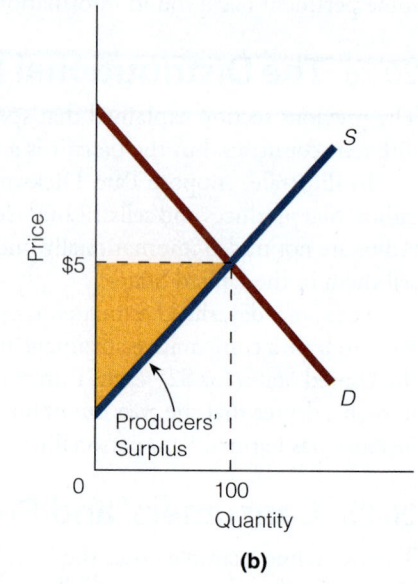

(a)   (b)

FINDING ECONOMICS

While Negotiating the Price of a House Robin is negotiating the price of the house she wants to buy from Yakov. Her last offer for the house was $478,000, and he countered with $485,000. She is thinking about offering $481,000. Where is the economics?

Obviously, in this negotiation each person is trying to increase his or her surplus at the expense of the other. The lower the price Robin pays, the higher her consumers' surplus will be and the lower Yakov's producers' surplus will be. Alternatively, the higher the price Yakov receives, the higher his producers' surplus will be and the lower Robin's consumers' surplus will be.

20-2c The Benefits and Costs of Trade Restrictions

Of the numerous ways to restrict international trade, tariffs and quotas are two of the more common. We use the tools of supply and demand to discuss these two methods, concentrating on two groups: U.S. consumers and U.S. producers.

Tariff
A tax on imports.

Tariffs A **tariff** is a tax on imports. The primary effect of a tariff is to raise the price of the imported good for the domestic consumer. Exhibit 4 illustrates the effects of a tariff on cars imported into the United States. The world price for cars is P_W, as shown in part (a). At this price in the domestic U.S. market, U.S. consumers buy Q_2 cars, as shown in part (b). They buy Q_1 cars from U.S. producers and $Q_2 - Q_1$ (the difference of Q_2 and Q_1) cars from foreign producers. In other words, U.S. imports at P_W are $Q_2 - Q_1$.

EXHIBIT 4

The Effects of a Tariff

A tariff raises the price of cars from P_W to $P_W + T$, decreases consumers' surplus, increases producers' surplus, and generates tariff revenue. Because consumers lose more than producers and government gain, there is a net loss due to the tariff.

	Consumers' Surplus	Producers' Surplus	Government Tariff Revenue
Free trade (No tariff)	$1 + 2 + 3 + 4 + 5 + 6$	7	None
Tariff	$1 + 2$	$3 + 7$	5
Loss or gain	$- (3 + 4 + 5 + 6)$	$+3$	$+5$

Result of tariff = Loss to consumers + Gain to producers + Tariff revenue

$$= - (3 + 4 + 5 + 6) \quad +3 \quad +5$$

$$= - (4 + 6)$$

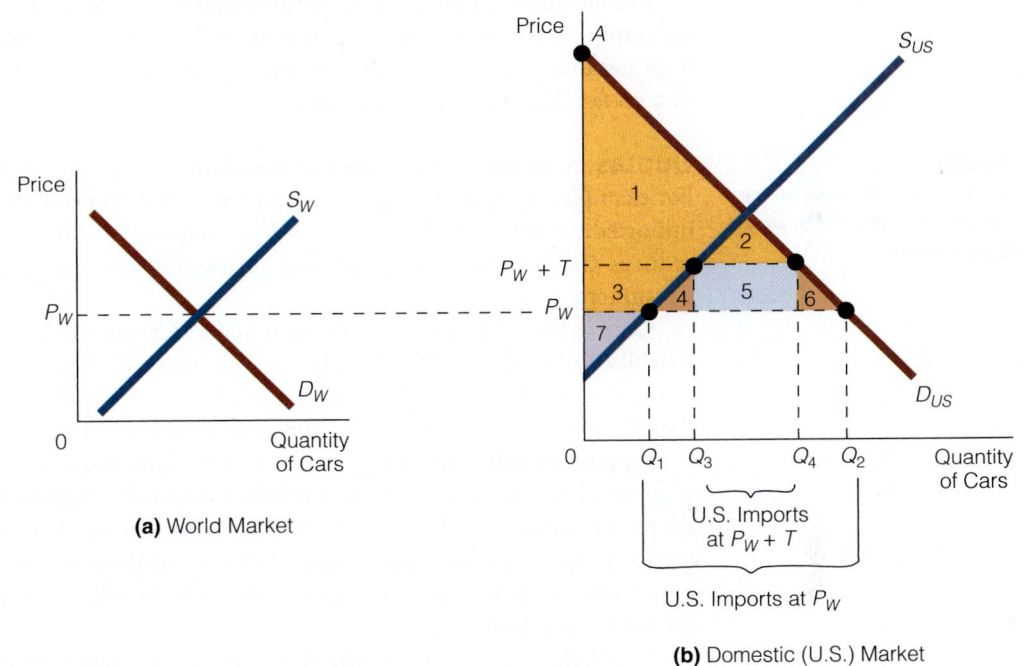

(a) World Market

(b) Domestic (U.S.) Market

In this situation, consumers' surplus is the area under the demand curve and above the world price, P_W: the sum of the areas 1, 2, 3, 4, 5, and 6 in part (b). Producers' surplus is the area above the supply curve and below the world price, P_W: area 7.

Now, suppose a tariff is imposed. Then the price for imported cars in the U.S. market rises to $P_W + T$ (the world price plus the tariff). At this price, U.S. consumers buy Q_4 cars: Q_3 from U.S. producers and $Q_4 - Q_3$ from foreign producers. U.S. imports are thus $Q_4 - Q_3$, a smaller number of imports than at the pretariff price. An effect of tariffs, then, is to reduce imports. After the tariff has been imposed, at price $P_W + T$ consumers' surplus consists of areas 1 and 2, and producers' surplus consists of areas 3 and 7.

Clearly, consumers receive more consumers' surplus when tariffs do not exist and less when they do exist. In our example, consumers received areas 1 through 6 in consumers' surplus when the tariff did not exist but they receive only areas 1 and 2 when the tariff exists. Because of the tariff, consumers' surplus was reduced by an amount equal to areas 3, 4, 5, and 6.

Producers, though, receive less producers' surplus when tariffs do not exist and more when they do exist. In our example, producers received producers' surplus equal to area 7 when the tariff did not exist, but they receive producers' surplus equal to areas 3 and 7 with the tariff. Because of the tariff, producers' surplus increased by an amount equal to area 3.

The government collects tariff revenue equal to area 5. This area is obtained by multiplying the number of imports $(Q_4 - Q_3)$ by the tariff, which is the difference between $P_W + T$ and P_W.[1]

In conclusion, the effects of a tariff are a decrease in consumers' surplus, an increase in producers' surplus, and tariff revenue for government. Because the loss to consumers (areas 3, 4, 5, and 6) is greater than the gain to producers (area 3) plus the gain to government (area 5), *a tariff results in a net loss*. The net loss is areas 4 and 6.

Quota

A legal limit imposed on the amount of a good that may be imported.

Quotas A **quota** is a legal limit imposed on the amount of a good that may be imported. For example, the government may decide to allow no more than 100,000 foreign cars to be imported, or 10 million barrels of OPEC oil, or 30,000 Japanese television sets. A quota reduces the supply of a good, and raises the price of imported goods, for domestic consumers.

Once again, we consider the situation in the U.S. car market. (See Exhibit 5.) At a price of P_W [established in the world market for cars—see part (a)], U.S. consumers buy Q_1 cars from U.S. producers and $Q_2 - Q_1$ cars from foreign producers. [See part (b).] Consumers' surplus is equal to the sum of areas 1, 2, 3, 4, 5, and 6. Producers' surplus is equal to area 7.

Suppose now that the U.S. government sets a quota equal to $Q_4 - Q_3$. Because this quantity is the number of foreign cars U.S. consumers imported when the tariff was imposed (Exhibit 4), the price of cars rises to P_Q in Exhibit 5 (a price equal to $P_W + T$ in Exhibit 4). At P_Q, consumers' surplus is equal to areas 1 and 2, and producers' surplus consists of areas 3 and 7. The decrease in consumers' surplus due to the quota is equal to areas 3, 4, 5, and 6; the increase in producers' surplus is equal to area 3.

However, area 5 is not transferred to government, as was the case when a tariff was imposed. Rather, it represents a gain earned by the importers (and sellers) of $Q_4 - Q_3$ foreign-made cars. Before the quota, importers were importing $Q_2 - Q_1$ cars, but only part $(Q_4 - Q_3)$ of that total quantity is relevant because $Q_4 - Q_3$ number of cars is the quantity of imports now that the quota has been established. Before the quota was established, the dollar amount that the importers received for $Q_4 - Q_3$ cars was $P_W \times (Q_4 - Q_3)$. Because of the quota, the price rises to P_Q, and they now receive $P_Q \times (Q_4 - Q_3)$. The gain is area 5.

In conclusion, the effects of a quota are a decrease in consumers' surplus, an increase in producers' surplus, and a gain for importers. Because the loss to consumers (areas 3, 4, 5, and 6) is greater than the increase in producers' surplus (area 3) plus the gain to importers (area 5), there is a *net loss as a result of the quota*. The net loss is equal to areas 4 and 6.

---

[1] For example, if the tariff is $100 and the number of imports is 50,000, then the tariff is $5 million.

EXHIBIT 5

The Effects of a Quota

A quota that sets the legal limit of imports at $Q_4 - Q_3$ causes the price of cars to increase from P_W to P_Q. A quota raises the price, decreases consumers' surplus, increases producers' surplus, and provides a gain to importers. Because consumers lose more than producers and importers gain, there is a net loss due to the quota.

	Consumers' Surplus	Producers' Surplus	Gain to Importers
Free trade (No quota)	$1 + 2 + 3 + 4 + 5 + 6$	7	—
Quota	$1 + 2$	$3 + 7$	5
Loss or gain	$-(3 + 4 + 5 + 6)$	$+3$	$+5$

Result of quota = Loss to consumers + Gain to producers + Gain to importers
$$= -(3 + 4 + 5 + 6) \quad +3 \quad +5$$
$$= -(4 + 6)$$

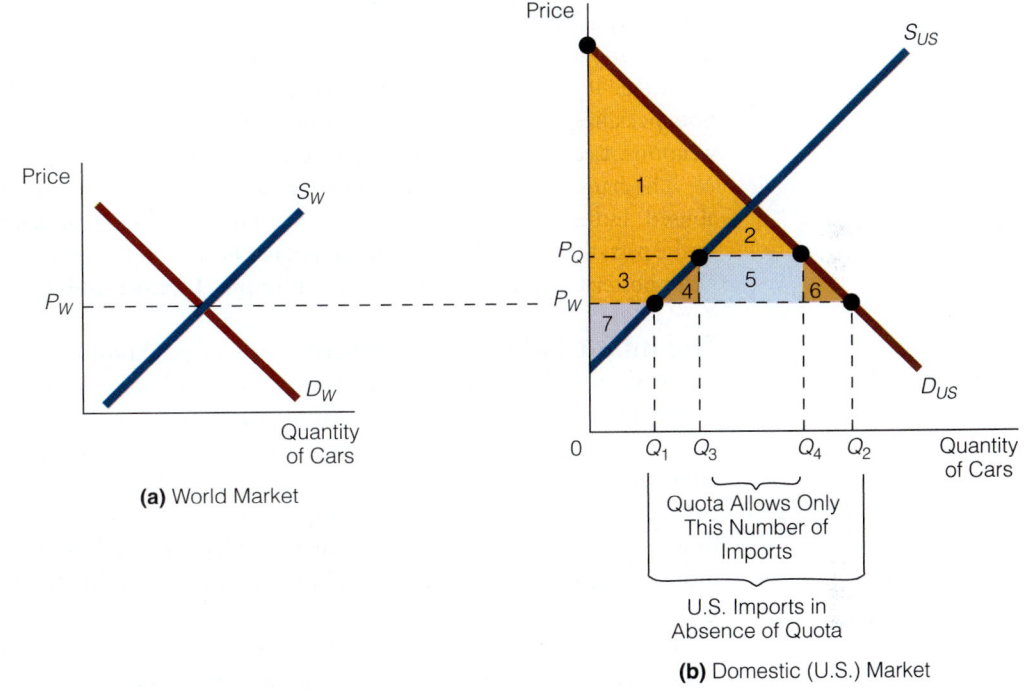

(a) World Market

(b) Domestic (U.S.) Market

FINDING ECONOMICS

In a Policy Debate   There is a debate tonight at the college Irina attends, with four people on either side of the issue: Should the United States practice free trade? Irina attends the debate and comes away thinking that both sides made good points. The side opposing free trade argued that, because other countries do not always practice free trade, neither should the United States. The side in favor of free trade argued that free trade leads to lower prices for U.S. consumers. Where is the economics?

Most of the debate, we believe, will fit into our discussion of Exhibits 4 and 5. These two exhibits show what happens to consumers and producers, and to society as a whole, as the result of both free and prohibited trade. The diagrams show (1) the benefits of prohibited free trade to domestic producers; (2) the costs of prohibited trade to domestic consumers; (3) tariff revenue to government, if such revenue exists; and (4) the overall net costs to prohibited trade.

20-2d Why Nations Sometimes Restrict Trade

If free trade results in net gain, why do nations sometimes restrict trade? The case for free trade (no tariffs or quotas) so far in this chapter appears to be a strong one. The case for free trade has not gone unchallenged, however. Some persons maintain that, at certain times, free trade should be restricted or suspended. In almost all cases, they argue that doing so is in the best interest of the public or country as a whole. In a word, they advance a public-interest argument. Other persons contend that the public-interest argument is only superficial: down deep, they say, it is a special-interest argument clothed in pretty words. As you might guess, the debate between the two groups is often heated.

The sections that follow describe some arguments that have been advanced for trade restrictions.

The National Defense Argument

Certain industries—such as aircraft, petroleum, chemicals, and weapons—are necessary to the national defense. Suppose the United States has a comparative advantage in the production of wheat and country X has a comparative advantage in the production of weapons. Many Americans feel that the United States should not specialize in the production of wheat and then trade wheat to country X in exchange for weapons. Leaving weapons production to another country, they maintain, is too dangerous.

The national defense argument may have some validity, but even valid arguments may be abused. Industries that are not really necessary to the national defense may maintain otherwise. In the past, the national defense argument has been used by some firms in the following industries: pens, pottery, peanuts, papers, candles, thumbtacks, tuna fishing, and pencils.

The Infant Industry Argument

Alexander Hamilton, the first U.S. secretary of the treasury, argued that so-called infant, or new, industries often need protection from older, established foreign competitors until they are mature enough to compete on an equal basis. Today, some persons voice the same argument. The infant industry argument is clearly an argument for temporary protection. Critics charge, however, that after an industry is protected from foreign competition, removing the protection is almost impossible: the once infant industry will continue to maintain that it isn't old enough to go it alone. Critics of the infant industry argument say that political realities make it unlikely that a benefit, once bestowed, will be removed.

Finally, the infant industry argument, like the national defense argument, may be abused. All new industries, whether or not they could currently compete successfully with foreign producers, would argue for protection on infant industry grounds.

The Antidumping Argument

Dumping is the sale of goods abroad at a price below their cost and below the price charged in the domestic market. If a French firm sells wine in the United States for a price below the cost of producing the wine and below the price charged in France, it is dumping wine in the United States. Critics of dumping maintain that it is an unfair trade practice that puts domestic producers of substitute goods at a disadvantage.

In addition, critics charge that dumpers seek only to penetrate a market and drive out domestic competitors, after which they raise prices. However, some economists point to the infeasibility of this strategy. After the dumpers have driven out their competition and raised prices, their competition is likely to return. For their efforts, the dumpers, in turn, would have incurred only a string of losses (owing to their selling below cost). Opponents of the anti-dumping argument also point out that domestic consumers benefit from dumping because they pay lower prices.

Dumping
The sale of goods abroad at a price below their cost and below the price charged in the domestic market.

ECONOMICS 24/7

Offshore Outsourcing, or Offshoring

Outsourcing is the term used to describe work done for a company by another company or by people other than the originating company's employees. Outsourcing entails purchasing a product or process from an outside supplier rather than producing it in-house. To illustrate, suppose company X has, in the past, hired employees for personnel, accounting, and payroll services, but now a company in another state performs these duties. Then company X has outsourced those work activities.

bikeriderlondon/Shutterstock.com

When a company outsources certain work activities to individuals in another country, it is said to be engaged in offshore outsourcing, or offshoring. Consider a few examples: A New York securities firm replaces 800 software engineering employees with a team of software engineers in India. A computer company replaces 200 on-call technicians in its headquarters in Texas with 150 on-call technicians in India.

The benefits of offshoring for a U.S. firm are obvious: It pays lower wages to individuals in other countries for the same work that U.S. employees do for higher wages. Benefits also flow to the employees hired in the foreign countries. The costs of offshoring are said to fall on persons who lose their jobs as a result, such as the software engineer in New York or the on-call computer technician in Texas. Some have argued that offshoring is a major political issue and that it could bring with it a wave of protectionism.

Offshoring will undoubtedly have both proponents and opponents. On a net basis, however, are there more benefits than costs or more costs than benefits? Consider a U.S. company that currently employs Jones as a software engineer, paying her $x a year. Then, one day, the company tells Jones that it has to let her go; it is replacing her with a software engineer in India who will work for $z a year (and, yes, $z < x$).

Why doesn't Jones simply agree to work for $z, the same wage as that agreed to by the Indian software engineer? Well, obviously, that's because Jones can work elsewhere for some wage between $x and $z. Assume that this wage is $y. So, even though offshoring has moved Jones from earning $x to earning $y, $y is still more than $z.

In short, the U.S. company is able to lower its costs from $x to $z and Jones's income falls from $x to $y. The U.S. company lowers its costs more than Jones's income falls because the difference between $x and $z is greater than the difference between $x and $y.

If the U.S. company operates in a competitive environment, its lower costs will shift its supply curve to the right and lower prices. In other words, offshoring can reduce prices for U.S. consumers. The political fallout from offshoring might, in the end, depend on how visible, to the average American, the employment effects of offshoring are relative to the price reduction effect.

The Foreign Export Subsidies Argument Some governments subsidize firms that export goods. If a country offers a below-market (interest rate) loan to a company, it is often argued, the government subsidizes the production of the good the firm produces. If, in turn, the firm exports the good to a foreign country, that country's producers of substitute goods call foul. They complain that the foreign firm has been given an unfair advantage that they should be protected against.[2]

[2.] Words are important in this debate. For example, domestic producers who claim that foreign governments have subsidized foreign firms say that they are not asking for economic protectionism, but only retaliation, reciprocity, or, simply, tit for tat—words that have less negative connotation than those their opponents use.

Others say that consumers should not turn their backs on a gift (in the form of lower prices). If foreign governments want to subsidize their exports and thus give a gift to foreign consumers at the expense of their own taxpayers, then the recipients should not complain. Of course, the recipients are usually not the ones who are complaining. Rather, the complainers are the domestic producers who can't sell their goods at as high a price because of the so-called gift that domestic consumers are receiving from foreign governments.

The Low Foreign Wages Argument

Some argue that American producers can't compete with foreign producers because American producers have to pay high wages to their workers and foreign producers pay low wages. The American producers insist that international trade must be restricted or they will be ruined. However, the argument overlooks why American wages are high and foreign wages are low in the first place: productivity. High productivity and high wages are usually linked, as are low productivity and low wages. If an American worker, who receives $20 per hour, can produce (on average) 100 units of good X per hour, working with numerous capital goods, then the cost per unit may be lower than when a foreign worker, who receives $2 per hour, produces (on average) 5 units of X per hour, working by hand. In short, a country's high-wage disadvantage may be offset by its productivity advantage, and a country's low-wage advantage may be offset by its productivity disadvantage. High wages do not necessarily mean high costs when productivity and the costs of nonlabor resources are included.

The Saving Domestic Jobs Argument

Sometimes, the argument against completely free trade is made in terms of saving domestic jobs. Actually, this argument has cropped up before in its different guises. For example, the low foreign wages argument is one form of it: If domestic producers cannot compete with foreign producers because foreign producers pay low wages and domestic producers pay high wages, domestic producers will go out of business and domestic jobs will be lost. The foreign export subsidies argument is another version: If foreign government subsidies give a competitive edge to foreign producers, not only will domestic producers fail, but as a result of their failure, domestic jobs will be lost.

Critics of the saving domestic jobs argument (in all its guises) counterargue as follows: If a domestic producer is being outcompeted by foreign producers and if domestic jobs in an industry are being lost as a result, the world market is signaling that those labor resources could be put to better use in an industry in which the country holds a comparative advantage.

THINKING LIKE AN ECONOMIST

Economics Versus Politics International trade often becomes a battleground between economics and politics. The simple tools of supply and demand and of consumers' and producers' surpluses show that free trade leads to net gains. On the whole, tariffs and quotas make living standards lower than they would be if free trade were permitted. On the other side, though, are the realities of business and politics. Domestic producers may advocate quotas and tariffs to make themselves better off, giving little thought to the negative effects on foreign producers or domestic consumers.

Perhaps the battle over international trade comes down to this: Policies are advocated, argued, and lobbied for largely on the basis of their distributional effects as opposed to their aggregate or overall effects. On an aggregate level, free trade produces a net gain for society whereas restricted trade produces a net loss. But economists understand that, even if free trade in the aggregate produces a net gain, not every single person will benefit more from free trade than from restricted trade. An example in this chapter showed how a subset of the population (producers) gains more, in a particular instance, from restricted trade than from free trade. In short, economists realize that the crucial question in determining real-world policies is more often, "How does it affect me?" than "How does it affect us?"

SELF-TEST

1. Who benefits and who loses from tariffs? Explain your answer.

2. Identify the directional change in consumers' surplus and producers' surplus when we move from free trade to tariffs. Is the change in consumers' surplus greater than, less than, or equal to the change in producers' surplus?

3. What is a major difference between the effects of a quota and the effects of a tariff?

4. Outline the details of the infant industry argument for trade restriction.

OFFICE HOURS

"Should We Impose Tariffs if They Impose Tariffs?"

STUDENT: Here is a problem I have with our discussion of free trade and prohibited trade. Essentially, I am in favor of free international trade, but I think the United States should have free trade with countries that practice free trade with us. In other words, if country X practices free trade with the United States, then the United States should practice free trade with it. But if country Y places tariffs on U.S. goods that enter country Y, then the United States ought to place tariffs on country Y's goods that enter our country.

INSTRUCTOR: Many people feel the same way you do, but this opinion overlooks something that we showed in Exhibits 4 and 5: The losses of moving from free trade to prohibited trade (where either tariffs or quotas exist) are greater than the gains. Remember? There is a net loss to society in that move.

STUDENT: I just think it is only fair that other countries get what they give. If they give free trade to us, then we ought to give free trade back to them. If they place tariffs and quotas on our goods, then we ought to do the same to their goods.

INSTRUCTOR: You need to keep in mind the price the United States has to pay for this policy of tit for tat.

STUDENT: What do you mean? What price does the United States have to pay?

INSTRUCTOR: It has to incur the net loss illustrated in Exhibits 4 and 5. If you look back at Exhibit 4, for example, you'll notice that moving from free trade to prohibited trade (1) decreases consumers' surplus, (2) increases producers' surplus, and (3) raises tariff revenue. But when we count up all the gains of prohibited trade and compare them with all the losses, we conclude that the losses are greater than the gains. In other words, prohibited trade leads to a net loss.

STUDENT: But suppose our practicing tit for tat (giving free trade for free trade and prohibited trade for prohibited trade) forces other countries to move away from prohibited trade. In other words, what I am saying is this: We need to look at this issue of free versus prohibited trade over time. Maybe the United States has to practice prohibited trade today (with those countries that impose tariffs or quotas on the United States) in order to force those countries to practice free trade tomorrow. Couldn't it work out that way?

INSTRUCTOR: It could work out that way. Or, then, things could escalate toward greater prohibited trade. In other words, country A imposes tariffs and quotas on country B, then country B raises its tariffs and quotas even higher on country A, so country A retaliates and raises its tariffs and quotas on country B, and so on.

STUDENT: So, what is your point? Is it that free trade is the best policy to practice no matter what other countries do?

INSTRUCTOR: That is what many economists would say, but that is not really the point I am making here. I am rather making two points with respect to the discussion. First, in response to your position that the United States ought to practice tit for tat (give free trade for free trade, tariffs for tariffs, quotas for quotas), I am simply drawing your attention to the net loss Americans incur if they practice prohibited trade—no matter what other countries are doing. In other words, there is a net loss for Americans, regardless of whether other countries are practicing free or prohibited trade. Second, with respect to your second point about prohibited trade today leading to free trade tomorrow, I am saying that we can't be sure that prohibited trade today won't lead to greater prohibitions on trade tomorrow. This is not to say that you can't be right: It is possible for prohibited trade today to lead to less prohibited trade tomorrow.

Points to Remember

1. A country that imposes tariffs or quotas on imported goods incurs a net loss, no matter what another country is doing—whether it is practicing free or prohibited trade.

2. We cannot easily predict the outcome of the United States' practicing tit for tat in international trade.

CHAPTER SUMMARY

SPECIALIZATION AND TRADE

- A country has a comparative advantage in the production of a good if it can produce the good at a lower opportunity cost than another country can.

- Individuals in countries that specialize and trade have a higher standard of living than they would if their countries did not specialize and trade.

- Government officials do not analyze cost data to determine what their country should specialize in and trade. Instead, the desire to earn a dollar, peso, or euro guides individuals' actions and produces the unintended consequence that countries specialize in and trade the good(s) in which they have a comparative advantage. However, trade restrictions can change this outcome.

TARIFFS AND QUOTAS

- A tariff is a tax on imports. A quota is a legal limit on the amount of a good that may be imported.

- Both tariffs and quotas raise the price of imports.

- Tariffs lead to a decrease in consumers' surplus, an increase in producers' surplus, and tariff revenue for the government. Consumers lose more through tariffs than producers and government (together) gain.

- Quotas lead to a decrease in consumers' surplus, an increase in producers' surplus, and additional revenue for the importers who sell the amount specified by the quota. Consumers lose more through quotas than producers and importers (together) gain.

ARGUMENTS FOR TRADE RESTRICTIONS

- The national defense argument states that certain goods—such as aircraft, petroleum, chemicals, and weapons—are necessary to the national defense and should be produced domestically whether the country has a comparative advantage in their production or not.

- The infant industry argument states that infant, or new, industries should be protected from free (foreign) trade so that they have time to develop and compete on an equal basis with older, more established foreign industries.

- The antidumping argument states that domestic producers should not have to compete (on an unequal basis) with foreign producers that sell products below cost and below the prices they charge in their domestic markets.

- The foreign export subsidies argument states that domestic producers should not have to compete (on an unequal basis) with foreign producers that have been subsidized by their governments.

- The low foreign wages argument states that domestic producers cannot compete with foreign producers that pay low wages to their employees when domestic producers pay high wages to their employees. For high-paying domestic firms to survive, limits on free trade are proposed.

- The saving domestic jobs argument states that foreign producers will be able to out-compete domestic producers through low foreign wages or government subsidies (or dumping and similar practices) and that, therefore, domestic jobs will be lost. For domestic firms to survive and domestic jobs not to be lost, limits on free trade are proposed.

- Not everyone accepts the arguments for trade restrictions as valid. Critics often maintain that the arguments can be and are abused and that in most cases they are motivated by self-interest.

KEY TERMS AND CONCEPTS

Comparative Advantage	Tariff	Quota	Dumping

QUESTIONS AND PROBLEMS

1. Although a production possibilities frontier is usually drawn for a country, one could be drawn for the world. Picture the world's production possibilities frontier. Is the world positioned at a point on the PPF or below it? Give a reason for your answer.

2. If country A is better than country B at producing all goods, will country A still be made better off by specializing and trading? Explain your answer. (*Hint*: Look at Exhibit 1.)

3. The desire for profit can end up pushing countries toward producing goods in which they have a comparative advantage. Do you agree or disagree? Explain your answer.

4. Whatever can be done by a tariff can be done by a quota. Discuss.

5. Neither free trade nor prohibited trade comes with benefits only. Both come with benefits and costs. Therefore, free trade is no better or worse than prohibited trade. Comment.

6. Consider two groups of domestic producers: those which compete with imports and those which export goods. Suppose the domestic producers that compete with imports convince the legislature to impose a high tariff on imports—so high, in fact, that almost all imports are eliminated. Does this policy in any way adversely affect domestic producers that export goods? If so, how?

7. Suppose the U.S. government wants to curtail imports. Would it be likely to favor a tariff or a quota to accomplish its objective? Why?

8. Suppose the landmass known to you as the United States of America had been composed, since the nation's founding, of separate countries instead of separate states. Would you expect the standard of living of the people who inhabit this landmass to be higher, lower, or equal to what it is today? Why?

9. Even though Jeremy is a better gardener and novelist than Bill, Jeremy still hires Bill as his gardener. Why?

10. Suppose that a constitutional convention is called tomorrow and that you are chosen as one of the delegates from your state. You and the other delegates must decide whether it will be constitutional or unconstitutional for the federal government to impose tariffs and quotas or to restrict international trade in any way. What would be your position?

11. Some economists have argued that, because domestic consumers gain more from free trade than domestic producers gain from (import) tariffs and quotas, consumers should buy out domestic producers and rid themselves of costly tariffs and quotas. For example, if consumers save

$400 million from free trade (through paying lower prices) and producers gain $100 million from tariffs and quotas, consumers can pay producers something more than $100 million but less than $400 million and get producers to favor free trade too. Assuming that this scheme were feasible, what do you think of it?

12. If there is a net loss to society from tariffs, why do tariffs exist?

WORKING WITH NUMBERS AND GRAPHS

1. Using the data in the accompanying table, answer the following questions:

   a. For which good does Canada have a comparative advantage?
   b. For which good does Italy have a comparative advantage?
   c. What might be a set of favorable terms of trade for the two countries?
   d. Prove that both countries would be better off in the specialization–trade case than in the no-specialization–no-trade case.

Points on Production Possibilities Frontier	Canada		Italy	
	Good X	Good Y	Good X	Good Y
A	150	0	90	0
B	100	25	60	60
C	50	50	30	120
D	0	75	0	180

2. In the accompanying figure, P_W is the world price and $P_W + T$ is the world price plus a tariff. Identify the following:

   a. The level of imports at P_W
   b. The level of imports at $P_W + T$
   c. The loss in consumers' surplus as a result of a tariff
   d. The gain in producers' surplus as a result of a tariff
   e. The revenue received as a result of a tariff
   f. The net loss to society as a result of a tariff
   g. The net benefit to society of moving from a tariff to no tariff

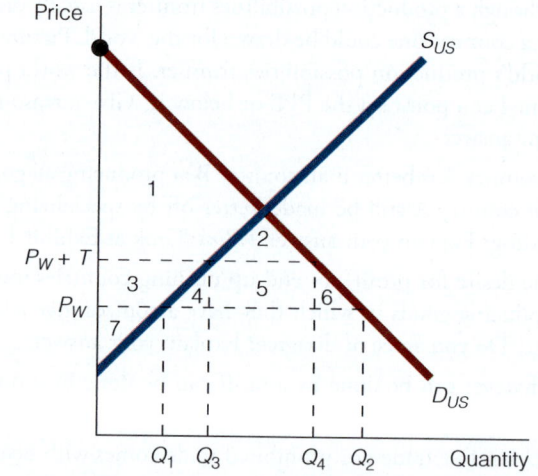

INTERNATIONAL FINANCE

Ellen Isaacs/Alamy Stock Photo

INTRODUCTION

When people travel to a foreign country, they buy goods and services in the country, whose prices are quoted in yen, pounds, euros, pesos, or some other currency. For example, a U.S. tourist in Germany might want to buy a good priced in euros and to know what the good costs in dollars and cents. The answer depends on the current exchange rate between the dollar and the euro, but what determines the exchange rate? That is just one of the many questions answered in this chapter.

21-1 THE FOREIGN EXCHANGE MARKET

The United States imports and exports goods and services. The difference between the value of its exports and the value of its imports is called *net exports*. Net exports are sometimes referred to as the **trade balance** (or balance of trade). If the value of exports is greater than the value of imports, a country is said to be running a **trade surplus**; if the value of imports is greater than the value of exports, the country is running a **trade deficit**.

One thing that can affect the trade balance of a country is the value of its currency in relation to other currencies. Currencies of different countries are exchanged (bought and sold for a price) in the **foreign exchange market**. The price that currencies are bought and sold for is called the **exchange rate**. For instance, it might take $1.08 to buy a euro and 13 cents to buy a Mexican peso.

In this section, we explain why currencies are demanded and supplied in the foreign exchange market. Then we discuss how the exchange rate expresses the relationship between the demand for, and the supply of, currencies.

Trade Balance
The value of a country's exports minus the value of its imports; sometimes referred to as net exports.

Trade Surplus
The condition that exists when the value of a country's exports is greater than the value of its imports.

Trade Deficit
The condition that exists when the value of a country's imports is greater than the value of its exports.

Foreign Exchange Market
The market in which currencies of different countries are exchanged.

Exchange Rate
The price of one currency in terms of another currency.

21-1a The Demand for Goods

To simplify our analysis, we assume that there are only two countries in the world: the United States and Mexico. Thus, there are only two currencies in the world: the U.S. dollar (USD) and the Mexican peso (the abbreviation for the Mexican peso is MXN). We want to answer the following two questions:

1. What creates the demand for, and the supply of, dollars on the foreign exchange market?

2. What creates the demand for, and the supply of, pesos on the foreign exchange market?

Suppose an American wants to buy a couch from a Mexican producer. Before he can purchase the couch, the American must buy Mexican pesos; hence, Mexican pesos are demanded. The American buys Mexican pesos with U.S. dollars; that is, he supplies U.S. dollars to the foreign exchange market and demands Mexican pesos. So, *the U.S. demand for Mexican goods leads to (1) a demand for Mexican pesos and (2) a supply of U.S. dollars on the foreign exchange market.* [See Exhibit 1(a).] Thus, the demand for pesos and the supply of dollars are linked:

Demand for pesos ↔ Supply of dollars

The result is similar for a Mexican who wants to buy a computer from a U.S. producer. Before she can purchase the computer, the Mexican must buy U.S. dollars; hence, U.S. dollars are demanded. The Mexican buys the U.S. dollars with Mexican pesos. So, *the Mexican demand for U.S. goods leads to (1) a demand for U.S. dollars and (2) a supply of Mexican pesos on the foreign exchange market.* [See Exhibit 1(b).] Thus, the demand for dollars and the supply of pesos are linked:

Demand for dollars ↔ Supply of pesos

21-1b The Demand for, and Supply of, Currencies

Exhibit 2 shows the market for pesos. The quantity of pesos is on the horizontal axis, and the exchange rate—stated in terms of the *dollar price per peso*—is on the vertical axis. In Exhibit 2(a), the demand curve for pesos is downward sloping, indicating that, as the dollar price per peso declines, the quantity demanded of pesos (by Americans) rises. To illustrate, if Americans have

---

EXHIBIT 1

The Demand for Goods and the Supply of Currencies

EXHIBIT 2

The Demand for, and Supply of, Pesos on the Foreign Exchange Market

(a) The demand for pesos. As the dollar price of a peso falls, the quantity demanded of pesos rises. (b) The supply of pesos. As the dollar price of a peso rises, the quantity supplied of pesos rises.

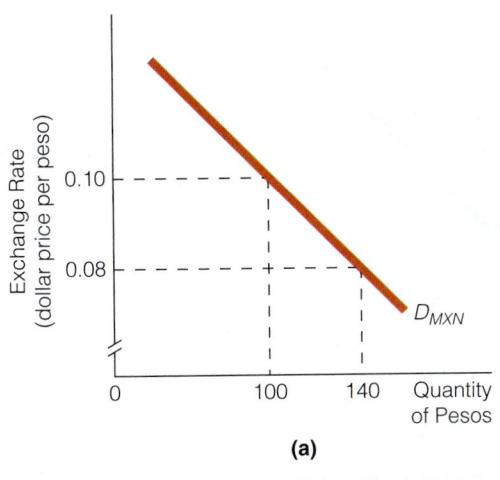

(a)

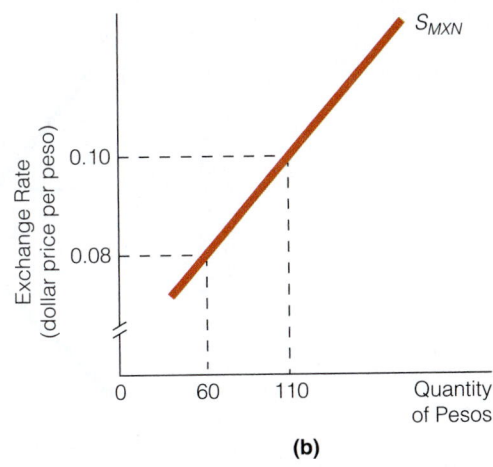

(b)

to pay 10 cents to buy a peso, they might offer to buy 100 pesos, but if Americans have to pay 8 cents to buy a peso, they might offer to buy 140 pesos.

The supply curve for pesos in Exhibit 2(b) is upward sloping, indicating that, as the dollar price of a peso rises—that is, as Mexicans receive more for a peso—the quantity supplied of pesos (by Mexicans) rises. To illustrate, at 8 cents for a peso, Mexicans might offer to sell 60 pesos, but at 10 cents for a peso, they might offer to sell 110 pesos.

21-2 FLEXIBLE EXCHANGE RATES

In this section, we discuss how exchange rates are determined in the foreign exchange market when the forces of supply and demand are allowed to rule. Economists refer to this dynamic as a **flexible exchange rate system**. In the next section, we discuss how exchange rates are determined under a fixed exchange rate system.

Flexible Exchange Rate System
A system whereby exchange rates are determined by the forces of supply and demand for a currency.

21-2a The Equilibrium Exchange Rate

In a completely flexible exchange rate system, the forces of supply and demand determine the exchange rate. In our two-country–two-currency world, suppose the equilibrium exchange rate (dollar price per peso) is 0.10 USD = 1 MXN, as shown in Exhibit 3. At this dollar price per peso, the quantity demanded of pesos equals the quantity supplied. There are no shortages or surpluses of pesos. At any other exchange rate, however, either an excess demand for pesos or an excess supply of pesos exists.

At the exchange rate of 0.12 USD = 1 MXN, a surplus of pesos exists. As a result, downward pressure will be placed on the dollar price of a peso (just as downward pressure will be placed on the dollar price of an apple if there is a surplus of apples). At the exchange rate of 0.08 USD = 1 MXN, there is a shortage of pesos and upward pressure will be placed on the dollar price of a peso.

EXHIBIT 3

A Flexible Exchange Rate System

At 0.12 USD = 1 MXN, there is a surplus of pesos, placing downward pressure on the exchange rate. At 0.08 USD = 1 MXN, there is a shortage of pesos, placing upward pressure on the exchange rate. At the equilibrium exchange rate, 0.10 USD = 1 MXN, the quantity demanded of pesos equals the quantity supplied of pesos.

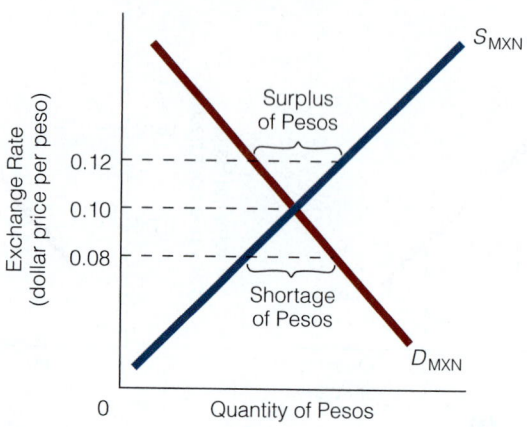

21-2b Changes in the Equilibrium Exchange Rate

A change in the demand for pesos, in the supply of pesos, or in both will change the equilibrium dollar price per peso. If the equilibrium dollar price per peso rises—say, from 0.10 USD = 1 MXN to 0.12 USD = 1 MXN—the peso is said to have **appreciated** and the dollar to have **depreciated**. A currency has appreciated in value if it takes more of a foreign currency to buy it. A currency has depreciated in value if it takes more of it to buy a foreign currency.

For example, a movement in the equilibrium exchange rate from 0.10 USD = 1 MXN to 0.12 USD = 1 MXN means that it now takes 12 cents instead of 10 cents to buy a peso, so the dollar has depreciated. The other side of the coin, so to speak, is that it takes fewer pesos to buy a dollar, so the peso has appreciated. That is, at an exchange rate of 0.10 USD = 1 MXN, it takes 10 pesos (1.00/0.10 = 10) to buy $1, but at an exchange rate of 0.12 USD = 1 MXN, it takes only 8.33 pesos (1.00/0.12 = 8.33) to buy $1.

Appreciated
An increase in the value of one currency relative to other currencies.

Depreciated
A decrease in the value of one currency relative to other currencies.

Does It Matter to You . . .
If the Dollar Depreciates?

On Monday, October 24, 2016, one British pound could be purchased for $1.22 and one euro could be purchased for $1.08. This means if you were an American in London on October 24, 2016, and wanted to buy a British-made sweater priced at £60, you would need to pay $73.20. Or if you were an American in Paris on October 24, 2016, and wanted to buy a French-made shirt priced at €30, you would need to pay $32.40.

Now does it matter to you if the dollar depreciates? We know that if the dollar depreciates, it will take more dollars and cents to buy one British pound and one euro. Let's suppose the dollar depreciates such that it takes $1.50 to buy a pound. What would the British-made sweater priced at £60 now cost you in terms of dollars and cents? The answer is $1.50 times 60 or $90. What once cost $73.20 now costs $90. Does dollar depreciation matter to you if you are buying a good in London? It does. It means that you will end up paying more (in dollars and cents) for everything you buy in London.

Now, let's change things. Suppose that instead of going to London and buying different goods and services, you simply have a savings account in a British bank, and the balance of the savings account is £5,000. If you want to close that savings account down, and covert pounds to dollars, you will get $6,100 from that savings account

if one pound trades for $1.22. But if one pound trades for $1.50, you will get $7,500 from that savings account. Since you had a savings account denominated in pounds, and because the dollar depreciated in value, the pound obviously appreciated. Your pound-denominated savings account obviously fetches more dollars and cents at $1.50 a pound than $1.22 a pound.

We return to our question: Does it matter to you if the dollar depreciates? If you are an American in London buying goods and services, the dollar depreciation makes those goods and services more expensive. If you are an American, with a pound-denominated savings account in London, then you are going to get more dollars and cents for each pound you have in that savings account.

21-2c Factors That Affect the Equilibrium Exchange Rate

If the equilibrium exchange rate can change owing to a change in the demand for, and supply of, a currency, then understanding what factors can change demand and supply is important. This section presents three such factors.

A Difference In Income Growth Rates An increase in a country's income will usually cause the nation's residents to buy more of both domestic and foreign goods. The increased demand for imports will result in an increased demand for foreign currency.

Suppose U.S. residents experience an increase in income, but Mexican residents do not. As a result, Americans want to buy more Mexican goods, so the demand curve for pesos shifts rightward, as illustrated in Exhibit 4. This shift causes the equilibrium exchange rate to rise from 0.10 USD = 1 MXN to 0.12 USD = 1 MXN. Because Americans must now pay 12 cents instead of 10 cents to buy a peso, the dollar has depreciated and the peso has appreciated.

Differences in Relative Inflation Rates Suppose the U.S. price level rises 10 percent at a time when Mexico experiences stable prices. Then an increase in the U.S. price level (in the face of a stable price level in Mexico) will make Mexican goods relatively less expensive for Americans and U.S. goods relatively more expensive for Mexicans. As a result, the U.S. demand for Mexican goods will increase and the Mexican demand for U.S. goods will decrease.

EXHIBIT 4

The Growth Rate of Income and the Exchange Rate

If U.S. residents experience a growth in income but Mexican residents do not, U.S. demand for Mexican goods will increase, and with it, the demand for pesos. As a result, the exchange rate will change: The dollar price of pesos will rise, meaning that the dollar depreciates and the peso appreciates.

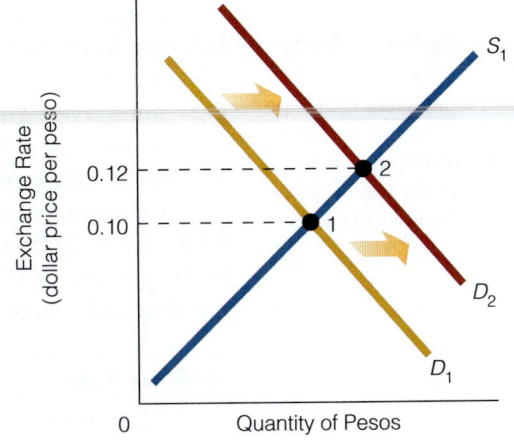

As a result of the rising U.S. demand for Mexican goods, the demand for pesos rises, as shown in Exhibit 5. As a result of the falling Mexican demand for U.S. goods, the demand for dollars decreases and therefore the supply of pesos decreases too. Exhibit 5 also shows the supply of, and the decline in, pesos. [Remember that the Mexican demand for U.S. goods is tied to the Mexican demand for U.S. dollars and, in turn, the Mexican demand for U.S. dollars is tied to the Mexican supply of pesos—see Exhibit 1(b).]

As Exhibit 5 shows, the result of an increase in the demand for Mexican pesos and a decrease in their supply constitutes an *appreciation* of the peso and a *depreciation* of the dollar. It now takes 11 cents, instead of 10 cents, to buy 1 peso (depreciation of the dollar); it now takes 9.09 pesos, instead of 10 pesos, to buy $1 (appreciation of the peso).

EXHIBIT 5

Inflation, Exchange Rates, and Purchasing Power Parity (PPP)

If the price level in the United States increases by 10 percent while the price level in Mexico remains constant, then Mexican goods become cheaper for Americans and U.S. goods become more expensive for Mexicans. So, the demand for pesos rises and the supply of pesos declines. As a result, the exchange rate will change: the dollar price of pesos will rise, meaning that the dollar depreciates and the peso appreciates. PPP theory predicts that the dollar will depreciate in the foreign exchange market until the original price (in pesos) of American goods to Mexican customers is restored. In this example, the dollar is required to depreciate 10 percent.

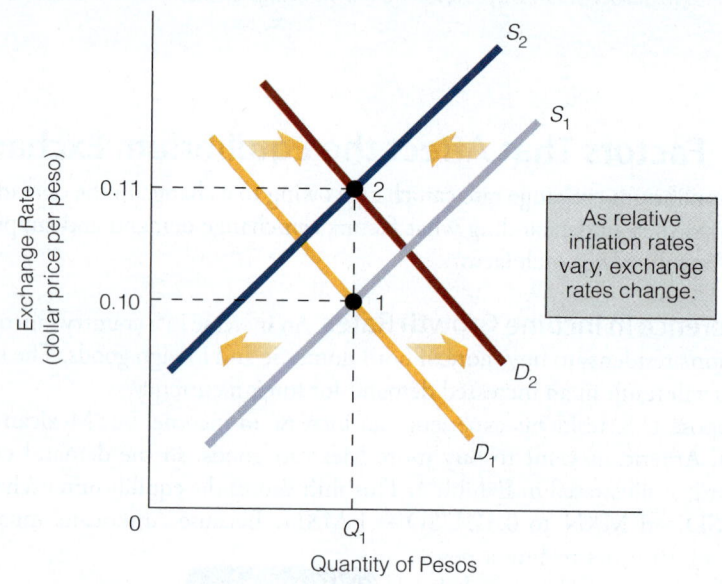

As relative inflation rates vary, exchange rates change.

Purchasing Power Parity (PPP) Theory

Theory stating that exchange rates between any two currencies will adjust to reflect changes in the relative price levels of the two countries.

An important question is how much will the U.S. dollar depreciate as a result of the rise in the U.S. price level? (Mexico's price level does not change.) The **purchasing power parity (PPP) theory** predicts that the U.S. dollar will depreciate by 10 percent as a result of the 10 percent rise in the U.S. price level. This prediction requires the dollar price of a peso to rise to 11 cents (0.10×10 cents = 1 cent, 10 cents + 1 cent = 11 cents). A 10 percent depreciation of the dollar restores the *original relative prices of American goods to Mexican customers*.

To illustrate, consider a U.S. car with a price tag of $20,000. If the exchange rate is 0.10 USD = 1 MXN, a Mexican buyer of the car will pay 200,000 pesos. If the car price increases by 10 percent, to $22,000, and the dollar depreciates 10 percent (to 0.11 USD = 1 MXN), the Mexican buyer of the car will still pay only 200,000 pesos:

Exchange Rate	Dollar Price	Peso Price
0.10 USD = 1 MXN	20,000 USD	200,000 MXN [(20,000 ÷ 0.10) MXN]
0.11 USD = 1 MXN	22,000 USD	200,000 MXN [(22,000 ÷ 0.11) MXN]

In short, the PPP theory predicts that *changes in the relative price levels of two countries will affect the exchange rate in such a way that 1 unit of a country's currency will continue to buy the same amount of foreign goods as it did before the change in the relative price levels.* In our example, the higher U.S. inflation rate causes a change in the equilibrium exchange rate and leads to a depreciated dollar, but 1 peso continues to have the same purchasing power it previously did.

The PPP theory of exchange rates has made some accurate predictions and some not-so-accurate ones. Many economists suggest that the theory's predictions are not always accurate because the demand for, and the supply of, a currency are affected *by more than the difference in inflation rates between countries.* For example, as noted, different income growth rates affect the demand for a currency and therefore the exchange rate. In the *long run*, however, and particularly when the *difference in inflation rates across countries is large*, the PPP theory does predict exchange rates accurately.

Changes in Real Interest Rates More than goods flow between countries. Financial capital also moves between countries. The flow of financial capital depends on different countries' *real interest rates*—interest rates adjusted for inflation.

To illustrate, suppose that the real interest rate is 3 percent in both the United States and Mexico. Suppose further that the real interest rate in the United States then increases to 4.5 percent. As a result, Mexicans will want to purchase financial assets in the United States that pay a higher real interest rate than do financial assets in Mexico. The Mexican demand for dollars will increase, and therefore Mexicans will supply more pesos. As the supply of pesos increases on the foreign exchange market, the exchange rate (the dollar price per peso) will change: fewer dollars will be needed to buy pesos. In short, the dollar will appreciate and the peso will depreciate.

FINDING ECONOMICS

In the President Speaking to an Economic Advisor The president of the United States is speaking to an economic advisor. The president asks, "What are the effects of the rather large budget deficits?" In response, the advisor might say that large budget deficits can affect interest rates, the value of the dollar, exports and imports, and the trade balance. "How so?" the president asks. Big deficits, the advisor answers, mean that the federal government will have to borrow funds, and the borrowing will increase the demand for credit, in turn pushing up the interest rate. Then, as the U.S. interest rate rises relative to interest rates in other countries, foreigners will want to purchase financial assets in the United States that pay a higher return. This desire will increase the demand for dollars, the dollar will appreciate, and foreign currencies will depreciate, in turn affecting both import and export spending.

ECONOMICS 24/7

The U.S. Dollar as the Primary Reserve Currency

Today, the U.S. dollar is the primary (i.e., the main) reserve currency. A *reserve currency* is a currency that central banks and major financial institutions hold in significant quantities as part of their foreign exchange reserves. For example, in 2015 the U.S. dollar accounted for 64 percent of foreign exchange reserves held by central banks, whereas the euro accounted for 23 percent. Also, major products bought and sold in the world market are usually denominated in the primary reserve currency. In other words, the U.S. dollar serves as the so-called unit of account of major global products. For this reason, and because governments and major financial institutions are willing to hold U.S. dollars, the demand for dollars on foreign exchange markets is higher than it would be if dollars weren't the major global reserve currency.

So, what would happen to the value of the U.S. dollar on foreign exchange markets if it were no longer the primary reserve currency? Obviously, the demand for dollars would decline, and subsequently, so would the exchange rate value of the dollar.

One of the advantages to a country whose currency is the primary reserve currency is that it can borrow at lower interest rates than other countries can. For example, in August 2011 China held approximately $2 trillion of its $3.2 trillion in foreign exchange reserves in dollars. Most of these dollar holdings were in the form of U.S. government bonds. (In fact, the U.S. dollars that foreign central banks keep in reserve are mostly in the form of U.S. government bonds.) In effect, because of the dollar's primary reserve currency status, China was more willing (than it would have been had the dollar not been the primary reserve currency) to buy

dollar-denominated U.S. government bonds. But, of course, heightened demand for U.S. government bonds means that the U.S. government can fetch a higher price when selling those bonds and therefore pay a lower interest rate on them.[1]

Will the U.S. dollar remain as the primary reserve currency over the next decade? Economists debate this question. Some argue that the dollar will likely remain the primary reserve currency. Others think that either the euro or renminbi (the official currency of the People's Republic of China) will displace it.

---

[1] To see that the price of bonds and the interest rate on the bond are inversely related, take a bond with the face value of $10,000 that is sold for $9,000 and matures in one year. The interest rate on this bond is found by solving for i in the following equation: $\$9,000 = \$10,000/(1 + i)^1$. This solving gives us an interest rate of 11.11 percent. Now, if the price of the bond had been higher, at, say, $9,500, we would change the price of the bond in the earlier equation accordingly and again solve for i. This result would give us an interest rate of 5.2 percent. In other words, the price of the bond and the interest rate are inversely related: As the price of the bond rises, the interest rate declines.

SELF-TEST

(Answers to Self-Test questions are in Answers to Self-Test Questions at the back of the book.)

1. In the foreign exchange market, how is the demand for dollars linked to the supply of pesos?

2. What could cause the U.S. dollar to appreciate against the Mexican peso on the foreign exchange market?

3. Suppose that the U.S. economy grows and that the Swiss economy does not. How will this difference affect the exchange rate between the dollar and the Swiss franc? Why?

4. What does the purchasing power parity theory say? Give an example to illustrate your answer.

Fixed Exchange Rate System
A system whereby a nation's currency is set at a fixed rate relative to all other currencies and central banks intervene in the foreign exchange market to maintain the fixed rate.

21-3 FIXED EXCHANGE RATES

The major alternative to the flexible exchange rate system is the **fixed exchange rate system**, which works the way it sounds: Exchange rates are fixed; they are not allowed to fluctuate freely in response to the forces of supply and demand. Central banks buy and sell currencies to maintain agreed-on exchange rates. The workings of the fixed exchange rate system are described in this section.

21-3a Fixed Exchange Rates and Overvalued or Undervalued Currency

Once again, we assume a two-country–two-currency world, but this time the United States and Mexico agree to fix the exchange rate of their currencies: Instead of letting the dollar depreciate or appreciate relative to the peso, the two countries agree to set the price of 1 peso at $0.12; that is, they agree to the exchange rate of 0.12 USD = 1 MXN. Generally, we call this the fixed exchange rate, or the *official price*, of a peso.[2] Because we will include more than one official price in our discussion, 0.12 USD = 1 MXN is official price 1 (Exhibit 6).

EXHIBIT 6

A Fixed Exchange Rate System

In a fixed exchange rate system, the exchange rate is fixed, and it may not be fixed at the equilibrium exchange rate. The exhibit shows two cases: (1) If the exchange rate is fixed at official price 1, the peso is overvalued, the dollar is under-valued, and a surplus of pesos exists. (2) If the exchange rate is fixed at official price 2, the peso is undervalued, the dollar is overvalued, and a shortage of pesos exists.

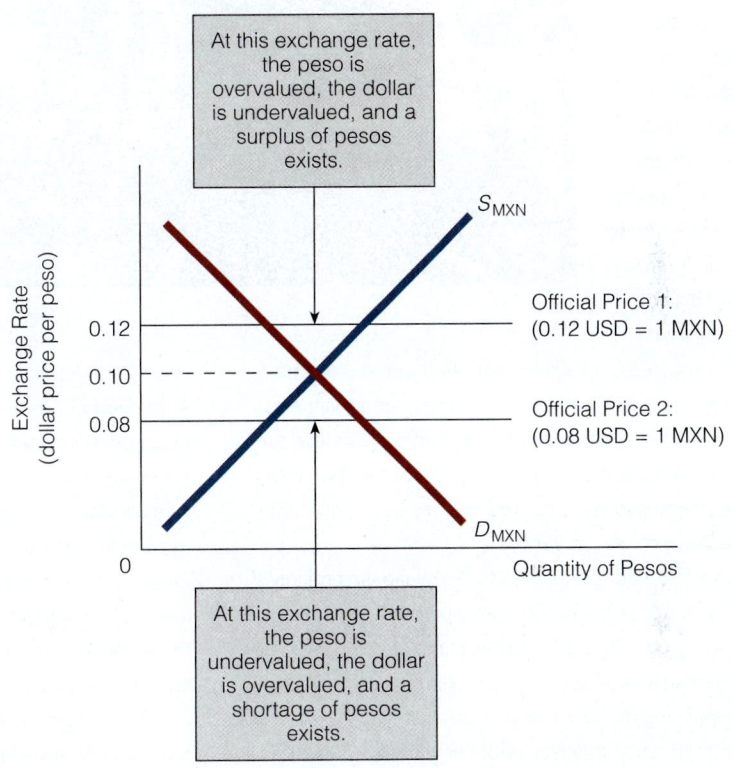

At this exchange rate, the peso is overvalued, the dollar is undervalued, and a surplus of pesos exists.

S_{MXN}

Official Price 1: (0.12 USD = 1 MXN)

Official Price 2: (0.08 USD = 1 MXN)

D_{MXN}

Quantity of Pesos

At this exchange rate, the peso is undervalued, the dollar is overvalued, and a shortage of pesos exists.

Exchange Rate (dollar price per peso)

If the dollar price of pesos is above its equilibrium level (as it is at official price 1), then a surplus of pesos exists and the peso is said to be **overvalued**. In other words, the peso is fetching more dollars than it would at equilibrium. For example, if 1 peso trades for $0.10 at equilibrium, but 1 peso trades for $0.12 at the official exchange rate, then the peso is said to be overvalued.

If the peso is overvalued, then the dollar is undervalued; that is, it is fetching fewer pesos than it would at equilibrium. For example, if $1 trades for 10 pesos at equilibrium, but $1 trades for 8.33 pesos at the official exchange rate, then the dollar is **undervalued**.

Overvalued

A currency is overvalued if its price in terms of other currencies is above the equilibrium price.

Undervalued

A currency is undervalued if its price in terms of other currencies is below the equilibrium price.

[2] If the price of 1 peso is $0.12, then the price of $1 is approximately 8.33 pesos. Thus, setting the official price of a peso in terms of dollars automatically sets the official price of a dollar in terms of pesos.

ECONOMICS 24/7

Chinese Imports and the U.S. Economy

Almost all countries occasionally intervene in foreign exchange markets to maintain the value of their currency vis-à-vis other countries. However, some countries do this more than others. China is one country that has intervened to a large extent.

China wants to promote its exported goods; that is, it wants the goods produced in China to be bought widely throughout the world. One way to promote its exported goods is to keep their prices low. And one way to keep the prices low is to deliberately undervalue its currency, the renminbi. (The renminbi is the official Chinese currency, but the yuan is the main unit of account of the renminbi. Thus, a person would not say, e.g., "You owe me seven renminbi," but rather, "You owe me seven yuan.")

At the time of this writing, $1 traded for 6.38 yuan. Accordingly, if a Chinese good was priced at, say, 100 yuan, a person would have to pay $15.67 for the good (100 yuan ÷ 6.38 yuan per $1 = $15.67). When the dollar was trading for 6.38 yuan, many economists argued that China was manipulating the yuan's value—that is, deliberately taking actions to keep its currency undervalued. Without such actions, the free-market exchange rate would have been about $1 = 4 yuan. Of course, at the free-market exchange rate, the Chinese good priced at 100 yuan would have cost an American (who uses dollars) $25 instead of $15.67. The higher dollar price for the Chinese-produced goods would have caused Americans to buy fewer of them.

So, as the argument goes, by manipulating the value of its currency, China is helping its producers sell their goods around the world. At the same time, it is hindering its competitors, such as the U.S. producers who produce and sell goods in the domestic market.

saiko3p/Shutterstock.com

As seen in our earlier example, the undervalued Chinese currency could harm U.S. companies selling goods in the United States that competed with imported goods from China, as well as indirectly adversely affecting the workers in those companies. But, of course, U.S. consumers would certainly benefit from the cheaper Chinese imports.

With both the benefits and costs of imports from China in mind, consider the research undertaken by two sets of economists. One group—David Autor, David Dorn, and Gordon Hanson—looked at the effect of Chinese import competition on regional employment and wages. For the period 1990–2007, they found that every $1,000 of additional exposure per worker to imported products from China was associated with a lowering of the U.S. employment rate by 0.77 percent. They also found that U.S. regions that faced more competition from Chinese imports had higher unemployment rates and lower wages. Note that this is not necessarily to say that Chinese imports are, on net, costly for the United States.

Another group of economists—Nicholas Bloom, Mirko Draca, and John Van Reenen—found that imports from China were associated with not only a lower price of goods for consumers, but also a lower cost of inputs for domestic firms, an increase in the variety of products those firms sold, and perhaps also a rise in U.S. productivity. These economists found that every 10 percent rise in Chinese imports was associated with increases of 3.2 percent in patent filings, of 3.6 percent in spending on information technology, and of 12 percent in carrying out research and development. And, according to the economists, 15 percent of the technical change in Europe during the period 2000–2007 was due to competition from imported products from China.

Similarly, if the dollar price of pesos is below its equilibrium level (as it is at official price 2 in Exhibit 6), then a shortage of pesos exists and the peso is undervalued; that is, the peso is not fetching as many dollars as it would at equilibrium. If the peso is undervalued, then the dollar must be overvalued. In sum,

$$\text{Overvalued peso} \leftrightarrow \text{Undervalued dollar}$$
$$\text{Undervalued peso} \leftrightarrow \text{Overvalued dollar}$$

21-3b What Is So Bad about an Overvalued Dollar?

You read in the newspaper that the dollar is overvalued and that economists are concerned about the overvalued dollar. They are concerned because the exchange rate, and hence the value of the dollar in terms of other currencies, affects the amount of U.S. exports and imports.

To illustrate, suppose the demand for pesos and the supply of pesos are represented by D_1 and S_1, respectively, in Exhibit 7. With this demand curve and supply curve, the equilibrium exchange rate is $0.10\,\text{USD} = 1\,\text{MXN}$. Let's also suppose that the exchange rate is fixed at this equilibrium exchange rate. In other words, the equilibrium exchange rate and the fixed exchange rate are initially the same.

Now, time passes, and eventually the demand curve for pesos shifts to the right, from D_1 to D_2. Under a flexible exchange rate system, the exchange rate would rise to $0.12\,\text{USD} = 1\,\text{MXN}$. But a fixed exchange rate is in effect, not a flexible one, so the exchange rate stays at $0.10\,\text{USD} = 1\,\text{MXN}$. Thus, the fixed exchange rate ($0.10\,\text{USD} = 1\,\text{MXN}$) is below the new equilibrium exchange rate ($0.12\,\text{USD} = 1\,\text{MXN}$).

Recall that, when the dollar price per peso is below its equilibrium level (as it is now), the peso is undervalued and the dollar is overvalued. To illustrate, at equilibrium (point 2 in Exhibit 7), 1 peso would trade for 0.12 dollars, but at its fixed rate (point 1), it trades for only 0.10 dollars, so the peso is undervalued. At equilibrium (point 2), $1 would trade for 8.33 pesos, but at its fixed rate (point 1), it trades for 10 pesos, so the dollar is overvalued.

What is bad about an overvalued dollar is that it makes U.S. goods more expensive for foreigners to buy, possibly affecting U.S. exports. For example, suppose a U.S. good costs $100. At the equilibrium exchange rate ($0.12\,\text{USD} = 1\,\text{MXN}$), a Mexican would pay 833 pesos for the good, but at the fixed exchange rate ($0.10\,\text{USD} = 1\,\text{MXN}$), he will pay 1,000 pesos:

EXHIBIT 7

Fixed Exchange Rates and an Overvalued Dollar

Initially, the demand for, and supply of, pesos are represented by D_1 and S_1, respectively. The equilibrium exchange rate is $0.10\,\text{USD} = 1\,\text{MXN}$, which also happens to be the official (fixed) exchange rate. In time, the demand for pesos rises to D_2, and the equilibrium exchange rate rises to $0.12\,\text{USD} = 1\,\text{MXN}$. The official exchange rate is fixed, however, so the dollar will be overvalued.

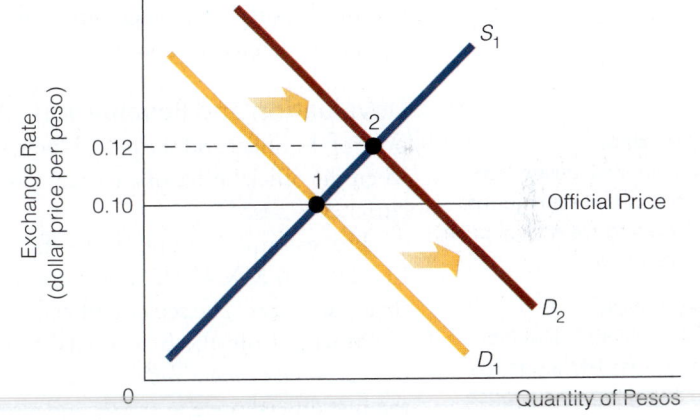

Exchange Rate	Dollar Price	Peso Price
0.12 USD = 1 MXN (equilibrium)	100 USD	833 MXN [(100 ÷ 0.12) MXN]
0.10 USD = 1 MXN (fixed)	100 USD	1,000 MXN [(100 ÷ 0.10) MXN]

The higher the prices are of U.S. goods (exports), the fewer of those goods Mexicans will buy, and, as just discussed, an overvalued dollar makes U.S. export goods higher in price.

21-3c Government Involvement in a Fixed Exchange Rate System

Suppose the governments of Mexico and the United States agree to fix the exchange rate at 0.12 USD = 1 MXN, as shown in Exhibit 6. At this exchange rate, a surplus of pesos exists. To maintain the exchange rate at 0.12 USD = 1 MXN, the Federal Reserve System (the Fed) could buy the surplus of pesos with dollars. As a result, the demand for pesos will increase and the demand curve will shift to the right, ideally by enough to raise the equilibrium rate to the current fixed exchange rate.

Alternatively, instead of the Fed's buying pesos (to "mop up" the excess supply of pesos), the Banco de México (the central bank of Mexico) could buy pesos with some of its reserve dollars. (It doesn't buy pesos with pesos, because using pesos would not reduce the surplus of pesos on the market.) This action by the Banco de México will also increase the demand for pesos and raise the equilibrium rate.

Finally, the two actions could be combined; that is, both the Fed and the Banco de México could buy pesos.

21-3d Options Under a Fixed Exchange Rate System

Suppose there is a surplus of pesos in the foreign exchange market, indicating that the peso is overvalued and the dollar is undervalued. Suppose also that, although the Fed and the Banco de México each attempt to rectify this situation by buying pesos, their combined action is not successful: The surplus of pesos persists for weeks, along with an overvalued peso and an undervalued dollar. Then, a few options are still available.

Devaluation
A government action that changes the exchange rate by lowering the official price of a currency.

Revaluation
A government action that changes the exchange rate by raising the official price of a currency.

Devaluation and Revaluation Mexico and the United States could agree to reset the official price of the dollar and the peso. Doing so entails *devaluation* and *revaluation*. A **devaluation** occurs when the official price of a currency is lowered. A **revaluation** occurs when the official price of a currency is raised.

For example, suppose the first official price of a peso is 0.10 USD = 1 MXN, or 1 USD = 10 MXN. Then, Mexico and the United States agree to change the official price of their currencies. The second official price is 0.12 USD = 1 MXN, or 1 USD = 8.33 MXN.

Moving from the first official price to the second means that the peso has been revalued, because it takes *more dollars to buy a peso* (12 cents instead of 10 cents). Of course, moving from the first official price to the second also means that the dollar has been devalued, because it takes *fewer pesos to buy a dollar* (8.33 pesos instead of 10 pesos).

One country might want to devalue its currency, but another country might not want to revalue its currency. For example, if Mexico wants to devalue its currency relative to the U.S. dollar, U.S. authorities might not always willingly comply, because, if they do, the United States will not sell as many goods to Mexico. As explained earlier, revaluing the dollar means that Mexicans have to pay more for it; instead of paying, say, 8.33 pesos for $1, Mexicans might have to pay 10 pesos. At a revalued dollar (a higher peso price for a dollar), Mexicans will find U.S. goods more expensive and not want to buy as many. Americans who produce goods to sell to Mexico may see that a revalued dollar will hurt their pocketbooks, so they will argue against it.

Protectionist Trade Policy (Quotas and Tariffs)
To deal with, say, an overvalued dollar (and, say, an undervalued Chinese renminbi), the United States can impose quotas and tariffs on Chinese goods in order to reduce U.S. consumption of them. (An earlier chapter explains how both tariffs and quotas meet this objective.) A drop in U.S. consumption of Chinese goods goes hand in hand with a decrease in the demand for the Chinese renminbi. In turn, a decline in the demand for the Chinese renminbi can affect the value of the U.S. dollar. In this case, it can eliminate an overvalued dollar.

Economists are quick to point out, though, that overvalued currencies are sometimes used as an excuse to promote trade restrictions, many of which simply benefit special interests (e.g., U.S. producers that compete for sales with foreign producers in the U.S. market).

Changes in Monetary Policy
Sometimes, a country can use monetary policy to support the exchange rate or the official price of its currency. Suppose the United States is continually importing more than it exports. To remedy this imbalance, the United States might enact a tight monetary policy to retard inflation and drive up interest rates (at least in the short run). The tight monetary policy will reduce the U.S. rate of inflation and thereby lower U.S. prices relative to prices in other nations. This effect will make U.S. goods relatively cheaper than they were before (assuming that other nations don't also enact a tight monetary policy), thereby promoting U.S. exports and discouraging foreign imports. It will also generate a flow of investment funds into the United States in search of higher real interest rates.

Some economists argue against fixed exchange rates because they think it unwise for a nation to adopt a particular monetary policy simply to maintain an international exchange rate. Instead, they believe that domestic monetary policies should be used to meet domestic economic goals, such as price stability, low unemployment, low and stable interest rates, and so forth.

SELF-TEST

1. Under a fixed exchange rate system, if one currency is overvalued, then another currency must be undervalued. Explain why this statement is true.

2. How does an overvalued dollar affect U.S. exports and imports?

3. In each of the following cases, identify whether the U.S. dollar is overvalued or undervalued:

   a. The fixed exchange rate is $2 = £1, and the equilibrium exchange rate is $3 = £1.

   b. The fixed exchange rate is $1.25 = €1, and the equilibrium exchange rate is $1.10 = €1.

   c. The fixed exchange rate is $1 = 10 pesos, and the equilibrium exchange rate is $1 = 14 pesos.

4. Under a fixed exchange rate system, why might the United States want to devalue its currency?

21-4 FIXED EXCHANGE RATES VERSUS FLEXIBLE EXCHANGE RATES

As in many economic situations, any exchange rate system has both its costs and its benefits. This section discusses some of the arguments and issues surrounding fixed exchange rates and flexible exchange rates.

21-4a Promoting International Trade

Which are better at promoting international trade, fixed or flexible exchange rates? This section presents the case for each.

The Case for Fixed Exchange Rates Proponents of a fixed exchange rate system often argue that fixed exchange rates promote international trade whereas flexible exchange rates stifle it. A major advantage of fixed exchange rates is certainty. Individuals in different countries know from day to day the value of their nation's currency. With flexible exchange rates, individuals are less likely to engage in international trade because of the added risk of not knowing from one day to the next how many dollars, euros, or yen they will have to trade for other currencies. Certainty is a necessary ingredient in international trade; flexible exchange rates promote uncertainty, which hampers international trade.

Economist Charles Kindleberger, a proponent of fixed exchange rates, stated that having fixed exchange rates is analogous to having a single currency for the entire United States instead of having a different currency for each of the 50 states. One currency in the United States promotes trade, whereas 50 different currencies would hamper it. In Kindleberger's view,

> The main case against flexible exchange rates is that they break up the world market…. Imagine trying to conduct interstate trade in the USA if there were fifty different state monies, none of which was dominant. This is akin to barter, the inefficiency of which is explained time and again by textbooks.[3]

The Case for Flexible Exchange Rates As noted, advocates of flexible exchange rates, maintain that it is better for a nation to adopt policies to meet domestic economic goals than to sacrifice domestic economic goals in order to maintain an exchange rate. Also, the chance is too great that the fixed exchange rate will diverge greatly from the equilibrium exchange rate, creating persistent trade problems for some countries (with import spending continually greater than export spending) and thus leading them to impose trade restrictions (tariffs and quotas) that hinder international trade.

The Current System Today's international monetary system is described as a managed flexible exchange rate system, sometimes referred to more casually as a **managed float**. In a way, this system is a rough compromise between the fixed and flexible exchange rate systems. The current system operates under flexible exchange rates, but not completely: Now and then, nations intervene to adjust their official reserve holdings to moderate major swings in exchange rates.

21-4b Optimal Currency Areas

An **optimal currency area** is a geographic area in which exchange rates can be fixed or a *common currency* used without sacrificing domestic economic goals, such as low unemployment. The concept of an optimal currency area originated in the debate over whether fixed or flexible exchange

Managed Float
A managed flexible exchange rate system under which nations intervene now and then to adjust their official reserve holdings in order to moderate major swings in exchange rates.

Optimal Currency Area
A geographic area in which exchange rates can be fixed or a common currency used without sacrificing domestic economic goals, such as low unemployment.

[3.] Charles Kindleberger, International Money (London: Allen and Unwin, 1981), p. 174.

rates are better. Most of the pioneering work on optimal currency areas was done by Robert Mundell, winner of the 1999 Nobel Prize in Economics.

Before discussing an optimal currency area, we need to look at the relationships among labor mobility, trade, and exchange rates. *Labor mobility* means that the residents of one country can move easily to another country.

Trade and Labor Mobility Suppose there are only two countries: the United States and Canada. The United States produces calculators and soft drinks, and Canada produces bread and muffins. Currently, the two countries trade with each other, and there is complete labor mobility between them.

One day, the residents of both countries reduce their demand for bread and muffins and increase their demand for calculators and soft drinks. In other words, relative demand changes: Demand increases for U.S. goods and falls for Canadian goods. Business firms in Canada lay off employees because their sales have plummeted. Incomes in Canada begin to fall, and the unemployment rate begins to rise. In the United States, prices initially rise because of the increased demand for calculators and soft drinks. In response to the higher demand for their products, U.S. business firms begin to hire more workers and increase their production. Their efforts to hire more workers drive wages up and reduce the unemployment rate.

Because labor is mobile, some of the newly unemployed Canadian workers move to the United States to find work, easing the economic situation in both countries. The movement of labor will reduce some of the unemployment problems in Canada, and, with more workers in the United States, more output will be produced, thus dampening upward price pressures on calculators and soft drinks. Clearly, then, changes in relative demand pose no major economic problems for either country if labor is mobile.

Trade and Labor Immobility Now let's suppose that relative demand has changed but that labor is *not* mobile between the United States and Canada, perhaps because of political or cultural barriers. If people cannot move, then what happens in the economies of the two countries depends largely on whether exchange rates are fixed or flexible.

If exchange rates are flexible, the value of the U.S. currency will change vis-à-vis the Canadian currency. If Canadians want to buy more U.S. goods, they will have to exchange their domestic currency for U.S. currency. Now, the demand for U.S. currency on the foreign exchange market will increase at the same time that the supply of Canadian currency increases. Consequently, U.S. currency will appreciate, and Canadian currency will depreciate. Then, because Canadian currency depreciates, U.S. goods become relatively more expensive for Canadians, so they buy fewer of them. And because U.S. currency appreciates, Canadian goods become relatively cheaper for Americans, so they buy more Canadian goods. As a result, Canadian business firms begin to sell more goods, so they hire more workers, the unemployment rate drops, and the bad economic times in Canada begin to disappear.

If exchange rates are fixed, however, U.S. goods will not become relatively more expensive for Canadians and Canadian goods will not become relatively cheaper for Americans. Consequently, the bad economic times in Canada (high unemployment) might last for a long time, indeed, instead of beginning to reverse. Thus, if labor is immobile, changes in relative demand may pose major economic problems when exchange rates are fixed but not when they are flexible.

Costs, Benefits, and Optimal Currency Areas In addition to benefits, flexible exchange rates have costs. Exchanging one currency for another (say, U.S. dollars for Canadian dollars or U.S. dollars for Japanese yen) incurs a charge, and the risk is greater of not knowing what the value of one's currency will be on the foreign exchange market on any given day. For many countries, the benefits outweigh the costs, so they have flexible exchange rate systems.

Now, suppose some of the costs of flexible exchange rates could be eliminated while maintaining the benefits. Then, if labor is mobile between the two countries, they could have a fixed exchange rate or adopt a common currency and retain the benefits of flexible exchange rates. In that case, they do not have to have separate currencies that float against each other because resources (labor) can move easily and quickly in response to changes in relative demand. The two countries can either fix exchange rates or adopt the same currency.

When labor in countries within a geographic area is mobile enough to move easily and quickly in response to changes in relative demand, the countries are said to constitute an *optimal currency area*. Countries in such an area can either fix their currencies or adopt the same currency and thus keep all the benefits of flexible exchange rates without incurring any of the costs.

The states of the United States are commonly said to constitute an optimal currency area. Labor can move easily and quickly between, say, North Carolina and South Carolina in response to relative changes in demand. Some economists have argued that the countries that compose the European Union make up an optimal currency area and, therefore, adopting a common currency—the euro—benefits these countries. Other economists disagree. They argue that, although labor is somewhat more mobile in Europe today than in the past, certain language and cultural differences make labor mobility less than sufficient to constitute a true optimal currency area.

OFFICE HOURS

"Why Is the Depreciation of One Currency Tied to the Appreciation of Another?"

STUDENT: I know that when the dollar depreciates, some other currency appreciates. Is this just the way it is? For example, if $1 dollar equals €1 euro, and then $1.25 equals €1, the arithmetic of exchange rates tells me that now $1 will fetch only €0.8. Is that all there is to it?

INSTRUCTOR: Not exactly. You're focusing on the arithmetic of exchange rates to the exclusion of the economics. There is an economic reason that dollar appreciation is linked to euro appreciation.

STUDENT: What is that economic reason?

INSTRUCTOR: Think of what can lead to the dollar's depreciating. Suppose you want to travel to Germany, where the euro is used. You take your dollars and buy euros with them. In other words, you do two things: You (1) buy euros by (2) supplying dollars. Now think of how you are affecting the market for euros and the market for dollars. You are increasing the demand for euros in the market for euros, and you are increasing the supply of dollars in the market for dollars. In other words, your demand for euros is linked to your supply of dollars. So, if you increase the demand for euros, you are automatically increasing the supply of dollars.

STUDENT: I'm used to thinking that my buying something affects only one market. For instance, when I buy more books, the purchase affects only the market for books. You seem to be telling me that this is not the case when I buy a currency, such as the euro. To buy euros is to supply dollars.

INSTRUCTOR: That's right. So when you increase the demand for euros, you automatically increase the supply of dollars. And then we have to ask ourselves what happens in each of the two markets: the market for euros and the market for dollars.

STUDENT: Well, if I increase the demand for euros, the price of a euro in terms of dollars will rise. Also, if I increase the supply of dollars, the price of a dollar in terms of euros will fall.

INSTRUCTOR: And what do you call it when the price of a euro has risen in terms of dollars?

STUDENT: We say the dollar has depreciated, because it now takes more dollars and cents to buy a euro.

INSTRUCTOR: And what do you call it when the price of a dollar has fallen in terms of euros?

STUDENT: We say the euro has appreciated, because it now takes fewer euros to buy a dollar.

INSTRUCTOR: So, let's go back to your original query. You wondered whether the dollar's depreciating and the euro's appreciating were just matters of arithmetic. Now we know that they aren't. They are a matter of curves shifting in different markets.

Points to Remember

1. To buy a currency is to affect two markets, not just one. If you buy euros, you affect the euro market. But by selling dollars to buy euros, you also affect the dollar market.

2. The fact that, when one currency depreciates, another appreciates is a matter of curves shifting in two currency markets.

CHAPTER SUMMARY

THE FOREIGN EXCHANGE MARKET

• The market in which currencies of different countries are exchanged is called the foreign exchange market. In this market, currencies are bought and sold for a price: the exchange rate.

• When the residents of a nation demand a foreign currency, they must supply their own currency. For example, if Americans demand Mexican goods, they also demand Mexican pesos and supply U.S. dollars. If Mexicans demand American goods, they also demand U.S. dollars and supply Mexican pesos.

FLEXIBLE EXCHANGE RATES

• Under flexible exchange rates, the foreign exchange market will equilibrate at the exchange rate for which the quantity demanded of a currency equals the quantity supplied of the currency; for example, the foreign exchange market equilibrates when the quantity demanded of U.S. dollars equals the quantity supplied of U.S. dollars.

• If the price of a nation's currency increases relative to a foreign currency, the nation's currency is said to have appreciated. For example, if the price of a peso rises from 0.10 USD = 1 MXN to 0.15 USD = 1 MXN, then the peso has appreciated. If the price of a nation's currency decreases relative to a foreign currency, the nation's currency is said to have depreciated. For example, if the price of a dollar falls from 10 MXN = 1 USD to 8 MXN = 1 USD, then the dollar has depreciated.

• Under a flexible exchange rate system, the equilibrium exchange rate is affected by a difference in income growth rates between countries, a difference in inflation rates between countries, and a change in (real) interest rates between countries.

FIXED EXCHANGE RATES

Under a fixed exchange rate system, countries agree to fix the price of their currencies. The central banks of the countries must then buy and sell currencies to maintain the exchange rate that was agreed on.

THE CURRENT INTERNATIONAL MONETARY SYSTEM

Today's international monetary system is described as a managed flexible exchange rate system, or managed float. For the most part, the exchange rate system is flexible, although nations periodically intervene in the foreign exchange market in order to adjust rates. Because today's system is a managed float system, it is difficult to tell whether nations will emphasize the float part or the managed part in the future.

KEY TERMS AND CONCEPTS

Trade Balance

Trade Surplus

Trade Deficit

Foreign Exchange
   Market

Exchange Rate

Flexible Exchange Rate
   System

Appreciation

Depreciation

Purchasing Power Parity
   (PPP) Theory

Fixed Exchange Rate System

Overvalued

Undervalued

Devaluation

Revaluation

Managed Float

Optimal Currency Area

QUESTIONS AND PROBLEMS

1. Explain the link between the Mexican demand for U.S. goods and the supply of pesos. Next, explain the link between the U.S. demand for Mexican goods and the supply of dollars.

2. The lower the dollar price of a peso, the higher is the quantity demanded of pesos and the lower is the quantity supplied of pesos. Do you agree or disagree? Explain.

3. What does it mean to say that the U.S. dollar has depreciated in value in relation to the Mexican peso? What does it mean to say that the Mexican peso has appreciated in value relative to the U.S. dollar?

4. Suppose the United States and Japan have a flexible exchange rate system. Explain whether each of the following events will lead to an appreciation or depreciation of the U.S. dollar and Japanese yen:

   a. U.S. real interest rates rise above Japanese real interest rates.

   b. The Japanese inflation rate rises relative to the U.S. inflation rate.

   c. An increase in U.S. income combines with no change in Japanese income.

5. Give an example of how a change in the exchange rate alters the relative price of domestic goods in terms of foreign goods.

6. What are the strong and weak points of the flexible exchange rate system? What are the strong and weak points of the fixed exchange rate system?

7. Explain the details of the purchasing power parity (PPP) theory.

8. A country whose currency is the primary reserve currency can likely borrow at lower interest rates than it could if its currency were not the primary reserve currency. Do you agree or disagree? Explain.

9. What does it mean to say that a currency is overvalued? undervalued?

10. Under a flexible exchange rate system, if the equilibrium exchange rate is 0.10 USD = 1 MXN and the current exchange rate is 0.12 = 1 MXN, will the U.S. dollar appreciate or depreciate? Explain.

11. Under a fixed exchange rate system, setting the official price of a peso in terms of dollars automatically sets the official price of a dollar in terms of pesos. Do you agree or disagree? Explain.

12. Country X wants to lower the value of its currency on the foreign exchange market. Under a flexible exchange rate system, how can it do that?

13. What is an optimal currency area?

14. Country 1 produces good X, and country 2 produces good Y. People in both countries begin to demand more of good X and less of good Y. Assume that there is no labor mobility between the two countries and that a flexible exchange rate system exists. What will happen to the unemployment rate in country 2? Explain.

15. How important is labor mobility in determining whether an area is an optimal currency area?

16. If everyone in the world spoke the same language, would the world be closer to or further from being an optimal currency area? Explain.

WORKING WITH NUMBERS AND GRAPHS

1. Use the following information to answer (a)–(c):

	U.S. Dollar Equivalent		Currency per U.S. Dollar	
	Thurs.	Fri.	Thurs.	Fri.
Russia (ruble)	0.0318	0.0317	31.4190	31.5290
Brazil (real)	0.3569	0.3623	2.8020	2.7601
India (rupee)	0.0204	0.0208	48.9100	47.8521

a. Between Thursday and Friday, did the U.S. dollar appreciate or depreciate against the Russian ruble?

b. Between Thursday and Friday, did the U.S. dollar appreciate or depreciate against the Brazilian real?

c. Between Thursday and Friday, did the U.S. dollar appreciate or depreciate against the Indian rupee?

2. If $1 equals ¥0.0093, what does ¥1 equal?

3. If $1 equals 7.7 krone (Danish), what does 1 krone equal?

4. If $1 equals 31 rubles, what does 1 ruble equal?

5. If the exchange rate is 0.08 = 1MXN, what is the cost in dollars of a Mexican table priced at 500 pesos?

SELF-TEST APPENDIX

Chapter 1

CHAPTER 1, PAGE 4

1. False. It takes two things for scarcity to exist: finite resources and infinite wants. If people's wants were equal to or less than the finite resources available to satisfy their wants, scarcity would not exist. Scarcity exists only because people's wants are greater than the resources available to satisfy their wants. Scarcity is the condition resulting from infinite wants clashing with finite resources.

2. Because of scarcity, there is a need for a rationing device. People will compete for the rationing device. For example, if dollar price is the rationing device, people will compete for dollars.

3. Because our unlimited wants are greater than our limited resources—that is, because scarcity exists—some wants must go unsatisfied. We must choose which wants we will satisfy and which we will not.

CHAPTER 1, PAGE 15

1. Every time a student is late to history class, the instructor subtracts one-tenth of a point from the person's final grade. Economists predict that, if the instructor raises the opportunity cost of being late to class by subtracting one point from the final grade, then fewer students will be late to class. In sum, the higher the opportunity cost is for being late to class, the less likely people will be late to class.

2. Yes. To illustrate, suppose the marginal benefits and marginal costs (in dollars) are as follows for various hours of studying:

Hour	Marginal Benefits	Marginal Costs
First Hour	$20.00	$10.00
Second Hour	$14.00	$11.00
Third Hour	$13.00	$12.00
Fourth Hour	$12.10	$12.09
Fifth Hour	$11.00	$13.00

Clearly, you will study the first hour, because the marginal benefits are greater than the marginal costs. Stated differently, studying the first hour has a net benefit of $10

(the difference between the marginal benefits of $20 and the marginal costs of $10). If you stop studying after the first hour and do not proceed to the second hour, then you forfeit the net benefit of $3 for the second hour. To maximize your net benefits of studying, you must proceed until the marginal benefits and the marginal costs are as close to equal as possible. They never actually reach equality—in the language of calculus, they approach each other asymptotically—however, economists speak of the equality of the two for convenience. In this case, you should study through the fourth hour. You would not study the fifth hour because it is not worth it: The marginal benefits of studying the fifth hour are less than the marginal costs, and, therefore, has a net cost.

3. You might be sleepy the next day, less alert while driving, and so on.

CHAPTER 1, PAGE 19

1. The purpose of building a theory is to explain something that is not obvious. For example, the reason for changes in the unemployment rate is not obvious, so the economist would build a theory to explain this.

2. A theory of the economy seeks to explain why certain things in the economy happen. For example, a theory of the economy might try to explain why prices rise or why output falls. A description of the economy is simply a statement of what exists in the economy. For example, we could say that the economy is growing or contracting, or that more jobs are available this month than last month. A description doesn't answer questions; it simply tells us what is. A theory tries to answer a question, such as, "Why are more jobs available this month than last month?"

3. If you do not test a theory, you will never know whether you have accomplished your objective in building the theory in the first place. In other words, you will not know whether you have explained something accurately. We do not simply accept a theory just because it sounds right, as what sounds right may actually be wrong. For example, during the time of Columbus the theory that the earth was flat might have sounded right to many people, and the theory that the earth was round might have sounded ridiculous. However, what sounded right turned out to be wrong—the earth is round.

4. Unless stated otherwise, when economics instructors identify the relationship between two variables, they implicitly make the *ceteris paribus* assumption. In other words, the instructor is really saying, "If the price of going to the movies goes down, people will go to the movies more often—assuming that nothing else changes, such as the quality of movies, and so on." Instructors don't always state "*ceteris paribus,*" because if they did, they would be using the term every minute of a lecture. So the instructor is right; although a student who is new to economics might not know what the instructor is assuming but not saying.

Chapter 2

CHAPTER 2, PAGE 49

1. A straight-line PPF represents the constant opportunity costs between two goods. For example, for every unit of X produced, one unit of Y is forfeited. A bowed-outward PPF represents increasing opportunity costs. For example, we may have to forfeit 1 unit of X to produce the 11th unit of Y, but we have to forfeit 2 units of X to produce the 100th unit of Y.

2. A bowed-outward PPF is representative of increasing costs, because the PPF would not be bowed otherwise. To prove this statement, look back at Exhibits 1 and 2. In Exhibit 1, costs are constant (not increasing) and the PPF is a straight line. In Exhibit 2, costs are increasing and the PPF is bowed outward.

3. The first condition is that the economy is currently operating *below* its PPF. It is possible to move from a point below the PPF to a point on the PPF and get more goods. The second condition is that the economy's PPF shifts outward.

4. False. Take a look at Exhibit 5. All of the numerous productive efficient points lie on the PPF.

Chapter 3

CHAPTER 3, PAGE 69

1. Popcorn is a normal good for Sandi, and prepaid telephone cards are an inferior good for Mark.

2. Asking why demand curves are downward sloping is the same as asking why price and quantity demanded are inversely related (as one rises, the other falls). Two reasons for this inverse relationship are mentioned in this section: (1) As price rises, people substitute lower priced goods for higher priced goods. (2) Because individuals receive less utility from an additional unit of a good they consume, they are only willing to pay less for the additional unit, which is a reflection of the law of diminishing marginal utility.

3. Suppose only two people, Bob and Alice, have a demand for good X. At a price of $7, Bob buys 10 units and Alice buys 3 units; at a price of $6, Bob buys 12 units and Alice buys 5 units. One point on the market demand curve represents a price of $7 and a quantity demanded of 13 units; another point represents $6 and 17 units. A market demand curve is derived by adding the quantities demanded at each price.

4. A change in income, preferences, prices of related goods, the number of buyers, and expectations of future price can change demand. A change in the price of the good changes the quantity demanded of it. For example, a change in *income* can change the *demand* for oranges, but only a change in the *price* of oranges can directly change the *quantity demanded* of oranges.

CHAPTER 3, PAGE 74

1. Increasing the quantity supplied of houses over the next 10 hours would be difficult, so the supply curve in (a) is vertical, as in Exhibit 7. Increasing the quantity supplied of houses over the next 3 months is possible, so the supply curve in (b) is upward sloping.

2. a. The supply curve shifts to the left.

   b. The supply curve shifts to the left.

   c. The supply curve shifts to the right.

3. False. If the price of apples rises, then the *quantity supplied* of apples will rise—not the *supply*. We are talking about a *movement* from one point on a supply curve to a point higher up on the supply curve, not about a shift in the supply curve.

CHAPTER 3, PAGE 90

1. Disagree. In the text, we plainly saw how supply and demand worked at an auction. Supply and demand are at work in the grocery store too, even though no auctioneer is present. The essence of the auction example is that the auctioneer raises the price when there is a shortage and lowers the price when there is a surplus. The same thing happens at the grocery store. For example, given a surplus of cornflakes, the manager of the store is likely to run a sale (lower prices) on them. Many markets without auctioneers act *as if* auctioneers were raising and lowering prices in response to shortages and surpluses.

2. No. It could be the result of a higher supply of computers. Either a decrease in demand or an increase in supply will lower price.

3. a. Lower price and lower quantity.

   b. Lower price and higher quantity.

   c. Higher price and lower quantity.

   d. Lower price and lower quantity.

4. At the equilibrium quantity, the maximum buying price and the minimum selling price are the same. For example, in Exhibit 15, both prices are $40 at the equilibrium quantity of 4. The equilibrium quantity is the only quantity at which the maximum buying price and the minimum selling price are the same.

5. $44; $34.

Chapter 4
CHAPTER 4, PAGE 97

1. A rationing device is necessary because scarcity exists. If scarcity did not exist, a rationing device would not be needed.

2. If (dollar) price is the rationing device used, then individuals have an incentive to produce goods and services, sell them for money (for the dollar price), and then use the money to buy what they want. If another rationing device were used (say, first come, first served or "need"), then the incentive to produce would be dramatically dampened. Why produce a good if the only way you can "sell" it (i.e., ration the good) is by way of first come, first served?

3. Price conveys information about the relative scarcity of a good. In the orange juice example, a rise in the price of orange juice transmitted information relating to the increased relative scarcity of orange juice due to a cold spell in Florida.

CHAPTER 4, PAGE 109

1. Yes, if nothing else changes—that is, yes, *ceteris paribus*. However, if other things change, they may not. For example, if the government imposes an effective price ceiling on gasoline, Jamie may pay lower gas prices at the pump but have to wait in line to buy the gas (because of first-come, first-served rationing of the shortage). Whether Jamie is better off paying a higher price and not waiting in line or paying a lower price and waiting in line is not clear. The point, however, is that buyers don't necessarily

prefer lower prices to higher prices unless everything else (quality, wait, service, etc.) stays the same.

2. Disagree. Both long-lasting shortages and long lines are caused by price ceilings. First, the price ceiling is imposed, creating the shortage; then the rationing device of first come, first served emerges because price isn't permitted to fully ration the good. Every day, shortages occur that don't cause long lines to form. Instead, buyers bid up the price, so that output and price move to equilibrium, and there is no shortage.

3. Buyers might argue for price ceilings on the goods they buy, especially if they don't know that price ceilings have some effects they may not like (e.g., fewer exchanges, first-come, first-served rationing devices). Sellers might argue for price floors on the goods they sell, especially if they expect their profits to rise. Employees might argue for a wage floor on the labor services they sell, especially if they don't know that they may lose their jobs or have their hours cut back as a result.

CHAPTER 4, PAGE 113

1. $1A = \frac{2}{3}B$ and $1B = 1.5A$.

2. The statement is correct in the sense that good X has a higher money price than it used to have. It is misleading because a higher money price doesn't necessarily mean a higher relative price. For example, if the absolute (money) price of good X is $10 and the absolute price of good Y is $20, then the relative price of X is ½ unit of Y. Now, suppose the absolute price of X rises to $15 while the absolute price of Y rises to $60. Then the new relative price of X is ¼ unit of Y. In other words, the absolute price of X rises (from $10 to $15), while its relative price falls (from ½ Y to ¼ Y). Thus, good X can become more expensive in money terms as it becomes cheaper in terms of other goods.

Chapter 5
CHAPTER 5, PAGE 117

1. Yes, we would expect that the demand for a U-Haul in Texas (going to California) would be less than the demand for a U-Haul in California (going to Texas). Therefore, all things remaining constant, we would expect the U-Haul rate going from California to Texas to be higher than the U-Haul rate going from Texas to California.

2. The demand for, and supply of, houses is not the same in all cities and, as a result, house prices are not likely to be the same in all cities.

CHAPTER 5, PAGES 119

1. No. In Exhibit 1, the two demand curves are parallel because the subsidy is always $1 and the vertical distance between the two curves is $1. With a different subsidy for different units of good X (a larger subsidy for the first unit than for the second and so on), the vertical distance between the two demand curves (the one with the subsidy and the one without the subsidy) is not always going to be the same. Therefore, the two demand curves will not be parallel.

2. The subsidy will cause the demand for solar panels to rise and, as a result, the price of solar panels will likely rise.

CHAPTER 5, PAGE 120

1. Answers will vary. Students sometimes say that it is fairer if everyone is charged the same price. Is it unfair, then, that moviegoers pay less if they go to the 2 p.m. movie than if they go to the 8 p.m. movie?

2. We learned about price ceilings in the previous chapter. Specifically, we learned that a price ceiling creates a shortage. In the application dealing with the 10:00 a.m. class, the university charged a below-equilibrium price for the 10:00 a.m. class, leading to a shortage of such classes.

CHAPTER 5, PAGE 122

1. If supply and tuition are constant and demand rises, the shortage of openings at the university will become greater. The university will continue to use its nonprice-rationing devices (GPA, SAT scores, and ACT scores) but will have to raise the standards of admission. Instead of requiring a GPA of, say, 3.5 for admission, it may raise the requirement to 3.8.

2. Not likely. A university that didn't make admission easier in the face of a surplus of openings might not be around much longer. When tuition cannot be adjusted directly—in other words, when the rationing device (price) cannot be adjusted—it is likely that the nonprice-rationing device (standards) will be.

CHAPTER 5, PAGE 124

1. The price of food will rise along with the premium for food insurance.

2. The new demand curve would be between D_1 and D_2.

CHAPTER 5, PAGE 125

1. A possible answer: Of two cities, one has clean air and the other has dirty air. The demand to live in the city that has clean air is higher than the demand to live in the city that has dirty air. As a result, housing prices are higher in the city that has clean air.

2. Ultimately, the person who owns the land in the city with good weather receives the payment. Look at it this way: People have a higher demand for houses in cities that have good weather than they do for houses in cities that have bad weather. As a result, house builders receive higher prices for houses built and sold in cities that have good weather. Because of the higher house prices, builders have a higher demand for land in cities that have good weather. In the end, higher demand for land translates into higher land prices or land rents for landowners.

CHAPTER 5, PAGE 127

1. The airline company will likely use the rationing device of first come, first served. The people who book their reservations early get their pick of seats; those who do not book early have to take the left-over seats.

2. The equilibrium price of the window seat is less than the equilibrium price of the aisle seat; the equilibrium price of the middle seat is less than the equilibrium price of the window seat. For example, if the equilibrium price of the aisle seat is $300, then the equilibrium price of the window seat might be $280, with the equilibrium price of the aisle seat even lower at $250.

CHAPTER 5, PAGE 128

1. Suppose that University X gives a full scholarship to every one of its football players (all of whom are super athletes), and the full scholarship (translated into wages) is far below the equilibrium wage of each of the football players. (Each football player gets a wage, or full scholarship, of $10,000 a year, when his equilibrium wage is $40,000 a year.) Paying lower than the equilibrium wage will end up transferring dollars and other benefits from the football players to the university, and by extension to the new field house and track, and perhaps to you, if you use the track for exercise.

2. If paying student athletes a wage above the full scholarship lowers consumers' demand for college athletics, then the equilibrium wage for college athletes is not as high as is shown in Exhibit 7.

CHAPTER 5, PAGE 129

1. Yes. For example, suppose a 30 percent down payment, instead of a 10 percent down payment, was needed to

obtain a mortgage loan. Due to the increase in the down payment requirement fewer individuals would be able to obtain a loan to buy a house, which would lower the demand for houses, and drive down house prices.

2. Yes. Reducing one's taxes because one has purchased a house makes buying a house more attractive, which would lead to a higher demand for houses. The higher demand for houses raises the equilibrium price of houses.

CHAPTER 5, PAGE 130

1. A speculator seeks to buy low and sell high. If she does so, she benefits. But by buying low and selling high, a speculator can reallocate supply and change prices in a way that benefits consumers. To illustrate, suppose a tornado threatens to reduce the wheat crop in the Midwest. Speculators translate this possibility into a future decrease in the supply of, and rise in the price of, wheat. So, they buy wheat today (before the tornado strikes and when it is relatively cheap) and sell it later (after the tornado has struck and the price is relatively expensive). In the process, they reallocate some of the supply of wheat from today to the future; and as supply changes, so does price. As for the buyers of wheat and wheat products, they may prefer to spread out the price-related pain of the tornado by paying a relatively higher price for wheat today and a relatively lower price for wheat in the future. For example, without the speculators reallocating some wheat, wheat prices might be $4 a bushel before the tornado and $9 after. But with the speculators, wheat prices might be $6 before the tornado and $7 after the tornado.

2. Without speculation, the price of good X is $40 on Monday through Thursday, and $50 on Friday through Sunday. In this instance, good X can be moved. Suppose that speculators buy some of good X on Monday through Thursday at the lower price, and sell it on Friday through Sunday at the higher price. This difference in price should last only a short while, because, in their attempts to buy low and sell high, speculators are reallocating some of the supply of good X from Monday through Thursday to Friday through Sunday. The lower supply on Monday through Thursday will raise the price of good X on these days, and the higher supply on Friday through Sunday will lower the price of good X on these days. In the end, it is likely that

the same price for good X will exist Monday through Sunday.

CHAPTER 5, PAGE 132

1. Any price above 70¢.

2. Assuming that tolls are not used, freeway congestion will worsen. An increase in driving population simply shifts the demand curve for driving to the right.

CHAPTER 5, PAGE 134

1. Moving from a system in which patients cannot sue their HMOs to one in which they can give patients something they didn't have before (the right to sue) at a higher price (higher charges for health-care coverage). The "free lunch"—the right to sue—isn't free after all.

2. If the students get the extra week and nothing else changes, then the students will probably say that they were better off. But if, as a result, the professor grades their papers harder than she would have otherwise, then some or all of the students might say that they weren't made better off by the extra week.

Chapter 6
CHAPTER 6, PAGE 148

1. $E_d = 1.44$.

2. If there is a change in price, the quantity demanded will change (in the opposite direction) by 0.39 times the percentage change in price. For example, if the price rises 10 percent, then the quantity demanded will fall 3.9 percent. If the price rises 20 percent, then the quantity demanded will fall 7.8 percent.

3. a. Total revenue falls.

   b. Total revenue falls.

   c. Total revenue remains constant.

   d. Total revenue rises.

   e. Total revenue rises.

4. Alexi is implicitly assuming that demand is inelastic. If, however, she is wrong and demand is elastic, then a rise in price will actually lower total revenue.

CHAPTER 6, PAGE 154

1. No. Moving from 7 to 9 substitutes doesn't necessarily change demand from being inelastic to elastic. It simply leads to a rise in price elasticity of demand, *ceteris paribus*. For example, if price elasticity of demand is 0.45 when good

X has 7 substitutes, it will be higher when there are 9 substitutes, *ceteris paribus*. Higher could be an elasticity of 0.67. If this is the case, demand is still inelastic (but less so than before).

2. a. Dell computers

   b. Heinz ketchup

   c. Perrier water

In all three cases, the good with the higher price elasticity of demand is the more specific of the two goods; therefore, it has more substitutes.

CHAPTER 6, PAGE 164

1. An income elasticity of demand of 1.33 means that the good in question is a normal good, and that it is income elastic; that is, as income rises, the quantity demanded rises by a greater percentage. In this case, quantity demanded rises by 1.33 times the percentage change in income. Thus, if income rises by 10 percent, the quantity demanded of the good will rise by 13.3 percent.

2. A change in price does not change the quantity supplied.

3. Tax revenue is equal to the tax times the quantity sold. If demand is inelastic, then the higher price brought about by the tax will result in a smaller cutback in quantity sold.

4. Under the condition that the demand for computers is perfectly inelastic or that the supply of computers is perfectly elastic.

Chapter 7
CHAPTER 7, PAGE 172

1. The paradox is that water, which is essential to life, is cheap, and diamonds, which are not essential to life, are expensive. The solution to the paradox depends on knowing the difference between total and marginal utility and the law of diminishing marginal utility. By saying that water is essential to life and diamonds are not essential to life, we signify that water gives us high total utility relative to diamonds. However, price is not a reflection of total utility, it is a reflection of marginal utility. The marginal utility of water is less than that of diamonds. How can the total utility of water be greater than that of diamonds, but the marginal utility of water be less than that of diamonds? According to the law of diminishing marginal utility, there is so much more water relative to diamonds that the next (additional) unit of water gives us less utility (lower marginal utility) than the next unit of diamonds.

2. If total utility declines, marginal utility must be negative. For example, if total utility is 30 utils when Lydia consumes 3 apples and 25 utils when she consumes 4 apples, then the fourth apple must have a marginal utility of −5 utils. Chapter 1 explains that something that takes utility away from us (or gives us disutility) is called a *bad*. For Lydia, the fourth apple is a bad, not a good.

3. The total and marginal utilities of a good are the same for the first unit of the good consumed. For example, before Tomás eats his first apple, he receives no utility or disutility from apples. Eating the first apple, he receives 15 utils. So the total utility (TU) for 1 apple is 15 utils, and the marginal utility (MU) for the first apple is 15 utils. Exhibit 1 shows that TU and MU are the same for the first unit of good X.

CHAPTER 7, PAGE 178

1. Alessandro is not in the consumer equilibrium, because the marginal utility per dollar of X is 16 utils and the marginal utility per dollar of Y is 13.14 utils. To be in equilibrium, a consumer has to receive the same marginal utility per dollar for each good consumed.

2. It means that the marginal utility–price ratio for one of the goods is higher than the ratio for the other good.

CHAPTER 7, PAGE 188

1. Yes, Brandon is compartmentalizing. He is treating the $100 that comes from his grandmother differently from the $100 that comes from his father.

2. The endowment effect relates to individuals valuing X more highly when they possess it than when they don't but are thinking of acquiring it. Friedman argues that, if we were to go back in time to a hunter–gatherer society when there were no well-established property rights (no rules as to what is mine and what is yours), we would find individuals who would fight hard to keep what they possessed but would not fight as hard to acquire what they did not possess. These individuals would have a higher probability of surviving than those who would fight hard in both cases and, therefore, put themselves at more risk. Those who would fight hard only to keep what they possessed and, therefore, put themselves at less risk, would have a higher probability of reproductive success. The characteristic of holding onto what you have has been passed down from generation to generation, and, although it may not be as important today as it was in a hunter–gatherer society, it still influences behavior.

Chapter 8

CHAPTER 8, PAGE 207

1. No. Individuals will form teams or firms only when the sum of what they can produce as a team or firm is greater than the sum of what they can produce working alone.

2. The person earning the low salary has lower implicit costs and so is more likely to start a business. She gives up less to start a business.

3. Accounting profit is larger. Only explicit costs are subtracted from total revenue in computing accounting profit, but both explicit and implicit costs are subtracted from total revenue in computing economic profit. If implicit costs are zero, then accounting profit and economic profit are the same. Economic profit is never greater than accounting profit.

4. A business owner can be earning a profit but not covering costs when he is earning (positive) accounting profit but his total revenue does not cover the sum of his explicit and implicit costs. For example, suppose Brad earns a total revenue of $100,000 and has explicit costs of $40,000 and implicit costs of $70,000. His accounting profit is $60,000, but his total revenue of $100,000 is not large enough to cover the sum of his explicit and implicit costs ($110,000). Brad's economic profit is a negative $10,000. In other words, although Brad earns an accounting profit, he takes an economic loss.

CHAPTER 8, PAGE 214

1. No. The short run and the long run are not lengths of time. The short run is that period during which some inputs are fixed and, therefore, the firm has fixed costs. The long run is any period during which no inputs are fixed (i.e., all inputs are variable) and, thus, all costs are variable costs. The period during which there are no fixed inputs can be shorter than the period during which there are fixed inputs.

2. The law of diminishing marginal returns holds only when we add more of one input to a given (fixed) quantity of another input. The statement does not identify one input as fixed (it says that both increase), so the law of diminishing marginal returns is not relevant in this situation.

3. When MC is declining, MPP is rising; when MC is constant, MPP is constant; and when MC is rising, MPP is falling.

CHAPTER 8, PAGE 225

1. $ATC = TC/Q$ and $ATC = AFC + AVC$.

2. Yes. Suppose a business incurs a cost of $10 to make a product. However, before it can sell the product, the demand for it falls and moves the market price from $15 to $6. Does the owner of the business say, "I can't sell the product for $6 because I'd be taking a loss"? If she does, she chooses to let a sunk cost affect her current decision. Instead, she should ask herself: will the market price of the product rise, or will it fall further? If she thinks that it will fall further, she should sell the product today for $6.

3. Unit costs are another name for average total costs (ATC), so the question is, "what happens to ATC as MC rises?" You might be inclined to say that, as MC rises, so does ATC, but this is not necessarily so. (See region 1 in Exhibit 6(b).) What matters is whether MC is greater than ATC. If it is, then ATC will rise. If it is not, then ATC will decline. This is a trick question of sorts. There is a tendency to misinterpret the average-marginal rule and to believe that, as marginal cost rises, average total cost rises and that, as marginal cost falls, average total cost falls. But the average-marginal rule actually says that when MC is above ATC, ATC rises, and when MC is below ATC, ATC falls.

4. Yes. As marginal physical product (MPP) rises, marginal cost (MC) falls. If MC falls enough to move below unit cost, which is the same as average total cost, then unit cost declines. Similarly, as MPP falls, MC rises. If MC rises enough to move above unit cost, then unit cost rises.

CHAPTER 8, PAGE 229

1. Suppose it currently takes 10 units of X and 10 units of Y to produce 50 units of good Z. Let both X and Y double to 20 units each. As a result, the output of Z more than doubles to 150 units. When inputs are increased by some percentage and output increases by a greater percentage, economies of scale are said to exist. When economies of scale exist, unit costs fall, and another name for unit costs is average total costs.

2. The $LRATC$ curve would be horizontal. When there are constant returns to scale, output doubles if inputs double. But unit costs stay constant, so the LRATC curve is horizontal.

3. Unit costs must have been lower when the firm produced 200 units than when it produced 100 units. That is, there were economies of scale between 100 units and

200 units. To explain further, profit per unit is the difference of price per unit and cost per unit (or unit costs): Profit per unit = Price per unit − Cost per unit.   Suppose the unit cost is $3 when the price is $4, giving a profit per unit of $1. There are economies of scale as the firm raises output from 100 units to 200 units. Unit costs must fall—let's say, to $2 per unit. If the price is $3, then there is still a profit of $1 per unit.

Chapter 9

CHAPTER 9, PAGE 238

1. It means that the firm cannot change the price of the product it sells by its actions. For example, if firm A cuts back on the supply of what it produces and the price of its product does not change, then firm A cannot control the price of the product it sells. In other words, if price is independent of a firm's actions, that firm does not have any control over price.

2. The easy, and incomplete, answer is that a perfectly competitive firm is a price taker because it is in a market in which it cannot control the price of the product it sells. But why not? The complete answer is that the firm is in a market in which (1) its supply is small relative to the total market supply, (2) it sells a homogeneous good, and (3) all buyers and sellers have all relevant information about prices, product quality, sources of supply, and so forth.

3. If a perfectly competitive firm tries to charge a price higher than the equilibrium price, all buyers will know that it is trying to do so (assumption 3). These buyers will then simply buy from another firm that sells the same (homogeneous) product (assumption 2).

4. No. A market doesn't have to perfectly match all assumptions of the theory of perfect competition for it to be labeled a perfectly competitive market. What is important is whether the market acts as if it is perfectly competitive. "If it walks like a duck and it quacks like a duck, it's a duck." If it acts like a perfectly competitive market, it's a perfectly competitive market.

CHAPTER 9, PAGE 247

1. No. Whether a firm earns profits depends on the relationship between price (P) and average total cost (ATC). If $P > ATC$, then the firm earns profits. To understand this relationship, remember that profits exist when total revenue (TR) minus total cost (TC) is a positive number. Total revenue is simply price times quantity $(TR = P \times Q)$, and total cost is average total cost times quantity

$(TC = ATC \times Q)$. Because quantity (Q) is common to both TR and TC, if $P > ATC$, then $TR > TC$ and the firm earns profits.

2. In the short run, whether a firm should shut down depends on the relationship between price and average variable cost (AVC), not between price and ATC. It depends on whether price is greater or less than average variable cost. If $P > AVC$, the firm should continue to produce; if $P < AVC$, it should shut down.

3. As long as $MR > MC$—for example, $MR = \$6$ and $MC = \$4$—the firm should produce and sell additional units of a good because doing so adds more to TR ($\$6$) than it does to TC ($\$4$). Whenever you add more to TR than you do to TC, the gap between the two becomes larger.

4. We start with the upward-sloping market supply curve and work backward. First, market supply curves are upward sloping because they are the "addition" of individual firms' supply curves, which are upward sloping. Second, individual firms' supply curves are upward sloping because they are the portion of their marginal cost curves above their average variable cost curves, and this portion of the MC curve is upward sloping. Third, marginal cost curves have upward-sloping portions because of the law of diminishing marginal returns. Therefore, market supply curves are upward sloping because of the law of diminishing marginal returns.

CHAPTER 9, PAGE 258

1. According to the theory of perfect competition, the profits will draw new firms into the market. As these new firms enter the market, the market supply curve will shift to the right. As a result of a larger supply, price will fall. As price declines, profit will decline until firms in the market are earning (only) normal (or zero economic) profit. When there is zero economic profit, firms no longer have an incentive to enter the market.

2. No. The market is in long-run competitive equilibrium only when firms have no incentive to (1) enter or exit the industry, (2) produce more or less output, or (3) change their plant size. If any of these conditions is not met, then the market is not in long-run equilibrium.

3. Initially, price will rise. Recall from Chapter 3 that, when demand increases, *ceteris paribus*, price rises. In time, though, price will drop because new firms will enter the industry because of the positive economic profits generated by the higher price. How far the price drops depends

on whether the firms are in a constant-cost, an increasing-cost, or a decreasing-cost industry. In a constant-cost industry, price will return to its original level; in an increasing-cost industry, price will return to a level above its original level; and in a decreasing-cost industry, price will return to a level below its original level.

4. Maybe initially, but probably not after certain adjustments are made. If firm A really has a genius on its payroll and, as a result, earns higher profits than firm B, then firm B might try to hire the genius away from firm A by offering him or her a higher income. To keep the genius, firm A will have to match the offer. As a result, the costs of firm A will rise, and if nothing else changes, its profits will decline.

CHAPTER 9, PAGE 259

1. It depends on how many firms in the market witness higher costs. If it is only one, then the market supply curve is not likely to shift enough to bring about a higher price. If, however, many firms in the market witness higher costs, then the market supply curve will shift left and price will rise.

2. No. Perfectly competitive firms that sell homogeneous products will not advertise individually, but the industry might advertise in the hope of pushing the market (industry) demand curve (for their product) to the right.

CHAPTER 10

CHAPTER 10, PAGE 266

1. Let's assume that any product a firm sells has some close substitutes. The question, however, is how close the substitute has to be before the theory of monopoly is not useful. For example, a "slightly close" substitute for a seller's product may not be close enough to matter. The theory of monopoly may still be useful in predicting a firm's behavior.

2. Economies of scale exist when a firm doubles inputs and its output more than doubles, lowering its unit costs (average total costs) in the process. If economies of scale exist only when a firm produces a large quantity of output and one firm is already producing this output, then new firms (that start off producing less output) will have higher unit costs than those of the established firm. Some economists argue that these higher unit costs will make the new firms uncompetitive compared with the established firm. In other words, economies of scale will act as a barrier to entry, effectively preventing

firms from entering the industry and competing with the established firm.

3. In a monopoly, there is a single seller of a good that has no close substitutes and the barriers to entry are extremely high. If a movie superstar has so much talent that the moviegoing public puts her in a class by herself, she might be considered a monopolist. Anyone can try to compete with her, but she may have such great talent (relative to everyone else) that no one will be able to compete. Her immense talent acts as a barrier to entry in the sense that, even if others try to compete with her, they won't be a close enough substitute for her.

CHAPTER 10, PAGE 273

1. The single-price monopolist has to lower price in order to sell an additional unit of its good. (This condition is what a downward-sloping demand curve necessitates.) As long as it has to lower price to sell an additional unit, its marginal revenue will be below its price. A demand curve plots price (P) and quantity (Q), and a marginal revenue curve plots marginal revenue (MR) and quantity (Q). Because $P > MR$ for a monopolist, its the demand curve will lie above its the marginal revenue curve.

2. No. Profit depends on whether price is greater than average total cost. A monopolist could produce the quantity of output at which $MR = MC$, charge the highest price per unit possible for the output, and still have its unit costs (ATC) greater than the price. In this case, the monopolist incurs losses, and does not earn profits.

3. No. The last chapter explains that a firm is resource allocative efficient when it charges a price equal to its marginal cost ($P = MC$). The monopolist does not do this, but rather charges a price above marginal cost. Profit maximization ($MR = MC$) does not lead to resource allocative efficiency ($P = MC$) because, for the monopolist, $P > MR$. This is not the case for the perfectly competitive firm, for which $P = MR$.

4. A monopolist is searching for the highest price at which to sell a product. In contrast, the perfectly competitive firm doesn't have to search; it simply takes the equilibrium price established in the market. For example, suppose Nancy is a wheat farmer. She gets up one morning and wants to know at what price she should sell her wheat. She simply turns on the radio, listens to the farm report, and finds out that the equilibrium price per bushel of wheat is $5. Being a price taker, she knows that she can't sell her wheat for a penny more than $5 (the highest

price), and she won't want to sell her wheat for a penny less either. The monopoly firm doesn't know what the highest price is for the product it sells. It has to search for it and experiment with different prices before it finds the highest price.

CHAPTER 10, PAGE 283

1. Monopoly has at least the following three costs, or shortcomings:

   a. A monopoly firm produces too little output relative to the output of a perfectly competitive firm; this difference causes the deadweight loss of monopoly.

   b. The profits of the monopoly are sometimes subject to rent-seeking behavior. Rent seeking, while rational for an individual firm, wastes society's resources. Society receives no benefit if one firm expends resources to take over the monopoly position of another firm. Resources that could have been used to produce goods (e.g., computers, software, shoes, and houses) are used to transfer profits from one firm to another instead.

   c. A monopolist might not produce products at the lowest possible cost. Again, failure to do so wastes society's resources.

2. An example helps to illustrate this concept. Suppose a perfectly competitive firm produces 100 units of good X, but a monopoly firm produces only 70 units, which is a difference of 30 units. Buyers value these 30 units by more than it would cost the monopoly firm to produce them, yet the monopoly firm chooses not to produce the units. The net benefit (benefits to buyers minus costs to the monopolist) of producing these 30 units is said to be the deadweight loss of monopoly. It represents how much buyers lose because the monopolist chooses to produce less than the perfectly competitive firm would.

3. If a seller is not a price searcher, then it is a price taker. A price taker can sell its product at only one price: the market equilibrium price.

CHAPTER 11

CHAPTER 11, PAGE 292

1. A monopolistic competitor is like a monopolist in that (1) it faces a downward-sloping demand curve, (2) it is a price searcher ($P > MR$), and (3) it is not resource allocative efficient. It is like a perfect competitor in that (1) it

sells to many buyers and competes with many sellers, and (2) entry into and exit from the market are easy.

2. Essentially, they face downward-sloping demand curves. Because the demand curve is downward sloping, it cannot be tangent to the lowest point on a U-shaped ATC curve. (See Exhibit 3.)

CHAPTER 11, PAGE 295

1. The incentive in both cases is the same: to increase their profits. After the cartel is formed, however, each firm has an incentive to break the cartel to increase its profits even further. (See Exhibit 5.) If there is no cartel agreement, the firm is earning zero profits by producing quantity q_1. After the cartel is formed, it earns $CP_C AB$ in profits by producing quantity q_C. But it can earn even higher profits ($FP_C DE$) by cheating on the cartel and producing quantity q_{CC}.

2. An oligopolistic firm is a price searcher. A price searcher faces a downward-sloping demand curve. Also, an oligopolistic firm has some control over the price it charges. Such control is the hallmark of a price searcher.

CHAPTER 12

CHAPTER 12, PAGE 318

1. How a market is defined will help determine whether a firm is considered a monopoly. If a market is defined broadly, it will include more substitute goods, so the firm is less likely to be considered a monopoly. If a market is defined narrowly, it will include fewer substitute goods, so the firm is more likely to be considered a monopoly.

2. The four-firm concentration ratio is 20 percent; the Herfindahl index is 500. The formulas in Exhibit 1 show how each is computed.

3. The Herfindahl index provides information about the dispersion of firm size in an industry. For example, suppose the top four firms in an industry have 15 percent, 10 percent, 9 percent, and 8 percent market shares, respectively. The four-firm concentration ratio will be the same for an industry with 15 firms as it is for an industry with 150 firms. The Herfindahl index will be different in the two situations.

CHAPTER 12, PAGE 325

1. Average cost pricing is the same as profit regulation. The regulators state that the natural monopolist must charge a price equal to its average total cost ($P = ATC$). Under this pricing policy, there is no incentive for the natural

monopolist to keep costs down. In fact, there may be an incentive to deliberately push costs up. Higher costs—in the form of higher salaries or more luxurious offices—simply mean higher prices to cover the higher costs.

2. No matter the motive for initially regulating an industry, the regulating agency will eventually be captured by the special interests (the firms) in the industry. In the end, the regulatory body will not so much regulate the industry as serve the interests of the firms in it.

3. According to the capture theory, the outcomes of the regulatory process will favor the regulated firms. According to the public choice theory, the outcomes of the regulatory process will favor the regulators.

4. Sometimes they favor regulation, and at other times they do not. Economists make the point that regulation involves both costs and benefits, and whether a particular regulation is worthwhile depends on whether the costs are greater or less than the benefits.

CHAPTER 13
CHAPTER 13, PAGE 335

1. $MRP = MR \times MPP$. For a perfectly competitive firm, $MR = P$, so MR is $10. MPP in this case is 19 units. It follows that $MRP = 190.

2. There is no difference between MRP and VMP if the firm is perfectly competitive. In this situation, $P = MR$, and because $MRP = MR \times MPP$ and $VMP = P \times MPP$, the two are the same. If the firm is a price searcher—a monopolist, a monopolistic competitor, or an oligopolist—$P > MR$; therefore, $VMP > MRP$.

3. A factor price taker can buy all that is wanted of a factor at the equilibrium price, and will not cause the factor price to rise. For example, if firm X is a factor price taker in the labor market, it can buy all the labor it wants at the equilibrium wage, and it will not cause this wage to rise.

4. It should buy the quantity at which the MRP of labor equals the MFC of labor.

CHAPTER 13, PAGE 348

1. The MRP curve is the firm's factor demand curve. $MRP = P \times MPP$ for a perfectly competitive firm; so, if either the price of the product that labor produces rises, or the MPP of labor rises (reflected in a shift in the MPP curve), the factor demand curve shifts rightward.

2. It means that, for every 1 percent change in the wage rate, the quantity demanded of labor changes inversely by 3 times this

percentage. For example, if wage rates rise 10 percent, then the quantity demanded of labor falls 30 percent.

3. The short answer is because supply-and-demand conditions differ among markets. The question of why supply-and-demand conditions differ is answered in Exhibit 11.

4. We can't answer this question specifically without more information. We know that, under four conditions, wage rates would not differ: (1) The demand for every type of labor is the same; (2) the jobs have no special nonpecuniary aspects; (3) all labor is ultimately homogeneous and can costlessly be trained for different types of employment; and (4) all labor is mobile at zero cost. Wage rates differ when one or more of these conditions are not met. For example, perhaps labor is not mobile at zero cost.

CHAPTER 14
CHAPTER 14, PAGE 361

1. The demand for union labor is lowered by a decline in (a) the demand for the product that union labor produces, (b) the price of substitute factors, and (c) the marginal physical product of union labor.

2. A closed shop requires an employee to be a member of the union before being hired; a union shop does not. The union shop requires employees to join the union within a certain period after becoming employed.

3. The purpose of a strike is to prove to management that union members will not work for a wage rate that is lower than the rate specified by the union. In terms of Exhibit 3, it is to prove that union members will not work for less than W_2.

CHAPTER 14, PAGE 367

1. A monopsonist cannot buy additional units of a factor without increasing the price it pays for the factor. A factor price taker can.

2. The minimum wage can increase the number of people working under the following conditions: (1) The firm hiring the labor is a monopsonist, and (2) the minimum wage is above the wage it is already paying and below the wage that corresponds to the point where $MFC = MRP$. In Exhibit 4(c), suppose the firm is currently purchasing Q_1 quantity of labor and paying wage W_1. Then W_2 becomes the minimum wage the monopsonist can pay to workers. Now it hires Q_2 workers. Notice, however, that if the monopsonist had to pay a wage higher than the wage that equates MFC and MRP, it would employ fewer workers than Q_1.

3. If the higher wage rate reduces the number of people working in the unionized sector and the people who lose their jobs in the unionized sector move to the nonunionized sector, then the supply of labor will increase in the nonunionized sector and wage rates will fall. (See Exhibit 6.)

CHAPTER 15

CHAPTER 15, PAGE 376

1. Government can change the distribution of income through transfer payments and taxes. Look at this equation: Individual income = Labor income + Asset income + Transfer payments − Taxes. By increasing one person's taxes and increasing another person's transfer payments, government can change people's incomes.

2. The statement is true. For example, two people can have unequal incomes at any one point in time and still earn the same total incomes over time. For example, suppose that in year 1 Patrick earns $40,000 and Francine earns $20,000. Then in year 2, Francine earns $40,000 and Patrick earns $20,000. In each year there is income inequality, but over the 2 years Patrick and Francine earn the same income ($60,000).

3. No. Individual income = Labor income + Asset income + Transfer payments − Taxes. Smith's income could come entirely from labor income, and Jones's income could come entirely from asset income. The same dollar income does not necessarily come from the same source.

CHAPTER 15, PAGE 380

1. No. The income shares a total of 105 percent.

2. A Gini coefficient of 0 represents perfect income equality, and a Gini coefficient of 1 represents complete income inequality. Thus, we are sure that country A has neither perfect income equality nor complete income inequality. Saying anything further is difficult. Usually, the Gini coefficient is used as a comparative measure. For example, if country A's Gini coefficient is 0.45 and country B's is 0.60, we could say that country A has a more equal (less unequal) distribution of income than country B.

CHAPTER 15, PAGE 383

1. The simple fact that Jack earns more than Harry is not evidence of wage discrimination. We do not know whether wage discrimination exists. For example, we do not know whether Jack and Harry work the same job, how productive each is, and so on.

2. It could affect it negatively or positively. The probability of both higher and lower incomes is greater if a person assumes a lot of risk than if a person plays it safe. Suppose Nancy has decided that she wants to be an actress, although her parents want her to be an accountant. The chances of her being successful in acting are small, but if she is successful, she will earn a much higher income than if she had been an accountant. (A top actress earns more than a top accountant.) Of course, if she isn't successful, she will earn less income as an actress than she would have as an accountant. (The average actress earns less than the average accountant.)

CHAPTER 15, PAGE 385

1. Whether poor people always exist depends on how we define poverty. If we define it in relative terms and we assume no absolute income equality, then some people must fall into, say, the lowest 10 percent of income earners. We could refer to these persons as poor. Remember, though, that these persons are relatively poor—they earn less than a large percentage of the income earners in the country—but we do not know anything about their absolute incomes. In a world of multimillion-dollar income earners, a person who earns $100,000 might be considered poor.

2. 13.5 percent.

3. An African American or Hispanic female who is the head of a large family, who is young, and has little education.

CHAPTER 16

CHAPTER 16, PAGE 395

1. Because there is a monetary incentive for them to be equal. Suppose the return on capital is 12 percent and the price for loanable funds is 10 percent. In this case, a person could borrow loanable funds at 10 percent and invest in capital goods to earn the 12 percent return. In the meantime, though, the amount of capital increases and its return falls. If the interest rates are reversed and the return on capital is lower than the price for a loanable fund, no one will borrow to invest in capital goods. Over time, then, the stock of capital will diminish and its return will rise.

2. Because the real interest rate is the rate paid by borrowers and received by lenders. For example, a person who borrows funds at a 12 percent interest rate when the inflation rate is 4 percent will be paying only an 8 percent (real) interest rate to the lender. Stated differently, the lender

has 8 percent, not 12 percent, more buying power by making the loan.

3. $907.03. The formula is $PV = \$1,000/(1 + 0.05)^2$.

4. No. The present value of $2,000 a year for 4 years at an 8 percent interest rate is $6,624.25. [$PV = \$2,000/(1 + 0.08)^1 + \$2,000/(1 + 0.08)^2 + \$2,000/(1 + 0.08)^3 + + \$2,000/(1 + 0.08)^4$]. The present value is less than the cost of the capital good, so the purchase is not worthwhile.

CHAPTER 16, PAGE 400

1. Jones earns $2 million a year as a news anchor for KNBC. His next-best alternative in the news industry is earning $1.9 million a year as a news anchor for KABC. If Jones were not working in the news industry, his next-best alternative would be as a journalism professor earning $100,000 a year. Within the news industry, Jones earns $100,000 economic rent (the difference between $2 million and $1.9 million). Outside the news industry, Jones earns $1.9 million in economic rent (the difference between $2 million and $100,000).

2. It is $0.

3. When a firm competes for artificial rents, it expends resources to transfer economic rent from another firm to itself. In other words, resources are used to bring about a transfer. No additional goods or services are produced as a part of the process. But when a firm competes for real rents, resources are used to produce additional goods and services.

CHAPTER 16, PAGE 405

1. A probability cannot be assigned to uncertainty; a probability can be assigned to risk.

2. Many theories purport to explain profit. One theory states that profit exists because uncertainty exists—no uncertainty, no profit. Another states that profit exists because of arbitrage opportunities (the opportunities to buy low and sell high) to which some people are alert. Still another theory states that profit exists because some people (entrepreneurs) are capable of creating profit opportunities by devising a new product, production process, or marketing strategy.

3. Profit can be a signal, especially if it is earned in a competitive market. Specifically, profit signals that buyers value a good (as evidenced by the price they are willing and able to pay for the good) more than the factors that go into making the good.

4. (1) Produce a good or service that satisfies an unmet demand. (2) Reduce the transaction costs of making trades.

CHAPTER 17

CHAPTER 17, PAGE 414

1. The market output does not reflect or adjust for either external costs (in the case of a negative externality) or external benefits (in the case of a positive externality). The socially optimal output does.

2. Certainly, if no costs are incurred by moving from the market output to the socially optimal output, the answer is yes. But this isn't likely to be the case. The economist considers whether the benefits of moving to the socially optimal output are greater than or less than the costs of moving to the socially optimal output. If the benefits are greater than the costs, then yes; if the benefits are less than the costs, then no.

CHAPTER 17, PAGE 419

1. Internalizing an externality means adjusting the private cost by the external cost. To illustrate, suppose that someone's private cost is $10 and the external cost is $2. If the person internalizes the externality, the external cost becomes his or her cost, which is now $12.

2. Transaction costs are associated with the time and effort needed to search out, negotiate, and consummate an exchange. These costs are higher for buying a house than for buying a hamburger. It takes more time and effort to search out a house to buy, negotiate a price, and consummate the deal than it takes to search out and buy a hamburger.

3. Under certain conditions, no. Specifically, if transaction costs are zero or trivial, the property rights assignment that a court makes is irrelevant to the resource-allocative outcome. Of course, if transaction costs are not zero or trivial, then the property rights assignment a court makes does matter.

4. Given a negative externality, there is a marginal external cost. The marginal external cost (MEC) plus the marginal private cost (MPC) equals the marginal social cost (MSC): $MSC = MPC + ME$. If a tax (t) is to adjust correctly for the marginal external cost associated with the negative externality, it must be equal to the marginal external cost; in other words, tax $= MEC$. With this condition fulfilled, $MPC + \text{tax} = MSC = MPC + MEC$.

CHAPTER 17, PAGE 423

1. Under a system in which each polluter eliminates the same amount of pollution, both the polluters that have a high cost of eliminating pollution and the polluters that have a lost cost of eliminating pollution have to eliminate the same amount of pollution. Under a tradable pollution permits system, it is primarily the low-cost polluters that end up eliminating most of the pollution.

2. Under an emissions tax, polluters know what price they have to pay to pollute but the government doesn't know how much pollution will be generated. Under a tradable pollution permits system (cap and trade), the government knows the amount of pollution but polluters don't immediately know what the price to pollute will be.

3. Under an emission tax, the price to pollute is the tax; under a tradable pollution permits system, the price to pollute is the price of the pollution permit.

CHAPTER 17, PAGE 427

1. After a nonexcludable public good is produced, the individual or firm that produced it wouldn't be able to collect payment for it. When a nonexcludable public good is provided to one person, it is provided to everyone. Because an individual can consume the good without paying for it, he is likely to take a free ride. Another way of answering this question is simply to say, "The market fails to produce nonexcludable public goods because of the free-rider problem."

2. (a) A composition notebook is a private good. It is rivalrous in consumption: if one person is using it, someone else cannot. (b) A Shakespearean play performed in a summer theater is an excludable public good. It is nonrivalrous in consumption (everyone in the theater can see the play) but excludable (a person must pay to get into the theater). (c) An apple is a private good. It is rivalrous in consumption: if one person eats it, someone else cannot. (d) A telephone in service is a private good. One person using the phone (e.g., in your house) prevents someone else from using it. (e) Sunshine is a nonexcludable public good. It is nonrivalrous in consumption (one person's consumption of it doesn't reduce its consumption by others) and nonexcludable (people cannot be excluded from consuming the sunshine).

3. A concert is an example. If one person consumes the concert, others can still consume it to the same degree. However, people can be excluded from consuming it.

CHAPTER 17, PAGE 432

1. The sellers of a fictional product X know that the good could, under certain conditions, cause health problems, but they do not release this information to the buyers. Consequently, the demand for good X is likely to be greater than it would be if there was symmetric information. The quantity consumed of good X is likely to be higher when there is asymmetric information than when there is symmetric information.

2. In the used-car market discussed in the text, if there is asymmetric information for two types of used cars—good used cars and lemons—the market price for a used car may understate the value of a good used car and overstate the value of a lemon. This discrepancy will induce sellers of lemons to enter the market and sellers of good cars to leave it. (The owners of good used cars will not want to sell their cars for less than their cars are worth.) In theory, the used-car market may eventually consist of nothing but lemons. In other words, a used-car market for good cars no longer will exist.

3. A college professor tells her students that she does not believe in giving grades of D or F. As a result, her students do not take as many precautionary measures to guard against receiving low grades. Does your example have the characteristic of this example—namely, one person's assurance affecting another person's incentive?

CHAPTER 18

CHAPTER 18, PAGE 446

1. No. The model doesn't say every politician has to do these things; it simply predicts that politicians who do these things have an increased chance of winning the election in a two-person race.

2. Voters may want more information from politicians, but supplying that information is not always in the best interests of political candidates. When they speak in specific terms, politicians are often labeled as being at one end or the other of the political spectrum. But, generally, this is not how elections are won.

3. Yes. In the cost equation of voting, we included (1) the cost of driving to the polls, (2) the cost of standing in line, and (3) the cost of filling out the ballot. Bad weather (heavy rain, snow, and ice) would likely raise the cost of driving to the polls and standing in line, thereby raising the cost of voting. The higher the cost of voting is, the less likely it is that people will vote, *ceteris paribus*.

3. *Ceteris paribus*, the dollar will depreciate relative to the franc. As incomes for Americans rise, the demand for Swiss goods rises. Rising demand for Swiss goods increases the demand for francs and the supply of dollars on the foreign exchange market. In turn, the dollar depreciates and the franc appreciates.

4. The theory states that the exchange rate between any two currencies will adjust to reflect changes in the relative price levels of the two countries. For example, suppose the U.S. price level rises 5 percent and Mexico's price level remains constant. According to the PPP theory, the U.S. dollar will depreciate 5 percent relative to the Mexican peso.

CHAPTER 21, PAGE 515

1. The terms *overvalued* and *undervalued* refer to the equilibrium exchange rate: the exchange rate at which the quantity demanded and the quantity supplied of a currency are the same in the foreign exchange market. Let's suppose the equilibrium exchange rate were 0.10 USD = 1 MXN. This is the same as saying that 10 pesos = $1. If the exchange rate were fixed at 0.12 USD = 1 MXN, which is the same as 8.33 pesos = $1, the peso would be overvalued and the dollar would be undervalued. Specifically, a currency is overvalued if 1 unit of it fetches more of another currency than it would in equilibrium; a currency is undervalued if 1 unit of it fetches less of another currency than it would in equilibrium. In equilibrium, 1 peso would fetch $0.10, and at the current exchange rate it fetches $0.12, so the peso is overvalued. In equilibrium, $1 would fetch 10 pesos, and at the current exchange rate, it fetches only 8.33 pesos, so the dollar is undervalued.

2. An overvalued dollar means that some other currency— let's say the Japanese yen—is undervalued. On the one hand, an overvalued dollar makes U.S. goods more expensive for the Japanese, so they buy fewer U.S. goods and the United States exports less. On the other hand, an undervalued yen makes Japanese goods cheaper for Americans, so they buy more Japanese goods and the United States imports more. Thus, an overvalued dollar reduces U.S. exports and raises U.S. imports.

3. a. Dollar is overvalued.

   b. Dollar is undervalued.

   c. Dollar is undervalued.

4. When a country devalues its currency, it makes it cheaper for foreigners to buy its products.

Web Chapter 22
CHAPTER 22, PAGE 527

1. He calculates the *MB/MC* ratio of producing and the *MB/MC* ratio of stealing. If the first ratio is greater than the second, then he devotes the next hour to producing rather than stealing, because the return from producing is greater than the return from stealing. He continues to devote more time to producing until the two ratios are the same.

2. Once Jack and Jill have agreed to stop stealing, each has an incentive to steal from the other. In terms of the payoff matrix in Exhibit 1, Jack and Jill may initially be in box 4. They make an agreement to stop stealing so that they can move to box 1. But once in box 1, each person can make himself or herself better off by moving to a different box. Jack is better off moving from box 1 to box 2, and Jill is better off moving from box 1 to box 3. They are likely, then, to break the agreement (not to steal) and try to move to their respective superior boxes, especially when no one can punish them for making the move. Jack and Jill can't move themselves from box 4 to box 1 because there is no enforcer of the agreement. However, the government may later come along to fill the role of enforcer of the agreement between Jack and Jill.

3. Disagree. Whether the government makes parties in a prisoner's dilemma setting better off by removing them from the setting depends on how much each party gains by being removed, compared with how much each party pays in tax to the government. If the gain from being removed from the setting is $2 and the tax is $3, then a person is made worse off with government than without. If the gain is $2 and the tax is $1, then the person is made better off. If the gain is $2 and the tax is $2, then the person is made neither better or worse off.

CHAPTER 22, PAGE 530

1. With respect to a negative externality, if the government can set the tax equal to the marginal external cost, then it can change an inefficient market outcome into an efficient one. With respect to a positive externality, if the government can set the subsidy equal to the marginal external benefit, then it can change an inefficient market outcome into an efficient one.

2. Individuals might want certain nonexcludable public goods, which the market will not produce because it cannot overcome the free-rider problem. Because nonexcludable public goods, once produced, cannot be denied to anyone, no one will have an incentive to pay for the good. Instead, individuals will choose to be free riders. Knowing this, no market participant will produce the good. The government can overcome the free-rider problem by taxing individuals and then using the tax monies either to produce the nonexcludable public good itself or to pay someone else to produce it.

CHAPTER 22, PAGE 532

1. The tax credit lowers the overall cost of buying a house; that is, a person who buys a house finds that his or her taxes are lowered. As a result, the demand to buy a house rises. As house demand rises, so do house prices.

2. Yes. When buying a house, the purchaser has to consider many factors: the interest rate on a mortgage loan, the taxes paid as a result of buying the house, the price of the house, and so on. In the tax credit policy example in this section, the tax credit initially lowered the overall cost of buying a house because it reduced the taxes a person would pay as a result of buying a house. But because it made buying a house less expensive, more people became homebuyers. In other words, the demand for houses increased. Because the demand for houses increased, house prices increased, all other things remaining constant.

CHAPTER 22, PAGE 537

1. 1,000 times larger.

2. Group B would be less willing to advocate growth policies over transfer policies. The smaller the slice of the economic pie the group receives, the less they receive from any economic growth and the less willing they would be to advocate growth over transfers.

Web Chapter 23

CHAPTER 23, PAGE 549

1. 30.

2. Stocks are purchased either for the dividends that the stocks may pay, the expected gain in the price of the stock, or both.

3. Yield equals the dividend per share of the stock divided by the closing price per share.

4. A P/E ratio of 23 means that the stock is selling for a share price that is 23 times its earnings per share.

CHAPTER 23, PAGE 554

1. A bond is an IOU, or a promise to pay. The issuer of a bond is borrowing funds and promising to pay back those funds with interest at a later date.

2. $0.07x = \$400$, so $x = \$400 \div 0.07$, or $\$5,714.29$.

3. $\$1,000/\$9,500 = 10.53$ percent.

4. A municipal bond is issued by a state or local government, and a Treasury bond is issued by the federal government.

CHAPTER 23, PAGE 557

1. A futures contract is a contract in which the seller agrees to provide a good to the buyer on a specified future date at an agreed-upon price.

2. You can buy a call option, which sells for a fraction of the cost of the stock. A call option gives the owner of the option the right to buy shares of a stock at a specified price within the time limits of the contract.

3. A put option gives the owner the right, but not the obligation, to *sell* (rather than buy, as in a call option) shares of a stock at a strike price during some specified period.

GLOSSARY

A

Absolute (Money) Price The price of a good in money terms.

Abstract The process (used in building a theory) of focusing on a limited number of variables to explain or predict an event.

Accounting Profit The difference between total revenue and explicit costs.

Adverse Selection A phenomenon in which the parties on one side of the market have information not known to others and self-select in a way that adversely affects the parties on the other side of the market.

Antitrust Law Legislation passed for the stated purpose of controlling monopoly power and preserving and promoting competition.

Appreciation An increase in the value of one currency relative to other currencies.

Arbitrage Buying a good at a low price and selling it for a higher price.

Asymmetric Information Information that either the buyer or the seller in a market exchange has and that the other does not have.

Average Fixed Cost (AFC) Total fixed cost divided by quantity of output: $AFC = TFC/Q$.

Average Total Cost (ATC) Total cost divided by quantity of output: $ATC = TC/Q$.

Average Variable Cost (AVC) Total variable cost divided by quantity of output: $AVC = TVC/Q$.

average–marginal rule When the marginal magnitude is above the average magnitude, the average magnitude rises; when the marginal magnitude is below the average magnitude, the average magnitude falls.

B

Bad Anything from which individuals receive disutility or dissatisfaction.

Bond An IOU, or a promise to pay.

Budget Constraint All the combinations, or bundles, of two goods a person can purchase, given a certain money income and prices for the two goods.

Business Firm An entity that employs factors of production (resources) to produce goods and services to be sold to consumers, other firms, or the government.

C

Capital Produced goods, such as factories, machinery, tools, computers, and buildings that can be used as inputs for further production.

Capture Theory of Regulation A theory holding that, no matter what the motive is for the initial regulation and the establishment of the regulatory agency, eventually the agency will be captured (controlled) by the special interests of the industry being regulated.

Cartel An organization of firms that reduces output and increases price in an effort to increase joint profits.

Cartel Theory A theory of oligopoly in which oligopolistic firms act as if there were only one firm in the industry.

Ceteris Paribus A Latin term meaning *all other things constant* or *nothing else changes*.

Closed Shop An organization in which an employee must belong to the union before he or she can be hired.

Coase Theorem The proposition that private negotiations between people will lead to an efficient resolution of externalities, as long as property rights are well defined and transaction costs are trivial or zero.

Collective Bargaining The process whereby wage rates and other issues are determined by a union bargaining with management on behalf of all union members.

Comparative Advantage The situation in which someone can produce a good at lower opportunity cost than someone else can.

Complements Two goods that are used jointly in consumption.

Concentration Ratio The percentage of industry sales (or assets, output, labor force, or some other factor) accounted for by x number of firms in the industry.

Conglomerate Merger A merger between companies in different industries.

Constant Returns to Scale The condition when inputs are increased by some percentage and output increases by an equal percentage, causing unit costs to remain constant.

Constant-Cost Industry An industry in which average total costs do not change as (industry) output increases or decreases when firms enter or exit the industry, respectively.

Consumer Equilibrium The equilibrium that occurs when the consumer has spent all of his or her income and the marginal utilities per dollar spent on each good purchased are equal: $MU_A/P_A = MU_B/P_B = \ldots = MU_Z/P_Z$, where the letters A–Z represent all the goods a person buys.

Consumers' Surplus (CS) The difference between the maximum price a buyer is willing and able to pay for a good or service and the price actually paid. (CS = Maximum buying price – Price paid)

Contestable Market A market in which entry is easy and exit is costless, new firms can produce the product at the same cost as current firms, and exiting firms can easily dispose of their fixed assets by selling them.

Cross Elasticity of Demand A measure of the responsiveness in quantity demanded of one good to changes in the price of another good.

D

Deadweight Loss of Monopoly The net value (the value to buyers over and above the costs to suppliers) of the difference between the competitive quantity of output (where $P = MC$) and the monopoly quantity of output (where $P > MC$); the loss due to not producing the competitive quantity of output.

Deadweight Loss The loss to society of not producing the competitive, or supply-and-demand determined, level of output.

Decisions at the Margin Decision making characterized by weighing the additional (marginal) benefits of a change against the additional (marginal) costs of a change with respect to current conditions.

Decreasing-Cost Industry An industry in which average total costs decrease as output increases and increase as output decreases when firms enter and exit the industry, respectively.

Demand Curve The graphical representation of the law of demand.

Demand Schedule The numerical tabulation of the quantity demanded of a good at different prices. A demand schedule is the numerical representation of the law of demand.

Demand The willingness and ability of buyers to purchase different quantities of a good at different prices during a specific period.

Depreciation A decrease in the value of one currency relative to other currencies.

Derived Demand Demand that is the result of some other demand. For example, factor demand is derived from the demand for the products that the factors go to produce.

Devaluation A government action that changes the exchange rate by lowering the official price of a currency.

Diamond–Water Paradox The observation that things with the greatest value in use sometimes have little value in exchange and things with little value in use sometimes have the greatest value in exchange.

Directly Related Two variables are directly related if they change in the same way.

Diseconomies of Scale The condition when inputs are increased by some percentage and output increases by a smaller percentage, causing unit costs to rise.

Disequilibrium A state of either surplus or shortage in a market

Disequilibrium Price A price other than the equilibrium price. A price at which the quantity demanded does not equal the quantity supplied.

Disutility The dissatisfaction one receives from a bad.

Dividends A share of the profits of a corporation distributed to stockholders.

Dow Jones Industrial Average (DJIA) The most popular, widely cited indicator of day-to-day stock market activity; a weighted average of 30 widely traded stocks on the New York Stock Exchange.

Dumping The sale of goods abroad at a price below their cost and below the price charged in the domestic market.

E

Economic Profit The difference between total revenue and total cost, including both explicit and implicit costs.

Economic Rent Payment in excess of opportunity costs.

Economics The science of scarcity; the science of how individuals and societies deal with the fact that wants are greater than the limited resources available to satisfy those wants.

Economies of Scale Economies that exist when inputs are increased by some percentage and output increases by a greater percentage, causing unit costs to fall.

Efficiency Exists when marginal benefits equal marginal costs.

Elastic Demand The demand that occurs when the percentage change in quantity demanded is greater than the percentage change in price. Quantity demanded changes proportionately more than price changes.

Elasticity of Demand for Labor The percentage change in the quantity demanded of labor divided by the percentage change in the wage rate.

Entrepreneurship The talent that some people have for organizing the resources of land, labor, and capital to produce goods, seek new business opportunities, and develop new ways of doing things.

Equilibrium Equilibrium means "at rest." Equilibrium in a market is the price–quantity combination from which buyers or sellers do not tend to move away. Graphically, equilibrium is the intersection point of the supply and demand curves.

Equilibrium Price (Market-Clearing Price) The price at which the quantity demanded of a good equals the quantity supplied.

Equilibrium Quantity The quantity that corresponds to the equilibrium price. The quantity at which the amount of the good that buyers are willing and able to buy equals the amount that sellers are willing and able to sell, and both equal the amount actually bought and sold.

Excess Capacity Theorem A monopolistic competitor in equilibrium produces an output smaller than the one that would minimize its costs of production.

Exchange (Trade) The giving up of one thing for something else.

Exchange Rate The price of one currency in terms of another currency.

Excludable A characteristic of a good whereby it is possible or not prohibitively costly to exclude someone from receiving the benefits of the good after it has been produced.

Explicit Cost A cost incurred when an actual (monetary) payment is made.

Externality A side effect of an action that affects the well-being of third parties.

F

Face Value (Par Value) Dollar amount specified on a bond; the total amount the issuer of the bond will repay to the buyer of the bond.

Factor Price Taker A firm that can buy all of a factor it wants at the equilibrium price. Such a firm faces a horizontal (flat, perfectly elastic) supply curve of factors.

Fixed Costs Costs that do not vary with output; the costs associated with fixed inputs.

Fixed Exchange Rate System A system whereby a nation's currency is set at a fixed rate relative to all other currencies and central banks intervene in the foreign exchange market to maintain the fixed rate.

Fixed Input An input whose quantity cannot be changed as output changes.

Flexible Exchange Rate System A system whereby exchange rates are determined by the forces of supply and demand for a currency.

Foreign Exchange Market The market in which currencies of different countries are exchanged.

Free Rider Anyone who receives the benefits of a good without paying for it.

Futures Contract An agreement to buy or sell a specific amount of something (a commodity, a currency, a financial instrument) at an agreed-on price on a stipulated future date.

G

Game Theory A mathematical technique used to analyze the behavior of decision makers who try to reach an optimal position for themselves through game playing or the use of strategic behavior, who are fully aware of the interactive nature of the process at hand, and who anticipate the moves of other decision makers.

Gini Coefficient A measure of the degree of inequality in the income distribution.

Good Anything from which individuals receive utility or satisfaction.

Gross Domestic Product (GDP) The total market value of all final goods and services produced annually within a country's borders.

H

Herfindahl Index An index that measures the degree of concentration in an industry, equal to the sum of the squares of the market shares of each firm in the industry.

Horizontal Merger A merger between firms that are selling similar products in the same market.

Human Capital Education, development of skills, and anything else that is particular to the individual and that increases personal productivity.

I

Implicit Cost A cost that represents the value of resources used in production for which no actual (monetary) payment is made.

In-Kind Transfer Payments Transfer payments, such as medical assistance and subsidized housing, that are made in a specific good or service rather than in cash.

Income Elastic The condition that exists when the percentage change in quantity demanded of a good is greater than the percentage change in income.

Income Elasticity of Demand A measure of the responsiveness of quantity demanded to changes in income.

Income Inelastic The condition that exists when the percentage change in quantity demanded of a good is less than the percentage change in income.

Income Unit Elastic The condition that exists when the percentage change in quantity demanded of a good is equal to the percentage change in income.

Increasing-Cost Industry An industry in which average total costs increase as output increases and decrease as output decreases when firms enter and exit the industry, respectively.

Independent Two variables are independent if, as one changes, the other does not.

Indifference Curve Map A map that represents a number of indifference curves for a given individual with reference to two goods.

Indifference Curve The curve that represents an indifference set and that shows all the bundles of two goods giving an individual equal total utility.

Indifference Set A group of bundles of two goods that give an individual equal total utility.

Inelastic Demand The demand that occurs when the percentage change in quantity demanded is less than the percentage change in price. Quantity demanded changes proportionately less than price changes.

Inferior Good A good for which demand falls (rises) as income rises (falls).

Initial Public Offering (IPO) A company's first offering of stock to the public.

Internalizing Externalities An externality is internalized if the persons or group that generated the externality incorporate into their own private or internal cost–benefit calculations the external benefits (in the case of a positive externality) or the external costs (in the case of a negative externality).

Interpersonal Utility Comparison Comparing the utility one person receives from a good, service, or activity with the utility another person receives from the same good, service, or activity.

Inversely Related Two variables are inversely related if they change in opposite ways.

Investment Bank A firm that acts as an intermediary between the company that issues the stock and the part of the public that wishes to buy it.

L

Labor The work brought about by the physical and mental talents that people contribute to the production process.

Land All natural resources, such as minerals, forests, water, and unimproved land.

Law of Demand As the price of a good rises, the quantity demanded of the good falls, and as the price of a good falls, the quantity demanded of the good rises, *ceteris paribus*.

Law of Diminishing Marginal Returns As ever larger amounts of a variable input are combined with fixed inputs, eventually the marginal physical product of the variable input will decline.

Law of Diminishing Marginal Utility Over a given period, the marginal (or additional) utility or satisfaction gained by consuming equal successive units of a good will decline as the amount consumed increases.

Law of Increasing Opportunity Costs As more of a good is produced, the opportunity costs of producing that good increase.

Law of Supply As the price of a good rises, the quantity supplied of the good rises, and as the price of a good falls, the quantity supplied of the good falls, *ceteris paribus*.

Least-Cost Rule Rule that specifies the combination of factors that minimizes costs and so requires that the following condition be met: $MPP_1/P_1 = MPP_2/P_2 = \ldots MPP_N/P_N$ where the subscript numbers stand for the different factors.

Loanable Funds Funds that someone borrows and another person lends, for which the borrower pays an interest rate to the lender.

Lock-In Effect The situation in which a product or technology becomes the standard and is difficult or impossible to dislodge from that role.

Logrolling The exchange of votes to gain support for legislation.

Long Run A period during which all inputs in the production process can be varied. (No inputs are fixed.)

Long-Run (Industry) Supply (*LRS*) Curve A graphic representation of the quantities of output that an industry is prepared to supply at different prices after the entry and exit of firms are completed

Long-Run Average Total Cost (LRATC) Curve A curve that shows the lowest (unit) cost at which a firm can produce any given level of output.

Long-Run Competitive Equilibrium The condition in which $P = MC = SRATC = LRATC$. Economic profit is zero, firms are producing the quantity of output at which price is equal to marginal cost, and no firm has an incentive to change its plant size.

Lorenz Curve A graph of the income distribution that expresses the relationship between the cumulative percentage of households and the cumulative percentage of income.

M

Macroeconomics The branch of economics that deals with human behavior and choices as they relate to highly aggregate markets (e.g., the market for goods and services) or the entire economy.

Managed Float A managed flexible exchange rate system under which nations intervene now and then to adjust their official reserve holdings in order to moderate major swings in exchange rates.

Managerial Coordination The process in which managers direct employees to perform certain tasks.

Marginal Benefits (MB) Additional benefits; the benefits connected with consuming an additional unit of a good or undertaking one more unit of an activity.

Marginal Cost (MC) The change in total cost that results from a change in quantity of output: $MC = \Delta TC/\Delta Q$.

Marginal Costs (MC) Additional costs; the costs connected with consuming an additional unit of a good or undertaking one more unit of an activity.

Marginal Factor Cost (MFC) The additional cost incurred by employing an additional factor unit.

Marginal Physical Product (MPP) The change in output that results from changing the variable input by one unit, with all other inputs held fixed.

Marginal Productivity Theory Marginal productivity theory states that firms in competitive or perfect product and factor markets pay their factors their marginal revenue products.

Marginal Rate of Substitution The amount of one good that an individual is willing to give up to obtain an additional unit of another good and maintain equal total utility.

Marginal Revenue (MR) The change in total revenue (*TR*) that results from selling one additional unit of output (*Q*).

Marginal Revenue Product (MRP) The additional revenue generated by employing an additional factor unit.

Marginal Social Benefits (MSB) The sum of marginal private benefits (*MPB*) and marginal external benefits (*MEB*): $MSB = MPB + MEB$.

Marginal Social Costs (MSC) The sum of marginal private costs (*MPC*) and marginal external costs (*MEC*): $MSC = MPC + MEC$.

Marginal Utility The additional utility a person receives from consuming an additional unit of a good.

Market Any place people come together to trade.

Market Coordination The process in which individuals perform tasks, such as producing certain quantities of goods, on the basis of changes in market forces, such as supply, demand, and price.

Market Failure A situation in which the market does not provide the ideal or optimal amount of a good.

Market Structure The environment whose characteristics influence a firm's pricing and output decisions.

Median Voter Model A model suggesting that candidates in a two-person political race will attempt to match the preferences of the median voter.

Microeconomics The branch of economics that deals with human behavior and choices as they relate to relatively small units: an individual, a firm, an industry, a single market.

Minimum Efficient Scale The lowest output level at which average total costs are minimized.

Monitor A person in a business firm who coordinates team production and reduces shirking.

Monopolistic Competition A theory of market structure based on three assumptions: many sellers and buyers, firms producing and selling slightly differentiated products, and easy entry and exit.

Monopoly A theory of market structure based on three assumptions: There is one seller, it sells a product that has no close substitutes, and the barriers to entry are extremely high.

Monopsony A single buyer in a factor market.

Moral Hazard A condition that exists when one party to a transaction changes his or her behavior in a way that is hidden from and costly to the other party.

N

Natural Monopoly The condition in which economies of scale are so pronounced that only one firm can survive.

Negative Externality The condition in which a person's or group's actions impose a cost (an adverse side effect) on others.

Network Good A good whose value increases as the expected number of units sold increases.

Neutral Good A good for which demand does not change as income rises or falls.

Nominal Interest Rate The interest rate determined by the forces of supply and demand in the loanable funds market.

Nonexcludable A characteristic of a good whereby it is impossible or prohibitively costly to exclude someone from receiving the benefits of the good after it has been produced.

Nonrivalrous in Consumption Said of a good whose consumption by one person does not reduce its consumption by others.

Normal Good A good for which demand rises (falls) as income rises (falls).

Normal Profit Zero economic profit, the level of profit necessary to keep resources employed in a firm. A firm that earns normal profit is earning revenue equal to its total costs (explicit plus implicit costs).

Normative Economics The study of *what should be* in economics.

O

Oligopoly A theory of market structure based on three assumptions: few sellers and many buyers, firms producing either homogeneous or differentiated products, and significant barriers to entry.

Opportunity Cost The most highly valued opportunity or alternative forfeited when a choice is made.

Optimal Currency Area A geographic area in which exchange rates can be fixed or a common currency used without sacrificing domestic economic goals, such as low unemployment.

Option A contract that gives the owner the right, but not the obligation, to buy or sell shares of a stock at a specified price on or before a specified date.

Overvalued A currency is overvalued if its price in terms of other currencies is above the equilibrium price.

Own Price The price of a good. For example, if the price of oranges is $1, this is its own price.

P

Perfect Competition A theory of market structure based on four assumptions: (1) There are many sellers and buyers; (2) the sellers sell a homogeneous good; (3) buyers and sellers have all relevant information; (4) entry into, and exit from, the market is easy.

Perfect Price Discrimination A price structure in which the seller charges the highest price that each consumer is willing to pay for the product rather than go without it.

Perfectly Elastic Demand The demand that occurs when a small percentage change in price causes an extremely large percentage change in quantity demanded (from buying all to buying nothing).

Perfectly Inelastic Demand The demand that occurs when quantity demanded does not change as price changes.

Positive Economics The study of *what is* in economics.

Positive Externality The condition in which a person's or group's actions create a benefit (a beneficial side effect) for others.

Positive Rate of Time Preference A preference for earlier over later availability of goods.

Poverty Income Threshold (Poverty Line) The income level below which people are considered to be living in poverty.

Present Value The current worth of some future dollar amount of income or receipts.

Price Ceiling A government-mandated maximum price above which legal trades cannot be made.

Price Discrimination A price structure in which the seller charges different prices for the product it sells and the price differences do not reflect cost differences.

Price Elasticity of Demand A measure of the responsiveness of quantity demanded to changes in price.

Price Elasticity of Supply A measure of the responsiveness of quantity supplied to changes in price.

Price Floor A government-mandated minimum price below which legal trades cannot be made.

Price Searcher A seller that has the ability to control, to some degree, the price of the product it sells.

Price Taker A seller that does not have the ability to control the price of the product it sells; the seller "takes" the price determined in the market.

Producers' (Sellers') Surplus (*PS*) The difference between the price sellers receive for a good and the minimum or lowest price for which they would have sold the good. (*PS* = Price received − Minimum selling price.)

Production Possibilities Frontier (PPF) The possible combinations of two goods that can be produced during a certain span of time under the conditions of a given state of technology and fully employed resources.

Productive Efficiency The situation in which a firm produces its output at the lowest possible per-unit cost (lowest *ATC*).

Productive Efficient The condition in which the maximum output is produced with the given resources and technology.

Productive Inefficient The condition in which less than the maximum output is produced with the given resources and technology. Productive inefficiency implies that more of one good can be produced without any less of another being produced.

Profit Maximization Rule Profit is maximized by producing the quantity of output at which $MR = MC$.

Profit The difference between total revenue and total cost.

Public Choice The branch of economics in which economic principles and tools are applied to public sector decision making.

Public Choice Theory of Regulation A theory holding that regulators are seeking to do—and will do through regulation—what is in their best interest (specifically, to enhance their power and the size and budget of their regulatory agencies).

Public Franchise A firm's government-granted right that permits the firm to provide a particular good or service and that excludes all others from doing so.

Public Good A good whose consumption by one person does not reduce its consumption by another person—that is, it is nonrivalrous in consumption.

Public Interest Theory of Regulation A theory holding that regulators are seeking to do—and will do through regulation—what is in the best interest of the public or society at large.

Purchasing Power Parity (PPP) Theory Theory stating that exchange rates between any two currencies will adjust to reflect changes in the relative price levels of the two countries.

Pure Economic Rent A category of economic rent such that the payment is to a factor that is in fixed supply, implying that the factor has zero opportunity costs.

Q

Quota A legal limit imposed on the amount of a good that may be imported.

R

Rational Ignorance The state of not acquiring information because the costs of acquiring it are greater than the benefits.

Rationing Device A means for deciding who gets what of available resources and goods.

Real GDP The value of the entire output produced annually within a country's borders, adjusted for price changes.

Real Interest Rate The nominal interest rate adjusted for expected inflation; that is, the nominal interest rate minus the expected inflation rate.

Regulatory Lag The period between the time that a natural monopoly's costs change and the time that the regulatory agency adjusts prices to account for the change.

Relative Price The price of a good in terms of another good.

Rent Seeking Actions of individuals and groups that spend resources to influence public policy in the hope of redistributing (transferring) income to themselves from others.

Residual Claimant Persons who share in the profits of a business firm.

Resource Allocative Efficiency The situation in which firms produce the quantity of output at which price equals marginal cost: $P = MC$.

Revaluation A government action that changes the exchange rate by raising the official price of a currency.

Rivalrous in Consumption Said of a good whose consumption by one person reduces its consumption by others.

Roundabout Method of Production The production of capital goods that enhance productive capabilities.

S

Scarcity The condition in which our wants are greater than the limited resources available to satisfy those wants.

Screening The process employers use to increase the probability of choosing good employees on the basis of certain criteria.

Second-Degree Price Discrimination A price structure in which the seller charges a uniform price per unit for one specific quantity, a lower price for an additional quantity, and so on.

Shirking The behavior of a worker who is putting forth less than the agreed-to effort.

Short Run A period during which some inputs in the production process are fixed.

Short-Run (Firm) Supply Curve The portion of the firm's marginal cost curve that lies above the average variable cost curve.

Short-Run Market (Industry) Supply Curve The horizontal sum of all existing firms' short-run supply curves.

Shortage (Excess Demand) A condition in which the quantity demanded is greater than the quantity supplied. Shortages occur only at prices below the equilibrium price.

Slope The ratio of the change in the variable on the vertical axis to the change in the variable on the horizontal axis.

Socially Optimal Amount (Output) An amount that takes into account and adjusts for all benefits (external and private) and all costs (external and private); the amount at which $MSB = MSC$. Sometimes referred to as the efficient amount.

Special-Interest Groups Subsets of the general population that hold (usually) intense preferences for or against a particular government service, activity, or policy and that often gain from public policies that may not be in accord with the interests of the general public.

Spontaneous Order The spontaneous and unintended emergence of order out of the self-interested actions of individuals; an unintended consequence of human action, with emphasis placed on the word "unintended."

Stock A claim on a corporation's assets that gives the purchaser a share of ownership in the corporation.

Strike The union employees' refusal to work at a certain wage or under certain conditions.

Subsidy A monetary payment by government to a producer of a good or service.

Substitutes Two goods that satisfy similar needs or desires.

Sunk cost A cost incurred in the past that cannot be changed by current decisions and therefore cannot be recovered.

Supply Schedule The numerical tabulation of the quantity supplied of a good at different prices. A supply schedule is the numerical representation of the law of supply.

Supply The willingness and ability of sellers to produce and offer to sell different quantities of a good at different prices during a specific period.

Surplus (Excess Supply) A condition in which the quantity supplied is greater than the quantity demanded. Surpluses occur only at prices above the equilibrium price.

T

Tariff A tax on imports.

Technology The body of skills and knowledge involved in the use of resources in production. An advance in technology commonly increases the ability to produce more output with a fixed amount of resources or the ability to produce the same output with fewer resources.

Theory An abstract representation of the real world designed with the intent to better understand it.

Third-Degree Price Discrimination A price structure in which the seller charges different prices in different markets or charges different prices to various segments of the buying population.

Tie-in Sale A sale whereby one good can be purchased only if another good is also purchased.

Total Cost (TC) The sum of fixed costs and variable costs.

Total Revenue (TR) Price times quantity sold.

Total Surplus (TS) The sum of consumers' surplus and producers' surplus. ($TS = CS + PS$.)

Total Utility The total satisfaction a person receives from consuming a particular quantity of a good.

Trade Balance The value of a country's exports minus the value of its imports; sometimes referred to as net exports.

Trade Deficit The condition that exists when the value of a country's imports is greater than the value of its exports.

Trade Surplus The condition that exists when the value of a country's exports is greater than the value of its imports.

Transfer Payments Payments to persons that are not made in return for goods and services currently supplied.

Transitivity The principle whereby, if A is preferred to B and B is preferred to C, then A is preferred to C.

Trust A combination of firms that come together to act as a monopolist.

U

Undervalued A currency is undervalued if its price in terms of other currencies is below the equilibrium price.

Union Shop An organization in which a worker is not required to be a member of the union in order to be hired but must become a member within a certain time after being employed.

Unit Elastic Demand The demand that occurs when the percentage change in quantity demanded is equal to the percentage change in price. Quantity demanded changes proportionately to price changes.

(Upward-Sloping) Supply Curve The graphical representation of the law of supply.

Util An artificial construct used to measure utility.

Utility A measure of the satisfaction, happiness, or benefit that results from the consumption of a good.

V

Value Marginal Product (VMP) The price of a good multiplied by the marginal physical product of the factor: $VMP = P \times MPP$.

Variable Costs Costs that vary with output; the costs associated with variable inputs.

Variable Input An input whose quantity can be changed as output changes.

Vertical Merger A merger between companies in the same industry but at different stages of the production process.

W

Wage Discrimination The situation in which individuals of equal ability and productivity (as measured by their contribution to output) are paid different wage rates.

X

X-Inefficiency The increase in costs, due to the organizational slack in a monopoly, resulting from the absence of competitive pressure to push costs down to their lowest possible level.

INDEX